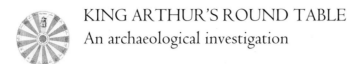

KING ARTHUR'S ROUND TABLE
An archaeological investigation

Frontispiece – The Round Table after cleaning in 1978

King Arthur's Round Table
An archaeological investigation

Martin Biddle

with

Sally Badham, A. C. Barefoot, Beatrice Clayre,
G. R. Coleman, Roger Davey, John V. Fleming,
David Haddon-Reece, Brian J. Heard, Cecil Hewett,
Simon Jervis, Michael Morris, R. L. Otlet, Susan J. Read,
Stephen Rees Jones, Pamela Tudor-Craig,
Clive Wainwright, and A. J. Walker

THE BOYDELL PRESS

First published 2000

ISBN 0 85115 626 6

A catalogue record for this book is available
from the British Library

Library of Congress Cataloging-in-Publication Data applied for

The Boydell Press is an imprint of Boydell & Brewer Ltd
P O Box 9, Woodbridge, Suffolk IP12 3DF, UK
and of Boydell & Brewer Inc.
P O Box 41026, Rochester, N Y 14604-4126, USA

This publication is printed on acid-free paper

Printed in Hong Kong

Contents

LIST OF COLOUR PLATES

Frontispiece The Round Table after cleaning in 1978 (photograph, IBM)

Between pages 92 and 93

Between pages 236 and 237

LIST OF FIGURES

LIST OF TABLES

Preface and Acknowledgements

The vast wooden disk known throughout the world as King Arthur's Round Table has hung on the wall of Winchester Castle hall for more than six hundred years. But what is it? Was it ever a table? When was it made? Why is it hanging on the wall? When was it painted with the famous image it now bears? Why is it called 'King Arthur's Round Table'? And why is it at Winchester?

In 1976 the Round Table was taken down from the wall and thoroughly examined by a team of historians and scientists assembled by the Winchester Research Unit on behalf of the Hampshire County Council. In this book they show how the history, structural archaeology and iconography of the Winchester Round Table reveal its changing use as a symbol of royal power in different generations.

The County of Hampshire has been the guardian of the Round Table and of the Great Hall in which it hangs since the beginning of the seventeenth century, initially through the Justices of the Peace, who administered the county through the Court of Quarter Sessions, and since 1889 as the Hampshire County Council. It is due entirely to the vision and generosity of the County Council, its elected members and officers, that the investigations recorded in this book have been possible. The County Council gave an immediate welcome to the suggestion of the Winchester Excavations Committee that the restoration of the Great Hall from 1974 onwards should include a thorough investigation of the condition and history of the Round Table. The County's officers undertook all the arrangements for the delicate tasks of taking the table down from the wall, fixing it in a position from which investigations and conservation could be undertaken, and in due course seeing the table safely rehung on the wall. Many of the illustrations in this book are reproduced from manuscripts and engravings in the care of the Council's Hampshire Record Office whose staff have assisted the project with enthusiasm at every stage. The records arising from every aspect of the investigation are now in the care of the Record Office where they may be consulted in the normal way.

A great debt is owed to the contributors to this volume, all of whom have given their time without stint over many years to the investigation, writing, and illustration of their own chapters and to help in other ways, not least for the patience with which they have endured the very long wait which has intervened between the start of the project and the publication of this volume.

The Winchester Excavations Committee under its successive chairmen, Mrs Dilys Neate and Mr David Ball, and latterly especially through its Executive Sub-Committee, has given every encouragement to the staff of its Winchester Research Unit to make the administrative and other arrangements for the research on which this book is based, particularly Derek Keene, Caroline Raison, and Chip Vincent, many of whose photographs appear in the pages which follow. The whole volume was word-processed by June Lloyd, assisted by David Lloyd, and this book, like the Committee's series of *Winchester Studies*, has been set from the disks they prepared with their customary flair and attention to detail. A most important debt, reflected in the dedication, is due to Dr Arnold Taylor for the intense interest he has taken in the project since the start. Dr Taylor has read and re-read several of the chapters, has carried out special searches in the Public Record Office in relation to the possible roles of Edward I and Edward III in the history of the table, and has corresponded at length on many of the problems involved. As a member of the Excavations Committee since its inception in 1962, Arnold Taylor has been an ever-present source of encouragement and inspiration, most particularly expressed in his support for and involvement in the investigation of the Round Table.

The Courtauld Institute of Art has played a special role in photographing the front and back of the table and in the radiography (by Portable X-rays Ltd.) and analysis of the painting reported by Professor Rees Jones in Chapter 7 and reflected in the reproduction here of many of the photographs taken by James Austin.

A special debt of thanks is due to the Atomic Energy Research Establishment at Harwell who undertook as a contribution to the project the radiocarbon dating reported by Bob Otlet and Jill Walker in Chapter 6.

I owe a particular debt to Hertford College and its Fellows, many of whose names appear in the list which follows, for their interest and support over the last eleven years, and not least to Mr David Astor under the terms of whose generous endowment of my fellowship this book was completed.

Many other bodies and individuals have made important contributions to the work over the years or provided illustrations. Many are acknowledged elsewhere in the book, but they are named here as an expression of gratitude for the range and importance of such collaboration in an investigation as varied, complex and long drawn-out as that of the Round Table: BBC 'Horizon', Peter Begent, Richard Bradley, Charlotte Brewer, Sarah Brown, Julia Briggs, Christopher Bronk Ramsey, C. N. L. Brooke, Robert Bruce-Gardner, Catherine Ridder Byerly, Geert H. H. Claassens, John Crook, Elisabeth Crowfoot, the late Edward Croft-Murray, P. L. Dickinson (Richmond Herald), Eamon Duffy, the late R. M. Eldredge, Ellis Evans, Geoffrey Fisher, Christopher Foley, Ian Friel, Paloma García-Belledo, Kate Gilbert,

Malcolm Godden, Ian Gourlay, Nicholas Griffiths, Pat Hewett, Martin Holmes, David Howlett, Lisa Jefferson, David F. Johnson, Birthe Kjølbye-Biddle, Phillip Lindley, Michael Metcalf, W. M. Ormrod, Ray Page, Kenneth Painter, Bob Pendreigh, Roger Pensom, Rosemary Pinches, Pauline Plummer, Susana Puch, Stephen Rees-Jones (junior), John Reynolds, Eva Rhys, Gill Rushton, Richard Sawyer, J. S. G. Simmons, Alison Tinniswood, Barbara Thompson, Jim Thorn, Mike Tite, Caroline Villers, Robert K. Vincent jr., Jane Wainwright, Jeff Wallis, Stephanie West, Gruffydd Aled Williams, Christopher Wilson, and Robert Yorke.

The many libraries, museums, and other institutions and individuals who have provided photographs of objects in their care or taken by them and have given permission for them to be reproduced are gratefully acknowledged individually in the lists of plates and figures.

A final and most important debt is owed to Richard Barber, whose role in the final appearance of this book has been crucial. As both an Arthurian scholar and as a publisher his contribution has been generous and exceptional and I (and we) are all deeply indebted to him.

Martin Biddle
Hertford College, Oxford

1 September 2000

Abbreviations

Add. MS.	Additional MS. (BL class reference)
AERE	Atomic Energy Research Establishment, Harwell
ALMA	Roger Sherman Loomis (ed.), *Arthurian Literature in the Middle Ages: a Collaborative History* (Oxford, 1959; reprinted 1961)
Art.	Article
Bk(s).	Book(s)
BL	British Library, London
BN	Bibliothèque nationale, Paris
Bodleian	Bodleian Library, Oxford
Cal Close R	*Calendar of Close Rolls*
Cal Lib R	*Calendar of Liberate Rolls*
Cal Pat R	*Calendar of Patent Rolls*
cap.	chapter in a MS or early printed text
CSP	*Calendar of State Papers (Domestic, Spanish, Venetian)*
DNB	*Dictionary of National Biography*
ed.	edited, editor(s)
edn	edition
EETS	Early English Text Society
HRO	Hampshire Record Office, Winchester
ill. (illus.)	illustration (illustrated)
LP Henry VIII	*Letters and Papers of Henry VIII*
MS. (MSS.)	Manuscript(s)
n. (nn.)	note(s)
orig.	original
os	old series
PMLA	*Publications of the Modern Language Association of America*
PRO	Public Record Office, Kew
ser.	series
Sig.	Signature of a quire or page (in an early printed book)
RIBA	Royal Institute of British Architects

The Contributors

Sally Badham is the author of many publications on medieval church monuments. Her main areas of research are epigraphy and typological analysis. Her latest book, with the late Malcolm Norris, is *Early Incised Slabs and Brasses from the London Marblers* (London, 1999).

A. C. Barefoot is Professor Emeritus of University Studies and of Wood and Paper Science, North Carolina State University, Raleigh N.C., and since 1964 has been dendrochronologist with the Winchester Research Unit . He is the author (with F. W. Hankins) of *Identification of Modern and Tertiary Woods* (Oxford, 1982).

Martin Biddle led excavations at Winchester from 1961 to 1971 and has been Director of the Winchester Research Unit and general editor of *Winchester Studies* since 1968. He is Professor of Medieval Archaeology at Oxford and Astor Senior Research Fellow and Tutor in Archaeology at Hertford College. He is the principal author of *Object and Economy in Medieval Winchester*, Winchester Studies 7.ii (Oxford, 1990).

Beatrice Clayre graduated MA, PhD in Prehistoric Archaeology from Edinburgh University, and also studied at the University of Freiburg, and in Barcelona and Lisbon. She has been associated with the Winchester Research Unit since 1975 and is author (with Martin Biddle) of *Winchester Castle*, Winchester Studies 6.i (Oxford, forthcoming).

Graham Coleman, formerly with the Building Research Establishment at Princes Risborough, is now an independent consultant specialising in dampness and timber infestation problems. He is the author of *Guide to the Identification of Dampness in Buildings* (rev. edn, Wessex Publishing, 1991)

Roger Davey was Deputy County Archivist of Hampshire 1971–1981, where he gained an interest in the history of the Winchester Castle area. He was County Archivist of East Sussex from 1982–2000. He is the author of *East Sussex Sentences of Transportation at Quarter Sessions, 1790–1854* (Lewes, 1998).

John V. Fleming, Professor of English at Princeton University, graduated Ph.D. Princeton '63. He is the author of *The Roman de la Rose: A Study in Allegory and Iconography* (Princeton, 1969); *Classical Imitation and Interpretation in Chaucer's Troilus* (Nebraska, 1990); and is currently working on Columbus and Ovid.

David Haddon-Reece was formerly at the Ancient Monuments Laboratory of English Heritage where he was particularly concerned with the co-ordination of tree-ring investigations. He is the author of many papers on tree-ring dating and an authority on the study and conservation of early clocks.

Brian J. Heard, formerly Deputy Head of the Metropolitan Police Forensic Laboratory , New Scotland Yard, is Head of the Forensic Firearms Examination Bureau of the Hong Kong Police. He is the author of *Handbook of Firearms and Ballistics: Examining and Interpreting Forensic Evidence* (J. Wiley, 1997) .

Cecil Hewett (1926–98) trained in Arts and Crafts and taught in Essex schools for nineteen years. He joined the GLC Historic Buildings Division in 1972, moving to Essex County Council Historic Buildings Division in 1974 until 1981. His published books include *English Historic Carpentry* (Phillimore, 1980) and *English Cathedral and Monastic Carpentry* (Phillimore, 1985).

Simon Jervis is President of the Society of Antiquaries of London, Chairman of the Furniture History Society, and Director of Historic Buildings for The National Trust. He was formerly Director of The Fitzwilliam Museum, Cambridge, and Deputy Keeper of the Furniture and Woodwork Department at the Victoria & Albert Museum. He is the author of *Woodwork of Winchester Cathedral* (Winchester, 1976) and many other works.

Michael Morris was Assistant County Architect responsible for the care and conversion to new uses of Hampshire County Council's stock of Historic Buildings from 1974–1991. He devised and directed all technical means and operational programmes employed to lower, transport and present the Round Table for investigation in 1976 and rehang it in 1980. He has a particular interest in Victorian art, design and engineering and the appreciation of 19th- and 20th-century architecture.

Bob Otlet has more than 30 years experience of radiocarbon measurements and at the time of the Round Table investigation, was head of the Isotope Measurements Laboratory, AERE Harwell. Jill Walker also worked at Harwell at this time and they have published numerous papers on different aspects of radiocarbon and for the past 10 years have run a private laboratory at RCD Lockinge carrying out low level 14C and 3H measurements.

Susan Read was at the Natural History Museum, London, and subsequently with the Biodeterioration Section of the Building Research Establishment at Princes Risborough. She is the author of papers on the taxonomy of butterflies and on wood preservatives.

Stephen Rees Jones (1909–96) was Emeritus Professor of the History of Technology of Art at the Courtauld Institute of Art, University of London, and Professor of Chemistry at the Royal Academy of Arts, London.

Pamela Tudor-Craig [Pamela Lady Wedgwood] is a medievalist who has divided her working life between conservation (cathedrals, Westminster Abbey, churches, wall paintings, etc.), teaching and research. She is the founder of the Harlaxton Symposium and author of *Richard III*, the catalogue of an exhibition at the National Portrait Gallery (2nd edn, Boydell Press, 1977).

Jill Walker was at the Isotope Measurements Laboratory, AERE Harwell, at the time of the Round Table investigation. She has published numerous papers with Bob Otlet with whom she now runs a private radiocarbon laboratory .

Clive Wainwright (1942–99) was Senior Research Fellow at the Victoria and Albert Museum . He had joined the museum in 1966 and since 1996 had also been Visiting Professor in the History of Art at Birkbeck College. He published extensively including *The Romantic Interior: the British Collector at Home 1750–1850* (Yale, 1989).

For

ARNOLD TAYLOR

historian of Edward I's castles

who discovered Edward's tournament

of April 1290 in Winchester

KING ARTHUR'S ROUND TABLE

An archaeological investigation

Problem and Context

Shortly after seven on the morning of Friday, 27 August 1976, a ten-ton mobile crane turned into Winchester High Street. It drove uphill, worked its way around West Gate, and turned into Peninsula Barracks. There, on the site of the medieval castle, it backed up to the high gable wall at the west end of the Great Hall, and came to a halt. With its stabilizers spread and carefully adjusted, the crane's hydraulic jib was extended, and its head gently inserted through the central light of the thirteenth-century triple window high in the gable of the hall. Within a few hours, 'King Arthur's' Round Table was lowered to the floor of the Great Hall inside, suspended from the jib of the crane outside.

Thirteen years earlier, archaeological excavations had begun on the site of the Assize Courts then shortly to be rebuilt by the Hampshire County Council. By 1967 work had advanced from the site of the new courthouse, built partly over the medieval castle ditch, to the site of the castle itself. Here, immediately north of the Great Hall, the only building from the medieval castle still standing, excavations took place each year until 1971. Gradually the history of the castle was worked out. William the Conqueror had taken over a deep salient at the south-west corner of the Roman town. Using the Roman town wall on three sides, he dug a line of rampart and ditch to form the east side of the castle. Here, on the highest ground within the city, the Conqueror thus established the castle which his sons were to develop into one of the greatest strongholds of the kingdom. The buildings of a royal palace were gradually erected within the castle walls. As early as Easter 1072, in a chapel discovered in our excavations 898 years later, William himself, Matilda his wife, Hubert the papal legate, and the archbishops and bishops of England had agreed to the supremacy of Canterbury over York. Here by about 1100 the royal treasury was kept, and with it Domesday Book, and here in the following years the apparatus of exchequer government first began to emerge. A century later, in 1207, the Conqueror's great-great-great-grandson was born in the castle, and in 1216, in his minority as Henry III, he began its almost complete reconstruction. The Great Hall, built between 1222 and 1235, was one of King Henry's greatest architectural achievements. It stands today, perhaps the finest medieval aisled hall to survive in England.

During the excavation seasons in the summers of 1967–71 in Castle Yard, the Great Hall was in regular use as a crown court. It was the scene in these years of a series of high-security trials, the arrangements for which posed serious problems for Winchester, as they did for the conduct of the excavations immediately outside the hall. Throughout these summers, we became more and more aware of the great interest of the public not only in our work, but especially in the Round Table hanging within the hall on the wall above the judge's bench. The County, as keepers of the hall, did their best to provide access for the public, who were able to get in, between sittings and at weekends, to stare up at the table on the wall and to wonder what it was really all about.

In 1974, the new courthouse was opened by Viscount Hailsham. Immediately arrangements were put in hand to clear the medieval Great Hall, to open its beautiful prospect up to view for the first time since 1938, and to restore to the public one of the finest public buildings in the country. At once the problem of the Round Table came to the front. How safely was it attached high on the wall? What condition was it in—its timbers, its painting? Above all, what was it? And in particular, how old was it? Was it really King Arthur's Round Table? Could it possibly have been made made in the 'Dark Ages'? Or was it much more recent, and if so, when and for what purpose had it been made? Had it indeed ever been a real table, or was it just a great symbol, not unlike the huge discs bearing the names of Allah, Mohammed, and the first four caliphs which hang from the walls of Santa Sophia in Istanbul?

A good deal could be surmised, but almost nothing was known for certain. The tales told to visitors were many and various, and whether credulous or sceptical were little different from what people had been told since the time of the first Elizabeth, if not before. The time had clearly come to try to answer some of these questions, not least because the safety and conservation of the table demanded attention without delay. The Winchester Research Unit proposed and the Hampshire County Council accepted that an investigation of the table should form a major element in the restoration of the Great Hall. The Round Table would be taken down from the wall for the first time in just over a century. It would be X-rayed, measured, and photographed. It would be dated by radiocarbon and tree-ring analysis. Its significance as a work of carpentry, as a piece of furniture, as a painting would be assessed, and its place in English history and literature and in the history of medieval symbols would be resolved, if at all possible.

To do this, a considerable team was brought together, most of whom have contributed to the making of this book. With the world's press, radio, and television already intrigued, the BBC 'Horizon' team decided to record the whole process and made a memorable film, repeated several times in Britain alone, and shown throughout Europe and further afield.

Our objective was to bring to bear on one of the world's great symbols all the various approaches, scientific, literary, historical, and technical, which could contribute to an understanding of its origin and subsequent vicissitudes. But first, we had to try to understand the context of the table. When and how did the idea of the Round Table appear in the stories of King Arthur and his knights, and what did it signify? To what extent was this idea realized in the work of medieval artists, or made real in the furniture of the Middle Ages? And was the Great Hall of Winchester Castle an appropriate setting for such a symbol, both in the High Middle Ages, and through subsequent centuries, as taste and historical and literary attitudes changed?

In the first chapter, Professor John Fleming of Princeton University describes the growth of the story of King Arthur and his knights, and explores the origin of the legend of the Round Table, as an object, an institution, and an event. This is the context in myth and literature in which the Winchester table might have been made and was later painted.

In the hierarchic order of medieval society, the idea of a round table was almost subversive. The great tables of the Middle Ages, their use and how they are shown in manuscript paintings and engravings forms part of Chapter 2 by Mr Simon Jervis, then Deputy Keeper of the Department of Furniture and Interior Design at the Victoria and Albert Museum. His investigation of the surviving tables, both rectangular and round, and the ways in which they were sometimes painted, demonstrates the unique character of the Winchester Round Table.

The setting of the Round Table in the Great Hall of Winchester Castle is explored in Chapter 3, by Dr Beatrice Clayre, the historian of the castle, and by myself. In the second part of this chapter Mr Michael Morris then of the Hampshire County Architect's Department sets the changing character of the Great Hall from 1600 to the present day in the context of change in architectural taste. As the architect in charge of the restoration of the Great Hall in 1974–6, and the man charged with the delicate task of lowering the Round Table in 1976, and putting it back up again in 1980, Mr Morris concludes Chapter 3 with a first-hand account of the events of August 1976.

1

The Round Table in Literature and Legend

Of all the enduring and powerful myths of medieval literature, it is the story of Arthur of Britain, 'once and future king', which has most conspicuously captured the imaginations of English readers and writers since the publication in London half a millennium ago of the book which is its classic English statement, the *Morte Darthur*. The publisher of that volume, William Caxton, described it simply as 'a book of the noble hystoryes of the sayd Kynge Arthur and of certeyn of his knyghtes'; and he claimed to print it 'after a copye vnto me delyuerd, whyche copye Syr Thomas Malorye dyd take oute of certeyn bookes of Frensshe and reduced it into Englysshe'.[1]

It is this Arthurian anthology, brought together by a mysterious English knight in the turbulent twilight of English chivalry that has, more than any other single book, made Arthur and his Round Table live for English readers and writers of the last five hundred years. The response to the literary Arthur has been varied but fruitful. One may not wish to call the Arthur of Spenser's *Faerie Queen* a 'living presence', but he is nonetheless present in that work and thematically necessary to it. Arthur's vitality to the poets of the nineteenth century is beyond question and generally recognized. We see it clearly in such works as Morris's *The Defence of Guenevere*, the most imaginative product of Victorian Arthurianism, and in Tennyson's *Idylls of the King*, its most famous triumph. The makers of the modernist tradition, including Eliot, have flirted and sometimes more than flirted with Arthurian themes, and the currently popular wave of 'fantasy' literature, some of it of contemporary invention and some revived from an earlier generation, claims an Arthurian ancestry by adoption if not always by blood.

[1] *Caxton's Malory*, ed. James W. Spisak (Berkeley and Los Angeles, 1983), i, p. 2.

The perennial vitality of the Arthurian legend springs no doubt from varied sources, but among them is its peculiar richness of powerful structuring images, which are at once brilliantly articulate and open-ended, and which at once capture and stimulate the reader's imagination. The themes of Arthurian romance include the quest, the fatal union of adulterous love, the deep pathos of internecine strife, and the ambiguous majesty of kingship itself; but the structuring metaphor *par excellence*, which binds together the disparate 'histories' of the legend and provides some focus for its diffuse moral energies, is that of the Round Table, with its suggestion of both good fellowship and tragically flawed chivalric order. 'The Rounde Table at Wynchestre beganne', wrote the chronicler Hardyng in the fifteenth century, 'And ther it ende, and ther it hangeth yet'.[2] What, exactly, it may be that 'hangeth yet' in the Great Hall of Winchester Castle is the general subject of this book. The aim of this chapter is to suggest some of the ways in which the literary history of the Round Table may be relevant for that larger task.

The existence of an 'historical Arthur' is doubtful, although the question continues to be heatedly debated.[3] He is mentioned a few times by the Anglo-Latin historians of the pre-conquest period, particularly by Nennius in the ninth century, who tells of his victorious battles against the Saxons. The date implied for these triumphs is the late fifth century. An 'Arthur' also appears, indistinctly, in early Welsh poetry. From one point of view it is fortunate that these murky matters have no demonstrable relevance to the literary history of the Round Table. A dense and swirling mist descends upon British history in the Anglo-Saxon period. Into this fog the 'historical Arthur' disappears and from it, some centuries later, emerges the Arthur of medieval legend. Between the time of the collapse of a coherent British 'nation' and the emergence in England of the Norman monarchy there almost certainly circulated throughout the country, principally in oral form, songs and stories about King Arthur, but we can know nothing specific about them. What does seem clear is that the invention of the Arthurian legend, destined to become one of the great 'matters' of European literature, owed much more to England's later inhabitants than to its earlier peoples.

An interest in British antiquity, reflected in a taste for history of the sort that our age might be happier to call historical fiction, became something of a fashion among the Anglo-Norman aristocracy of the twelfth century. It is easy enough to suggest

---

[2] *The Chronicle of Iohn Hardyng*, ed. Henry Ellis (London, 1812), p. 146. See below, p. 21–2.

[3] See K. H. Jackson, 'The Arthur of History', in *ALMA*, pp. 1–11. The most elaborate case for a 'historical Arthur' is made by Leslie Alcock, *Arthur's Britain. History and Archaeology, A.D. 367–634* (London, 1971). A quite different view can be found in David N. Dumville, 'Sub-Roman Britain: History and Legend', *History* 62 (1977), 173–92.

plausible explanations for this development in literary taste. The establishment of a national myth, particularly one which in some ways legitimated the usurpation of Anglo-Saxon institutions, was clearly desirable for the grandchildren of the knights – 'pirates, the sons of pirates' – who had won the day at Hastings. There is some parallel here, however inexact, with the cultivation of the supposed 'Tudor myth' in a later century. It will not do, however, to torture the texts too cruelly with modern historical 'methodology'. Many in the Middle Ages made no great distinction between the truths of the poets and those of the chroniclers, and saw both the prosaic *memorabilia* of Livy or Orosius and the more remarkable events of sacred and secular legend in a similar light.[4] The city fathers of Chaucer's London called their town 'Trinovant', 'New Troy', and they assiduously cultivated the belief that the cultural traditions and high destiny of the ancient city, and the *pietas*, the sense of respect and duty it deserved, had through the *translatio studii* become their birthright.[5] We shall find the same idea expressed poetically in the opening lines of *Sir Gawain and the Green Knight*.

We need to keep this flexible attitude towards history in mind as we turn to the real father of the medieval Arthurian legend, Geoffrey of Monmouth.[6] Geoffrey's origins are obscure. We may guess that he was born around the year 1100; but although he is called 'of Monmouth', it is not certain that he was a Welshman. His father's name was Arthur, a name (like his own) rare in Wales but fairly common in Brittany. Whether Geoffrey was Briton or Breton, his public career was not associated with any Celtic land, but with Oxford in England, where he was a clerk and, possibly, a teacher in a monastic school. It was at Oxford that he came into contact with the archdeacon Walter, from whom he claims to have had 'a most ancient book in the British tongue' which he translated into Latin. This Latin book came to be known as the *Historia Regum Britanniae*, or *The History of the Kings of Britain*.

Readers from Geoffrey's own time down to this have been unsure what to make of the *Historia*. Did Geoffrey believe uncritically in the story of Arthur as he wrote it? Was he the creator of an essentially literary work? Or did he, as some have suggested, deliberately introduce legendary and fabulous elements among the more sober

---

[4]   Not all medieval historians were so undiscriminating, least of all William of Newburgh, whose attack on Geoffrey of Monmouth's *History* and his account of Arthur has been described as 'a masterly piece of destructive historical criticism': P. G. Walsh and M. J. Kennedy (ed.) *William of Newburgh: The History of English Affairs*, Book I (Warminster, 1988), pp. 6–8, 28–37.

[5]   D. W. Robertson, *Chaucer's London* (New York, 1968), p. 2.

[6]   See J. J. Parry and R. A. Caldwell, 'Geoffrey of Monmouth', *ALMA*, pp. 72–93; the most thorough study of Geoffrey is J. S. P. Tatlock, *The Legendary History of Britain* (Berkeley and Los Angeles, 1950). Christopher Dean, *Arthur of England* (Toronto, 1987), pp. 3–31, surveys the tradition of Arthurian historiography begun by Geoffrey.

historical 'facts', for purposes of parody or propaganda? Central to these concerns is the 'ancient book' which Geoffrey claimed to have translated. Many Arthurian scholars, believing that all or nearly all of the important features of the Matter of Britain reflect lost or transformed Celtic 'sources', have taken this claim more or less at its face value. My own opinion is that we shall find the Celtic 'original' of Geoffrey's British history when we find the Latin 'Lollius' whom Chaucer affects to follow in *Troilus and Criseyde* – which is to say never.[7] The appeal to a fictive authority is an ancient and honourable device, and one frequently employed in a literary climate in which what we call plagiarism was a high form of compliment. Geoffrey *did* have sources, of course. Some of them, such as Gildas and Bede, he names; others he plunders silently. And he almost certainly would indeed have had, from Walter or otherwise, old Welsh tales and songs. Yet what emerged in the *Historia Regum Britanniae* was in no familiar sense of the word a 'translation', but a triumph of the scholarly imagination. The book is a history of British antiquity which includes fabulous topographies and genealogies and some of the most enduring features of the 'British myth' as they were devoutly believed by Englishmen until at least the time of Henry VIII. It also included the fabulous journey of Brutus and the founding of 'Trinovant', later to be London, but its rhetorical and narrative centre-pieces are its stories of Merlin and of Arthur, son of Uther Pendragon, great warrior, mighty conqueror.

The importance of the *Historia Regum* for the development of the Arthurian legend in literature would be difficult to exaggerate; Tatlock rightly calls it 'one of the most influential books ever written, certainly one of the most influential of the Middle Ages'.[8] But although he launched the Matter of Britain into the stream of international courtly literature, Geoffrey said nothing at all about the Round Table itself. In the *Historia* King Arthur's court is the gathering place of chivalric celebrities from many lands; its atmosphere is reminiscent of that in *Culhwch and Olwen* in the *Mabinogion*. Geoffrey clearly went to some trouble in scouring genealogies for plausible names for his knights, yet for anything the author tells us we could assume that when they sat down to eat they did so at a rectangular table. For the first clear statement that matters were otherwise, we must turn to another clerical historian, Wace of Jersey, Geoffrey's contemporary admirer and popularizer.

---

[7] Recent scholarly opinion, while generally rejecting the idea that Geoffrey's work is simply a translation, ranges from those who believe that the 'ancient book' was a sheer fabrication (Valerie I. J. Flint, 'The *Historia Regum Britanniae* of Geoffrey of Monmouth', *Speculum* 54 (1979), 447–68) to supporters of the theory that there was a source, now lost, for the Arthurian material (Geoffrey Ashe, "A Certain Very Ancient Book": Traces of An Arthurian Source in Geoffrey of Monmouth's *History*', *Speculum* 56 (1981), 301–23.

[8] Tatlock, *Legendary History*, p. 4.

The life of Wace is also very sketchy, although he has left some solid autobiographical evidence in his *Roman de Rou*, a verse chronicle of the dukes of Normandy.[9] He was born in Jersey and removed as a lad to Caen, where he studied 'letters', which almost certainly means the grammar of a monastic school. He travelled in the Île de France and perhaps also to the West Country of England, of which he seems to reveal some close knowledge; but his religious and literary careers belong to the Norman mainland. He wrote some hagiographical works in *romanz*, as well as the two 'historical' books for which he is better known. Wace is a poet of some considerable if self-advertised accomplishment, and his 'translation' into French of Geoffrey's *Historia*, usually called the *Roman de Brut*, or simply *Brut*, seems totally to have supplanted the translation which had been undertaken by a certain Gaimar in the 1140s.

Wace's *Brut* was finished in 1155, the year in which Geoffrey of Monmouth died. The 'translation' of the *Historia* into vernacular poetic form would have been an important stage in the development of the Arthurian legend under any circumstances; but Wace made certain positive original contributions himself which make his work even more remarkable. The most important of these was the Round Table, which he mentions by name three times. 'Fist Artur la Roünde Table', writes Wace, 'Dunt Bretun dient mainte fable'. Thus the Round Table appears for the first time in surviving literary tradition. It may be useful to have the relevant passages before our eyes:

> Pur les nobles baruns qu'il out,
> Dunt chescuns mieldre estre quidout,
> Chescuns se teneit al meillur,
> Ne nuls n'en saveit le peiur,
> Fist Artur la Roünde Table
> Dunt Bretun dient mainte fable.
> Illuec seeient li vassal
> Tuit chevalment e tuit egal;
> A la table egalment seeient
> E egalment servi esteient;
> Nul d'els ne se poeit vanter
> Qu'il seiüst plus halt de sun per,
> Tuit esteient assis meain,
> Ne n'i aveit nul de forain. (lines 9747–60)

---

[9] See Charles Foulon, 'Wace', *ALMA*, pp. 94–103.

De cels ki en la curt serveient
Ki des privez le rei esteient,
Ki sunt de la Roünde Table,
Ne vuil jo mie faire fable. (lines 10283–5)

Dunc peri la bele juvente
Que Arthur aveit grant nurrie
E de plusurs terres cuillie,
E cil de la Table Roünde
Dunt tel los ert par tut le munde. (lines 13266–70)[10]

Because of these noble lords about his hall, of whom each held himself to be the best, and none would count himself the least praiseworthy, Arthur made the Round Table, concerning which the Bretons tell many stories. This Round Table was ordained of Arthur that when his fair fellowship sat to meat their chairs should be high alike, their service equal, and none before or after his comrade. Thus no man could boast that he was exalted above his fellow, for all were seated alike, and there was none outside. . .

[... of such knights as were of the king's house] and served him about his court, who were his chosen friends, who are of the Round Table, of those I cannot tell more. . .

There perished the comely young whom Arthur had nourished and gathered from so many lands, and those knights of the Table Round, whose praise had rung through all the world.[11]

In the literary and historical documents of the twelfth and thirteenth centuries we shall find three quite separate if cognate meanings for the term 'round table'. Two of them appear in the passages in the *Brut*. The literal sense of the term, a dining board, is the one which most sharply engages the attention of this study. It is clearly an actual table, a piece of furniture, which, according to Wace, Arthur made or had made. Yet this meaning, which we may regard as the simplest the term could bear, is also demonstrably the rarest in Arthurian texts. The second and much more common meaning of 'round table' appears in the next two citations from the *Brut*. Here the Round Table means the *chivalric institution* established by Arthur, his circle of knights. Its numbers vary – fifty, one hundred, one hundred and fifty, 'sixteen hundred and

---

[10] Wace, *Le Roman de Brut*, ed. I. Arnold, 2 vols. (Paris, 1938–40).

[11] Translation adapted from Eugene Mason, *Wace and Layamon: Arthurian Chronicles* (London, 1912; repr. 1996), pp. 55, 64, 113.

more' according to Layamon – but it is always as it were an order or society to which the valorous and the noble are chosen or appointed. In the romances of the Matter of Britain, the idea of the Round Table thus conceived provides the context for a hundred different tales; and, with its internal divisions, the fellowship of the Round Table often becomes the arena of poignant tragedy. There is a third meaning, absent from Wace's *Brut* but found easily enough in the later romances and in descriptions of actual chivalric ceremonies alike. Here 'round table' means a formal chivalric meeting. In the romances King Arthur 'holds' Round Table at Whitsun with tourneys and jousts and the expectation, rarely disappointed, of strange adventures.

The fictional chivalric 'meets' of Arthurian romance were imitated in real life in the courtly gatherings called in Latin '*tabula rotunda*', and it has frequently and plausibly been suggested that the Winchester table may have been constructed in connection with some such festivities. We can easily enough find Arthurian and other literary inspiration behind a wide range of chivalric entertainments – tournaments, pageants, feasts, regal epiphanies – which ranged in their ambition from the relatively simple to the sumptuous court masques of the Renaissance.[12] Jean I of Beirut, on the occasion of the dubbing of his two sons in Cyprus in 1223, threw a grand fête, notable for its lavishness, the sumptuous dispensation of gifts, and the re-enactment of Arthur's adventures.[13] Walter of Guisborough reports, without elaboration, that in 1281 'a Round Table was held magnificently at Warwick'.[14]

Such references are sufficiently numerous to suggest the relative frequency of such theatrical 'round tables', but they are also unfortunately too laconic to give the phrase a very specific meaning. That it had specific and defining characteristics seems clear from the report in the *Abbrevatio chronicorum Angliae* of the unfortunate death in 1252 of Sir Ernald of Munteinni, 'not in that jousting called a tournament, but rather in that military sport known as the round table'.[15] Yet other writers use

---

[12] See Lewis F. Mott, 'The Round Table', *PMLA*, 20 (1905), 231–65, and Roger Sherman Loomis, 'Arthurian Influence on Sport and Spectacle', *ALMA*, pp. 553–9.

[13] Philippe de Novare, *Mémoires, 1218–1243*, ed. C. Kohler, Classiques françaises du moyen âge 10 (Paris, 1913), p. 7.

[14] 'Eodem anno tabula rotunda tenebatur sumptuose apud Warewick': *The Chronicle of Walter of Guisborough*, ed. Harry Rothwell, Camden Society 3rd ser. 99 (London, 1957), p. 218; and see further below, Ch. 10. The chronicler was formerly known as Walter of Hemingford or Hemingbrugh.

[15] '... non ut in hastiludio, quod Torneamentum dicitur, sed potius in illo ludo militari, qui Mensa Rotunda dicitur': *Matthaei Parisiensis ... Monachi Sancti Albani Historia Angliae*, ed. F. Madden, Rolls Series 44, pt. 3, (London, 1869), p. 124; cited by Mott, 'Round Table', p. 237. For further examples see Hermann Reichert, 'King Arthur's Round Table: sociological implications of its literary reception in Scandanavia,' in *Structure and Meaning in Old Norse Literature*, ed. John Lindow, Lars Löggroth, and Gerd Wolfgang Weber (Odense University Press, 1986), pp. 403–4.

the term to denote not merely the military games, but also the social and ceremonial setting in which they took place. To 'hold Round Table' thus meant to put on a show, to remember, almost in sacramental imitation, a glorious chivalric past in order to make its energies immediate and relevant to a needy present. Nor is it improper to insist on a certain confusion, or overlay, of secular and religious ideas in the Arthurian myth, for it is precisely this confusion which gives the myth its particular richness and glory.

To create a convincingly Arthurian atmosphere, the medieval Round Tables almost certainly involved a more or less elaborate *mise en scène*, with stage settings, costumes, and 'props' of various kinds, including round tables. That the Winchester Round Table is such a stage property from a chivalric *tabula rotunda* of the Plantagenet era, decorated at a considerably later time in an antiquarian style and in a spirit of veneration, sincere or politic, is an attractive possibility.[16]

But what of the Round Table at its first literary appearance, in the pages of the *Brut?* The salient features concerning the institution of the Round Table would seem to be four, according to Wace. It was in the first place an actual table. Secondly, Arthur himself made it or had it made (as *fist* could also be taken to mean). Furthermore, the clearly implied motive for the table's construction was to avoid problems of protocol in seating a group of knights 'each of whom held himself to be the best'. A final point is that the table was already well known in Breton story at the time Wace wrote.

Concerning Wace's testimony there have been, broadly speaking, two opinions; the first honours his veracity, the other his poetic inventiveness. Professor Loomis and others who give credit to the literal statement that 'the Bretons tell many stories [about the Round Table]' find in it clear evidence of an ancient Celtic oral tradition in which, to a greater or lesser degree, the legend of the Round Table was already formed.[17] They point out that, on the whole, Wace follows his written source (Geoffrey's *Historia Regum*) closely and even scrupulously. Furthermore, the rest of his

[16] As suggested, for example, by E. K. Chambers, *Arthur of Britain* (London, 1927; repr. Cambridge, 1964), pp. 131–2; Roger Sherman Loomis and Laura Hibbard Loomis, *Arthurian Legends in Medieval Art* (London and New York, 1938), pp. 40–1. The excellent article in Du Cange, *Glossarium* (Paris, 1678, and later edns.), under the heading 'Tabula, seu Mensa Rotunda', includes evidence about the Winchester table used elsewhere in the present book, especially in Chapters 10 and 11. For other examples of round tables, depicted or extant, see Chapter 2.

[17] Loomis's theory of the development of the Round Table motif is most succinctly outlined in *Arthurian Tradition and Chrétien de Troyes* (New York, 1949), pp. 61–70. On the question of Celtic origins see also A. C. L. Brown, *The Round Table Before Wace*, [Harvard] Studies and Notes in Philology 7 (1900), pp. 183–205; James Douglas Bruce, *The Evolution of Arthurian Romance from the Beginnings down to the Year 1300* (Göttingen, 1928), i, p. 82 *et seq.*; and Tatlock, *Legendary History*, pp. 471–5.

known *oeuvre*, the hagiographic poems and the *Roman de Rou*, are the works of an historian rather than a novelist. Although Geoffrey of Monmouth says nothing about the Round Table, he, too, strongly suggests that he is working from ancient Celtic tales — Wace's *fables*, perhaps, among them. The idea of a Celtic source for the Round Table, furthermore, is consistent with the motive which Wace attributes to Arthur at its institution, for it accords, in a general way, with the Celtic 'analogues' which have been suggested.

This theory may be correct, but I must say that I doubt it. The supposition of a Celtic source is neither necessary nor, to my mind, compelling; and in particular I see little to recommend Loomis's conclusion that the Round Table 'originated in the Celtic seating arrangement in a banquet hall — a king on his couch, with twelve warriors on their couches around him'.[18]

The possibility that Wace, who *was* after all a poet, has made, with his idea of the Round Table, a significant poetic invention seems to me no less implausible. Thirty-five years ago, however, a French scholar, M. Delbouille, developed a rather ingenious middle position, according to which Wace, while actually inventing the Round Table, *thought* he was following Geoffrey of Monmouth.[19] Delbouille's argument rests on a technical point. Geoffrey's *Historia* was circulated in distinctly variant versions, and it is possible that a phrase in the text which Wace probably studied (*coepit familiam suam augmentare tantamque facetiam in domo sua habere,* **ut emulationes longe positis populis ingereret,** '[Arthur] began to enlarge his company and to develop such a code of courtliness in his household that he inspired some even among those peoples living far away to imitate him') may have suggested to him, on a mistaken quick reading, the idea of 'the envy of those who sat at a distance from the king'. This is a witty suggestion, and there is a certain wry satisfaction to be got from the possibility that the Round Table is simply a marvellous mistake, a schoolboy's howler like Cinderella's glass slippers.

It is only fair to say, since I have confessed scepticism about Celtic origins, that the motive implied by Wace and possibly by Geoffrey himself — to obviate the quarrelsome jealousies of a court of temperamental barons — is indeed a plausible one in the light of early literary tradition. But the motif of the quarrelsome court will be found not merely in the Celtic analogues adduced by Loomis and others, but also in the classical epic tradition. There is a hint of it in Old English literature in the slanging match between Brecca and Beowulf, and much more than a hint in Layamon's *Brut*.

---

[18] Loomis, *Arthurian Tradition*, p. 66.
[19] M. Delbouille, 'La legende arthurienne', *Romania* 74 (1953), 185 *et seq.*.

Layamon was an English poet who, around the year 1200, set out to do for Wace what Wace had done in his time for Geoffrey of Monmouth. In 'translating' the French work into English, Layamon doubled its length, partly by means of remorseless rhetorical puffing, and partly by means of major narrative additions to the plot. One such addition explains that the Round Table was made by a Cornish carpenter as the direct result of a serious quarrel over seating precedence which broke out at Arthur's Christmas feast.[20] Many scholars believe that the story told by Layamon is one of the Breton *fables* alluded to by Wace. Layamon's *Brut* cannot have been a very influential poem, for it has survived in only two manuscripts. It does, however, show that there was an English-speaking audience for the Matter of Britain at an early date; and some of its narrative details — important action set in Winchester, for example — are conceivably of specific relevance to the Winchester table.

Unfortunately, neither in the *Brut* of Wace nor in that of Layamon do we find the detail which might suggest what the Round Table actually looked like. Their statements, scanty though they be, were certainly enough to nourish the imaginations of a later generation of romancers. But if we ask ourselves precisely what sort of a round table Wace imagined, or might have expected his readers and imitators to visualize, the answer is by no means easy. His statement that 'all were seated alike, and there was none outside' is actually rather cryptic. Layamon's attempt to render that idea into English makes particularly heavy weather of it:

> 'Al turn abuten.
> þat nan ne beon wið-uten
> wið-uten and wið-inne
> mo to-ȝaeines monne'.[21]

Layamon offers two other suggestions about the physical nature of the table, neither of them particularly helpful. The first, already mentioned, is that the table accommodates upwards of 1600 knights. The second is that it is portable; Arthur takes it with him wherever he goes. This notion, as implausible as it may strike us, would have seemed less remarkable to a medieval audience, for most medieval tables were, in a quite literal sense, 'boards' set up on trestles and removed when not actu-

---

[20] *Brut*, ed. G. L. Brook and R. F. Leslie, EETS (I, [no. 250], 1963; II [no. 277], 1978), lines 11345–11421, pp. 593–6, II, p. 597. See Loomis, 'Layamon's *Brut*,' *ALMA*, p. 109. Elizabeth J. Bryan ('Truth and the Round Table in Lawman's *Brut*,' *Quondam et futurus*, 2 (1992), no. 4, 27–35), suggests that in the notorious imprecision of Layamon's language, which implies but does not state that the table is *round*, we find already a blurring Arthur's table with that of the Last Supper (see below).

[21] *Brut*, ed. Brook and Leslie, lines 11435–6 (II, p. 596).

ally in use.[22] Stationary tables were sufficiently remarkable to command a special Middle English word, 'table-dormant'. Chaucer's Franklin kept one in his hall.[23]

Wace's importance is not merely that of the historical pioneer. His *Brut* was widely read and widely admired. From it the greatest of all Arthurian romancers, Chrétien de Troyes, may have learned what he knew of the Round Table. Yet if in Chrétien's magnificent poems we begin to see the fuller dramatic and psychological possibilities of the flawed fellowship of Arthur's knights, we shall still not find the more remarkable features of the legend of the table itself, through which the energies of a secular, regal myth were joined to those of sacred history.

The idea of a circular table around which a high and solemn fellowship gathered, however striking or novel it may have been in the courtly literature of the twelfth century, had one obvious precedent in sacred history and iconography. By widespread and ancient tradition, medieval Christian artists often imagined the table of the Last Supper, at which Christ had instituted the great sacrament of the Eucharist, as circular in form (Fig. 3). In the most important historical and iconographic essay yet published on the motif of the Round Table Beate Schmolke-Hasselmann has summarized both the arguments that have been used to make a connection between 'secular' and 'sacred' round table and those advanced to deny it.[24] The Last Supper was a topic widely illustrated in a variety of media, but especially in illuminated gospel books. Furthermore, the dramatic situation of the Last Supper has some affinities with that suggested, for example, by Wace's treatment of the Round Table; for it includes an argument (*contentio*) among the disciples as to 'which of them should be accounted the greatest' (Luke 22:24). It is not necessary to agree with Mrs Loomis's suggestion that

---

[22] See Alwin Schultz, *Das höfische Leben zur Zeit der Minnesinger* (Leipzig, 1889), i, pp. 80, 432. The table's portability seems already in the early thirteenth century to be a subject of levity in the *Parzifal* of Wolfram von Eschenbach (6.309), where it is perhaps a lace tablecloth!

[23] Geoffrey Chaucer, *The Canterbury Tales*, General Prologue, in *The Works of Geoffrey Chaucer*, ed. F. N. Robinson, 2nd edn. (London, 1957), p. 20, line 353.

[24] Beate Schmolke-Hasselmann, 'The Round Table: Ideal, Fiction, Reality', *Arthurian Literature*, 2 (1982), 41–75. The chief early proponent of a theory of 'Christian origins' was Laura Hibbard [Loomis]. Schmolke-Hasselmann cites with approval the refutation of Hibbard's work by Hildegard Eberlein-Westhues, 'König Arthurs "Table ronde". Studien zur Geschichte eines lieterarischen Herrschaftszeichen', in *Der Altfranzösische Prosaroman: Funktion, Funtionswandel und Ideologie am Beispiel des Roman de Tristan en prose*, ed. Ernstpeter Ruhe and Richard Schwaderer (Munich, 1979), 184–269. Though Eberlein-Westhues does correct important aspects of Hibbard's argument, her essay cannot, in my opinion, convincingly deny a probably conscious ideographic connection between the Arthurian and Grail tables in writers anterior to Robert de Boron. Schmolke-Hasselmann's admirable essay also provides an excellent bibliography and an important dossier of visual illustrations. Another important iconographic essay is that of Emmanuèle Baumgartner, 'La couronne et le cercle: Arthur et la Table Ronde dans les manuscrits du Lancelot-Graal,' in *Texte et Image* [Actes du Colloque internationale de Chantilly, 13 au 15 octobre 1982], (Paris, 1984), 191–200.

the table of the Last Supper provided a positive *source* for the Round Table of Arthurian tradition – it could indeed have had its origin in a discrete tradition, Celtic or otherwise – to see the importance of the connection. For if we set aside the question of ultimate origins, fascinating to the early giants of Arthurian study but tangential to our topic, there is no question but that in the thirteenth century writers of romance clearly thought of Arthur's table and the table of the Lord as similar if not identical objects, and those who illustrated these works, then and later, emphasized this association visually (Plate I, Figs. 1–2). This tradition passed through the so-called 'Vulgate cycle' of Grail romances and came, eventually, to Malory. It was the tradition accepted and transmitted by the chronicler Hardyng, our first witness to the Winchester table. So far as surviving evidence would indicate, this tradition begins at the turn of the twelfth and thirteenth centuries with the Burgundian poet Robert de Boron.[25]

Robert de Boron wrote a trilogy of poems about the history of the Holy Grail, the cup used by Christ at the Last Supper. Only one of these three works, sometimes called *Joseph d'Arimathie* and sometimes the *Roman de l'estoire dou Graal*, has survived in a complete poetic text. The two others, *Perceval*, which has been entirely lost, and *Merlin*, of which a major fragment has perished, are nonetheless known through their contemporary prose redactions.

These texts have presented philologists and literary historians with a particularly rich repertory of interpretive problems, not all of which have by any means been solved to the general satisfaction of modern Arthurian scholars; but even in their imperfect and problematic state they show clearly enough that Robert de Boron deserves the credit, or perhaps the blame, for the very complex religious associations which the Round Table attracts in the romances of the thirteenth century. In Robert's work, indeed, three quite distinct tables merge in a fruitful but unresolved poetic suggestion: the actual round table of Arthur's court, the table of the Last Supper, and the table of the Holy Grail.[26] And it was Robert who apparently introduced two special features of the Round Table which are of particular importance to the Winchester table, the *siège perilleux* and the magical writing of the knights' names.

The *Estoire dou Graal*, although its subject matter is really the fabulous history of Joseph of Arimathea, the supposed evangelist of Britain, begins with the scriptural evocation of the institution of the Eucharistic sacrament at the Last Supper. On divine instruction, Joseph sets out to find a table *like* that of the Last Supper. There he is to establish Bron, the Fisher King, next to his own seat, and to set down the

---

[25] See Pierre le Gentil, 'The Work of Robert de Boron and the *Didot Perceval*', *ALMA*, pp. 251–62.

[26] See A. Micha, 'La table ronde chez Robert de Boron et dans la "Queste del Saint Graal"', in R. Nelli (ed.), *Lumière du Graal* (Paris, 1951), pp. 119–33, an admirable article. See further Ginna L. Greco, 'From the Last Supper to the Arthurian Feast: *Translatio* and the Round Table,' *Modern Philology*, 96 (1998), 42–7.

Grail itself. One of the relevant features of this Grail table is that it has thirteen places, one of which is kept vacant in memory of the defection of Judas. Later, Joseph entrusts the Grail 'and all' to Bron, who takes it away to the West, where we shall find it again in the romance known as *Perlesvaus*.[27]

It is in the romance of *Merlin* that Robert de Boron gives his account, or rather his accounts, of the establishment of Arthur's Round Table; accounts which ascribe to this table supernatural features associated with the table of the Last Supper and the table of the Grail. As Alexandre Micha has written, the Round Table of Robert de Boron shares nothing with Wace's table but the name.[28] It is Merlin, not Arthur, who makes or commissions the table for King Uther. Throughout the course of the work, its size and composition vary; but at its inception it has fifty-two places – a seat for the king, seats for fifty knights, and a vacant 'Judas seat'. In the latter section of the *Merlin* there is what could be called a revised history of the institution of the table. The scene is an extraordinary one, rich with a density of imaginative detail which is the peculiar joy of Robert de Boron's narrative at its best. The Round Table has been reduced by battle to a hundred knights, and Arthur commands Merlin to appoint fifty new ones to bring it up to full complement. Merlin chooses forty-eight new knights, leaving one space for the king and another, vacant, as the Judas seat. Here the Judas seat has become the *siège perilleux*, the dangerous seat. No one must sit in it until the chosen one comes, 'that most excellent knight who will bring to completion the most marvellous adventures of the Kingdom of Logres'. In the Didot *Perceval*, the prose redaction of Robert's lost poem on this theme, it is Perceval who occupies the seat, and with unhappy results. In the *Queste del Saint Graal*, another version of the story, it is Galahad who claims the seat, mysteriously prepared for him by divine decree.[28a]

The institution of the table in the *Merlin* has deeply religious, nearly sacramental overtones. Merlin introduces the new knights to their more experienced brethren, and calls in the 'bishops and archbishops' for the blessing of the company. The knights exchange a kiss of peace. Then, as each knight rises to do homage to Arthur, Merlin sees that the name of each appears miraculously written at his seat – a sign which confirms the divine pleasure at the establishment of the Round Table.[29]

The pseudo-sacramentalism of the Grail legend gained a very wide audience indeed through the stories of the Vulgate cycle, and particularly through the *Queste*

---

[27] Loomis, *Arthurian Tradition*, pp. 63–4.

[28] Micha, 'La Table Ronde', p. 120.

[28a] On this motif see Liliane Dulac, 'L'épreuve du siège vide: equisse d'une lecture croisée d'un épisode du *Joseph* et du *Merlin* de Robert de Boron,' in *Rewards and Punishments in the Arthurian Romances and Lyric Poetry of Mediaeval France: Essays Presented to Kenneth Varty*, ed. Peter V. Davies and Angus J. Kennedy (Cambridge, 1987) esp. pp. 32–4.

[29] *Merlin, roman en prose du xiiiᵉ siècle*, ed. Gaston Paris and Jacob Ulrich (Paris, 1886), ii, pp. 66–7.

1 The 'Round' Table and the Holy Grail with Galahad in the Siege Perilous. French, 1463

2 Arthur feasting at the Round Table. French, 1488

3 The Last Supper. Scriptorium of the Holy Sepulchre, Jerusalem, *c.*1135.

del Saint Graal, a marvellous work of the early thirteenth century, written under the influence of a profound Cistercian spirituality, in which the energies of the Matter of Britain were masterfully bent to the purposes of Christian allegory. In that great prose romance there is an explicit statement of the sacred origins of the Round Table. An anchoress explains to Perceval:

> You are well aware that the world has seen three great tables. The first was the Table of Jesus Christ, where the apostles often ate. ... After that table there was another built like it and in remembrance of it. That was the table of the Holy Grail. ... After that table there was the Round Table built by Merlin, which was not established without a high spiritual meaning. That it is called 'The Round Table' suggests the roundness of the earth, the spheres of the planets, and the elements of the firmament ... so that one can justly say that the Round Table means the world.[30]

It was from this French source that Malory would build 'th'istory of the Sancgreal ... whiche is a story chronycled for one of the truest and the holyest that is in thys world'.[31]

There was already in the fourteenth century an elaborate iconography of Arthurian materials in ivory carving, ceramics, textiles, mural painting, and, above all, book illustration.[32] The decorator of the Winchester table would almost certainly have been familiar with at least certain features of that iconographic tradition, and there are three features of what might be called the 'standard' illustration of the Grail legend in particular which are of specific relevance to the Winchester table. The first of these, already discussed, is the round shape of the table. Second, there is the detail of the inscribed names. Finally, there is an iconographic detail which has no basis in the text itself, the canopy over the *siège perilleux*. A fine late fourteenth-century manuscript of the *Queste* in the National Library of France (Plate II) suggests the obvious analogies of conception in the illustration of the Grail legend and the decoration of the Winchester table.

The French romances of the Vulgate cycle – the 'certeyn bookes of Frensshe' of which Caxton speaks – bring us back to England and to the *Morte Darthur* of Thomas Malory, although in this instance it will be a disappointing homecoming. There is, however, one intermediary step to be taken, and that is to examine the testimony of the chronicler John Hardyng, our first recorded witness to the existence of the

---

[30] *La Queste del Saint Graal*, ed. Albert Pauphilet (Paris, 1975), pp. 74–6.

[31] *Caxton's Malory*, as above, note 1, p. 505, lines 31–33.

[32] See Loomis and Loomis, *Arthurian Legends in Medieval Art*, as above, note 16, and Muriel Whitaker, *Legends of King Arthur in Art*, (Woodbridge, 1990).

Winchester table. 'At Wynchestre beganne' the Round Table, he writes; 'And ther it ende, and ther it hangeth yet'.[33]

In a single sentence Hardyng uses the term 'round table' in two of its three different senses. The table which 'beganne and ... ende' is, clearly enough, the chivalric institution; that which there 'hangeth yet' is equally clearly the physical relic which is the object of our study. That it was already *hanging* on display as an object of antiquity and curiosity, clearly implied in the lines, is full of suggestion, although we may wish that the chronicler had said something of its decoration. Perhaps vague suggestion is all that Hardyng has to offer our investigation, but I think there may be more. In the first place, Hardyng may have had a quite particular reason for an interest in the antiquities of Winchester and their association with the heroic and kingly figure of Arthur (see below, pp. 394–5, 417–18). In this regard it is of interest that his chronicle, more than that of any other historian of his age, owes much to romance materials.[34] Moreover, he has something more to say about the Round Table than simply to connect it with Winchester: he follows the tradition of Robert of Boron's *Estoire dou Graal* in connecting the table with Joseph of Arimathea.[35] We may probably assume that the romance history which Hardyng brings to the table would have been familiar to many others in the fifteenth century, and later.

A similar intervention of literary expectation almost certainly accounts for the confusing and tantalizing statements of Diego de Vera, a Spanish historian who described the table in the course of an account of the royal marriage of Mary Tudor and Philip II of Spain at Winchester in 1554. He reported that the table was made up of twenty-five compartments painted in green and white, meeting in a point in the centre, and increasing in size towards the circumference, and that in each part was written the name of the knight, and of the king.[36] Diego de Vera, who worked under the patronage of Cardinal Sandoval, archbishop of Toledo in the mid seventeenth century, cannot have seen the table himself. He could have, and apparently did, read the Vulgate cycle romances.[37]

The debt of the Winchester table to medieval literary tradition, although unambiguous, is of a general and derivative nature, and it has not been possible for me to

---

[33] Ellis, *Chronicle of Iohn Hardyng*, p. 146. See below, pp. 393–5.

[34] Robert H. Fletcher, *The Arthurian Material in the Chronicles* (Boston, 1906), p. 251.

[35] Ellis, *Chronicle of Iohn Hardyng*, p. 120.

[36] 'Epítome cronológico, real, y universal de todos los imperios y monarquías del mundo desde el primer instante del tiempo hasta el año de 1650 de nuestra salud', Madrid, Biblioteca Nacional, MS. 1300, fol. 237v. On Diego de Vera and the comparable description by Julian del Castillo, see below, Chapter 14.

[37] See Charles B. Millican, *Spenser and the Table Round: A Study in the Contemporary Background for Spenser's Use of the Arthurian Legend* (Cambridge, Mass., 1932), p. 36 and p. 162, n. 98.

identify a single specific literary 'source' for the particular assembly of knights whom the table honours. For purposes of poetic justice the source of the table's inspiration *should* be Sir Thomas Malory, the fifteenth-century editor, translator, and remaker of the disparate works of French Arthuriana in circulation in his day. The unique manuscript of the *Morte Darthur*, the classic English expression of the Arthurian myth, was found, seventy years ago, in the library of Winchester College, a short walk from the Great Hall where the table hangs. Its discovery was, indeed, perhaps the greatest literary 'find' of the century, and one would especially welcome a demonstration of its relevance to our artefact (see below, pp. 278–9, 282).

The inscriptions and iconography of the Winchester table are dealt with in Chapters 8 and 9; I shall concern myself here only with certain possible connections between the table's decoration and specific literary traditions. Even a superficial discussion of the list of knights as it appears on the table today, however, must begin with an admission that conclusions drawn from its lexical and calligraphic features must be tentative. This is so for two reasons. In the first place it seems unlikely that William Cave and his son William junior, who repainted the table in 1789, were fully confident in their use of the inscriptional black-letter. Even less likely is it that they had an independent knowledge of the variations and peculiarities of Arthurian proper names. Second, the testimony of modern written and pictorial evidence, which begins with John Aubrey in the 1670s and the engraving by Benning after a drawing of 1743 (Fig. 120), and extends to the line engraving published by the Winchester Archaeological Congress of 1845 (Fig. 165) is never wholly reliable and often becomes something of a game of visual Chinese whispers. For example, the reading 'Sater' (Name 15; see below Table 15), reproduced in all the modern illustrations of the Winchester table, is a mistake obvious to anyone at all familiar with the Arthurian legend, and almost certainly never appeared on the table.[38]

Even so, peculiar forms of the names of certain of the knights have been very scrupulously preserved through the repainting. The spelling 'Galahallt' (Name 1), in particular, is remarkable and almost certainly reflects a reliance, in this specific instance, on Malory. Loomis, who made many acute observations about the table, thought that 'Malory was the source of most of the names, as we should expect'.[39] I think this goes too far. In fact, neither in their number nor in their particular grouping do the knights of the Winchester table reflect a single, specific literary debt.

[38] The early records of the inscriptions and their evidence are discussed in Chapter 8.
[39] Loomis and Loomis, *Arthurian Legends in Medieval Art*, as above, n. 16, p. 41.

'This is the rownde table of kyng Arthur with xxiiii of his namyde knyttes'. The wording of the inscription at the centre of the table, particularly the word 'namyde', is a little odd, but there seems to be no claim that twenty-four is either the total number of Arthur's knights or the total capacity of the Round Table – merely that this table manifests 'named' knights to that number. It is possible to provide from Celtic tradition a precedent, or at least an analogue, for the twenty-four knights;[40] and there is at least one place in the *Morte Darthur* where that number make up the table.[41] This is hardly a literary tradition, however, and in no major branch of the Arthurian legend will we find the institution of a table of twenty-four. Given the relationship between the idea of the Round Table, if not the Winchester table itself, and the founding of the Order of the Garter, it is worth noting that in Edward III's letters patent for the endowment of St George's Chapel, Windsor, monies are provided for 'twenty-four poor knights'.[42] Finally, of course, it has to be said that the twenty-five places at the Winchester table more or less exhaust the actual seating space at a table of this size. The illustrator of the *Queste del Saint Graal* (Plate II) imagined a banquet of about the same size, perhaps slightly smaller.

One must be equally inconclusive about the actual roster of knights. The decorator began, working clockwise from the figure of the king, with the 'stars' of Arthurian romance, Galahad, Launcelot, Gawain, Percival, Lionel, Tristram, and Gareth. Most of these names were literally 'household words', for they actually appear as given Christian names among the more avant-garde members of the aristocracy. Beginning at least with 'plomyd' (Name 12), however, the list becomes more eclectic, although it never abandons major *dramatis personae*. Given the vast riches of Arthurian pedigree, the list is a very conservative one.

Two of the knights offer special problems, Sir Degore (Name 20) and Sir Lybyus Dysconyus (Name 22). There is indeed a hero of a Middle English romance named Degore, but he appears nowhere in connection with King Arthur. That he should be given a seat at the Round Table is, therefore, peculiar. It is possible that the name Degore does not refer to our English hero at all, but is an ellipsis for one of the many Arthurian knights known as 'de Gorre', that is, 'from the land of Gorre' (but see below, p. 280). Sir Lybyus Dysconyus, the happy child of calligraphic error, has long been the mystery knight of the table. This is fitting, since that is precisely

---

[40] Anon., 'Arthur and his Knights', *Archaeologia Cambrensis* 1 (1846), 48–9.

[41] *The Works of Sir Thomas Malory*, ed. Eugène Vinaver, 2nd rev. edn. (Oxford, 1973), ii, p. 1048.

[42] Elias Ashmole, *The Institution, Laws, and Ceremonies of the Most Noble Order of the Garter* (London, 1672), fol. Kv, in the appendix. The statutes for the institution of the Order proper stipulate *twenty-six* knights (fol. Ar). For further discussion of the relationship between the Round Table and the Garter, see below, Chapters 9 and 11, and Appendix I.

the role he played in Arthurian romance (although not in Malory), where he was 'the handsome stranger', *li biaus desconu*.

We must not, I think, demand too much of the Winchester table as a literary text. It is either a decorated relic or a fake antique or both; and what is written on it is dictated partly by considerations of visual design, as well as by literary tradition. Its calligraphic programme, in particular, suggests a rigorous draughtsman's control. The knights with lengthy names requiring two lines are distributed among the lighter-coloured buff panels, where the letters stand out as they would not against the dark of the green. Furthermore, they are distributed in such a way that the long names (Lancelot du Lake, Bors de Ganys, and so on) appear on *every other* buff panel in harmonious display.

The inscribed names of the knights and the prominence of a conspicuous canopied figure have obvious if oblique connections with the iconographic tradition of the Round Table in illustrations of the Vulgate cycle romances, particularly that of the *Queste del Saint Graal*. A representation of King Arthur *on*, rather than seated *at*, a table would seem to be unique, although not entirely without a certain literary warrant. An important group of texts (best represented in English by the fourteenth-century alliterative poem called the *Morte Arthure*) describe a remarkable dream in which Arthur saw himself, in the company of the others of the Nine Worthies, mounted upon Fortune's wheel. The dream turns to nightmare when Arthur, temporarily raised to the top of the wheel, sees himself hurled from it and crushed below. Whether or not this specific episode is positively related to the iconography of the Winchester table, it would be difficult to ignore the formal compositional similiarities between it and the very common medieval iconography of the Wheel of Fortune.

This pictorial image, expanded from the merest textual suggestion in the incalculably influential *De consolatione philosophiae* of Boethius, appears in several forms, but it often includes the four regal figures — *Regno, Regnavi, Sine Regno Sum* and *Regnabo* ('I rule, I have ruled, I have no kingdom, I shall rule') — who exemplify the fickle and cyclical ebb and flow of worldly prosperity. This image was extremely popular in book painting, in mural decoration, and in an elegantly witty form of architectural decoration in which sculpted figures were placed on an exterior wall at the quadrants of a wheel which was also a window. The concept of Fortune's wheel, and its visual illustration, entered the world of courtly literature in the thirteenth century not merely through numerous translations and adaptations of Boethius (Plate III), but also through such enormously influential 'secular' works as the *Roman de la Rose* and the *De casibus* of Boccaccio (Figs. 4–6). We know from the chancellor's roll for 20 Henry III (1236) that a Wheel of Fortune was in fact painted in the Great Hall and

4 The Wheel of Fortune. French, late 14th or 15th century

5 The future Emperor Charles V about to topple Fortune from her Wheel. Flemish, 1515

6 The Wheel of Fortune, from the title page of a Spanish edition of Boccacio's *Fall of Princes*, 1552

that there was also a *mappa mundi* – a world map – painted there shortly afterwards where the table later hung.[43] There is no trace of either painting today, but it is possible that the visual form of a medieval Wheel of Fortune existing on one wall of the hall may have influenced the Winchester designer in positioning the figure of the king. Similar examples of iconographic 'lateral contamination' are easy enough to find.

It is entirely possible that the decoration of the Winchester table, dating, as it seems to do, from the Tudor period, did not depend directly on medieval literary tradition at all. The history of the Round Table in literature does not end with Malory. There is a perceptible if moderated vogue for Arthurian materials throughout the Continent in the late Renaissance. Much of this is antiquarian and pseudo-historical in nature, rather like the work of Hardyng. Some of it is quite elaborately detailed. There appeared at Paris in the early sixteenth century, possibly in 1520, for example, an elaborate Arthurian armorial called *La devise des chevaliers de la Table Ronde*. This had woodcut illustrations, with descriptions, of the arms of no fewer than 168 Arthurian knights, as well as the arms of eight more 'whose names have been lost'.[44] And the latter-day and rather extravagant adventures of the Round Table were among the fictions which excited the mania of Don Quixote. But it was in England, understandably enough, that the antiquarian taste became something of a state cult. In the Tudor period, beginning with the quite sharply nationalistic policies of Henry VII and encouraged by the insular direction taken by the English Reformation under Henry VIII and Elizabeth, the literary cult became pronounced.

The history of Tudor Arthurianism is still being written.[45] Its evidences, though scattered, are impressive and varied, and they include shows and pageants, serious works of history, antiquarian chivalric orders, and the like. At least one full-blown Arthurian romance dates from the period – Middleton's *Famous History of Chinon of England* – and Spenser includes a bowdlerized Round Table in the *Faerie Queen*. The evidence concerning the credence commanded by the 'historical Arthur' in the English Renaissance is, to be sure, ambiguous and at times whimsical. There were numerous sceptics and debunkers like Polydore Vergil, but there were also those for

---

[43] See Edward Smirke, 'On the Hall and Round Table at Winchester', *Proceedings of the Annual Meeting of the Archaeological Institute ... at Winchester, September MDCCCXLV* (London, 1846), p. 64. See also below, pp. 74–5.

[44] *La Devise des Chevaliers de la Table Ronde qui estoient du temps du tresnomme et vertueux Artus roy de la grante Bretaigne avec la description de leurs armoires.*

[45] See, however, Millican, *Spenser and the Table Round*; James D. Merriman, *The Flower of Kings: A Study of the Arthurian Legend in England between 1485 and 1835* (Lawrence, 1973), esp. pp. 31 *et seq.*; and especially T. D. Kendrick, *British Antiquity* (London, 1950). See further below, Chapter 12.

whom the invocation of Arthur and the Round Table was no gesture to a politically useful fiction but the practice of a lively faith.

The attitude of the famous antiquary Leland, who published his *Assertio inclytissimi Arturi* in 1544, is one of polemical, nearly religious belief. Leland specifically mentions the Winchester table as one of the proofs of Arthur's existence: 'At Venta Symeno alias Winchester in the castle most famously knowne, standeth fixed the table at the walle side of the kinges Hal, which (for the maiesty of Arthure) they cal the rounde table'. He goes on to associate 'that rounde order of Knightes' with the institution of the Garter.[46] Richard Robinson, 'citizen of London' and toxophile, translated Leland's *Assertio* in 1582 as the *Assertion of King Arthure* and, in the following year, published an engaging book called *The Avncient Order, Societie, and Unitie, Laudable of Prince Arthure and His knightly Armory of the Round Table*. It is an abridged and amended version of the *Devise des Chevaliers de la Table Ronde* mentioned above.[47] Robinson prefaced the work with a brief history of the Round Table, which he traced to Kenilworth in 1279 and down through the Order of the Garter. It is of some interest that he placed Edward III's 'building known as The Round Table' not in Windsor but in Winchester.[48]

Robinson associated the idea of the Arthurian 'order' not merely with an antique chivalry but with the manly arts of defense and with a quasi-religious sense of fellowship. He takes as the epigraph of his book the *Ecce quam bonum* of Psalm 133 (Vulgate 132), reduced to Protestant doggerel:

> O how happy a thyng it is and ioyfull for to see
> Brethren together fast to hold the Band of Amitie.

The author of the *Queste del Saint Graal* had referred to the same verses three centuries before.

Further examples of an Arthurian vogue, half historical in character and half literary, could easily be adduced. The political fable of the 'once and future king' was undoubtedly a useful one. We need not be too cynical about it, however. The claims of the English monarchs, even when the 'Tudor myth' had fully matured, were comparatively modest. The French king was annointed with a chrism made in Heaven. The English, as usual more sober, claimed no such extravagant relic; but

---

[46] John Leland, *Assertio ... Arturi* (London, 1544), reprinted with Richard Robinson's English paraphrase, which is quoted here, in *The Famous Historie of Chinon of England, together with The Assertion of King Arthure*, ed. William Edward Mead, EETS os 165 (London, 1925), p. 36. See further below, pp. 94, 483–4.

[47] Richard Robinson, *The Avncient Order ... of the Round Table* (London, 1583).

[48] Ibid., fourth page of 'Epistle Dedicatory' (unpaginated).

they did claim a noble lineage which reached back through epochs of a legendary history to Camelot and Trinovant.

In his preface to the *Morte Darthur* Caxton explains how certain gentlemen pressed him to publish a book about the deeds of the great King Arthur.

> To whom I answerd that dyvers men holde oppynyon that there was no such Arthur and that alle such bookes as been maad of hym ben but fayned and fables, bycause that somme cronycles make of hym no mencyon ne remembre hym noothynge, ne of his knyghtes.

These gentlemen dismissed this attitude as outright folly, which flew in the face of the

> many evydences of the contrayre. Fyrst, ye may see his sepulture in the monasterye of Glastyngburye ... item, in the castel of Dover ye may see Gauwayns skulle and Cradoks mantel; at Wynchester, the Rounde Table; in other places Launcelottes swerde and many other thynges.[49]

Material relics illustrative of literary legend filled the churches and shrines of medieval Europe. Laura Hibbard Loomis, in arguing her case for the connection between the Round Table and the table of the Last Supper, rightly made much of the fact that the English pilgrim Sæwulf was shown such a table in Jerusalem in 1102. But he could have seen another in the church of St John Lateran at Rome. Even in the Middle Ages many found such a situation absurd or scandalous, as did Erasmus in the dawn of the Reformation; and since then most people who have talked or written about medieval relics at all have been content to do so in terms of the fraud and venality of clerics and the ignorance and gullibility of laymen. Such explanations would in many cases no doubt be correct, but not in every case; and it seems certain that many relics began their careers as pious rather than criminal counterfeits: nails *like* the nails which pierced Christ's hands; a whip *like* the one used to scourge Him. Such may very well have been the case as well with the Arthurian relics cited by Caxton: Gawain's skull, Craddoc's mantle, Lancelot's sword, and 'at Wynchester, the Rounde Table'.

---

[49] *Caxton's Malory,* as above, note 1, pp. 1–2.

2

The Round Table as Furniture

Nowadays the piece of furniture called the Round Table evokes notions of conviviality and comradeship, infused perhaps with distant Arthurian echoes. In the late Middle Ages, however, a round table was not merely an offence against protocol, it embodied a contradiction of the rigidly hierarchical system in which the received understanding of political reality was enshrined. The significance of such a table is encapsulated in this French couplet:

> A ce rond qui n'a point de bout
> La place d'honneur est partout.[1]

> At this circle without end
> Every seat does honour lend.

That this tripping formula records a Gordian solution to a real problem is most vividly expressed in Layamon's *Brut* of around 1200, where Layamon interpolates into Wace's comparatively anodyne account of the invention of the Round Table a tale of pride, envy and slaughter.[2]

Most of our detailed information about medieval etiquette and systems of precedence dates from the late fifteenth century or later. But Alienor of Poitiers's *Les Honneurs de la Cour*, of about 1484, perhaps the most elaborate manual of manners, records observations of her mother, Isabelle of Souza, who in turn had derived much of her knowledge from traditions passed on by Jeanne of Namur, born in 1372.[3] The *Ménagier de Paris*, written in 1393, contains an account of a dinner probably given in 1379 where precedence was clearly of primary importance:

[1] Quoted from 'un poète' in Blavignac, *Histoire des enseignes* (Geneva, 1877), p. 431.
[2] *Layamon's Brut*, ed. G. L. Brook and R.F. Leslie, EETS os 277 (Oxford, 1978), ii, pp. 592–9; see above, pp. 9–10.
[3] M. Paul Lacroix, 'Cérémonial', *Le Moyen Age et la Renaissance*, iii (Paris, 1850), fol. xiii.

Note that Monseigneur de Paris had three esquires of his own to serve him and he was served apart with covered dishes. And Monseigneur the President had one esquire and was served apart, but not with covered dishes. Item, at the bidding of Monseigneur the President the Procureur du Roi was seated above the Avocat du Roi.[4]

The 1261 *Ordinatio hospicii et familiae* of Louis XI of France (later St Louis), although it does not record any details of etiquette, is evidence that the problems of establishing formal hierarchies in a feudal household were already objects of thought and action in the thirteenth century.[5] A crude but effective statement of the basic problem is provided by Doon of Mayence:

And if you have a valet, take care not to seat him at the table by you, or take him to bed with you; for the more honour you do to a low fellow, the more he will despise you.[6]

The chosen system of precedence, which aimed at expressing and reinforcing the feudal order, had to be seen to operate to be effective, and one of the main occasions when this order was made visible was at meals. Bishop Grosseteste's *Household Statutes*, written in the middle of the fifteenth century in a time of change, contain a clause which demonstrates the contemporary consciousness of the real importance to a lord of having his household eat together and the danger of his failing to do so:

The xvij commaundee ȝe dineris and sapers prively in hid plase be not had, & be they forbeden that there be no suche dyners nother sopers oute of the halle, for of suche comethe grete destr[u]ccion, and no worshippe therby growythe to the lorde.[7]

The basic division in the hall, as in Oxbridge colleges even now, was between the high table and the body of the hall, although precedence, as decided by the marshal, was observed throughout. To quote from *The Boke of Curtasye* of about 1460:

[4] *The Goodman of Paris*, ed. Eileen Power (London, 1928), p. 237.
[5] Joinville, *Histoire de Saint Louis*, ed. C. Du Cange (Paris, 1668), p. 108.
[6] Quoted by Thomas Wright, *A History of Domestic Manners and Sentiments* (London, 1862), p. 105.
[7] Bishop Grosseteste's Household Statutes', in *The Babees Book*, ed. F. J. Furnivall, EETS os 32 (London, 1868), p. 331.

In halle marshalle alle men schalle sett
After here degré, with-outen lett.[8]

The high table was rectangular or square and those using it sat, as a rule, on one side facing the body of the hall. How the guests at the high table were to be seated was a theme on which infinite variations could be played, because the estate of each participant, which determined his precedence, could be overridden by other considerations, depending on the circumstances of the meal. Thus at the banquet given in 1378 by King Charles V of France for the Emperor Charles IV and his son, Wenceslas, the King of the Romans, all three sat side by side, each beneath a 'cloth of estate' (a canopy over a throne); but the King of France occupied the central seat, the place of honour, which in theory was the prerogative of the emperor (Plate IV).[9] A later instance of the workings of precedence is given by Sir John Finett, Master of the Ceremonies to Charles I, describing how in 1626 the Duke of Buckingham, giving an entertainment at York House for the French ambassador, Monsieur Bassampierre,

> had his Feast honoured with the Presence of bothe Their Majesties, the King sitting towards the end of the Table with the Queen at his right hand, the Ambassador was (as soon as they were set) invited by his Majesty to sit downe at the end of the Table on that hand which might seem to be the upper end, but was held the lower because next the doore, and furthest from the fire.[10]

In the seventeenth century the standard practice was for the king to eat apart, as is evident from a reported exchange between Marais and Louis XIII:

> 'Il y a deux choses à votre mestier dont je ne me pourrois accomoder'.
> 'Hé quoi?'
> 'De manger tout seul et de ch ... en compagnie'.[11]

> 'There are two things I couldn't put up with in your job'.
> 'Oh, what?'
> 'Eating alone and sh ... ing in company'.

[8] 'The Boke of Curtasye', in Furnivall, *Babees Book*, p. 311, lines 403–4.

[9] Claire Richter Sherman, *The Portraits of Charles V of France* (New York, 1969), fig. 35.

[10] *Finetti Philoxensis: Som Choice Observations of Sr John Finett Knight, and Master of the Ceremonies to the Two Last Kings* (London, 1656), pp. 191–2.

[11] Henry Havard, *Dictionnaire de l'ameublement* (Paris, n.d.), iv, col. 1118; quoting from Gédéon Tallemant des Réaux, *Les historiettes*, 3rd revised edn. (Paris, 1862), ii, p. 72.

7 Louis XIII dining with the Chevaliers de Saint Esprit at Fontainebleau, 1633

8 The Canterbury Pilgrims at table, from Caxton's Chaucer, 1483

An engraving of 1633 shows Louis XIII dining with the Chevaliers de Saint Esprit at a separate high table with a cloth of estate (Fig. 7).[12] In a plate from Elias Ashmole's *Order of the Garter* Charles II is shown in the same solitary pre-eminence, dining with the Garter knights at Windsor in 1664.[13] It is difficult to be precise about when it became orthodox for the highest estate present to eat apart. Solomon is certainly shown being ceremoniously served, separate from his wives, in P. Stephan Fridolin's *Der Schatzbehalter* of 1491.[14] John Russell, writing of the highest estates in his mid fifteenth-century *Book of Nurture*, prescribes that

> Vche Estate syngulerly in halle shalle sit adowne[15]

and elsewhere the high table may be referred to specifically as the 'lordis borde', the 'souereignes table', or more generally as the 'hye borde', 'the principall tabill'.[16] What seems to have been normal in the fifteenth century was for the lord, or the lord and his wife, to eat apart at the high table on ordinary occasions, but to allow guests of the highest estate to eat at the high table on festive occasions. If a guest's estate did not transcend the claims to precedence of his host, his importance could nonetheless be marked by symbols of honour. Thus when John of Gaunt was entertained by the King of Portugal on the Galician border in 1386, the king took precedence both as host and king.[17] A late fifteenth-century illustration of this event shows the king seated in the place of honour on a *bench* under a cloth of estate, while John of Gaunt is at the right end of the table on a high-backed *chair*, presumably as a visible compensation for his lack of precedence.[18] What seems certain is that any admission to the high table, whether the lord regularly ate apart or in company, was regarded as a mark of special favour.

On exceptional occasions the use of round tables is recorded. They were set up in the streets in the fifteenth and sixteenth centuries for general feasting, but this was only to celebrate such momentous real-life or fictional events as the solemn entry to

[12] Illus. Bernard Champigneulle, *Le règne de Louis XIII* (Paris, 1949), p. 57.

[13] Elias Ashmole, *The Institutions, Laws & Ceremonies of the Most Noble Order of the Garter* (London, 1672), opp. p. 593.

[14] *Der Schatzbehalter* (Nuremberg, 1491), fig. 68.

[15] Furnivall, *Babees Book*, p. 189, line 1074.

[16] Furnivall, *Babees Book*, p. 8, line 196; p. 131, line 229; p. 329; p. 366.

[17] Sir John Froissart, *Chronicles ...*, trans. Thomas Johnes (London, 1855), ii, p. 187.

[18] Jean de Mavrin, 'Chronique d'Angleterre', BL, Royal MS. 14 E.iv, fol. 244v. Illus. Eric Mercer, *Furniture 700–1700* (London, 1969), pl. I.

9 Job feasting with his children. English, early 15th century

10 The Round Table and the Holy Grail with Galahad in the Siege Perilous. French, 1479–80

Paris in 1467 of Charlotte of Savoy or Pantagruel's victory over the giants of the city of Amaurotes.[19] Illustrations of the use of round tables occur both in situations where an iconographic link with the Last Supper may be indicated and on the rare occasions when informality, rather than precedence, reigned. In the first category is an early fifteenth-century depiction of Job feasting with his children (Fig. 9);[20] in the second, woodcuts of the Canterbury pilgrims published by William Caxton in 1483 and by Richard Pynson in 1526.[21] The Caxton illustration, suggestively in the Winchester context, shows twenty-four pilgrims squeezed round the table (Fig. 8). Only in the seventeenth century did round and oval tables come into use for dining on normal occasions.[22] And even in the eighteenth century the need was still felt for curious compromises between informality and protocol. Thus a fan of 1758–9 shows a dinner party given by Louis XV at Versailles, at which the table is shaped like a dumbbell with a curved bar.[23] The diners, seated along one side of the 'bar' and two-thirds of the way round the 'weights', are placed for intimate conversation, but none faces or obstructs the king in his place of honour in the centre.

But although a monumental round table on the Winchester scale is an historical anomaly, it is relevant to record that three standard types of small round table do regularly occur in illustrations in fifteenth- and sixteenth-century manuscripts and printed books. One variety has a round base, tapering and expanding below and above a central knop, like a Gothic chalice; these seem often to have been used as chess tables. A table of this type, grossly overscaled, is shown as a Round Table supporting the Grail in a miniature of 1479–80 by Evrard d'Espingues (Fig. 10).[24] Another type of small round table had three broad planks as legs, set face outwards, but leaning inwards and tapering towards the table-top; they are sometimes connected by massive stretchers in a T-formation. Such tables were sometimes used for gaming, but also for dining alone, informally, or even in a small company (Fig. 11). In the Hours of Catherine of Cleves, of about 1438, the Israelites are seen eating their Passover lamb and unleavened bread from such a table, a scene which prefigures the Last Supper, and therefore the Round Table. Another prefigurement of the Last Supper was the table prepared for the psalmist by the Lord in Psalm 22

[19] Quoted in Havard, *Dictionnaire*, as above, n. 11, iv, cols. 1132–3.

[20] Bodleian, MS. C.C.C. 161, p. 58. Illus. Colin Platt, *The English Medieval Town* (London, 1976), p. 101.

[21] Illus. *William Caxton* (British Museum, 1976), fig. 57, and Edward Hodnett, *English Woodcuts 1480–1535* (Oxford, 1973), fig. 151. I am indebted to Pamela Tudor-Craig (Lady Wedgwood) for calling my attention to the Caxton illustration.

[22] Havard, *Dictionnaire*, as above, n. 11, iv, col. 1133.

[23] Illus. *Apollo* 105 (1977), 407.

[24] Loomis and Loomis, *Arthurian Legends in Medieval Art* (as above, p. 12, note 16), p. 111 and fig. 296.

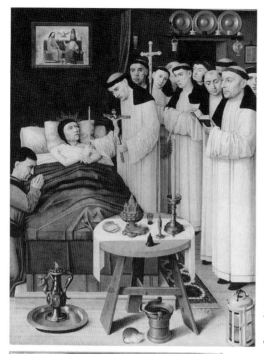

11 A round table for the Last Rites: The Death of St. Augustine. Flemish, *c.*1500, National Gallery of Ireland.

12 Dining alone at a round table. Flemish, 1473–83? (above left).
13 The round table in the Chapter House, Salisbury Cathedral. English, 14th century (above right).

(23), 'The Lord is my shepherd': it may be significant that in the ninth-century Utrecht Psalter and later copies thereof this table is depicted as round.[25] The third type of late medieval small round table had two end-supports connected by a stretcher, and was also used for individual dining and other occasional uses (Fig. 12).[26] It sometimes had a tip-up mechanism, as did the type with three legs.

None of these round tables approaches the scale of the one at Winchester. In the chapter house of Salisbury Cathedral, however, there survives a round table with a massive architectural base formed of eight columns separated by cusped arches (Fig. 13).[27] Expanded, such a base could certainly support a table of the Winchester size, but there seems no relationship between the structures of the two. Indeed, for the size of its top, the under-framing of the Salisbury table is unnecessarily massive, and it is certainly a curiosity in the context of the chapter house, where the only congruous position for a single round table would be around the central pillar. (In the seventeenth century there was a table around a pillar in the hall at Bolsover Castle, a comparable position and in a medievalizing building.)[28] The question arises whether the base of the Salisbury table, whose top is not necessarily original, may not originally have served a quite different function. A possible explanation is that it was once the base for a pulpit.

The only other surviving medieval round table of any grandeur is the elaborate late Gothic example made in 1506 by Tilman Riemenschneider for the Rathaus in Würzburg, specifically designed to carry a large Sohnhofer stone slab, with armorial engraving (Fig. 14).[29]

This short review has demonstrated that the Winchester Round Table bears little similarity to other medieval round tables, resembling neither the standard types nor the few extant tables of comparably large size. But the table's most glaring abnormality is of course its contrast with standard rectangular tables of the Middle Ages. Usually these had separate tops, which were supported on trestles. An early fifteenth-century French manuscript on the life of Bertran of Guesclin shows two such tables, one standing and the other fallen, its trestles askew.[30] Numerous references in books of household management and elsewhere make it clear that it was

[25] *The Hours of Catherine of Cleves*, ed. John Plummer (London, 1966), p. 76. For an example of a round table used in an illustration of Psalm 22 (23), see BN, MS. Latin 8846, fol. 39. Illus. G. Zarnecki *et al.* (ed.), *English Romanesque Art 1066–1200* (London, 1984), p. 127.

[26] BL, Royal MS. 14 E.vi, fol. 294r. Illus. Ralph Edwards, *Dictionary of English Furniture*, iii (London, 1954), p. 209.

[27] Illus. Henry Shaw, *Specimens of Ancient Furniture* (London, 1836), pl. XLVI, drawn by J. C. Buckler in 1833.

[28] P. A. Faulkner, *Bolsover Castle, Derbyshire* (London, 1972), p. 21.

[29] Heinrich Kreisel, *Die Kunst des deutschen Möbels*, i, *Von den Anfängen bis zum Hochbarock* (Munich, 1968), fig. 71.

[30] Illus. H. P. Kraus, *Monumenta Codicum Manu Scriptorum* (New York, 1974), no. 31, 'Livre historial des fais de ... Bertran de Guesclin'.

14 Round table made by Tilman Riemenschneider at Würzburg in 1506; Solnhofen stone top on wooden base

15 Folding table in the Rathaus at Lüneburg, Lower Saxony, painted folding top, 14th century; supports, 15th century.

usual for tables, trestles, and benches to be set up and cleared away before and after eating:

> The marshall in the mornyng ought to come into the hall and se that it be clene of all maner thyng that may be fond vnhoneste ther in: the stolis trestelles or elles formys yef ony be, that they be set in ther owne places at melis at the bordes, and afore and aftur melis in corners farthest from encombrance ...[31]

But it was also possible for such tables to be 'dormant', that is, permanent, fixed structures.[32] In the great hall of the king's palace in Paris there was a quite exceptional dormant high table, described by Jean de Jandun in his *De laudibus Parisiis* of about 1323:

> Sed et marmorea mensa, sue politissime planitiei uniformitate refulgens, quod occidentalium vitrearum lumine fixa, sic tamen quod ad oriens respiciunt convivantes, tante profecto magnitudinis existit, quod, si mensuram ejus absque probatione proponerem, timerem michi non credi.[33]

> There is also a marble table there, set so that it reflects the light of the western windows in its smooth and highly polished surface while the guests sit facing east. It is so large in fact, that I fear I would not be believed were I to give its measurements without offering some kind of proof.

On 16 December 1431 Henry VI dined at this table after his coronation as king of France.[34] In his *Description de la ville de Paris* of 1434 Guillebert of Metz described it as 'de neuf pieces';[35] it was destroyed by fire in 1618.[36] In the reign of Edward I there seem to have been two marble tables in Westminster Hall. For the coronation of Edward II in 1308 a new piece of marble was supplied for one of them. In 1399 it was mended and provided with a new stone trestle. Fragments excavated in the dais confirm that this table existed, and it is known from a description of 1734 that it was 19 feet long and 3 feet wide (5.8 by 0.9 metres) (Fig. 21).[37] Add to these

---

[31] *A 15th Century Courtesy Book*, ed. R. W. Chambers, EETS os 148 (London, 1914), p. 11.

[32] Interestingly, 'dormer' came to be a term used for trestles. See, for example, *Ingatestone Hall in 1600, An Inventory* (Chelmsford, 1954), p. 13.

[33] Le Roux de Lincy and L. M. Tisserand, *Paris et ses historiens* (Paris, 1867), pp. 48–9.

[34] Ibid., quoting the *Journal d'un bourgeois de Paris*.

[35] Ibid., p. 158.

[36] M. Bonnardot, *Études sur Gilles Corrozet* (Paris, 1848), p. 24.

examples a surviving table of the early fourteenth century in the Rathaus at Lüneburg, 22 ft. 6 in. (6.85 metres) long (Figs. 15, 16),[38] and there seems some basis for suggesting that in the Middle Ages important public halls, where royal entertainments were held, and government and justice were transacted, may have regularly contained rectangular high tables of abnormal size, permanence, and elaboration. The Great Hall of Winchester Castle certainly fits into the category of buildings appropriate for such a suggested special class of rectangular table. If this argument is valid, then the Round Table at Winchester may be seen in its context not as *sui generis*, but as a specific variation, in a notoriously Arthurian site, on a recognised type. It would also follow that no particular historic occasion need be adduced to account for its provision (but see further, Chapter 10).

But elsewhere the pull of the standard rectangular table was such that several manuscript illustrations show the Round Table as rectangular, for example a French *Queste* of about 1316 (Fig. 17)[39] and the *Queste del Saint Graal* completed by Pierart dou Tielt in 1351.[40] A compromise solution is shown in a French *Tristan* of 1463,[41] where a rectangular table has been bent into a semicircle. This solution is taken even further in an Italian *Queste del Saint Graal* of the late fourteenth century[42] in which the Round Table is shown as a rectangle bent around almost into a circle, leaving a narrow entrance free for the servants (Plate II). The logical but absurd conclusion of this mode of depicting the Round Table is to be found in a *Livre de Lancelot du Lac* acquired by Jean, Duke of Berry, in 1405, but revised in about 1460 for Jacques of Armagnac, Duke of Nemours.[43] This shows the Round Table as a complete circle with a hole in the centre, inaccessible to servants, but occupied by two hovering angels who support the Grail. The same formula is more elaborately rendered in another *Lancelot*, also owned by Jacques, completed in 1470 (Plate I).[44] The reason for these depictions of the Round Table as rectangular or pseudo-rectangular was doubtless that this solution reduced the affront to medieval notions of precedence inherent in a 'realistic' representation, and allowed servants to face their masters at

---

[37] H. M. Colvin (ed), *The History of the King's Works* ii, *The Middle Ages*, (London, 1963), p. 544; and information from the Inspectorate of Ancient Monuments, especially from Dr A. J. Taylor, who directed the first reconstruction of the table in 1965–70, and Mr J. L. Thorn, who produced the new reconstruction first published here.

[38] Heinrich Kohlhaussen, 'Bildertische', *Germanisches Nationalmuseum Anzeiger 1936–39* (Nuremberg, 1939), p. 43, n. 2. See p. 51.

[39] Loomis and Loomis, *Arthurian Legends in Medieval Art*, p. 98, fig. 242.

[40] Ibid., p. 123, fig. 341.

[41] Ibid., p. 109, fig. 295.

[42] Ibid., p. 119, fig. 330.

[43] Ibid., p. 107, fig. 187.

[44] Ibid., pp. 110–11. Illus. Elizabeth Jenkins, *The Mystery of King Arthur* (London, 1975), p. 96.

16 The Judgement of Solomon, painted roundel with flanking bands of shields, detail from the painted top of the table in the Rathaus, Lüneburg, 14th century.

la ueille de la pentecou
ste qnt tout li compaig
non de la table ronde fu

17 Arthur's Pentecost feast, at a rectangular table. French, *c.*1316

18 Round table with raised rim and tablier. French, 12th century.

19 The Last Supper, ivory panel. Catalan, *c.* 1100.

20 The Last Supper. Bavarian, 12th century

the high table, as etiquette demanded. But the contrivance also subverted the entire reason for creating the Round Table in the first place: to escape the constraints of precedence. Medieval ideas about hierarchy and protocol died hard.

The back of the Winchester Round Table shows that it was once a real table standing on a base (Chapter 4), but its structure has no direct parallels in surviving medieval furniture. The only free-standing pieces of comparable size and shape are cope chests such as those preserved at York, Salisbury, Gloucester, and Wells. But one feature of the Winchester table, its raised rim, may be explained by reference to depictions of tables, both round and rectangular, of about 1200 or earlier. Viollet-le-Duc observed that a raised rim, or 'gallery', was a feature of tables shown in Herrade of Landsberg's 'Hortus Deliciarum' of 1175 to 1205 and elsewhere.[45] Two illustrations in the 'Hortus' appear to show this raised rim with, below, a rod with rings supporting a valance or apron, arranged in formalised folds, which Viollet identified as a *tablier* (Fig. 18). The rod and rings are rarely found in tables illustrated elsewhere; indeed not all the tables in the 'Hortus' possess it. But a common feature in depictions of tables of this period is an evident difference in colour and/or pattern between the cloth on the top of the table and the *tablier*, which is invariably shown as presenting a regular pattern of folds. Moreover the top and the *tablier* are usually separated in manuscript illustrations by one or more bold lines (Plate V).[46] What do these lines signify? One answer would be that they represent a sewn joint, or even two sewn joints with an intervening strip of material. Another answer would be to describe these lines as a purely formal device, the equivalent of leading in glass or a *cloison* in enamel. A third possibility, which may be relevant in the Winchester context, is that these lines are a formula for representing an applied rim which both held the *tablier* down and masked the join between *tablier* and top cloth. The only unequivocal evidence which seems to exist for the use of such a rim is a Spanish ivory of the Last Supper from San Millán de la Cogolla, dating from about 1100 (Fig. 19).[47] This shows an unmistakeable moulding all around a rectangular table apparently holding down the top of the *tablier*. Two other ivory Last Suppers,[48] one in Narbonne Cathedral, the other in the Wernher Collec-

[45] E. Viollet-le-Duc, *Dictionnaire raisonné du mobilier français*, i (Paris, 1858), pp. 254–5.

[46] Examples: Madrid, Biblioteca Nacional, Biblia de Ávila, Vit. 15–1, fol. 349v; Nuremberg, Germanisches Nationalmuseum, Codex Aureus Epternacensis, fol. 52v; Leyden, Universitätsbibliothek, St Louis Psalter, MS. BPL 76A, fols. 20v and 27; Boston Museum of Fine Arts, *Last Supper* from S. Dandelio de Berlanga; Cambridge, St John's College, MS. 231 (K26), fol. 18r; Erlangen, Universitätsbibliothek, Gumbertus Bible, MS. 1, fol. 355v; Cambridge, Pembroke College, MS. 120, fol. 2r; Barcelona, Museo de Arte de Catalunya, Altar frontal of St Michael from Soriguerola, Urtx, Last Supper (Plate V).

[47] Illus. Adolph Goldschmidt, *Die Elfenbeinskulpturen*, iv (Berlin, 1926), pl. XXXII, no. 98d.

[48] Illus. ibid., i (Berlin, 1914), pl. XV, no. 31, and ii (Berlin, 1918), pl. XXIX, no. 87.

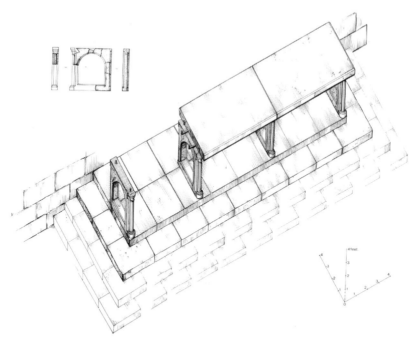

21 The high table of Purbeck marble in Westminster Hall: a reconstruction. English, 13th century.

22 Seven persons dining at a round table. Flemish, 1514

tion, also have tables whose edges are moulded, but in both cases the mouldings are beaded. Whether this beading is intended to depict nails driven through a moulding or directly into the edge of the table to support a *tablier*, or whether it has another practical or purely formal function, it is difficult to tell. An illustration in the mid twelfth-century Lambeth Bible showing a row of circles along the top edge of a table is equally hard to interpret with certainty, but a row of nails seems the most plausible reading.[49] The feature identifiable as a rim seems to die out after about 1200: thenceforth in illustrations the table-cloth is shown to fall over the edge of the table to replace the *tablier*. If the scientific analysis of the table is correct (Chapters 5 and 6), the rim was almost certainly added to a pre-existing table in 1516. Perhaps it represented a survival of an earlier tradition of raised rims, or more plausibly it may have been a conscious revival of this feature, an antiquarian gesture appropriate in an Arthurian context.

As nothing survives of the base of the Winchester Round Table its detailed reconstruction must be speculative. The basic structure must have been a large column in the centre and smaller legs nearer the circumference, and indeed twelve mortises for the smaller legs survive (Chapter 4). Most early illustrations of tables are uninformative or, at best, imprecise about the form of their supports. However, a Last Supper in a *Perikopenbuch* of the early twelfth century from Kloster Altomünster (Fig. 20) does appear to show a conformation of legs similar to that required to support the Winchester table, which could have been influenced by such a model.[50] The only surviving support for a table on the Winchester scale is on display in the Jewel Tower in Westminster.[51] It is a massive Purbeck marble slab with an arched opening in the centre and an engaged column on its front edge (Fig. 21). As it supported the thirteenth-century rectangular table of Purbeck marble in Westminster Hall, it does not provide a very close analogy for the Round Table. But it raises the possibility that the Round Table might, as a comparably massive and permanent table in a public setting, have had a stone support.

The question of the original form of seating used with the Round Table may be dismissed quickly. The only evidence, that to be found in medieval depictions of tables, is so various as to make it impossible to suggest a specific solution. Short straight benches, with and without backs; curved benches; turned stools, with or without backs; box stools; chests; slab-ended stools; X-framed chairs and stools; high-backed chairs; and stall-like structures, all are found (Plates I, II, X, Figs. 8–10,

---

[49] Illus. C. M. Kauffmann, *The Bible in British Art* (London, 1977), cover.

[50] Munich, Staatsbibliothek, Clm. 2939. Illus. E. F. Bange, *Eine Bayerische Malerschule des XI und XII Jahrhunderts* (Munich, 1923), pl. 58, fig. 161.

[51] See above, p. 41 and note 37.

22).[52] However as the place names of the knights, albeit added later, provide exactly the right space for a seated diner, it seems fair to conclude that the table was originally sat at, whatever the participants sat upon.

Whereas the form of seating associated with the Round Table can only be a matter of speculation, its painting in the early sixteenth century can be placed in an historical context. Normally tables were covered with a cloth, and surface decoration was unnecessary. The exposed table ends not covered by the cloth were sometimes decorated with carved or incised ornament. To cite an example from an Arthurian context, a table in the Castle of the Holy Grail, in a French illustration of about 1330 for *Le Conte de Graal* of Chrétien of Troyes, has two lines with a band of round-headed arcading at each end.[53] More elaborate tracery is visible in the same positions on the Table of Honour occupied by the Knights of the Star, an order created by Jean II of France in 1351, as depicted in the 'Grandes Chroniques de France'.[54]

Tables decorated with painting are uncommon, but two significant groups exist from the fourteenth to sixteenth centuries. Before these are discussed two early examples must be noted. First, there is the table that Charlemagne left to the church of Ravenna in his will, a round table with a view of the city of Rome, which was one of several exceptional tables ('mensas') in his possession.[55] The second example is what appears to be a rectangular table with a border consisting of squares containing

---

[52] Tilman Riemenschneider, *Blutaltar* (1499–1504), St Jacobskirche, Rothenburg ob der Tauber. Illus. Loomis and Loomis, *Arthurian Legends in Medieval Art*, as above, p. 12, note 16, fig. 200; H. W. Davies, *Early German Books in the Library of C. Fairfax Murray* (London, 1913), no. 416 (Brussels, 1514); Douglas Ash, 'Gothic', in *World Furniture*, ed. Helena Hayward (London, 1965), figs. 55 and 84; Mercer, *Furniture*, p. 10, pl. I; Loomis and Loomis, *Arthurian Legends in Medieval Art*, as above, p. 12, note 16, fig. 287.

[53] BN, MS. Fr. 12577, fol. 18v. Illus. Richard Barber, *King Arthur in Legend and History* (London, 1973), fig. 17. Similar decoration is shown in a fourteenth-century representation of St Louis serving a learned monk, 'Grandes Chroniques de France', BN, MS. Fr. 2813, fol. 265. Illus. *Horizon Book of the Middle Ages* (London, 1969), p. 55.

[54] BN, MS. Fr. 2813, fol. 394r. Illus. André Maurois, *An Illustrated History of France* (London, 1960), p. 20.

[55] Einhard and Notker the Stammerer, *Two Lives of Charlemagne*, ed. Lewis Thorpe (Harmondsworth, 1969), p. 89; *Einhardi Vita Karoli Magni*, ed. G. H. Pertz, MGH, 3rd ed. (Hannover, 1863): 'Inter caeteros thesauros atque peccunias tres mensas argenteas et auream unam praecipuae magnitudinis et ponderis esse constat. De quibus statuit atque decrevit, ut una ex his, quae forma quadrangula, descriptionem urbis Constantinopolitanae continet, inter caetera donaria quae ad hoc deputata sunt, Romam ad Basilicam beati Petri apostoli deferantur, et altera, quae forma rotunda Romanae urbis effigie decorata est, episcopio Ravennatis ecclesiae conferatur. Tertiam, quae caeteris et operis pulchritudine et ponderis gravitate multum excellit, quae ex tribus orbibus conexa, totius mundi descriptionem subtili ac minuta figuratione complectitur, et auream illam, quae quarta esse dicta est, inter haeredes suos, atque in elemosinam dividendae partis augmentum esse constituit'.

heads of kings, depicted as part of the treasure deposited in the Temple at Jerusalem by Solomon, in Herrade of Landsberg's 'Hortus Deliciarum'.[56]

The first of the two significant groups of painted tables consists of two extant German examples. One, in the Fürstensaal of the Rathaus in Lüneburg, is a rectangle about 22 ft. 6 in. (6.85 metres) long painted with five medallions enclosing Old Testament scenes: the Sacrifice of Abraham, the Brazen Serpent, David and Goliath, the Judgment of Solomon, and Samson and the Lion. (Figs. 15, 16)[57] The whole table is bordered by forty heraldic shields and helms, by which it can be dated with reasonable certainty to about 1330 and, although the arms of France and England are included, located in Lower Saxony. As all the biblical scenes face one of the long sides of the table it seems likely that it was intended for use on ceremonial occasions in the Lüneburg Rathaus at which those presiding sat on one side only. The second table in this first group was acquired by the Musée de Cluny in Paris in 1864.[58] Again rectangular, although only 15 feet (4.55 metres) long, it is decorated with four painted scenes in quatrefoil frames, once more directed to one side only. The subjects are proverbial and biblical: an Ass in Bed, Four Things Hard to be Known (*Proverbs* 30:18), the Fable of the Mouse and the Lion, and the Judgement of Solomon. These quatrefoil scenes alternate with eight large shields and crested helms, arranged as three pairs flanking the inner arms with singletons at each end, while the border of the table contains forty-four small shields, German, European, exotic, and fanciful. On the basis of heraldry this table has been dated to about 1358 and located, like the Lüneburg example, in north Germany. It seems probable that the Cluny table was intended to serve a similar function; apart from other resemblances the width of both tables is almost identical.

'It is well known that among his other treasures and property there were three silver tables as well as one gold table of extraordinary size and weight. He ordered and decreed that one of these, whose four-cornered top encloses a picture of the City of Constantinople, should be taken with other gifts allotted for this purpose to Rome to the the church of the Blessed Apostle Peter; and that another whose round top is distinguished by a likeness of the City of Rome should be conveyed to the bishop of the church of Ravenna. He resolved that the third table, which far surpasses the other two both in beauty of workmanship and in weight, and which is made up of three linked circles and represents in fine and extraordinary detail the arrangement of the whole universe, should go with that gold table, mentioned further above, to increase the lot which is to be divided between his heirs and for charitable purposes'. On Charlemagne's tables, see now Eberlein-Westhues, 'König Arthurs "Table ronde" ', as above, p. 15, note 24, pp. 232–5.

[56] Viollet-le-Duc, *Dictionnaire raisonné*, as above, n. 45, i, p. 260.

[57] Kohlhaussen, 'Bildertische', as above, n. 38, pp. 12–13; p. 43, no. 2.

[58] Ibid., pp. 12–17; p. 43, no. 3. See also no. 9, which strongly suggests that the provenance of the Cluny table may have been Kloster Wienhausen.

The second significant group of painted tables is much larger. The earliest surviving example seems to be a table painted by Hieronymus Bosch in about 1490 (Plate VI).[59] It depicts the Seven Deadly Sins and is now in the Prado Museum in Madrid, but from 1574 it was in the Escorial, in the bedroom of Philip II of Spain, who also owned a lost companion piece of the Seven Sacraments. The Prado table is 4 by 5 feet (1.20 by 1.50 metres), and its strongly geometric composition consists basically of a large central medallion with a smaller medallion in each corner. In the Österreichisches Museum für angewandte Kunst in Vienna there is a contemporary table of similar dimensions, 3 ft. 10 in. (1.16 metres) square, but with a wholly irregular composition, a patchwork of scenes of the Passion, of the Risen Christ, of the Ten Thousand Virgins, and of scattered plants, animals, and figures, some of the latter engaged in hunting and fighting.[60] A similar scatter of figures, although of much higher artistic quality, appears on a table, now in the Schweizerisches Landesmuseum in Zürich, long attributed to Hans Holbein the Younger but known to have been painted by Hans Herbst in 1515 for Hans Baer, the standard-bearer of the city of Basel, who was killed in the same year at the battle of Marignano.[61] Its dimensions are 3 ft. 4 in. by 4 ft. 6 in. (1.02 by 1.36 metres). The formula of the Vienna and Zürich tables, both with light figures on a dark background, is repeated on a table of 4 feet by 3 ft. 8 in. (1.22 by 1.12 metres) in the Bayerisches Nationalmuseum, Munich, sprinkled with all manner of flora and fauna.[62]

In the Germanisches Nationalmuseum, Nuremberg, there is another table-top of similar proportions, 4 feet by 3 ft. 7 in. (1.22 by 1.10 metres), which is dated 1518, close to the painting of the Winchester Round Table.[63] The Nuremberg table is decorated with a painted representation of Charlemagne's legendary battle against the Huns before Ratisbon, attributed to a master in the circle of Albrecht Altdorfer. In 1518 the Emperor Maximilian attempted to have his grandson, King Charles of Spain, elected King of the Romans at the Diet of Augsburg. Although this attempt failed, the date 1518 combined with the presence of the double-headed eagle of the King of the Romans makes it probable that the Nuremberg

---

[59] Charles de Tolnay, *Hieronymus Bosch*, 2nd ed. (Baden-Baden, 1966), p. 338.

[60] Kohlhaussen, 'Bildertische', as above, note 38, pp. 17–19.

[61] Kohlhaussen, 'Bildeutische', pp. 19–28; Lucas Wütrich, *Der Sogenannte 'Holbein-Tisch'* (Zürich, 1990) Mitteilungen der Antiquarischen Gesellschaft in Zürich, 57.

[62] Kohlhaussen, 'Bildertische', pp. 28–30.

[63] Ekkehard Schenk zu Schweinsberg, 'Eine gemalte Tischplatte von 1518', *Pantheon* 30 (1972), 133–43; Arno Schönberger, 'Keysers Karls streyt vor der stat regenspurg geschehen', ibid., 211–16; Ekkehard Schenk zu Schweinsberg, *Die letzte Schlacht Karls D. Gr.*, Hefte des Kunstgeschichtlichen Instituts der Universität Mainz 1 (Mainz, 1972).

table was produced in connection with this abortive dynastic manoeuvre. Maximilian's interest in Charlemagne, the founder of his empire, may be seen as a direct analogy to Henry VIII's interest in his predecessor, King Arthur, an interest shared by Maximilian himself.[64]

At the Abbey of Berne at Heeswijk in Holland is a table of about the same date as that at Nuremberg, although larger by a quarter, 3 ft. 7 in. by 4 ft. 8 in. (1.10 by 1.43 metres) and originally probably 4 ft. 8 in. (1.43 metres) square.[65] It continues the tradition of the Hieronymus Bosch table in Madrid, with scenes, in this case all biblical, set in a symmetrical pattern of medallions, originally seventeen in number and thus forming a fairly elaborate geometric construction. The medallions are supported by foliate ornament and by abbreviated quotations from the Vulgate in black letter on scrolls, the first significant inscriptions so far noted on a table.

[64] See *Karl der Grosse, Werk und Wirkung* (Aachen, 1965), catalogue nos. 746–9 and 765–6, for examples of this cult. Maximillian's cult of his ancestry led him in 1512 to commission the scholar Jacob Mennel, whom he had known since 1498 and employed continuously since 1505, to write a genealogical history of the Habsburgs, the *Fürstliche Chronik gennant Kayser Maximilians Geburtsspiegel.* (*Maximilian I, 1459–1519*, Österreichische Nationalbibliothek, Vienna, 1959, p. 57). The task took until 1517, and the decorations of the five books (six volumes in manuscript) were executed in 1518. Also in 1518 Mennel produced a volume of watercolours by the 'Mennel-Meister', who illustrated several of his works, to accompany his *Geburtsspiegel*: it was entitled *Kayser Maximilians besonder buch genannt der Zaiger* (ibid., p. 55). One watercolour shows Mennel handing over the five books of his *Geburtsspiegel* to Maximilian (here Fig. 161). The scholar is shown standing in front of a large wheel-like disk, in whose outer border the five books seem to revolve, and whose centre is decorated with the rays of the sun. (The sun is also etched on a Hungarian shield probably made for Maximilian by Hans Laubermann in 1515 and reoccurs in a clock included in a scene of Maximilian jousting by an artist close to Altdorfer in the manuscript *Die Historia Friderici et Maximiliani* of about the same date (ibid., p. 183, fig. 83, and pp. 115–6, fig. 51). The *Zaiger* also includes a watercolour in which the clerical members of the Habsburg family, from hermits to popes, are shown ascending a golden ladder to a sun heaven. In other watercolours secular Habsburgs climb a silver ladder to a moon heaven, while a jewelled ladder leads to the uppermost zone of heaven, reserved for saints of the Habsburg family. Several of these, including Adalbert, Edgar, both Edwards, Martyr and Confessor, Oswald and Thomas of Canterbury, were English, and there were three British saints, 'Sant Lütz Künig in Bryttania', 'Sant Ursula die hochgelobt Künigs tochter von Brittania' and 'Sant Jos Künigs sun in Brittania' (Simon Laschitzer, 'Die Heiligen aus der 'Sipp-, Mag, und Schwägerschaft' des Kaisers Maximilian I' *Jahrbuch der kunsthistorischen Sammlungen des allerhöchsten Kaiserhauses*, 5 (1887) p. 208. For Maximilian's interest in Arthur, see further below, Chapter 12, pp. 463–72.

[65] *Antiek* 4 (1969), whole issue with articles by B. Dubbe, 232–64 and 274–80; H. van Bavel and O. Praem, 265–73; and N. J. M. van Rosmalen, 281–4.

Four further tables in this group need only be mentioned briefly here. The first, painted in Strasbourg in 1530 by Hans Baldung Grien, bears a variety of scenes.[66] The second, dated 1531, is decorated with a map of Bavaria.[67] The third, painted in 1533 by Martin Schaffner, represents the Seven Liberal Arts.[68] The final table in this group was painted in 1534 by Hans Sebald Beham for Cardinal Albrecht of Brandenburg, and depicts four scenes from the life of King David.[69]

All the tables mentioned thus far in the second significant group are high-quality specimens of painting, and all are approximately square. At the Museum für Kunst und Kulturgeschichte in Dortmund, however, there is a small round table, 3 ft. 5 in. (1.04 metres) in diameter from Schloss Cappenburg, crudely painted with a sundial based on a calendar published in 1493 (Plate VII). The table, which cannot be much later than that date, is of considerable interest in the Winchester context because of its shape.[70] Moreover, the painted sundial with a sun in the centre corresponds formally to the radiating scheme of the Winchester table.

On 20 September 1486 the first son of Henry VII and Elizabeth of York was born at Winchester. He was baptised Arthur in Winchester Cathedral, as part of his father's policy to legitimate the new Tudor dynasty by stressing its links with King Arthur. In 1501, when Catherine of Aragon arrived in London to be married to Prince Arthur, she was greeted by ceremonies and pageants full of Arthurian symbolism. The cosmic machine incorporating a figure of Arthur, the signs of the zodiac, and armed knights, which was the main feature of the fourth pageant, is likely to have borne some formal resemblance to the Dortmund table.[71] It may also have recalled the white *rose en soleil*, or rose surrounded by the sun, which was a favourite badge of Prince Arthur's grandfather, Edward IV.[72] It has been suggested that the circles and wheels of fan vaulting reflect Tudor attitudes to kingship, the sun, and the cosmos.[73] The ceremonies

---

[66] Kohlhaussen, 'Bildertische', as above, note 38, pp. 29–33.

[67] Ibid., pp. 33–5. See also Paul Wescher, 'Ein weiteres Jahreszeitenbild zum Wertinger-Zyklus', *Münchener Jahrbuch der bildenden Kunst* 8 (1957), 101–14. This table includes an informal company sitting on one side of a round table in a garden, derived from Sebald Beham, *The Feast of Herodias*, woodcut, *c*.1530 (illus. Wescher, 'Ein weiteres Jahreszeitenbild', fig. 3). In the Rijksmuseum, Amsterdam, is a *round* map of Spain, executed in *verre eglomisé*, of the second half of the sixteenth century, ascribed to Wenzel Jamnitzer's Nuremberg workshop. It has a gilt base and was presumably intended to stand on a table, perhaps a round table. Diameter 61 cm.

[68] Kohlhaussen, 'Bildertische', pp. 35–9.

[69] Ibid., pp. 39–42.

[70] Kreisel, *Kunst des deutschen Möbels*, i, p. 36 and fig. 76.

[71] Francis Grose, *The Antiquarian Repertory*, ii (London, 1808), p. 315; Sydney Anglo, *Spectacle, Pageantry and Early Tudor Policy* (Oxford, 1969), pp. 77–85.

[72] Nicholas Harris Nicholas, *Privy Purse Expenses of Elizabeth of York: Wardrobe Accounts of Edward the Fourth* (London, 1830), p. 244.

[73] Walter C. Leedy, *Fan Vaulting: a Study of Form, Technology, and Meaning* (London, 1980), pp. 31–4.

of 1501 are said to have been devised by Richard Fox, who became bishop of Winchester in that year.[74] Fox was still bishop in 1516, when the Round Table was probably painted following the visit to Winchester of Henry VIII, Prince Arthur's younger brother. It seems likely that Fox had some involvement in this project and could then have looked back to 1501 and therefore to formal and symbolic sources comparable to those expressed in the Dortmund table, however apparently disparate an artefact (see Chapters 9 and 12).

A reference in a 1569 Essex inventory to 'the hutch that is painted with a St Catherine wheel' is evidence that in England the painting of furniture with geometric late Gothic subjects was not confined to the Round Table at Winchester.[75] In Switzerland, moreover, there are two large circular paintings of the seventeenth century which resemble the Winchester Round Table. The earlier of the two, known as the Grosse Ratsrose, was painted in 1651 by Hans Bildstein for the large council chamber in the Rathaus of Appenzell, where it remains (Plate IX).[76] The second, the Kleine Ratsrose, was painted in 1688 for the small council chamber, possibly by Johann Martin Geiger; it is now in the Schweizerisches Landesmuseum in Zürich (Plate VIII).[77] In 1679–80 the painter Hans Jacob Ulrich was paid for repairing the 'Grossen Röss' in the Rathaus in Zürich:[78] this was presumably a similar object which no longer exists. The two surviving Ratsrosen are identically laid out. Each has an allegorical scene in the centre, a middle band containing the arms of the nine 'Rhjoden' or local administrative divisions, and an outer border with the arms of the twenty-five members of the privy council, identified in black letter (*textura*). The 1651 Ratsrose originally had red cloth hanging from it, and has therefore been interpreted as a canopy to hang over the seat of the presiding officer. But the alternative suggestion, that it was a table with a cloth valance, around which the council could sit in Swiss equality, is attractive in the Winchester context. The Ratsrosen both have separate rim mouldings, that on the 1651 example painted barber-pole fashion, which could have been used to secure a *tablier* in the same way as has been suggested above for the Winchester table. Any direct connection is highly unlikely, but in view of the scarcity of parallels the Appenzell Ratsrosen certainly bear mention and investigation.

[74] E. K. Chambers, *The Mediaeval Stage* (Oxford, 1903), ii, p. 171.

[75] Quoted by F. G. Emmison, *Elizabethan Life: Home, Work & Land* (Chelmsford and Plymouth, Massachusetts, 1976), p. 20.

[76] Rainald Fischer, 'Die Malerei des 17. Jahrhunderts in Appenzell Innerrhoden', *Zeitschrift für Schweizerische Archäologie und Kunstgeschichte* 34 (1977), 34–6.

[77] Ibid., pp. 35–6.

[78] Konrad Escher, *Die Kunstdenkmäler des Kantons Zürich*, iv, *Die Stadt Zürich*, pt. 1 (Basel, 1939), p. 321.

When the Round Table was horizontal it was self-evidently a piece of furniture. When it was hung vertically and was painted it equally evidently ceased to be a functional table. But it did not cease to be a piece of furniture. It became, in effect, a cloth of estate, an essential means of marking precedence. Normally of course a cloth of estate was of cloth and comprised a dosser or dossal hanging vertically behind and above the person in the place of honour, and a canopy projecting from the wall, composed of celure and valance.[79] Both forms and nomenclature could vary considerably, but there can be no doubt that cloths of estate were a conspicuous element of display and ceremony during the visit of Charles V to England in 1522. When the emperor was staying at Henry VIII's lodging at Greenwich his Spanish retinue wondered at the rich hangings 'and specially at the riche cloth of estate'; and there were 'three clothes of estate' at the upper end of the hall at Greenwich. Particularly relevant was the pageant at Cornhill prepared for the emperor's entry to London : 'under a riche clothe of estate sat Kyng Arthur at a round table & was served with X Kynges, Dukes and erles all bearing Targettes of their arms'. As Henry and Charles approached, a poet proclaimed verses culminating in the hexameter 'Illustrat fortes Arthuri fama Britannos' ('Arthur's renown adorns the British brave').[80]

On 8 December 1523 Ferdinand, archduke of Austria, Charles V's younger brother, was invested with the Order of the Garter in Nuremberg by, among others, Sir Thomas Wriothesley, Garter King of Arms from 1504 to 1534. Wriothesley subsequently had this event commemorated in a miniature which shows Ferdinand at dinner, seated at a square table (Plate X*b*) under a cloth of estate. He paired this illustration with one showing Charles and Ferdinand's grandfather, Maximilian, King of the Romans and later Emperor Elect, at dinner on 12 September 1490, the day of his investiture (Plate X*a*). Among others at the table are Sir Thomas Wriothesley's father and predecessor as Garter King of Arms, John Writhe. Maximilian is shown under a cloth of estate at a round table, where precedence seems to be strictly observed. The miniature is highly unlikely to represent an attempt at accurate visual reportage more than thirty years after the event, but as it must date from soon after 1523 and is thus fairly close in date to the visit of Ferdinand's brother, Charles, in 1522, it is tempting to suggest that the pairing of cloth of estate and round table may be an echo of the pageant in Cornhill.[81]

---

[79] Nicholas, *Privy Purse Expenses*, p. 66.

[80] Edward Hall, *Chronicle*, ed. Sir Henry Ellis (London, 1809), pp. 635, 637, 639. See further below, Chapter 12, p. 427.

[81] College of Arms, MS. Vincent 152, fol. 178. Illus. Sir Anthony Wagner, *Heralds and Ancestors* (London, 1978), pl. 10

The decoration of cloths of estate could be as varied as their form, but for obvious reasons coats of arms were particularly favoured. It seems reasonable to argue that in the Great Hall of Winchester Castle the quasi-heraldic painted Round Table took on the role of the 'tableau armoyé de ses armes' which hung above the seat of Philip the Good, duke of Burgundy, at the first feast of the Golden Fleece in 1431.[82] In 1522 Charles V, Philip's great-great-grandson and the successor of Charlemagne, would have been fully conscious of the resonances of the Round Table acting as a cloth of estate above the place of his host, Arthur's successor Henry VIII, at Winchester. The irony involved in using the Round Table, instituted to abolish precedence, as a mark of precedence may however have been lost on both king and emperor.

It must by now be apparent that an analysis of the Winchester Round Table as a piece of furniture must be highly speculative. Much of this essay has been taken up with suggestions rather than facts. Those suggestions which attempt to define the table within its specific context as a piece of furniture may be crudely summarised thus. The Round Table at Winchester is an example of a recorded type of large cere- monial table found in public halls. Its rim is a reference to earlier tables, particularly those depicted in representations of the Last Supper. Its painting was part of a continuing tradition of painted tables, others of which, including examples labelled in black letter and executed for noble and royal patrons, provide both iconographic and formal parallels. And finally, the Round Table was transmuted into a cloth of estate. But the Winchester Round Table defies categorization. There exists no other monumental thirteenth-century table. There exists no other late medieval painted table on this scale. There is no other table which represents a large act of public propaganda in which antiquarianism, politics, and diplomacy are compounded. There is no other medieval table whose roundness is not an occasional attribute but constitutes, by its contradiction of the rectangular norm, its very definition. As furniture, in sum, the Winchester Round Table is unique.

---

[82] Havard, *Dictionnaire*, as above, note 11, i, col. 171.

3

The Setting of the Round Table: Winchester Castle and the Great Hall

Castle and fortress[1]

I n November 1066, barely a month after the Battle of Hastings, Winchester opened its gates without a struggle to the forces of William the Conqueror. This act delivered into his hands intact the principal city ('capital' has little meaning at this date) of the English kingdom, with the royal treasure, the records of government (such as they were), the ancient palace of the Anglo-Saxon kings, the cathedral, and two other royal monasteries. The surrender of the city opened the way for a flank march around London and William's coronation in Westminster Abbey on Christmas Day.

In the early weeks of 1067 William secured his hold on Winchester by ordering the construction of a castle within the city walls and by stationing there his principal military commander, William fitzOsbern, with the task of defending the left flank of the Norman bridgehead in south-east England against attack from the still unconquered Mercian English to the north.

The western defences of Winchester had been laid out in the late first century AD and surviving portions remained an obvious feature in the townscape until the nineteenth century. The West Gate, which still marks their line, has been the site of one of the city gates for nineteen hundred years. South of West Gate the Roman defences had swung west to form at the south-western corner of the city a large salient, 200 feet (60 metres) wide and 800 feet (245 metres) from north to south.

---

[1] The results of the excavations in Castle Yard in 1967–71 and in the 1980s, and elsewhere in the castle in 1990 and 1995–6, with a study of the documentary sources relating to the building and repair of the castle and Wren's King's House, which succeeded it on the same site, will be found in Martin Biddle and Beatrice Clayre, *Winchester Castle*, Winchester Studies 6.i (Oxford, forthcoming). A short account is Martin Biddle and Beatrice Clayre, *Winchester Castle and the Great Hall* (Winchester, 1983; new edition, Winchester, 2000).

This salient enclosed the highest ground within the city walls, but is otherwise unexplained. A stone wall was added to the city defences shortly after AD 200. It followed the line of the early rampart around the salient and remained in use throughout the Anglo-Saxon period and even later.

William built his castle in the salient, digging a line of bank and ditch to cut the area off from the rest of the city to the east. The Roman town wall, still in use, became the castle wall to north, west, and south; the new earthworks crowned by a timber palisade formed the fourth side. The area enclosed was just over four acres (Fig. 23a).

The strengthening of the castle began almost as soon as it was built. Our detailed knowledge is still confined to developments at the north end, north of the present Great Hall, where the construction of a royal chapel was followed immediately, perhaps as early as c.1071–2, by the piling up of an earthen mound or 'motte' revetted with timber. This mound was the first in a long sequence of structures at the northern apex of the castle designed to form a strong point to control the West Gate of the city. Within a very few years the timber revetment was replaced by a stone wall which continued down the east side of the castle on the line of the Conqueror's bank. In the early twelfth century, a great stone keep, comparable in size to that at Portchester, was built on the mound, and an extension of the latter buried the early royal chapel. At the south end of the castle there was from an early date a second and even larger earthen mound which later formed the upper ward or *dunione*, the strong-point of the whole fortress (Fig. 23 *inset*; cf. Fig. 24).

In 1141, Henry de Blois, bishop of Winchester and brother of the imprisoned King Stephen, with the help of Stephen's queen and her supporters, laid siege to the Empress Matilda, who held most of the walled city and was herself in Winchester Castle. In August and September 1141 the city was burnt, and Matilda was forced to abandon the castle and flee west to Wherwell. The castle was again under siege in 1216 when it was captured by Louis, son of Philip II of France, and the magnates in rebellion against John. A fortnight's pounding by siege engines broke great gaps through the walls and damaged buildings. After capturing the castle the French tried to plug the breaches with oak palisades and to clear the ditches,[2] but they were unable to prevent its recapture in 1217 in the name of Henry III.

The first task of the young king's advisers, who included Peter des Roches, bishop of Winchester, was to repair and strengthen the castle. The great square keep at the north-east angle was pulled down and its mound levelled. It was replaced in about 1222 by a splendidly built and immensely strong round tower equipped with sally-port passages. The great gate, which faced west towards Romsey and Salisbury, was

---

[2] Françoise Michel, *Histoire des ducs de Normandie et des rois d'Angleterre* (Paris, 1840), p. 192.

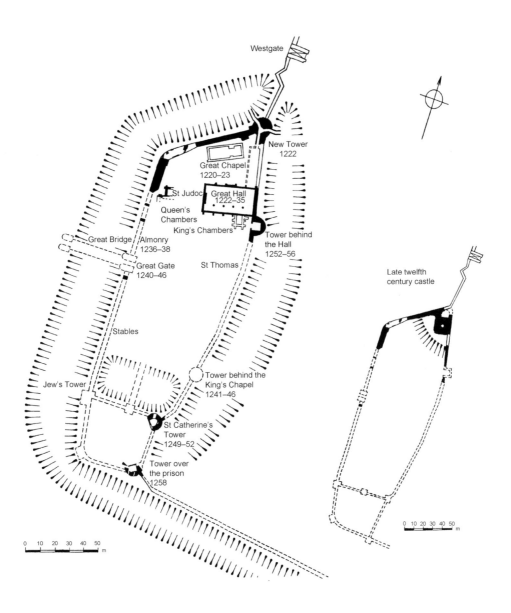

Westgate

New Tower
1222

Great Chapel
1220–23

St Judoc Great Hall
1222–35

Queen's
Chambers

King's Chambers

Tower behind
the Hall
1252–56

Great Bridge Almonry
1236–38

Great Gate
1240–46

St Thomas

Stables

Jew's Tower

Tower behind the
King's Chapel
1241–46

St Catherine's
Tower
1249–52

Tower over
the prison
1258

Late twelfth
century castle

0 10 20 30 40 50
m

0 10 20 30 40 50
m

0 10 20 30 40 50
m

23 Winchester Castle in the thirteenth century; *inset right*, the castle in the twelfth century. Outline reconstruction plans based on documentary, topographical, and archaeological evidence.

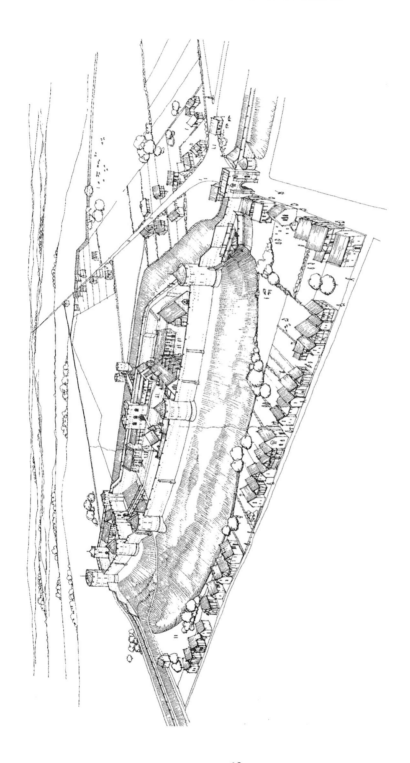

24 Winchester Castle as rebuilt by Henry III (1216–72). Perspective reconstruction, looking south-west.

rebuilt along with its bridge in 1240. In 1243 the castle ditch was widened and by 1258 all the towers on the east side of the castle facing the city had also been rebuilt. The total cost of these defensive works was around £6,000, but the castle successfully withstood siege when the city was captured by Simon de Montfort the younger in 1265 during the troubles between Henry III and the barons (Figs. 23c, 24).

Edward I continued to maintain the defences. In 1287 the great bridge outside the main gate of the castle was rebuilt by Master Peter the carpenter.[3] In 1294 a team of workmen worked on the castle walls from May to September, and more repairs were carried out in 1301.[4] After Edward I, maintenance became more sporadic. The threat of a French invasion in 1339 led to hasty repairs to the defences of both city and castle, and the garrison of the castle was increased, but the crisis was soon over.[5]

From the earliest days, the sheriff of Hampshire had usually been the constable of the castle, responsible to the king for its maintenance. This changed in 1383 when Robert Cholmeley was granted the office of constable for life, with the fees, wages, and profits belonging to it.[6] From this time until the castle passed into private hands in 1607, its maintenance was the responsibility of the constable. Within a short time of Cholmeley's appointment, a systematic programme of repairs was instituted. In 1387 these were in the hands of John Thorpe, who also had responsibility for the Southampton town walls and for works at Carisbrook Castle on the Isle of Wight. In 1389 three of the king's master craftsmen, William Wynford and Henry Yevele, masons, and Hugh Herland, carpenter, were working in Winchester on two of the great projects of the bishop, William of Wykeham. One of these was the continuing transformation of the cathedral nave from the Romanesque to the Perpendicular style; the other was the building of St Mary's College, now Winchester College, which William had founded in 1382. In 1390 these three craftsmen were appointed for seven years by writ under the great seal to repair the walls, turrets, gates, and bridges of 'the castle and the houses within which had not fallen'. The forty marks a year (£26 13s. 4d.) assigned for this purpose were to be paid by the bailiffs of the city out of the annual tax, or 'fee farm', which they owed to the crown. The repairs recorded during this period, which was renewed for a further seven years in 1397,[7] may have been linked to the provision of adequate accommodation for the constable. For the first time a distinction is made in the

---

[3] PRO, E101/561/1. For Edward I's works, see further below, Chapter 10, pp. 358, 364–7.
[4] PRO, E101/491/18; E372/147, rot. 7d.
[5] *Cal Close R 1339–41*, pp. 7, 33, 57, 324, 346.
[6] *Cal Pat R 1381–5*, p. 363.
[7] *Cal Pat R 1388–92*, p. 237; *Cal Pat R 1391–6*, p. 98; *Cal Pat R 1396–9*, p. 116.

records between the sheriff's ward, presumably based on the Great Hall at the north end of the castle, and the upper or constable's ward, which must be identified with the thirteenth-century *dunione*, or donjon, at the south end. In 1424 the bailiffs were ordered to spend some of the income from their fee farm for another period of seven years on repairs to the castle.[8]

By 1559 the importance of the castle as a royal fortress had declined so much that the queen readily granted the petition of the City of Winchester for its custody.[9] For the next forty-five years the ditches and the Castle Green were let out for pasture, and for a time the *dunione* at the south end was used as a house of correction.[10] In 1607 the castle passed into private ownership, when James I granted it (excluding the Great Hall) to Sir Benjamin Tichborne.[11] He and subsequent owners seem to have been intent on turning the *dunione* enclosure into a mansion house (see below, Chapter 13).

When the Civil War broke out in 1642, the castle belonged to Sir William Waller, who joined the parliamentary army and became colonel, later sergeant-major-general, of a regiment of horse. In December 1642 Winchester Castle became a refuge for royalist troops fleeing from Waller, but they soon surrendered when Waller's men were observed preparing to fire the castle gate. It was probably on this occasion that the Round Table was used for target practice (see below, Chapter 4), because after taking the castle Waller's men, who were months behind in their pay, proceeded to loot the city. In 1643 the castle was seized for the royalists by Sir William Ogle, who immediately set about fortifying and provisioning it. Ogle held the castle until October 1645, despite an attempt by Waller to retake it following his victory at the Battle of Cheriton in March 1644. On Sunday, 28 September 1645, Oliver Cromwell arrived in Winchester. The city was difficult to defend and surrendered to him. Cromwell then laid siege to the castle. For a week it held out, but a heavy mortar bombardment terrified and demoralized the garrison and severely damaged Waller's house. One mortar is said to have landed in the Great Hall, killing three men. Heavy canon fire had meanwhile opened a wide breach in the north wall. Ogle surrendered and Cromwell and Waller entered the castle on Monday, 6 October.[12]

In 1649 the Council of State, concerned that Winchester Castle should never again pose a serious threat to the Commonwealth, resolved that its defences should

[8]   *Cal Pat R 1422–9*, p. 199.
[9]   PRO, C66/946 [35].
[10] Biddle and Clayre, Winchester Studies 6.i, Gazetteer, s.v. House of Correction.
[11] PRO, C66/1697.
[12] Biddle and Clayre, Winchester Studies 6.i.

be dismantled. The county was at first reluctant to proceed in the matter but finally in 1651 under the supervision of Cromwell's in-law, Richard Major of Hursley Park, many of the castle walls and towers were thrown down.[13] For some years the castle remained no more than an imposing ruin. In 1656 Waller sold the site of the castle 'as it now stands defaced and erased' to the City of Winchester.[14]

The site returned to the crown in 1682 when the city granted it to Charles II, who had decided to build a hunting lodge on the site to a design by Sir Christopher Wren.[15] Charles died in 1685 before the building was complete, and for a century it remained 'little more than a carcass of a house' known as the King's House, serving at various times as a prison for enemy soldiers during the Seven Years' War and the American War of Independence, and as a refuge for French clergy fleeing the Revolution.

After the outbreak of war with France in 1793 the King's House became a particularly useful barracks for accommodating a large number of troops near to their ports of embarkation. By 1807 Winchester was the chief barracks in the south-west district, accommodating as many as 3,000 infantry at one time. The King's House was renovated and remodelled at a cost of more than £73,000 in 1809–11, and for the next eighty years it served as one of the principal depots of the British Army. It was destroyed by fire on the night of 19 December 1894; the Great Hall, containing the Round Table, was only ten feet (3 metres) from the fire and was saved with difficulty.[16] After the fire Long Block and Short Block were built as replacement barracks, using stone and a coat of arms salvaged from the King's House. The army continued to occupy the buildings until 1985 when the Winchester depot was moved from the site of the old castle to Flowerdown north of the city. This move brought to an end some nine centuries of crown occupation.

Castle and palace

The principal royal residence in Winchester at the time of the Norman conquest was in the centre of the city, just west of the cathedral, where it had been for centuries. About 1070 William extended this Anglo-Saxon royal palace north to the High Street, doubled its size, and erected a new hall and other buildings. This building

---

[13] *CSP Domestic 1649–50*, pp. 180, 197, 241, 243, 245, 272, 294, 304–5, 320, 323; *CSP Domestic 1650*, pp. 178, 471, 479, 488; *CSP Domestic 1651*, pp. 11, 57.

[14] PRO, C54/3888.

[15] HRO, W/F2/5, fols. 370–1.

[16] *Hampshire Chronicle* 22 Dec. 1894.

programme strongly suggests that William himself had no intention of replacing the ancient palace in the city centre by the new castle on the hill. Nevertheless, the role of the new castle was soon to change: by the early years of Henry I's reign, if not before William Rufus's death in 1100, it had come to combine the functions of residence and fortress.

In the castle, a royal chapel (whose walls still stand buried below the north side of the Great Hall) was already in existence by Easter 1072. In that year William and his queen, the papal legate, and the archbishops of Canterbury and York attended a council in the chapel to discuss a dispute between the archbishops over the primacy.[17] Where there was such a chapel and such a gathering, there almost certainly were a royal hall and other apartments, and there may also have been a prison, for Archbishop Stigand is said to have been held prisoner in the castle earlier in the same year.

When William Rufus was killed while hunting in the New Forest in August 1100, Henry I rode within hours to Winchester to secure the royal treasure, which was by then apparently in the castle. Within a decade the practice by which the Norman kings wore their crown in the cathedral at Easter each year they were in England was abandoned, and the old royal palace, conveniently close to the cathedral for such ceremonial, fell into disuse and passed into the hands of the bishop. A plea heard before the queen in the 'treasury' in the castle about 1110 may be the first indication of the existence of the exchequer, and suggests that the castle was by then the principal royal seat in the city. Here too during the twelfth century Domesday Book was also kept.

Little is known of the buildings in the castle until the mid twelfth century, when expenditure on works at the castle was recorded almost annually in the pipe rolls of the Exchequer. These records show that there was then concentrated within the castle 'that complex of halls, chambers, and chapels which constituted a medieval palace'.[18] Apart from work on the walls in 1169–71 and further strengthening of the defences two years later almost all the later twelfth-century activity was concentrated on the royal 'houses', perhaps partly because Eleanor of Aquitaine was confined here after her sons' rebellion. Work is recorded on the king's chamber and hall, the queen's chamber, a new chapel of St Thomas the Martyr (1174–7), the 'pentice where the young queen hears mass' (1174–5), the chapel of St Judoc (a Breton saint whose relics were at Hyde Abbey), a chamber for the king's clerks, a herb garden, a bird house, the treasury, and a new gaol.[19] Henry II's expenditure on houses and

---

[17] Martin Biddle (ed.), *Winchester in the Early Middle Ages*, Winchester Studies 1 (Oxford, 1976), p. 302 and n. 4.

[18] H. M. Colvin (ed.), *The History of the King's Works* ii, *The Middle Ages* (London, 1963), p. 855.

[19] Biddle and Clayre, Winchester Studies 6.i.

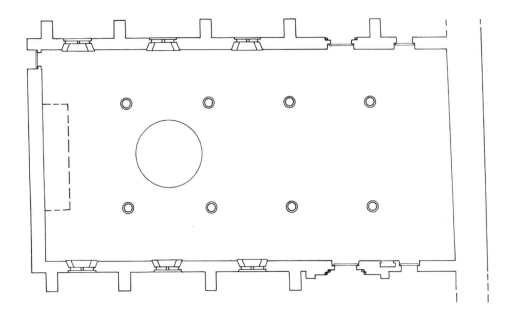

25 The Great Hall, as built by Henry III between 1222 and 1256. The circle shows the space which would have been occupied by the Round Table had it stood in this position. The rectangle against the west wall marks the position of the dais.

chapels at Winchester far outstripped his outlay on defence. Winchester Castle was now more residence than fortress, and had completely subsumed the role of the former royal palace in the middle of the town.

Henry III, often called 'Henry of Winchester' because he was born in the castle in 1207 and baptized in the cathedral, was nine years old when he became king. He was a frequent visitor to Winchester, passing eighteen Christmases in the city during his long reign. In addition to his expenditure on refurbishing the defences of the castle, he also spent some £4,000 extending and improving the royal apartments. Henry II's hall was pulled down in 1222 and work began on its replacement – the present Great Hall. To the south and west of the hall, the king's and queen's chambers were renovated, extended, and made more comfortable and attractive by the addition of fireplaces, glazed windows, tiled floors, wooden panelling, and latrines. Many of the chambers were painted, often green or green with gold stars, and were decorated with biblical scenes. Dovecots were built and lawns or herb gardens established. Several projects of reconstruction and decoration were carried out in the three chapels which already existed in the castle at the beginning of Henry's reign. In addition, two new chapels were built: a small one, near the king's bed, and the great chapel of St Mary to the north of the Great Hall, which may have been intended for the use of officials and visitors. For most of Henry's reign these chapels were served by five chaplains.[20]

Henry's works, which continued throughout his reign, established the final form of the medieval castle, for after his death there was no new building of any significance. The excavations in Castle Yard in 1967–71 and a study of contemporary and later documentary sources have allowed us to reconstruct the layout of the castle in the late thirteenth century (Figs. 23–5). At the southern end of the castle there was a quadrangular enclosure, usually referred to in the thirteenth century as the *dunione*. It had a tower at each corner – two rounded, facing the city, and two square, facing west – and a gatehouse facing north across a ditch which separated the *dunione* from the rest of the castle. Between the *dunione* and the complex of royal apartments which clustered around the Great Hall at the northern end of the castle, there was about an acre of open ground which in the sixteenth century was known as the Castle Green. Stables lined the castle walls and facing west was the imposing main gate, approached across a wooden bridge which in about 1390 was described as the *pluis beale pounte dengleterre fait de boys de chastell ou de ville* ('the most beautiful wooden bridge of any castle or town in England').[21] Access to the castle from the city was probably by

---

[20] Ibid.

[21] PRO, E28/6. The great bridge was rebuilt in 1287 and 1289, in 1355, and possibly again in 1425–9.

means of small postern gates, one in the *dunione* and the other leading to the Great Hall through the round tower at the north-east angle of the castle.

Edward I, although he spent less time in Winchester than his father had done, nevertheless continued to maintain the castle and royal apartments. The work carried out during his reign seems to have consisted mostly of roofing, glazing, and repairing walls. From February to October 1289 an extensive programme of repairs costing more than £70 was carried out, probably in preparation for the tournament to be held the following year (see Chapter 10). Slaters worked throughout the period on royal apartments such as the queen's great chamber and the chapel of St Thomas, and on domestic buildings such as the scullery, almonry, and the stables, working on the latter for nine weeks. The chamber of Richard Foun, the master of the king's horse, was also repaired. Glaziers worked from May to August, the Great Hall and the king's chapel of St Thomas receiving particular attention. From late May to late July, carpenters, sawyers, masons, plumbers, and labourers were all employed in repairing the hall in the *dunione*.[22] In 1301, the substantial sum of £279 7s. 9d. was spent on repairs, but no details survive.[23]

This steady programme of maintenance came to an end in 1302 when a fire — from which the king and queen barely escaped with their lives — severely damaged the royal apartments. A later survey of the king's and other chambers gutted in the fire concluded that the damage was so severe it was impossible to estimate the cost of repairs.[24] The work was never done, and after 1302 it was rare for a royal visitor to stay in the castle. In 1330, although Edward III ordered chambers to be prepared for him to stay in the castle when parliament met there, the queen stayed at the bishop's palace of Wolvesey on the opposite side of the city.[25] Edward I's queen had already stayed at Wolvesey in 1306 when she gave birth to their third child. When Henry IV married Joan of Navarre in Winchester Cathedral in 1403, they stayed at Wolvesey and held their marriage feast there, to judge from the damage caused by the king's men in the great hall at Wolvesey. Contrary to popular opinion, Henry V received the French Ambassador at Wolvesey and not at the castle on the eve of the Agincourt War in 1415. Henry VI often stayed at Winchester College. Henry VIII and the Emperor Charles V stayed at Wolvesey in 1522, and Mary Tudor stayed there for her marriage to Philip II of Spain in 1554. Philip was accommodated in the Prior's Hall, now the Deanery, but the marriage feast following their wedding in

---

[22] PRO, E101/491/17. See further below, Chapter 10, pp. 364–7.

[23] PRO, E372/147, rot. 7d.

[24] PRO, C145/74/22.

[25] *Cal Close R 1330–3*, p. 5; for this and subsequent references to Wolvesey, see also Martin Biddle, *Wolvesey Palace*, Winchester Studies 6.ii (Oxford, forthcoming).

the cathedral was held at Wolvesey. The Prior's Hall was also the scene in 1486 of the birth of Prince Arthur, the eldest son of Henry VII. Not until 1683, when Charles II began to build his palace on the site of the demolished castle, was there any prospect of a return to royal residence in Winchester.

The Great Hall from 1222 to c.1600

By the early thirteenth century there were two halls in Winchester Castle. One was in the tower or *dunione* at the southern end of the castle.[26] The other was in the bailey near the royal apartments,[27] and was almost certainly the one repaired for the young king Henry's Christmas visits to Winchester.[28] Its exact location is unknown but the complex of royal apartments of which it formed a part was situated to the west and south of the present Great Hall, and south of the keep built at the north-east angle of the castle in the early twelfth century. When, following the siege of 1216, the keep was demolished and replaced by the round tower which henceforth formed the northern bastion of the castle, its mound was levelled and the opportunity seized to rebuild the hall and repair the royal apartments. In 1222 orders were given for the hall within the bailey to be demolished and its timbers to be saved.[29] The following year quarrymen at Haslebury, near Bath, were paid 16s. 8d. to extract stones from their quarry for the buttresses of the hall within the bailey.[30] Between 1223 and 1228, however, progress seems to have been slow, and there is only one reference to work on the new hall. This may have been partly due to the difficult nature of the site chosen. In 1969 excavation on the north side of the Great Hall showed that it was built on steeply sloping layers of soil which covered the buried remains of the early Norman chapel and formed part of the mound and filled the adjacent ditch (p. 60). In 1985, a cursory investigation of the area outside the south door, before the construction there of the present garden, revealed that the porch had been built over an earlier structure, possibly a gatehouse at the southern outer end of a stone bridge leading up the mound to the twelfth-century keep. Some idea of the difficulty of building on the site is shown by the wall at the south-east internal angle of the hall, which continues to a depth of eleven feet (3.3 metres) below the floor. From 1228,

---

[26] H. M. Colvin, *The Building Accounts of Henry III* (Oxford, 1971), p. 126.

[27] Ibid., pp. 126, 138.

[28] T. D. Hardy (ed.), *Rotuli Litterarum Clausarum in Turri Londinensi Asservati* i, *1204–1224* (London, 1833), pp. 409, 483.

[29] Colvin, *Building Accounts*, p. 138.

[30] Ibid., p. 128.

however, progress was steady until the completion of the hall in 1235. It cost over £500, of which £200 was lent by Peter des Roches, the bishop of Winchester.[31]

The new hall in the bailey soon became known as the king's hall, or the Great Hall (Figs. 25–7). It was built in the Early English style of Gothic architecture, which first appeared in England towards the end of the twelfth century in such cathedrals as Canterbury, Wells, and Lincoln. At Winchester it was seen first in the cathedral where Bishop Godfrey de Lucy (1189–1204) removed the Norman Lady chapel to build the present retrochoir in the new style. Perhaps the most famous example of the Early English style is Salisbury Cathedral, where Elias of Dereham (1180–1245) had been in charge of the building works since its foundation in 1220. Elias was associated with many other architectural works of the early thirteenth century, such as the shrine of Thomas Becket and the great hall of the archbishops at Canterbury,[32] and in 1233 he appears in charge of the king's works in Winchester Castle and thus of the completion of the Great Hall.

The hall, 'the finest surviving aisled hall of the 13th century',[33] measures 111 feet in length from east to west and 55 feet in width (34 by 16.8 metres). It is divided by two rows of Purbeck marble columns into a nave and two aisles. The columns, each enhanced by four slender shafts, divide the length of the hall into five bays. In the easternmost bay there were formerly two small service doors, the one on the north leading to the buttery and pantry and the one on the south leading to the salsary and the great kitchen. Both have been blocked up. The second bay from the east was occupied by two large doors. The north door, blocked in 1789 (see p. 87), led directly into a courtyard across which lay the great chapel of St Mary. The great south door, with its fine Purbeck marble mouldings, led out through a grand porch towards other royal apartments. Between the two doors on the south, a small door probably once led by a small spiral staircase to the king's chamber above the porch and perhaps to a musicians' gallery.

In the hall as originally built there was no window over the south door and the windows over the three other doors at the east end were short. The other six windows were long, two-light openings, each with transoms, a quatrefoil in the head, and a circular light above. Each window was covered by an individual gable rising between overhanging eaves, the original roof being steeply pitched from the ridge down to the level of the window transoms and covered with oak shingles (Fig. 27a). There was a small three-light window in the east gable, and possibly another in the west.

[31] *Cal Close R 1231–4*, p. 234.
[32] John Harvey, *English Medieval Architects*, 2nd edn., (Gloucester, 1984), pp. 81–2.
[33] Margaret Wood, *The English Mediaeval House* (London, 1965), pp. 39–40.

a

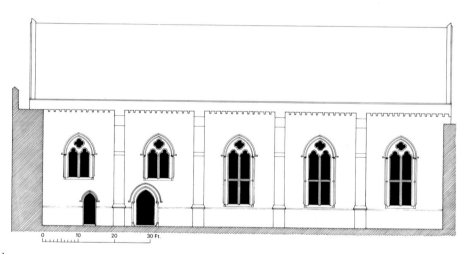

b

26 The north elevation of the Great Hall: *a*, as originally built in 1222–35; *b*, as reconstructed in the 14th century (?1348).

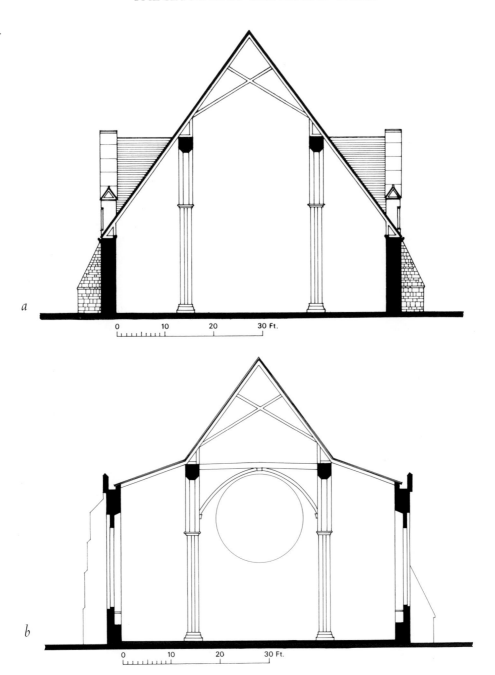

27 The section of the Great Hall, looking east: *a*, as originally built in 1222–35; *b*, as reconstructed in the 14th century (?1348), the circle showing the Round Table hung on the wall.

The internal layout of the hall would have been typical of the period, but little structural evidence for it has survived. The service and main doors, where there would have been constant traffic and consequent draughts, were located at the lower end of the hall, in this case at the east end, and were probably screened off in some way. The high seat would have been situated on the dais at the other end of the hall, in this case at the west end, where the remains of a later dais can still be seen (Fig. 25). At Winchester some confusion has arisen from the fact that the pipe roll account for making the royal seat in the hall refers to it as being *ad capud aule Regis Winton versus orientem*, a phrase which has sometimes been interpreted as meaning at the east end of the hall. But there can be no doubt that the head of the hall was at the west, so that *versus orientem* must be understood as meaning 'looking east'.[34] Further confirmation that the dais lay at the west end is provided by the existence of the small but elaborate private doorway of Purbeck marble at the north end of the west wall. This would have allowed the royal party to reach the dais, which can only have occupied the width of the nave, from their private apartments.

The chancellor's roll for 1235–6 shows that the internal walls of the hall were plastered and whitewashed, the windows glazed, and the capitals and wooden bosses gilded, and that there was a high seat with a chair for the king at the west end. On the gable above this seat, also facing east (*versus orientem*), there was a painting of the Wheel of Fortune.[35] The hall was well maintained throughout the reign of Henry III, and from the frequent references to the work done we learn that the doors and windows were painted with the king's arms, that heads were made above the dais and were gilded, and that the floor was paved and the dais tiled. In 1239, a writ addressed to the guardians of the bishopric of Winchester (the bishop, Peter des Roches, having died the previous year) instructed them to have a map of the world (*mappam mundi*) painted in the hall. Elias of Dereham, who was in charge of works at the castle when the hall was completed and the Wheel of Fortune painted, was also an executor of Bishop Peter des Roches and may have been consulted about this painting because he appears to have been interested in cosmographical theories as a circular drawing of a windrose *secundum magistrum Eliam de Derham* ('according to Master Elias of Dereham'), copied by Matthew Paris, suggests.[36]

[34] PRO, E352/29, rot. 15; E372/80, rot. 10d. *Versus*, with the meaning 'turned towards', 'facing', was used by classical writers such as Livy: see Charlton T. Lewis and Charles Short, *Latin Dictionary* (Oxford, 1966), p. 1978. This usage would be appropriate for someone standing in the hall.

[35] PRO, E352/29, rot. 15.

[36] For the painting of the map, see *Cal Lib R 1226–40*, p. 405. For the windrose, see Richard Vaughan, *Matthew Paris*, 2nd edn. (Cambridge, 1979), p. 255 and pl. xxd.

The map of the world, which would have been a circular design similar to the one known from Hereford Cathedral, was probably painted on the east wall of the hall above the screens passage and opposite the Wheel of Fortune above the dais. It would appear to have been the work of Nigel, 'chaplain and painter in the king's hall and chapel', who in 1240 and again in 1241 received of the king's gift a robe costing 16s., paid for out of the revenues of the bishopric of Winchester.[37] In 1260 the sheriff of Hampshire was ordered to renew the paintings in the hall,[38] but whether this included the Wheel of Fortune or map of the world we do not know.

There is no sign that the main door on the north side of the hall ever had a porch. It seems rather to have opened directly into a courtyard, opposite the chapel of St Mary. Beyond that again was the round tower built in the 1220s at the north-east angle of the castle, through which there was almost certainly a way into the city (Fig. 24).

On the other side of the hall, the south door led to a two-storey porch of exceptional size and elevation. In 1239 four images were ordered for this porch.[39] In 1256 an image of St George was ordered to be made and placed on the wall 'over the entrance to the hall' and in 1268–9 an image of St Edward was to be carved, painted, and set 'at the door of the hall',[40] descriptions which probably both refer to the more important south door leading towards the king's apartments and the royal chapel of St Thomas. An attempt to restrict or control access through this entrance seems to have been made in 1238, when two posts with a chain were ordered to be set up before the porch together with some kind of wooden barrier (*licias*).[41] The plan of the south porch of the Great Hall shown in Fig. 23 is identical in outline and scale with the great north porch of Salisbury Cathedral, the main entrance, above which is a chamber known as the Parvis Room. The association of Elias of Dereham with both works explains this similarity, but of the two the Winchester porch seems to have been the more elaborate, being decorated with a series of statues rather than with the single figure of Christ.[42] The king's chamber on the upper floor was fitted with a fireplace and from here the king may have had a view of the hall through a well placed window or squint.[43]

---

[37] *Cal Lib R 1226–40*, p. 438; *Cal Lib R 1240–5*, p. 26; PRO, E372/85, rot. 3 (episcopal vacancy account, 14 June 1238 – 15 April 1240).

[38] *Cal Lib R 1251–60*, p. 526; PRO, E372/104, rot. 3.

[39] *Cal Lib R 1226–40*, p. 405.

[40] *Cal Lib R 1251–60*, pp. 307–8; *Cal Lib R 1267–72*, p. 89 (no. 784).

[41] *Cal Lib R 1226–40*, p. 350; PRO, E372/83, rot. 1.

[42] Roy Spring, *Salisbury Cathedral*, The New Bell's Cathedral Guides (London and Sydney, 1987), pp. 40–1 and plan, p. 62.

[43] *Cal Lib R 1226–40*, p. 432.

Under Edward I both halls in the castle were kept in repair. More than 4,000 shingles were bought for roofing the Great Hall in 1283 and in 1289, the year before the tournament, masons were working on the walls and entrance of the hall, while glaziers repaired the windows. In the same year the hall in the *dunione* was extensively repaired.[44]

The hall escaped the fire which devastated the royal apartments in 1302, and a survey of the castle taken in 1314 stated rather surprisingly that the hall needed repairs only to the value of 100s.[45] After 1302 its use for royal visits was very limited (see above, p. 69). Parliament met in Winchester from time to time, but only Edward III in 1330 recorded a wish to stay in the castle. The locations where the triers of petitions met in 1393, 'in the chapel of the middle chamber' and 'in the chapel of the withdrawing chamber', make no sense in the context of the castle as revealed in other documentary records, and should perhaps be set in Winchester College or at Wolvesey. The king and queen were twice in Winchester that year to visit the bishop, William of Wykeham, and on both occasions they are known to have stayed at Wolvesey.

During the fourteenth and fifteenth centuries the hall became more important as a legal and administrative centre. After the appointment of Robert Cholmeley as constable of the castle in 1383 (see above, p. 63), the sheriff administered the county from the Great Hall, now in 'the sheriff's ward'. The increasing use of the hall must also have resulted from the statutes passed in 1344 and 1350 requiring the appointment of justices of the peace who were to meet at least four times a year to hear and determine felonies and trespasses done against the peace of the county.[46]

Some time during these two centuries, the hall underwent a major reconstruction, when the separate gables over the windows were removed, the aisle walls heightened, and the aisles separately roofed (Figs. 26*b*, 27*b*). This is often thought to have happened in 1393–4 (following the meeting of parliament in Winchester), when a certain great hall in the upper ward of the castle was *de novo constructo* ('built from new') by the mason, Walter Ufford.[47] The hall in the upper ward must, however, be the hall in the *dunione*, then part of the constable's ward at the south end of the castle; a great hall in the constable's ward is recorded as being roofed in 1396–7.[48] This would be consistent with a refurbishment of the *dunione* or upper ward for

---

[44] PRO, E101/491/15; PRO, E101/491/17; see further below, Chapter 10, pp. 364–6.

[45] PRO, C145/74/22.

[46] Danby Pickering (ed.), *The Statutes at Large from the Fifteenth Year of King Edward III to the Thirteenth Year of King Henry IV inclusive* ii (Cambridge, 1762), pp. 11, 35.

[47] PRO, E364/28.

[48] PRO, E364/31.

28 Badges: *a, b,* 16-point rayed roses from the tie-beams of the Great Hall, 14th century (?1348); *c, rose-en-soleil* from Thurbern's Chantry, Winchester College, carved in 1484–5.

the constable's use (see above, p. 64). In 1394–5 the Winchester bailiffs recorded work on the Great Hall in the sheriff's ward and the constable's counter-roll for the same year mentions masons' work on the repair of walls and windows of the Great Hall in the sheriff's ward, in Munesies tower, and on other walls of the castle, as well as lead roofing work on the hall.[49] Since annual expenditure on these repairs was limited between 1390 and 1404 to £26 13s. 4d., it seems unlikely that there was enough money to cover the cost of a major reconstruction of the hall as well.

The only other occasion during this period when a considerable sum appears to have been spent on the hall was in 1348–9, when orders were given for the hall to be re-roofed. Other buildings were also involved, but the work took longer than expected and the costs increased to over £300, the initial allowance having been for £100.[50] The heightening of the aisle walls of the hall at this time would be particularly interesting in the context of Bishop Edington's contemporaneous work in beginning the transformation of the nave of the cathedral from the heavier Romanesque to the lighter Perpendicular style. The impetus for change could have been the increasing use of the Great Hall following the appointment of justices of peace in 1344. By this time the Round Table would have been a considerable inconvenience at floor level, no longer being required for royal feasts, and this may have been the moment when the table was hung on the east gable, thereby protecting it from daily concourse in the hall (see Chapter 11).

The existing tie-beams of the roof, with the archbraces and panelled spandrels still surviving below them, may have been inserted during this reconstruction (Figs. 27b, 29). The panelling in the spandrels looks like high-quality court-school work in the Perpendicular style of the mid fourteenth century.[51] But this dating raises considerable problems. The badges carved on the underside of the tie-beams and integral with them are usually identified as displaying the *rose en soleil* and attributed to Edward IV (1461–83; Fig. 28). This is a very late date for the panelling of the spandrels, and there is in fact no record of any work on the hall during Edward's reign. (An allowance of £80 made in 1450 for work at the castle does not mention the hall). Henry IV also used the (red) *rose en soleil* badge, and this might suggest that the tie-beams were inserted as part of the programme of maintenance undertaken between 1390 and 1404, but this badge is not found in contemporary buildings at the cathedral or the college, although a more sophisticated badge with a double rose

---

[49] PRO, E364/29; PRO, E101/491/25.

[50] *Cal Close R 1346–9*, pp. 450, 574; *Cal Close R 1349–54*, p. 125.

[51] Dr Christopher Wilson kindly discussed this point, drawing a compelling parallel between the panelling of the Great Hall spandrels and the panelling in the lower part of the lantern at Ely Cathedral, constructed by the king's master carpenter William Hurley in 1334–40.

29 Tracery panels in a spandrel below one of the tie-beams of the Great Hall, 14th century (?1348).

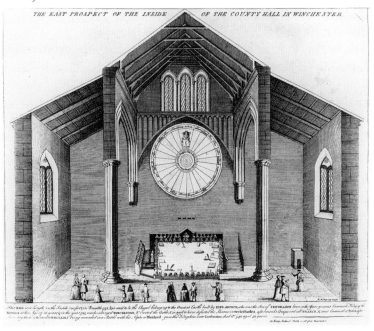

30 The east end of the Great Hall, *c*.1743, showing the Nisi Prius Court and the Round Table (cf. Fig. 120).

does occur in both places. The rose found on the badges in the Great Hall is a conventional heraldic form with five displayed petals (one has four and one has six), with intervening spaces between the petals, and it may be an earlier form. Moreover, an account of 1389 which refers to repairing the lead on the two aisles of the Great Hall suggests that their walls had already by then been raised: only after the reconstruction would the low pitch of the aisle roofs have required their shingles to be replaced by lead.[52] On balance, therefore, it seems better to date the alteration of the hall, with the raising of the aisles and the re-roofing of the nave, to 1348–9, and to suspect that the badges could also have been used in the reign of Edward III (see below, Chapter 11).

Between 1425 and 1428 the Great Hall was completely re- roofed with 48,000 shingles. After this date and until 1559, when the city sucessfully petitioned for custody of the castle, there are few references to the castle or to the Great Hall. Many repairs to the hall were carried out during the last forty years of the sixteenth century, however. The south aisle was repaired at the crown's cost, the 'middle roffe' at the city's, and liability for the repair of the north aisle 'which was so decayed as to be in danger of falling' became the subject of litigation (see below, Chapter 13).

The Great Hall from c.1600 to the present day

The sixteenth century saw an awkward transition in English architecture, from the perfection of medieval Perpendicular to a clumsy use of the ill-understood forms of the Renaissance. Ever since Henry VIII had become interested in the new style, it had increasingly ousted native architectural traditions based on the use of the pointed arch. But it was only in the early years of the next century that Renaissance models were finally accepted and fully understood.

In 1603, the very year of Queen Elizabeth's death, the architect and painter Inigo Jones (1573–1652) returned from Italy equipped with a thorough knowledge and appreciation of the principles of classical architecture. This he derived from long observation of examples of ancient architecture and from a study of the works and writings of the Italian architect Andrea Palladio. Jones first established his reputation by devising the masques for which the court of King James I and his queen, Anne of Denmark, became famous. But his other talents, in painting and especially in architecture, were fully appreciated, and in 1615 he became the Surveyor of the King's Works and Buildings, a post he held until ejected by Parliament in 1643. In his designs for the Queen's House at Greenwich from 1616 and the Banqueting

[52] PRO, E364/29d.

House at Whitehall in 1619–22 Jones demonstrated for the first time in England the proper use of the elements of classical architecture.[53] Through them he brought about the complete and decisive break with the past which made possible the work of Wren and the English architects of the eighteenth century.

Within the space of a decade the architecture of the pointed arch and the mullioned window was wholly superseded by the architecture of the classical orders and came to be seen as barbarous by comparison. By the middle of the seventeenth century it had begun to be fashionable to suggest its crudity and uncouthness by use of the newly invented word 'Gothic', a word whose derivation underlines the contempt it was originally meant to convey.[54] In the eyes of Sir Henry Wotton, writing in 1624, pointed arches were devices which,

> both for the naturall imbecility of the sharpe *Angle* it selfe, and likewise for their very *Vncomelinesse*, ought to bee exiled from judicious eyes, and left to their first inventors, *the Gothes*, or *Lumbards*, amongst other *Reliques* of that barbarous Age.[55]

Barely twenty years later, following his successful siege in 1645, Oliver Cromwell ordered Winchester Castle to be disgarrisoned. Save for the Great Hall, which Sir William Waller had sold to the Justices of the Peace for Hampshire in 1642 for the use of the county, the castle was eventually rendered defenceless and was partly demolished in 1651. By this time the architecture of the Great Hall had almost certainly come to be of little interest, or cause for excitement and wonder, to any but a handful of antiquarian scholars. In another hundred years just what the hall had originally been was quite forgotten.

Among the many ceremonial and social uses to which the Great Hall would have been put from the first, the regular sitting of courts of law would have been one of the most important. Many famous trials took place within its walls, including that of Sir Walter Raleigh in 1603, when the courts which normally sat in Westminster were transferred to Winchester to avoid the plague in London.

It was for such public use that the hall had been sold to the justices by Sir William Waller for £100 in 1642, but he retained the right to its use when not

---

[53] For Inigo Jones, see John Summerson in H. M. Colvin (ed.), *The History of the King's Works* iii, *1485–1660*, pt. 1 (London, 1975), pp. 121–59. The proportions of the Whitehall Banqueting House, which has been described as the 'handsomest room in England', are strikingly similar to the Winchester Great Hall: 110 x 55 x 56 feet, compared to 111 x 56 x 55 feet.

[54] Sir Kenneth Clark, *The Gothic Revival* (London, 1928; reprint, Harmondsworth, 1964), p. 3.

[55] Sir Henry Wotton, *Elements of Architecture* (London, 1624), p. 51; also quoted by Clark, *Gothic Revival*, pp. 3–4.

required for the public service. Such incidental uses continued for a long time. As late as 1733 the justices in the Michaelmas Session ordered:

> that the Hall keeper doe not for the future permitt or suffer any person or persons to put, lay or thresh any Wheat, Barley, Oats, Beans, Pease or other Grain Whatsoever into the County Hall.[56]

To accommodate trials, simple but apparently permanent structures were erected at each end of the hall, occupying only the central portion of each end bay. As early as the 1640s, the Nisi Prius Court (or 'barre') for trying civil causes sat at the east end of the hall, below the Round Table: in a furious comment on the sentence of death passed on Captain John Burleigh in the Great Hall in 1648 for attempting to rescue Charles I from Carisbrooke Castle in the Isle of Wight, the *True and Brief Relation* of his suffering supposed

> my Lorde himselfe whilst he is determining a Cause between party & party, at the Nisi Prius barre, should be beaten down with King Arthurs round Table & so crushed under the weight of it that he perish, ...[57]

Burleigh was presumably tried in the Crown Court, the criminal court, at the other end of the hall from the table, although there seems to be no other evidence for its separate existence before the re-arrangements of 1765. Even after the works ordered in 1723 and 1727 to make the accommodation for the 'sitting and standing' of counsel and juries more convenient, the furnishings of the court (or courts, if there were already two) interfered little with the open layout of the hall, to judge from the engraving made by Richard Benning in or after 1743 (Fig. 30).[58]

Indeed the arrangements shown in this engraving, entitled *THE EAST PROS-PECT OF THE INSIDE OF THE COUNTY HALL IN WINCHESTER* (a wording which will be referred to later in another context), appear so barely adequate that the next and perhaps most regrettable chapter in the history of the hall was hardly surprising. Melville Portal (1819–1904), the historian of the hall and himself a Hampshire justice, described the changes with some feeling:

---

[56] Michaelmas Session Book 1733, HRO Q1/12, fol. 56v.

[57] *A True & Brief Relation of the Araignment, Condemnation and Suffering of Capt. John Burleigh, who was drawn, hang'd and quartered at Winton* (1648), p. 2 (BL, E.426. (1.)).

[58] For the authorship and date of the drawing on which this engraving is based, see p. 480.

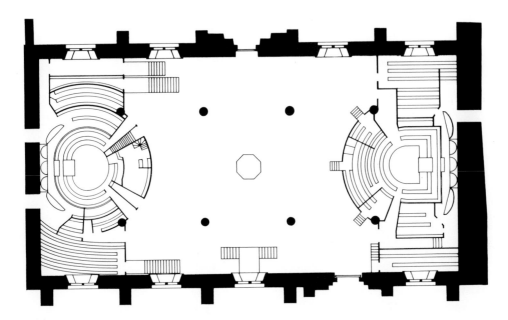

31 The courts in the Great Hall, 1765–1873: *left*, Crown Court; *right*, Nisi Prius Court.

32 The central bay of the Great Hall in the ?early 19th century, showing the Georgian flat corniced ceiling, the relocated roundels, the half-blocked windows, and the ?14th century timberwork of the south aisle roof. Drawn by Edward Blore (1787–1879).

at the Michaelmas Sessions, of 1764, in consequence of a Presentment made by the Grand Jury at the last assizes, an order was made that two new Courts should be erected in the County Hall ... In carrying out the work but little regard was paid to the claims of antiquity, architectural beauty, or historic association. The old Hall was sacrificed to utilitarian views: its two ends were partitioned off for the respective purposes of the Crown and Nisi Prius Courts, and its main architectural features were concealed behind wooden galleries and plaster adornments. Whitewash and stucco were triumphant. The whole work presented an admirable example of the debased taste of the Georgian Era; the Royal Arms were made to supplant the Old Round Table, in the place which it had occupied for centuries on the west wall, as if, with bitter irony, to mark the precise date of the reign of ugliness.[59]

Few drawings or photographs exist of these structures, but a plan made in 1865 of the arrangement established in 1765 and modified in 1789 shows that the Crown Court, laid out in a compressed circle of tiered seats, occupied the west bay of the hall and the Nisi Prius Court, arranged in a horseshoe, occupied the east bay, as it had done previously (Fig. 31). The back walls of the two courts bulged into the space remaining in the middle of the hall. A photograph taken in 1873 when the Round Table was lowered shows that the back wall of the Nisi Prius Court at the east end of the hall was of wooden construction covered with lath and plaster up to the underside of the roof, which was ceiled; simple wooden panelling extending to a height of some fifteen feet above the floor (Fig. 34). A drawing by the architect Edward Blore (1787–1879) made early in the nineteenth century shows the central area of the hall with a flat corniced ceiling between the trusses, but gives no indication of the court structures which then existed to either side (Fig. 32). Even when every allowance is made for Melville Portal's prejudiced view of Georgian taste, and considering that almost nothing made between 1700 and 1780 could by today's standards be truly described as ugly, there is little doubt these structures detracted considerably from the magnificent interior of the medieval hall. In his old age in 1921, the Winchester architect Thomas Stopher remembered them as 'hideous'.

Ironically, at this very time the revival of interest in Gothic architecture had begun. In 1762 Horace Walpole had written as if to refute Sir Henry Wotton:

---

[59] Melville Portal, *The Great Hall, Winchester Castle* (Winchester and London, 1899), pp. 68–9. Portal refers to the Royal Arms over the Crown Court having replaced the Round Table at the west end of the hall because he had convinced himself (wrongly) that the table had hung there in the Middle Ages. The problem lies in the interpretation of the Latin descriptions, see above, p. 74.

The pointed arch, that peculiar of Gothic architecture, was certainly intended as an improvement on the circular, and the men who had not the happiness of lighting on the simplicity and proportion of the Greek orders, were however so lucky as to strike out a thousand graces and effects, which renders their buildings magnificent, yet genteel, vast yet light, venerable and picturesque.[60]

The early years of the eighteenth century saw a diversification and slackening in the cultural impulse of the Renaissance and the emergence of the new ideas, attitudes, and moods which by the end of the century were to interlock and form the complex jigsaw of the Romantic Movement. One manifestation of this movement, initially perhaps its most serious, was the extension of the study of classical culture to the investigation of its origins in ancient Greece. Another, rather less serious to begin with, was the study and appreciation of ruins, ready to hand for study in England in a great many semi-derelict cathedrals and tumbledown country churches and in the crumbling piles of the monasteries dissolved by Henry VIII. In architecture, the first was to give rise to the Greek Revival; out of the second grew slowly but surely the revival of Gothic.

The Society of Antiquaries was founded in 1707. The development of scholarly studies and archaeology which it encouraged balanced nicely the considerable volume of work produced by writers, poets, and painters, inspired by the same subjects, which treated the past with greater licence and much sentimentality. By the time Walpole wrote on the pointed arch in 1762 the renaissance of Gothic had begun and a number of buildings, including Walpole's own extraordinary house, Strawberry Hill at Twickenham, had been built or decorated in imitation of medieval models.

Inasmuch as it was reasonably well preserved and in regular use at this time, the Great Hall was probably more fortunate than the great majority of major medieval buildings. As Lord Clark put it:

> The great Gothic buildings had been neglected for almost two centuries, and when once more they became a subject of interest they were found to have decayed. This discovery was met in two ways: either the buildings were restored, or they were closed and utterly deserted, that their collapse might not endanger human life. The former course was certainly the more disastrous, even when a building was really in danger of falling down; and often restoration took place where none was needed. These restorations were called

---

[60] Horace Walpole, *Anecdotes of Painting* (Strawberry Hill, 1762), i, p. 107; also quoted by Clark, *Gothic Revival*, p. 30.

improvements, and arose from the fact that the eighteenth century's conception of Gothic did not always agree with the evidence of actual examples.[61]

Dr John Milner, one of the most learned scholars of Gothic architecture living at the end of the eighteenth century and the builder in Winchester in 1792 of the chapel regarded by many as the first ecclesiastical building in the Gothic Revival style, believed that the Great Hall had been an ancient church or chapel.[62] If a person of Milner's scholarship could be so mistaken, little reliable knowledge can have existed. Delightful though much of the architecture of the early Gothic Revival may be, little of it displays any serious understanding of the principles of medieval building. For Lord Clark, indeed, Milner's Winchester chapel was 'the grubby Gothic of the Commissioners' churches, perhaps the most completely unattractive architectural style ever employed'.[63]

A water-colour by Francis Grose of about 1780 shows the north side of the Great Hall with the entrance in its original position in the second bay from the east, and the original stone plate-tracery still in place in the three central windows (Plate XI). In the windows at either end which lighted the two courts, the plate-tracery has been replaced by elaborate 'Gothick' tracery, probably in wood. Even in the three central windows only the upper lights are glazed, the lower lights and quatrefoil light at the top apparently being walled up.[64] The level of the ground outside the hall is shown considerably raised above the level inside, as it is known to have been already a century earlier.[65]

In 1789 the main entrance on the north side was removed from its original position to the central bay, an arrangement which better suited the new layout of the courts, but which also brought an uncharacteristic symmetry to the exterior and a disturbing lack of relationship internally between the door and window openings on

---

[61] Clark, *Gothic Revival*, p. 64.

[62] John Milner, *The History ... of Winchester* 2nd edn. (Winchester, 1809), ii, p. 182. For his Winchester chapel, see ibid., pp. 240–59 and pl. between pp. 240 and 241. For Milner, see now M. N. L. Couve de Murville, *John Milner 1752–1826*, Archdiocese of Birmingham, Historical Commission publication (Birmingham, 1986).

[63] Clark, *Gothic Revival*, p. 89, a harsh judgement attributable in part at least to the state into which the chapel had fallen by 1927–8. It was gutted in 1953, but was restored in 1988.

[64] The walling up of the lower lights can also be seen in Blore's drawing, reproduced here as Fig. 32.

[65] 'Went to Winchester into the Hall and Arbour to see the choice of Knights of the Shire. Jarvis, Henly and Fleming stood. It came to the Pole, I offer'd my Voice, but was refus'd because I would not lay my hand on and kiss the book, though I offer'd to take my Oath. My Rapier was broken short off, I suppose coming down the steps into Hall.' M. Halsey Thomas (ed.), *The Diary of Samuel Sewall 1674–1729* (Massachusetts Historical Society, New York), i, *1674–1708*, p. 196 (19 Feb. 1689).

opposite sides of the hall. The new doorway was shielded by an incongruous brick porch in a Georgian style.

No further work was done until the early years of Queen Victoria's reign, but it is not difficult to imagine that during the first forty years of the nineteenth century – a period which saw, according to Melville Portal, 'the revival of taste' – the hall became for more and more people a building of much curiosity and interest. To further this revival of taste locally, the great stone choir screen in Winchester Cathedral, designed by Inigo Jones in 1634 in the classical style, was dismantled and removed. In two centuries the needle of taste had swung almost full circle. Gothic was looked upon not as a style but as a religion.[66]

The thorough restoration of the Great Hall in Queen Victoria's reign was carried out in two stages. The first was the restoration of the exterior begun by O. B. Carter, a Winchester architect, in 1845. The second was the restoration of the interior by T. H. Wyatt. This followed his construction over the castle ditch at the east end of the Great Hall in 1872–3 of a new court building designed to allow the hall finally to be freed of the court structures which had for so long disfigured it.

Owen Browne Carter (1806–59) was an able architect of considerable talent and sensitivity and an especially skilled draughtsman. His most notable work in Winchester was the Corn Exchange in Jewry Street, now used as a public library. A number of exquisite drawings of the Great Hall made by Carter in 1843 reveal his thorough knowledge of the building's form and construction, both inside and out, and show his understanding of the original position and probable design of the main entrance.[67]

Carter restored both the stonework of the parapets and gables and the medieval plate-tracery windows, removing the 'Gothick' wooden frames which since 1789 had been fitted to all the windows on the north side of the hall. He also replaced the Georgian doorway and brick porch in the centre of the north wall by a porch and door of Gothic design. The windows of the Great Hall as restored by Carter in 1845 are generally regarded to be among the finest examples of plate-tracery to be found (Pl. XIII), and his doorway, although perpetuating the incorrect relocation of 1789, is a bold essay in Early English Gothic, a style little used by architects at this time.

When Carter was preparing this work he had as a pupil in his office the young G. E. Street, who was to become one of the towering figures in the later years of the Gothic Revival. The Great Hall would most certainly have impressed Street deeply.

---

[66] Clark, *Gothic Revival*, p. 106.

[67] Robin Freeman, *The Art and Architecture of Owen Browne Carter (1806–1859)*, Hampshire Papers 1 ([Winchester], 1991), pp. 14–16.

In a statement made to T. H. Wyatt many years later, Street claimed to have drawn the new north doorway.[68] Whether by 'drawn' he meant 'designed', is a tantalizing question which cannot be answered.

A scheme to remodel the Great Hall was prepared in 1856 by W. B. Moffat (1812–87), a collaborator on occasion with Sir Gilbert Scott in the design of churches.[69] Moffat's scheme shows the hall extended at each end by a chancel-like structure containing a court, all in the Middle Pointed style popular among architects at this time. Although it did not go ahead, the realization of Moffat's scheme might have been extremely interesting, if destructive. It would have meant moving the Round Table from the east wall, through which a large pointed arch was to be formed. A similar arch was proposed in the west wall, leaving the blank wall over the doorway in the south wall as the only place remaining to hang the Round Table. Perhaps the thickness of the east wall was one of the reasons the scheme was not carried out, for although shown on Moffat's drawings to be some four feet thick, in reality it was in places more than eight.

In 1871 Melville Portal, whom we have already met as a justice and the historian of the hall and who also served as chairman of the Quarter Sessions, made a presentment to the Court at the mid-summer session that the Great Hall was in need of repair and restoration and that a new court building was required for the holding of the Assizes and Sessions. At the following Michaelmas session an order was made for the restoration of the hall and the erection of a new court building and offices. A three-man building committee, under Portal's chairmanship, chose Thomas Henry Wyatt (1807–80) to prepare the design for the new court building and to restore the hall. Wyatt had had a long and honourable career. He was a past president of the Royal Institute of British Architects and in 1873 was to be the recipient of the Institute's Gold Medal. Among his many buildings were the Exchange at Liverpool, the old Knightsbridge Barracks, and the remarkable church of St Mary and St Nicholas at Wilton in Wiltshire, which had been designed in collaboration with David Brandon in 1843 for the Hon. Sidney Herbert in an Italian Lombardic style absolutely foreign to its setting.

The design of the new court building caused Wyatt many problems: the only site available to him, the old castle ditch at the east end of the hall, was some thirty feet below the floor of the hall. Construction was to cause him even greater anxieties. The ground was found to be so poor that the foundations of solid concrete had to

---

[68] 'On The Old Hall and New Assize Courts at Winchester', paper read by T. H. Wyatt, 20 April 1874, in R.I.B.A. *Sessional Papers* 10 (1873–4), at p. 168.

[69] Charles L. Eastlake, *A History of the Gothic Revival* (London, 1872), pp. 69–70. Moffat's designs are in the HRO, 31M60/1, nos. 1–4.

33 The Round Table lowered in 1873. Photograph by William Savage.

34 The Round Table being moved out of the Nisi Prius Court in 1873. Photograph by William Savage.

be sunk in some places to a depth of thirty-six feet. But despite settlement during its construction, the new court building was completed in 1873 and the restoration of the Great Hall put in hand. The new building was linked to the old by the construction of two rib vaults within the considerable thickness of the east wall of the hall, framed on each side by paired pointed arches. It was the formation of these lofty vaulted openings which required Wyatt to move the Round Table from the east wall to the west.

> An effort was now made to efface indignities which had been offered to the old Hall; and though its original purpose had passed away, there was an earnest endeavour to restore the fabric, as nearly as might be, to its former grandeur. The unsightly partitions, which had been created in 1764 [*sic*], were now removed, and the full length of the Hall was again displayed in all its beauty. The modern ceiling was taken down, and the old timbers of the roof once more exposed to view. The Purbeck shafts were restored, the plaster removed from the walls, and the interesting remains of the doors, jambs, shafts, and dais ... which contain in themselves a complete key to the architectural history of the Hall, were again revealed. ...

> ... All that was old was carefully preserved, no new work or other innovation was attempted, and with tender and almost reverential care, the ancient Hall was restored, as far as circumstances would admit, to its earlier and beautiful proportions.[70] (Plates XII, XIII).

In directing Wyatt's restoration Melville Portal evidently relied heavily on the excellent paper 'On the Hall and Round Table at Winchester' read by Sir Edward Smirke to the Winchester Meeting of the Archaeological Institute in September 1845.[71] Smirke drew attention for the first time to the considerable works carried out on the hall in the reign of Richard II at the end of the fourteenth century (but for uncertainty over this date, see above, p. 76–80). Much of Wyatt's activity consisted in fact of restoring these fourteenth-century works, but by removing all the plaster from the walls he found undeniable evidence that the roof of the hall had originally been quite different in shape, with the windows once rising as

[70] Portal, *Great Hall*, pp. 69–70, 72.

[71] *Proceedings at the Annual Meeting of the Archaeological Institute ... at Winchester, September MDCCCXLV* (London, 1846), pp. 44–80. Melville Portal's own copy of this paper, inlaid page by page on larger sheets, grangerized with further illustrations, including photographs of the table as lowered in 1873 (Figs. 33 and 34, here), and specially bound, containing his book-plate, is in the possession of Mr Richard Sawyer of Horsebridge, who very kindly allowed copies of the photographs to be made for this book.

I The Round Table and the Holy Grail with Lancelot in the Siege Perilous. French, *c.* 1470

II Arthur's Pentecost feast. North Italian, *c.* 1380–1400

III The Wheel of Fortune. From Boethius, *De consolatione philosophiae*.
North Italian, *c.* 1390–1400

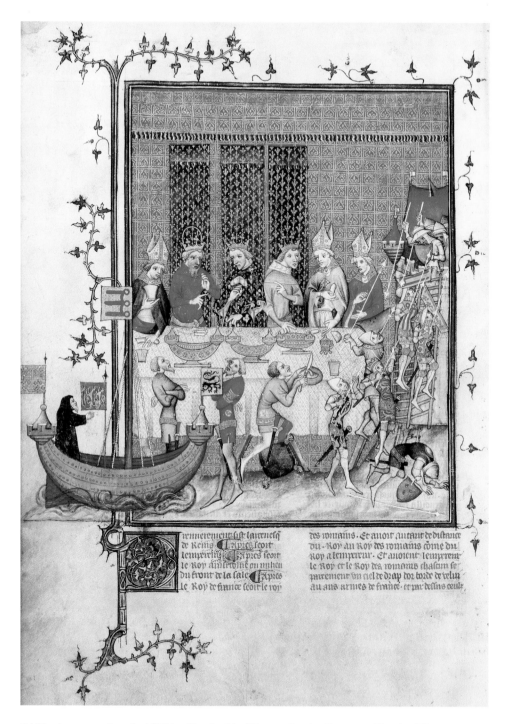

IV The banquet given in 1378 by Charles V of France for the Emperor Charles IV
and his son, Wenceslas, King of the Romans. French, 1378–9

V The Last Supper. Altar frontal. Catalan, *c.* 1300

VI The Seven Deadly Sins, a table painted by Hieronymus Bosch, *c.* 1490

VII Folding round table from Schloss Cappenburg, painted with a sundial based on a calendar published in 1493. Westfalen, *c.* 1500

VIII The Kleine Ratsrose, painted by Johann Martin Geiger (?) in 1688 for the Rathaus, Appenzell, Switzerland

IX The Grosse Ratsrose, painted by Hans Bildstein in 1651 for the Rathaus,
Appenzell, Switzerland

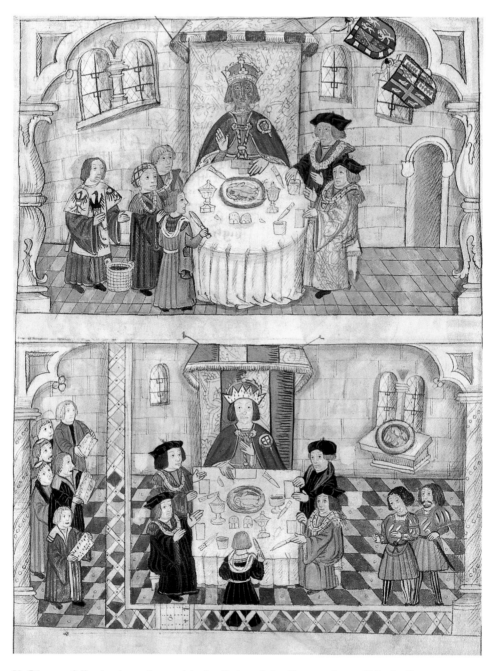

X Dinners following investiture with the Order of the Garter: *above*, of Maximilian,
King of the Romans (later Emperor), on 12 September 1490; *below*, of Ferdinand,
Archduke of Austria (later Emperor), on 8 December 1523. English, *c.* 1525

XI The Great Hall of Winchester Castle, water-colour of the exterior looking south-west, by Francis Grose, *c*. 1780

XII The Great Hall of Winchester Castle, the interior looking west following the restorations of 1974–80 and 1997–8

XIII The Great Hall of Winchester Castle, the interior looking south-west following the restorations of 1974–80

XIV The Round Table ready to be lowered, 27 August 1976

XV Looking behind the Round Table for the first time, 27 August 1976

XVI The rotten brackets which had supported the Round Table from 1874 until August 1976

XVII An English oak blown down in the great wind of 15/16 October 1987, looking towards the root. The sawn section shows the sequence of bark, cambium, sapwood, heartwood and pith identified in Fig. 92b

XVIII Radiocarbon samples taken for dating the Round Table: plank 22, showing the shallow rectangular areas (22A and 22A) removed for radiocarbon dating from either side of a groove cut for tree-ring dating (cf. Figs. 79 and 81). The massive timber appearing at a diagonal to the right is vertical 131, with the notch and rope-hole showing immediately below the number (cf. Fig. 43)

XIX Bob Otlet of AERE, Harwell, holding the loose insert 125A from behind which the radiocarbon samples of the rim, shown in Fig. 81, were taken

XX Stephen Rees Jones examining the X-ray of the painting of the head
of King Arthur from the Round Table, in the Great Hall on the afternoon
of 27 August 1976

dormers above much lower eaves, and with circular openings in the gable of each window (Fig. 26a). As we have seen, this was the form of the Great Hall as originally built by Henry III between 1222 and 1235. The external appearance of such an arrangement of walls, roof, and dormers must have been altogether much more lively and attractive than the rather forbidding external aspect of the hall today. (Fig. 26b).[72]

The removal of the plaster also revealed the remains of two features of which we shall have more to say in a moment: a fine doorway framed in Purbeck marble in the north-west corner of the hall, and an opening and duct in the west wall assumed to be a communicating tube between the dais and the chambers on the other side of the wall.

The other main work of Wyatt's restoration was the complete rebuilding of the roof of the hall, there being not one pair of rafters in the old structure sufficiently sound to save. This reconstruction of the roof did not extend to the massive oak tie-beams and archbraces, which still survive and which carry on their bosses the rayed-rose badge (Fig. 28a, b and see above, p. 80).

Wyatt described the restoration of the Great Hall in a paper read to the Royal Institute of British Architects on 20 April 1874, at a meeting presided over by Sir Giles Gilbert Scott, R.A. (1811–78), perhaps the most representative architect of the Victorian era.[73] In explaining how he had taken the Round Table down from the east wall of the hall and rehung it on the west wall (Figs. 33–4), Wyatt sought to suggest that this had been its original position by referring to two features which appear in Richard Benning's engraving of THE EAST PROSPECT OF THE INSIDE OF THE COUNTY HALL IN WINCHESTER, mentioned earlier (Fig. 30). One feature was the strip-like object shown on the wall below the table (see Fig. 120) and the other was the small structure shown in the right-hand corner of the hall.

By convincing himself that the strip-like object below the table was the opening and duct he had found in the west wall, and that the small structure in the right-hand corner was the doorway he had discovered in the north-west corner, Wyatt was able to suggest that the engraving was 'intended to represent the western wall of the Hall, as seen from the east end'.[74] In fact the strip below the table was perhaps the illegible remains of the inscription placed there in honour of the visit to the hall in 1522 of Henry VIII and the Emperor Elect Charles V (see below, p. 431, 473), while the small structure in the right-hand corner was almost certainly a privy. The high sills of the windows show clearly that this was the easternmost bay of the hall,

---

[72] T. H. Wyatt, drawing of supposed restoration of dormer windows (1874), HRO, 31M60/2, no. 30.

[73] Wyatt, 'On the Old Hall'.

[74] Ibid., p. 159.

where doorways below these shallower windows had originally led to the kitchens and serveries.

We need not doubt that Benning's engraving depicts the east wall of the hall, and the likelihood is that until 1873 the Round Table had always hung there. Hardyng did not say on which wall it hung, but in 1544 the antiquary John Leland wrote that the table 'standeth fixed ... at the walle side of the kinges Hal' (see above, p. 29), where he will have seen it on his visit to Winchester in 1540 in the course of his *Laboriouse Journey* through England. By 'walle side' Leland can only mean the east end where the castle wall forms the end of the hall. A good reason for this might be that at this end of the hall the wall-walk of the eastern battlements ran just below the triple lancets of the gable, which at this end rose above the outer wall of the castle (Fig. 26). Here on the wall-walk it would have been a simple matter to arrange a winch to raise or lower the table from outside.

With the rehanging of the Round Table on the west wall of the Great Hall Wyatt's work was complete: including a new oak roof and the restoration of the Purbeck marble it had cost some £3,500.

The stained glass which fills the windows of the restored hall was designed and made by John Hardman and Co. of Birmingham, under the direction of Melville Portal, between 1876 and 1880.[75] It displays the heraldic arms (whether actual or invented) of persons connected with Hampshire who had contributed to the fame of the county from the earliest times to the end of the seventeenth century. John Hardman had made the windows for the Houses of Parliament to Pugin's designs for Sir Charles Barry, and his firm had at this time a considerable reputation for the manufacture of stained glass and metalwork.

The same firm was employed by Portal to decorate the east wall of the hall, now that the Round Table had been removed to make room for the double arched opening into the new courts. The scheme of decoration, which includes motifs based on traces of medieval decoration found by Wyatt on the original plaster,[76] consists of an elaborate tree of the Knights of the Shire, the parliamentary representatives of Hampshire, monarch by monarch, from Edward I to Victoria.

With the installation of the last of Hardman's stained glass in 1880 the restoration of the hall was complete (Plates XII, XIII). To exactly what it had been restored it is difficult to say. Henry III, Richard II, and even Henry VIII might, if they could have stood together in the restored hall, have wondered just where they

---

[75] 'Stained Glass: Winchester', *The Builder*, 19 May 1876, p. 819; 31 July 1880, p. 1561.

[76] T. H. Wyatt, drawings of discovered decorations on original plaster (1874), HRO, 31M60/2, nos. 21, 24–5.

were. The feature most familiar and recognizable to them all would have been the Purbeck columns and the arcades above them.

Deploring the practices of restoration he saw going on all around him, William Morris had written in 1877:

> but every change, whatever history it destroyed, left history in the gap, and was alive with the spirit of the deeds done amidst its fashioning. The result of all this was often a building in which the many changes, though harsh and visible enough, were by their very contrast interesting and instructive, and could by no possibility mislead. But those who make the changes wrought in our day under the name of Restoration, while professing to bring back a building to the best time of its history, have no guide but each his own individual whim to point out to them what is admirable and what contemptible: while the very nature of their task compels them to destroy something, and to supply the gap by imagining what the earlier builders should or might have done. Moreover, in the course of this double process of destruction and addition, the whole surface of the building is necessarily tampered with; so that the appearance of antiquity is taken away from such old parts of the fabric as are left, and there is no laying to rest in the spectator the suspicion of what may have been lost; and in short, a feeble and lifeless forgery is the final result of all the wasted labour.[77]

These words of Morris have had a profound effect on the practice of restoration; as profound as other of his words have had in many fields. It is impossible today not to be grateful to Portal and Wyatt for the work which they did to allow the magnificent proportions of the interior of the hall to be seen again. But if they had been a little less relentless in their pursuit and exposure of archaeological evidence, and had left in place some material to suggest the accumulation of history, with its conflicts of style and taste, the Great Hall today would be a place of even richer interest than it is.

Wyatt's new courts were short lived. In November 1932 the County Council learnt that extensive repairs to the south and east external walls were necessary because of weaknesses caused by using mortar of inadequate strength. The masonry at the south-east corner of the building was reported to have become completely detached for a height of more than forty feet. The advice of a consulting engineer was taken and the building was braced with steel framing, but in November 1936 it was reported that movement was still occurring. In February 1938 the County Council was told that the consultant had pronounced the building unsafe; that it had

---

[77] William Morris, 'Statement Issued on the Foundation of the Society for the Preservation of Ancient Buildings' (1877), quoted in J. W. Mackail, *The Life of William Morris* (London, 1899), pp. 343–4.

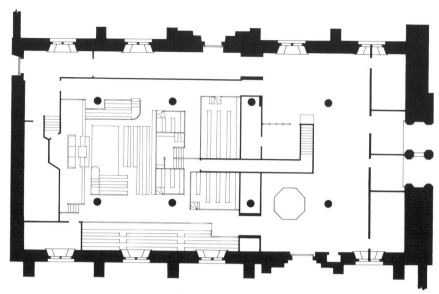

35 The Crown Court in the Great Hall, 1938–74.

36 The Crown Court and the Round Table, 1938–74, looking west.

been closed; and that interim arrangements had been made for a court to sit in the Great Hall, while designs for a new Assize Court were prepared and a new building erected. A new building was designed by the County Architect, but although detailed drawings and bills of quantities were prepared, the 1939–45 war intervened. Meanwhile, the demolition of Wyatt's courts began in the middle of 1938 and was complete in February 1939.

The scheme prepared for the new courts was abandoned after the war. Eventually, in the 1960s, a much larger and more elaborate scheme was prepared by the architectural firm of Louis de Soissons and Partners. Construction of their new courts began in 1968 and was finished in 1974. The emergency arrangements made in 1938 continued to be used, with some modifications, until the new courts came into use in 1974.

The temporary court of 1938–74 was laid out in the three western bays of the hall, recalling the arrangements of earlier centuries (Fig. 35). This area was shut off by a partition of woodwool slabs on a framework of scaffolding which rose from the floor to the underside of the roof. The furnishings were taken from one of Wyatt's courts, and the judge sat beneath the Round Table, as his predecessors had once sat in the Nisi Prius Court at the other end of the hall (Fig. 36). Since 1910 the massive bronze statue of Queen Victoria, the work of Alfred Gilbert R.A., commissioned by W. I. Whitaker to commemorate the Queen's Golden Jubilee in 1887, had stood at the west end of the hall. The statue was now moved to a position in the south arcade in front of the rear doorway. A block of cells two storeys high, built of brick and concrete, was erected in the easternmost bay of the hall, necessitating the removal of the stained glass from the windows in this bay. If Melville Portal could have seen the Great Hall in 1970 he might have been forced to admit that the Georgian courts he had railed against so bitterly were by comparison a model of elegance and refinement.

With the opening of the new courts in 1974, the structures which had made little more than a makeshift of the Great Hall for nearly forty years were removed, and work was put in hand to restore, as it were, the restoration of the hall so thoroughly carried out a century before (Plates XII, XIII).

When T. H. Wyatt took the Round Table down from the east wall of the hall in 1873 he relied, to judge from the photographs taken at the time (Figs. 33–4), upon stout cordage, a pulley block or two, and a few doughty Victorian workmen. He probably also had, to judge from the same photographs, the considerable advantage of having been able to remove the roof at this end of the hall.

When the time came in 1976 to take the Round Table down again from the west wall of the hall after just over a century, the operation was devised to ensure

37 Devices for lowering the Round Table, 1976.

38 Crane in position outside the west wall of the Great Hall for lowering the Round Table, 27 August 1976.

39 The Round Table being lowered, 27 August 1976.

that the table remained absolutely vertical at all times. Nothing was known of the physical condition of the wood, and we were concerned that the weight of the central square of the framing visible on the back of the table in the photographs taken in 1873 might, if the table were allowed to move out of the vertical, cause the surface to bulge or hollow, with disastrous consequences for the painting and even for the integrity of the whole table. We had therefore to minimize any redistribution of the stresses in its surface and framing. This required the use of rather more elaborate devices than T. H. Wyatt had employed (Fig. 37). Supported on two massive oak cantilever brackets built into the wall, and held back at the top by two wrought-iron cramps which locked it immovably on the west wall, the table lay below the medieval tie-beam and arched braces of the end truss of the roof. Two substantial wrought-iron hangers fastened to the central uprights of the table's framework passed above and behind the tie-beam in the small gap between the beam and the wall. The tie-beam effectively prevented a direct lift from above and the hangers made it impossible to move the table forward without lowering it first. As the table had to remain vertical at all times, a steel frame was designed with a suspension point in front of the tie-beam. This frame could be raised into position by a crane and fastened to the table, which could then be lowered while attached to the frame.

As the crane could not be brought into the hall, it had to be positioned outside the west wall, with its jib passing through the central lancet in the gable (Fig. 38), and its operator receiving instructions by radio from inside the hall. The operating clearances for the jib head through the lancet and under the collars of the roof trusses were little more than one inch horizontally to left and right and less than two inches vertically. At a height of more than forty-five feet above the floor of the hall, these had to be maintained under varying conditions of loading at different stages of the operation. The design of the frame was of necessity eccentric, and when suspended it had to be maintained in a vertical position before and after receiving the weight of the Round Table by carefully located counterweights. The distribution of its own weight enabled these to be relatively small, which made it easy to trim the loaded frame and keep the table vertical at all times. To remove the oak brackets supporting the table, a steel gantry was designed to support it temporarily and also to locate the frame accurately when it was raised into position. The transfer of the weight of the table on to this gantry was effected by hydraulic flat jacks. The amount of pressure required to expand these and lift the table indicated that it weighed approximately 1¼ tons. To transport the table to the position in which it was to be examined after having been lowered, the frame was fitted with low friction roller shoes which dropped into steel channels laid out as a railway on the floor of the hall.

As any sort of trial run was out of the question, the final operation was not without some moments of anxiety. But each element proved equal to its task and contributed to the control and precision with which the Round Table was lowered for the first time in more than a century to the floor of the Great Hall shortly after mid-day on 27 August 1976 (Fig. 39).

The Table

With the Round Table safely lowered to the floor and moved forward on its tracks, it was possible to look behind it for the first time since 1873 (Plate XV). In each of the twelve radial spokes we could see a mortise for fixing what can only have been a leg, confirming at once the conclusion reached during the Victorian move that the great disk had indeed originally been the top of a table. After this first quick look, the frame holding the table was rolled still further forward until it rested between the western pair of Purbeck marble columns. Here it was firmly fixed for the duration of the investigation. There was now free access to both sides of the table, with enough distance to stand back for photography and plenty of space for the ladders and scaffold towers needed to reach the top of an object fully the height of an ordinary two-storey house (Fig. 97). In the next few days platforms were built on both sides of the table and securely decked at the level of the lowest point of the rim.

Investigations started at once. The X-raying of the table began the afternoon of the lowering (Chapter 7; Plate XX). Even before that, Cecil Hewett, author of *English Historic Carpentry* and pioneer of the method of dating timber-work by analysis of the development of jointing techniques, had begun his examination, which enabled him to make the drawings and model illustrating Chapter 4.

It was good to have settled from the start that the Round Table had indeed once been a table, but the question uppermost in everyone's mind was its date. By the second day Cecil Hewett had concluded that the carpentry looked as if it belonged to the second half of the thirteenth or first half of the fourteenth century – to the time of Henry III or the first three Edwards. Other methods of dating were to take much longer. The Atomic Energy Research Establishment at Harwell had agreed to date the wood of the table by the radiocarbon method. The work was done by the Isotope Measurements Laboratory under the direction of Bob Otlet. Chapter 6 gives his account of the series of experiments which over the next ten years became the largest radiocarbon project ever mounted on a single object.

In the 1970s the technique of radiocarbon dating could only offer about the same degree of accuracy as that obtainable from dating by carpentry technology. Statistical techniques developed in the 1980s and 1990s for the calibration of radiocarbon dates have however made it possible to arrive at a narrower date. The method which theoretically offered the possibility of assigning the construction of the table to a single calendar year was tree-ring dating. Since 1964, Professor A. C. Barefoot, then Head of the School of Forest Resources at State University, North Carolina, Raleigh, and universally known as 'A. C.', had been developing for the Winchester Excavations Committee a tree-ring curve based on oak timbers taken solely from the Winchester/Hampshire region. Beginning with recently felled oaks in Hursley Park, whose last year of growth was known, Professor Barefoot built his chronology backwards from the present, using Hampshire timbers from HMS *Victory*'s refit of 1814–15, and progressively older timbers from houses, churches, and other structures of known date, such as the brewhouse of Winchester College and the choir stalls of the cathedral (Fig. 78). In Chapter 5 he describes the principles behind tree-ring dating (dendrochronology) and sets out the steps by which he discovered both the number of trees used to provide the oak for the table, and the date of the latest ring surviving on any of the timbers of its original structure.

The results of the tree-ring and radiocarbon dating programmes are compared and discussed in Chapter 10 in relation to the indications provided by carpentry technology and the written sources.

4

Carpentry, Condition, and Sequence

The back of the Round Table reveals far more than the front about the nature and history of the object (Plate XV, Fig. 40). There are three layers of super-imposed timber-work, and in this stratification the principal events in the life of the table are revealed (Fig. 41). The timbers have been numbered for reference (Figs. 42–3), but for clarity these numbers are used as sparingly as possible on the diagrams which accompany this description.

The layers of timber-work are as follows:

I   The original structure, timbers 1–121; made entirely of oak fastened with wooden pegs (treenails), except in the joints of the felloes, where iron nails were used.
II Vertical timbers 130–5, added to strengthen the table when hung on the wall (plus the addition of a raised rim to the front of the table, timbers 122–9); also of oak but fastened throughout with iron nails.
III An outer ring of flat boards and other additions, 136–49; all of softwood (deal) and fastened with steel screws.

The original structure

The carpentry of the original structure is described by Cecil Hewett.

This artefact is a flat, circular frame of timber with a planked surface, measuring approximately 18 feet in diameter and weighing in its present condition 1 ton 4 cwt. It is formed entirely in oak and proves on examination to have been the top of a circular table, the legs of which were roughly broken out, presumably when it was being got ready to hang on the wall.

40 The back of the Round Table.

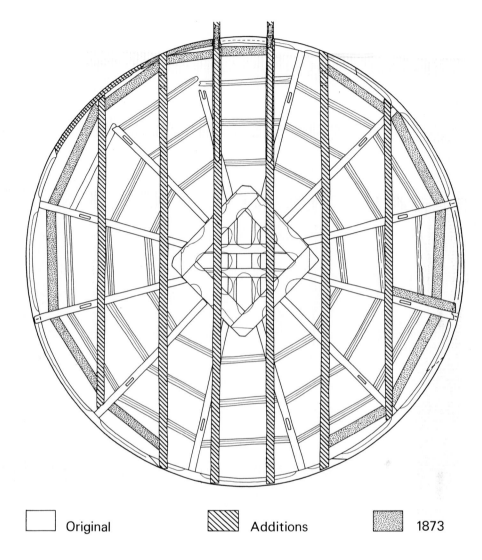

Original   Additions   1873

41 The stratification of the back of the Round Table.

THE ROUND TABLE   WINCHESTER CASTLE

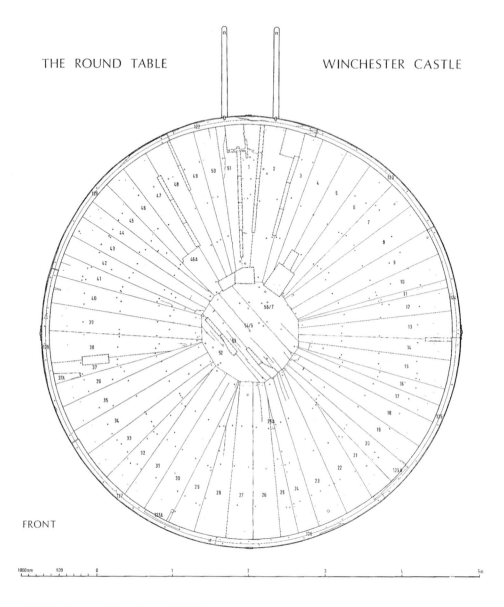

FRONT

42 The front of the Round Table: a survey.

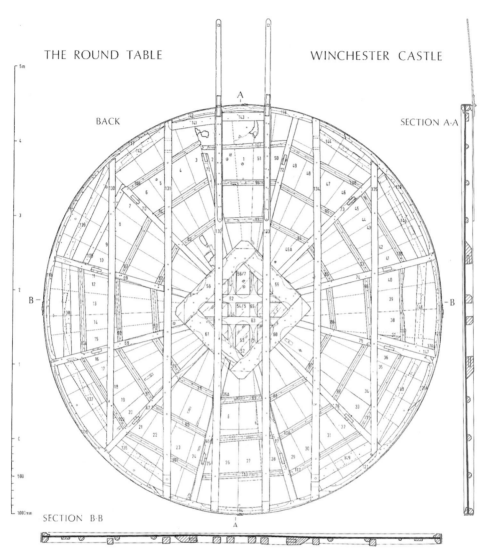

43 The back of the Round Table: a survey.

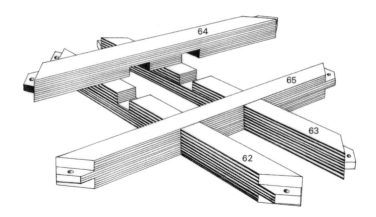

44 The Round Table: the clasp-arm assembly.

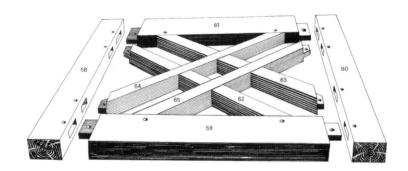

45 The Round Table: the central square assembly.

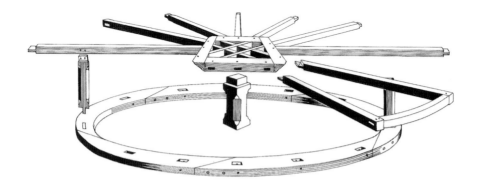

46 The Round Table: the assembly of the frame.

Having determined and doubtless drawn his design, the carpenter began by framing a heavy square with a void central area. This square was made of oak sawn at 10 x 4 inches and laid flatly in place. The corners were jointed by means of *haunchless*[1] tenons of reduced widths, in order to achieve strong closed mortises for the assembly (Fig. 45). Within the square four clasp-arms were fitted, cross-halved together, and chase-tenoned into the interior edges of the square (Fig. 44). The unit was finally secured by driving twelve pegs from face to face – the holes for which are shown in Fig. 45.

The central pedestal and circular stretcher were assembled during this time, but their structure can only be guessed at today (Fig. 46). The circular table-top was then formed around the central square, by setting out twelve radial timbers or 'compass-arms' resembling the spokes of a wheel. These spokes are so arranged that one leaves the centre of each of the four sides of the square at 90°, while the remaining eight leave at 120° from close to its corners. The spokes are jointed with accurately cut squint, or square, stub-tenons, each of which is placed closer to the upper surface of the spoke than to its centre of depth. The spokes were then mortised on their under-surfaces with auger and chisel at points 6 ft. 8 in. from the centre of the square assembly, to coincide with the presumed mortises in the stretcher and to provide both top and base mortises for the twelve table-legs. Fig. 47 shows the fitting and assembly, but before final assembly the circumference of the rim would have been scribed on to the twelve spokes, and their end-joints cut.

The actual steps taken to build the rim of the frame are shown in Fig. 47, in which the numbering indicates a plausible order of assembly. It is a curiosity of this that three spokes were mortised for the rim felloes, while the remainder were tenoned and the felloes mortised. There is no obvious explanation for this, and no apparent reason to change the design from what must have been the original intention to mortise the spokes. The splayed scarfs of the rim felloes were transfixed radially to the circumference with iron nails (Fig. 62), a method of fixing such small joints or scarfs noted elsewhere. The frame being assembled and pegged, the craftsmen turned their attention to chamfering its arrises, for the traditional and best of all reasons: to reduce the weight of the construction without impairing its strength or stability, and thereby to enhance its mechanical efficiency.

This chamfering of the arrises of the central assembly produced the interesting pattern shown in Figs. 48 and 49, which includes 'spherical triangles', architectural devices with which the late thirteenth century was much preoccupied. Even the four

[1] For this and other technical terms used here to describe carpentry joints, see C. A. Hewett, *English Historic Carpentry* (London and Chichester, 1980), pp. vii-xii, and compare pp. 279–83 with figs. 290–309; see also pp. 286–7.

corners of the square central frame were reduced by cutting to a flat, splayed plane at 45° to the adjacent sides. The thorough application of this treatment to all the arrises emphasises the small and ultimately central square which is alone left square-edged on the inside. This strongly suggests the presence of a central pedestal, which would indeed have been necessary to prevent the ton of framing from sagging in the middle under its own weight when in use as a table.[2]

The work would have looked at this stage somewhat as shown in Fig. 50, and the next step was to fit the ledges into the frame for the support of the planking. The ledges were let into arris trenches on the upper faces of the spokes, the trenches being sufficiently offset to avoid excessive weakening of the spokes. This is why the three concentric rings of ledges are each formed of twelve tangents to their respective circles. The joints employed are diminished laps (Fig. 51), a fact which shows that the ledges were intended to resist pressure only from above. This virtually proves that the object was intended as a table-top, since it was specifically designed to support a flat surface, although at what height above the floor is obviously unknown. The cross-section of the ledges is reminiscent of similar ledges on the inner faces of cathedral doors made during the thirteenth century.[3]

The surface is formed of fifty-one oak planks (plus four in the centre) which were sawn or split on the quarter at one-inch thickness and to various widths – the latter determined by the size of the tree trunks available. The planks were cut into converging four-sided figures and so arranged as to cover the circular frame. As Fig. 52 shows, the sections of plank were tapered as little as possible, and dart-shaped pieces, or 'gores', were used to fill the gaps. These gores were almost certainly the off-cuts produced when the major planks were sawn into their tapering shapes. The planks were then pegged edge-to-edge, about seven times each so far as one can see. The type of pegs and the method of using them is shown in Fig. 53. The pegs themselves are of square section and examination of one of them, which can be removed bodily from its socket, has shown that they were first pointed, and then driven into holes bored in the edges of the planks. Their protruding ends were then marked on to the edge of the immediately adjacent plank and sharpened, holes were drilled, and the two planks forced together. By this means the top was *probably* assembled into four quadrants, of tolerably rigid planking, after which the process would have been repeated four more times to assemble the whole circle.

---

[2]   This figure omits the approximate weight of the added verticals and rim.

[3]   C. A. Hewett, *English Cathedral Carpentry* (London, 1974), pp. 94–5 and fig. 84. Many of these were chamfered after the surface planks had been pegged on, but the cuts left on the planks do not indicate clearly the type of cutting tool used.

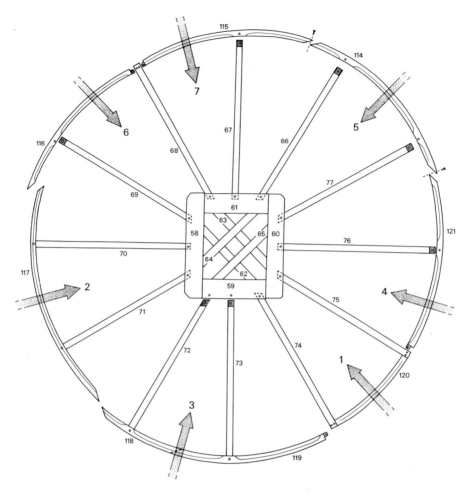

47 The Round Table: the sequence of assembly of the felloes to form the rim of the frame.

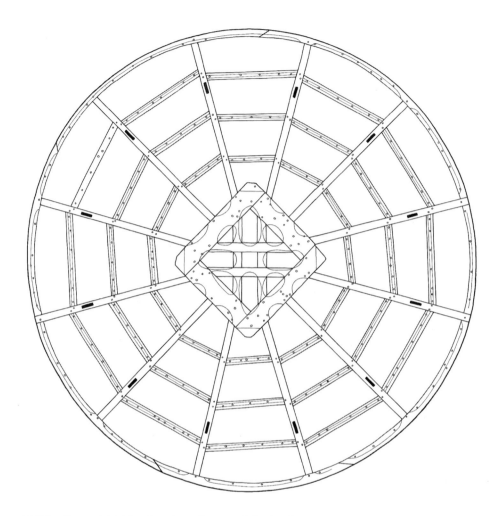

48 The Round Table: the chamfering of the back.

49 The Round Table: the central square assembly.

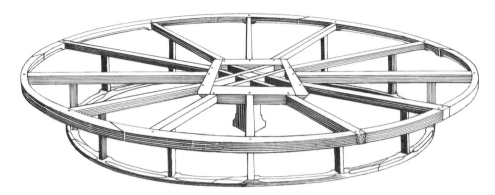

50 The Round Table: the frame assembled.

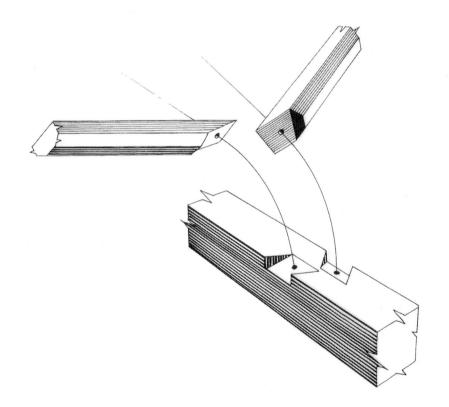

51 The Round Table: the jointing of the ledges to the spokes.

When all this had been done and the top assembled as a circle, it was drilled for pegging both to the rim of the frame and to the ledges. On the ledges there is an average of one peg to each plank crossing it, and the holes for these pegs must have been drilled from beneath — i.e. first through the ledge and then upward through the plank. The pegs were then driven downward from the planked surface, cut neatly flush on top, and roughly trimmed below. The polygonal void at the centre of the surface was cut into a dodecagon at some stage not determined, either when the top was in several large sectors or when it was finally in position. It is interesting that the gores are set roughly over the spokes, and that the angles of the dodecagon were set to meet the gores, as shown in Fig. 52. The dodecagon was then filled with four planks pegged down by twenty-four pegs which penetrated fully the four-inch-thick timbers of the square frame and produced on its underside a dodecagonal pattern. This bears no structural relationship to the spoke assembly, despite appearing to do so (Fig. 52; compare Fig. 48).

At this point two features must be observed: first, the edges of the planks are 'straight', 'true', and 'square', the carpenter's trinity, and this suggests that they were planed. Second, the four large areas of assembled edge-to-edge planking were smoothed on both faces after they had been pegged to the frame. This is logical, since if they had been smoothed before assembly irregularities might have been introduced when the planks were edge-pegged one to another. The smoothing of the under-face was probably done with an adze rather than a very convex plane, which would have been difficult, if not impossible, to use in the awkward spaces of the frame. This smoothing, which left clear but shallow 'fluting' running across the planks of the under-face (Fig. 54), could have been carried out from underneath if the table was raised on a scaffold, but there is the alternative possibility that the table (including the top) was assembled upside-down. The ledges were all then chamfered with a broadaxe, which left a series of characteristic cut-marks and removed most of the assembly numbers (see below, p. 127 and Figs. 60–1). Finally, the upper faces of the planks were 'shot' across their grain with a well-set plane, the signature of which is still visible today through the paint. A scale model of the table, constructed to demonstrate the various features revealed by this examination and to show the sequence of construction, is shown in Fig. 55.

The indications of date provided by the style of the carpentry and the types of joint suggest that the table was made sometime in the century 1250 to 1350. The surprisingly elaborate design possibly indicates that the carpenter responsible was confronted with a relatively unfamiliar problem. To solve it he either studied, or had previously studied or been employed upon, the construction of large wooden wheels of the kind which were early in use for numerous purposes: military engines like the

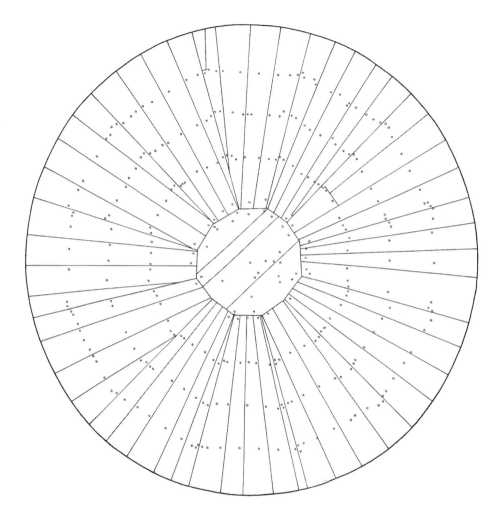

52 The Round Table: the planking of the top.

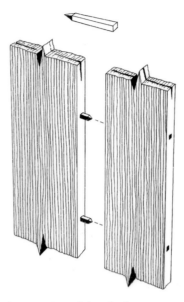

53 The Round Table: the edge pegging of the planks.

54 The back of the Round Table: adze or plane signatures running from plank to plank (in this case from planks 26 to 27).

mangonel; windlasses for raising building materials for major works in cathedrals and castles (Fig. 56);[1] or the wheels of windmills and water-mills (Fig. 57).[2] In the light of these comparisons, the design of the framing is highly significant, for it refutes the much-publicized view that 'clasp-arms' first appeared about 1550. The term refers to the way in which four timber 'arms' can be framed together (Fig. 44) to clasp an axle, thus allowing a wheel to be made without the need to weaken the axle by cutting mortises in it to take the spokes. It has been generally accepted for many years that the earliest published illustration of such clasp-arms was in Agricola's *De re metallica*, first printed in 1556 (Fig. 58).[3] About 1225–50 Villard de Honnecourt had, however, already drawn a clasp-arm wheel of similar design in his sketchbook, noting by it that it showed how to frame a wheel without cutting (i.e. weakening) the axle (Fig. 59).[4] The generally accepted dating of this innovation must therefore be revised, and indeed its appearance on the Round Table provides what is at present perhaps the earliest known surviving example of its actual use.

Thus far, Cecil Hewett on the original construction of the table. Once finally assembled, it was never again taken apart. The smoothing of the planks provides clear evidence of this, for the table could never have been reassembled so exactly that the signatures of adze and plane would have matched as precisely as they do from plank to plank (Fig. 54). Any such dismantling and reassembly would also have left traces wherever pegs were knocked out and reinserted, but there are no such traces. It

---

[1] Hewett, *Cathedral Carpentry* (as above, n.3), pp. 67–73, esp. fig. 57 (Salisbury) and fig. 58 (Beverley Minster).

[2] For clasp-arm assemblies used in the head or brake wheels of windmills, see Rex Wailes, *The English Windmill* (London, 1954), pp. 121–2 and figs. 13 and 25; and Rex Wailes, *A Source Book of Windmills and Watermills* (London, 1979), pp. 58–9 and figs. on pp. 58 and 60–2. For clasp-arm assemblies on water-wheels, see, for example, Wootton Mill in J. Kenneth Major, *The Mills of the Isle of Wight* (London, 1970), pp. 94–5, or the Woodbridge tide mill in Neil Cossons, *The BP Book of Industrial Archaeology* (Newton Abbot, 1975), pp. 14–5. Clasp-arm assemblies were also used for pit-wheels operating tilt hammers, as at Abbeydale Forge, Sheffield: Brian Bracegirdle, *The Archaeology of the Industrial Revolution* (London, 1973), p. 100 and pl. 27c; and for donkey-wheels: Hugo Brunner and J. Kenneth Major, 'Water Raising by Animal Power', *Industrial Archaeology* 9 (1972), 117–51, and fig. on p. 120. Mr K. A. Falconer of the Royal Commission on the Historical Monuments of England kindly provided information on clasp-arms in industrial structures.

[3] Georg Bauer (known as Agricola), *De re metallica libri XII* (Basle, 1556). Clasp-arm assemblies of the developed type (where the four clasp-arms form chords to the circle of the wheel) are shown in Book VI (Miners' tools and machines) on pp. 132–3, 142, 145–7 (reproduced here as Fig. 58), 155, 158, and 164, and in Book VIII on p. 254. The wheels are overshot and undershot water-wheels and treadwheels, used for mine drainage and ventilation and for stamp-mills. Further examples of Agricola's wheels are reproduced in C. Singer *et al.* (eds.), *A History of Technology*, ii (Oxford, 1956), figs. 19, 20, 22.

[4] Alain Erlande-Brandenburg *et al.* (eds.), *Carnet de Villard de Honnecourt* (Paris, 1986), pl. 45b and see p. 125.

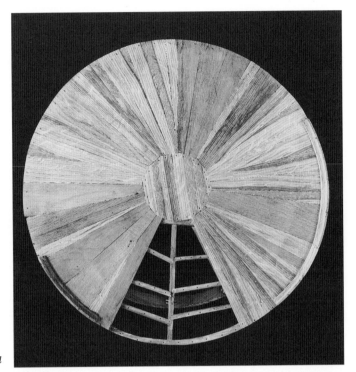

a

b

55 The carpentry of the Round Table: an explanatory model made by Cecil Hewett. *a*, the front of the table; *b*, the back of the table.

56 Beverley Minster: treadmill windlass with clasp-arm assembly.

57 Woodbridge tide mill: water-wheel with clasp-arm assembly (before reconstruction).

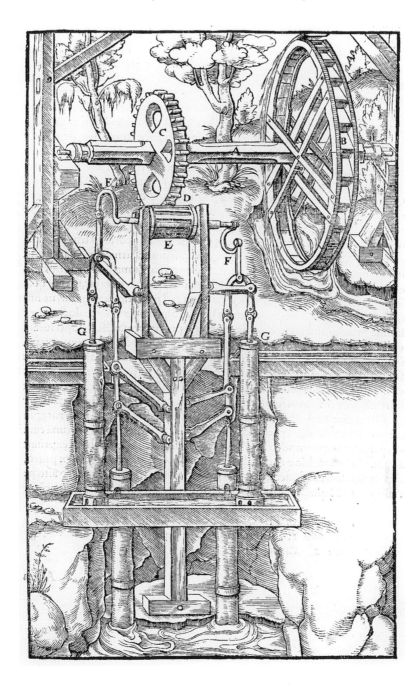

58 Mine drainage: overshot water-wheel with clasp-arm assembly driving a set of pumps, from Agricola, *De re metallica* (1556).

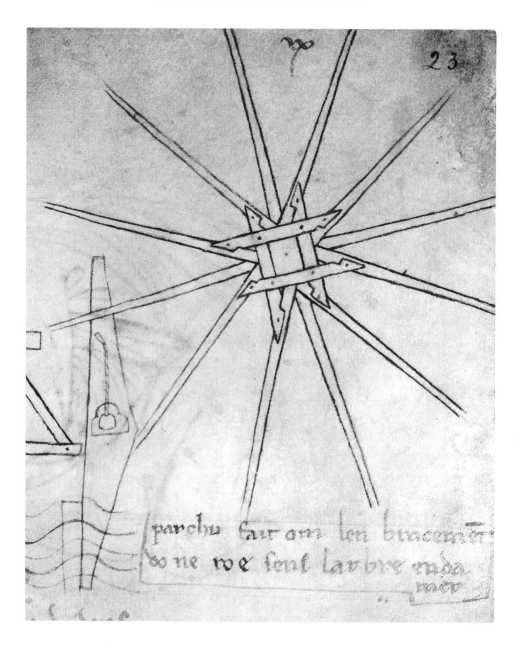

59 Villard de Honnecourt's clasp-arm assembly: 'How to assemble a wheel without cutting into the axle'. French, 1225–50.

60 Assembly marks on the Round Table: *a*, III on ledge 104; *b*, VII on ledge 108; *c*, VIII on ledge 109; *d*, XXIV on ledge 101; *e*, V on felloe 119; *f*, ⊣ on radial 68.

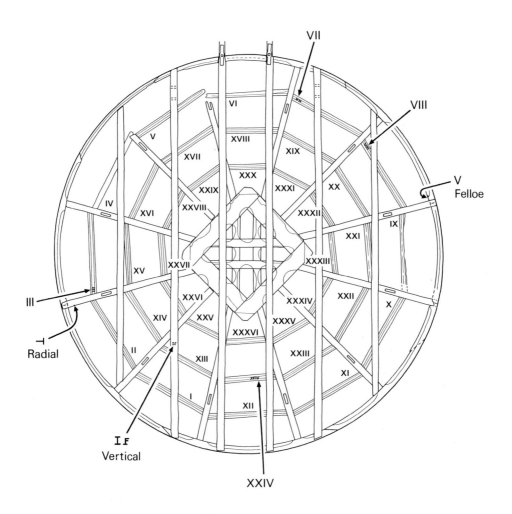

61 Assembly marks on the Round Table. The surviving marks are identified outside the table. Numbers of ledges reconstructed inside the table: outer ring, I–XII; middle ring XIII–XXIV; inner ring, XXV–XXXVI (see p. 127).

would also have required each piece of timber to be lettered or numbered for reassembly, but there are no such secondary marks.

There are the remains of an earlier system of assembly marks, but most of these were drilled through for the insertion of pegs or smoothed off in the final assembly (Fig. 60). They belong therefore to a stage in the original assembly, not to a system applied to guide reassembly.

The location of the surviving marks is shown in Fig. 61. There is a 'V', presumably the Roman numeral, on one of the felloes (119), probably part of a series related to the felloes, of which no other examples survived decay or chamfering. There is a 'T'-like mark on one of the radials (68), but no others were noted. The fullest series is on the ledges: 'III' (on ledge 104), 'VII' (108), 'VIII' (109), and 'XXIV' (101) belong to a sequence which numbered the outer ring of ledges from I to XII, the middle ring from XIII to XXIV, and (presumably) the inner ring from XXV to XXXVI, as shown on Fig. 61.

Although a particularly complex example, such a system of carpenter's marks is normal medieval and later practice. It implies that the table was 'framed' elsewhere. That is to say, the timbers were cut, the joints formed and fitted but not pegged, and the pieces marked to show which fitted where, before the whole assembly was taken apart and carried to the place where it was finally put together, pegged, and finished. Hugh Herland framed the great hammerbeam roof of Westminster Hall at Farnham in Surrey in 1393–5 in just this way, to quote only the most famous of examples.[5] So too with the Round Table, which must have been framed in the carpenters' shop before being brought into the Great Hall for its final assembly – for if Cecil Hewett's suggested date of 1250–1350 for the carpentry is accepted, the hall was already standing when the table was made.

One final point needs to be made about the original structure. X-ray examination showed the presence of a large number of small nails hammered in radially around the edge of the table (see below, p. 246; Figs. 103–4). These are concealed by the iron collar put round the edge in 1874 and so cannot be directly examined. They do not seem, however, to strengthen or repair the edge, as far as one can make out, and are therefore unlikely to belong to any period after the original use of the table had been abandoned. Their most likely function was perhaps to attach a cloth hung around the edge of the table when in use, a practice for which there is plenty of contemporary evidence, as Simon Jervis has shown in Chapter 2 (Figs. 18–20). Possibly, however, they may have attached a cloth or other cover stretched *over* the table (see below, Chapter 11).

---

[5] H. M. Colvin (ed.), *The History of the King's Works* i, *The Middle Ages* (London, 1963), pp. 529–30.

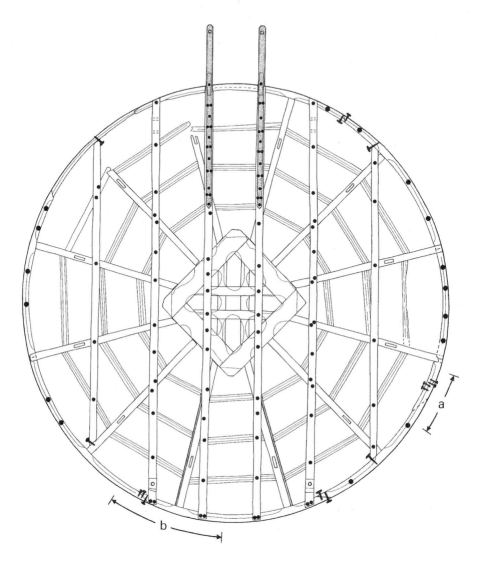

62 Nailing and other ironwork on the back of the Round Table. For areas *a* and *b* see Figs. 103–4. Note that the softwood boards put on in 1873 with steel screws are omitted (cf. Figs. 41, 43).

63 The back of the Round Table, upper right, showing rope holes (arrowed) in vertical 134, mortice for leg in radial 72, and iron suspension strap on vertical 133.

The addition of the vertical timbers and the raised rim

Six oak spars of square section, 4¼ x 4¼ inches, are fixed vertically to the back of the table by large iron nails or spikes (Figs. 41, 62). These verticals are laid tight up to the back of the planks, and to achieve this have been halved over the ledges, and roughly halved *into* the radials and *into* the timbers of the central assembly (Figs. 43, 49, 63). The outer verticals (130 and 135) butt up against the inner face of the original felloes, but the inner four have been halved *into* the felloes, so deeply at the junction of vertical 134 with felloe 118, that the latter has broken in two. This symmetry extends to the treatment of the fixing of their lower ends: the four inner spars are fixed with two nails apiece straight into the felloes, while the outer pair are nailed diagonally from the side into the adjacent radial or felloe. Elsewhere, there is usually a nail at each point where a vertical crosses a ledge or radial, with two nails used at intersections with the broad timbers of the central square and at places where the crossing is especially oblique; but as one might expect, the nailing is not entirely consistent (Fig. 62).

Wrought-iron straps are nailed to the upper ends of the inner pair of vertical timbers (Figs. 62–3, 67). These straps project 3 ft. 9 in. (1.14 metre) above the top of the table and near the top are pierced by square holes. There is no reason to doubt that the straps are contemporary with the verticals. They were designed to pass up the narrow space between the wall and eastern timber truss of the hall, where they (and the table) would have hung from bars passing through the holes and resting at one end on the top of the truss and at the other on the window sill. Although this arrangement was designed to work at the east end of the hall, it worked equally well at the west end after 1873, and was found in use when we came to lower the table in 1976. It was probably never intended that these straps should take the full weight of the table, but they would have served the double task of taking some of the weight off the brackets below, while holding the top of the table tight and vertical against the wall.

The upper ends of the middle pair of vertical timbers (131 and 134) are each pierced horizontally from side to side by two drilled holes, one above another, each about 1 inch in diameter (Figs. 62–3). The mouths of these holes are somewhat worn and there seems little doubt that they were intended to take the ropes by which the table was hoisted into position on the east wall of the hall after the fixing of the verticals. A pair of windlasses, set on the wall-walk outside the outer lights of the triple window in the east gable, would have served, as Michael Morris suggests on p. 94, to raise the table into position. These holes show how the ropes were fixed and also how they could easily be withdrawn when the job was done. They were not used in the lowering of 1873, as the photograph of that operation shows (Fig. 34), because their existence would have been unknown. Whether they were used when the table was hoisted up the west wall, we do not know: it seems unlikely that this would then have been regarded as a safe procedure.

The lower ends of the same pair of verticals (131 and 134) are also each pierced horizontally, but from front to back, by a single drilled hole about 1 inch in diameter. The two holes penetrated the surface of the table through planks 23 and 30, where they were subsequently filled with wooden plugs. The backs of the verticals are notched horizontally at the same level (Figs. 43, 62). These lower holes, in the same pair of vertical timbers as the upper holes, seem likely also to have had something to do with hoisting the table back into position on the east wall of the hall. A single rope might have passed through both these lower holes, while the notches would have prevented it fouling against the wall once the table was tight against the face, thus allowing the rope to be withdrawn. It was perhaps in the process of pulling the rope out, that a piece of plank 30 near the name 'bors' (in 'bors de ganys') came away and had to be replaced (Fig. 112). A rope passing through these lower holes might have acted as a stay to hold the table away from the wall as it was hoisted up, but it might also have served to secure a series of lashings such as were used in 1873–4 (Figs. 33–4).

The Round Table was already in a bad way when the vertical timbers were fixed to its back (Fig. 66). The outer end of radial 70 has been destroyed by brown rot (see pp. 136–8), and since vertical 130 is not halved to take this radial, the damage must have taken place before the verticals were added. In addition, felloe 117 is neither mortised nor halved to receive radial 70, and shows no sign of the stop-chamfers which flank the junctions of all the other radials to the felloes (except on felloe 142, which is a Victorian replacement, as we shall see). Felloe 117 must therefore be a replacement. In fact this whole sector of the table seems to have been in bad condition when the verticals were added, for although brown rot has affected verticals 132 and 133, showing that rot continued after the addition of the verticals, the latter are for the most part in much better condition than the original timbers, not only in this area, but also in those other parts of the table affected by rot.

As Cecil Hewett has pointed out earlier in this chapter, there are anomalies in the construction of the rim of the frame, notably the way in which some radials are tenoned and others mortised to the felloes. To these oddities can be added the behaviour of stop-chamfers to either side of the splayed scarfs between felloes — usually present, sometimes not. But the mortises at the outer ends of radials 68, 74, and 75 must be original, since each of these radials is also mortised to take a leg.

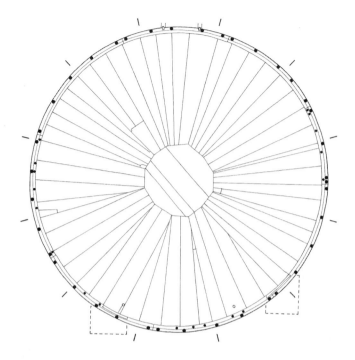

64 Nailing of the rim to the front of the Round Table, with the probable position of the pre-1873 brackets suggested by cutouts 125A and 127A in the rim.

65 The wooden brackets which supported the table, examined by Martin Biddle (left) and Michael Morris.

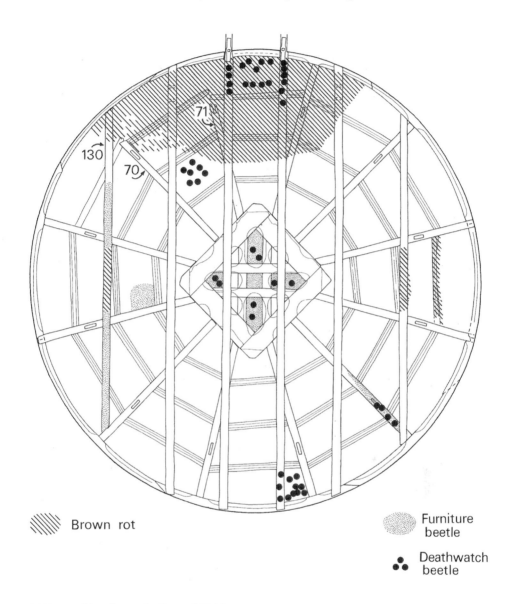

66 Rot and beetle on the Round Table.

There is thus no reason to suppose that these anomalies indicate the replacement of any of the felloes except 117 and 142.

Several of the felloes are however transfixed by iron nails driven in from the back of the table, sometimes two nails between each pair of radials, but once four and in several cases none (Fig. 62). The significance of this pattern is not clear, but the nails must have been intended to fix the rim of the frame more firmly to the raised rim added to the front of the table. Had these nails been intended solely to secure the surface planks to the frame, they would have been driven in from the front, not the back.

These nails take us to the front of the table, where a raised rim of eight oak segments of unequal length is fixed around the edge by iron nails or spikes (Fig. 64). The inner edge has a hollowed section, but this would have done little to mitigate the awkwardness of such a raised rim when the table was in use, as Simon Jervis points out in Chapter 2. But we can in fact be reasonably sure that this raised rim was only added later, when the table was already an ikon hung on the wall, and that its function was partly (like the verticals) to prevent further distortion of an object raised from its intended horizontal to a vertical plane, partly to hide and repair the decay of the original edge, and partly to provide a frame for the painting (see below, pp. 441–2). The best indication of the contemporaneity of the raised rim and the verticals lies in the lavish use of large iron spikes or nails to secure them both. On the rim there are five spikes through the flat surface of each segment, except for 124, which has four. There are in addition smaller nails in the hollow of 124 and 126–8, perhaps to fasten planks which were still loose after the addition of the rim. The nails hammered through the felloes from the back of the table may have served a similar purpose.

Two small areas on the inner edges of the raised rim, on segments 125 and 127, have been cut out and filled with carefully cut matching pieces (Fig. 64; see also Plate XVIII). These patches are not level with each other, but they seem nevertheless to have something to do with the placing of the brackets which supported the table at these points before 1789. On John Carter's drawing of about that date (Fig. 163), the brackets are shown at different levels, just as these patches imply. Presumably they remained as shown on Carter's drawing until 1873. If so, the patches were perhaps inserted then to reinstate the rim, but one cannot be sure. Equally, they might mark the position of earlier abortive seatings for the brackets, wrongly sited (as comparison of the actual positions of the brackets shown on Carter's drawing with the painted names might suggest), and therefore patched when this was discovered, as soon as the table was hoisted into position after fixing the verticals and the rim.

67 The back of the Round Table, top centre, showing damage by rot and missile fire. The areas rotted away are covered with tin-plate and the missile holes plugged with bottle corks.

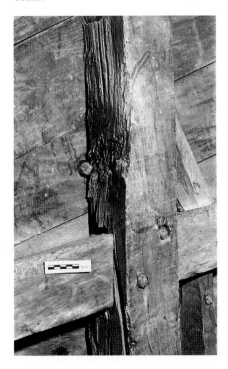

68 The scar of a missile angling up against the side of vertical 134. The hole in the plank is plugged with a bottle cork.

Rot and beetle

One of the reasons for examining the table in 1976 was to check its condition, and the condition of the wooden brackets on which it rested. These brackets were taken out of the wall as soon as the weight of the table had been taken by a steel frame inserted below it, and were found to be badly rotted (Fig. 65). When the back of the table was examined, clear traces of rot were found in the upper part, behind the king's head, in addition to areas of both rot and beetle damage elsewhere. Mr Graham Coleman and Mrs Susan J. Read of the Biodeterioration Section of the Building Research Establishment at Princes Risborough examined the table within a month of the lowering and described its condition as follows:

Before 1873 the Round Table hung on the east wall of the hall, beneath three lancet windows. It was taken down in 1873, repaired, and replaced on the west wall. At some time leakage had occurred from one of the windows above the table, for there was evidence of wetting of the reverse of the table behind the king's head.

Decay. Severe fungal infection of the brown rot type was observed in the area wetted by the leaking window (Fig. 66). Parts of the rim, the ends of two of the radials, and some of the ledges were badly decayed. A number of the planks also showed signs of decay (Fig. 67).

The heavy wooden brackets which had been embedded in the west wall to support the table were extensively damaged by the fungus *Polyporus sulphureus* (a brown rot), the mycelium of which was visible on their surface. The wood was a deep red-brown colour and showed typical cuboidal cracking (Fig. 65).

Polyporus sulphureus causes heart rot in old standing oaks and is common in Europe and America. It is able to continue its growth after the tree has been felled, as long as the timber remains sufficiently moist. It is often present in old buildings and was one of the causes of decay in the hull of HMS *Victory*. Brown rots attack the cellulose of the wood and its associated pentosans, but the lignin remains relatively unaffected, so causing some darkening of the wood. Cracks running parallel with the grain of the decayed timber also appear; these are due to shrinkage.

Readings taken during the inspection at various points in the under-surface of the table showed a moisture content of between 10 and 14 per cent, which is well below the threshold of 20 per cent necessary to support the growth of wood-destroying fungi. The planking of which the table is composed is sufficiently thin to have allowed dampness within the wood to evaporate after its relocation in 1873 on the drier west wall, and it seems likely that the fungal attack dates from before that time.

Insect damage. The emergence holes of death-watch beetles were present in the area damaged by brown rot, as well as scattered elsewhere in the planks, in one of the radials, and in one of the vertical strengthening timbers (Fig. 66). The death-watch beetle (*Xestobium rufovillosum* Deg) is commonly associated with fungal attack in ancient hardwoods, preferring timber decomposed by fungal action.

Damage in one of the radials and in the square central structure was mostly caused by *Anobium punctatum* Deg, the common furniture beetle. One of the vertical strengthening timbers had been particularly infested by *Anobium* but damage was generally scattered throughout the table (Fig. 66).

The upper side of the table showed larval tunnels and exit holes which had been filled with paint when the table was repainted in 1789. As no new exit holes were observed perforating the painted surface, it is reasonable to suppose that the insect attack was extinct before 1789 and has remained inactive ever since. The exit holes visible on the underside of the table are dirt-stained with age, and no fresh clean holes were observed.

Conclusions. The present fungal damage appears to be extinct, and as long as the timbers can be maintained below 20 per cent moisture content no further fungal deterioration will occur. The timber has apparently remained free from insect infestation for at least the past two hundred years and, provided that the table is displayed under conditions of temperature and humidity essentially similar to those prevailing over the recent past, no further insect infestation is likely and no insecticidal treatment need be undertaken.

We have already seen that much of the damage by brown rot took place before the vertical spars were added to the back of the table (above, p. 131). It also took place before the table was painted for the first time, for on the badly decayed areas at the top of the table the original paint was laid down directly on to planks which were already in placed reduced by rot to less than half their former thickness. This can be seen on a loose fragment of plank 51 found behind the tin-plate which had been nailed to the front of the table before repainting in 1789, to cover the worst areas of decay. Behind the tin-plate, stretches of the original paint remain intact (Fig. 107). The fragment shows that this paint was applied only after most of the thickness of the plank had rotted away. The marks of a tool used to pare down to good wood in preparation for painting are clearly visible (Figs. 105–6, and see further below, p. 251).

The fact that the worst of the rot lies at the top of the table, as presently hung, suggests that the table was hanging in a similar way before the verticals were added and that water coming through the gable windows was already then wetting what is still the upper part of the table. Brown rot continued when the table was rehung, for some of the vertical timbers are also decayed, but not to anything like the same degree. Irregular expenditure on repairing the roofs and windows of the hall shows how real was the danger of damp (see above, pp. 78, 80; below, pp. 357–9, 477).

The edge of the table has also suffered, as the replacement of felloes 117 and 142 and the strengthening of several of the other felloes with screws in 1873 both show. In 1548 Paolo Giovio, probably relying on a description made by someone who had seen the table at the time of the emperor Charles V's visit in 1522, recorded that decay had formerly eaten it away badly around the edge (see below, p. 405). A century and a half later in 1672, Elias Ashmole recalled that even before the Civil War it was already 'half ruined through age' (see below, p. 141). Damage by death-watch and furniture beetle affected the original timbers and the vertical spars about equally, and may of course have begun before the verticals were added. It was apparently at an end before the painting of 1789.

We can thus reconstruct the sequence of decay: brown rot, principally but not entirely *before* the verticals were added; followed by beetle attack, mainly, but perhaps not entirely, *after* the verticals were in place, and at an end by 1789. Most important of all, the brown rot at the top of the table suggests that the Round Table was already hung up below the leaking window before the verticals were added; and that the present upper part of the table was at the top then also.

Bullet holes

When we were able to examine the back of the table in 1976, we were surprised to find a number of bottle corks filling holes in the planks. A scar angling up against the side of vertical 134 from one of these holes showed that it must have been caused by a missile, and incidentally that the verticals were already in place when this happened (Fig. 68). This seemed to require the help of the police, so Mr Brian J. Heard, then Deputy Head of the Firearms Section, Metropolitan Police Forensic Science Laboratory, New Scotland Yard, came to the scene of the incident and made the following report:

> Examination of the rear of the table revealed forty-five easily discernible missile exit holes. These were of several different sizes, ranging in diameter from 0.5 to 0.9 inches. The radiographs taken of the table also showed the presence of what could be a further five missiles, within the same size range, still embedded in the thicker central beams. The distribution of the holes shows clearly that the table was used as a target, with the king's head and the centre rose used as the aiming marks (Figs. 69–70).

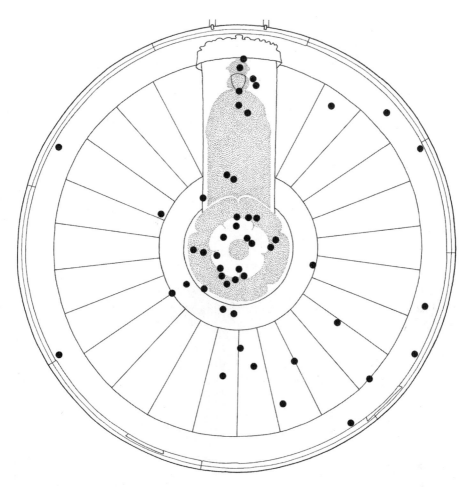

● Missile entry holes

69 The Round Table as target: missile holes in the front of the table.

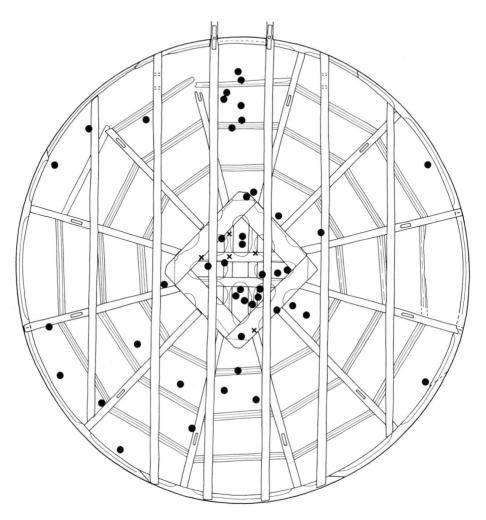

● Missile exit holes × Possible sites of missiles shown
 by radiographs

70 The Round Table as target: missile holes in the back of the table.

During the early part of the seventeenth century the military were armed with a wide variety of weapons ranging in calibre from 0.6 to 1.0 inches. The foot soldier was nearly always armed with a simple smooth-bore matchlock musket and the cavalryman with a wheel-lock pistol or carbine. This situation was standardized by an order of 1673, when the calibre of the service musket was fixed at 12 bore (0.729 inch). If the damage to the table was inflicted by military troops, this probably therefore took place before the last quarter of the seventeenth century, when weapons of several different calibres were in use at the same time.

A clue as to who might have been responsible for this incident is provided by John Milner's comment in 1799 that the Round Table was 'perforated with many bullets, supposed to have been shot by Cromwell's soldiers'.[6] The table was repainted in 1789 (see below, p. 142), so assuming that the corks were inserted from the front at that time to prepare the surface for repainting, Milner's reference to the bullet holes ten years later may have been drawn from memory. He gives no source for the supposition that Cromwell's soldiers were to blame. This may have been a local tradition, or it may have been based on the account given by Elias Ashmole in 1672 in *The Institution, Laws & Ceremonies of the most Noble Order of the Garter*, a book to which Milner might have had access, although he does not refer to it.

> At the upper end of the great Hall in *Winchester Castle*, I remember to have seen a large Round Table hung against the wall, called King *Arthurs Round Table*. ... This old Monument was broken to pieces (being before half ruined through age) by the Parliaments Soldiers, in the beginning of the late unhappy War, because looked upon as a relique of Superstition (as were those little gilded Coffers with Inscriptions, that did preserve the bones of some of the *Saxon* Kings and Bishops, deposited by Bishop *Fox* in the top of the Walls on both sides the upper part of the Quire of the Cathedral Church of that City) though guilty of nothing but the crime of reverend Antiquity.[7]

The abridged edition published in 1715 as *The History of the Most Noble Order of the Garter* gives the impression of greater precision. The table, it says, 'was destroy'd in

---

[6] John Milner, *The History Civil and Ecclesiastical, and Survey of the Antiquities, of Winchester*, 1st edn. (Winchester, 1798–9), ii, p. 171. This comment was repeated verbatim in the two subsequent editions and in many of the nineteenth-century guidebooks to Winchester.

[7] Elias Ashmole, *The Institution, Laws & Ceremonies of the Most Noble Order of the Garter* (London, 1672), p. 95.

the rebellious Times of Forty One',[8] but this is presumably just an (erroneous) reference to the period which followed the outbreak of trouble in 1642. The city of Winchester fell to a Parliamentary force under Sir William Waller on 12 December 1642; the castle surrendered the next day. Castle and city were regained for the king in October 1643, but were again taken by Parliament in 1645, the city surrendering on 29 September and the castle opening its gates on 6 October after a short siege under Cromwell's personal command.[9] It was on the first occasion in 1642 that the cathedral was ransacked and the burial chests of the Anglo-Saxon kings and bishops broken open,[10] and it was then, if we are to follow Ashmole, that the Round Table was defaced. Milner's tradition supposed it was Cromwell's soldiers who fired the shots. This may suggest that the incident took place after the siege of the castle in 1645, when Cromwell was himself present, but is probably no more than a reflection of those tales which attribute to Cromwell all destruction in the Civil War. Ashmole is quite specific that the damage took place 'in the beginning of the late unhappy War', and we should accept his contemporary evidence, even if he exaggerated the damage and had clearly not seen the table since.

The trajectories of the missiles can be traced by comparing the positions of their entry and exit holes (Fig. 71). Many of the shots came from below and to the right, suggesting that a tightly grouped bunch of soldiers, having burst into the Great Hall through the south door (the principal entry before the demolition of the castle in 1650–1), fired impulsively up at the twin targets presented by the king's head and the central rose. Before many of them had a chance to move across the floor for a straighter shot, they were brought in hand by a cooler head, doubtless some corporal or sergeant.

Repainting in 1789

The Round Table was repainted in 1789 by the firm of Cave and Son (Fig. 97, and see below, Chapter 7 and pp. 319–22, 480). There is no sign that it was taken down from the wall at that time, and no evidence of any repairs except to the painted surface. Here the missile holes were plugged from the front with bottle corks, as already

---

[8] Elias Ashmole, *The History of the Most Noble Order of the Garter*, 1st edn. (London, 1715), pp. 50–1. The work was prepared posthumously, Ashmole having died in 1692, and in these words probably represents no more than the editor's paraphrase. Ashmole's own interleaved copy of *The Institution* (Bodleian, MS. Ashmole 1742, p. 95) has no corrections or additions to his original text at this point.

[9] G. N. Godwin, *The Civil War in Hampshire (1642–45)*, 2nd edn. (Southampton and London, 1904), pp. 45–50, 123–4, 333–43.

[10] Godwin, *Civil War*, pp. 47–50; John Vaughan, *Winchester Cathedral. Its Monuments and Memorials* (London, c.1919), pp. 15–28.

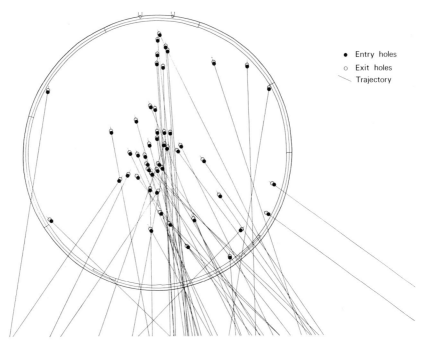

- ● Entry holes
- ○ Exit holes
- ╲ Trajectory

71 The Round Table as target: missile trajectories reconstructed by comparing the position of the entry and exit holes shown in Figs. 69 and 70. Entry holes ●, exit holes ○.

72 'Repaired by George Blake April 14th 1873': pencil inscription on the back of plank 45.

described. The worst areas of rot and other damage were covered with pieces of tin-plate carefully nailed down over the surviving paint and in one place secured by an iron T-bar (Plate XXII, Fig. 107). The repaired surface was then repainted.

Additions and repairs in 1873

The softwood boards fastened to the back of the table in a concentric ring between the outer ledges and the felloes were added in 1873 (Figs. 41, 43, Nos. 136–49). An inscription written in pencil on plank 45 and subsequently hidden behind board 145 provides the precise date: *Repaired by George Blake April 14th 1873* (Fig. 72).

This ring of boards was fixed down in a most efficient fashion with two or three steel screws into each plank of the surface, but strangely some gaps were left, between 143 and 144 at the top, and between 136 and 149 at the bottom. In addition, 147 was fixed alongside the weakened felloe 75, and part of the rim of the frame was replaced at the top, where felloe 142 is a softwood replacement, scarfed into 117 and fixed with screws. Screws were also inserted at various points around the rim of the frame, and in other places as required, to secure weak points (see Figs. 103–4). In the lower half of the table iron straps were screwed on to the outer sides of the inner pair of verticals and down the adjacent radials (Fig. 62). Since the table hangs from these verticals, the straps helped to spread the weight throughout the original framework. Finally, early in 1874, the whole structure was clamped firmly together by passing an iron band like the tyre of a wheel around the circumference. This band, hinged at top and bottom, was fastened to either side at three and nine o'clock with folding wedges, by means of which it was tightened (Figs. 73, and see below, p. 481–2). The iron straps were also fixed more firmly to the top of the table by cramps which gripped the front edge of the table and were secured behind by nuts bolted down over long washers.

For the actual move of the table in 1873 horizontal battens were fastened across the back (Fig. 34), but these were removed before the table was raised into position on the west wall.

The surface was subsequently varnished. Whether this was done in 1789 or later is not known, but in 1834 a certain T. K. Drown pencilled his name and initials, together with the date, several times on the king's left and right hands and on his sword (Fig. 133). These grafitti came away when the varnish was removed in 1978, showing that they had been written on top of the varnish and that the varnish itself was already in place in 1834. It would have been impossible to reach this high without a ladder, so the grafitti may reflect some 'official' action such as varnishing, but Drown has not been traced and he was not apparently a member of the present-day Bond Street firm of picture restorers of the same name.

73 The iron band put on around the edge of the Round Table in 1874: one of the two pairs of folding wedges by which the band was tightened.

More recent events

The century and a quarter since 1873 is in some ways the most obscure in the history of the Round Table. Throughout the investigations of 1976 and later, tales of events in the table's recent history were always cropping up: how it had been taken down for one event or another; how it had been repainted yet again; and so forth. Many of these stories proved to be baseless. Others had their source in distant childhood recollections of replicas of the Round Table, some of them quite large, made as gifts to distinguished persons, as specially commissioned furniture, as pageant properties, or as tourist souvenirs. Each story had to be followed up because it was important to know whether the table had been treated in recent times with preservative compounds which might have affected the radiocarbon dating programme (see Chapter 6).

There seems to have been only one such treatment. In 1938, when the courts were being reinstated in the Great Hall (see above, p. 97), Stanley Richardson, head of the well-known Winchester firm of Richardson and Starling which specialized in timber preservation, was asked by the County Architect's Department to inspect the table. Mr Richardson examined the painted surface all over from a step-ladder or scaffold, but found no evidence of active beetle or decay. Mr A. L. Roberts, the County Architect, requested that the table should nevertheless be sprayed as a preventive measure against insect attack. This was done by Mr Richardson's men, although not in his presence, using chloronaphthalene wax. The painted surface would certainly have been sprayed, and the back could also have been sprayed using the extension rods then in use. Mr Richardson remembered that in 1938 he also observed the timber 'strengthening framework' on the back of the table. For this to have been visible, the table must have been lifted a few inches over the upturned ends of the brackets and pulled away from the wall. Mr Richardson thought the table was supported on trestles for this purpose, but it could not have been pulled very far away from the wall, for there was not much room in which to look and Mr Richardson did not see the empty mortises for the legs. His recollection that the back of the table appeared to be clean can be explained by the fact that he was looking up from below.

Mr Richardson also remembered someone telling him at the time that the table was probably made for a festival or a tournament. This may well have been the distinguished American Arthurian scholar R. S. Loomis, who held this view and may have taken the opportunity of Mr Richardson's inspection to peer around the back of the table. 'An inspection', Loomis wrote in 1938, 'of the back of the board shows that it originally had legs, and the most plausible account of its origin is that it was constructed for one of those festivities ... called Round

Tables'.[11] But was Loomis referring to an inspection of his own, or to the one made in 1873, a drawing of which was to be found in the book by Melville Portal to which Loomis refers?[12]

In 1948 Mr (later Sir) Walter Oakeshott, a leading scholar of early medieval painting who was then headmaster of Winchester College, suggested to the County Council that an examination ought to be made to see if there was an earlier painting below the present design:

> One would reckon that an earlier inscription would be quite different in form, and that, *if* it were necessary to destroy a little bit of the surface paint, in order to find out if there'd been earlier painting, it might be necessary to destroy a letter or two of the inscription. An earlier date would be a promising sign, and one feels that such a very preliminary action could easily be restored, if a good photograph of the existing surface were available.[13]

As a result of this suggestion the Duke of Wellington, then chairman of the council's Winchester Castle Committee, held discussions with the directors of the National Gallery and the Victoria and Albert Museum, and decided to commission an 'expert restorer' to make an inspection and report. Scaffolding was in position by the end of April, and by 28 June the Duke was able to report back to his committee that he had received the report. Extensive enquiries have failed to reveal who the expert or experts may have been, but the gist of their advice is clear: 'the removal of the top coat of paint would destroy the original painting'. It was decided to take no action, and the scaffolding was removed. The committee noted that the table was in good condition, and that the opportunity had been taken to have it cleaned down.

Nothing more was done until the table was lowered in 1976 for our own investigation. During 1978 the painting was cleaned by Pauline Plummer, who removed the accumulated grime and varnish, and brought the painting to its present condition (*frontispiece*; compare e.g. Figs. 97, 100). In February 1980, after an interval of three and a half years during which it was again visited by a reigning monarch (Fig. 168), the Round Table was rehung on the west wall of the Great Hall. (Fig. 169).

---

[11] Roger Sherman Loomis and Laura Hibbard Loomis, *Arthurian Legends in Medieval Art* (London and New York, 1938), p. 41.

[12] Melville Portal, *The Great Hall, Winchester Castle* (Winchester, 1899), pp. 89–90.

[13] Letter to the author, 6 Dec. 1983; HRO (modern records centre), H/CX1/55/1, 26 January and 28 June 1948. See also *Hampshire Chronicle*, 15 May 1948.

Sequence of events

The three layers of timber-work and the relationship of the other observable features to these three stages and to each other allow us now to reconstruct the sequence of events through which the Round Table has passed since its original construction. Some of these events can be dated directly by external evidence; others – especially the original construction and the addition of the vertical spars and raised rim – can only be dated by more elaborate methods (Chapters 5 and 6). The state of knowledge at this stage of the investigation can be set out as follows:

1	Table made	Oak, wooden pegs	Date? (1250–1350? see Chapter 10)
2	Legs broken out, table hung up		Date? (1348? see Chapter 11)
3	Brown rot appears in upper part of table as hung		Date? (before repairs)
4	Table repaired, strengthened with vertical spars, raised rim added, painted, rehung with same sector uppermost	Oak, iron nails	Date? (1516?, see Chapter 12)
5	Brown rot and insect attack		16th–17th century
6	Table used as a target		1642 (?1645)
7	Rot and insect attack ?continue		17th–18th century
8	Table repainted		1789
9	Painting varnished		before 1834
10	Table taken down from east wall, repaired and strengthened, rehung on west wall	Pine, steel screws	1873–4
11	Table sprayed against further insect attack		1938
12	Painting examined for possibility of removing 1789 repainting		1948
13	Investigation		1976
14	Painting cleaned		1978
15	Table rehung		1980

5

Tree-ring Dating the Round Table [1]

The Work of 1976–1980

Dendrochronology and radiocarbon dating

In the early 1960s dendrochronologists in England and elsewhere began their search for modern and ancient tree-ring sequences with which to build dated 'tree-ring chronologies'. It was their hope that wooden artefacts from archaeological excavations, or panel paintings, or ships, for example, could be dated by comparing the widths of tree rings in the artefact with those of growth periods of known date. Tree-ring data from dated paintings on wood, muniment chests, wall panelling, ships of war, chapels, timber-framed buildings, modern trees, and other available sources were gathered for the purpose of building standard chronologies. On the European continent, several successful exercises of this kind were undertaken about the same time.[2]

---

[1] I am grateful to Fred Hughes, now retired from the Forest Department, Oxford, his wife, Doris; to the Richardson family of Winchester, the late Stanley, his wife, Phyl; his son, Barry, and his wife, Janet; to Ian Gourlay; Lewis Woodhouse; and especially John and Maude Long; and many others too numerous to mention; not forgetting Martin and Birthe Biddle (who really made this whole adventure possible) for the many professional and personal courtesies extended to me during the entire scope of my 'Winchester' tree-ring studies. North Carolina State University and its College of Forest Resources and the Division of Multidisciplinary Studies of the College of Humanities and Social Sciences made this study possible through their many means of financial and moral support. I particularly thank Nan and Randolph Bulgin for use of their e-mail, while proofing this chapter in the Mountains of North Carolina.

[2] See, for example, Bruno Huber and Veronika Giertz-Siebenlist, 'Unsere tausendjährige Eichen-Jahrringchronologie durchschnittlich 57 (10–150)–fach belegt', in *Sitzungsberichten der Österreichischen Akademie der Wissenschaften, Mathem.-Naturw. Kl.*, Abt. I, Bd. 178, Heft 1–4 (1969), 37–42. See also B. Kolchin, 'Dendrochronological Method in Archaeology', *VI International Congress of Prehistory and Protohistory Sciences*, Academy of Sciences of the USSR, Institute of Archaeology (Moscow, 1962).

In 1964 the Round Table hanging in the Great Hall of Winchester Castle became an artefact of unusual interest to dendrochronologists involved with archaeological investigations in Winchester. They thought that the table might contain a wealth of ancient tree-ring information for southern England. Moreover, speculation about its date of construction, the type of wood used, and the preparation of the wood had intrigued both historians and lay people for many years. The greatest impediment in immediately examining the table-top in 1964 lay in its inaccessible position on the wall of the Great Hall. There was the hope, nevertheless, that some day the table would be available for examination.

With removal of the table from the wall in 1976, and with approval by the county authorities of the proposed sampling procedures, a dendrochronology study was at last feasible. There was, in addition, an unparalleled opportunity to coordinate an examination of the wooden planks in the table and correlate their age as estimated by radiocarbon and tree-ring dating. The concurrent development of these approaches would make a significant contribution not only to knowledge of dendrochronology in southern England but also to the implications of dating ancient artefacts by radiocarbon.

It was thought important to use the two dating techniques in order to reach independent estimates of the ages of the planks used in construction of the table. But the two approaches were soon seen as complementary: dating by tree rings could be expedited if radiocarbon could provide an estimated age as a starting point; and afterwards, the inexactness of the radiocarbon results could be gauged by the preciseness of the tree-ring matches.

Before dating by tree rings could be attempted, however, there were other concerns to be considered by both the radiocarbon scientists and the dendrochronologists. These included the genus and species of timber used for the planks and frame of the table, the quality of the wood, its state of seasoning at the time of construction, and the character of the workmanship exhibited. Later changes to the wood due to environmental and human activities, and the number of trees from which the planks in the table-top may have come, had also to be taken into account. Finally, dendrochronologists were most interested in whether they could use the tree-ring width data to establish a standard tree-ring chronology suitable for dating other artefacts.

With these technical concerns in mind, the joint tree-ring/radiocarbon dating programme was undertaken. The resulting study and its story provide a striking example of the value of interdisciplinary cooperation in a scientific investigation.

Wood technology

All the ancient wood used in the Round Table came from oak trees, *Quercus* spp., either *Q. robur* and/or *Q. petraea* or their hybrids, that is to say English oak, in which a layer of wood is laid down each year on the trunk of the tree. These layers, as seen in a cross-section of the trunk, form rings which vary in width each year, depending principally on the climate of the growing season during a given year (Plate XVII).

As an English oak matures and adds rings of growth year by year, a central core of the tree is impregnated with extractives deposited in the cells by the living tree. This central core, brownish in colour, is termed 'heartwood' to distinguish it from the outer, still whitish, last formed rings of 'sapwood' just beneath the bark. The heartwood is highly resistant to decay and insect attack. By contrast, the sapwood, not having the toxic depositions, is easily attacked by wood-boring insects and (unless kept quite dry or saturated with water) is susceptable also to destructive decay organisms. The craftsmen building the table must have been well aware of these facts. They trimmed off virtually all the sapwood.

As can be easily appreciated from the above, the presence of sapwood is necessary to estimate the year of felling the tree from which a given wood sample was taken. A mature tree of 150 to 300 years of age will, by volume and ring count, be mostly heartwood. The outer rim of sapwood, the most recently formed rings, will usually be of about 20 to 30 rings and will only increase slightly in number as the tree grows. Indeed for most purposes one may consider that the sapwood of English oak around Winchester is composed of about 25 rings. If an artefact has bark with the last formed ring in place, it may therefore be possible to date the exact year of felling the tree. If only a portion of the sapwood is present, an estimate, plus or minus say five years, of the felling date may be arrived at by assuming that the tree had 25 rings of sapwood and estimating the date by adding the 'missing' rings of sapwood. Obviously, if no sapwood is present the felling date is not readily available unless the artefact may be related to other wood from the same tree. Fortunately, some small amounts of sapwood, although too severely deteriorated for measurement, but providing a count of rings of sapwood, were present on a few boards of the table (Table 1, p. 166). From these, once the planks had been correctly cross-dated (Tables 2–5), the felling dates of those planks could be deduced or estimated (Table 6, p. 193).

Two principal types of boards, or planks, can be manufactured from logs: flat-sawn and quartersawn (Fig. 74*a* and *b*, respectively). Quartersawn boards are those in which the annual rings are kept, as far as possible, at right-angles to the wide surface of the boards. More flatsawn boards of usable width can be produced from a given log than quartersawn boards, but the outer flatsawn boards are far more liable to warp and shrink more in width than quartersawn boards. This is so because wood shrinks more in the tangential direction around the rings than across the rings. Thus, flatsawn boards or even ones with obliquely sawn rings, say at a 45° angle or less to the surface of the board will exhibit differential shrinkage and will therefore warp upon drying. Quartersawn boards are the more expensive in time and materials to produce, but they are the best for furniture construction or for wall or picture panelling, because differential shrinkage across the board, plank, or panel is less than in fully flatsawn stock, hence shrinkage and warping are at a minimum. The craftsmen who built the table must have known that the choice material for constructing panels and flat furniture surfaces, including table-tops, was the quartersawn oak planks from the heartwood of the tree: dimensionally stable and resistant to decay and insects; the superior working, long lasting wood!

An additional observation should be noted here. The greatest crack between the planks in the table, most likely due to shrinkage after construction of the table, is of the order of ¼ inch (6 to 8 mm); most cracks are far narrower, ¹⁄₁₆ to ³⁄₃₂ inch (2 to 3 mm). These cracks, of the order of 1 to 3 per cent, if they existed at all beforehand, presumably widened to these dimensions only after central heating was installed in the hall in 1825[3] and additional drying of the wood took place. The original moisture content was probably in equilibrium with conditions in the hall at the time of the table's manufacture. In other words, the boards were most likely very well seasoned at the time of use to an EMC, Equilibrium Moisture Content, for the conditions they were to encounter in the early years without central heating. Prior to the actual sawing, fitting and planing of the boards in the table, the seasoning process could well have been deliberately extended over several years to ensure the dimensional stability of the planks when finally in use.

The boards are otherwise remarkably free of defects. Large knots are not present, although the grain deviations due to them are. Indeed, small knots, when present at all, are of an insignificant, unnoticeable size. Again, this is an indication of the selection of superior material of the highest quality for construction of an important, significant, symbolic object: the Round Table.

Fortunately then for tree-ring studies of the table, the craftsmen selected quartersawn material of a high quality known to have long life, durability, strength, and stability for constructing what must have been a very special article of furniture. Also fortunately for dendrochronology, trimming was done sparingly, and some otherwise undesirable sapwood remained on the boards at the time of construction. The quartersawn planks of the table thus provided an excellent year-by-year record of the

---

[3] For this date, see below, Chapter 13, p. 481.

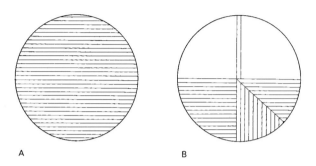

A   B

74 Flatsawn (*a*) and quartersawn (*b*) boards. There are several possible methods of quarter sawing, only two of which are shown here (cf. Fig. 85).

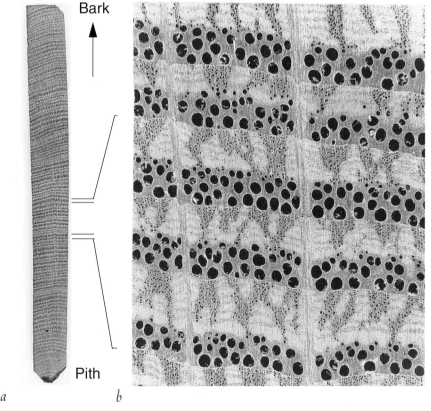

75 Cross-sections of English Oak (*Quercus sp.*), showing the annual rings and the rays which radiate from the pith towards the bark: *a*, section of a gun-deck plank, scribed '1815', from a refit of HMS Victory; *b*, photomicrograph of five rings of another sample (not from HMS Victory).

153

growth of the trees from which they came, and it proved possible to compare growth records among the planks and ultimately with other dendrochronological reference curves. In addition, the sapwood present allowed for the calculation of felling dates with reasonable precision. Likewise, an excellent record became available for positioning the radiocarbon samples within the tree-ring sequence contained in each board.

In recording this year-by-year pattern, a V-shaped groove was cut across the back of the boards with a portable, but well sharpened, router to expose the growth rings. This was necessary because the iron band rimming the edge of the table was not allowed to be removed to expose the widest part of the wedge-shaped boards where the maximum number of rings could have been observed. The authorities therefore granted the compromise position allowing cuts to be made in the most inconspicuous places possible on the back of the table. As a result, the maximum account of information stored in the boards has not been obtained. There is still data for some future dendrochronologist to obtain when a full sampling becomes available, if ever. In recording the tree-ring widths it was necessary to determine the proper orientation of the boards in relation to the direction of the tree's growth. In oak trees the centre and bark directions of quartersawn boards are relatively easily determined by considering the patterns of springwood, summerwood, and flame-like dendritic structures formed in the annual rings of the planks. The large springwood pores (the light-coloured earlywood bands of Fig. 75*b* form first in any given ring, and afterwards the pores of summerwood (the progressively smaller pores in the darker, flame-like, dendritically marked latewood bands of Fig. 75*b*). In specimens such as these, the evidence shows that the centre of the tree is on the springwood side of the ring and the bark on the summerwood side. Ring-width measurements were then obtained, as described later, for the entire ring composed of spring and summer portions, from the centre toward the bark, so that years of growth would follow each other in their proper chronological series.

The principles of tree-ring dating

Each tree ring, with its combination of spring and summer growth, is a reflection of the environmental factors affecting wood production in a given year. Dating wooden objects by dendrochronology relies on the hypothesis that the trees of a particular location will respond similarly to the variable climatic and growth conditions of each year by producing rings of similar relative width. If that is so, it should be possible to match, year by year, the ring-width data from two or more trees, especially trees growing in the same region with similar soil, soil water and plant enviroments. 'Noise' in the tree-ring data due to unknown causes does occur and complicates the comparison process even for trees growing nearby to each other. One of the first steps in dating a wooden object is therefore to measure each of the rings in a cut section and to plot the widths, or their standardized values[4], on a graph such as the one shown in Fig. 76*a* and 76*b*, respectively, where the pattern of wide and narrow annual rings appears as a series of peaks and valleys. The Round Table, with more than four dozen individual planks to test, yielded many such graphs of plotted measurements, called 'curves'. Theoretically, the planks, if they came from trees which grew near one another, should have produced curves which could be matched to the year. And indeed, as the ten curves in Fig. 77 show, there were striking similarities in some of the patterns. Not all of the curves match as neatly as the ones shown in Fig. 77, however, because not all trees respond identically to the growing conditions each year. Some oaks may put their energy into mast (acorn) production rather than into wood. Some may be attacked by insects or disease. Some may be freed temporarily of adjacent tree competition if an adjacent tree is blown over by wind, dies, or is felled. In hardwood trees caused to lean, by wind for example, relatively wide rings (tension wood) are formed until the lean is corrected. Other unknown influences may also disrupt normal growth. For ancient wood virtually all of these influences are unknown to dendrochronologists, since all they have in hand are the actual ring widths. Discrepancies in the data can therefore also be seen in Fig. 77.

It is unlikely that any two trees will, in fact, produce exactly identical ring patterns. Indeed, while patterns may differ within a tree from one side of the trunk to the other, these are the curve patterns which can be expected to be most similar – sometimes, but certainly not always, almost line by line duplicates of each other. The role of the dendrochronologist is to look for similarities in the growth patterns, to sort out the incongruities, to make allowances for the discrepancies, to correct errors in the data collection process, to identify the matching points of ring sequences within these variable patterns, and finally to combine the data from several trees to produce an average curve.

The initial step in making matches in a set of unknown, previously unstudied tree-ring sequences involves looking for and learning the characteristics which exist in the growth pattern of the trees from which the planks came. This procedure requires study of the ring formations in the wood itself, study of the plotted curves, and 'statistical' analysis. For the latter, a modification of the Baillie and Pilcher 'CROS'

---

[4]   A. C. Barefoot, 'A Winchester Dendrochronology for 1635–1972 A.D. Its Validity and Possible Extension', *Journal of the Institute of Wood Science* 7 (1975), 25–32.

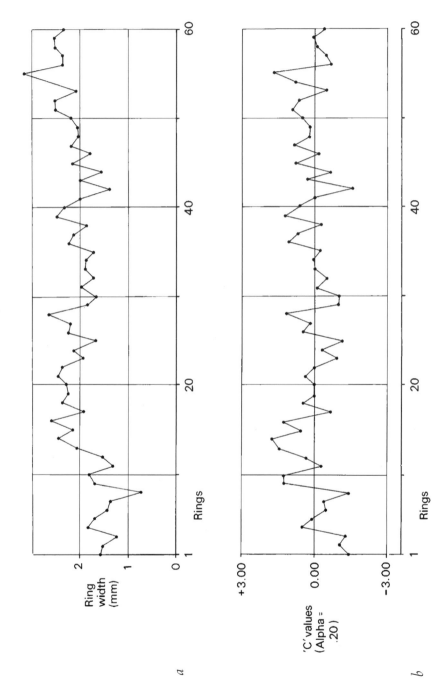

76 Plotting the ring-widths of Round Table plank 2: (*a*) above, the raw ring-widths in mm; (*b*) below, the 'C' values.

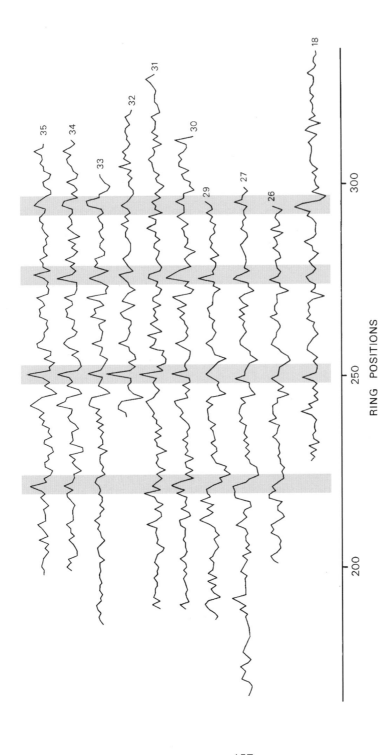

77 Statistically standardized curves from ten of the twenty-five wide-ringed planks of the Round Table, shown in their matching positions.

computer programme was used which calculated the product-moment correlation coefficient 'r' between two curves at every position of overlap.[5] Each 'r' value is 'tested' with Student's 't' test, where values of 't' greater than 2.0 to 3.5 are deemed to be indicative of possible matching positions for the two ring series[6]. Usually the greater the value of 't', the more likelihood of a fit. Note, a word of warning; the one on one comparison of all possible fitting positions in this usage is not a valid use of "t" as a statistical probability statement. Therefore, visual comparisons of the two curves must be made of the plotted data at the several candidate positions to select the one position that is, or appears, to be the best fit. Also, the raw data may need editing for missing rings or the inclusion of a duplicate measurement of a single ring, for example. Some times, many times, the choice is obvious. And, certain patterns become such strong signatures that the 't' test is not even needed; such was the situation with many of the curves from the Round Table (see Fig. 77). The 't' screening serves best in helping fit the less obvious patterns, but ones which will still exhibit the signature positions, if not so strongly recognizable immediately. For this situation there are no statistically valid probability statements which can be stated for the results of the comparing of every possible one on one position. It is the visual comparison which takes precedence over statistical numbers. To give a valid probability assessment to the 't' test, an *a priori* (with reason) hypothesis must be stated which tests a specific, single pre-selected matching position. For this reason it is the experience and mental judgements of the researcher which must finally be brought to bear in making matching comparisons starting from raw data curves. Sometimes the job of matching is easy, as noted above for a few of the graphs from the table (Fig. 77). At other times, even the most sophisticated statistical analyses are unhelpful, and it is impossible to decide which are the matching positions. It is at this time that the mind of the dendrochronologist must watch for errors in the data. In the data collecting and measuring process rings may be missed or included twice. The researcher then must make honest steps to reconcile the data; the curve patterns must be corrected (edited) before including the sequence in an average curve.

To be as objective as possible in matching, the Round Table tree-ring data was standardized by a mathematical procedure which uses an exponentially weighted smoothing scheme and conversion of the raw ring-width to a 'chronology' value, 'C'.[7]

[5]   M. G. L. Baillie and J. R. Pilcher, 'A Simple Cross-Dating Program for Tree-Ring Research', *Tree Ring Bulletin* 33 (1973), 7–14.

[6]   'Student' was the pen-name of W. S. Gosset, who invented the t-test in 1908. For Student and his work, see now E. S. Pearson, *Student: a Statistical Biography of William Sealy Gosset* (Oxford, 1990). See Table 5 for probabilities of 't'.

[7]   Barefoot, 'A Winchester Dendrochronology for 1635–1972 AD'.

The data as plotted, therefore, actually fluctuates by about the same amount of ± three values on either side of a zero mean line (Fig. 76b). With these calculations and the plotting of the 'C' values, wide-ring trees and narrow-ring trees can be compared visually on the same scale. Other workers have chosen to tackle these problems in somewhat different ways.[8] Once the comparison decisions have been made, the individual ring sequences are averaged together to form an undated chronology, which can then be compared with and positioned on dated chronologies derived from the dendrochronological study of other timbers.

Ideally data from at least ten and preferably thirty to forty trees are desirable to establish a valid chronology. It is not always possible to gather this much information, however. For example, the Choir Stall chronology specially constructed for this study as one of the reference, or comparison, curves does not include that many panels, let alone so many trees. Individually, some other reference curves used here also have limitations which will seriously impede an accurate dating for the Winchester region, but taken together (Table 4) they provide good and well corrobated evidence for dating the Round Table curve for the purpose of estimating a construction date.

Reference curves

Previous work had established a tree-ring curve for Winchester for the period AD 1051–1972; indeed the curve might be extended back to 866, but the earlier portion is based upon the measurement of one plank in Westminster Abbey and may not necessarily contribute to a Winchester chronology.[9]

The modern portion of this chronology, from 1635 to 1972, is based on tree-ring sequences of thirty-six trees felled after 1960 and data from the five 'trees' squared-up to serve as the large gun-deck beams for HMS *Victory*.[10] The ends of the *Victory* beams were being replaced because of deterioration and were found to date from the repair of the damage following the Battle of Trafalgar. The beams were dated to the 1813–15 refit of HMS *Victory*. Including 14 rings of sapwood, their tree-rings span the period 1640 to 1800, so that the overlapping match fell entirely, and wonderfully well, onto the modern tree data, which extended back to 1635. The accuracy of this portion of the curve is unquestioned.

[8]   H. C. Fritts, *Tree Rings and Climate* (London and New York, 1976), pp. 261–81.

[9]   A. C. Barefoot, W. L. Hafley, and J. F. Hughes, 'Dendrochronology and the Winchester Excavation', in *Dendrochronology in Europe*, ed. John Fletcher, National Maritime Museum Archaeological Series 4, British Archaeological Reports, International Ser. 51 (Oxford, 1978), pp. 160–72.

[10]   Barefoot, 'A Winchester Dendrochronology for 1635–1972 AD'.

By a series of such overlapping matches the chronology was extended backwards by 'bridging' (Fig. 78). A series of panels from 126 High Street, Winchester, extended the chronology back to 1391; a series from the Langton Chapel in Winchester Cathedral pushed it back to 1188, and a final series from the choir stalls in the cathedral took it back to 1051.[11] These earlier portions of the Winchester curve are still subject to some minor adjustment of years, if trials with other data show this to be necessary. If, as hoped, the tree-ring data from the table proved amenable to analysis, this could well help to provide a significant medieval chronology for the Winchester area.

Comparative data have also been made available by the authors of two other curves:

1.   the curves known as 'Ref. 5', developed by the late Dr John Fletcher.[12]
2.   'Chronology II', built up by Dr J. Bauch.[13]

These two curves also have limitations for our purposes, Bauch's curve relates to another geographical region, the southern Netherlands, while Fletcher's curve may be based mainly on material from a district of England other than Winchester. Nevertheless, the use of these two and the Winchester curve with the table data appeared to give consistent results, and they were therefore used as the comparison curves for dating purposes.

Inasmuch as these curves were not (in 1980) 'proved' adaptable for southern England in the periods anticipated, the carbon-14 investigation was undertaken to provide both an independent estimate of the age of the table and an indication of the period to which the tree-ring data of the table should be referred.

Thus, if the tree-ring data from the table proved amenable to analysis, these data could well provide a significant early chronology for the Winchester region. Equally important, they could contribute to an understanding of carbon-14 dating by providing an accurate age for comparison of medieval carbon-14 dates. Thus the Round Table had significant unknown scientific, as well as historical, facets in its cultural origins.

---

[11]   Barefoot *et al.*, 'Dendrochronology and the Winchester Excavation'.

[12]   J. M. Fletcher, 'Tree-Ring Chronologies for the Sixth to Sixteenth Centuries for Oaks of Southern and Eastern England', *Journal of Archaeological Science* 4 (1977), 335–52; idem, 'Oak Chronologies for Eastern and Southern England: Principles for Their Construction and Application: Their Comparison with Others in North-West Europe', in *Dendrochronology in Europe*, ed. Fletcher, pp. 139–56. For subsequent discussion of these chronologies, see below, pp. 180–1, 184, and Table 4, n. 3.

[13]   J. Bauch, 'Tree-Ring Chronologies for the Netherlands', in *Dendrochronology in Europe*, ed. Fletcher, pp. 133–7.

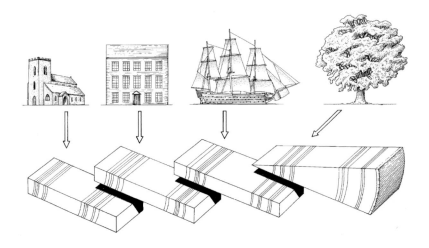

78 Cross-dating a series of tree-ring curves, adapted to suit the Winchester exercise from M. G. L. Baillie, *Tree-ring Dating and Archaeology* (1982).

79 An area of the back of the Round Table, showing grooves cut in planks 33 to 36 for tree-ring dating. Wherever possible the grooves were cut below one of the Victorian pine boards which were removed for this purpose and subsequently replaced (see p. 164). In this photograph, the shadow of board 148 can be seen to either side of the grooves. For the rectangular cut on the right-hand plank (here bearing the provisional chalk number 10) made for radiocarbon dating, see below, p. 213 and Fig. 81.

80 Simulation of the method used to mark the rings observed in the grooves cut into the Round Table planks: under illuminated magnification Ian Gourlay marked each ring boundary by cutting with a scalpel into a white card pinned against the groove.

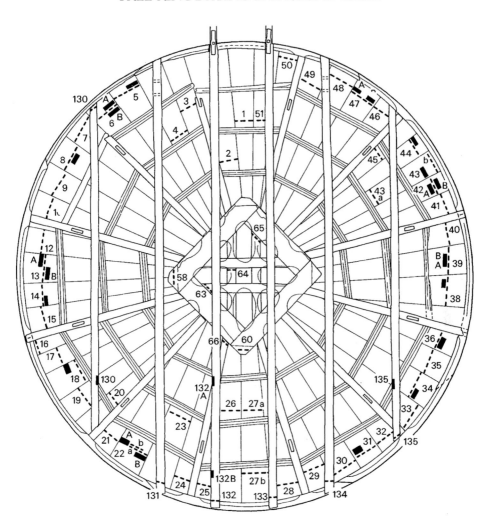

◼ Carbon 14 sample   - - - - Dendrochronology groove

FRONT

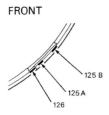

125 B
125 A
126

81 The Round Table, showing the positions from which radiocarbon (Carbon-14) samples were taken and the location of tree-ring dating (dendrochronology) grooves.

Specimen preparation and data collection

To read tree rings accurately for dendrochronological purposes one must usually first have a clean-cut, prepared cross-section. Preferably the entire section should be mountable under a microscope, especially when extremely narrow rings are being examined. However, because the iron band around the table could not be removed to expose the ends of the boards and because the planks could not be cut through to obtain samples, these conditions could not be satisfied. Perhaps some future dendrochronologist may have access to the ends of each board for obtaining the full information from the table. Also, for obvious aesthetic reasons, all the tree-ring and radiocarbon samples had to be taken from the back of the table. For the tree-ring studies, access to the end-grain structure was obtained by cutting shallow 'V' grooves on the back of the boards with a portable router (Fig. 79). Each groove was approximately ¼ to ⁷/₁₆ inch (5 to 10 mm) wide at the top and about the same depth. Unless very good reasons dictated otherwise – insect damage, decay, or problems of access – the sampling groove was cut in an area covered by one of the Victorian deal boards which had been removed for this study (Fig. 79). A scalpel was used to obtain a clean-cut surface to the edges of the groove, which was then examined *in situ* under a simple hand-held microscope of 5x to 20x magnification (Fig. 80). For relatively wide-ringed material, there were few difficulties other than access or good positioning of the worker's body while marking the rings, although because the table was vertical, most of the work had to be done from scaffolding. Narrow-ringed planks, however, often required the use of at least a 20x hand lens with a very short working distance in order to distinguish the ring boundaries. Under these circumstances, the limitations of physical access and, more prevalently, the presence of wood which had been damaged by insect holes and decay often made interpretations tedious and subject to error, particularly in these zones of extremely narrow rings. Some ring sequences were reworked and rechecked several times.

Dendrochronological samples from forty-nine of the fifty-one radial planks forming the surface of the table were prepared by Ian Gourlay, of the then Department of Forestry, University of Oxford, who also recorded and measured most of the sequences. The planks and ring sequences were identified by the Winchester Research Unit (WRU) numbers assigned to the timbers of the table (Fig. 81; cf. Figs. 42–3). When any question about interpretation, or accuracy of ring count, or measurement was involved, Gourlay and Barefoot consulted together and checked each other's work. Even so, they were and are not confident of error-free work on some of the highly damaged, narrow-ringed specimens.

The ring sequence of a plank was recorded by transferring the ring-width record to a thin white card mounted along the prepared groove (Fig. 80). The positions of the rings were cut into the edge of the card with a sharp scalpel. For rings which were 1/32 to 3/16 inch (1 to 5 mm) in width, the experimental error of transfer should have been, and we assume was, relatively small and insignificant. For the sequences of narrow rings less than 1/32 inch (1 mm) in width, extreme care was necessary to minimize ring-width errors and to avoid omitting or inventing rings. It was not always successful to do this at the table, even for the wide-ringed planks. Missing rings, due to initial poor surface preparation, worm-holes or decayed sections, became evident when the data was examined in the matching of ring series. Several planks had to be re-measured completely or examined to justify including suspected missing rings. Although a 20x hand lens was used in these situations to delineate the ring for cutting the record, a most tedious procedure, it was not possible to be as accurate as would have been liked in recording the ring count or ring widths.

After the ring records were cut and any appropriate remarks recorded on the card while cutting in the rings, the cut card record was mounted under a measuring microscope at the then Department of Forestry in Oxford. The microscope was equipped with a digitizer which produced a paper tape of data ready for all subsequent computer computations and plotting. The device used gave measurements to 0.001 mm, a degree of precision higher than was necessary. The data and plots were prepared following the procedures described above (pp. 155–9).

There are fifty-one wedge-shaped planks or boards, radiating outward from the centre of the table. Of these, forty-nine were sampled for tree-ring dating. Two boards, 11 and 37, were so awkwardly placed and so narrow that they were not measured at all. The timbers of the square central assembly and some of the vertical spars were also measured, but contained too few rings for reliable dating. They are not discussed further in this chapter, but the positions where the timbers were cut are shown on Fig. 81.

The characteristics of the rings in the portion of each plank measured are given in Table 1. Because of constraints on sampling, the full ring information was not always available from each plank. Often only one-third or so of a plank was available because of the presence of vertical or radial members (see the comments in Table 1). There was sufficient data, however, for tree-ring analysis.

TABLE 1
Characteristics of rings in measured portions of the Round Table planks
(*Boards which formed the 25-plank curve)

Plank no.	Width		Ring count	Rings per mm	Rings per in.	Comments
	mm	in.				
1.	214	8⁷⁄₁₆	212	0.99	25.1	Not measured at widest point
2.	224	8¹³⁄₁₆	66	0.29	7.5	A narrow portion measured
3.	203	8	186	0.92	23.3	Not measured at widest point
4.	249	9³⁄₁₆	208	0.84	21.2	A narrow portion
5.	328	12⁵⁄₁₆	255	0.78	19.7	A full, wide cut
6.	305	12	269	0.88	22.4	A full, wide cut
7.	342	13½	140	0.41	10.4	One-third of plank not measured
8.*	345	13⁹⁄₁₆	143	0.41	10.5	A full, wide cut
9.*	318	12¹⁷⁄₃₂	126	0.40	10.1	A full, wide cut
10.	265	10¹⁵⁄₃₂	135	0.51	12.9	A full, wide cut; pith side under radial
11.	NOT MEASURED					
12.	281	11³⁄₃₂	172	0.61	15.5	A full, wide cut
13.*	330	13	132	0.40	10.2	Sapwood on plank but not at sample point
14.	406	8⅛	213	0.52	13.3	A full, wide cut
15.*	208	8³⁄₁₆	103	0.46	12.6	Short on cambium side under radial
16.	157	6³⁄₁₆	169	1.08	27.3	Pith side under radial
17.	209	8¼	116	0.56	14.1	A full, wide cut
18.*	287	11⁹⁄₃₂	114	0.40	10.1	Approximately 10 rings of sapwood present but unmeasurable due to insect damage
19.	262	10⁵⁄₁₆	183	0.70	17.7	A full, wide cut
20.*	171	6¾	78	0.46	11.6	Pith side under radial
21.*	233	9⁵⁄₃₂	110	0.47	12.0	Cambium side under radial
22.*	364	14⁵⁄₁₆	140	0.38	9.8	Sapwood near sampling point
23.*	296	11⅝	133	0.45	11.4	No sap noted
24.*	204	8¹⁄₁₆	102	0.50	12.7	Pith side under radial
25.*	176	6³¹⁄₃₂	71	0.40	10.2	Pith side under radial

Plank no.	Width mm	in.	Ring count	Rings per mm	Rings per in.	Comments
26.*	254	10	101	0.40	10.1	Pith side under radial, a short cut
27.*	323	12²³⁄₃₂	139	0.43	10.9	Not fully cut
28.*	255	10¹⁵⁄₃₂	121	0.47	12.1	Cambium side under vertical
29.*	272	10¹¹⁄₁₆	117	0.43	10.9	Cambium side under radial
30.*	301	12¼	131	0.44	11.1	One-third pith side under radial
31.*	316	12⁷⁄₁₆	147	0.47	11.8	A full, wide cut
32.*	222	8¾	81	0.36	9.3	Pith side under radial
33.*	318	12¹⁷⁄₃₂	125	0.39	10.0	Pith side under radial and vertical
34.*	320	12⁹⁄₁₆	120	0.38	9.5	A full, wide cut
35.*	315	12¹³⁄₃₂	120	0.38	9.5	A full, wide cut
36.*	235	9⁹⁄₃₂	111	0.47	12.0	Sapwood on plank but not at sampling point
37.	NOT MEASURED					
38.	373	14¹¹⁄₁₆	292	0.78	19.9	A full, wide cut
39.*	334	13⅛	155	0.46	11.8	Sapwood on plank but not at sampling point
40.*	240	9⁷⁄₁₆	96	0.40	10.2	Cambium side under radial, edge soft
41.	250	9²⁷⁄₃₂	236	0.94	24.0	Pith side under radial
42.	228	9	213	0.93	23.7	A full, wide cut
43.	268	10⁹⁄₁₆	177	0.66	16.8	A narrow cut on a wide plank
44.*	193	7¹⁹⁄₃₂	131	0.68	17.2	Approximately 12–13 rings of sapwood at sample
45.	167	6½	79	0.47	12.0	Pith side under radial
46.	213	8⅜	159	0.75	19.0	Cambium side under vertical
47.	330	13	306	0.93	23.6	A full, wide cut; sapwood about 6 in. from cut
48.	311	12¼	229	0.74	18.7	Cambium side under vertical
49.	286	11¼	236	0.83	21.0	Pith side under radial
50.	209	8⁷⁄₃₂	139	0.67	16.9	Cambium side under radial
51.	137	5⅜	97	0.71	18.0	Cambium side under vertical

Matching of the plotted tree-ring sequences for tree-ring analysis

Very fortunately, the initial study of the wide-ringed sequences revealed several easily recognized patterns which could be matched rapidly (see Fig. 77). Within a day, sixteen of the curves had been matched and their data had been merged into an average curve. Not too long after that, twenty-three curves had been matched. Following the subsequent rechecking of two planks back at the table itself, an average curve of twenty-five planks was obtained for the wide-ringed material. Later, following more careful comparisons of all the individual curves to the 'master' curve of all 25 boards (to ensure absolutely correct cross-dating), two additional ring series were checked back at the table and adjusted by adding rings to the series to give a final position fit to reflect correctly the date of the last ring of the board. These corrections were usually at worm holes that had been incorrectly marked in the original ring-marking of the planks. Confidence in the correctness of the matching of these 25 edited curves and in the construction of their average curve is of the highest order.

Adding the narrow-ringed trees to this first curve proved most vexing. However, a pattern in six planks enabled a curve to be developed consisting of fourteen individual narrow-ringed sequences.[14] Note: the six curves were from planks with extensive decay and insect damage. Cross-dating of high confidence was not possible. This composite narrow-ringed curve of fourteen planks was found to compare with the 25-plank curve at a position where the narrow-ringed curve extends four rings beyond the end of the average of the 25-plank curve. The combination of these two curves into a 39-plank curve allowed the addition for dating purposes only of the remaining ten planks into the 'Great Table' curve, which ends five rings beyond the end of the 25-plank curve. It must again be emphasized that these data are matched and included in the Great Table curve for dating purposes only, but with far less confidence than in the 25-plank average.

The Great Table curve

This final curve now consisted of the merged data from forty-nine planks out of the fifty-one in the top surface of the table. The greatest span of rings in any single plank was 292, but with overlaps the total number of rings spanned by the curve was 353.

---

[14]   The six planks are nos. 4, 5, 42, 43, 47, and 48, as indicated on Tables 2 and 3.2. When the table is next examined, these six planks should be more intensively sampled in order to create carefully cross-dated curves for these and any other planks judged to be critical for a better understanding of the dating of the table.

TABLE 2
The matching positions of the rings in the Round Table planks
(*Boards which formed the 25-plank curve)
([+]The six boards next matched most easily after the 25-plank curve had been created, see p. 168)

Plank no.	Beginning position[1]	Ending position[1]	Number of rings[2]	Plank no.	Beginning position[1]	Ending position[1]	Number of rings[2]
1.	136	340	205	27.*	166	299	132
2.[3]	167	225	59	28.*	179	292	114
3.	90	268	179	29.*	186	295	110
4.[+]	74	281	208	30.*	189	312	124
5.[+]	105	352	248	31.*	189	328	140
6.	90	351	262	32.*	239	319	81
7.	183	315	133	33.*	185	302	118
8.*	190	325	136	34.*	199	311	113
9.*	221	339	119	35.*	198	310	113
10.	204	331	128	36.*	228	331	104
11.	NOT MEASURED			37.	NOT MEASURED		
12.	170	334	165	38.	67	351	285
13.*	216	340	125	39.*	190	337	148
14.	148	353	206	40.*	226	314	89
15.*	186	281	96	41.	124	352	229
16.	133	294	162	42.[+]	99	311	213
17.	93	201	109	43.[+]	102	278	177
18.*	228	335	107	44.*	191	314	124
19.	78	260	183	45.[3]	51	122	72
20.*	257	327	71	46.	71	222	152
21.*	188	290	103	47.[+]	1	306	306
22.*	213	345	133	48.[+]	14	242	229
23.*	223	348	126	49.	96	324	229
24.*	238	332	95	50.	18	149	132
25.*[3]	225	288	64	51.	127	223	97
26.*	201	294	94				

[1]The final curve was 353 years in length; the position numbers refer to the placing of the planks in this ring series between 1 and 353.
[2]The 'C' values for rings 1–7 of some, but not all, the planks were omitted from the curve data.
[3]Some of the short series, such as these two, may be wrongly positioned because of insufficient rings.

Each position on the curve, representing one year, was given a number between 1 and 353, with 353 the latest in the series. Table 2 gives the position numbers of the beginning and ending ring of each plank, as originally measured or as subsequently corrected in cross-dating the series. Figs. 82–4 represent the relative positions of all forty-nine planks. The locations of the radiocarbon samples taken from the planks are also shown, and these are fully discussed in the next chapter.

For the purpose of ascertaining the number of trees which might have contributed to the planks in the table-top, Fig. 85 is a representation of the cross-section of a log sawn into planks of about the sizes found in the table. One can see that the maximum number of boards from one log of one tree, of the high quality used in the table, would be well below forty. Indeed, using all the evidence before us, our best guess is that at least four, and possibly up to seven or eight, trees are likely to have been used to produce the planks forming the table-top (Table 3). When the possible allotment of the planks to individual trees is applied to the relative positions of the forty-nine planks in the table itself, the result looks far from random. This is clear when the planks are rearranged in order of the earliest (rather than the latest) ring surviving on each (Fig. 84), and especially so when this information is applied to the distribution of the planks in the table-top itself (Fig. 86).

Implications of the relative positioning of the planks and trees

A most surprising result came from examining the positions of those planks which retain sapwood. Fig. 87 shows the end of the Great Table curve. Located in this figure are the ending positions of several planks and their assignment to trees, with estimated, although relative, felling dates. The spread in felling dates between Tree 3 and Tree 4 can be seen to be about 35–40 years, possibly up to 55 years (Table 6). Yet all these planks and trees appear in the 25-plank curve. We believe that these sequences are not subject to any of the errors which might be possible for the remaining narrow-ringed series. If Tree 2 of the narrow-ringed material is considered, the spread in felling dates may perhaps be extended to greater than fifty years.

Such a result is delightful to contemplate. It suggests that on someone's thoughtful command, high-quality boards were laid aside and stored for making objects which would in the future require the use of superior materials. It suggests that the boards were well protected and well seasoned before use. And when the boards came to be used, Fig. 86 suggests that they were worked up systematically in batches in a way which seems to relate rather closely to the probable sequence in which Cecil Hewett has suggested the table-top was put together (see Chapter 4).

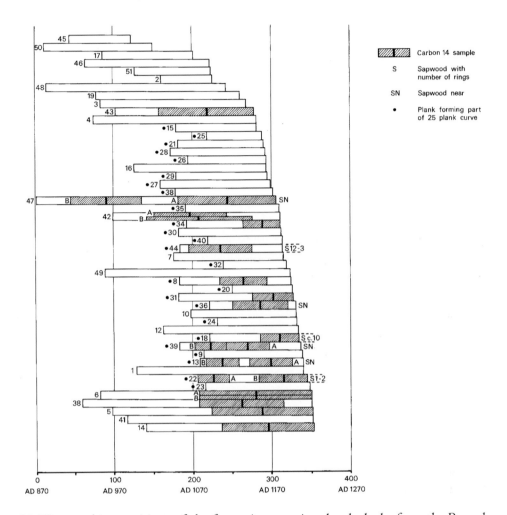

82 The matching positions of the forty-nine tree-ring dated planks from the Round Table, arranged in descending order of the *latest* surviving ring. The positions of the twenty-two radiocarbon (Carbon-14) samples are also shown. Dates as assigned 1980; revised 1990 as four years earlier (see below, pp. 188–92 and Table 5).

171

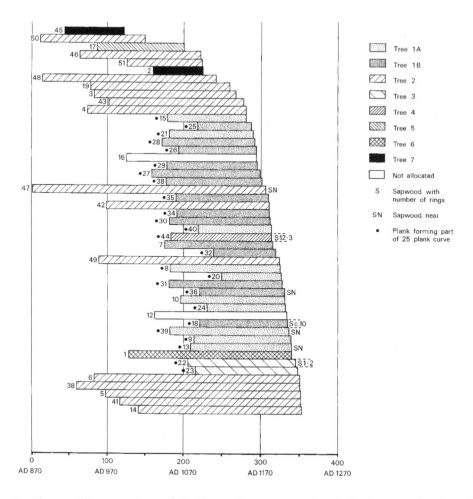

83 The matching positions of the forty-nine tree-ring dated planks from the Round Table, arranged in descending order of the *latest* surviving ring (as Fig. 82), but shaded to indicate proposed allocation of planks to 'trees' (cf. Figs. 84 and 86). Dates as assigned 1980; revised 1990 as four years earlier (see below, pp. 188–92 and Table 5).

172

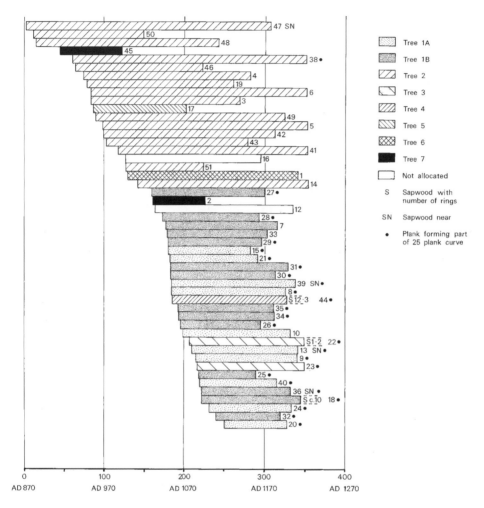

84 The matching positions of the forty-nine tree-ring dated planks from the Round Table, arranged in descending order of the *earliest* surviving ring (contrast Figs. 82 and 83) and shaded to indicate proposed allocation of planks to 'trees' (cf. Figs. 83 and 86). Dates as assigned 1980; revised 1990 as four years earlier (see below, pp. 188–92 and Table 5).

173

TABLE 3

The grouping of ring series for determining tree sources of the Round Table planks:

3.1 Grouping of planks according to rings per inch

Rings per in.	6.7–9.7	9.7–12.7		12.7–15.7	15.7–18.7	18.7–21.7	21.7–24.7	24.7+
	2	7	27*	10	19	5	6	1
	32*	8*	28*	12	43	38	41	16
	34*	9*	29*	14	44*	46	42	
	35*	13*	30*	17	48	49	47	
		15*	31*		50			
		18*	33*		51			
		20*	36*					
		21*	39*					
		22*	40*					
		23*	45					
		24*						
		25*						
		26*						

*Boards which formed the 25-plank curve.

TABLE 3

The grouping of ring series for determining tree sources of the Round Table planks:

3.2 Grouping of planks according to visual comparisons of data and graphs[1]

			'Trees'				
1A[2]	1B[2]	2[3]	3	4	5	6	7
8*	7	3	22*	44*	47	1	2
9*	18*	4[+]	23*				45
10	25*	5[+]					
13*	26*	6					
15*	27*	14					
20*	28*	19					
21*	29*	38					
24*	30*	41					
39*	31*	42[+]					
40*	32*	43[+]					
	33*	46					
	34*	47[+]					
	35*	48[+]					
	36*	49					
		50					
		51					

*Boards which formed the 25-plank curve.
[+]The six boards which next matched most easily after the 25-plank curve had been created (see p. 168)

[1]These are subjective groupings that rely on comparisons of the recorded data, including the original 'nicked' cards with their visual characteristics noted on them at the time of 'working' the table, rather than on in-hand, side-by-side comparisons of the planks, which were not feasible. The assignments are thus inevitably speculative.

[2]Trees 1A and 1B may be one tree, although there appeared to be differences in the gross growth patterns between them. Certain of the planks could have been assigned to either group.

[3]Tree 2 might also have been divided into two series.

From these observations, *one might also conclude that the planks came from locally produced timber rather than from imported wood*, a view entirely in agreement with southern England's wealth in timber at this date.[15] These facts also imply that it was known that several years must follow felling before the boards would be dried to equilibrium with atmospheric conditions. Apparently the craftsmen of those days knew the virtue of well-manufactured and well-seasoned boards free of major growth defects, including sapwood. The presence of small amounts of sapwood left in some areas of curved grain indicates, however, that economy in trimming was also duly observed. This evidence and the table itself contribute greatly to our understanding of wood procurement and wood manufacturing knowledge in those earlier years of hand-crafting furniture. The people who built the table were highly knowledgeable, skilled craftsmen who must have known that they were selecting material for an object of the greatest importance. The material they used certainly justifies such an opinion.

One final note: One can only speculate as to whether this particular production exhausted the supply of high-quality boards in storage at the time. (*I suspect that it did.*) If more wood of this quality had been available, the carpenters would most probably have trimmed off all the sapwood and eliminated more of the extremely *curly* grain in some of the boards.

From all these observations, one can be certain that felling of the last tree used in the construction of the table took place many years after the end of the Great Table's position 353 (Fig. 87): probably indeed after position 380; but more probably after position 385. The time needed to season the last timber harvested must also be added to these position numbers, as well as an estimate of the number of rings under the rim, not measured, setting the time of construction of the table after position 400 perhaps.

Dating the rings

Up to this point, all the work – measuring the rings, plotting their widths, matching the curves, and averaging the data – had been directed towards producing the composite Great Table curve, on which each position number represents one year of growth. At this stage, however, the curve itself was undated. In order to assign actual years to the positions on the curve, it was necessary to match the Great Table curve to other known and dated curves, based on entirely different specimens of wood.

---

[15] John Perlin, *A Forest Journey. The Role of Wood in the Development of Civilization* (New York and London, 1989), pp. 163–5, 204, and (for problems of transport) pp. 222–3.

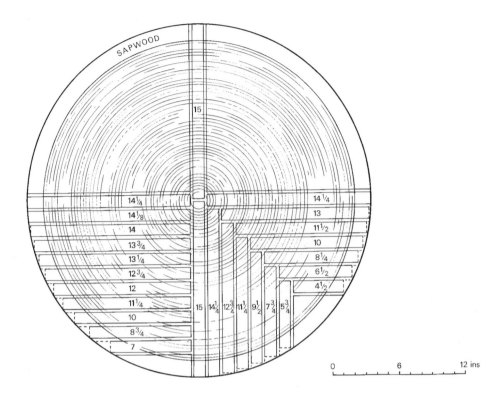

85 Diagram of the theoretically possible number of quartersawn planks to be obtained from one log, using two of the methods of quarter sawing (cf. Fig. 74).

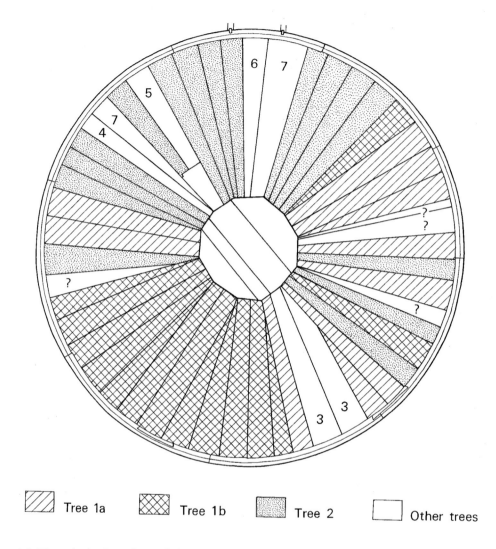

| | Tree 1a | | Tree 1b | | Tree 2 | | Other trees |

86 The planked surface of the Round Table, showing the proposed allocation of planks to 'trees'.

Year AD	Ring no.	Plank no. at year of last ring	Comment	Great Table Curve	'Tree' & ring width	Suggested felling date of 'tree' on year scale
	305				5 narrow	
		47	No sapwood Estimate 25 to 50+ rings missing			
1180	310					
	315	44	Plus 12 or 13 rings missing		4 medium	
1190	320					
	325					
1200	330	36	Sapwood up the board			
	335	18	Plus about 10 rings of sapwood		1B wide	
		39	Sapwood up the board			
1210	340	9	No sapwood noted			'Tree' 4 : 1209±
		13	Sapwood up the board		1A wide	
	345	22	Sapwood near cut			
		23	Sapwood near cut		3 wide	'Tree' 5 : 1218 ±
1220	350	6, 38	See Plank 14		2 narrow	
		5	No sapwood			
		14	With 6 and 38 no obvious sapwood			
	355					
1230	360					'Tree' 1B : 1228±
	365					
1240	370					'Tree' 1A : 1238±
						'Tree' 3 : 1243±
	375					
1250	380					
	385					'Tree' 2 : 1250-55±

87 The last fifty years of the Great Table curve, showing the ending position of certain planks, together with their proposed allocation to 'trees' (Table 3.2). Dates as assigned 1980; revised 1990 as four years earlier (see below, pp. 188–92 and Table 5).

The ring dates of these 'reference' curves had been 'authenticated' to the best known possibility in 1980.

As described above (p. 160), the three dendrochronologies used for comparative purposes were the Choir Stall curve from Winchester Cathedral, Fletcher's 'Ref. 5', and Bauch's Chronology II for the southern Netherlands. Besides their relevance for the task of dating the table, these exercises gave us the opportunity to test the data in independent ways.[16]

TABLE 4

Comparison by A. C. Barefoot in 1980 of the 25-plank curve and the 49-plank curve with three previously dated curves[1]

4.1 The 25-plank curve compared with:	Student's 't'[2]	Years of overlap	Calendar date of last ring[3]
Choir Stall curve	3.07	170	1220
Fletcher's 'Ref. 5'	3.03	73	1219
Bauch's 'Chronology II'	3.76	53	1219

4.2 The Great Table curve of 49 planks compared with:	Student's 't'[2]	Years of overlap	Calendar date of last ring[3]
Choir Stall curve, best fit	2.34	173	1223
Choir Stall curve, alternative fit	2.09	175	1225
Fletcher's 'Ref. 5'	3.21	78	1224
Bauch's 'Chronology II'	3.80	58	1224

[1]The original data supplied for Fletcher and Bauch curves were standardized according to our procedures before 't' comparisons were made.
[2]The probability of a value of 't' greater than 2.00 = 0.05; greater than 3.00 = 0.005; greater than 3.50 = 0.001.
[3]The difference of one year in compared dates is unexplainable at this time except that Fletcher's and Bauch's curves are for different geographical regions. See above p. 160. For subsequent correction of the art-historical chronologies of Fletcher, see below, p. 184 and n. 21.

[16] In the absence in 1979–80 of a definitively tested curve, or curves, for southern England, it was thought best to use as many reputable, established curves as possible for making data comparisons. We felt, moreover, that until such a curve (or curves) could be established, the dates selected here would have to retain a certain tentativeness which would allow for a future minor adjustment in the final date. This was exactly the case by 1990, as David Haddon-Reece shows in his contribution discussed at the end of this chapter (pp. 188–92 and Table 5).

Table 4 gives the results of comparing the 25-plank curve and the Great Table curve of forty-nine planks to the three reference curves, using the Student's 't' statistic produced by the program of Baillie and Pilcher.[17] The 25-plank curve correlates with an end-date of 1220 on the Choir Stall curve and 1219 on the Fletcher and Bauch curves. Since the Great Table curve of forty-nine planks extends five rings beyond the end of the 25-plank curve for the wide-ringed boards, the expected results in matching the 49-plank curve to the three comparison curves should have been end-dates of 1225 and 1224 respectively. As Table 4 shows, this is indeed the case.

However, one anomaly, as yet unexplainable, creeps in: the year 1223 also appears to be a possible statistical fit for the Great Table curve on the Choir Stall chronology. This may be due to the use of an insufficient data base in forming the Choir Stall chronology or to errors in compiling the data of the narrow-ringed sequences on the table. Since the overlap of the Great Table curve is much greater on the Choir Stall chronology than on the Fletcher or Bauch curves, the statistical result is more likely to be due to errors in the data, arising from the difficulty of recording the narrow-ringed material *in situ* on the table (see above pp. 164–5). The resolution of this issue will require further analysis.

In any event, selection of the years 1223 to 1225 provides the only position at which all the curves can be consistently compared and therefore seems to be a reasonably sound choice for the end-date of the Great Table curve. At this position visual comparison of the curves is also acceptable. There is one further statistical note to be reported. A strong matching (a high 't' value) of the narrow-ringed 14-plank curve (described above, p. 168) occurred on the Choir Stall curve at an end-date of about 1290. In the absence of corroborative data from Fletcher's and Bauch's curves, this result was dismissed as one of the statistical quirks frequently noted in working data of this type. It is due perhaps to the inadequacy of the Choir Stall data.

Based upon this evidence, the year of growth of the last ring available in 1976 from the Round Table can be dated with some confidence to 1224 ±1 year. (Table 4)[18] To this date must be added the rings not counted or measured due to the inability to sample the rings under the outer iron rim. As argued above the earliest date for felling of this tree could be position 385 = AD1256. If the rings are greatly increased by considering those missed under the rim, then the date could be much later.

---

[17] Baillie and Pilcher, 'Cross-Dating Programme' (as above, n. 5).
[18] And see Table 4, n. 3.

Implications for the date of construction of the Round Table

Given the dating of the last available tree ring to *c.*1224, allowing for continued uncertainty about the number of sapwood rings on any tree and for the unknown number of heartwood rings removed from Tree 2 (Figs. 83–4 and 87), and considering the period of several years necessary to season the wood before it was used, the construction date of the table may be estimated as lying well after 1250 to 1265 at the earliest. If the guesses on the number of missing rings are too small and the allowance for seasoning too short, the actual time of construction could well have been much later. This is especially true if the periods of up to forty years spent in store are recalled for some of the planks before they were used (Fig. 87 and above, p. 170). Although, it is not known how long Tree 2 was kept in seasoning, or if it was stored for any long length of time at all beyond seasoning, a date for construction would not be expected to have been much beyond 1275 to 1280. If Tree 2 was in store for any eqivalent time, construction could have been much later, to 1290 or 1300 even. Including the unlikely felling date of 1290, the outside limit would be 1320 or so. But the wood evidence at this time weighs most heavily in favour of selecting the years 1250 to 1280 as the earliest time of construction of the table.

Conclusions

For most people, the dating of the construction of the table to late in the thirteenth century (or less likely, the early fourteenth century) is probably the most interesting conclusion to have been reached. In arriving at this date, however, the spread in the felling dates of the trees was seen to be on the order of at least 35–40, but more likely 50 years. This finding led to several hypotheses which serve to enlighten us about procurement, drying, storage, and use of wood in medieval England. The choice of high-quality, defect-free material, the technological care and craftsmanship exhibited in fabricating the table, and the absence of further major technological defects in the quartersawn boards indicate a superb knowledge of 'wood technology' in those days. The widespread insect and decay damage present today on the table are due to lack of thought and care in later generations; but the survival of the table in spite of this deterioration still speaks to the skill and knowledge of the original craftsmen.

To provide such material for what must have been unknown future uses, a positive and forward-thinking policy for the accumulation of these superior boards must have been established by responsible authorities. The commitment of a large portion of the stores so accumulated must have been a most deliberate and solemn decision.

The superior materials, the use of a special store of these high-quality materials accumulated over a long period of time, the implied knowledge of wood technology, and the craftsmanship exhibited, all point to the most important conclusion for us, as dating technicians. This was a unique table, well built and dedicated to a most high purpose.

Subsequent Analysis of Data in 1989–1990

I brought my study of the tree-rings of the Round Table to the point above early in 1980. Since then dendrochronology has made great advances in Britain, notably in the hands of M. G. L. Baillie, working in Belfast. His results and those of several other workers, especially Ruth Morgan and Jennifer Hillam at Sheffield, have been assembled together with a suite of up-to-date programs and data in a computerised data-base by David Haddon-Reece, formerly of the Ancient Monuments Laboratory of English Heritage in London. It is now possible to take curves such as those produced from the tree-ring data of the Round Table and to compare them with great speed against a large body of material covering almost the whole of the British Isles and north-western Europe. In the section which follows, David Haddon-Reece's work in matching the Round Table data against those curves which had been compiled by 1990 is considered.[19]

In many ways I am grateful for the almost two decade delay in publishing the original work. The time lapse has allowed for the accumulation of many well-established and authenticated reference curves. The work of David Haddon-Reece in compiling these curves and using them to test the Round Table data is in the best of scientific tradition. I am pleased with the final outcome.

Results of the 1990 Data Analysis

The extensive use of indentation in the following discussion indicates the direct lifting of material from the personal communication of David Haddon-Reece to Martin Biddle. My inserted wording is placed to provide a condensed bridge of his complete report.

To begin, he refers to having read the 1980 draft of the above work and says,

---

[19] David Haddon-Reece, pers. comm to Martin Biddle detailing his work in comparing the Round Table data to 35 reference curves (1990). See Table 5.

..., Professor A. C. Barefoot describes his dating of the forty-nine Round Table timbers and presents statistically derived estimates of felling date ranges for both the components of his '25-timber master' and the remaining twenty-four timbers.[20] He explains that since the work was done at a time when very few reference chronologies ('curves') were available for English timbers, his final dates are necessarily tentative. Indeed, this can be seen, as A. C. Barefoot himself observes, in the discrepancy between the final dates produced by the alignment of his table curves with the reference curves of Fletcher[21] and Bauch and his own Choir Stall chronology.

..., A. C. Barefoot's date, although inevitably of a pioneering nature, was remarkable in being generally correct despite the paucity (and inaccuracy) of the available reference curves. Working practically single handed, he was able to collect sufficient Hampshire timber to build a reference chronology backwards in time from the present day to the period of the table and then to produce a date range for the felling the Round Table timbers, which remains valid even after the minor adjustment in felling date resulting from a 1990 comparison to more reference curves.

In the years since A. C. Barefoot's work, extensive research by dendrochronologists has produced a wide and well-corroborated corpus of reference chronologies, including the re-alignment of the art-historical chronologies (bringing them four years nearer the present).[22] This ... presents the comparison of the table curves with English and European reference chronologies ... in 1990.

Retrieving and using the ring-curve data

After Professor Barefoot had worked on the data, all unedited, original and non-cross-dated ring-width readings had been stored as punched paper tape and left in the care of Ian Gourlay at the Commonwealth Forestry Institute at Oxford. With the help of Dr Kit Bailey, Computer Manager for the Forestry School, a large boxful of paper

---

[20] 'C' values for the curves can be obtained from the author at North Carolina State University, Division of Multidisciplinary Studies, PO Box 7107, Raleigh, NC 27695–7107, USA. Raw ring-width data is available from the Ancient Monuments Laboratory, English Heritage, Fortress House, 23 Savile Row, London W1X 2AA, England. The edited and cross-dated original tree-ring data for the author's 25-plank-curve are available from the International Tree-Ring Data Bank, National Geophysical Data Center, NOAA, 325 Broadway, E/ GC, Boulder, CO 80303, USA.

[21] Fletcher later corrected his curve by four years (see Table 4, n.3 and this page, n. 22).

[22] M. G. L. Baillie, 'Some Thoughts on Art-Historical Dendrochronology', *Journal of Archaeological Science* 11 (1984), 371–93, and J. M. Fletcher's reply, 'Dating of Art-Historical Artefacts', *Nature* 320, no. 6061 (1986), 466.

tapes was transferred, not without some restoration of their sellotape splices, on to a standard 3.5 inch computer 'floppy disc'. Using an IBM-compatible Toshiba T1200 microcomputer as intermediary, the information on the disc was then 'entered' into the memory of the Torch Sequent computer at the Ancient Monuments Laboratory of English Heritage. This computer already held a huge data bank of tree-ring curves and an extensive suite of programs for processing them, and it was here that much of the subsequent work was done. On checking the data, it was found that the transcription process had introduced some 'noise', i.e. corrupt readings, and the first task was to correct this manually by checking the final computer version against a typed copy of data on the punched tape.

Unfortunately, as Haddon-Reece later notes in his report himself, he could not access the table to correct and edit for missing or duplicate rings. For this reason, his work cannot be an exact duplicate of the original analysis; but, as one will see, it is remarkably close and more than adequate in the final analysis. As a result of being unable to correct and edit the tree-ring data of Plank No. 23, Haddon-Reece decided to omit it from his 24-timber curve. Whether he did so in re-creating the 25-plank curve is not entirely clear. One has to assume he included the original (incorrect and unedited series) data versions of all 25 planks. It is just as well that he titles his 25-curve as a '25-timber master' to distinguish it from my 25-plank curve since there are slight differences in matching due to his use of the unedited data.

In his consideration of 'cross-matching' , Haddon-Reece remarks as follows:

> ... the basic principle of dendrochronology is beautifully but deceptively simple: the annual growth increment (ring) of a tree reflects the weather during the growing season, and, therefore, all trees of the same species growing under the same climatic conditions will produce identical series of wide and narrow annual rings. By comparing the ring-width series from two trees, it should therefore be possible to find a unique position at which they fit; if one series is of known date, the cross-match will date the other precisely.

> ... Due to variability in the tree, the annual ring is by no means a perfect circle, so that two radii from the same cross-section will vary slightly (sometimes quite markedly). Furthermore, the ring-width measurements will, by the nature of measurement, include some imprecision ... Fortunately, the component errors in the ring-width ... are randomly distributed about the 'true' value ...

For these reasons, methods for curve comparison need to emphasize the 'climatic signal' and reject the noise. The visual method involves drawing each series as a graph showing the ring-widths as vertical distances above a baseline spaced at regular intervals in the horizontal direction. The sample curve is slid along the master curve until the maximum number of troughs and peaks correspond (as relative ups and downs and without regard to absolute size); eye and brain are the arbiters.

The standard statistical cross-matching programs also slide one ring-width series past another, producing an objective measure of the strength of cross-match at each position of overlap, and a significance factor which indicates the probability that so strong a cross-match could have occurred by chance alone. If that chance is less than 1 in 1000, then the match is [*sic* highly] significant, and if it is corroborated by other cross-matchings may be deemed acceptable. This is the approach used by A. C. Barefoot. The two series of numbers representing the master and sample curves are moved past each other, and at every successive position of overlap, the computer calculates the product-moment correlation coefficient, r, and a corresponding statistical significance value, Student's 't'.[23] The ring-width series can be tested against a previously dated sequence, or it may be compared with other undated sequences in the same batch, combined with them, and then compared as a site 'master'.

Long term trends in tree growth must be removed to avoid scaling effects. To continue with Haddon-Reece:

... A. C. Barefoot's ... approach is to apply exponential smoothing, a process which modifies each ring-width by the incorporation of a factor based on the combination of the previous year's growth and its own modification factor ... arguably a more realistic model of a tree's true behaviour ... Before correlation, the data is again standardized, producing A. C. Barefoot's 'C' values as described in his papers on a Winchester regional curve.[24] ...

Cross-matching: practical work on the Round Table data

In my work on the Round Table data, I used Baillie's CROS program to compute the cross-product correlation coefficients and their associated Student's 't'-values, as explained above.[25] For consistency with A. C. Barefoot's calculations, I also converted the curves into A. C. Barefoot's C-indices and tested the cross-matching in that form

[23] See above, n. 6.

[24] See above, nn. 4, 9 and 20.

[25] See above, n. 5.

rather than allowing the CROS program to apply the high frequency filter as usual. The calculation of correlation and Student's 't' was the same in each case.

One of the great advantages of using the C-indices lies in the ease of comparison of two or more plots of tree-ring data. This advantage lies in the ability to lay one plot upon another and have the same standardized scales for all the data. For the most part the data is centered on a zero line plotted on the paper and confined mostly within lines plotted at ± three index values. Therefore, for visual comparison of the data the plot of the C-indices makes the comparisons so much easier than using plots of the raw, non-standardized, data. The eye and brain can see all the data patterns at once and the memory of patterns of previously studied curves helps in the matching procedures. This was the situation in many of the curves in the 25-plank average. Once the C-curves were plotted and compared, it was not necessary always to calculate 't' values to see the correct matching positions or to see obvious data points to examine for errors.

In his report, Haddon-Reece makes another significant observation, he says:

It was evident that in the final cross-matchings of 'tree' groups and the table master curve against reference curves, better t-values were obtained by not C-indexing either the table masters or the references. This is because the averaging of so many constituent members has already smoothed the curve sufficiently and further C-indexing will remove information.

In addition, I observed another difference between C-indexed and high-pass-filtered cross-matching. At a correct position of overlap in the list of successive t-values, the high-frequency filter method usually shows the match as a strong t-value bordered by low values. The C-indices produce a high(er) t-value at that position, but often with non-zero (and sometimes significant) t-values on either side...

... it is possible that the method of measurement may have missed rings or introduced false ones, which would inevitably place one portion of a faulty curve at least one year out of alignment. As A. C. Barefoot says, he had to return to the table on several occasions to try to correct this effect.

Although he could not access the table to check for errors, Haddon-Reece's use, presumably, of the raw unedited data and the data of plank 27A rather than the longer 27B (which I include), the omission of planks 23 and 44 and the inclusion of plank 10 to form his average 24-timber curve proved to confirm the 1976–1980 25-plank average. His presumed (by ACB) use of the incorrect data would be masked to some extent in the statistical averaging by the over-whelmingly correct ring-data of the ring series not needing editing.

Haddon-Reece's analysis of the 25-plank curve

Haddon-Reece began his work on the ring-data by reassembling the data using the ending dates given in Table 2. He re-names my '25-plank curve' usuage to a '25-timber curve'; technically a mis-nomer but perhaps that is just as well as it provides a distinction between the two '25-curves'; his 25-timber curve is not an exact duplicate of my 25-plank curve. (In the timber trade, a plank or board usually does not exceed 2½" in thickness; a timber, technically, exceeds 4½" in thickness.) The boards, or planks of the 'table' top are far less than 2½" in thickness.

To pick up on his analysis, he tells how he created his 25-timber curve, thusly:

> ... Using the ending dates given in Table 2, the 25 curves...(were)... averaged into a 'floating', i.e. undated, curve... Comparisons between this curve and the reference curves immediately indicated a cross-match of strong and highly significant correlation when year 345 was aligned at AD 1211. This was reinforced by a strong visual correlation between the 25-timber curve and the master curves. The results are shown in Table 5. It must be noted that Fletcher himself found it necessary to shift by four years the absolute date of some of his chronologies.[26]

I further presume his choice of the 345 position to test in the 't' comparisons of the stored reference curves is a result of his decision to omit plank 23, which had its end-point at position 348. I shall choose to use plank 23 for my last end-point in the 25-plank curve. The resulting date for position 348 is AD 1214.

Also, because David Haddon-Reece is not readily available to me to defend or explain his final writing on this subject, I must regretfully presume his 'now 24-timber curve' stored at the 'Ancient Monuments' is incomplete at best. It certainly does not provide all possible information in the current data holdings.

Haddon-Reece then proceeds to look at the matter of trees making up the table. He proceeds to explain:

> ... the two sub-groups of 'tree 1' were examined. Each group matched strongly with reference curves and with each other, but several members of each group matched

[26] See above, n. 22.

more highly with the other group... As A. C. Barefoot suggests, the cross matches are in some instances ... so high that a common source from one tree is almost certain ...

To this observation, I agree.

The remaining timbers

The next stage was to check the remaining timbers. As expected from Professor Barefoot's findings, results here were not so good as for the 25- (now 24-) timber master. [*sic*: the 24-timber master referred to here is his average curve resulting from his omitting the (corrected) plank 23, which I had edited and found to be a good and correct fit. ACB.] In fact, the t-values from cross-matching at the positions indicated by Table 2 were generally so low as to be unacceptable on statistical grounds alone, although as A. C. Barefoot explains, there was a considerable degree of visual similarity, particularly in the earlier portions of some curves. To a certain extent then, this was expected ... , but it was hoped that the greatly increased corpus of reference curves since 1980 would help to find dates, particularly where it was thought a timber might span a time period before the start of the 25- (now 24-) timber master.

Professor Barefoot says that the next curves to be matched were 4, 5, 42, 43, 47, and 48. These were tested, paying special attention to the early portions, both visually and statistically. He adds that he still has 'considerable reservations about the total goodness' of these curves. From my examination of the data, I must share this reservation. There is no doubt that they do not match adequately, either with each other or with reference curves....

Not having seen the timber, I find it impossible to comment on the appropriateness of adding or deleting rings [*sic*: we did edit the data, A. C. B.], but the evidence points both to missing (or extra) rings and to noisy data. As Professor Barefoot reports, the wood was damaged by rot and death-watch beetle; recording conditions were difficult – poor lighting, difficult access, and so on. It is not unknown to miss rings even in laboratory conditions, or to create them by imagining a ring boundary in a particularly wide cluster of early wood vessels in an otherwise cramped series of rings. Without sight of the wood, I could not judge the relevance of these suppositions, but I was able to examine some of the cards cut to record the rings on the upright members.[27] It appears that errors could arise from variations in direction of cut, raggedness of the edge of the cut, and indecision introduced by the thickness of the scalpel blade, as well as the possibilities mentioned by A. C. Barefoot.

[27] Professor Barefoot currently has custody of the 'cut' plank cards for all 49 planks, including many of the remeasured sequences. Also he has the original typed out ring-data from the raw measurements. All these data will be archived in due course with the rest of the Round Table records.

TABLE 5

Cross-matching by D. Haddon-Reece in 1990 of Round Table 25- (now 24-) timber master at AD 1211 with 35 British and North-west European reference curves of which 28 match significantly

North-west European curves [1]	Student's 't' [2]
t <2.00	
S Scotland (MGLB) 946–1975	0.00
Yorkshire 2 (JH) 1192–1663	1.23
MK53 Netherlands (JB/DE) 1115–1643	1.41
Dunstable (MCB) 1172–1302	1.44
Beverley, Lurk Lane (JH) 1137–1236	1.46
Ref. 1 (JMF) 1103–1623	1.66
Merton, Warden's Hall (DHR) 1163–1246	1.98
t =2.00[2]	
Shrewsbury SHR10 (CG) 1174–1268	2.00
Zouche Chapel (RM/JMF) 1114–1382	2.08
Ref. 4 (JMF) 1124–1403	2.19
Oxford, jetty 17 (DHR *et al.*) 1164–1348	2.55
Zacharias, Oxford, 16-timber mean (DHR *et al.*)	2.55
England (JH) 404–1216	2.77
Droitwich (JH) 1178–1415	2.80
t = 3.00[2]	
MC13 Trichay St., Exeter (JMF) 811–1170	2.99
Bishop's Throne, Exeter (MCB) 1102–1284	3.17
Stafford (CG) 884–1255	3.29
Ref. 7 (JMF)	3.48
t = 3.50[2]	
Dublin (ex JMF) 895–1306	3.53
Reading Waterfront (JH *et al.*) 1160–1407	3.66

North-west European curves [1]	Student's 't' [2]
Wigan (CG) 1029–1205	3.73
Bredon Barn (VG) 1176–1330	4.02
Nantwich (PL) 930–1330	4.37
Central Europe (EH) (part) 801–1975	5.06
Bradwell Abbey (MCB) 1083–1279	5.07
Gt Coxwell Barn (JMF *et al.*) 1043–1267	5.21
Beverley (CG) 858–1310	5.46
Oxford mean (DHR *et al.*) 1043–1740	5.51
Exeter Cathll (CM) 1137–1332	5.80
East Midlands (NTRG) 882–1981	6.23
MC14 chests/boards (JMF) 902–1261	6.54
Glastonbury Abbey Barn (MCB/DHR) 1095–1334	7.60
England (MGLB/JP) 404–1981	7.85
Ref. 6 (JMF) 778–1199	9.46
Ref. 7/5 (JMF) 845–1298	10.26

[1]Sources: MGLB, M. G. L. Baillie; JB, J. Bauch; MCB, M. C. Bridge; DE, D. Eckstein; JMF, J.M. Fletcher; VG, V. Giertz; CG, C. Grove; DHR, D. Haddon-Reece; JH, J. Hillam; EH, E. Hollstein; PL, P. Leggett; CM, C. Mills; RM, R. Morgan; NTRG, Nottingham University Tree-Ring Group; JP, J. Pilcher.

[2]Student's 't': the probability of a value of 't' greater than $2.00 = 0.05$; greater than $3.00 = 0.005$; greater than $3.50 = 0.001$.

[continued from p. 189]

In some cases, there are low t-values matches, but these are neither strong enough nor sufficiently consistent to base confident dating on using the criteria applied to the 25- (now 24-) timber group. In the light of the remarks above, the noisiness of the data may mask a situation which is in fact correctly but dimly seen and is therefore impossible to disprove by conventional methods. That the tentative dating is in general correct is confirmed by the radiocarbon, but as Professor Barefoot says, the dates for the remaining timbers will have to be left tentative. As he hopes, re-examination of the Round Table and re-measurement at some future date may resolve the problems.

The year date of the last ring in the 25-plank curve

I accept the date of AD 1211 as the correct date for position 345 of the 24-timber curve. The date then of position 348 (due to the inclusion of plank 23), the end ring of the 25-plank curve, would be AD 1214 and the end date for the 'Great Table' curve would be 1219. This date is five years earlier than my 1976–1980 analysis of 1224. The supposition has to be that there were missing rings in the reference curves used in the earlier analysis and this was reflected in the earlier date of AD 1219 for the 25-plank curve. It is with a great deal of satisfaction that we can report that a solid base of data curves all agree upon a single date of AD 1214 for the last measured ring of great confidence in the Round Table; a date so close to my original that I am pleased with the outcome of Haddon-Reece's study confirming the basic accuracy of the earlier work.

Felling Dates

Estmated felling dates are given in Table 6 for a few of the trees. These dates are based upon the following premises. (1) For a tree with bark edge (i.e., all sapwood rings present), the felling date may be given not only for the year but the season of cutting. None of the 25 planks met this criteria. (2) With some sapwood present an estimate of missing rings may be added to give an estimated felling date. This was the situation with a few planks, fortunately. (3) Finally, if no sap rings are available, as Haddon-Reece puts it, '...the best that can be obtained is a *terminus post quidcunque* – a definite date after which felling must have taken place, although at some undefinable period therafter.'

As indicated earlier, the estimate chosen to represent sapwood rings near Winchester was 25 rings. A statistical estimate to obtain this average, was based upon actual counts of rings by the author (ACB) of 29 modern trees between the ages of 70 and 350 from the Hampshire region. By fitting a linear regression to these data, it was found that sapwood rings increased on the average from 22 to 29 sapwood rings as the age increased over the range 70–350 and had a 95 per cent confidence band of 12 to 35 rings at age 125. Using data supplied by me, Haddon-Reece further calculated the 95 per cent confidence band for these 29 trees 'as 12 to 33 rings'.

From the notes on the cut-cards indicating the presence of sapwood, its ring position (or its proximity to the location of the V-cut) and the dating records, the estimated felling dates of the 'trees' having sapwood were estimated as given in

Table 6. Given the uncertainties of seasoning time and subsequent storage times, these felling dates do not substantially change the estimates of the earliest construction dates postulated in the 1976–1980 analysis of the table data, i.e. AD 1250 to 1280.

TABLE 6

Estimated felling dates and felling-date ranges for Round Table planks with an identifiable heartwood/sapwood boundary, arranged in order of date
from early to late

Plank no.	Start ring[1]	End ring[1]	Start year[2]	End year[2]	Notes[3]	Heartwood/ sapwood boundary	Felling-date range		'Trees' (see Fig. 87)
							Sapwood estimate: c.25 rings	Sapwood estimate: 12–33 rings	
44	191	314	1056	1180	Approx. 12–13 rings of sapwood after ring 314, unmeasured	1180	c.1205	c.1192–1213	Tree 4
18	228	335	1094	1201	Approx. 10 rings of sapwood after ring 335, unmeasured	1201	c.1226	c.1213–1234	Tree 1b
36	228	331	1094	1197	Sapwood up plank, about 10 rings beyond ring 331	c.1207	c.1232	c.1219–1240	Tree 1b
39	190	337	1055	1203	Sapwood up plank, about 5 rings beyond ring 337	c.1208	c.1233	c.1220–1241	Tree 1a
22	213	345	1078	1211	Approx. 1–2 rings of sapwood after ring 345, unmeasured	1211	c.1236	c.1223–1244	Tree 3
23	223	348	1089	1214	Sapwood present very near cut: i.e. at or close after ring 348	c.1214	c.1239	c.1226–1247	Tree 3
13	216	340	1081	1206	Sapwood up plank c.5–10 rings beyond ring 340	c.1211–1216	c.1236–1241	c.1223–1249	Tree 1a
14[4]	148	353	1014	1219	No sapwood; add 5–10 rings heartwood	c.1224–1229	c.1236–1257	c. 1241–1262	Tree 2

[1]From Table 2.
[2]Accepting Ring 345 as dating to AD 1211 (Table 5).
[3]From Table 1.
[4]Plank 14 is neither in the 25-plank curve nor has a sapwood/heartwood boundary. It is included so that Tree 2, the last tree felled for making the Round Table (see Fig. 87), is represented here for comparison and discussion.

6

Radiocarbon Dating the Round Table

Introduction

R adiocarbon dating of the Round Table was first suggested in early 1976 when it formed part of the combined study of the history of the table. Although it was felt at this time that the radiocarbon date might not be as precise as the study required, it would nevertheless be of value in establishing a broad period within which the other inquiries could be concentrated. This was particularly important at the time for the dendrochronological studies where it was necessary to establish an approximate date in order to exclude possible false correlations with tree-ring matches of other periods. Just two samples were taken in this first phase, one from a radial plank in the table top and one from the rim and these gave results initially interpreted as AD 1330 ± 70 and AD 1480 ± 100 respectively. These dates were shown in the BBC TV Horizon programme of 1976 but, although they dispelled any belief that the table could possibly have belonged to King Arthur in the fifth to sixth centuries AD, the date for the radial plank was not precise enough to help place the table in its true historical context.

A second stage radiocarbon dating programme was soon afterwards adopted in which the specific objective was to obtain a much more precise date, both as a 'stand-alone' result (meaning a result which did not rely upon separately determined dendrochronological alignments) and as a dendrochronological adjusted result. The strategy to obtain a more precise result from the available measurement techniques, which at the time could not be expected to give results for individual measurements significantly better than ± 70 years, was to take a number of replicate samples, which, when combined, would provide a closer estimate of the randomly occurring uncertainties. The precision of measurement was also examined through the results of a number of duplicate samples (pairs) taken and processed at separated times and to improve confidence in the overall accuracy of the technique a series of 'known age' samples from the Winchester area was also included in the programme.

195

This chapter is primarily concerned with the sampling, measurement strategy, results and interpretation of this second phase of the experiment, with particular reference to the radial planks. It also includes details of the dating of two other timber elements of the table, the raised rim and vertical members, which were thought to be later additions. For these radiocarbon was the only technique able to provide specific dates, since the available timbers contained far too few annual rings for dendrochronological dating. No scientific dating was needed, however, for the strengthening-pieces, which had been fitted concentrically at right angles to the radial planks. On removing the screws which held them, it was discovered that the carpenter had thoughtfully written in pencil behind one of the pieces his name and the exact date they were fitted, *Repaired by George Blake April 14th 1873* (Fig. 72; see above, p. 144).

Before looking in detail at the dating of the Round Table an outline description is given of the more general principles which underlie the radiocarbon method of dating, and some of the ways in which the raw data obtained must be adjusted to give useful results.

Radiocarbon dating

Principles

The invention and first development of the method was by the American, W. F. Libby, in the late 1940s, a discovery for which he was awarded the Nobel Prize in 1953.[1] It emerged from the realisation, by Libby, that the radioactive isotope ^{14}C (also referred to as radiocarbon) was, and presumably always had been, a minutely abundant but natural constituent of atmospheric carbon dioxide, the life-source at the head of the food-chain of the entire living world. He predicted that ^{14}C is produced continuously by the interaction at high altitude of neutrons, a secondary product of high energy cosmic particles, with atoms of atmospheric nitrogen. The single ^{14}C atoms so produced are chemically highly reactive and quickly form carbon dioxide ($^{14}CO_2$) which combines with the more abundant forms of atmospheric carbon dioxide at lower altitude where its incorporation in all living material begins. The proposition that this contribution of ^{14}C in atmospheric carbon dioxide has been at a constant level throughout all time is one of the important assumptions of the original Libby theories and is discussed in more detail later, together with its

---

[1] W. F. Libby, *Radiocarbon Dating* (Chicago, 1952).

application to the dating of timber and its relevance to the integrity of ^{14}C in tree-rings.

The ultimate fate of the ^{14}C, once the living material has died and the incorporation of ^{14}C has ceased, is demonstrated in Fig. 88. In the inset is given the 'disintegration' scheme of a ^{14}C nucleus in which it is seen to decay from its unstable radioactive form ^{14}C back to the stable form ^{14}N. In making this transition an electron is emitted and is the sole radioactive ß⁻ particle emission of ^{14}C. It is the interaction of this particle in a nuclear detector which enabled the presence of ^{14}C to be identified originally and provided the methods by which its concentration could be measured.

Precisely when any particular ^{14}C nucleus will disintegrate is entirely unpredictable. On a 'macro' scale, however, the reduction in the amount of ^{14}C present follows natural statistical rules which give rise to a consistent rate of decay, typical of the isotope. This is usually described in terms of the isotope's 'half-life'; the best known value for which for ^{14}C is 5,730 years. A 'half-life' is the period of time over which the number of radioactive nuclei present initially falls to exactly half that original value. In Fig. 88 the decay of the ^{14}C in once living material, having a radioactivity emission rate of 14 disintegrations per minute per gram of carbon (14 dpm/g C) is plotted over a period of four half-lives. At one half-life (5,730 years) the level is seen to have fallen to 7 dpm/g, i.e. half the value at which it began. This is the pattern which repeats indefinitely, but in practice the level becomes indistinguishable from zero after seven to eight half-lives, 40,000 to 50,000 years, the practical limit for radiocarbon dating.

Assumptions and need for calibration to 'true age'

In dating, the decay of carbon-14 has to be assessed from the opposite point of view to that expressed in the graph (Fig. 88). What is observed in a sample to be dated is the residual, decayed, level of ^{14}C and the age is determined by considering how long it will have taken to come down to this point from its assumed original 'living' level. For a precise date, it is important that this original level should be accurately predicted. In the initial theories on radiocarbon dating Libby assumed that the living (modern) level had always remained constant but it is now known that his assumption was only partially valid and that considerable error in the dating results would result if correction for the variation were not made.

In addition, there was the uncertainty in the accuracy of the estimated half-life of ^{14}C. Originally a best value for the ^{14}C half life of 5,568 years was adopted.

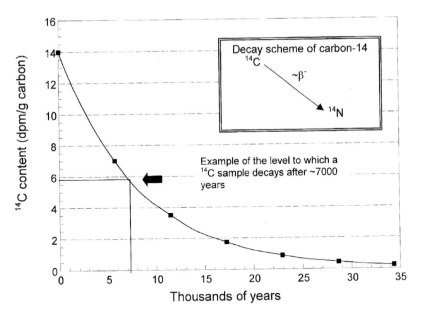

88 Radioactive decay of carbon-14 (^{14}C).

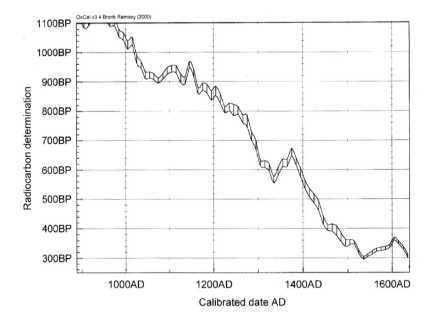

89 Radiocarbon calibration curve for the period of the Round Table (INCTAL98).

Today this value has been updated to 5,730 years following more sophisticated attempts at its measurement.[2]

A convenient way out of the double problem of 'original level' and 'half-life' emerges from measurements of residual ^{14}C preserved in the annual rings of long-lived trees. A tree adds to its girth one specific layer of wood (tree-ring) in every year it is alive. The radiocarbon level in the carbon of the components that make up the wood (cellulose, lignin, etc.) is characteristic of the radiocarbon level of the year in which that ring was added and there is good evidence that this level does not mix with neighbouring rings. Thus, in the individual tree-rings of any tree there is preserved the decaying record of the original level of radiocarbon contemporary with the year in which each ring grew. The unravelling of this contemporary level as it varies from year to year is accomplished by selecting a slice of a suitably long-lived tree, marking off the exact years (simply by counting the rings year by year from the known date at which the tree was felled), and then cutting off suitable sections for individual radiocarbon measurements.

From these measurements a practical calibration curve can be constructed, an example of which, for the period relevant to the Round Table, is given in Fig. 89. In theory by using the curve a given level of residual radiocarbon, measured in any convenient radiocarbon units and plotted on the vertical axis, can be read off along the horizontal axis in terms of the calendar year it represents. Because of the uncertainty range associated with radiocarbon determinations, application to the calibration curve usually needs a more sophisticated overlay of the radiocarbon range on to the calibration curve as discussed below (pp. 202–4). However, the general principle is upheld, i.e. by using a valid calibration curve a calendar age is obtained which is independent of any prior knowledge of the original level of radiocarbon in the atmosphere or its half-life.

The establishment of an irrefutable calibration curve is a work which has taken many years to complete. It began with the investigations of de Vries who, on taking radiocarbon measurements at intervals through a section of a long-lived tree, demonstrated that variations as large as 1% in the contemporary level had certainly occurred since AD 1500.[3] In 1960 a systematic curve going back over the last 1300 years was produced from measurements of an American Giant Redwood.[4] This showed that even larger variations, of up to 3%. had occurred. Subsequently, curves

---

[2] H. Godwin, 'Half-life of Radiocarbon,' *Nature* 195 (1962), 984.

[3] H. de Vries, 'Variations in Concentration of Radiocarbon with Time and Location on Earth,' *Koninklijke Nederlandse Akademie van Wetenschappen, Amsterdam B*, 61 (1958), 1–9.

[4] E. H. Willis, H. Tauber, and K. O. Munnich, 'Variations in the Atmospheric Radiocarbon Concentration over the past 1300 Years', *Radiocarbon* 2 (1960), 1–4.

going back to approximately 6500 BC were developed from overlapping sections of living and dead samples of a very long-lived tree, the bristlecone pine, which grows in the White Mountains of California.[5]

Lack of agreement upon a common interpretation of the bristlecone pine tree-ring radiocarbon measurements made by the three principal laboratories (Suess,[6] Ralph,[7] and Damon[8]) unfortunately meant an unequivocal master calibration-curve did not emerge from this work. The presence of very short-term variations superimposed on a longer-term trend was hotly debated. Only with the advent of much higher measurement precision facilities, brought about by considerable refinements in the original gas counting and later liquid scintillation counting, both of which used decay counting methods, and together with a number of independent tree chronologies (not just bristlecone), agreement was eventually reached. Thus a result can now be obtained with much better confidence for the Round Table than could have been possible at the time when the original measurements were made.

Measurement Procedures

The precise measurement of the levels of ^{14}C in natural materials by decay counting, i.e. counting the particles emitted in the decay process over a measured time period, raises certain specific challenges. In the first place, the emitted beta-particle is rather weak which results in only a very reduced number of particles compared to the total being emitted passing through the 'window-wall' of any conceivable conventional nuclear detector. Furthermore the normal background count-rate of most detectors, due to cosmic rays and other naturally occurring radiation, even when enclosed within thick lead shielding, may still swamp the numbers occurring by a beta-particle emission from a natural carbon sample containing ^{14}C.

For these reasons alone, ^{14}C measurements can never be made *in situ* using an ordinary nuclear particle measuring device, e.g. a simple Geiger Muller Counter. To enable a measurement to be made with a certainty of better than ± 1% (equivalent

---

[5] For example, the curve produced by H. E. Suess, 'Bristlecone Pine Calibration of the Radiocarbon Time-scale 5200BC to the Present,' in I. U. Olsson (ed.), *Radiocarbon Variations and Absolute Chronology* (New York, 1970), pp. 303–12.

[6] As n. 5.

[7] E. K. Ralph, H. N. Michael, and M. C. Han, 'Radiocarbon Dates and Reality', *MASCA Newsletter* 9.1 (1973), 1–20.

[8] P. E. Damon, A. Long, E. I. Wallick, 'Dendrochronologic Calibration of the Carbon-14 Time-scale,' in T. A. Rafter and T. Grant-Taylor (ed.), *Proceedings of the Eighth International Radiocarbon Conference, Lower Hutt, New Zealand, 1972* (Wellington, 1973), i, pp. 429–57.

to approximately 80 years in age terms), specially developed detectors and procedures must be used and these are only practical on a laboratory scale.

Up to the time when the Round Table determinations were made (1976 to 1978) only two practical systems had emerged, these were gas-counting and liquid-scintillation counting. For gas-counting the sample to be dated is converted to a gas, e.g. carbon dioxide (CO_2) or methane (CH_4), and is introduced into the counter as the gas filling which it needs for its operation. Self-absorption and transmission losses are thereby avoided and the whole system is enclosed in an elaborately shielded system specially designed to minimise cosmic-ray background.

In the second process, liquid-scintillation counting, the sample is converted to a liquid, organic solvent, benzene. This is mixed in solution form with a similar solvent into which has been dissolved a solute of a suitable fluorescent substance. On decay, the beta-emission from the ^{14}C imparts energy to the solvent molecules within a suitable transparent vial and these in turn hand it on to the solute molecules causing them to fluoresce, that is, to emit light quanta (flashes). These light quanta are transmitted through the vial and are detected by sensitive photomultiplier tubes, shielded in a light-tight compartment, and counted electronically.

This latter process was used for the Round Table measurements. The ideal size of sample required for this system was one that would produce about 6 ml. of benzene (equivalent to 5 g of pure carbon). In the case of dry wood this amount was obtained from around 15 to 20 g. of initial material.

Fundamental to obtaining a reliable result from any counting system is that an adequate total number of counting events should be observed in each measurement. A total of 40,000 counts was collected from each Round Table sample dated, giving a relative precision (standard deviation, counting statistics only) of ± 0.5%, equivalent to ± 40 years in terms of the resulting date. However when all other possible uncertainties were included, the full, replicate sample-reproducibility of all the samples dated was estimated to be approximately ± 70 years.[9] To improve on this single-sample, single-count, precision repeat/replicates samples were taken and processed as independently as possible at different times, and counted both together and separately in repeated counting sequences.

[9]   R. L. Otlet, 'An Assessment of Laboratory Errors in Liquid Scintillation Methods of ^{14}C,' in R. Berger and H. E. Suess (ed.), *Proceedings of the Ninth International Radiocarbon Dating Conference, Los Angeles and La Jolla, 1976* (Berkeley, 1979), pp. 256–67. One uncertainty which can be allowed for is the isotopic fractionation that occurs in the photosynthetic process by which carbon for the plant's (tree-rings') growth is absorbed from atmospheric carbon-dioxide and during which the plant discriminates against ^{14}C. The correction is based on the comparable discrimination against ^{13}C with respect to ^{12}C (δ^{13}C) and although the corrections are rarely larger than an equivalent of 16 years error, every sample in the Round Table programme was individually corrected for its specific, measured δ^{13}C value.

Current status and techniques of calibration

The conversion of the laboratory ^{14}C measurement to a real historical calendar date is a step necessarily accomplished using a calibration curve developed from sequential ^{14}C measurements of 'known-age' tree rings. The initial available curves of Suess,[10] Ralph,[11] and Damon[12] were developed from the measurement of tree-ring sections taken from ordered chronologies of timbers of the long-lived bristlecone pine but problems with the apparent differences between these curves and especially upon how they should be used caused enormous difficulties. For many years, therefore, even in the period which extended beyond the Round Table programme of dating, the principles of calibration were well understood, universally recognised as a necessary solution, but there was no clear answer to the question of which of the published interpretive curves it was best to use in any given case.

The publication of a completely independent curve by Stuiver in 1982 represented a considerable breakthrough out of this confusion.[13] Stuiver's curve covered the period from the present to approximately 2000 years before the present (BP) and was produced from a chronology constructed from overlapping sections of entirely different trees, Douglas Fir from the Pacific Northwest for the period from the present day back to AD 730, with an overlapping sequence of Sequoia from California covering AD 940 back to AD 1.

In comparison with the earlier bristlecone pine curves the new curve did not need interpretive smoothing techniques to enable its use, the ^{14}C measurements having been carried out to much greater precision in newly developed measurement systems. These employed large volume gas proportional counters operated specially for high precision measurements. By 1985 these measurements had been combined with a comparable sequence obtained by Pearson (Belfast) using Irish bog oaks with measurements carried out by him on a dedicated high precision liquid scintillation counter system. The definitive calibration curve for the period, so produced, was recommended by the Twelfth International Radiocarbon Conference that year.[14]

Although the calibration curve to use is now agreed, the procedure for using it still needs some consideration. The expression of a radiocarbon date determination in terms of a mean and plus or minus standard deviation is a useful shorthand way of defining the probability ranges within which the true date is likely to lie. However

---

[10] As n. 5.

[11] As n. 7.

[12] As n. 8.

[13] M. Stuiver, 'A High Precision Calibration of the AD Radiocarbon Time Scale,' *Radiocarbon* 24.1 (1982), 1–26.

[14] M. Stuiver and G. W. Pearson, 'High Precision Calibration of the Radiocarbon Time Scale AD 1950–500 BC,' *Radiocarbon* 28 (2B) (1986), 805–38

the full range of probabilities is a Gaussian (bell shaped) distribution as shown on the y-axis in Fig. 90a. Something more than a point to point read-off on the calibration curve of the mean ^{14}C result is clearly involved. For the 95 per cent confidence range, it is necessary to consider all the likely calibration values occurring in the interval from minus two standard deviations to plus two standard deviations about the mean date. The calibrated result then emerges as a single, or multiple, probability range(s), in some cases demonstrating distinctly asymmetric probability regions. Stuiver originally suggested that these results should be expressed in terms of the full range of probabilities taking the result from the left-hand side of the uncertainty band of the calibration curve at the minus end of the range as the lower limit, and the right-hand side of the band at the other end as the upper limit. This intercept method is the one used here for the Round Table. The problem with this procedure is that the result, which is then a probability range (or worse still, ranges), does not readily lend itself to the required further computations, i.e. making the appropriate corrections for growth-allowance and the amalgamation of groups of results to determine a single date range (Fig. 90a).

The technique known as 'wiggle matching' has been used to try to overcome this problem (Fig. 91a). The principle is that for a set of radiocarbon results separated by well defined age differences a best fit can be made of the whole group, arranged in order of their age spacing, when overlain correctly on the actual calibration curve. The match can be made either by hand using a simple transparent paper overlay or mathematically, i.e. by finding the place where the sums of the squares of the deviations of the data (above and below the actual curve) are minimised. The technique has been shown to work very successfully with precisely measured ^{14}C data matched on to a section of the calibration curve where distinctive 'wiggles' are clearly seen to occur. Because of the lower precision of the Round Table measurements (possibly compounded by additional uncertainties in the age separators) the matches are less precise and although extreme positions where the fits are improbable may be clear (even by eye) additional criteria are required to quantify the most probable regions within the range. Two available calibration packages which include wiggle matching procedures have been used in the analysis of the Round Table data, these are OxCal[15] and Groningen.[16] An example using the Groningen package is given in Fig. 91a. It shows the individual ^{14}C results of a selected set (Group 1) of Round

[15] C. Bronk Ramsey, OxCal v.3.4 (2000). For the OxCal calibration package, see C. Bronk Ramsey, 'Analysis of Chronological Information and Radiocarbon Calibration: the Program OxCal', *Archaeological Computing Newsletter* 41 (1994), 11–16; and C. Bronk Ramsey, 'Radiocarbon Calibration and Analysis of Stratigraphy: the OxCal Program', *Radiocarbon* 37(2), 425–30.

[16] J. van der Plicht, CAL25 (1998), Centre for Isotope Research, Groningen.

Table dates plotted, with their 2σ error bars, on the relevant portion of the curve. This set of results fits well upon the curve, other groupings are much more scattered and difficult to place visually. Even in this case, however, the optimum positioning is best obtained by using the y-axis 'Goodness of Fit' statistic from the program. This statistic is derived from the least squares sum of the y-axis residuals in each position as the set is moved through the possible region for a match. The associated 'goodness of fit' statistic is seen plotted in Fig. 91b. The arbitrary boundary points have been set at around AD 1215 (left) and AD 1275 (right) where the Goodness of Fit statistic becomes very large, nearly double the minimum.

The OxCal package provides the data as new probability distributions, which represent the earliest date in the set. The OxCal result for the same data set is shown in Fig. 92a and with the growth allowance added the 68.2% and 95.4% ranges give comparative values of AD 1218 to AD 1269 and AD 1174 to AD 1313.

Radiocarbon dating of the Round Table

Sampling objectives and strategy

The programme began with the initial simple objective of establishing an approximate time frame within which other studies, in particular the dendrochronological dating work could concentrate. The early dendrochronological examination suggested that only a limited number of trees had gone into making the planked surface of the table. Some planks were seen clearly to have come from the same tree and it seemed therefore unnecessary to sample each and every plank, so only one sample was taken. The expansion of the programme followed in the next phase where the declared objective was to obtain, as independently as possible from the dendrochronological work, as precise a date by radiocarbon as the methods of the time could provide. The essence of the programme then was to date as many different pieces (individual planks) as the budget would allow with the objective of finding the most precise mean date from a larger distribution of the individual results. In all cases every attempt was made, in the sampling and measurement procedures, to remove common factors so that the effects which might produce variation should occur randomly and not produce a particular bias in a particular direction.

The precision of the radiocarbon measurements, whether considered singly or combined, was an underlying problem since the normal estimate made at this time for samples of the approximate period of the Round Table, was $\pm$ 70 years, expressed as one sigma standard deviation (1σ). This was a measure of the full sample-reproducibility and not just of its counting statistics.[17] It meant that the possible range of a single result was intolerably large for the application, giving a 95.4% confidence range ($\pm 2\sigma$) equivalent to 280 years. Because of this possible 280-year spread, comparisons of individual radiocarbon results with specific tree-ring values would have been meaningless. Two procedures were employed in an attempt to reduce this range. The first was to extend the counting time on a given sample: this reduced the uncertainty deriving from the counting statistics and from the instrumental drift in the counting apparatus, but did nothing to reduce the contribution of the random errors common to the individual sample preparation procedure. The second was multi-sampling, i.e. dividing the initial sample so as to make a set of fully replicated, independent measurements. The new error estimate was then taken as the standard deviation on the means, which, if the individual standard deviations were correctly allowed for, is mathematically consistent with the individual standard deviation divided by the square root of the number of separate samples included in the mean. Undoubtedly, there is a limit to the ultimate precision which can be achieved, since it is implicit in such a combination that all errors are random and that there are no common systematic contributions. Although this is unlikely to be the case absolutely, a better precision is achieved and in the end it is the variability of the results themselves that indicates the actual precision attained.

Timber dating and its application to the Round Table

The growth of a tree, which adds one new layer of wood (tree-ring) to its girth for every year it is alive, has already been described (see p. 151). Certain factors have to be considered when radiocarbon dating a wood sample taken by cutting a section from a large timber. These are (Fig. 92*b*):

1. the position of the sample as it once existed in the tree relative to the last ring produced prior to felling, i.e. the outermost (bark-edge) ring
2. the number of years (i.e. rings) spanned by the cut sample
3. the eventual calibration of the raw data measurements.

All had to be taken into account in the sampling, measurement and interpretation of the Round Table samples.

---

[17] See above, n. 9.

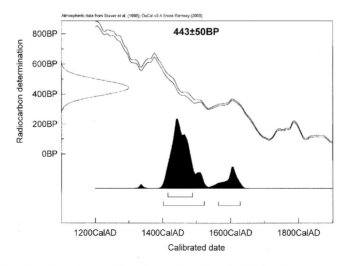

90*a* Example of radiocarbon calibration using Oxcal (Oxford).

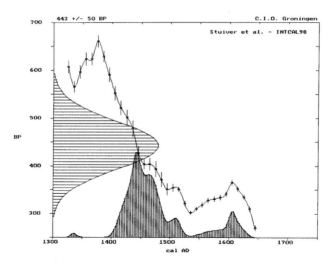

90*b* Example of radiocarbon calibration using CAL25 (Groningen).

The example given is for the Winchester College shutter (see below, p. 217 and Table 9). It shows how the Gaussian curve of the radiocarbon determination can be transformed into multiple probability ranges depending upon the shape of the calibration curve in that period.

The growth allowance is added to the ranges after calibration and, as would be expected since both packages use the same calibration data, the results are virtually identical: OxCal   AD1484–1556 (68.2% probability), CAL25   AD1485–1555 (68.2% probability)

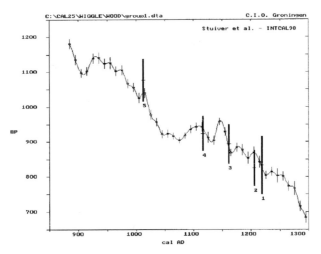

91*a* 'Wiggle-matching' by CAL25 of the radiocarbon results of the Group 1 samples (cf. Table 7). 1, RAD 18; 2, RAD 22B; 3, RAD 47A; 4, RAD 22A; 5, RAD 47B.

The radiocarbon determinations are shown with 2σ error bars. The horizontal distance between the determinations represents the number of rings separating each sample, thus sample 5 (RAD 47B) has the greatest growth allowance (rings to sapwood edge) and sample 1 (RAD 18) the smallest.

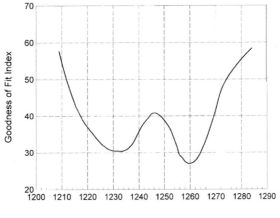

91*b* Goodness-of-fit statistic for 'wiggle-matching' the radiocarbon results of the Group 1 samples shown in Fig. 91a.

The best fit of the sample data to the calibration curve is given by the minimum goodness of fit index.

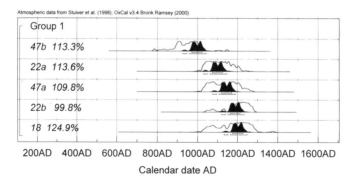

Atmospheric data from Stuiver et al. (1998); OxCal v3.4 Bronk Ramsey (2000)

92*a* OxCal probability distribution produced by 'wiggle-matching' the radiocarbon results of the Group 1 samples (cf. Figs. 91*a* and 91*b*).

The radiocarbon determinations in the group are fitted to the calibration curve in a similar manner to that shown in Figure 91*a*. The OxCal package then calculates a new probability distribution (shown black in the figure) which is compared with the individual distributions.

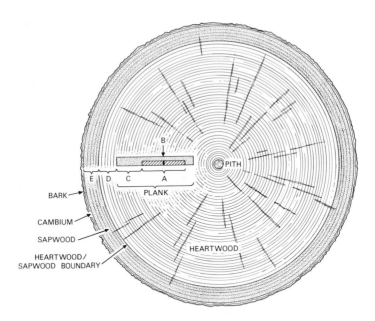

92*b* The growth allowance (see p. 209): A, number of rings spanned by a radiocarbon sample within a plank; B, central ring of the radiocarbon sample; C, known number of rings between the outer edge of the radiocarbon sample and the outer edge of the plank (Table 7); D, additional number of rings between the outer edge of the plank and the heartwood/sapwood boundary (Table 7); E, number of sapwood rings.

Sample position (see Fig. 92*b*, Letters A–E)

For a timber which includes sapwood a precise correction to the heartwood-sapwood boundary can be made simply by counting the number of annual rings separating the ring at the centre of the cut sample (B) from the beginning of the sapwood ((A ÷ 2) + C + D). The full 'growth-allowance' is then completed by adding to this count an assumed, nominal, 'sapwood-allowance' for the total of the sapwood rings (E). The figure generally taken for the mature oak is 25, although Baillie has recommended 32 ± 9.[18]

This tree-ring 'growth-allowance' is quite a different proposition from the technique of dendrochronological dating since factors such as ring-widths, or the matching of ring-width patterns to a known-age master tree-ring curve, are in no way involved.

When there is no sapwood present on the timber from which the radiocarbon sample is cut, a growth-allowance can only be made by counting the number of rings up to the surviving edge of the plank (C + (A ÷ 2)). The radiocarbon date in this situation must always earlier than the felling date by an amount equal to the sum of the sapwood allowance plus the missing rings (D) between the edge of the plank and the start of the sapwood.

The alternative to the growth allowance method is to estimate the position of the sample relative to the felling date of the tree through a dendrochronological alignment, i.e., by matching the ring-pattern of the plank sampled to a developed master chronology which covers the full range of timbers used.

Samples from the Round Table provided a mixture of possibilities for the final analysis. In the case of samples taken from the radial planks, some came from timbers which had visible sapwood along a direct line to the edge of the board at the point the sample was cut (Group 1). For others, it was known that sapwood was present not far from the direct line, although not in a position to which a ring-by-ring count could be made with absolute precision (Group 2). The final group (Group 3) consisted of samples taken from planks which had no evidence of sapwood at all. These samples are all listed in Table 7.

---

[18] M. G. L. Baillie, *Tree-ring Dating and Archaeology* (London and Canberra, 1982), pp. 53–60.

Table 7

Summary by Groups 1–3 of all data used to estimate radiocarbon 'stand-alone' felling dates for the radial planks of the Round Table (see Table 12)

Radiocarbon sample	Radiocarbon age BP	Calibrated radiocarbon age range AD (68.2% probability)	Growth allowance, i.e. rings to add to plank edge	Additional rings to correct to heartwood/ sapwood boundary	Tree Number (cf. Table 3.2)	Sapwood and condition notes (cf. Table 1)
Group 1 Planks with identified sapwood						
RAD 22A	924 ± 49	1036 to 1160	120	−2	3	Soft, possibly 1 to 2 rings of sapwood near sampling point
RAD 22B	825 ± 51	1163 to 1272	31	−2		
RAD 18	833 ± 83	1065 to 1279	26	−10	1b	Approximately 10 rings of sapwood (not measured)
RAD 47A	893 ± 56	1042 to 1212	63	5	5	Sapwood further down plank, possibly 5 rings away
RAD 47B	1077 ± 61	895 to 1019	217	5		
RAD 44	603 ± 51	1303 to 1400	80	−12	4	In 12 rings of sapwood
Group 2 Planks with possible sapwood						
RAD 39A	834 ± 36	1166 to 1257	69	5	1a	Soft further up plank, possible sapwood
RAD 39B	747 ± 57	1222 to 1296	116	5		
RAD 13A	773 ± 52	1220 to 1284	42	5	1a	Soft further up plank, possible sapwood
RAD 13B	820 ± 52	1164 to 1274	104	5		
RAD 36	880 ± 52	1044 to 1217	47	5	1b	Soft further up plank, possible sapwood
Group 3 Planks with no evidence of sapwood						
RAD 8	780 ± 55	1215 to 1285	62	10	1a	
RAD 34	813 ± 52	1189 to 1277	24	10	1b	
RAD 31	850 ± 54	1070 to 1260	27	10	1b	
RAD 38	890 ± 56	1042 to 1214	90	10	2	
RAD 42A	840 ± 49	1160 to 1262	116	10	2	
RAD 42B	743 ± 51	1224 to 1296	104	10		
RAD 6A	793 ± 51	1212 to 1282	72	10	2	
RAD 6B	820 ± 56	1163 to 1276	72	10		
RAD 14	940 ± 57	1027 to 1158	59	10	2	

Radiocarbon sample	Radiocarbon age BP	Calibrated radiocarbon age range AD (68.2% probability)	Growth allowance, i.e. rings to add to plank edge	Additional rings to correct to heartwood / sapwood boundary	Tree Number (cf. Table 3.2)	Sapwood and condition notes (cf. Table 1)
RAD 5	888 ± 65	1040 to 1216	65	10	2	Much damaged
RAD 43	915 ± 67	1035 to 1186	61	10	2	Much damaged

Full growth allowance corrections were not possible for the samples cut from the rim and vertical members, and the final results are necessarily less precise (see Table 8 and below, pp. 214–15, 231–2).

Ring span

Strictly, because of the nature of radioactive decay, it is an approximation to take the central position of the total rings spanned in a cut sample as the point in time that has been dated. However, from the practical point of view of cutting the Round Table samples it was of more importance to ensure that the quantity of wood removed from each ring was approximately even. In general the required weight of sample (minimum 16 g) could be obtained from a volume of about 25 cm^3, which is roughly equivalent to half the solid volume of a pocket-size matchbox. Care was taken when cutting the samples from the radial planks not to cut too deeply for fear of breaking through to the front face of the table. Sections cut from radials (Plate XVIII; cf. Figs. 79 and 81) were typically 12 cm long by 4 cm wide and 0.5 cm deep. Fortunately, the radius of curvature on the rings in the regions where the samples were cut was relatively even, so that it was only necessary to ensure that the depth of the cut was as regular as possible.

Calibration

The fact that the cut sections of timber spanned a number of rings (years) was considered an advantage at the time of the dating programme. The existence of short-term variations in the level of radiocarbon in the atmosphere had caused considerable controversy in the derivation of a universally acceptable calibration curve and it was generally accepted that the 'lifetime' of a wood sample should span enough years to smooth out the 'shortest-term' variations. Ten to twenty years was considered a long enough 'lifetime' and Round Table samples were always more than this, their spans ranging from 40 to 144 years.

The latest, precise, dendrochronological calibration measurements clearly show that short-term variations did occur in certain periods and the form they give to the calibration curve can sometimes be used to obtain a very accurate result for a chronological series of dates from a timber through the technique of 'wiggle' matching which is described later.

A further consideration given to the selection of samples was to disperse their mean positions throughout the lifetime of the tree (or trees) to which they originally belonged. Some were deliberately taken near to the very centre of the tree (the pith), some were at, or close, to the heartwood-sapwood boundary, and others lay between. The point of this was to ensure that a range of different calibration possibilities was invoked, thus ruling out overall dependence on the accuracy of calibration in a particular period.

Finally, when calibrating results from timbers, it must be remembered that the calibration applies to the age of the rings of the cut sample and that **growth allowances, however derived, must be added after calibration**. This was particularly important when interpreting the results of the Round Table radial planks.

Sampling Programme

The programme comprised four categories of samples. Three of these represent timber members of the table itself, the radial planks, the vertical timbers, and the raised rim. The other consists of 'equal-age' samples. The latter came from different locations in the Winchester area and all had dates suggested by the historical record. Samples in the four categories are discussed in detail below.

Radials

Although the procedure of multi-sampling could not be applied in all cases, compared with most dating projects the dating of the radial planks provided a virtually unique opportunity to exploit the principle. Time was available for extended counting and there was no shortage of raw material for multi-sampling. However, of the multi-sampling carried out, only those samples taken in pairs from adjacent positions (i.e. identical rings) were strictly true replicates (Table 7). The others, the pseudo-replicates, comprised those samples whose results were brought to a common value through growth allowances added after calibration of their individual measured result.

Fig. 81 shows the positions from which the twenty-two radial (and the four vertical and the three rim) samples were taken. All the radial samples came from the rear face of the table and lay along the grooves cut in making the dendrochronological measurements. Plate XVIII shows in detail the areas removed for the two radiocarbon samples (RAD 22A and RAD 22B) alongside the groove cut for counting the tree rings of this plank. The areas of wood removed for radiocarbon dating all lay entirely behind the strengthening boards added in the Victorian period which were specially removed for these investigations (Nos. 136–49; Fig. 43, cf. Fig. 79). When these boards were replaced at the end of the work, the cuts for the radiocarbon samples were entirely hidden.

Following the single original sample from RAD 22A, 22 samples were taken from a total of 16 planks in four batches throughout the period September 1976 to November 1977. Originally the sampling strategy was designed around the preliminary grouping of the planks into two sets, thought to represent two trees, and was based on dating only those which had sapwood and/or some obvious visual matches from their dendrochronological patterns. Later in the project all suitable planks showing evidence of sapwood were added, together with a number which were proving otherwise difficult to place. This policy was continued into the final batch, but extra pairs were also included to allay concern that some of the early samples might have been affected by wood preservative, possibly transferred from the Victorian boards (Nos. 136–49) from beneath which the samples were cut or applied in 1938 (see above, pp. 146–7). These samples were from RAD 6B, 42B, 39B, and 13B and in the second sampling the top surface of the timber was discarded. No significant difference between the A and B samples was however eventually observed (Tables 10 and 11).

Table 7 also includes ring-counting data and sapwood notes for each sample provided by Ian Gourlay, Department of Forestry, University of Oxford. Sapwood was identified by him on or very close to the line of the samples on four of these planks (which produced six samples forming Group 1) and was believed to lie within five to ten rings of the plank edge at the point sampled on another three planks (a further five samples, Group 2). In these three latter cases sapwood was present elsewhere on the edge of the planks and, although not on the line of the samples, was sufficiently close for him to estimate the position of the samples in relation to the heartwood-sapwood boundary. The remaining eleven samples were taken from nine planks, none of which showed any traces of sapwood (Group 3).

Table 13 includes the ring correction data necessary in the second method of data analysis to align each radiocarbon result to the datum of the master dendrochronological curve. Values given represent the number of years which Professor A. C. Barefoot recommends should be added to the calibrated mean radiocarbon date to bring the result for each plank to the datum for the hypothetical last ring of the tree-ring chronology, i.e. Ring 380. This value is calculated in three stages. First, to the radiocarbon result is added the number of rings counted between the mean position of the radiocarbon sample and the plank edge (or estimated heart-wood-sapwood boundary, where appropriate). Second, the number of rings between the plank edge and Ring 355 of the master dendrochronological curve is added. Third, the nominal sapwood allowance of twenty-five years is added to bring each value to the notional last ring of the last tree felled, i.e. Ring 380 (cf. Fig. 92*b*).

The result of this procedure is to correct all the radiocarbon dates to the same point in time, i.e. to adjust them as if they were all multiple dating results of the same tree ring. The validity of the procedure relies completely on the dendro-chronologist (i) to identify to which tree of those used in the construction of the table each radiocarbon sample belonged and (ii) to align accurately each of the trees in the order they were felled. It has to be recognised that much of the inde-pendence of the radiocarbon date is, therefore, lost in the final answer calculated this way.

Verticals

The vertical timbers fastened to the back (under surface) of the table were sampled to establish the date of what was shown by the stratigraphy of the woodwork to be a secondary phase in the history of the table (Nos. 130–5; see Figs. 41 and 43). Four samples were cut from these vertical timbers: VRT 130, VRT 132A, VRT 132B, and VRT 135 (Fig. 81). Growth allowance corrections were possible for samples VRT 130, VRT 132A, and VRT 132B, but could not be attempted for VRT 135. The results are given in Table 8.

Table 8

Radiocarbon determinations of samples taken from the rim and vertical timbers of the Round Table

Radiocarbon sample	Radiocarbon age BP	Mean radiocarbon age BP	Calibrated radiocarbon age range AD 68.2% probability (95.4% probability)	Rings spanned by sample	Additional rings to correct to felling date (including 25 years sapwood)	Sapwood notes
Verticals						
VRT 130	310 ± 54		1452 to 1616	16	28	5 rings in sapwood
VRT 132A	490 ± 52	380 ± 30	(1442 to 1630)	8	29	7 rings in sapwood
VRT 132B	360 ± 54			25	31	7 rings in sapwood
VRT 135	715 ± 58		1243 to 1386 (1212 to 1398)	*	*	No sapwood evident
Rim						
RIM 125A	530 ± 117		1413 to 1446	*	25	No sapwood evident
RIM 125B	485 ± 55	476 ± 37	(1401 to 1480)	*	25	No sapwood evident
RIM 126	455 ± 56			*	25	No sapwood evident

* Impossible to count number of rings spanned due to inaccessibility of the timber.

Rim

The rim framing the face (upper surface) of the table was also thought to represent a secondary phase in the history of the table, possibly contemporary with the addition of the vertical timbers to the back. Sampling from the rim posed problems, however, as the outer edge and back of the rim were inaccessible and cutting anywhere else would obviously damage the visible surface. Fortunately a single loose section of the rim was discovered. This section (Plate XIX) was removed and samples were taken from the adjacent pieces of the rim (Nos. 125 and 126), where they were overlapped by the loose section (Fig. 81). The portions cut away for the samples were completely covered when the loose piece was replaced. The original sample taken from No. 125 was small and did not give a satisfactory radiocarbon result (RIM 125A), but the two later samples were completely adequate for the measurement process (RIM 125B, RIM 126). No growth allowance corrections were possible, however, due to the small number of the rings and their inaccessibility for counting and no sapwood was evident. The results are given in Table 8.

Equal-age samples

These samples, from other local sources, were introduced in the course of the measurement programme as a gross check on the overall accuracy of the laboratory results (Table 9). Although the other laboratory checks kept watch and enabled quantification of sources of imprecision of the measurement procedure, they would not show presence of a common systematic error (e.g. a laboratory standard offset) which would affect all the results equally. The equal-age samples were intended to be from securely dated historical contexts and of values covering approximately the same ranges of dates as the samples taken from the table (before growth allowance and calibration corrections). In practice, it was more difficult than expected to find samples to meet these specifications. Details of the six samples obtained by Dr Derek Keene, then of the Winchester Research Unit, are given briefly below.

Minster Café

The wood used was taken from the building once known as Minster Café, 9 Great Minster Street, which is estimated on architectural grounds to have been erected in the mid or later sixteenth century.[19] The wood, which was dry, was taken from a post which contained forty-five rings up to the sapwood. Two samples were cut from adjacent sections which spanned the twelve earliest heartwood rings.

Winchester Cathedral

This wood came from the south side of the choir stalls in Winchester Cathedral. The stalls are datable on stylistic and historical grounds to the early fourteenth century,[20] with an expected felling date for the timber of about 1300. Two adjacent samples were taken from a seating beam which appeared to have been cut along the full radius of the tree; although sapwood was not present, the outer edge of the beam was probably not far from the latest heartwood ring. The beam contained about sixty-eight rings, the samples spanning its earliest eighteen rings.

---

[19] Derek Keene, *Survey of Medieval Winchester*, Winchester Studies 2 (Oxford, 1985), p. 588, tenement **178**.

[20] Charles Tracy, 'The 14th-century Choir-stalls,' in John Crook (ed.), *Winchester Cathedral: Nine Hundred Years* (Chichester and Winchester, 1993), pp. 193–206, at pp. 194–5: work on the stalls had begun before 1308 and was then still in progress.

Cathedral Green (*RF 1594* and *RF 1576*)

The samples were taken from the bottom timbers (all oak) of a deep cess-pit dug adjacent to the Anglo-Saxon Old Minster between *c*.980 and 1020.[21] Two adjacent samples were taken from *RF 1594*, both covering 90 rings immediately inside the sapwood. A third sample was taken from a re-used timber, *RF 1576*, from the same timber-lined well, covering 40 rings immediately inside the sapwood.

36 Middle Brook Street

This sample came from a timber-framed building at 36 Middle Brook Street, Winchester, believed to have been erected in either 1420 (written evidence) or about 1470 (architectural evidence).[22] The joist from which the sample was taken formed part of the original structure and covered thirty-eight rings to the sapwood. The sample spanned the earliest eighteen heartwood rings.

Winchester College

This sample was taken from one of the planks which formed part of a broken shutter near the painted panel of the Trusty Servant hanging in the west range of Chamber Court. The shutter was thought to date from the first period of the college buildings created in 1387–94, but information received from John Harvey after the radiocarbon measurement had been made suggests the possibility that the shutter may have belonged to any time between 1390 and 1530, although *c*.1390 is still the most probable period. The sample spanned forty-five rings. Ten rings were trimmed off the outside of these rings during sampling and it is estimated that sapwood was approximately ten rings further away.

Validation of the radiocarbon method

A very significant part of the project was to demonstrate the confidence that should be given to the radiocarbon dating results. This was planned in three ways, by the evidence of repeat counting throughout the period to demonstrate continuity of the

---

[21] Martin Biddle and Birthe Kjølbye-Biddle, *The Anglo-Saxon Minsters of Winchester*, Winchester Studies 4. i, Part II, Chapter XI, forthcoming.

[22] Keene, *Survey* (as above, n. 19), pp. 158, 738 and n. 26 (which refers to this radiocarbon date), Fig. 84.

measurement systems, by the dating of replicate pairs of samples taken and measured at different times to demonstrate full sample to sample reproducibility, and by selected measurements of local known age (historical records) samples to check the overall accuracy of the method.

Continuity of the measurement systems

In the full programme 38 samples were processed at different times throughout the period from October 1976 to April 1978 and measured by liquid scintillation counting. Ten batch counting sessions were devoted to these measurements, each batch comprising of the order of ten Round Table samples together with background and instrument calibration standards, following the laboratory procedures described elsewhere.[23] In each session every sample was measured to a counting precision (1σ) of $\pm$ 0.5%, equivalent to an age uncertainty of 40 years (counting only). Every sample was counted in at least two sessions, most were repeated three or four times, and some of the earliest processed were repeat counted throughout the whole period.

Of the 125 individual measurements of Round Table samples made in the period only two were rejected on grounds of the statistics of the sets of repeat counting, i.e. those which produced statistically unacceptable results, one just over three times the standard deviation of the others in the set and the other just over four times the standard deviation. The results of the first count of six other samples were not included because the initial counting data clearly showed that they had not been stored long enough before beginning the measurement to allow the natural Radon-222 (half-life 3.8 days) to die away. The conclusion from the analysis was that the constancy of measurement had been maintained throughout the period and that the repeat counting uncertainty equivalent to between $\pm$ 40 and $\pm$ 50 years was a valid estimate.[24]

The dating of replicate pairs

Eleven sample pairs were measured but as four of them were from significantly different ring positions within the radial planks only seven could be taken as exact sample replicates. The results of the others can also be compared but then only after

---

[23] R. L. Otlet and R. M. Warchal, 'Liquid Scintillation Counting of Low-level ^{14}C,' in M.A. Cook and P. Johnson (ed.), *Liquid Scintillation Counting 5* (London, 1978), pp. 210–18.

[24] Andrew Hewson (British Museum Research Laboratory) 1981, pers. comm.

calibration and growth allowance corrections. Table 10 shows the results obtained. The agreements between these pairs is seen to be between 14 years and 163 years, mean −58 ± 74 years, which reduces to −40 ± 63 when Minster Café is rejected, and to −22 ± 50 when VRT 132 is also rejected. Prediction of what should be expected requires an estimate to be made of an average, global, standard error of measurement applicable to the individual results of every pair. On the basis of the values in the table (except RIM 125a) the average value assigned is ± 52 years. With this value the predicted average RMS differences ($\sqrt{52^2 + 52^2}$) should be ~74 years. The result of 90 years would only be consistent with a global average standard error of ± 64 years which is significantly larger than the given estimates. Rejecting the most deviant result (Minster Café, 163 years difference), which is just beyond the 99% confidence range, taking all the differences as a set, reduces the average dramatically to 70 years which suggests a more reasonable global standard error of ± 55 years. Further rejections are not justified on the 3σ criterion. It is concluded that the procedure of estimating the precisions assigned to the radiocarbon results in this programme is demonstrated by these paired results to be valid.

The ring-separated replicates are listed in Table 11. Here the interpretation of the results is more difficult since before the comparison can be made of each pair the individual radiocarbon results require firstly calibration and secondly the addition of the growth allowances to a common datum (in this case plank edge). Differences between the probability ranges thus derived are given in the table simply as differences in the mid range positions and are seen to be between 16 to 96 years (mean 35 ± 46 years), which are considered entirely consistent with the conclusion.

Equal-age samples

Table 9 compares the results with the historically expected ages. In four, possibly five, of the six samples listed the agreement is extremely good. For the others, the differences could very well be due in part to the insecurity of the historically expected age but, even taking them at their face value, the results clearly suggest that agreement between the known age and the calibrated radiocarbon age has been established, but it is noted that the uncertainties are greater than was originally hoped.

Table 9

'Equal-age' samples: radiocarbon determinations of samples taken from Winchester timbers for comparison with the radiocarbon determination of samples taken from the Round Table

Source	Mean radiocarbon age BP	Growth allowance i.e. rings to add to plank age	Calibrated radiocarbon age range AD (95.4% probability)	Context and Comments
Minster Café, 9 Great Minster Street	388 ± 38	64	1502 to 1697	On architectural evidence the building is said to have been erected *c.* 1550 or somewhat later (see p. 216)
Winchester Cathedral, choir stalls	758 ± 36	84	1295 to 1385	Seating beam on south side. The choir stalls are known to have been under construction in 1308 (see p. 216)
Cathedral Green, Old Minster, CG *RF 1594*	1049 ± 39	70	960 to 1110	Cathedral Green, Feature 265, a cess-pit whose construction is dated to a range between 980 and 1020 (see p. 217)
Cathedral Green, Old Minster, CG *RF 1576*	913 ± 55	45	1070 to 1300	Same context as CG *RF 1594*. Although the result is not in such good agreement as obtained for CG *RF 1594*, if the raw radiocarbon ages of the two samples are combined before calibration an acceptable weighted mean result of 1004 ± 32 BP is obtained, which calibrates to AD 980 to 1157 (see p. 217)
36 Middle Brook Street	567 ± 55	54	1350 to 1490	Joist from the gallery of the original timber-framed structure. Architectural evidence suggests the building was constructed *c.* 1470, but written evidence indicates that the house on the property was rebuilt *c.* 1420. Both dates are within the 95.4% probability range (see p. 217)
Winchester College, shutter near the 'Trusty Servant' panel	443 ± 50	68	1460 to 1700	Shutter assumed to date to the first period of the College with a felling date for the timber *c.* 1390. The possibility that the date lies within a range *c.* 1390 to *c.* 1530 cannot be excluded (see p. 217)

Table 10

Analysis of paired samples: true replicates (i.e. where the same rings were dated twice)
(uncalibrated)

Radiocarbon sample	Radiocarbon age BP years	Age separation in years*
RAD 6A	793 ± 51	
RAD 6B	820 ± 56	+ 27
RAD 42A	840 ± 49	
RAD 42B	743 ± 49	–97
VRT 132A	490 ± 52	–130
VRT 132B	360 ± 54	
RIM 125A	530 ± 117	–45
RIM 125B	485 ± 55	
Minster Café A	473 ± 54	
Minster Café B	310 ± 52	–163
Cathedral Choir Stalls A	750 ± 50	
Cathedral Choir Stalls B	767 ± 51	+17
Cathedral Green, RF 1594A	1055 ± 51	
Cathedral Green, RF 1594B	1041 ± 59	–14

*Age separation calculated by subtracting first result from the second in all cases.

Average root mean square (RMS) differences:
for all dates: ~90 years, with Minster Café rejected: ~70 years

Table 11

Analysis of paired samples: ring-separated plank replicates (i.e. where the samples dated from the same plank are separated by a known number of rings)

Radiocarbon sample	Radiocarbon age BP	Growth allowance i.e. rings to add to plank edge	Calibrated radiocarbon age range AD with growth allowance added (68.2% probability)	Mid-range differences in years*
RAD 13A	773 ± 52	42	1262 to 1326	+29
RAD 13B	820 ± 52	104	1268 to 1378	
RAD 22A	924 ± 49	120	1156 to 1280	+31
RAD 22B	825 ± 51	31	1194 to 1303	
RAD 39A	834 ± 36	69	1235 to 1326	+95
RAD 39B	747 ± 57	116	1338 to 1411	
RAD 47A	893 ± 56	63	1105 to 1275	−16
RAD 47B	1077 ± 61	217	1112 to 1236	

*In all cases the differences in years are calculated by subtracting the mid-point of the A sample from the mid-point of the B sample range

Analysis of the Round Table dating results: radials

Following the original objectives of the programme, two radiocarbon 'pooled-mean' results for the felling dates of the radial planks were attempted as detailed below.

'Stand-alone' ^{14}C

By 'stand-alone' is meant to obtain a pooled mean result independently of the dendrochronological assignments or tree-ring alignments. For this the full 28 sample results are first considered as a single group. These are listed in Table 7 together with their associated calibrated age, 68.2% probability ranges, ring counting data of years separating the sample from the plank edge, and additional corrections to normalise all results to the heartwood/sapwood boundary. For information only at this stage, the assignment of each plank to a 'tree' proposed by Professor A. C. Barefoot and notes regarding the presence of sapwood rings provided by Ian Gourlay at the time the sample was cut, are also given.

The results were calibrated using the computer packages OxCal[25] and CAL25,[26] both of which use the latest recommended calibration data for this period, INTCAL98.[27] Essentially there was no difference between the calibrated results from either package but to avoid confusion only the data from OxCal are given in the tables. The values are then in agreement with that shown in the OxCal visual representation of the results and ranges (with overall growth allowance offsets added in and arranged in date order) given in Fig. 93.

The age results, which are all normalised to the felling date of each plank, are seen to spread fairly evenly over an astonishingly long period of nearly 500 years. It is inconceivable that this distribution over such a range could be attributed merely to the random spread of a set of radiocarbon results all originating from a relatively short time period. This assertion is borne out by the results obtained in the coincident tests of the programme with replicate samples and equal-age measurements discussed above (pp. 218–19). Attempts to wiggle-match this set of data by OxCal and CAL25 also confirm this conclusion. With CAL25, to obtain an acceptable fit, meaning a fit where all the tails of the 2-sigma (95.4% confidence) bars at least touched the calibration curve, required rejection of 7 of the total 28 results; OxCal required rejection of 6. The general conclusion was made that there existed too large a spread on the felling dates of the trees to obtain the 'stand-alone' date from all the results simply pooled together. The next move was to consider the pooled means of the individual groups, i.e.,

i.   those from planks which showed evidence of sapwood in the line of the ^{14}C sample
ii.   those from planks which were thought to be near the sapwood/heartwood boundary
iii.   a final group of all those from planks which showed no evidence of sapwood.

Table 12 lists the results for these groups. Most reliance must be given to the wiggle-match results derived from the OxCal and CAL25 packages, but to avoid total reliance on these 'black-box' procedures a comparative, weighted mean, result is also given. This mean is calculated simply from the mid-points of the overall cali-

[25] See above, n. 15.

[26] See above, n. 16, and below, next n.

[27] J. van der Plicht, 'The Groningen Radiocarbon Program', *Radiocarbon* 35(1) (1993), 231–8; upgraded with INTCAL98 dataset, M. Stuiver, P. J. Reimer, E. Bard, J. W. Beck, G.S. Burr, K. A. Hughen, B. Kromer, G. McCormac, J. van der Plicht, and M. Spurk , 'INTCAL 98 Radiocarbon Age Calibration, 24,000–0 cal BP', *Radiocarbon* 40(3) (1998), 1041–83.

brated ranges with each value weighted inversely as the magnitude of the range squared. Although this procedure and weighting applied to probability ranges can only be for arbitrary comparison, it was felt necessary to provide an alternative approach, and in this case the weighting was chosen to bias the results in favour of those which produced the smallest probability ranges. It was appreciated, however, that the magnitude of the probability ranges was only in part due to the original measurement uncertainties, but the similarity of the results given by the different techniques is encouraging.

The mean results of the groups is next considered, starting with Group 1 (Table 12). Except for RAD 44, which appears to be totally out of place even as a member in the complete set of radial measurements,[28] the Group 1 data gives a good wiggle-match (Fig. 91a) with a possible range of AD 1215 to AD 1275 as judged from the plot of the 'goodness of fit' statistic (Fig. 91b) or AD 1218 to AD 1269 from the OxCal 68.2% probability range. The original expectation was that because this grouping all comprised planks with definitely identified sapwood the pooled mean should give a felling date closest to the true construction date of the table. This is clearly not the case according to the radiocarbon dating when the means of the other two groups are considered and suggests the surprising conclusion that the Group 1 planks were felled some 60 years earlier than the others.

Table 12

Summary of 'stand-alone' radiocarbon determinations for Groups 1–3 of the radial plank samples from the Round Table (all dates AD; cf. Table 7)

	OxCal (68.4% probability)	CAL25	Weighted Mean
Group 1 with sapwood	1202 to 1272	1215 to 1274	1237 ± 60
Group 2 with possible sapwood	1310 to 1345	1300 to 1325	1317 ± 18
Group 3 with no sapwood	1299 to 1337	1295 to 1315	1324 ± 30
Groups 2 + 3	1307 to 1338	1295 to 1355	1330 ± 23

[28] RAD 44 turned out to be a problem result in all subsequent analyses and it is suggested that laboratory error cannot be ruled out. RAD 44 has therefore not been included from here on.

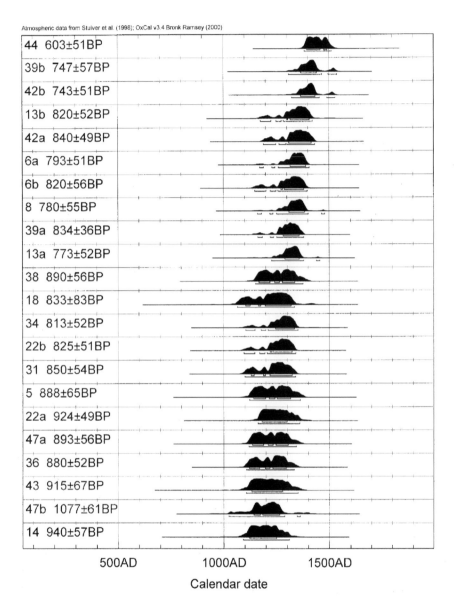

Atmospheric data from Stuiver et al. (1998); OxCal v3.4 Bronk Ramsey (2000)

44	603±51BP
39b	747±57BP
42b	743±51BP
13b	820±52BP
42a	840±49BP
6a	793±51BP
6b	820±56BP
8	780±55BP
39a	834±36BP
13a	773±52BP
38	890±56BP
18	833±83BP
34	813±52BP
22b	825±51BP
31	850±54BP
5	888±65BP
22a	924±49BP
47a	893±56BP
36	880±52BP
43	915±67BP
47b	1077±61BP
14	940±57BP

500AD   1000AD   1500AD

Calendar date

93 Age probabilities of all radial plank samples aligned with dendrochronological offsets to felling date.

Results for the radial planks are shown in ascending order of latest dates. Each result has been calibrated and then had its individual growth allowance to felling date added.

Table 13
Felling dates, by radiocarbon and tree-ring dating, of the trees from which the planks of the Round Table were cut

Tree Number	Plank Number (RAD)	Radiocarbon age BP	Calibrated radiocarbon age range AD (68.2% probability)	Growth allow- ance i.e. rings to add to plank edge	Additional rings to correct to heartwood / sapwood boundary	Total correction to Ring 380	Felling date ranges from 'wiggle- matching' 68.2% probability (95.4% probability) 25 years added for sapwood	Dendro- chronological felling date AD (Table 6; cf. Fig. 87)
1a	39A	834 ± 36	1166 to 1257	69	5	112	1330 to 1362 (1311 to 1371)	c. 1233 or c. 1236–41
	39B	747 ± 57	1222 to 1296	116	5	159		
	8	780 ± 55	1215 to 1285	62	10	117		
	13A	773 ± 52	1220 to 1284	42	5	82		
	13B	820 ± 52	1164 to 1274	104	5	144		
1b	31	850 ± 54	1070 to 1260	27	10	79	1245 to 1297 (1217 to 1327)	c. 1226 or c. 1232
	34	813 ± 52	1189 to 1277	24	10	93		
	36	880 ± 52	1044 to 1217	47	5	96		
	18	833 ± 83	1065 to 1279	26	−10	71		
2	38	890 ± 56	1042 to 1214	90	10	119	1298 to 1345 (1266 to 1366)	c. 1236–57
	42A	840 ± 49	1160 to 1262	116	10	185		
	42B	743 ± 51	1224 to 1296	104	10	173		
	43	915 ± 67	1035 to 1186	61	10	163		
	5	888 ± 65	1040 to 1216	65	10	93		
	6A	793 ± 51	1212 to 1282	72	10	101		
	6B	820 ± 56	1163 to 1276	72	10	101		
	14	940 ± 57	1027 to 1158	59	10	86		

Tree Number	Plank Number (RAD)	Radiocarbon age BP	Calibrated radiocarbon age range AD (68.2% probability)	Growth allowance i.e. rings to add to plank edge	Additional rings to correct to heartwood / sapwood boundary	Total correction to Ring 380	Felling date ranges from 'wiggle-matching' 68.2% probability (95.4% probability) 25 years added for sapwood	Dendro-chronological felling date AD (Table 6; cf. Fig. 87)
3	22A	924 ± 49	1036 to 1160	120	−2	155	1218 to 1307 (1179 to 1333)	c. 1236 or c. 1239
	22B	825 ± 51	1163 to 1272	31	−2	66		
5	47A	893 ± 56	1042 to 1212	63	5	137	1141 to 1268 (1131 to 1279)	c. 1214
	47B	1077 ± 61	895 to 1019	217	5	291		

Moving on to Groups 2 and 3 it is seen that, although the scatter on the values is unacceptably large for a set of radiocarbon results supposedly representing a single time event (i.e. the scatter is more probably due to real age differences in the plank edge dates), the two pooled means are hardly separable as belonging to separate groups. It is proposed, therefore, that the best value 'stand-alone', i.e. independent of dendrochronology, result has to be the pooled mean of the Groups 2 and 3 taken together. For this OxCal gives an all-in wiggle-match (68.2% probability range with offset to felling date) of AD 1307 to AD 1338. Strictly OxCal calls for 5 rejections from the set before an acceptable match is achieved (see also the CAL25 match in Fig. 94), but even making the rejections the range is constricted by less than 5 years at each end and does not therefore affect the general conclusion for the 'stand-alone' date. Of more importance is the consideration that because there was no sapwood identified on a significant number of planks, the arbitrary allowance of 10 years added to the nominal 25-year sapwood allowance may still leave the missing rings underestimated. In addition there is the unknown quantity of minimum seasoning time which has to be added after the felling date to the 'stand-alone' estimate to obtain the likely construction date.

Latest felling date from dendrochronological alignments

The agreement of the tree alignments with the combined radiocarbon results of the same trees is first considered. These are arranged for comparison in Table 13 in order of their closeness of fit. Trees 3 and 5 show best agreement, the agreement of the dendrochronological ages with the mid-point radiocarbon ranges being −20 and +24 years respectively. Trees 1b and 2 are within acceptable bounds (i.e. within the 95.4% probability range), but both differences are towards later dates than the dendrochronological placings. Tree 1a, however, shows no semblance of agreement, the dendrochronological placing being around 70 years earlier than the earliest limit of the 95.4% range and nearly 60 years earlier than the all-in probability range of the full suite of radiocarbon results (AD 1298 to AD 1341 at the 95.4% range).

Since the pooled mean for Tree 1a originates from five independent radiocarbon measurements (from three separate planks) the difference cannot be attributed to imprecision in the radiocarbon alone. The impact of this difference cannot be ignored since, on the radiocarbon placing, this tree becomes the very latest one of the series and, therefore, the most significant for the dating of the Round Table. Accordingly the pooled mean of Tree 1a (95.4% confidence, AD 1311 to 1371) becomes the first choice result for the range of the latest felling date. If the given dendrochronological alignments are maintained, however, the comparative felling date for Ring 380 is AD 1322 to 1350 using OxCal, but the program declares the agreement to be poor in 6 of the 21 dates entered. The scatter of the points and the obvious outliers are seen visually in Fig. 94 (CAL25 wiggle-match of the same data).

Date ranges for the Round Table from the radiocarbon results.

Felling dates of radial planks

The original objectives were to obtain two comparative radiocarbon-age results, one by ignoring any dendrochronological assignments regarding tree associations or alignments, called the 'stand-alone' date, and a second derived from the dendro-chronological alignments to Ring 380. From interpretation of the data a third possibility emerged, based on the dating of the individual trees. In this case only the relatively easier process of matching of planks which once belonged to the same tree is involved. From interpretation Tree 1a emerged as the most recent tree and has the highest recommendation for latest felling date and, therefore, the most relevant result for deciding the construction date of the table:

OxCal
(95.4% probability range)

Radiocarbon 'stand-alone' date   AD 1298 to AD 1341
(felling date for Groups 2 and 3 only)

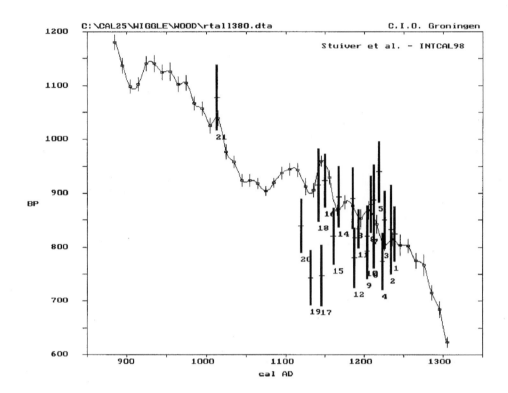

94 'Wiggle-matching' by CAL25 for all radial plank samples with dendrochronological alignments to Ring 380, the notional last ring of the last tree felled (see above, p. 214).

Samples identified sequentially as follows:
1, RAD 22B; 2, RAD 18; 3, RAD 31; 4, RAD 13A; 5, RAD 14; 6, RAD 34; 7, RAD 5; 8, RAD 36; 9, RAD 6A; 10, RAD 6B; 11, RAD 39A; 12, RAD 8; 13, RAD 38; 14, RAD 47A; 15, RAD 13B; 16, RAD 22A; 17, RAD 39B; 18, RAD 43; 19, RAD 42B; 20, RAD 42A; 21, RAD 47B.

229

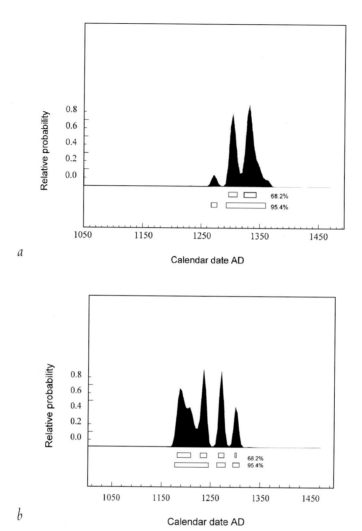

95 OxCal probability distributions for Tree 2 produced by 'wiggle-matching':
a using the radiocarbon determinations as measured by Harwell, *b* using the radiocarbon determinations adjusted by an offset of 0.5% in the older direction.

Comparison of the two distributions shows how an offset of 0.5% (~40 years)
causes the probability distribution to be extended by considerably more than this
in the older direction, due to the shape of the calibration curve for this period.
Felling dates for Tree 2 from these distributions are: with no offset, AD 1298 to
1345 (68.2% probability), with 0.5% offset, AD 1183 to 1303 (68.2%
probability).

Radiocarbon results aligned to Ring 380   AD 1298 to AD 1350

Felling date of Tree 1a   AD 1311 to AD 1371

In fact the three results are in relatively good agreement. The 'stand-alone' date is slightly earlier than the Tree 1a result but this is as expected since the planks were from a number of different trees, some earlier and some later than the latest tree felling date. The 'stand-alone' date, however, serves its original purpose of providing an overall check on the other procedures.

The date aligned to Ring 380 gives a fairly narrow range (52 years) but the agreement of the set of results was poor. OxCal gave 'poor' agreement indices for 5 of the 21 measurement results and poor overall agreement for the set.

The third result then becomes the recommended value. It is not possible to be more precise than this and, of course, seasoning time has to be added to the ranges. Although these results contradict the dendrochronological dating it is difficult to suppose they could be extended back to the earlier 13th century.

Felling dates for the rim and vertical timbers

Because the total estimated ring spans to the felling date for three of the vertical timber samples were essentially the same, the three radiocarbon ages were amalgamated before calibration (Table 8). The fourth sample (VRT 135) was not included as no growth allowance could be allocated. Its result, however, being earlier than that of the other three, is consistent with it having originated from an earlier portion of the (or a) tree. The recommended result for the vertical timbers is, therefore, the indicated mean calibrated range given in Table 8, plus the average rings (30 years) to correct to the estimated felling date, i.e. (at 95.4% probability range)

AD 1472 to AD 1660

The three radiocarbon results from the rim samples were also amalgamated before calibration and the date ranges are given in Table 8. To be consistent with the procedures used for radial samples in cases where no sapwood was evident, a nominal 10 rings of heartwood has been added, bringing the total correction to felling date to 35 years. This gives the recommended radiocarbon result for the rim of

AD 1436 to AD 1515.

Considering the ranges for these two different timbers, the rim appears to be slightly earlier than the verticals but given the overlap between the two ranges it is not possible to specify whether they do represent different phases in the history of the table.

Recalibration and Date Assessments, August 2000

The chapter described the objectives, programme design, procedures and results obtained from work carried out between 1976 and 1978. The dates were derived from the original measurement results using the most recent and now internationally accepted calibration data and methods of application. It is of some concern that the newly calibrated dates have tended to draw the radiocarbon results away from the dendrochronologically determined values with a movement of all the radiocarbon dates to more recent values. Of particular concern is the set of results for Tree 1a which gives the mean radiocarbon date for the set ~100 years more recent than its dendrochronological placing. A critical assessment of the radiocarbon methods used at the time is, therefore, considered.

A major feature of the radiocarbon dating on this project was the number of in-built validation tests of the method included at the time in the programme. These were:

1. *Extended tests to verify the stability of the ^{14}C measurement system throughout the two-year measurement period:*
   No evidence of steps or drifts in the instrument behaviour were identified in the repeated batch counting measurements

2. *Tests on the reproducibility of the dating of replicate samples, with processing carried out at separated times during the measurement period (Tables 10 and 11):*
   The measurement of sample pairs (radials and equal-age) provided the evidence that the full processing procedure was replicated within the estimated precision of measurement. Of the eleven pairs, only one seemed to be an outlier and the estimate of errors was, therefore, considered to be upheld.

3. *Tests on known-age ('equal-age') material as an overall check on the accuracy of the radiocarbon measurements (Table 9):*
   This was intended to identify any systematic error in the process, such as an error in the laboratory measurement standards, which would affect all the measurements similarly and could create a constant off-set in the final results.

Although the final comparison of the results of the six samples with their historical contexts shows good agreement in four (perhaps even five) cases, both the contexts and the calibrated date ranges are too wide to identify a small offset.

In general, therefore, the first two facets of the radiocarbon process tested appear to have been validated but the absolute 'accuracy' of the measurements could not be demonstrated completely satisfactorily. In the twenty years that have elapsed since the radiocarbon dating of the Round Table the radiocarbon community has made considerable efforts to improve both their precision and accuracy through regular intercomparison exercises[29] and as a result some laboratories identified minor offsets in their results. Harwell was not one of these and, indeed, it is thought unlikely as the laboratory was more than usually strict about the use of freshly made standards (NBS Oxalic Acid) on which the accuracy of the date results depend. For the sake of completeness and as an aid to those making an overall assessment of the table, the effect of a standardisation offset of approximately 0.5% offset (i.e. ~45 years) in the older direction has been considered, although even in 1977 this would have been considered a large offset (Fig. 95). Recalculation of the equal-age samples with this offset showed that good agreement would still be considered to have been achieved in four of the six samples and, because of the peculiarities of the calibration curve in this period, an extended range on a fifth (Winchester College, broken shutter near the Trusty Servant panel) allowed slightly better agreement than hitherto, but as evidence of an offset the situation was still inconclusive.

The same offset was applied to the results from the samples taken from the radial planks to consider its effect on the radiocarbon results for the individual tree felling dates, the 'stand-alone' date, and the dendrochronologically aligned date. The ranges obtained for the individual trees were significantly broader than before, again because of the peculiarity of the calibration curve in this period, in general extending more years in the earlier direction, as illustrated in Fig. 95, (a) with no offset and (b) with 0.5% offset. For Trees 1b, 2, 3 and 5 there was slightly better agreement between the radiocarbon and the dendrochronological placing, although the radiocarbon was now slightly skewed in a positive direction, i.e. earlier than the dendrochronological felling date, whereas before it was in a more pronounced negative direction, but the problem of Tree 1a remained, with the range mid-point and

---

[29] E. M. Scott, D. D. Harkness, and G. T. Cook, 'Interlaboratory Comparisons: Lessons Learned,' *Radiocarbon* 40(1)(1998), 331–40.

CAL25 minimum still lying some 60 to 70 years later than the dendrochronological placing. In order to gain alignment of Tree 1a with the dendrochronological placing an incredibly large offset of nearly 2% would be required and, in that case, the radiocarbon dates for all the other trees would then no longer agree with the dendrochronological placings.

In conclusion it is felt that, judging from the results of the felling dates of the individual trees, there is no sound evidence to suppose that there was any offset on the Harwell results at the time of this dating programme and the main conclusion for a 14th-century felling date based on the radiocarbon investigation is therefore upheld.

XXI Cross-sections of the microsamples of paint removed from the Round Table before cleaning and restoration in 1978

a and *b* are from a white petal of the rose. In *b*, all the original paint (3) and the chalk ground (2) have flaked away, so that the Cave repaint (4) lies directly on the wood (1). In *a*, the Cave repaint (4) lies on original paint (3). 1 oak, 2 chalk and size, 3 original white lead, 4 later white lead, 5 varnish.

c is from the detached fragment (compare, Pl. XXII*e*), free of overpaint. 1 oak, 2 chalk and size, 3 white lead, 4 charcoal black paint detail.

d is from an intersection of a red radial line and a black circumferential line. 1 oak, 2 chalk and size, 3 minium, 4 black, 5 orpiment plus realgar, 6 black. 3 and 4 are original, 5 and 6 are by Cave.

e is from the edge of the ermine robe. The original layer of white lead, with coarse particles of a pigment now faded, developed a crack which the Cave paint has penetrated. This effect is also to be seen in the radiographs where the intrusions are X-ray opaque. 1 oak, 2 chalk and size, 3 original white lead, 4 unknown, 5 orpiment and realgar repaint.

f is from the sword. The white is in two layers, the lower one having a blue tinge. Surface grime is visible between 3 and 4. 1 oak, 2 chalk and size, 3 original red minium, 4 retouching in white which extends marginally to the red.

Some of the sections are by chance in a transverse direction with respect to the planks, e.g. *c* and *f*, and this shows the pores typical of oak. The division in the ground chalk and size layer is due to a greater proportion of size in the upper layer. Assuming the table was horizontal when the ground was applied, as is the normal practice, the partial segregation could happen during drying. Otherwise it means that two separate coats were applied.

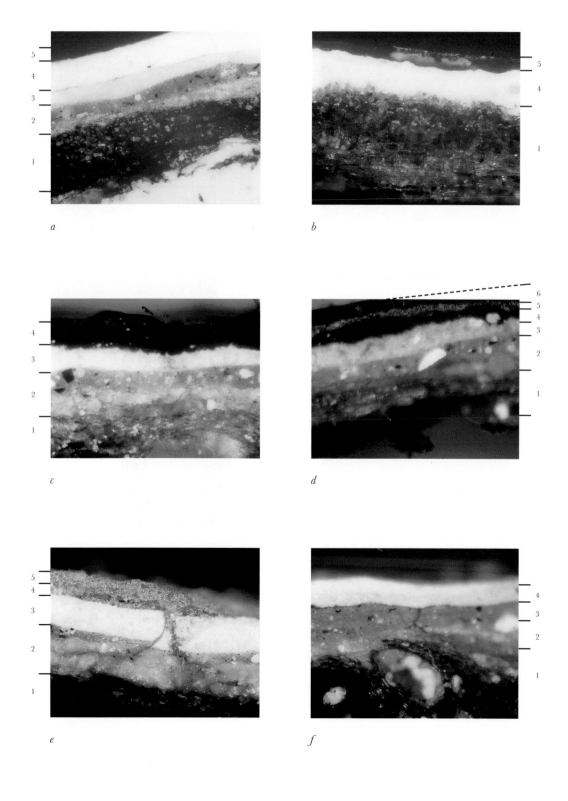

a

b

c

d

e

XXII Original paintwork of the Round Table revealed behind a tin-plate attached in 1789 (*a–d*), and preserved on a detached fragment (*e*):

   a tin-plate patch in position over the canopy to left of the king's head

   b the tin-plate patch prised off and folded down to reveal the original paintwork of the canopy. Compare with the blurred paintwork of 1789 in *a*

   c the original paintwork of the canopy: enlarged detail of *b*

   d the original paintwork of the canopy: enlarged detail of *b* and *c*, showing a crocket on the upper edge of the canopy

   e the detached fragment of Plank 51, originally filling the lower part of the hole partly visible on *b*. The diagonal lines on the fragment form part of the cross-hatching visible on *b*; the horizontal blue band at the top of the fragment corresponds with the horizontal line across the middle of the canopy seen on *b*. Cf. Plate XXIC and Figs. 105-6

XXIII The Round Table (detail): the canopied figure
of King Arthur

XXIV The Round Table (detail): the head of King Arthur

XXV The Round Table (detail): the rose and central inscription

XXVI Henry VIII and the Knights of the Garter, *c.* 1534

XXVII The meeting of Henry VIII and the Emperor Maximilian I at Thérouanne, 1513, artist unknown (detail)

XXVIII Charles V and Henry VIII, double portrait commemorating the signing of a treaty, either at Windsor on 16 June or at Waltham on 2 July 1522, artist unknown

The Painting

At the same time as the back of the table was revealing its structural history and being sampled for tree-ring and radiocarbon dating, the front was also being examined. Technological study of the painting was in the hands of Professor Stephen Rees Jones of the Courtauld Institute for the History of Art of the University of London (Chapter 7) whose task involved examination of the layers of paint, their composition, application, and condition. The methods used were cleaning tests, the removal of tiny samples for microscopic examination, and the X-raying of the entire painted surface of 254 square feet in a series of 224 films of the size used for chest X-rays. The radiography began on the afternoon of the lowering, with the films processed in the mobile darkroom provided by the contractors, Portable X-rays Ltd. The first results were available almost instantly (Plate XX). They provided perhaps the biggest surprise of the whole investigation: the present painting, clearly of Tudor date as shown by the red and white rose, is the only design ever to have been painted on the table. Since the table was already hanging in the hall by 1461–3, and possibly long before (Chapter 11), we had assumed that there was an earlier painting of a different design below the present picture. The X-rays showed otherwise. The only painting on the table is the one we see today through the veil of its repainting to the same design in 1789. The results of the radiography thus posed a problem for which there is still no certain explanation (Chapter 11).

The world knows the Round Table by its painted face. A design of dense content and great complexity, it yet presents a direct and compelling image, instantly recognizable. There are three principal components to examine, the wheel-like layout, the inscriptions, and the figure of the king in his canopy set above the central rose. The repainting of 1789 has blurred and muddied, so that everywhere allowance must be made for the distortions of the late eighteenth-century way of seeing (see below, pp. 319–22).

The wheel-like image with its expanding rays – what *Country Life* once disrespectfully called 'the world's largest dartsboard' – may be derived from the idea of the Wheel of Fortune which John Fleming has discussed in Chapter 1. There was in fact a Wheel of Fortune painted above the dais at the west end of the Great Hall in 1235–6 (see above,

p. 74). If this was still to be seen in the early sixteenth century, it may possibly have influenced the present design. Or the influence may have been less direct (Chapter 11).

The inscriptions identify the table. Their content and the precise form of the names is thus of fundamental importance. They should tell us the source or sources used by the artist – or perhaps more precisely, by the author – of the design. The form of the letters may indicate a broad date for the painting and the relationship of the inscriptions to comparable work elsewhere. But the problems are compounded by the overpainting of 1789. To what extent are the visible inscriptions accurate copies of the originals? In Chapter 8, Sally Badham, who has done much in recent years to define regional 'schools' in the craft of medieval monumental brasses, analyses the 'black-letter' (*textura*) script and provides a definitive reading of the inscriptions which can be seen today, while I examine the evidence we have for what was there before the repainting of 1789, as recorded in copies made by visitors and in the information provided by the X-rays described in Chapter 7. In fact the differences are slight. This allows me to go on to examine the relationship of the names on the table to lists of Arthurian names in Malory's *Morte Darthur* and other fifteenth- and early sixteenth-century sources. In the main this confirms John Fleming's view in Chapter 1 that the probable origins of the inscriptions lie in a generalized post-Malory Arthurianism typical of the sixteenth century but it provides some fresh insights into the sources and mind of the compiler of the inscriptions, and a perhaps unexpected hint of the date of the painting.

The figure of Arthur rules over the table. No trace here of that first among equals which is embodied in the idea of the Round Table. The peculiar significance of this representation of the king emerges from the detailed analysis which Dr Pamela Tudor-Craig (Lady Wedgwood) brings to the portrait and to each attribute of the figure, the canopy above, and the rose below, in the context of early Tudor iconography. The probable date of the painting is established by comparisons between each feature and datable parallels in manuscript paintings and sculpture, with some help from the detailed chronology of Henry VIII's beard. Finally, Dr Tudor-Craig, who includes the iconography of medieval kingship among her special fields of study, examines the political and dynastic circumstances – 'a context of some richness' – surrounding the creation of the painting.

96 Infra-red photograph of the Round Table.

97 The Round Table gridded for radiography, 27 August 1976.

7

Investigation of the painting

Preliminary visual inspection of the front of the Round Table before it was lowered from the west wall of the Great Hall showed immediately that the surface was extensively overpainted. It could be seen for example that no attempt had been made in 1789 by the presumed restorers, William Cave and his son William junior, to confine the repaint to actual areas of lost or damaged paint, or even to apply a filling to produce an even surface for the new paint. The surface was virtually a continuous film of repaint beneath a coat of varnish and a deposit of surface grime. It can be inferred that the need for this restoration arose, as is commonly the case with panel paintings, through loss of adhesion between the wood and the ground layer of the painting, and from the effect of many cycles of changing humidity on the dimensions of the wood. In several places, particularly in the upper sector carrying the image of the king, some rather crude repairs had been carried out before the repainting by nailing sheets of metal (tin-plate) over the gaps in the wood caused by the action of damp and rot, by the opening of joints between planks, and by missile fire (see above, Chapter 4).

Once the table had been taken down from the wall it was possible to investigate it in depth, by taking infra-red photographs and radiographs and by removing small samples of the paint for examination under the microscope. Infra-red photography (Figs. 96, 98) showed the paint surface more clearly through the grime and deteriorated varnish than it then appeared to the naked eye. The red letters and lines could not be seen in the photographs, however, since they have the same reflectance as the white background on which they are painted, and are thus indistinguishable from it.

As a subject for radiography, the Round Table has much in common with altar-pieces and other paintings on wood supports, but there were special problems due to its size and to its structure, which includes six vertical reinforcing timbers, each about four inches thick. Means had to be found to ensure that the beam from

98 The Round Table: infra-red photograph of King Arthur.

99 The Round Table: radiograph of King Arthur.

100 The Round Table: the head of King Arthur. Photograph taken in 1976 before conservation, cf. Fig. 98.

101 The Round Table: radiograph of the head of King Arthur.

the X-ray source, mounted behind the vertically held table, was precisely directed at the X-ray film placed in contact with the painted side for each of the many exposures required to cover the entire area of the table. The technicians from Portable X-rays Ltd. who carried out the radiography achieved this by using two identical metal frames which formed squares large enough to enclose the table's circle. To these were tied horizontal and vertical strings which formed reference grids (Fig. 97). With the two grids mounted and aligned on either side of the table, one to position the X-ray source and the other the film, 224 exposures were made covering the entire table. The film size was 17 x 14 inches, the focus film distance 48 inches, and the exposure 110 seconds, 50mA at 60kV. The radiographs gave a clear image of the structure and the paint layers, except where they were obscured by the thick supporting timbers at the back of the table and the metal sheets nailed to the front surface. The films covering the king are reproduced in Fig. 99, the head in Fig. 101, and some of the lettering in Fig. 102.

The radiographs and other investigations showed, contrary to expectation, that the composition now visible is the only one ever to have been painted on the planks of the table. Moreover, only one earlier version lay behind the repainting of 1789. Where small areas of the overpaint were removed with solvent, this original was found to have been more finely and precisely painted than its successor. This same superiority of technique could also be seen in the area behind the tin-plate patch which was carefully prised off to reveal the original layer of paint (Plate XXII; cf. Fig. 107). It was not possible to ascertain from these investigations whether errors were made in repainting the names of the knights and the central inscription in 1789 (but see Chapter 8). The Caves' method was to repaint the white background approximately up to the edge of the lettering and the boundary lines, and then to repaint the letters in black or red overlapping the new white ground. The X-ray image is thus simply that of the roughly applied white paint. Since the red lines and letters are in minium (red lead), they are hardly distinguishable in the radiographs from the white lead background.

The radiographs also show hidden details of the timber construction, such as wooden dowels, together with an assortment of iron nails and screws (Figs. 103, 104). Most of these obviously pertain to the various conservation measures of the past, but there is a series of nails driven in radially from the edge along the circumference which serve no such purpose. They often occur in groups of two or three at approximately five- to six-inch intervals and are about an inch long. As they are now headless and flush with the edge and have no function, it can only be assumed that they are the remains of headed nails which once secured a valance or some other cloth to the table-edge. A final observation is that there is damage to the left of the king's mouth made when the table was used as a target.

102 The Round Table: radiograph of the last four letters of the name 'plomyd(e?)'.

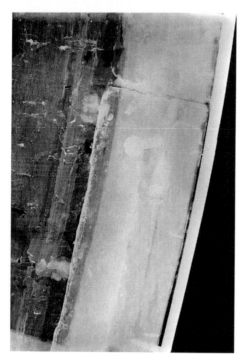

103 The rim of the Round Table, radiographs seen from the front: *a*, at the junction of rim 127 (left) and 126 on plank 28; *b*, on rim 126 at the junction of planks 23 (left) and 22 (cf. Fig. 104).

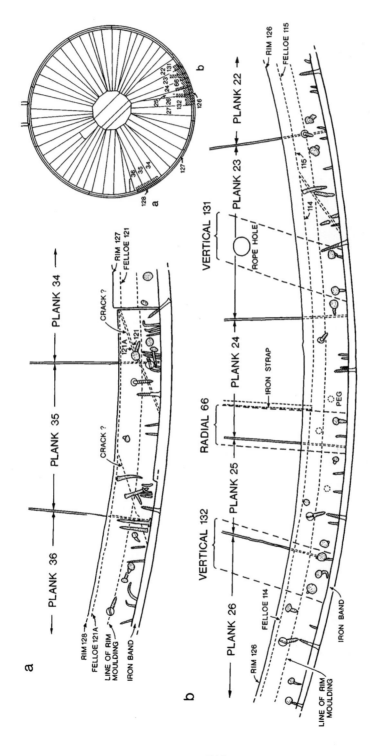

104 The rim of the Round Table, seen from the front: nails, screws, and other ironwork revealed by radiography in two sample sections of the rim.

249

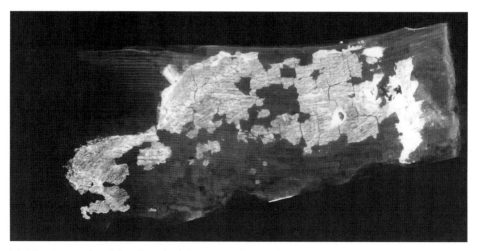

105 Radiograph of the detached fragment from Plank 51.

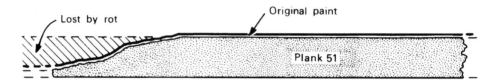

106 Section of the detached fragment from Plank 51.

107 Original paintwork of the Round Table revealed behind a tin-plate attached in 1789: *a*, the tin-plate in position; *b*, the tin-plate prised off to reveal the original paintwork of the canopy above the king (cf. Plate XXII).

The paint samples were embedded in blocks of synthetic resin and cut and polished to provide cross-sections through the paint layers for examination under 100 x magnification. A photomicrograph of a cross-section, such as those shown in Plate XXI, shows the sequence of layers from the wood up through the ground, the original paint, the Cave repaint, and the final varnish. Generally, the radiographs and cross-sections threw light on the painting technique, the condition, and some of the questions posed by the historians. These preliminary conclusions were fully supported when later tests were made by removing the overpaint with solvents in a small area and by prising off one of the metal repair patches (Fig. 107) in the course of the conservation operations described below. A loose fragment from one of the planks of the table, about 6½ inches long, was found behind one of the tin-plate sheets (Plates XXI*c*, XXII*e*). It had never been repainted. The radiograph (Fig. 105) and the cross-section drawing (Fig. 106) of this fragment provide visual evidence that the first painting of the table took place after the outer edge in this area had been severely affected by wood rot (see Chapters 4 and 11). The radiograph also provides an image for comparison with the repainted state of the table.

Thus it became clear that the wood had been prepared for painting in a way which was universal for panels in the sixteenth century and earlier, with a ground composed of chalk and animal glue. In the case of the table this ground is rather rich in glue medium and has consequently dried with the excess forming a skin containing little chalk (Plate XXI*a* and *c*). The pattern of small cracks ('craquelure') present over the entire surface is mainly due to the ageing of this glue medium. Incidentally, where the repaint contains a pigment opaque to X-rays the film shows how the later paint has filled the cracks, thus confirming the existence of the original layer.

On the ground there is one layer, or sometimes two, of original paint. The second layer may be a superimposed detail such as, for example, one of the red lines on a green background. The technique used in painting the king's red robe is simple, the modelling being achieved with an under-layer of creamy white followed by red of varying thickness and a transparent red glaze. No trace was found of metal leaf – of tin as a base for the sword, or gold for the jewellery and the crown – although the possibility cannot be completely ruled out on the basis of a few micro-samples. The pigments are commonplace and do not help with the dating, but it can be said that the quality of the paint and the radiographic evidence of the way it has been applied are found in English portraits from around 1500. To this conclusion must be added, however, that even in its pristine state the table was not in the same class as, say, a portrait by a court painter or a finely worked altar-piece. The absence of gold or tin leaf, while not in itself discriminatory, is a point to consider. The unadulterated painting to be seen on the detached fragment and where the

108 Radiograph positive of the right-hand end of rim 122 (as seen from the front), showing nails driven in from the edge of the table and textile remains trapped behind the rim.

metal plate was removed is freely done and lacks high precision. Panels in fine works have an even prepared surface and the ground is of even thickness: in the table the ground at its thickest is over four times its thinnest. This is presumably due to the table having served another purpose before becoming a support for the painting and to the damage by decay, facts which may also account for the many atypical details in the radiographs. It is worth noting however that the wood grain seen in the radiographs is mostly that of the best-quality radial-cut oak.

Conservation

Although the materials and technique used on the table — oak support, chalk and size ground, paint — are what is typically found in North European paintings, its dimensions and condition presented the conservator with exceptional problems. At the outset it was decided that the removal of previous restoration work to reveal the original paint was not feasible. Not only was the extent and condition of the surviving original work unknown at that stage; the scale of the restoration was a problem. It would be a very lengthy process to undertake complete restoration of the whole painted surface, an area of some 254 square feet (22 m²). There was also the problem posed by the tin-plate sheets, a curious restoration measure from 1789. What did they hide and should they be removed? However, the weak adhesion between the wood and the ground layer which had led to loss of paint in the past was still causing further flaking and needed treatment. Thus it was decided to consolidate, clean and restore the visible painting of 1789 rather than to attempt a complete restoration of the Tudor original beneath.

The task was undertaken by Pauline Plummer and her assistants, who proceeded as follows. The first step was to treat the loose paint using a wax/resin consolidant; each flake was gently pressed back into position with a hot spatula. With the paint surface secure the dust and debris could be removed from the back of the table and areas of decayed wood strengthened with a proprietary hardener and missing areas replaced with filling compound or pieces of wood cut to shape. The painted surface was solvent cleaned to remove the layers of discoloured varnish. After an exploratory attempt to remove one of the metal repair patches, it was decided to leave them in place, with their paint which was part of the 1789 restoration. Corrosion losses to the tin-plate sheets were made up with glass fibre and epoxy resin. After the various repairs and filling had been in-painted, the whole was sprayed with modern synthetic resin picture varnish.

Enough of the Tudor painting does probably survive beneath the repainting and tin-plate of 1789 to make it feasible one day to remove the repainting and reveal the original and much finer work. The problem of scale remains. It is a choice for some future generation to make.

8

Inscriptions in the Painting

T he painted inscriptions on the Round Table identify it and name the king and twenty-four of the men who were by tradition thought to have been seated round it. The inscriptions fall into three groups: first, the words around the Tudor Rose in the centre, which identify the table; second, the inscription on the royal portrait, identifying the king; and third, around the perimeter of the table, the names of the twenty-four knights, each of which is treated as a separate inscription. The inscriptions as currently painted read as follows, with omitted letters from abbreviated words in square brackets and incorrect or indistinct letters in parentheses:

Thys is the rownde table of kyng Arthur w[ith] xxiiii of hys namyde kny3ttes

kyng arthur

1. *S[ir] galahallt*
2. *S[ir] launcelot deulake*
3. *S[ir] gauen*
4. *S[ir] p[er]cyvale*
5. *S[ir] lyonell*
6. *S[ir] trystram delyens*
7. *S[ir] garethe*
8. *S[ir] bedwere*
9. *S[ir] blubrys*
10. *S[ir] lacotemale tayle*
11. *S[ir] lucane*
12. *S[ir] plomyd(e?)*

13. *S[ir] lamorak*
14. *S[ir] bor(s) de ganys*
15. *S[ir] Safer*
16. *S[ir] pelleus*
17. *S[ir] kay*
18. *S[ir] Ectorde mary(s)*
19. *S[ir] dagonet*
20. *S[ir] degore*
21. *S[ir] brumear*
22. *S[ir] lybyus dyscony[us]*
23. *S[ir] Alynore*
24. *S[ir] mordrede*

The inscriptions include some of the contractions and abbreviations in everyday use in writing until the late seventeenth century. Throughout the perimeter inscriptions the word 'Sir' is denoted by a majuscule 'S' crossed by a diagonal stroke, the accepted way of indicating 'Sir'. The accepted abbreviation for 'per' was 'p' with a short horizontal bar across the descender; the painter employed this convention in the name 'percyvale'. He also used 'w' with a superscript 't' to indicate the word 'with' in the central inscription and an abbreviation resembling the Arabic figure 9 to indicate 'us' in 'dysconyus' in the perimeter inscriptions.

Although the original painting can be dated with some probability to the latter part of 1516 (see below, Chapters 9 and 12), the table was repainted in 1789. An analysis of antiquarian copies of the inscription made in the seventeenth and eighteenth centuries demonstrates that the 1789 repainting was a quite faithful rendering (see below, pp. 272–3). Most of the letter shapes can, therefore, be trusted, and, indeed, can be paralleled in scripts on other objects. However, some errors evidently crept in on the repainting, possibly due to the workman being unfamiliar with the style of lettering and the forms of contraction and embellishment employed. Although where the Tudor painting can still be seen it is bright and would have provided a clear guide for the 1789 craftsman, the table was damaged and part of the paint surface lost by 1789. In part this damage was caused by missile entry holes made when the table was shot at by parliamentary troops in 1642, but there may well also have been flaking due to damp and rot in the upper right quadrant of the table. Where the original paint was lost, the workman would have had to reconstruct the letter forms to the best of his ability. He seems to have managed this remarkably well, but ten sections of the inscriptions are of doubtful accuracy:

a   In the name 'gauen' the letter 'g' straddles a gap between two planks of wood; when it was repainted the bottom part of the letter was imperfectly joined up (compare 'galahallt' and 'gauen' in Fig. 109).

b   In the name 'percyvale' the later workman has joined the descender of the letter 'y' to the preceding letter 'c'. He was probably confused by the omission of the 'er' and by the gap between the two planks of wood which comes at the extreme left-hand edge of the 'y' (see Fig. 110). That the error was made in 1789 is borne out by an infra-red photograph showing the alteration (see Fig. 96).

c   In the name 'garethe' the letters are imperfectly aligned horizontally and the upper part of the 't' is incomplete. These oddities appear to be due to missile damage; there is a missile entry hole where the top of the 't' would have been (see Fig. 111).

d   The second letter 'a' in the name 'lacotemale tayle' lacks the double horizontal bar found on other minuscule letter 'a's; again this is probably because the letter straddles two planks of wood which have shrunk apart.

e   In the name 'lucane' the second horizontal bar of the 'a' is missing, but there is no obvious explanation of why this happened.

109 Inscriptions: 'S[ir] gauen' and 'S[ir] galahallt'.

110 Inscription: 'S[ir] p[er]cyvale'.

111 Inscription: 'S[ir] garethe'.

112 Inscription: 'S[ir] bor(s) de ganys', showing problem caused by rope hole

113 Inscriptions: 'S[ir] Safer' and 'S[ir] pelleus'.

114 Inscription: 'S[ir] Ector de mary(s)', showing tin-plate patch at '...ys' of 'mary(s)'.

116 Central inscription: 'T' of 'Thys', suggested original form.

115 Central inscription: 'Thys' showing tin-plate patch at 'T'.

f   The last letter of 'plomyde' is not in its original form. Alone of all the perimeter inscriptions, 'plomyde' crosses the red line dividing each of the knights' names from the next. Moreover, the form of the terminal letter is unlike any of the other letter forms shown on the table. The most likely explanation is that originally the word ended with a composite 'de' like that of 'mordrede', or possibly a composite 'de' followed by an 's' to give 'plomydes'. The 'd' is against a plank edge; the separation of the planks may have caused part of the paint to flake off so that by 1789 only the upward curl of the 'e' remained distinct (Fig, 102).

g   In the name 'bors de ganys' the final letter of 'bors' now appears as an 'n', but with one too few scallops on the top edge. Clearly it was originally a terminal 's' of the type ending 'ganys' – the outlines at the top and bottom of the letters compare closely. The error evidently arose because of the rope-hole over the position of the upward curl of the 's' left when the table was hoisted into position after its initial painting in 1516. This hole was subsequently plugged with a wood stopper (see Fig. 112 and above, p. 131) but presumably the original artist did not stay on to make good such details, thus leaving the 1789 painter insufficient evidence of the original form.

h   The letters of the name 'Safer' appear to have been thickened, and the general appearance of the word is untidy and slightly blurred (compare 'Safer' and 'pelleus' in Fig. 113). There is no obvious explanation of this. The shapes of the individual letters, however, appear reliable.

i   In the name 'Ectorde marys' the terminal 's' has once again caused difficulty and its upper part is misformed. The explanation for this is that the right-hand ascender of the 'y' and virtually all of the 's' are painted on tin-plate nailed over especially badly damaged areas in 1789 (see Fig. 114).

j   The 'T' of 'Thys' in the inscription round the central Tudor Rose stands out as being entirely unlike the other letter forms and cannot be paralleled in contemporary inscriptions on other objects. However, there was a heavy fall of missiles in this area and the left-hand half of the letter is again painted on tin-plate (see Fig. 115). Consequently the 1789 painter had to use considerable imagination in reconstructing the letter. It is suggested that originally the 'T' was of the form shown in Fig. 116, a Lombardic-derived form still in common usage in the early sixteenth century.

Only three colours of paint are used for the inscriptions. The words 'kyng arthur' on the royal portrait are all in gold. For the remainder of the inscriptions black is used, except for the initial letter of each inscription, which is painted red.

The diamond-shaped stops between the words of the inscription around the Tudor Rose and the flourish at the end are also in red.

The style of the lettering employed is the formal display script traditionally known as black-letter but more properly termed *textura*, in which the letter forms are reduced as far as possible into straight lines, or 'minims'. *Textura* was commonly used from the mid fourteenth century until well into the sixteenth century. It was not an everyday business hand, and is not therefore normally found in documents, other than perhaps for the opening words, particularly of charters and chancery rolls.[1] It was, however, the standard lettering style in this period for manuscript books and for inscriptions on monuments, paintings, screens, metalwork, windows, seals, and even embroidery.

The development of *textura* falls into three phases. In the fourteenth century the letters are fairly rounded and well spaced, so that each is separated from the next, giving a script that is comparatively easy to read. By contrast, fifteenth-century *textura*, particularly that of the middle of the century, is much more angular and compressed; the letters, and even the words, are jammed closely together and the letters are formed as regularly as possible, without the variations of form necessary to distinguish one from another. The minims are frequently joined at both apex and base, irrespective of the letter form depicted. The practice of placing a dot (or, more usually, a tiny reversed S-shaped squiggle) over the letter 'i' dates from this time; otherwise words such as 'minimum', composed entirely of minims, without ascenders and descenders, would have been impossible to decipher. It was also common to use the letter 'y' rather than 'i', which helps legibility, although again a dot or reversed S-shaped squiggle was frequently placed over the 'y'. The overall impression given is usually one of extreme simplicity. Majuscule letters appear only sporadically – even names frequently begin with what is apparently a minuscule letter – but, where they are used, they are sometimes highly decorated, giving welcome relief from the austerity of the minuscule letters. Legibility improves once more by the early sixteenth century, as the letters become more widely spaced, incorporate curves and loops as well as straight lines, and are often more ornamented. This may have been the result of influence from the Netherlands, where, at least on incised slabs, a clearer, rounded, and more decorative form of *textura* had been employed since the second half of the fifteenth century.[2]

This chronology of *textura* script is generalised and the periods covered by the three phases of development very approximate. Fashions of lettering do not change

[1] Pamela Tudor-Craig (Lady Wedgwood), *Richard III*, National Portrait Gallery publication 132 (London, 1973), pls. 20, 22, 23. For *textura* generally, see S. Morrison, *'Black-letter' Text* (Cambridge, 1942), and N. Gray, *A History of Lettering* (Oxford, 1986), especially pp. 109–21.

[2] F. A. Greenhill, *Incised Effigial Slabs* (London, 1976), ii, pls. 74b, 76a, 83b, 84b.

117 The letter forms used in the Round Table inscriptions. Letters painted in red are hatched

118 The range and common forms of the letter 'A' in *textura* inscriptions.

as quickly, or as completely, as those of costume and it is not uncommon for a style of lettering to continue in use long after new forms have developed. Thus, Lombardic lettering, the display script which preceded *textura*, was commonly used by founders for inscriptions on bells well into the sixteenth century and even makes an occasional appearance in the place of majuscule letters on the inscriptions of sixteenth-century windows, monumental brasses, and incised slabs.[3] Individual workshops might well have adopted a style which appears old-fashioned in comparison with others of the same date, but it should not be assumed that they were deliberately aiming at an archaic effect. This adds to the difficulty of attempting any real chronology of *textura* inscriptions. Regional variants of lettering style can sometimes be identified, perhaps indicating a connection between workmen employed in apparently separate crafts. For example, the distinctive exaggeratedly cusped outlines of the lettering of monumental brasses from the Yorkshire 2 workshop, in operation between *c.*1435 and the 1470s, also appear on contemporary York glass, such as the Prick of Conscience window in All Saints, North Street, York, although there is little likeness in individual letter forms.[4] An even closer connection can be made between the 'double image' majuscule letters of monumental brasses from the Norwich 3 workshop, spanning the period *c.*1485–1505; locally painted glass, like the East Harling east window; and ecclesiastical woodwork, such as the pulpit at Horsham St Faith.[5] Where such links can be found, more precise dating may be possible, but they are as yet few and far between. Our knowledge of *textura* script is still at an elementary stage, and most inscriptions cannot be dated with any precision.

It is against this background that the lettering style of the Round Table must be viewed (see Fig. 117 for drawings of all the individual letter forms). It is a very elegant and well-executed form of *textura* termed *texturalis quadrata* with a strongly

---

[3] J. L'Estrange, *The Church Bells of Norfolk* (Norwich, 1874), *passim*; J. J. Raven, *The Church Bells of Suffolk* (London, 1890), *passim*; H. Read, J. Baker, and A. Lammer, *English Stained Glass* (London, 1960), pls. 63, 102; S. Badham, 'The Suffolk School of Brasses', *Transactions of the Monumental Brass Society* 13 (1980), 52, and pl. IVb; M. Norris, *Monumental Brasses: The Craft* (London and Boston, 1978), pl. 32; F. A. Greenhill, *Monumental Incised Slabs in the County of Lincoln* (Newport Pagnell, 1986), pls. 44, 45, 47, 48, 52.

[4] S. Badham, J. Blair, and R. Emmerson, *Specimens of Lettering from English Monumental Brasses* (London, 1976), figs. 252–70; S. Crewe, *Stained Glass in England 1180–1540* (London, 1987), pl. 33.

[5] R. Greenwood and M. Norris, *The Brasses of Norfolk Churches* (Norwich, 1976), p. 27; S. Badham, 'London Standardisation and Provincial Idiosyncrasy: the Organisation and Working Practices of Brass Engraving Workshops in England in the pre-Reformation Period', *Journal of the Church Monuments Society*, 5 (1990), 3–25; S. Badham, 'The Contribution of Epigraphy to the Typological Classification of Medieval English Brasses and Incised Slabs', in J. Higgitt, K. Forsyth and D. Parsons (ed.), *Roman, Runic and Ogham Medieval Inscriptions in the Insular World and on the Continent*, forthcoming.

vertical emphasis, the letters being exceptionally tall in relation to their width. The letters are packed tightly together, with the minims joined at apex and base. In the inscriptions around the perimeter of the table, even individual words are run together so that names appear to read 'launcelot deulake', 'trystram delyens' and 'Ectorde marys'. This type of *textura* is firmly in the fifteenth-century tradition, although, as explained above, the unconscious use of 'old' forms is not unusual. The *textura* script on the early sixteenth-century panel paintings at Chichester, although by no means identical, is also far from the forefront of fashion. Moreover, a similar compressed style, albeit with more decorative touches, can be seen on a group of monumental brasses made in Bury St Edmunds in the 1530s and 1540s.[6]

The main strokes of all the minuscule letter forms are emphatically angular. The painter has, for example, chosen the more angular form of 'a' in common usage at this time, rather than the type with a curved 'fish-head' top.[7] Such curved lines as were unavoidable are clearly subordinate to the strict angularity of the main strokes. The tail of the 'y' is unnaturally small in relation to the rest of the letter and is tucked neatly beneath. In only two cases is there any significant variation in the shape of different examples of the same letter. Two forms of 'r' can be seen in the inscriptions, a simpler form being used in 'garethe', 'blubrys', and 'bors' in the perimeter inscriptions and 'arthur' in the gold-painted inscription for the king's name. Three variants of the 's' are employed. The long form is used in the middle of words, as in 'trystram' and 'dyscony[us]'. The terminal 's' is normally of the closed form, e.g. on 'blubrys', but a wider, open form is used for 'lyens'. It is, however, common to find this variety of forms of 's' in a single inscription. One letter stands out from the rest, both for its relative unfamiliarity and its lack of angularity: the Middle English letter yogh (see Fig. 117), which is employed in the word 'knyʒttes'.

The decorative flourishes of the minuscule letters are exceptionally restrained and are not allowed to conflict with the overall impression of angularity and vertical emphasis. The ascenders of the 'b', 'h', 'k', 'l', and 't' are bifurcated at the top, but the points do not develop into a pair of outward-facing curls as is common on many inscriptions. The 'b' is frequently followed by a stroke rather like an apostrophe; sometimes this is joined to the right-hand point of the bifurcated ascender. The ascender of the 'l' occasionally also has a very short horizontal bar, as in 'table' and the double 'll' of 'lyonell'. The 'e' usually has a curl on the minor diagonal stroke and, where it is the terminal letter, two curls, but they are almost always small and tight. The same is true of the curls of the 'x' and the

---

[6] Badham, Blair, and Emmerson, *Specimens*, figs. 310–28.
[7] Ibid., fig. 278.

terminal 's'. All examples of the letter 'h' and the terminal 'n' of 'gauen' have a curved grace stroke continuing below the line of script; and all the examples of the 'a' have a second thin line below the main diagonal bar. The cross-stroke of the 'f' and 't' is embellished throughout by a pair of lines descending from it, often curved outwards at their base.

This restraint in the forms of the minuscule letters is in marked contrast to some of the majuscule letters. The latter appear far less frequently than the content of the inscriptions would allow, with most proper names beginning with a minuscule letter. The only uniformity in the use of the majuscule letters is that initial letters of inscriptions painted in red are always of the majuscule form; this gives us a majuscule form of 's' and 't'. Otherwise majuscule letters are used only for 'Arthur' in the central inscription, and for 'Safer', 'Ector', and 'Alynore' in the perimeter inscriptions; although the majuscule forms of 'A' and 'T' are used elsewhere in the inscriptions, the initial letters of 'arthur' on the royal portrait and 'trystram' on the perimeter inscriptions are in the minuscule forms.

The majuscule letters give more scope for comparison with lettering on other media. The letters painted in red are relatively plain forms. The 'S' of 'Sir', repeated twenty-four times round the perimeter of the table, is a simple rounded form in common use in the fifteenth and sixteenth centuries, which looks more modern than the remainder of the script but which was essentially based on the outdated Lombardic alphabet.[8] The 'T' of 'This', as reconstructed in Fig. 116, is another form derived from the Lombardic alphabet still in use in the sixteenth century.[9] The central curl has a foliated terminal, probably an oak-leaf, a device much in vogue on monumental brasses and in manuscripts around 1400 and seen in glass later in the fifteenth century, but not unknown in the sixteenth century.[10] Thus, for example, on the Chichester panel paintings the inscription on the scroll issuing from St Wilfrid's mouth begins with a majuscule letter with a foliated terminal.

The black-painted majuscule letters are far more elaborate and appear somewhat incongruous in comparison with the austerity of the remainder of the script. The 'S' of 'Safer' is of the same basic shape as the red 'S' of 'Sir', but is decorated with strap-work, an embellishment of Franco-Flemish origin which is a feature of the decoration of initial letters in important English legal documents from about 1430

[8] Ibid., fig. 31; compare Norris, *Monumental Brasses: The Craft*, pls. 32, 214; M. Norris, *Monumental Brasses: The Memorials* (London, 1978), figs. 179, 186, 238.

[9] Badham, Blair, and Emmerson, *Specimens*, fig. 32; compare Norris, *Monumental Brasses: The Craft*, pls. 32, 35; Norris, *Monumental Brasses: The Memorials*, fig. 300.

[10] S. Badham, *Brasses from the North East* (London, 1979), p. 20; Crewe, *Stained Glass*, pl. 46.

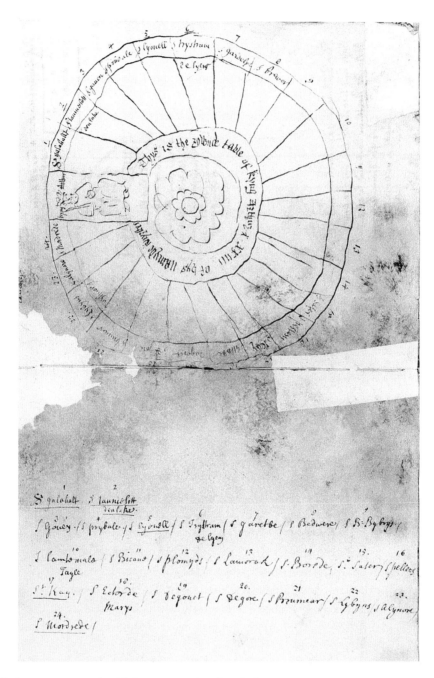

119 Anonymous early 18th-century sketch of the Round Table with a list of its inscriptions (see p. 270.

120 The Round Table and its inscriptions, detail from Richard Benning's engraving, probably after Robert Malpas's lost drawing of 1743 (cf. Fig. 30).

onwards.[11] Beginning in the late fifteenth century its use became extremely popular in the writing of inscriptions, and artists as well as scribes began to employ it. The feature was not limited to metropolitan artists; a particularly elaborate example begins the inscription on the locally produced incised slab of *c.*1470 to John Croxby at Howell, Lincolnshire.[12] A close parallel for the 'S' of 'Safer' appears in the decoration by the 'Master of the Decorated Documents' of the opening membrane of the plea roll for Michaelmas Term, 1485.[13]

The majuscule 'A' and 'E' are both characterised by a series of lozenges on the left-hand vertical stroke. This is a feature of late fifteenth- and sixteenth-century inscriptions, although two lozenges are more common than the four or five shown here; good examples appear on brasses from the London Series G and Yorkshire Series 3 brass engraving workshops.[14] The basic shape of the 'E' is the standard form in use at this time, but that of the 'A' is not. No one shape was universal, but the range of common forms is shown in Fig. 118. No exact parallel can be suggested for the 'A' of 'Arthur'. However, it is interesting that this letter has a looped cross-bar, seen best in the 'A' of 'Alynore' on the perimeter inscriptions. This tiny feature is the only pointer towards the less rigidly angular nature of the final phase in the development of *textura* script.

This study of the lettering of the inscriptions of the Round Table inevitably leads to disappointingly few firm conclusions. It is impossible to date the style of script with any precision. Even though the development of *textura* has received scant attention, what little we know shows that new and outmoded letter forms continued to be used, virtually side-by-side, for many years. Nor in the present state of knowledge is it possible to make a distinction between letter forms used in different media which would enable us to ascribe an inscription to a workman from a specific craft. All that we can say is that the style of script employed on the Round Table is consistent with a date of 1516 and that few alterations were made when the paint was renewed in 1789.

Our next task is to compare the inscriptions as they read today, established by Sally Badham in the first part of this chapter, with lists of the names recorded by antiquaries and other visitors before the repainting of 1789. Nine lists are known, made between about 1670 and 1789.

[11] Tudor-Craig, *Richard III*, pp. 33, 48, 49, and pls. 20–3; J. J. G. Alexander, *The Decorated Letter* (London, 1978), p. 27; P. Lasko and N. J. Morgan, *Mediaeval Art in East Anglia 1300–1520* (Norwich, 1973), p. 47, no. 68.

[12] Greenhill, *Monumental Incised Slabs*, pl. 41.

[13] Tudor-Craig, *Richard III*, pl. 20.

[14] Norris, *Monumental Brasses: The Craft*, pl. 34; Norris, *Monumental Brasses: The Memorials*, fig. 238; Badham, *Brasses from the North East*, figs. 34–8.

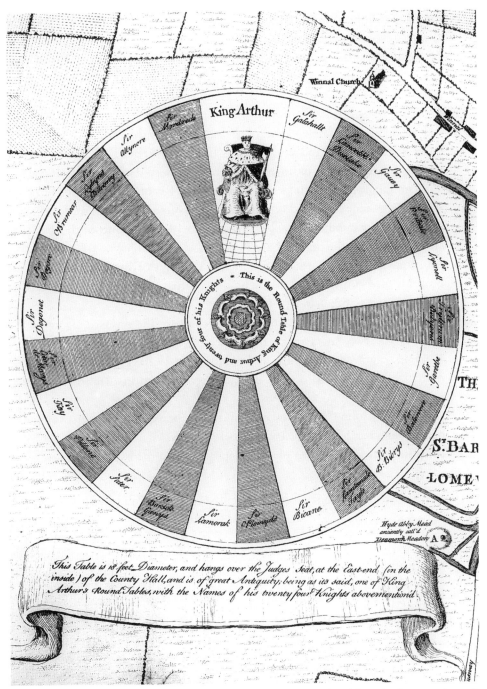

121 The Round Table and its inscriptions, detail from Richard Benning's engraving of William Godson's *Map of Winchester*, published in 1750.

A   list made by John Aubrey, possibly about 1670, and recorded in his *Monumenta Britannica* (see below, p. 492–3).

H   list made by Anthony Henley from a picture, presumably of the Winchester Round Table, in the possession of Lady Norton, and reported to John Aubrey in an original letter of 19 September [1670?] bound into the *Monumenta* (see below, p. 499).

Wd   A drawing by an unknown hand of the early eighteenth century bound up in a series of papers collected in the 1790s by the Reverend Richard Warner of Fawley for a History of Hampshire, now preserved among the Reverend William Bingley's collections in the Hampshire Record Office (Fig. 119).[15]

Wl   A list in the same hand and on the same piece of paper as the last, to which it is keyed by the numbers 1 to 24 (Names 9 to 14 appear only in this list; they are omitted from the drawing: see Fig. 119).[16]

M   An engraving by Richard Benning of the east end of the hall, undated, but probably after a drawing made by Robert Malpas in 1743 (Fig. 120; cf. Fig, 30; see above, p. 82; below p. 480).

G   An engraving closely related to the last (compare the reversed figure of the king on the two engravings), but appearing on William Godson's *Map of Winchester*, engraved by Benning and published in 1750 (Fig. 121; see p. 480).

P   A list by Dr Richard Pococke in 1754, recorded in his *Travels* (see below, p. 497).

Cd   A drawing by John Carter now in the British Library, originally in a volume of his drawings for 1789 (Fig. 163; see below, p. 503).[17]

Cl   A list in Carter's hand on a piece of paper stuck on the back of the last.[18]

Clearly, these lists are not all independent sources: Wd and Wl were made by the same person on the same occasion; M and G probably both derive from the same

---

[15] HRO, 16M 79/129, fol. 39r. On the verso of this leaf there is a sketch plan of the hall showing the north door in the position it occupied until 1789, and a sketch elevation of the east wall with the table held in position by the two lower brackets and by clamps to upper right and upper left. The outline of the table is filled by the words: 'The East End of the Inside of the Great Hall (as 'tis now call'd) upon the Castle Hill in the city of Winchester, ag'. which ye Fictitious Round Table of King Arthur is affix'd'. Below there is a note on the size of the hall and a suggestion that it was 'originally built for Divine worship'.

[16] HRO, 16M 79/129, fol. 38v.

[17] BL, Add. MS. 29,943, fol. 45 (originally fol. 17, later fol. 35), taken from BL, Add. MS. 29,928 (which was Vol. XI for 1789), where between fols. 101 and 102 there is a note of its extraction, and where fols. 99, 100, and 101 are drawings of the Winchester West Gate, the Great Hall from the castle ditch, and the Great Hall from Castle Hill, respectively.

[18] BL, Add. MS. 29,973, fol. 46 (originally fol. 35a).

drawing by Robert Malpas, and their texts usually agree; Cd and Cl again come from a single hand. There are other problems. H is derived second-hand from an otherwise unknown picture. P could be derived from the engravings M or G, but the differences from M and G in its readings suggest not, although it is difficult to know whether P's editor is transcribing these unusual names with complete accuracy. And it is impossible at this stage to be sure whether Cd and Cl of 1789 were made before or after the Caves' repainting in the same year (but see below, p. 274). Even so, these lists provide a minimum of five separate guides to how people read the inscriptions on the table up to 1789.

The easiest way to see the variations is to work through the names, using the letters set out above ('d' and 'l' indicate 'drawing' and 'list', respectively) to identify the spelling given by one or more of the sources. The present form as read by Sally Badham (see above, p. 255) is given first in bold, omitting 'S[ir]'.

kyng arthur [None correct]; kyng Arthur Wd; King Arthur M, G, P, Cl [Cd illegible; A, H, Wl omit]

1 **galahallt** Wd, Wl, Cd; Galahallt M, G, P, Cl; Galahalt A, H
2 **launcelot deulake** Cd; launcelott deu lake Wd, Wl; Launcelot du Lake H; Lancelot deu lake A; Lancelot Duelake M, G, P; Lancellot Duelake Cl
3 **gauen** Wd, Cd; Gauen A;[19] Gaven H; Gauey Wl, M, G, Cl; Gavey P
4 **p[er]cyvale** [None correct]; p[er]çviale Cd; Pribald P; Pribale M, G; prybale Wl; prudale Wd; Pulalo Cl; Poyvale A, H
5 **lyonell** Wd, Wl, Cd; Lyonell A, H, M, G, P, Cl
6 **trystram delyens** Wd, Cd; Trystram de Lyens A; Tristram de Lyens H; Tristram De lyens P; Tryltram de lyens Wl; Tryltram Delyens M, G; Tryltram Delyems Cl
7 **garethe** Cd; Garethe A, H; Garetbe M, G, Cl; garetbe Wl; Gavetbe P; gardelye Wd
8 **bedwere** Cd; Bedwere Wl, M; Bedewere G, P, Cl; Bedduere H; Beddvere A; brewer Wd
9 **blubrys** Cd; Blubrys A, H; B. Bibrys M, P, Cl; B: Bybrys Wl; B: Bibrys G [Wd omits]

---

[19] Aubrey refers again to 'S[ir] Gawen ... a Knight of ye Round-Table, as is to be read [seen *inserted above line in MS.*] in the Limbe [drawing] about the Round-Table in the Castle-hall at Winchester' in connection with Gawen's Barrow at Knowle Hill, Broad Chalke, Wilts.; see John Aubrey, *Monumenta Britannica*, ed. John Fowles (Milborne Port, 1980), ii, pp. 716–17, and compare pp. 712–13.

10 **Lacotemale tayle** Cd; Lacotemale Tayle H; Lacote maletayle A; Lamtemale Tayle Wl; Lamtemale Tayle G, Cl; Lamtemal Tayle M; Lametemale Tayte P [Wd omits]

11 **lucane** Cd [twice]; Bucane A, H; Bicane Wl, M, G, P, Cl, [Wd omits]

12 **plomyd(e?)** Cd [as name is now]; Plomyds Wl, M, G; Plomyd A, H; Oplomyds P; lomyds Cl [Wd omits]

13 **lamorak** [None correct]; Lamorak Wl, M, G, P, Cl; Lamorall H [A, Wd, Cd omit]

14 **bor(s) de gany** Cd [as 'bor(s)' now is]; Borsde Ganys M, G, Cl; Bors de gavys H; Boro de Ganys P; Bors de gauis A; Bors de ... Wl [Wd omits]

15 **Safer** A, Wd, Cd; Sater H, Wl, M, G, P, Cl

16 **pelleus** Cd; pellens Wd, Wl; Pellens A, H, M, G, P, Cl

17 **kay** Cd; Kay A, H, Wd, Wl, M, G, P, Cl

18 **Ectorde mary(s)** Cd; Ector de Marys Wl, M, G; Ector De Marys Cl; Ectorde marys A; Edorde Marys P; Sertor de Marys H; ettorde ... Wd

19 **dagonet** [None correct]; dagonett A; Dagonett H; dagoret Wd; degonet Wl; Degonet M, G, P, Cl; dagone Cd [confused with 'degore'?]

20 **degore** A, Wd, Wl, Cd; Degore H, M, G, Cl; Degare P

21 **brumear** Cd; Brumear A, H, Wl, G, P, Cl; brumer Wd; Brumer M

22 **lybyus dyscony[us]** [None correct]; lybyus dylony[us] Cd; Lybius dyscony A; Lybyus dyscuor[us] Wd; Lybyns d'yscony H; Lybyns Dilcony M, G; Lybyns Dileony Cl; Lybyns Dillong P; Lybyns Wl

23 **Alynore** Wl, Cd; alynare Wd; Alymare A, H; Allynore M, G, Cl; Allymore P

24 **mordrede** Cd; Mordrede Wd, Wl, G, P, Cl; Mordred A, H; Mordrod M

The words of the inscription around the Tudor Rose have not been detailed here since, as might be expected in a text of this length, all seven versions which include it (H and Wl omit) are slightly different, but the differences add nothing to our understanding of the text. The treatment of the number 'xxiiii' illustrates nicely the vagaries of antiquarian 'copying': xxiiii Wd, Cd; xxiiij A; 24 M; twenty four G, Cl; twenty-four P.

Perhaps the first point to make in reviewing this sad *mélange* is that the form of a name as it now appears on the table is often recorded in precisely, or almost precisely, the same form by one or another of the earlier recorders. Wd, Wl, A, and H are conspicuous here, but there is no case in which all four agree, and each is only too able to make a dreadful hash of one or more of the other names. When one looks at the kinds of variation appearing in the spelling of a single name, it becomes clear that these variations are due either to carelessness or to an inability to read accurately some of the more unusual *textura* forms. Overlying this is a difference in attitude: one expects too much in hoping for letter-for-letter accuracy in antiquarian copies of the later seventeenth and eighteenth centuries.

If we accept for the moment that there is sufficient evidence here to show that the words on the table were the same (or very much the same) before the repainting of 1789 as they are now, how often did these nine records get them right? The results are set out in Table 14: the figures in the second column relate to precisely accurate transcriptions, but those in the third take into account the fact that one cannot expect accurate capitalization and word-breaks in transcribing *textura* at this date.

TABLE 14
How antiquaries read the names on the Round Table:
the accuracy of nine records compared

Source	Names transcribed exactly	Names spelt correctly, ignoring capitals and word-breaks	Total
		Written lists	
A	2	9	11
H	–	7	7
Wl	4	7	11
P	–	6	6
Cl	–	9	9
		Drawings	
Wd	6	2	8
M	–	9	9
G	–	10	10
Cd	20	–	20

Even when such allowances are made, eight of the nine records fail to get even half the names 'right'. Apart from simple errors (e.g. the omission of 'lamorak' by A, Wd, and Cd; P's 'a' for 'o' in 'degore'; the omission of the third 'l' in 'galahallt' by A and H; or reading 'i' for 'y' in 'trystram'), the sources of the problems can all be seen on the table today. Most of them are due to difficulties inherent in reading *textura* letter forms, arising either from the unusual form of a letter or from the repetition of minims (see above, p. 261). In the first category come the reading of 'y' for 'n' in 'gauen', of 'l' for the long 's' in 'trystram', of '-dd-' for '-dw-' in 'bedwere', of 'Bu-' or 'Bi-' for 'lu-' in 'lucane', of 't' for 'f' in 'Safer', of 'All-' for 'Al-' in 'Alynore', or the omission of the final 'e' in 'mordrede'. In the second category come the omission of 'u' in 'launcelot', the reading '-mt-' for '-cot-' in 'lacotemale', or of '-ens' for 'eus' in 'pelleus'. All the recorders failed to understand some of the abbreviations, such as 'p[er]' in 'percyvale' or the '-us' in the form of an Arabic 9 at the end of 'dysconyus'. Some were misled by the dividing lines of the segments into adding an extra 't' to 'launcelot' or 'dagonet' or reading '-ll' for '-k' at the end of 'lamorak'. Finally, there were the damaged areas, 'p[er]cyvale', 'garethe', and 'plomyd(e?)', which still cause difficulty today (see above, pp. 256, 260).

There is nothing in this analysis to suggest that any of the names were significantly different prior to the repainting in 1789 – and much to suggest that the repainting is a very close reflection of the original. In one or two cases, the original may have been a little easier to read: the early recorders had little trouble with the final '-s' of 'bors', and all (who did not omit it) put an 's' at the end of 'plomyd(e?)'. But there is little else in their favour. The verdict must be that early antiquaries – and we have some famous names here – could not read *textura*.[20] There are extenuating circumstances: the table was high on the wall, behind the judge's seat; it was probably dirty; the light will not always have been good; and quite half the texts were sideways or upside-down. Eyesight, too, will have varied and spectacles may not have been much help at this distance. Above all, we cannot expect modern standards of accuracy.

John Carter was the exception. His drawing (Cd; Fig. 163) can be read today with almost complete confidence: twenty of the twenty-three names he gives are accurate. This, and his treatment of 'p[er]cyvale' (where the tail of the 'y' seems attached, as now, to the 'c'), 'plomyd(e?)', 'bors', and the initial 'T' of the central inscription, all suggest that he made his drawing after the Caves' repainting of 1789. Curiously, Carter's failure to transcribe the names properly in his list (Cl) only emphasises his accuracy as a draughtsman. He may not have been able to read *textura*, but he knew, and was able to reproduce, what he saw. Carter's errors in Cl, many of them in common with those made by earlier recorders, go far to support the view that their readings provide no sure guide to the pre-1789 names. It is the skill of the Caves' repainting which has preserved the best record of the names as originally painted in the sixteenth century.

[20] For the continued use of *textura* in the sixteenth century and after, and the ability to read it, see Keith Thomas, 'The Meaning of Literacy in Early Modern England', in Gerd Baumann (ed.), *The Written Word. Literacy in Transition*, Wolfson College Lectures 1985 (Oxford, 1986), pp. 97–131, at p. 99. I owe this reference to the kindness of my colleague, Julia Briggs.

With the spellings established, we can proceed to compare the form of the names on the table, their selection, and the sequence in which they appear with other early lists of Arthur's knights.

The first point to be made is that the names are English, not French (Table 15). This shows most clearly in spellings such as 'galahallt', 'garethe', 'bedwere', or 'bors', instead of 'Galehot', 'Gaheriet', 'Bedoier', and 'Bohors', but in fact is evident to some extent in most of the names.[21]

Eighteen of the twenty-four names can be found in French in one of the lists of 150 or more knights attached to *La forme quon tenoit des tournoys et assemblees au temps du roy uterpendragon et du roy artus*, ['The Manner of Holding Tourneys and Assemblies in the Time of King Utherpendragon and King Arthur'], written perhaps by Jacques d'Armagnac between 1452 and 1477.[22] The same number appear in Middle English on a slightly different roll-call, in R. W. Ackerman's *Index of Arthurian Names in Middle English*,[23] when the names found in Sir Thomas Malory's *Morte Darthur* are omitted (Table 16). Malory's work needs to be considered separately, because more of the names on the Round Table can be found there than in any other one source, twenty-one in all out of the twenty-four, with as many as nineteen or twenty in a single passage.[24]

[21] For the transfer of the names of Arthur's knights from French to English, see F. L. Utley, 'The Names of the Knights of the Round Table', *Names* 23 (1975), 194–214, at pp. 200–2

[22] Sixteen names can be found in each of two other versions of the list; all three versions are printed and discussed in Edouard Sundoz, 'Tourneys in the Arthurian Tradition', *Speculum* 19 (1944), 389–420.

[23] R. W. Ackerman, *Index of the Arthurian Names in Middle English* (Stanford, 1952), who omits, however, names such as Degore which are not strictly Arthurian.

[24] P. J. C. Field, 'The Winchester Round Table', *Notes and Queries* 223 (1978), 204, pointed this out, but his identifications and counting are bedevilled in part by reliance upon the erroneous readings of the names on the table given in a sixpenny booklet which used to be 'obtained from The Hall Keeper': Sir William W. Portal, *The Great Hall of Winchester Castle: a Summary* (Winchester, 1st edn. 1916; reprinted without change many times until at least 1971), p. 15. This relied in turn on Melville Portal, *The Great Hall, Winchester Castle* (Winchester and London, 1899), p. 90.

TABLE 15
The names of the knights on the Round Table as they are spelt in various possible sources

| Round Table names in clockwise sequence[1] | French Arthurian prose and verse romances[2] (selected forms only) | Middle English Arthurian sources (other than Malory)[3] | Malory's Morte Darthur | | | | |
| | | | Caxton's table of contents | | Book XIX, Chapter 11 | | |
			Caxton[4]	Wynkyn de Worde[5]	Winchester MS[6]	Caxton[7]	Wynkyn de Worde[8]
1. galahallt	Galehot Galahaut	Galath Galaad Galaaz	12. Galahalt Galahault	Galahalt Galahad	1. Galahalt	Galahalt	Galahalt
2. launcelot deulake	Lancelot del dou/du Lac, Lak	Launcelot de du Lake (*not* deu) (*MA, etc.*)	1. Launcelot (*usual*), never de/du Lake	Launcelot	5. Launcelot (de/du Lake)	Launcelot (de/du Lake)	Launcelot
3. gauen	Gauvain Gauvayn Gauven Gaven	*Many var. incl.* Gawen, Gauan, *but not* gauen	3. Gawayn Gauwayn	Gawayn(e)	2. Gawayne	Gawayne	Gawayne
4. percyvale	Perceval (*not i or y*)	*Many var., usually with i or e, rather than y;* Percyvell *is closest*	16. Percyuale, Pervyual Percyualles	Percyvale	14. Percivale (Percyuale)	Percyual	Percyuale
5. lyonell	Lionel Lyonel Lyonnel Lioniel Lyoniel	Lyonell (*MA, etc.*)	5. Lyonel (*always*)	Lyonel(l)	6. Lyonell	Lyonel (Lyonell)	Lyonell
6. trystram delyens	Tristan Tristens Tristram Trystram de Loenois Lyonois	Tristeran Tristren Tramtris Tristem Tristre Tristren *but not* de Lyens *or var.*	2. Trystram (*often*) de Lyones (VIII.[1])	Trystram Tristram (de Lyones)	17. Trystram (de Lyones)	Tristram, (Trystram de Lyones)	Tristram (de Lyones)
7. garethe	Gahenet, Gahaviet, Gariet	Gaheris (*the form* Gareth *does not occur before Malory*)	8. Gareth (*always*)	Gareth	4. Gareth (Garethe)	Gareth	Gareth
8. bedwere	Bedoi(i)er Bediver Bedu(i)er Bediuvers	Bedwere (*MA, LMA*)	20. Bedwere (XX.6)	Bedwere	16. Bedyvere (Bedwere)	Bedeuer(e) (Bedwere)	Bedever
9. blubrys	Bliob(l)eris Bleoble(e)ris Blyoberis Blioberis	Bleoberi(i)s Bliobel Blyobers Bleobers, *etc*	10. Bleoberys Bleoberis	Bleoberys Bleoberis	9. Bleoberys (Bleobrys)	Bleoberis (Bleoberys)	Bleoberys
10. lacotemale tayle	La Cote Mal Taillee	–	14. La Cote Male Tayle (IX.1, 2, 4, 5)	La cote male tayle	12. La Cote Male Tayle	La Cote Male Tayle	la cote male tayle
11. lucane	Lucan Lucain Lucant	Lucane (*LMA*)	–	–	15. Lucan	Lucan (Lucanere)	Lucan
12. plomyd(e?)	Palamedes Palamides	–	9. Palomydes Palamydes	Palomydes	18. Palomydes	Palomydes	Palomydes

| Round Table names in clockwise sequence[1] | French Arthurian prose and verse romances[2] (selected forms only) | Middle English Arthurian sources (other than Malory)[3] | Malory's Morte Darthur | | | | |
| | | | Caxton's table of contents | | Book XIX, Chapter 11 | | |
			Caxton[4]	Wynkyn de Worde[5]	Winchester MS.[6]	Caxton[7]	Wynkyn de Worde[8]
13. lamorak	Lamorat Lamourat	–	13. Lamorak (IX.14; X.24)	Lamorak	13. Lamorak	Lamorak	Lamorak
14. bor(s) de ganys	Bo(h)ort Bo(h)ors Bores, de Gaunes	Bors (LMA) de Gaways, Gawnes, not ganys	19. Bors (often), never de ganys or var.	Bors	8. Bors de Ganys	Bors de Ganys	Bors de Ganys
15. Safer	Saphar Sephar	–	18. Safer (X.83–4)	Safyr	(Safer)	(Safer)	(Safere, Safyr)
16. pelleus	Pellias	–	4. Pelleas (always)	Pelleas	19. Pelleas	Pelleas	Pelleas
17. Kay	Keu, Keux Ké , Kei, Key	Kay (common)	7. Kaye	Kay	11. Kay	Kay	Kay
18. Ector de mary(s)	Hector Ector Hestor	Ector (LMA), but not de marys	6. Ector (always)	Ector de Marys	7. Ector de Marys	Ector de Marys	Ector de Marys
19. dagonet	Daguenet, Daguenés Dangueneit	Dagenet, not dagonet	15. Dagonet (always)	Dagonet	(Dagonet)	(Dagonet)	(Dagonet)
20. degore	–	Degore (see p. 280)	–	–	–	–	–
21. brumear	Brunor le Noir [Brumant?]	–	11. Breunor	Brewnor	10. Brewne le Noyre (Brunor)	Bruyn le Noyre (Breunor)	Bruyn le noyre
22. lybyus dysconyus	Le Bel Desconneü , Le Biau Descouneü	Lybyus (LOZ) disconyus (CC)	–	–	–	–	–
23. Alynore	–	Alymere (MA)	–	–	–	–	–
24. mordrede	Mordret, Mordrés, Mordré	Mordrede (MA)	17. Mordred (always)	Mordred	3. Mordred (Mordrede)	Mordred	Mordred

[1]See above, p. 255.

[2]G. D. West, An Index of Proper Names in French Arthurian Verse Romances 1150–1300, Univ. of Toronto Romance ser. 15 (Toronto, 1969); G. D. West, An Index of Proper Names in French Arthurian Prose Romances, Univ. of Toronto Romance ser. 35 (Toronto, 1978).

[3]Robert W. Ackerman, An Index of the Arthurian Names in Middle English (Stanford, 1952), omitting Malory for the purposes of this table. Where the same spelling as on the Round Table is recorded, this is given with an indication of the source. Otherwise a range of the nearer variants is shown. A dash indicates that this name is not recorded by Ackerman.

[4]James W. Spisak (ed.), Caxton's Malory (Berkeley and Los Angeles, 1983). Where the spelling of the Round Table occurs in Caxton's table of contents, this is given with reference to the book and chapter heading, unless it is a frequent or invariable form. Variant forms are only given when no exact parallel occurs. The numbers give the sequence in which each name first appears in the table of contents. For Book XIX, Chapter 11, variant forms from elsewhere in the book are only given if these are closer to the Round Table form.

[5]A. S. Mott (ed.), Syr Thomas Malory, The Noble and Joyous Boke Entytled Le Morte Darthur (Oxford, 1933), printed from the unique copy of the 1498 edition in the John Rylands Library, Manchester. Variant forms are not given as there is no index of the name-spellings for this edition.

[6]Eugene Vinaver (ed.), The Works of Thomas Malory, 2nd edition., 3 vols, (Oxford, 1967; repr. 1973). Caxton's table of contents does not, of course, appear in the Winchester MS. The spellings are those of the list in Chapter 11. Where a spelling close to that of the Round Table appears elsewhere in the MS, this is given in parentheses, as are the two names which only occur elsewhere. The numbers give the sequence in which the names appear in the course of the list. The sequence is the same for Caxton and Wynkyn de Worde.

[7]Spisak (ed.), Caxton's Malory, see n. 4.

[8]Mott (ed.), Sir Thomas Malory, see n. 5.

TABLE 16

Knights named on the Round Table who occur in various possible sources

Medieval French verse	Medieval French prose	La forme quon tenoit des tourneys[3]			Middle English other than Malory[4]	Malory's Morte Darthur											
						Winchester MS.[5]				Caxton 1485[6]				Wynkyn de Worde 1498[7]			
		H	B	M		Table of contents	VII. 27.8	XVIII .3	XIX. 11	Table of contents	VII. 27.8	XVIII .3	XIX. 11	Table of contents	VII. 27.8	XVIII .3	XIX. 11
1150–1300[1]	1300–1500[2]																
15	21	16	16	18	17	–	16	12	19	20	15[11]	12	19	20	15[12]	12	19
					(18)[8]							(21)[9]	(21)[10]			(21)[9]	(21)[10]

[1] As Table 15, n. 2, *Verse Romances*. [2] As Table 15, n. 2, *Prose Romances*.

[3] As above, p. 275, n. 22, at pp. 403–8. H, B, and M refer respectively to the Harvard, de Blangy, and Morgan Library manuscripts of the list, all three of which are printed by Sandoz.

[4] As Table 15, n. 3. [5] As Table 15, n. 6. [6] As Table 15, n. 4.

[7] As Table 15, n. 5. [8] Add Degore, see p. 280.

[9] Add Safer and Dagonet from elsewhere in Malory for total of 21. [10] Add Lucan from elsewhere in Malory for total of 21.

[11] Bleobrys omitted by Caxton. [12] Caxton's omission of Bleobrys followed by Wynkyn de Worde.

There are eight major and many lesser lists of knights' names in the *Morte Darthur*, but only three need really concern us here (Table 16).[25] In Book VII, Chapters 27–8, sixteen of the names on the Round Table appear in a list of the fifty-one knights attending the tournament called by Lady Lyones; in Book XVIII, Chapter 3, twelve of the twenty-four knights at Queen Guinevere's dinner are also named on the table; and in Book XIX, Chapter 11, nineteen names on the table appear in the list of those who searched Sir Urré's wounds (the list is intended to number 110 but does not quite do so). With two additional names which occur elsewhere in the *Morte Darthur* we reach the total of twenty-one noted above. But the greatest number of names from the Winchester Round Table to be found together is in Caxton's 'Table or rubrysshe of the contente of chapytres' of the *Morte Darthur*, where there are twenty. This is a slightly different list from that in Book XIX, but with one name found elsewhere, we again reach a total of twenty-one.

Table 15 shows the forms of the names as they occur on the Round Table, in French romances, in Middle English sources other than Malory, and in Caxton's table of contents and Book XIX of the *Morte Darthur*. For the *Morte Darthur*, three variants are given: the Winchester manuscript discovered in 1934 by [Sir] Walter Oakeshott and published by E. Vinaver; Caxton's printing of 1485; and Wynkyn

[25] For these lists, see Utley, 'Names of the Knights', pp. 195–7. For the basis of the numerical correspondences given here and in Table 16, see the lists and sources in Table 15.

de Worde's edition (after Caxton) of 1498.[26] The main conclusion to be drawn is that the names on the Round Table are closer as a group to the names of the *Morte Darthur* than to anything which preceded it. Moreover, seven of the names (garethe, lacotemale tayle, plomyd(e?) (i.e. Palomides), lamorak, Safer, pelleus, and brumear (i.e. Breunor?), together with two of the bynames (de lyens, de mary(s)), are not to be found to judge by Ackerman's *Index* in any extant Middle English Arthurian sources before Malory. This would seem to mean that *a* version of Malory's *Morte Darthur* is a principal source of the names on the table. This conclusion stops short of claiming that the *Morte Darthur* is the only source. There is no correspondence between Malory and the painted names respecting the order in which the knights appear, and no obvious principle governing which names were selected for the table. Moreover, three of the table's names (degore, lybyus dysconyus, and Alynore) do not occur in the *Morte Darthur*, and there are several whose spelling is very different. We shall look at these problems in turn, but first, can we tell, assuming it was a source, which of the versions of the *Morte Darthur* may have been used? In fact, it is extremely difficult, if not impossible, to judge between them (Table 16). In view of the other difficulties, this may also tend to suggest that none of the versions of the *Morte Darthur* examined here, not even the Winchester manuscript itself, is a direct source.

Something has been said in Chapters 1 and 9 about the number of twenty-four chosen for the Winchester Round Table. In the present discussion, it is relevant that three of Malory's eight lists of knights come to twenty-four: Guinevere's dinner guests in Book XVIII, Chapter 3; Launcelot's war party in Book XX, Chapter 5 (although the text says the party numbered twenty-two); and the same band, whom Launcelot made great lords in France, in Chapter 19. The inscription around the rose at the centre of the Round Table seems to make it clear that the twenty-four are only some of a larger company whose names were known: 'Thys is the rownde table of kyng Arthur w[ith] xxiiij of hys namyde kny3ttes'. But the basis of the Winchester selection is elusive: while it certainly includes the greatest names, it also includes others not so prominent in Malory (Safer, pelleus, dagonet, for example), some who do not occur in Malory, even if well-known elsewhere (degore, lybyus dysconyus), and possibly one or two – Alynore (if he is not Alymere) and brumear (if he is not Breunor le Noir) – who are otherwise unknown. Selection or compilation, however, there has certainly been and not

---

[26] Wynkyn de Worde's edition of 1529 and Wyllyam Copland's edition of 1557 have also been examined (the former in the unique copy, BL, Dept. of Printed Books, G.10510; the latter in Bodleian, Douce A subt. 64). Where there are differences, 1529 and 1557 tend to agree together against Wynkyn de Worde 1498, whereas the latter tends to agree with Caxton.

entirely uninfluenced by both external and internal factors. The first six names on the Round Table occur in the same order in Caxton's prologue of 1481 to his printing of *Godeffroy of Boloyne*.[27] These are the great names, or some of them, but the spellings are different (e.g. 'ghalehot'), and so the selection and sequence may be chance. Still, this list of Caxton's serves to remind us that the immediate source or sources of the Round Table list may not have survived.

The need to arrange the names in groups of three followed by a longer name forming a double line in every fourth segment of the painting may also have affected the sequence of names on the table and perhaps their selection, although it is clear that there was room for manoeuvre by including or excluding bynames: Launcelot, Trystram, Bors, and Ector occur much more often in the *Morte Darthur* without their bynames; by contrast, bynames for percyvale, blubrys, lucane, kay, and brumear(?) could have been found if needed. Only lybyus dysconyus and lacotemale tayle had to spread over two lines.

Four names are particularly problematic. Sir Degore does not appear in Malory. It is perhaps possible that his name is a bungle, formed from the territorial byname of King Urien or King Baudemagus 'of the land of Gore', but it is much more likely that he is the hero of the Middle English metrical romance printed with the title *Syr Degore* by Wynkyn de Worde in 1512–13.[28]

Sir Lybyus Dysconyus, 'the happy child of calligraphic error', long an enigma of the Winchester table, has been identified by John Fleming in Chapter 1. Sir Lybyus – 'Le Bel Desconneü', 'the Fair Unknown' – is also absent from the *Morte Darthur*, but Chaucer knew him towards the end of the fourteenth century ('Sir Lybeux' in *Sir Thopas*) and so did the Tudor poet laureate John Skelton.[29] An account in Middle English of his adventures, probably composed by Thomas Chestre between 1375 and 1400, may have been printed early in the sixteenth century, but if so no copy of this printing has been discovered.[30]

[27] William Caxton (trans.), *Godeffroy of Boloyne, or The Siege and conquest of Jerusalem*, ed. M. N. Colvin, EETS extra ser. 64 (London, 1893), p. 2. The significance of this list in relation to the Round Table was pointed out by Sue Ellen Holbrook, 'Malory's Identification of Camelot as Winchester', in James W. Spisak (ed.), *Studies in Malory* (Kalamazoo, 1985), pp. 13–27, at p. 26 (note 22).

[28] A. W. Pollard and G. R. Redgrave, *A Short-Title Catalogue of Books Printed in England ... 1475–1640*, 2nd edn., (London, 1986), No. 6470. See also G. P. Faust, *Sir Degore. A Study of the Texts and Narrative Structures*, Princeton Studies in English 11 (Princeton, 1935), and 'Sir Degorré', in *Middle English Romances*, ed. A. V. C. Schmidt and Nicolas Jacobs, London Medieval and Renaissance ser. (London, 1980), ii, pp. 7–11, 57–88, 240–6.

[29] *The Canterbury Tales*, ed. N. F. Blake (London, 1980), p. 489, line 900; John Skelton, *The Complete English Poems*, ed. John Scattergood, Penguin English Poets (Harmondsworth, 1983), pp. 88 ('Phyllyp Sparowe', lines 649–50), 122 ('Agenst Garnesche' (i), line 17).

Sir Brumear is more of a problem. In that form his name appears to be unknown in Arthurian romance. But the middle part of the word 'brumear' is formed of a sequence of minims leaving, as Sally Badham stresses in the earlier part of this chapter (p. 261), much room for error, whether in the original painting or in the repainting of 1789. If this does explain the origins of this otherwise unknown knight, he is probably to be identified as Breunor le Noir, also spelt by Caxton Breunes, Breune, Bruyn, and Brewnor, and in the Winchester manuscript as Brunor and Brewne.[31] The range of spellings demonstrates the difficulty. There is, however, a further problem, for Breunor is the knight whom Sir Kay named La Cote Male Tayle. So if we adopt the solution of brumear as Breunor, the same knight appears twice on the table.

Sir Alynore poses a similar problem. Some have suggested he is an error for Astamore or Ascamour,[32] but this is not obvious. An easier solution might be to identify him as Alymere, a form which could be explained in terms of minims. But Alymere is a very rare knight, who appears only in Arthur's last battle in the alliterative *Morte Arthure*,[33] one of the main sources of Malory's *Morte Darthur*.

Clearly, these problems cannot all be solved with finality, but our investigation has revealed some new evidence of the eclectic nature of the names on the Winchester table. If we think of the names on the table as read clockwise from King Arthur at the top — the logical direction in which to read and the direction of the central inscription around the rose — it is interesting to observe that the more obscure names fall together in a single group near the end of the list, just as the great names come together at the start. These groupings may possibly have something to say of the process by which the list was formed (see below, Chapter 11).

There are four more knights on the Round Table who can be identified well enough, but whose names present special problems of spelling.

---

[30] *Lybeaus Desconus*, ed. M. Mills, EETS 261 (Oxford, 1969). For the suggestion that *LD* was printed early in the sixteenth century, see *Libeaus Desconus*, ed. Max Kaluza (Leipzig, 1890), pp. x–xi. This possibility is enhanced by John Scattergood's analysis of the sources of Skelton's 'Phyllyp Sparowe' which in this part of the poem (lines 614–723) can mostly, perhaps all, be plausibly derived from printed works (*Complete English Poems*, pp. 411–12). Since 'Phyllyp Sparowe' was probably composed up to line 844 before 1505 (*Complete English Poems*, p. 405) and 'Agenst Garnesche' in the summer of 1514 (ibid., p. 424), any printed version of *LD* would date at the latest from the first years of the century.

[31] Ackerman, *Index*, s.n. Breunor le Noir; Eugène Vinaver (ed.), *The Works of Sir Thomas Malory*, 2nd edn. (Oxford, 1967; repr. 1973), iii, index.

[32] E.g. Field, 'The Winchester Round Table'.

[33] *Morte Arthure* ed. Erik Björkman, Alt- und Mittelenglische Texte 9 (Heidelberg and New York, 1915), line 4078.

Bedwere is the single companion who stayed with Arthur to the end and afterwards returned the sword Excalibur to the Lady of the Lake. His name is more
usually spelt with the middle syllable: Bedivere, or the like. But the spelling of the
table is close to the form in which Bedwyr first appears in *Culhwch and Olwen*, and as
Bedwere it is found in the same alliterative *Morte Arthure* as Alymere,[34] as well as in
the Winchester manuscript of Malory and in Caxton's 'Table' (Table 15).

Blubrys is more difficult. Spelled Bliobers in French and Bleoberys in Malory,
his name caused great difficulty in Middle English (Table 15). The nearest spelling
to that of the Winchester table is the 'Bleobrys' of the Winchester manuscript of
Malory.[35] But there is no doubt who he is: Sir Bleoberys de Ganys, cousin of Sir
Bors.

Both gauen and pelleus are forms otherwise unknown, but their identification as
Gawain, the principal hero of Arthurian romance, and Pelleas, the noble knight,
beloved of Ettarde, is not in doubt. Likewise with plomyd(e?), who can scarcely be
other than the Saracen knight Palomides.

We are thus returned to the unresolved problem of sources. If anything, in the
crucial names the table is closest to the Winchester manuscript of the *Morte Darthur*
(Table 16), but it is a fine judgement, and in any case there are sufficient differences
and omissions to show that the Winchester manuscript cannot have been the sole
source. The author of the Round Table programme may have been relying on
memory for his list, but if he did so, he was remarkably well read in Arthurian
romance beyond Malory. The spellings and choices of names suggest rather that the
Winchester list was garnered by a piece of careful research which involved the use of
several books, some of them perhaps recently published. Having put together the
first part of his list quite easily, the author perhaps had more difficulty with the later
names and cast about for knights who, because of their recent appearance in print,
might reasonably be expected to have been present. If this is so, the choice of names
may provide some indication of the date of the painting. It must surely date from
after the availability in manuscript or print of Malory's *Morte Darthur*, that is, after
1469/70 and probably after 1485. Perhaps, however, the painting should be dated
more precisely to some time after the appearance of Wynkyn de Worde's *Syr Degore*
in 1512–13.[36] This can only be conjecture, but it is in agreement with other indications of date from the painting, as Pamela Tudor-Craig shows in Chapter 9.

---

[34] Ibid., lines 1162, 1264, etc.

[35] Vinaver, *Works*, i, 316 (Book VII, Ch. 13).

[36] For this date, see Pollard and Redgrave, *Short-Title Catalogue*, 2nd edn. (1985), no. 6470. H. S. Bennett, *English
Books and Readers, 1475 to 1557*, 2nd edn. (Cambridge, 1969), p. 247, preferred '1515?', but *STC* reflects the
latest knowledge of the chronology of Wynkyn de Worde's printing.

The first part of this chapter sought to establish a reliable text of the inscriptions on the Round Table. In this last part we have sought to go further, to enter in some sort into the mind of the devisor of the painting so as to see how, in solving his problem, he sought to recreate for Arthur the fellowship of twenty-four 'of his namyde kny3ttes'.

9

Iconography of the Painting

The object of this chapter is to put forward all the visual evidence afforded by the painted surface of the Round Table, with a view to establishing when it is likely to have been carried out. By and large, activities like the refurbishing of an ancient relic of this kind are usually precipitated by a special event, such as a royal birth, death, or state visit. In Tudor Winchester there were four such occasions within the possible time span of this painting:

the birth and christening of Prince Arthur in 1486
the visit of Henry VIII in 1516
the visit of Henry VIII with the Emperor Charles V in 1522
the marriage of Philip and Mary in 1554.

Set out below are the clues that have led me to reject the first and last of these opportunities in favour of the second or third. The features are simple and obvious, before the eyes of every observer. I have dealt in turn with every element of the design, other than the cartwheel and the lettering, which fall into other provinces (Chapters 1, 8, 11, and 12). I have brought to bear upon each feature a muster of comparative material which, in sum, makes my case for placing the picture. With a caveat about its present condition, I have then gone on to discuss the authorship of the painting, and lastly, the climate of thought of which it was an expression.

If my theory for its date is acceptable, then a context of some cogency and richness forms around the painting. As Tennyson invested the character of the Once and Future King with the virtues of the Prince Consort of his day, so I believe the painter of the Round Table attempted to give to his Arthur the features of the reigning sovereign.

Some may be disappointed that I cannot claim a more distant antiquity for this painting, or attribute it to a distinguished artist. But if I am near the truth, it was

122 *Arturus rex* as one of a series of figures from the legendary early history of York Minster. Painted window, York Minster, western choir clerestory, south side (S10), *c.* 1408–14.

123 *Rex Arturus conquestor inclitus*, one of eight figures of kings. Painted window, Coventry, St. Mary's Hall, *c*.1451–61.

a

b

124 The image of the king on the Tudor coinage: *a*, Henry VIII, gold sovereign, third coinage, 1544–7 (enlarged x 2); *b*, Henry VII, silver penny, York mint (enlarged x 4).

done to please Henry VIII: an embodiment of our ancient history, painted for a king who took that history very seriously, and painted by men half in love with the strange invincible antiquity of this country, as some of us are still.

The seated figure

An image of a king seated, wearing a red cloak lined with ermine over a blue garment with ermine cuffs, might seem an obvious solution to the problem of representing Arthur (Pl. XXIII). However, there are alternative approaches to the problem. In the great French tapestry of c.1385 of the Christian Heroes, Arthur's kingship was subordinate to his knighthood, and he appeared in full armour under a surcoat.[1] In the tapestry he is seated, but in his role as one of the nine Worthies or in series of kings, Arthur is usually represented standing (Figs. 122–3).[2] The seated image is often associated with the authority of rule: a classical concept found where classical ideas were paramount. So Henry III had introduced a gold penny (worth 20 silver pence) in 1257, and stamped it with an image of himself, seated on a throne, holding an orb and sceptre. Apart from the 'sovereign/martlets' type struck by Edward the Confessor, it was the first coin of such elaboration minted in this country since the Roman occupation. Edward III, nursing imperial pretensions,[3] used the seated, frontally posed figure for his gold florin of 1344, but with that exception, the idea did not reappear until Henry VII's gold sovereign of 1489. About the same time a penny with a somewhat abbreviated version of the same format was issued (Fig. 124b).[4] These coin types, with very slight modifications made in 1509 and 1526, were in currency until the issue of Henry VIII's third coinage in 1544 (Fig. 124a).[5] It is a factor worth consideration that the only visual model of a seated king readily available in this country was one

[1]   The Cloisters, Metropolitan Museum, New York. Illus. Geoffrey Ashe, Leslie Alcock, C. A. Ralegh Radford, Philip Rahtz, and Jill Racy, *The Quest for Arthur's Britain* (London, 1968), ill. 17.

[2]   For the Innsbruck statue of Arthur cast in 1513 by Peter Vischer for the tomb of the Emperor Maximilian and illustrated in Fig. 159, see further, p. 466–7 Among later examples, the figures across the east front of Montacute House (1588–1601) offer a parallel with the play within the play of *Love's Labour's Lost*. The representation of the Worthies most nearly apposite to the painting on the Round Table was their appearance among the decorations of the Tudor Triumph at the Field of Cloth of Gold.

[3]   For the early fourteenth-century development of the concept of imperial power, see Michael Wilks, *The Problem of Sovereignty in the Later Middle Ages* (Cambridge, 1963).

[4]   See D. M. Metcalf, *Sylloge of Coins of the British Isles, 23: Ashmolean Museum, Oxford. iii. Coins of Henry VII* (London, 1976), esp. Pls. XXXII, XL, and XLI.

[5]   See C. A. Whitton, 'The Coinages of Henry VIII and Edward VI in Henry's name', *British Numismatic Journal*, 26 (1949–51), 56–89.

which almost any Tudor Englishman would have found in his purse: a 'sovereign' penny. What is more, the fall of the drapery over the legs of the painted Arthur bears a closer resemblance to the formula used on that penny than to the more sophisticated sovereign coin itself – and a closer resemblance to the 1489–1544 penny than to any other drapery design so far matched against it.

A red cloak with an ermine lining and ermine cape was commonplace for royal images from the time of Henry VI. It appears in innumerable coloured images, and the markings of the ermine are a more or less uniform feature of drawn versions. The relatively wide cuffs of the undergarment with their ermine trimmings appear, for example, on the screen painted for Bishop Oliver King between 1485 and 1503 at St George's, Windsor,[6] and on the Plea Roll for Easter 1514.[7] Another source which would have illustrated the same fashion is the Nuremberg Chronicle of 1494.[8] In short, Arthur is presented here in a manner which would have seemed, to an early Tudor observer, virtually identical with the pose and costume in which he would expect to see his reigning monarch, with the slight proviso that by 1520 such a costume would have seemed traditional to the point of being perhaps deliberately old-fashioned.

The one feature about the image of the king which might have aroused comment is the jewel about the king's neck (Plate XXIV; Fig. 133). This appears to be of oval form, surrounded by smaller gems, the whole hanging from a gold chain. It is exceedingly rare to find a jewel hanging over an ermine cape. Further evidence of the detail of its design might emerge if it were stripped of overpaint. There was no tradition as to the form of the collar of knighthood worn by King Arthur's knights, although it was assumed in the early sixteenth century that they had worn collars of some sort. The details of the precise form of the Garter collar, and the obligation to wear the Lesser George at almost all times, were proclaimed at the Windsor Chapter in April 1522. Collars were thus in the public consciousness at this time.

---

[6]   Illus. Anthony Cheetham, *The Life and Times of Richard III* (London, 1972), pp. 100–1.

[7]   Erna Auerbach, *Tudor Artists* (London, 1954), Pl. 3a. This indispensable book ought to be reprinted. The same ermine-trimmed cuffs appear on a charter of Henry VI of 1446, ibid., Pl. 1c; and on the presentation page of the 'Dictes des Philosophes' (Lambeth Palace Library, MS. 265) of 1477, illus. Cheetham, *Life and Times*, p. 79.

[8]   I owe this reference to Mr Martin Holmes, for whose help in the preparation of this chapter I am most grateful. If the 'Pageant of Richard Beauchamp' (BL, Cotton MS. Julius E. IV, fol. 8v and *passim*) of 1480–5 is also cited, a case for the fashion's pre-eminence in the years before 1500 begins to build up. The Beauchamp Pageant has been published in full in two monographs: one edited by William, Earl of Carysfort, *The Pageants of Richard Beauchamp, Earl of Warwick*, Roxburghe Club 150 (Oxford, 1908); the other edited by Viscount Dillon and W. H. St John Hope, *Pageant of the Birth, Life and Death of Richard Beauchamp, Earl of Warwick, K.G., 1389–1439* (London, 1914).

125 The Round Table (detail): the rose and central inscription.

The rose

The double rose of the House of Tudor was adopted as soon as Henry VII had married Elizabeth of York, early in 1486.[9] The more usual way to represent it is with a red outer and white inner rose, as on the Round Table (Pl. XXV; Fig. 125). However, from the first the colours were interchangeable, as they remained on the Garter collar, as codified in 1522.[10] Elizabeth of York wears the roses in alternating form, white on red, red on white, in the contemporary version of her portrait at Holyrood House. The earliest surviving Garter of c.1489 shows the white rose with a red centre and gold stamens:[11] indeed, so simple a white rose with so small a red centre that it hardly departs from Yorkist tradition, when a white enamelled rose with a red jewelled centre was presented to Charles the Bold by Edward IV.[12] The rose on the Round Table is laid out with a vigorous simplicity which suggests that its designer was well versed in Tudor heraldic motifs. Iconographically it indicates a time span no shorter than 1486–1603. However, close visual parallels can be drawn with examples of the first thirty years of the sixteenth century. The rendering of the rose in the glass, now destroyed, of the west window of Henry VII's chapel at Westminster was similar.[13] The closest comparison is with the ceiling painting of roses in

[9] The evidence for the immediate use of the Tudor Rose is set out by Charles Ross, *The Wars of the Roses* (London, 1976), p. 15. The Croyland Chronicle, finished by April 1486, refers to the opposing roses.

[10] In the voussoirs of the arch from the north transept to the north choir aisle at Worcester there are traces of a band of white roses with red roses in their centres. This decoration may be associated with the chantry chapel built in the choir for Prince Arthur, d.1502. In the vault of the south-east chapel of Winchester Cathedral itself the roses are alternately red with white centres and white with red centres. The polychrome here has been heavily restored, but presumably the restoration followed ancient indications.

[11] In the collection of the National Trust at Anglesey Abbey. See Charles R. Beard, 'The Emperor Maximilian's Garter in the Collection of Lord Fairhaven', *Connoisseur*, 131 (1952), 108–9. Illus. D. Starkey (ed.), *Henry VIII: A European Court in England* (Greenwich, 1991), p. 98, No. VI.6. The heraldic drawing in BL, Harleian MS. 4632, fol. 237 gives a white rose with a red rose superimposed, the whole set against a Yorkist sunburst, and flanked by a red and a white rose. Illus. Ross, *Wars of the Roses*, p. 12. In the painting of the Field of the Cloth of Gold in the Royal Collection, the Tudor Roses in the spandrels of the arch into Henry VIII's temporary palace at Guisnes have five alternations: a red centre, white, red, white, and red again. See Starkey (ed.), *Henry VIII*, pp. 50–1.

[12] See my *Richard III*, National Portrait Gallery publication 132 (London, 1973 and 1978), Pl. 48.

[13] See Royal Commission on Historical Monuments, *London*, i, *Westminster Abbey* (London, 1924), Pl. 119. As the Commission suggests, one would expect the glazing of the chapel window to have been carried out near the end of the building operations, i.e. 1515–19. On the other hand, I have difficulty in accepting the thesis that a schema including, and including prominently, the feathers of the Prince of Wales would have been drawn up when there was no Prince of Wales. I would therefore prefer to assume that this window was designed, if not placed, before 1509. The same problem arises with the Fairford glass and the Rudhall frieze.

Bishop Sherborne's palace at Chichester, which must have been carried out before 1528 (see below, p. 327, and Fig. 126).[14]

The crown

Late medieval heraldry attributed to King Arthur a shield of three crowns, sometimes quartered with a statue of the Virgin.[15] The form of these crowns tended to follow contemporary fashion, so they do not help us in considering the crown worn by Arthur on the table (Plate XXIV; Fig. 127). This presents several features for examination.

The hoops: The arched ('imperial') crown was not represented on the English Great Seal until 1471.[16] From that date it became more or less invariable in representations of Tudor insignia. But there are important representations of the imperial crown before 1471, for example in the Coventry window of *c.* 1451–61 (Fig. 123). In Westminster Abbey, Henry V's chantry, built between 1437 and 1441, has two different representations of coronations. In the one facing the south ambulatory, the king wears a low, solid crown which has been assumed to represent St Edward's crown. In the scene facing north he wears a prominently hooped imperial crown which appears to be ornamented exclusively with fleurs-de-lys. This makes the point that the imperial type of crown was being adopted in France, if anything, slightly earlier than in England. I interpret these two scenes to represent the two crownings of Henry as king of England and symbolically as heir presumptive to the throne of

---

[14] See Edward Croft-Murray, 'Lambert Barnard: an English Early Renaissance Painter', *Archaeological Journal*, 113 (1956), 108–25, esp. p. 114 and Pl. XIXa. I am particularly grateful to the late Mr Croft-Murray for his generous help in the preparation of this chapter. The relationship between the roof at Chichester and the Round Table is further discussed under the heading of 'Artist', p. 322–7. Yorkist roses *en soleil* adorn the rood canopy at Rainham Church, Kent.

[15] For example, 'The Genealogy of Kingship' (Society of Antiquaries, MS. 501) of 1447–55 gives Arthur a red shield with three gold crowns. Many earlier examples, however, set the crowns against a blue ground. See Ashe *et al.*, *Quest for Arthur's Britain*, ill. 17, and compare ill. 5.

[16] For the Crown Imperial, see now Ronald Lightbrown, 'The English Coronation Regalia before the Commonwealth' in Claude Blair (ed.), *The Crown Jewels. The History of the Coronation Regalia in the Jewel House of the Tower of London*, 2 vols. (London, 1998), pp. 257–353, at pp. 293–5. See also A. J. Collins, *Jewels and Plate of Queen Elizabeth I: the Inventory of 1574* (London, 1955), Introduction, pp. 10–13, and pp. 264–6. For the representation of Edward the Confessor's crown, see Martin Holmes, 'The Crowns of England', *Archaeologia*, 86 (1937), 73–90; and 'New Light on St Edward's Crown', ibid., 97 (1959), 213–23. For the Great Seals, see A. B. Wyon and Allan Wyon, *The Great Seals of England* (London, 1887).

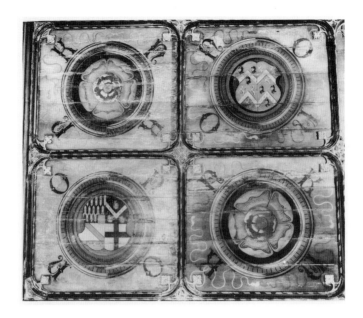

126 Chichester, the ceiling of the hall of the bishop's palace painted between 1524 and 1528(?) probably by Lambert Barnard.

127 The Round Table (detail): the crown and the head of King Arthur.

a   *b*

128 The Golden Bulla, 1527: *a*, obverse; *b*, reverse.

129 Plea Roll, Hilary 1520–1, initial letter 'P'.

a

130 The coronations of King Henry VI: *a*, at Westminster in 1429; *b*, at St. Denis in 1431. From *The Beauchamp Pageant*.

b

France. The adoption of imperial-type crowns was undertaken in France for the same reason as in England: it signified a declaration of autonomy.[17] That issue became a burning one in England in the 1510s and 1520s, as can be illustrated by the entirely new shape and emphasis of the imperial crown worn by Henry VIII on the Golden Bulla of 1527 (Fig. 128).[18] Here both the crown worn by the king on the recto and its representation on the verso rise (literally) to new heights. The hoops, it would appear, spring from the lower part of the rim and override the crosses and fleurs-de-lys. Does the crown represented on the Golden Bulla describe an actual crown made at that point in Henry VIII's reign? At the coronation of Edward VI in 1547, he was crowned three times: once with the crown of St Edward,[19] then with the imperial crown, and lastly with 'a very rich one made pourpously for his Grace'.[20]

The imperial crown was too large and too heavy for Edward VI and had to be held over the boy's head. Although crowns were altered for every occasion, it is nevertheless a possibility that this one had been made for Henry VIII before 1527. The Golden Bulla crown represents a *ne plus ultra* of imperial crowns (further reflected in Henry VIII's Great Seal of 1532, Fig. 134). However, a crown as emphatically hooped as the one on the Round Table occurs on the Plea Roll for Hilary 1520–1 (Fig. 129). It would not be an anachronism to read into the image on the Round Table the fully fledged imperial pretensions of Henry VIII, for by 1519 Cuthbert Tunstall had already told Henry that 'his own islands were an empire'.[21] In that same year the prime ship in Henry's fleet was called the *Henry*

[17]   There is a vigorous literature on the tension between lay and spiritual authority during the later Middle Ages. See Alistair Fox and John Guy, *Reassessing the Henrician Age: Humanism, Politics and Reform 1500–1550* (Oxford, 1986), especially John Guy's article on 'Thomas Cromwell and the Intellectual Origins of the Henrician Revolution', pp. 151–78.

[18]   For the Golden Bulla of Henry VIII and the one of Francis I, see Starkey (ed.), *Henry VIII*, No. V.33 and V.35, pp. 84–5 illus. There is much which is apposite to the problems of the table in Walter Ullmann, '"This Realm of England is an Empire"', *Journal of Ecclesiastical History*, 30 (1979), 175–203; and R. Koebner, '"The Imperial Crown of this Realm", Henry VIII, Constantine the Great, and Polydore Vergil', *Bulletin of the Institute of Historical Research*, 26 (1953), 29–52.

[19]   I believe that St Edward the Confessor's crown was of the solid, domed type, ornamented with ribs of decoration. Only thus can I square the evidence of his Great Seal (Wyon and Wyon, *Great Seals*, Pl. I, nos. 5 and 6) with Froissart's account of Henry VI's coronation, where he was crowned with the crown of St Edward, 'which is arched over like a cross' (quoted by Holmes, 'Crowns of England', p. 79). The imperial crown, on the other hand, has arched hoops meeting in the centre, and is worn over a red or purple velvet Cap of Maintenance. It is not always easy to distinguish between the solid and padded crowns in small images, but the crown on the Round Table is definitely imperial.

[20]   Janet Arnold, 'The "Coronation" Portrait of Queen Elizabeth', *Burlington Magazine*, 120 (1978), 729–41, esp. pp. 731–2.

[21]   For Henry's imperial hopes in 1516–19, see below, pp. 448, 473.

Imperial. The imperial precedent of King Arthur is described in Malory's *Morte Darthur*, the chief literary source for this image.[22] The Malory manuscript, which remained for centuries at Winchester, offers the fullest account of Arthur's triumphs. In its colophon we read that Arthur was 'Emperoure hymself thorow dygnyté of his hondys',[23] a text exalted enough for the seated figure on the Round Table, and one probably familiar to the king who commissioned it.

Imperialistic claims were to grow in magnitude as Henry VIII's reign progressed. However, as early as November 1515, Henry said that 'the kings of England in times past never had any superior but God'.[24] In view of the insistent visual imagery that marches with Henry VIII's growing claims of supremacy, Walter Ullmann in particular seems overcautious in his reading of the term 'imperial crown' as 'an abstract summary or short-lived device for that imperial function of a king'.[25] From the 1574 inventory of Queen Elizabeth's jewel house we learn that the 'Imperial Crown or King's Crown of Gold' weighed more than seven pounds.[26] None of Henry VIII's heirs could actually bear the weight of that English 'abstract summary'.

The crosses: Most early Tudor representations of the royal crown show it with crosses and fleurs-de-lys alternating. Occasionally one appears without the other. Is there any significance in the use here of the cross without the fleurs-de-lys? In the series of pictures known as the Beauchamp Pageant, which I have elsewhere suggested was made between 1480 and 1485,[27] there are two types of crown. In one picture the king of France is shown with a crown of fleurs-de-lys, with no hoops;[28] in another scene which shows the young Henry VI's coronation as king of France, he too wears this crown of fleurs-de-lys only (Fig. 130*b*).[29] On the other hand, Henry IV, Henry V, and their queens all wear crowns of crosses alternating with fleurs-de-lys, hooped, and Henry VI wears such a crown for his coronation at Westminster (Fig. 130*a*).[30] This differentiation suggests that in the standard

[22] Sir Thomas Malory, *The Works*, ed. Eugène Vinaver, 2nd edn., 3 vols, (Oxford, 1967).

[23] Ibid., i, p. 247.

[24] Ullmann, 'This Realm', p. 187.

[25] Ibid.

[26] Arnold, '"Coronation" Portrait', p. 732.

[27] See Dillon and St John Hope, *Pageant of Richard Beauchamp*, Pl. XXIV and my *Richard III*, pp. 57–8.

[28] Dillon and St John Hope, *Pageant of Richard Beauchamp*, Pl. XII (fol. 6b).

[29] Ibid. Pl. XLVII (fol. 24).

[30] Ibid. Pl. XLVI (fol. 23b).

Tudor crown of crosses interspersed with fleurs-de-lys, the fleurs-de-lys refer to British pretensions to the French throne. Arthur's reign antedated the medieval claim to the French throne. Could that be the reason why the fleurs-de-lys were omitted from his crown on the Round Table?

The points: Crowns with points, and nothing else but points, are commonly found on Roman imperial coins of the third century AD, not least on both official issues and copies minted in Roman Britain,[31] and the misunderstood fragments of similar crowns filtered down into the Anglo-Saxon coinage. If a genuine coin of King Arthur had survived, it might well have shown him wearing a crown so ornamented. Crowns of naked points reappear on the heads of the earlier kings – William I to Edward I – in the Elizabethan and Jacobean sets of portraits of English kings.[32] The prominent part paid by numismatic studies in Elizabethan antiquarianism may account for this feature. Is there any chance that the use of points on the crown of King Arthur at Winchester is a deliberate archaism of this kind? The spandrels of the painted 'framing' of the portrait of Richard III in the Royal Collection and its derivations are decorated with quatrefoils containing portraits of a lady and a king wearing a crown with spikes. These images, which I have suggested, may have been intended for Helena and Constantine, have been dated by tree-ring analysis to *c.*1518–23.[33] Henry VIII's psalter of 1540–2 shows King David with a crown consisting entirely of points.[34] The crown worn by Edward the Confessor on the grille of Henry VII's tomb at Westminster Abbey has points with knobs between its crosses and fleurs-de-lys (Fig. 131). This grille was begun by Thomas Ducheman in 1505, but was still unfinished in 1509.[35] Decorative scallops topped with trefoils also ornament the crowns used heraldically in the nave of King's College Chapel, Cambridge, carved by Thomas

---

[31] For example a coin of Carausius (287–93) from the London Mint; illus. in C. H. V. Sutherland, *Roman Coins* (London, 1974), no. 509, Pl. on p. 263. The earliest substantial image of Arthur, that in mosaic at Otranto Cathedral, dated 1166, shows him wearing a conspicuous crown of points; illus. in Richard Barber, *King Arthur in Legend and History* (London, 1973), Pl. 6.

[32] See the crowns worn in the prints from Godett's 'Chronicle', *c.*1562, illus. in T. D. Kendrick, *British Antiquity* (London, 1950), Pl. XI.

[33] See my *Richard III*, p. 44, Pl. 26.

[34] BL, MS. Roy. 2A XVI. See my article, 'Henry VIII and King David', in D. Williams (ed.), *Early Tudor England: Proceedings of the 1987 Harlaxton Symposium* (Woodbridge, 1989), pp. 183–205.

[35] See also Robin Gibson, 'The National Portrait Gallery's Set of Kings and Queens at Montacute House', *National Trust Yearbook 1975*, pp. 81–7. The earliest royal panel portrait, that of Rudolph IV of Habsburg, *c.*1365, wears a hooped crown of points: see *Europäische Kunst um 1400* (Vienna, 1962), Pl. 1 and Entry 80, p. 145.

131 Edward the Confessor, brass statue from the grille of the tomb of King Henry VII, Westminster Abbey, cast by Thomas the Ducheman, *c*.1505.

132 Crown and rose, from King's College Chapel, Cambridge, *c*.1508–15.

133 The Round Table (detail): the orb and sword.

134 Henry VIII's Second Great Seal, 1532.

135 Henry VIII's Third Great Seal, 1542.

Stockton in 1512–13 (Fig. 132).[36] Perhaps the most important precedent for the points on the crown of King Arthur are the points on the crowns above the tomb chests of the Anglo-Saxon kings and bishops reinterred *c.*1520 over the choir screen in Winchester Cathedral. These tomb chests (Fig. 149), in conjunction with the Anglo-Saxon bishops painted upon the backs of the wings of the Winchester altar-piece by 'T. G.' in 1526 (see below, p. 325, and Fig. 148), argue an exceptional interest in the antiquities of Winchester, presumably on the part of Bishop Fox. If an archaizing intention can be read into the form of the crown worn by King Arthur, then the bishop emerges as the likely source of antiquarian information.[36a]

The orb

The Great Seal of Henry VIII of 1532 (Fig. 134) marked the abandonment of a long-stemmed cross upon the orb in favour of a short-stemmed variety.[37] Henry VIII's first Great Seal of 1509 had been, to all intents and purposes, merely a repetition of his father's, established in 1485. Thus changes in fashion for the orb in the years preceding 1532 have to be followed in the Plea Rolls and charters of the first part of Henry VIII's reign. Some show the gobonée form,[38] others crosses crosslet.[39] It is doubtful whether the actual form of the royal orb was known to the artists.[40] A

[36] Lawrence Stone, *Sculpture in Britain: the Middle Ages*, Pelican History of Art (Harmondsworth, 1955), Pl. 187b and p. 229. The bosses of Prince Arthur's chantry at Worcester, dated by Stone (ibid., p. 227) to 1504–6, are of the same form. It is still found in Holinshed's 'Chronicle' of 1577 (illus. Holmes, 'New Light', Pl. LXXIXc).

[36a] For the mortuary chests on the choir screens at Winchester, see Martin Biddle, 'Early Renaissance at Winchester', in John Crook (ed.), *Winchester Cathedral: Nine Hundred Years 1093–1993* (Chichester and Winchester, 1993), pp. 257–304, at pp. 275–8. Biddle suggests that the chests may have been purchased, probably in London, in the mid 1520s, and that the lids, which are altogether simpler, may have been replacements of 1661. On the other hand, the lids could equally have been made locally in the 1520s to complete the Italian chests. The crowns are fixed to the lids.

[37] For a full account of all the Great Seals discussed here, see W. de Grey Birch, *Catalogue of the Seals in the British Museum* (London, 1887), vol. 1, and Wyon and Wyon, *Great Seals*. For this point, see especially Wyon and Wyon, Pl. XVIII, no. 99. As Henry VIII's first Great Seal repeated his father's, the 1532 design was the first opportunity for the short-cross orb to appear on the Great Seal.

[38] Patent for Cardinal College, Oxford, 5 May 1526, PRO, E24/6/1 (Fig. 136); illus. Auerbach, *Tudor Artists*, Pl. 12a. See also the drawing of the Confessor in the Islip Roll of 1532, in Westminster Abbey Library, illus. Holmes, 'New Light', Pl. LXXVI.

[39] Patent for Cardinal College, Oxford, 25 May 1529, PRO, E24/20/1; illus. Auerbach, *Tudor Artists*, Pl. 13a.

[40] For actual orbs in the royal regalia, see Collins, *Jewels and Plate*, pp. 16–18 and no. 3, p. 267; and Arnold, '"Coronation" Portrait', p. 731. For the orb, see now Lightbown, 'English Coronation Regalia' (as above, n. 16), pp. 322–8.

cross patée like the one on the orb on the Round Table (Plate XXIII; Fig. 133), although of less exaggerated form, appears on the Letters Patent for Cardinal College, Ipswich, of 20 August 1528 (Fig. 138).[41]

The manner in which the orb is carried by a seated figure is an important aspect of its representation. Is it held in the palm of the hand with only the fingertips showing?[42] Is it held against the body with most of the sitter's left hand seen in profile? Or is it resting on the knee with the hand above it, probably threading the cross between the fingers? This last might be considered the dramatic style, and is associated with the introduction of Michelangelesque seated poses.[43] The first known example of this pose, both more vital and more casual, is on the Golden Bulla of 1527, designed under the supervision of Cardinal Wolsey, whose Italianate taste is well known (Fig. 128a).[44] The Great Seal of 1542 marked the high point of this development (Fig. 135),[45] and attempts at the same swaggering pose are found in illuminations of the same year.[46] The hand is over rather than around or under the orb on the Plea Roll for Hilary 1541, but the artist was so ill-acquainted with the new convention that the orb is suspended in mid-air.[47] From 1542 onwards there are numerous examples of the orb balanced on the knee.[48] Elizabeth I is often shown with it tilted sideways, a fashion followed by Charles II. Here the subject passes beyond our present study. In earlier Tudor as in Plantagenet times the more common form shows the orb held in the palm of the hand. There are, however, several examples among the Plea Rolls of the years 1520–6 of a profile hand, as appears on the Round Table (Pl. XXIII; Fig. 133). The first, on the Plea Roll for Hilary 1520–1 (Fig. 129)[49] is clumsier than the Round Table pose. More sophisti-

---

[41] Auerbach, *Tudor Artists*, Pl. 10c.

[42] Plea Roll of Henry VIII, Michelmas 1535, PRO, KB27/1097; illus. Auerbach, *Tudor Artists*, Pl. 10d.

[43] Auerbach, *Tudor Artists*, Pls. 4b, 5, 8, 9, 10c, etc. However, the first definitive appearance in this country of Michaelangelo's grandiose seated pose, with one leg drawn back behind the chair and the extended arm of his Christ in the *Last Judgement*, was in the design for the triumphal arch to greet the coronation of Anne Boleyn in May 1533, where Holbein used it for the Apollo. Illus. in Roy Strong, *Holbein and Henry VIII* (London, 1967), Pl. 6.

[44] Wyon and Wyon, *Great Seals*, Pl. XIX, no. 103. The Golden Bulla of 1527 surely reflects the sophisticated taste of Wolsey. After his death there is a slump in the quality of royal imagery, as instanced by the Great Seal of 1532, ibid., Pl. XVIII, no. 99; a slump which lasted until Holbein entered royal service.

[45] Illus. Birch, *Catalogue*, Pl. III; and Wyon and Wyon, *Great Seals*, Pl. XIX, no. 101.

[46] For example the Plea Roll for Trinity 1542, PRO, KB27/1124; illus. Auerbach, *Tudor Artists*, Pl. 16.

[47] PRO, KB27/1118; illus. Auerbach, *Tudor Artists*, frontispiece.

[48] Letter Patent to the Dean and Chapter of Winchester Cathedral, 28 March 1541, Winchester Cathedral Muniments; illus. Auerbach, *Tudor Artists*, Pl. 15a.

[49] PRO, KB27/1038; illus. Auerbach, *Tudor Artists*, Pl. 12b.

136 Patent for Cardinal College, Oxford, 5 May 1526, initial letter 'H'.

137 Patent for Cardinal College, Oxford, 8 May 1526, initial letter 'H'.

138 Patent for Cardinal College, Ipswich, 20 August, 1528, initial letter 'H'.

139 Plea Roll, Hilary 1527–8, initial letter 'P'.

cated examples appear on the Plea Roll for Hilary 1525–6,[50] and the patent for Cardinal College, Oxford, of 8 May 1526 (Fig. 137).[51]

A certain dissatisfaction with the well-worn formula of the orb held in the palm of the hand is visible, therefore, in three drawings datable to 1520–6. The future might be said to have lain with the bolder solution of the orb balanced between hand and knee, probably first demonstrated in this country in the Golden Bulla of 1527. The position of the hand on the Round Table falls into the experimental period leading up to that resolution.

The sword

The fame of Excalibur, or Caliburn,[52] as it was still known to the author of the Black Book of the Garter incorporating material of before 1529[53] (although the fair copy is of 1534), was not so exalted as it was to become under the pen of Tennyson. From the early sixteenth-century viewpoint, it suffered from the disadvantage that, by its nature, it had left no relics.[54] We know, however, from Caxton and John Rastell that the impression of Arthur's seal hanging by the shrine at Westminster showed him carrying orb and *sceptre*,[55] so there was in any case another option open to the painter at Winchester or his advisers (Plate XXIII; Figs. 133, 142).

---

[50] PRO, KB27/1058; illus. Auerbach, *Tudor Artists*, Pl. 10a.

[51] PRO, E24/11/2; illus. Auerbach, *Tudor Artists*, Pl. 10b.

[52] Excalibur is called Caliburn or Caliburnus, from the Welsh 'Caledfwlch', in Geoffrey of Monmouth's *Historia Regum Britanniae* finished in 1135. See Richard Barber, *King Arthur in Legend and History* (Ipswich, 1973), pp. 25 and 40.

[53] The text includes references to Wolsey so fulsome they could hardly have been drafted after his downfall in 1529: for example, '... as that prudent and active Man, Cardinal Wolsey, then of the Council to this wise Monarch, with great Foresight and a good Omen foretold. ... To whose Mouth, he who gave a prophetick Utterance to Balaam, might give a prophetick Virtue also ...'. The text of the Black Book was published by J. Anstis, *The Register of the Most Noble Order of the Garter from its Cover in Black Velvet Usually Called the Black Book* (London, 1724), pp. 35–6. The entry (No. VI.5) for the Black Book of the Garter in Starkey (ed.), *Henry VIII*, pp. 94–5 illus. reads: 'begun in 1534, but incorporates material from an earlier register (now lost) started under Henry V ...'.

[54] Leland, however, relates that the bridge at Pontperlus was said to be the place from which Excalibur was thrown into the waters: T. Hearne (ed.), *Itinerary* (Oxford, 1710), i, p. 148, quoted by Kendrick, *British Antiquity*, p. 95.

[55] See Caxton's preface to his *Morte Darthur* (1485), and John Rastell's *The Pastyme of People* (1529), both quoted by Kendrick, *British Antiquity*, p. 96. The detail of Arthur seated on a rainbow suggests either that the design was altered from one of Christ in Judgement, or that it may have been related to one from the Byzantine empire, showing the emperor seated on a bow-legged throne. On the other hand, the bowed throne of classical origin is not unknown in the Gothic period. See for example the throne of Charles V between Spiritual and Temporal Power in 'Le Songe du Vergier' of 1378, BL, Royal MS. 19 C.IV, fol. 154; illus. George Warner and Julius P. Gilson, *Catalogue of the Western MSS. in the Old Royal and King's Collections in the British Museum*, ii (London, 1921), p. 334 and Pl. 110.

British royalty from Edward the Confessor to Henry III were shown on the rectos of their Great Seals seated, carrying orbs and swords. In 1259, when Henry III made peace with France, he exchanged the sword on his Great Seal for a sceptre. The peaceable significance of this gesture was appreciated at the time.[56] From that moment onwards, the sword was relegated to the versos of Great Seals, where it was brandished by the monarch on horseback, armed for battle. The implication was clear: enthroned, the king dispenses justice and mercy. In his more active capacity, he embodies might. On Plea Rolls and charters, where again the king is usually shown enthroned, the orb and sceptre are the norm. The sword makes a very occasional appearance, usually when the king is shown standing.[57] In 1554, when Philip and Mary had to be shown enthroned together, he carried the sword, and she the sceptre:[58] his might, her justice. In 1521 Pope Leo X presented to Henry 'One great Two handed Sworde garnyshed with syulver and guylte',[59] surely with reference to his new papal title as Defender of the Faith. That presentation and the title were fresh in the mind in 1522. A reference to it in terms of Excalibur on the Round Table would have been appropriate, if the painting was of that year. If it was done before the investiture then it conveyed the message of Arthur, emperor by right of battle – like Henry VIII (Pl. XXIII; Fig. 123).

The face and beard

Art history has paid too little attention to one of the most striking visual achievements of Henry VII's reign – the introduction, in 1504–5, of the profile head on his silver testoon.[60] In one gesture the nation was offered, in place of a full-face beardless image still surrounded by the curled hair of Edward III, the sophisticated profile

---

[56] See *Chronica Johanni de Oxenedes*, ed. H. Ellis (Rolls ser., 1859), p. 219; quoted by Michael Prestwich, *War, Politics and Finance under Edward I* (London, 1972), p. 14.

[57] e.g. Plea Roll for Edward IV, Hilary 1465–6, PRO, KB27/819; illus. Auerbach, *Tudor Artists*, Pl. 2a.

[58] Margaret Post, *Royal Portraits from the Plea Rolls, Henry VIII to Charles II* (London, 1974), Pl. 6.

[59] Collins, *Jewels and Plate*, p. 19, quoting Sir F. Palgrave, *The Ancient Kalendars & Inventories of the Treasury of His Majesty's Exchequer* (Record Commission, 1836), ii, p. 306. The inventories themselves are BL, Stowe MS. 558, fol. 70v, and BL, Add. MS. 12501, fols. 16v and 17.

[60] D. M. Metcalf, *Coins of Henry VII*, discussing the date and attribution of the profile design, pp. xiv–xvi and Pls. XLII *et seq*. This innovation was immediately reflected in the profile of Henry VII's head within a roundel on the *lattimo* vase which was probably brought to Henry VII by Castiglione in 1506. A coin must have been sent out to Italy for a model: see Starkey (ed.), *Henry VIII*, No. II.14, p. 35. The beardless face and bouffant hair of Edward III in 1344 had been repeated, with amazing disregard for fashion, for all small denominations of the coinage until 1500. Even Henry V, whose 'pudding basin' hair style is known to most twentieth-century British children, appeared on his groats with Edward III's curls.

of a Renaissance king, portrayed with the blend of idealization and fidelity which is the mark of a great numismatic designer. Nothing was done to modify this new face during the first fifteen years of Henry VIII's reign, but the groat and half-groat of Cardinal Wolsey's coinage of 1526 introduced the first unmistakeable profile portrait of Henry VIII himself, already full-jowled but at that moment beardless.[61] This in its turn went unrevised until 1542–3, when the first full-face image of the bearded and ageing king was put forward and rejected. In 1544 the familiar full-face was put into common currency.

The testimony of the Wolsey coins that Henry VIII was clean-shaven in 1526 is supported by a group of miniatures, all closely related, and in one case bearing an inscription dating it to his thirty-fifth year, i.e. 1525–6.[62] One of the four versions of this miniature departs from the others in showing a beard, suggesting that the king grew one while the image was being repeated. This is confirmed by the most curious and striking of all Plea Roll images of Henry VIII, that for Hilary 1527–8 (Fig. 139).[63] This drawing is unique among the Plea Rolls in showing the king to half length, within the indications of a frame of the type used at that time. Moreover, he is in profile and bearded. I am inclined to attribute the use of the profile to the influence of the Wolsey coinage, only then a year in circulation. The face is of a similar laborious truthfulness. But it appears the artist was sufficiently near to events to make the emendation of a beard. We can say, therefore, with some confidence that Henry VIII grew a beard early in 1526.[64] But was it for the first time?

If Henry VIII had one reason to cover his chin – a jowl which had become heavy, like the rest of him, before he reached thirty years[65] – the Habsburgs had another, in their characteristic underhung jaws. It is as well that Charles V had adopted a beard before Titian painted him,[66] but at some date, perhaps early in 1522, his jaw line was

---

[61] J. Alexander Parsons, 'Notes on the "Wolsey" Coins of Henry VIII', *British Numismatic Journal*, 25 (1945–8), 60–70 and Pl. opp. p. 64.

[62] See Graham Reynolds, 'Portrait Miniatures', *Connoisseur Period Guides: Tudor* (London, 1956), Pl. 69a. The dated version, which may be the best, is in the Fitz William Museum, Cambridge. Two of the others, one of them bearded, are in the Royal Collection, and the fourth is in the possession of the Duke of Buccleugh and Queensbury. The type is attributed to Lucas Hornebolte. See Roy Strong, *Artists of the Tudor Court*, Victoria and Albert Museum publication (London, 1983), pp. 34–44, esp. Cat. nos. 5 and 7. See also Daphne Foskett, *A Dictionary of British Miniature Painters*, i (London, 1972), p. 338 and ibid; ii, Pl. 170, no, 440.

[63] PRO, KB27/1066; illus. Auerbach, *Tudor Artists*, Pl. 11 and dust-jacket.

[64] The beard also appears on the Patent for Cardinal College, Oxford, for 5 May 1526, PRO, E24/6/1; illus. Auerbach, *Tudor Artists*, Pl. 12a (here, Fig. 136).

[65] For Henry VIII's progress in girth, observe his suits of armour, especially the difference between the suit of c.1512 and the one of 1515–20, illus. A. R. Dufty, *European Armour in the Tower of London* (London, 1968), Pls. X, XII, and XIII.

[66] In the Prado Museum, Madrid.

140 Henry VIII, *c.*1520, artist unknown (Anglesey Abbey).

141 Henry VIII: radiograph of the Anglesey Abbey portrait.

still painfully undisguised (Fig. 157).[67] It has been suggested that since we know Henry VIII was influenced in these matters by Francis I (see below, p. 314 and Fig. 158), he may also have adapted his chin to Charles V's. None of the Plea Rolls up to 1526–7 suggests a beard, but they are plainly copied one from another, showing some influence from other sources but without reference to the 'sitter'. The same is true of the charters so far examined. However, further evidence emerges from the study by the late Dr John Fletcher of a series of early portraits of Henry VIII.[68] He has identified as having been painted on boards cut from the same tree a group of portraits of the second decade of the sixteenth century with cusped borders, showing Henry as a very young man. They all show him beardless, with one exception, the example at Anglesey Abbey (Fig. 140). Here X-rays show that the portrait was indeed once beardless like the rest, but that a beard has been added later and the hair shortened (Fig. 141). Henry adopted shorter hair with his second beard, but for aesthetic reasons he might have done the same with an earlier beard. A portrait in the National Portrait Gallery showing Henry with a somewhat similar beard to that in the Anglesey Abbey alteration emerges, on tree-ring dating, to have been painted on a panel of *c.* 1511–16 *c.*1515–20. (Fig. 156)[69] Among other portraits of Henry, the ones formerly in the collections of Dudley Cutbill and H. Clifford Smith show a spade beard unlike the double goatee of early 1526.[70]

---

[67] See also the portrait from the studio of Bernaert van Orley, already in the Royal Collection by 1542, reproduced in colour in Jasper Ridley, *Henry VIII* (London, 1984), facing p. 129. Mr Martin Holmes has suggested to me that since Henry VIII grew his first beard in compliment to Francis I, at some time before the Field of Cloth of Gold, he may have shaved it off again to greet the smooth if jutting chin of Charles V in 1522, but the double portrait of Charles and Henry probably painted to celebrate the visit of 1522 shows both rulers bearded (Plate XXVIII).

[68] The Dendrochronology Exhibition at the National Portrait Gallery, 1977. The bearded portrait from Anglesey Abbey, on a panel cut *c.*1513–18 and painted between 1515 and 1521, appears under X-ray to have had the beard added. As it was cut from the same tree as a panel for another smooth-chinned version, this is consistent with their having been produced at the same time. For a fuller publication, see J. Fletcher, 'A Group of English Royal Portraits Painted Soon After 1513: a Dendrochronological Study', *Studies in Conservation*, 21 (1976), 171–8, especially p. 174 and Fig. 6. For the Anglesey Abbey portrait, now in the possession of the National Trust, see 'Three Royal Portraits in the Possession of Lord Fairhaven', *Connoisseur* 123 (1949), 98. For Fletcher's subsequent correction of his dating, making the panels four years earlier, see above Chapter 5, p. 184 and nn. 21–2. See also Roy Strong, *Tudor and Jacobean Portraits* (London, 1969), i, pp. 158–61 and ii. pl. 302.

[69] NPG 4690. For the tree-ring dating of this panel see John Fletcher, 'Tree Ring Dates for Some Panel Paintings in England', *Burlington Magazine*, 116 (1974), 250–8, esp. p. 256 and Table 2 but see last note for correction.

[70] Illus. *Connoisseur*, 122 (1948), Pl. 167; subsequently in the collection of N. Balchin and sold at Sotheby's, 2 December 1964 (Lot 103). For the fourth portrait of the bearded king belonging to this early group and once optimistically ascribed to Jean Perréal, see *Connoisseur* 123 (1949), 52–3, and James Lees-Milne, *Tudor Renaissance* (London, 1951), Fig. 5. This portrait, formerly in the collection of H. Clifford Smith, was last recorded at Christie's, 7 July 1967 (Lot 10).

So there are at least four portraits which may represent an early beard, although the evidence thus far is not conclusive enough to rule out their representing the beard of 1526. However the wrestling scene (which has not been altered) in the retrospective painting of the Field of Cloth of Gold shows both Henry VIII and Francis I with beards in 1520.[71] Even more significant is the report of the Venetian Ambassador Sebastiano Giustiniani written in the autumn of 1519, and covering the whole course of his four-year mission from April 1515 to July 1519. In this final despatch, Giustiniani says that Henry was then twenty-nine years old. Since the king's twenty-ninth birthday did not fall until June 1520, Giustiniani must have meant that he was then in his twenty-ninth year, which began on 28 June 1519. Giustiniani's description of Henry belongs therefore to the last month of his embassy: Henry, he wrote,

was much handsomer than any other Sovereign in Christendom, – a great deal handsomer than the King of France. He was very fair, and his whole frame admirably proportioned. Hearing that King Francis wore a beard, he allowed his own to grow, and as it is reddish, he then got a beard which looked like gold.[72]

So there is no doubt about it. Henry VIII had a beard by 1519. What we do not know is at what point between April 1515 and July 1519 he grew it.

[71] Roy Strong argues persuasively that the cycle of paintings which includes the Field of Cloth of Gold consists of Elizabethan copies of lost originals: *Holbein and Henry VIII* (London, 1967), pp. 25–6 (reprinted in *The Tudor and Stuart Monarchy*, i (Woodbridge, 1996)). David Starkey dates the painting to *c.*1545 ((ed.) *Henry VIII*, p. 51) which reconciles all elements. The dress of the yeomen of the guard suggests 25 years after the event. On the other hand it used to be plain in a slanting light that the face of Henry VIII in the central procession had been repainted. It may be that the evidence of repainting, which occupied a small circular area encompassing the full-face of the king, is not again legible since the tragic fire at Hampton Court. However it was clear when the picture was exhibited at the National Portrait Gallery in 1977. For what reason would the face have been altered, if not to bring it up to date with the full-face Holbein type to which it now conforms? Does that not in itself suggest that the picture as such existed before Holbein invented that type in 1538?

[72] Rawdon Brown (ed.), *Four Years at the Court of Henry VIII. Selection of Despatches Written by the Venetian Ambassador, Sebastian Giustinian and Addressed to the Signory of Venice, January 12th 1515, to July 26th 1519*, 2 vols. (London, 1854), ii p. 312; also in Rawdon Brown (ed.), *CSP Venetian*, ii, *1509–1519* (London, 1867), no. 1287 (p. 559); and précis in *Letters and Papers Henry VIII*, 3.i (1519–21), no. 402 (p. 142). Jasper Ridley, *Henry VIII*, p. 88, might be read as implying that Henry had grown his beard by the time of his first meeting with Giustiniani in April 1515, but Piero Pasqualigo's detailed description of the king's appearance on that occasion does not mention a beard and his words on the king's complexion seem to be positive evidence against it (Brown (ed.), *Four Years*, i. p. 86; compare *Letters and Papers Henry VIII*, 2.i (1515–16), no. 395. The limiting dates are thus April 1515 to July 1519. [M. B.].

There is also some uncertainty as to when he shaved it off. In August 1519 Sir Thomas Boleyn, the English ambassador to France, told Francis that Henry had resolved to wear his beard until they met, as a proof of his desire for their meeting. By November, however, Henry had shaved it off, apparently at Queen Catherine's insistence, for previously, when Henry 'hath worn long his beard, .., the Queen hath daily made him great instance, and desired him to put it off for her sake'. In France, the Queen Mother, appeased for this slight by Boleyn's assurance that Henry 'had greater affection for her son than any King living', remarked that 'the[ir love] is not in the berdes, but in the harts'.[73]

Be that as it may, diplomatic pressures seem to have led Henry to grow his beard again, in fulfilment of his promise to Francis, before their meeting at the Field of Cloth of Gold the next June. In addition to the evidence of the wrestling scene in the retrospective painting, just mentioned, there is the strictly contemporary evidence of *La Description et ordre du camp festins et ioustes*, written at Ardres on 11 June:

> led' Roy Dangleterre est mount beau prince & honneste hault & droit sa maniere doulce & benigne ung peu grasset & une barbe rousse assez grande qui luy advient tres bien.[74]

At some point between June 1520 and early in 1526, Henry again decided to shave off his beard. This was probably not until after the visit of Charles V in 1522 for both rulers are shown bearded in the double portrait which was probably painted to commemorate the signing of one of the treaties agreed during the visit (Plate XXVIII; see below Chapter 12, p. 447). By 1526 Henry had settled for the beard which he retained for the rest of his life.

It may be as well to summarise our present understanding of the history of Henry's beard:

First beard, summer to November 1519

Clean shaven, November 1519 to spring/early summer 1520

Second beard, by June 1520 until at least July 1522
(unless clean shaven in the meanwhile)

Clean shaven, from a date after July 1522 until early 1526

Third beard, from early 1526

---

[73] *Letters and Papers Henry VIII*, 3.i (1519–21), nos. 416, 514. [M. B.].

[74] Copy in BL, C.33.d.22 (2), unpaginated; reprinted with the same title (Paris, 1864), where the description quoted is on p. 20. [M. B.].

Of what importance to the Round Table are the vicissitudes of Henry VIII's jaw line between April 1515 and May 1526? King Arthur is always represented bearded.[75] Yes, but in early Tudor times beards, and especially white beards on elderly chins, were associated with relatively cadaverous cheeks, and were in themselves much longer than the one indicated at Winchester (Pl. XXIV; Fig. 100).[76] A bland unwrinkled face such as we see here, with no hollows beneath the cheek bone, and with a short squarish beard, was a relative novelty. English kings, by and large, had been clean-shaven since Henry IV. The square, but relatively youthful and short-bearded face which Henry VIII presented by 1519 was new (Fig. 147). It can be claimed that it finds some reflection in the Round Table. Obviously Arthur has to appear ancient, but nevertheless it could be said that he has been devised to meet the actuality of the royal appearance halfway. Surely any artist commissioned to give an account of the legendary founder figure of the Tudor dynasty for that dynasty's representative would attempt to build in a family likeness? Henry VIII inherited from his brother the obligation to reincarnate King Arthur.[77] It was surely the intention that he should find here a reflection of himself.

The canopy or celour

The provision of a canopy or celour, a housing around a real or represented figure of secular or sacred importance, has its roots in classical antiquity.[78] The way in which this tabernacling is rendered throughout the Middle Ages provides a touchstone of architectural and domestic fashion. The presence of thousands of empty niches in our churches can blind us to the equal importance of this framing for the human form in domestic settings such as regal or courtly interiors, where very few examples survive. For evidence of what these domestic canopies were like, we must turn to inventories and the painted interiors in

---

[75] As he appeared on the seal at Westminster Abbey: see Kendrick, *British Antiquity*, p. 96.

[76] For example, the faces and beards on the York pulpitum.

[77] See Antonia Gransden, *Historical Writing in England*, ii, *c. 1307 to the Early Sixteenth Century* (London, 1982), pp. 471–5. Starkey (*Henry VIII*, No. VI.5, p. 95) observed that in the illuminated initials of the kings in the Black Book of the Garter, Henry V, the greatest of them, is shown 'as a clear likeness of Henry VIII'. A quite different facial type for Henry V was well known: this can only have been deliberate.

[78] See John Summerson, *Heavenly Mansions and other Essays on Architecture*, (London, 1949), ch. 1: 'Heavenly Mansions: an Interpretation of Gothic'.

manuscripts.[79] In general they fall into two types: those of hard materials, most often wood – the equivalent of the gabling over choir stalls; and those which can best be described as soft furnishings. The first type grew markedly in importance during the fourteenth century, only to be supplanted to some degree during the fifteenth century by soft canopies made of exotic imported fabrics. The introduction of Renaissance forms which could not be executed in soft fabrics revived the popularity of canopies made from hard materials. Nevertheless, in a large proportion of the canopies shown in the Plea Rolls executed between the eighth and the fourteenth years of Henry VIII's reign (1516–22), the soft-furnishing form still predominated.[80] Two canopy forms, which might be termed the 'pelmet' and the 'lampshade' types, are prominent in this group of drawings. A number of designs are without canopy types at all, but the 'pelmet' appears three times, and the 'lampshade' twice. Many drawings and illuminations show how the 'pelmets' were suspended from the domestic ceiling by means of cords.[81] By the wit of the draughtsman, a canopy may hang from his initial letter.[82] The 'lampshade' type can be traced back at least as far as the early fifteenth century.[83] Although designed to display woven materials, this type demands an inner framework of a semi-domed shape. This type, with its affinities to tented pavilions, may be related to the onion-dome canopy, which appears in English art as early as the 1460s. Onion domes are used in the Hastings Chapel paintings at Windsor *c.*1485 and in the Great Malvern priory glass, executed before 1502, and become a strong element in early sixteenth-century design. Consider the pinnacles of Henry VII's chapel at Westminster (before 1518), the canopy over the tomb of Lady Margaret Beaufort therein (1511–12), or the pinnacles of Hengrave Hall (*c.*1525–30). All these have a feature in common with the Round Table canopy:

---

[79] For a full discussion of this vital aspect of medieval furnishings and in particular soft and portable embellishments, see Penelope Eames, 'Documentary Evidence Concerning the Character and Use of Domestic Furnishings in England in the Fourteenth and Fifteenth Centuries', *Journal of the Furniture History Society*, 6 (1970), 41– 60. The canopy over a seat is first cousin to the half celour over a state bed. The first such state bed in English royal records was that of Henry III at Westminster Palace: see H. M. Colvin (ed.), *The History of the King's Works*, i (London, 1963), pp. 497–8.

[80] Auerbach, *Tudor Artists*, has a number of illustrations.

[81] Most plainly, the dedication page of the *Receuil des Chroniques* of Jean de Waurin, BL, Royal MS. 15 E.IV, fol. 14; see Warner and Gilson, *Catalogue of Western MSS.* ii, p. 176.

[82] Letters Patent for Cardinal College, Ipswich, 20 August 1528, PRO, E24/12/1; illus. Auerbach, *Tudor Artists*, Pl. 10c (here, Fig. 138).

[83] The Trinity is shown housed under a 'lampshade' form of canopy in a missal, now in the Cluny Museum in Paris, executed for a member of the Montaigu Family *c.*1400. The Evangelists who occupy the angles of the illumination are seated at stalls with wooden canopies.

142 The Round Table (detail): the canopied figure of King Arthur.

143 Plea Roll, Michaelmas 1515, initial letter 'P'.

crockets along their ribs. But the general shape of the Round Table canopy is a different matter altogether (Plate XXIII; Fig. 142).

The most adventurous canopy designs of the early sixteenth century are to be found among the documents decorated for Cardinal Wolsey.[84] Every variation on the themes of swags and shell niches can be found among these dazzling essays in penmanship of the 1520s. But an actual dome does not appear until 1529, when it is fish-scaled and elaborately fringed.[85] We have yet to examine the Great Seals, however, which disseminated artistic fashion with the spectacular imprimatur of royal approval.

The first Great Seal to show an English monarch under a canopy was Edward III's, in use from 1327.[86] From that point, canopies are an indispensible feature of the design. The changeover from Gothic to Renaissance in their detailing takes place during Henry VIII's reign. His first Great Seal, in use 1509–32, merely repeated that of Henry VII, a Perpendicular design of 1485. His second (Fig. 134), in use 1532–41, is still ornamented with tabernacling in the Gothic spirit, but it shows a dome-shaped roof over the king's seat which can be compared with the one shown on the Round Table.[87] The third Great Seal, created in 1542, shows the full-blown classical form (Fig. 135). Three earlier seals anticipated the 1542 designer in some measure: that of Thomas Wolsey as cardinal (in use 1515–29), that of Stephen Gardiner (bishop of Winchester, 1531–50), and that attached to the Golden Bulla of 1527 (Fig. 128), which is far more in the continental fashion than the Great Seal of 1532. It is the Great Seal of 1532, however, which provides the closest comparison not only with the general low profile of the dome of the canopy on the Round Table, but also with the fluting with which it is decorated.

Only one drawing, however, exactly matches the flattened dome with the crocketed outline on the Round Table, and that one is much earlier. It appears on the Plea Roll for Michaelmas 1515 (Fig. 143).[88] In typological sequence, therefore, the Round Table canopy comes between 1515 and 1532 (Plate XXIII; Fig. 142).

---

[84] Illus. Auerbach, *Tudor Artists*, Pls. 10b, 10c, 12a, 13a, and 13b (the first three also here, Figs. 136–8). This dazzling series of illuminated documents is kept in one file at the Public Record Office. They deserve a monograph.

[85] Patent for Cardinal College, Ipswich, 26 May 1529, PRO, E24/2/1; illus. Auerbach, *Tudor Artists*, Pl. 13b.

[86] Wyon and Wyon, *Great Seals*, VIII, no. 53.

[87] Birch, *Catalogue*, pp. 43–4.

[88] PRO, KB27/1017; illus. Auerbach, *Tudor Artists*, Pl. 3b.

Condition

The traumas which the Round Table has undergone are unusually well documented. For our present purpose the most important are the seventeenth-century bullet holes and the 1789 restoration.

The bullet holes (see Chapter 4)

Alas, the rose and the face were the selected targets, so that the face in particular is likely to have suffered many losses. For that reason no conclusions have been drawn here from anything but its general outline. However, the method of repair, whereby large damaged areas were covered in sheets of metal and the metal painted in its turn, has offered a valuable bonus. Where the metal has been turned back – sadly, only in a small area of the canopy – the paint beneath it may be punctured with bullet holes, but in quite significant passages it is intact and not much discoloured (Pl. XXII). Clearly the patching was done at the first restoration, since there is nothing but the first painting beneath it. And as the paint over the metal is the same as that used on the rest of the surface, the evidence of the X-rays is confirmed, namely that there are but two paint layers, the original and that of one old restoration.

The 1789 restoration

The Round Table was repainted in 1789 by the Winchester firm of Cave and Son, comprising the artists William Cave senior (1737–1813) and his eldest son (c.1760–1816), who was also named William (see below, p. 480).[89] From the present painted surface of the Round Table it may be judged that the Caves belonged, like Thomas Stothard, to the group of late eighteenth-century and early nineteenth-century painters who, in their heavy dependence upon sentiment, antici-

[89] Barbara Carpenter-Turner, *Proceedings of the Hampshire Field Club*, 22.1 (1961), 30–4, with illustrations. The dates of birth and death given here and in Chapter 13 below have been revised where necessary by reference to the relevant obituaries in the *Hampshire Chronicle*.

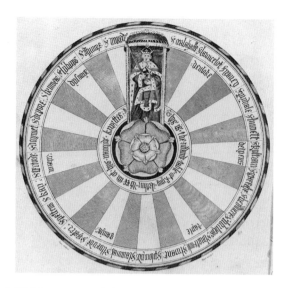

144 The Round Table, engraved by J. Pass after a drawing by James(?) Cave, published 1796.

145 Henry VIII, artist unknown, late 18th or early 19th century (Hatfield House).

pated the Victorian way of seeing. We also have an engraving by J. Pass of Pentonville after a drawing by James Cave, William junior's younger brother (c.1772–1834), showing another member of the family's idea of a facial type for King Arthur (Fig. 144).[90] And a very fluffy version of the King Arthur on the Round Table it is. This somewhat woolly treatment of the face can be compared with the similar off-focus effect of the portrait of Henry VIII at Hatfield (Fig. 145).[91] The Hatfield Henry, which is obviously based, at a polite distance, on the full-face Holbein type, is accompanied by a series of portraits of his wives. It is not certain whether the set is entirely of the Cave period, or whether they heavily overpaint earlier panels.

Now that so much well-meant restoration of the last two centuries has been removed from our pictures, it is difficult to find instances which parallel the sensation one gets from the Round Table of looking at a sixteenth-century painting through tinted spectacles. Hogarth's attempts in the seicento manner,[92] or more appositely his 1759 portrait of Meg Woffington as Mary Queen of Scots,[93] have something of this effect. The polite misunderstandings of Boydell's Shakespeare Gallery[94] or, at the other end of the scale, the reproductions of Old Masters put out by the first British generation of art historians[95] – these are the twilight regions of misrepresentation to which the present surface of the Round Table belongs. The vigorous brushwork of that part of the original canopy which was briefly revealed under the metal during our investigation would not have been acceptable

[90] This engraving was published in 1796, based on a drawing by 'Cave'. Since Pass was the engraver of all James Cave's drawings for John Milner's *History of Winchester* (1st edn., 2 vols., Winchester, 1798–9), and since these include a small engraving of the table (vol. 1, opp. p. 374) which is very similar to the larger engraving of 1796, it seems likely that James Cave was responsible for the drawing behind the 1796 engraving. As for the actual repainting of the table itself in 1789, it is impossible to tell which of the two William Caves, father or son, was responsible. James, born c.1772, was probably too young at about seventeen to have played a major role, although Milner's preface of 1798 (nine years after the painting of the table) calls him 'a young artist of great ingenuity and unwearied application' and *The British Critic*, April 1800, wrote of his plates in Milner's *History* that they were 'so ably executed as to reflect credit upon this or any other work to which they should be annexed'. [M. B.].

[91] See Erna Auerbach and C. Kingsley Adams, *Paintings and Sculpture at Hatfield House* (London, 1971), no. 12 (pp. 36–7). C. Lloyd and S. Thurley, *Henry VIII: Images of a Tudor King* (Oxford, 1990) devoted a whole section to 'Henry VIII and the Antiquarian Tradition', pp. 77–108.

[92] See Lawrence Gowing, *William Hogarth* (London, 1971–2), Pl. 211.

[93] Ibid., Pl. 202. Gainsborough's essays in the vein of Murillo come into the same category; see, for example, his *Two Shepherd Boys with Dogs Fighting*, exhib. R.A. 1783, best version at Kenwood House, London.

[94] For which see T. S. R. Boase, *English Art: 1800–70*, Oxford History of Art (Oxford, 1959), p. 2 *et passim*.

[95] For example the publications of the 'Masterpieces in Colour' series, edited by T. Leman Hare. Consider, for that matter, the nineteenth-century canon of the masterpieces of Leonardo da Vinci. Many of them are now known to be studio works.

in 1789.[96] Interesting though it is that we have here a restoration of a known date by known painters who have left us pictures made in their own right, nevertheless the Caves' work does effectively conceal an image created for the eye of Henry VIII. Comparable survivors on a large scale can be counted on the fingers of one hand. To remove the overpaint from the entire table would bring it back to its original freshness. On the other hand, it would be a laborious task, revealing perhaps little of major importance. If the removal of the whole cannot be undertaken, must we really leave the Tudor figure of the king himself under the Caves' bushel? The recent surface cleaning and brilliant varnish have robbed the table of a discreet veil of dirt. The Caves' skills cannot withstand so much limelight.

The artist

The arrival of sophisticated foreign artists in this country before Holbein came over in 1526 was a spasmodic affair. Torrigiano was here from 1511 to 1518. Giovanni da Maiano arrived in *c*.1521, and like Benedetto da Rovezzano, who was here from *c*.1524 to *c*.1535, he moved towards the circle of Cardinal Wolsey rather than that of the king. If da Rovezzano's design for Wolsey's tomb, of which the sarcophagus now houses the remains of Lord Nelson in the crypt of St Paul's, or Torrigiano's conception of a monument for Henry VIII himself, with its equestrian figure, had been fully executed, the English Renaissance would have moved far more deeply than it did into Italian waters.[97] As it is, we have to savour Wolsey's Italianism in the exquisite initials of his charters (Figs. 136–8), and Henry's in the scurrility of Girolamo da Treviso's *Four Evangelists Stoning the Pope*.[98] With Italianism even in the

---

[96] See David Pike Watts's comment in 1810 on Constable's *Christ Blessing the Sacrament* in St James's Church, Nayland: 'It is scarcely justifiable for any *Picture* to be shown so *raw*, unless a Testimony was affixed that the Artist dies before he could finish it; no other excuse can reconcile a Picture being affix'd for Public View in so uncultivated a state.' See also Leslie Parris, Ian Fleming-Williams, and Conal Shields, *Constable: Paintings, Watercolours and Drawings* (London, 1976), pp. 13–14.

[97] For this first stage of Italian infiltration, in which sculptors played so large a role, see M. D. Whinney, *Sculpture in Britain: 1530–1830*, Pelican History of Art (Harmondsworth, 1964), ch. 2: 'Renaissance Influence from Italy and France'. Martin Biddle's study of the Renaissance elements in Bishop Thomas Langton's chantry chapel of 1501–10 in Winchester Cathedral, and in Bishop Richard Fox's chantry chapel of 1513–18, charts some of the earliest evidences of an awareness of classical motifs outside London. He agreed with Anthony Blunt in finding the sources in direct contact with Gaillon and Cardinal Georges d'Amboise: Biddle, 'Early Renaissance at Winchester' (as above, n. 36*a*), pp. 257–9. These parallels are particularly apposite as they prove that Renaissance features, if only on a small scale, were circulating in Winchester at the time the Round Table was being painted.

[98] See Roy Strong, *The Elizabethan Image* (London, 1970), no. 7, with illustration, reprinted in *Tudor & Stuart Monarchy*, i.

architectural design of Hampton Court kept to the level of marginalia, it was possible for native artists to remain ignorant of all but the uneasy thought that they should introduce some Italian accent to prove that they were abreast with fashion. Italianism is represented on the Round Table by the canopy. The rest is as traditional as might be. This situation in itself points to a native artist, but the claim of the Flemish colony in England must not be overlooked. Trading connections were strong; the distance was relatively short. Flemings in search of provincial patronage came over in considerable numbers. As their names were quickly Englished, it is impossible to be sure how large an element they formed by *c.*1520 in the artistic population. Judging by surviving work, none would have made a great mark in his native land, unless it were in the field of stained glass. The vast pageant of the windows of King's College Chapel, Cambridge, the only lesser achievements of Fairford, of the Vyne, and of the east window of St Margaret's Westminster were the broadest visual statement of the Renaissance idiom under execution in Britain during the first quarter of the sixteenth century.[99]

If the artist of the Round Table knew of the contemporary activity in stained glass, it had no effect on him. The work of two other known painters, however, comes nearer home to Winchester. As Mr Croft-Murray demonstrated,[100] there are two groups of paintings with actual Winchester connections: the altar-piece from Winchester Cathedral, now at Knole, and the paintings at Chichester and Amberley which he found to be by the Barnard brothers. Lambert Barnard's patron, Bishop Robert Sherborne, was a Wykehamist and a friend of Bishop Fox of Winchester. The themes of the Chichester paintings and of the Winchester altar-piece are in striking conformity with that of the Round Table. All deal with

[99] For the windows of King's College Chapel, see Hilary Wayment, *The Windows of King's College Chapel, Cambridge,* Corpus Vitrearum Medii Aevi, suppl. 1 (London, 1972). For the Vyne, see G. McN. Rushforth, 'The Painted Windows in the Chapel of the Vyne', *Walpole Society,* 15 (1927), 1–20. For Fairford, see Hilary Wayment, *The Stained Glass of the Church of St. Mary, Fairford, Gloucestershire* (London, 1984). For St Margaret's Westminster, see Royal Commission on Historical Monuments, *London,* i, *West London excluding Westminster Abbey* (London, 1925), p. 102 and Pl. 153. *Pace* Sir Roy Strong (*Tudor and Jacobean Portraits,* pp. 39–40 and Pl. 72 from Drake's copy of 1921), I must agree with G. Scharf ('Remarks on Some Portraits from Windsor Castle, Hampton Court and elsewhere', *Archaeologia,* 39 (1863), 249 *et seq.*) that the portraits in the St Margaret's Westminster glass are of Henry VIII and Catherine of Aragon. The iconography, with St Catherine and pomegranate, admits of no alternative in her case. The strong probability, therefore, is that the original of St Catherine's face, now in the museum of Westminster Abbey, is a prime image of the queen. The conventional young king of the Westminster window is fully in accord with the early type for Henry VIII, and agrees with his representation in the glass at the Vyne. The figure is crowned, so it cannot be meant for his brother Arthur.

[100] E. Croft-Murray, *Decorative Painting in England 1530–1837* (London, 1962), pp. 30–1; idem, 'Lambert Barnard', as above, n. 14, with illustrations.

146 King Æthelstan (924–39), artist unknown, early 16th century (Society of Antiquaries of London).

subjects connected with British history. Bishop Sherborne was among those who escorted Charles V from Calais to London in 1522. Barnard's major works for him are the two paintings of *The South Saxon King Cædwalla Granting the See of Selsey to St Wilfrid* and its pendant, *Henry VIII Confirming to Sherborne the Royal Protection of Chichester Cathedral* (Fig. 147). Each subject is supported by a series of portrait medallions of the kings of England from the Conqueror, and of the bishops of Chichester from St Wilfrid. The event shown in the painting of Henry VIII does not seem to have actually taken place, so these works cannot be dated on the basis of their subject matter. There is, however, an old tradition that they were executed about 1519.[101] Mr Croft-Murray preferred a date *c.*1535–6, but I find 1519 still quite possible. The tentative form of the Garter collar worn by the king, and his splayed hat brim, favour a relatively early dating. Compare the hat with that in the Anglesey Abbey portrait (Fig. 140). The closeness of the script at Chichester to that on the Round Table would favour the earlier date. Of the quality of the painting itself it is as difficult to speak as in the case of the Round Table, and for the same reason.[102]

One board – that of an attendant holding a mitre – has been cleaned in recent times. It reveals passages of paintwork of greater sophistication than the drapery on the Round Table, but with certain features in common with another important commission of those years – the first painting of the frieze in Wolsey's closet at Hampton Court.[103] Both at Hampton Court and at Chichester the standard appears to have been higher than on the Round Table, going by what can be seen of the latter. The same is true when the Winchester altar-piece of 1526, signed 'T G', is brought into consideration. Although the front of this work is somewhat hackneyed, the back, with grisaille paintings of local saints, each standing under a canopy of classical forms but pointed arches (Fig. 148), is too accomplished to compare with the Round Table.

---

[101] Croft-Murray, *Decorative Painting*, p. 116, quotes George Vertue on this point.

[102] A heavy repainting was carried out in 1747, and there had been vandalism by Parliamentary troops in 1642; ibid., p. 115.

[103] I cannot agree with G. H. Chettle and John Charlton (*Hampton Court Palace* (London, 1975), p. 32, repeated in 1983 edition) that the lower layer of painting in Wolsey's closet is of the fifteenth century. Everything about it suggests Wolsey's time at Hampton Court (1515–29), with a repainting superimposed in Henry VIII's period. A Thomas Griffith was working on decorative painting at Hampton Court in 1515 (PRO, E36/236, pp. 128 *et seq.*, quoted by Auerbach, *Tudor Artists*, p. 166). A Steven Gosling was doing the same in 1532–4. This is not to say they were the authors of these schemes, but the documents do show that work was in hand at Hampton Court at the moments the pictures themselves suggest. A great deal of the earlier layout survives beneath the later. It is to be hoped that one day both may be displayed.

147 *Henry VIII Confirming to Sherborne the Royal Protection of Chichester Cathedral*, by Lambert Barnard, *c*.1519(?) (Chichester Cathedral).

148 Grisaille paintings of the three sainted Anglo-Saxon bishops of the see of Winchester, Birinus, Æthelwold, and Hædde, from the back of an altar-piece for Winchester Cathedral, by 'T.G.', 1526 (Knole, Kent).

The unusually full documentation for Lambert Barnard shows that, even though he was capable of elaborate and unprecedented figure subjects, he was still expected to execute relatively humble work, like the ceiling of the bishop's palace at Chichester. His rose there provides a striking comparison with the rose on the Round Table. The devices include an H and a K for Katherine, so the work must have been executed before Henry's estrangement from Katherine (Catherine) of Aragon in 1528 (Fig. 126). This ceiling is one of several heraldic examples of the earlier sixteenth century[104] which must have provided painters of relatively humble pretensions with plenty of work on which to depend.

The records of early Tudor royal patronage indicate a variety of such opportunities for scenic/heraldic painters, many of them less eminent than Lambert Barnard.[105] Starting with the heraldic painting for the funeral of Prince Arthur in 1502 and of his mother the following year, there followed the entertainments for foreign ambassadors in 1509; the Field of Cloth of Gold and the Round House at Calais in 1520; the revels at Greenwich in 1527; decorative painting at Hampton Court Palace in 1530 (the first stage of the new regime there); and a major painting of the king's coronation for Westminster Palace in 1531. One hundred and thirteen names occur, 27 of them of evident or probable foreign origin. Either the Thomas Grene or the Thomas Griffith listed could be responsible ('T. G.') for the Winchester altar-piece. Only 25 out of the 86 native-looking names appear more than once. Twelve men are mentioned only in connection with the heraldic painting for the funeral of Henry VII in 1509; 25 are listed only for the 1527 revels at Greenwich; and 29 appear only in connection with the works at Westminster Palace in 1531. Perhaps our Round Table man — or men, for nothing emerges more strongly than the size of the teams employed on these occasions — is to be found among those of whom we know at least a few sketchy facts. John Brown (who more fortunately named?), who held the office of King's Painter from 1511 until his death in 1532, is perhaps the most substantial candidate. His career marched in perhaps uneasy parallel with that of the Italian Vincent Volpe — but no Neapolitan came near the Round Table. We could just say that, at best, the painting on the Round Table might reflect the solid worth and professional conservatism of John Brown. Much depends on the handling of the actual surface. All that can be said from the evidence now visible is that it is not good enough for Lambert Barnard.

---

[104] See for instance the ceiling of the prior's room of the pele tower of the deanery of Carlisle Cathedral, executed for Simon Senhouse, prior 1500–20, and the ceiling of the parlour at Haddon Hall, c.1520.

[105] Fully published by Auerbach, *Tudor Artists*, Appendix 2b.

Iconography

> *Hostess*: Nay, sure, he's not in hell: he's in Arthur's bosom, if ever man went to Arthur's
> bosom ....
> *Henry V*, I.iii.line 9 (speaking of Falstaff).

As Mr Croft-Murray described, Lucas Eglimont painted in the chapel at Naworth in 1514 a tree of Jesse and in the Great Hall at Kirkoswald a 'greate portraite of King Brute, lying in the end of the roof of the hall, and of all his successors portraited to the waist ...'.[106] So talents, nurtured in the language of the Church, learnt secular usage. For Jesse substitute Brut; for Abraham read Arthur. Caritas moves into the place of the Virgin. Gog and Magog await, perhaps for the second time, the part of St Christopher. For the Kings of Judah exchange the Kings of Britain.[107] In this respect at least the new or revived imagery of the Renaissance was ready in the wings to serve the iconoclasm of the Reformation, an assortment of secular images which not only were unsusceptible to controversy, but also had a gloss of patriotism and even of the new learning about them.

It is striking that three of the most important painted schemes of the early sixteenth century in Britain were concerned with our ancient history:

1   The 'Saxon Kings' belonging to the Society of Antiquaries, which appear to depict the Anglo-Saxon kingdoms united under Æthelstan in 927 (Fig. 146).[108]

2   The Chichester cycle by Lambert Barnard, of Cædwalla granting the See of Selsey to St Wilfrid, with its Henrician parallel and its supporting casts of kings and bishops in roundels (Fig. 147).[109]

---

[106] Croft-Murray, *Decorative Painting*, pp. 158–9. It is likely that Lord Naworth owned the register of the Honour of Richmond which is now Bodleian, Lyell MS. 22; illus. O. Pächt and J. J. G. Alexander, *Illustrated MSS. in the Bodleian Library*, iii (Oxford, 1973), Pl. CVI. This manuscript is illustrated with a later fifteenth-century drawing of a knight kneeling before William the Conqueror. Perhaps there was a more than ordinary interest in British history at Naworth in early Tudor times.

[107] For this point see not only the Rous Rolls (College of Arms and BL, Add. MS. 48976) but also the Salisbury Roll in the collection of the Duke of Buccleugh and Queensbury; and compare Anthony Wagner, 'Medieval Rolls of Arms', *Aspilogia*, 1 (Oxford, 1950), pp. 103–4, *et seq.*

[108] From Baston House in Kent, for which see my forthcoming publication of the Society's pictures. The form of the 'A' on the cloak of Athelstan inclines the dating towards the first years of the sixteenth century. I am grateful to Mr John Goodall for this observation.

[109] Croft-Murray, *Decorative Painting*, pp. 23–25 and Pl. 35; and idem, 'Lambert Barnard', as above n. 14.

149 Mortuary chest containing the remains of King Eadred (946–55) in Winchester Cathedral, artist unknown, *c*.1525–30.

3   The grisaille Anglo-Saxon bishops on the back of 'T. G.'s' altar-piece for Winchester Cathedral (Fig. 148).

As we have seen, Robert Sherborne, bishop of Chichester from 1508 until 1536, and Richard Fox, bishop of Winchester from 1501 until his death in 1528, were in touch with one another.[110] Fox's own chantry chapel in Winchester Cathedral is one of the last essays in the pure Perpendicular manner, in strong contrast to that of his successor, Stephen Gardiner, bishop from 1531 to 1555, which is heavily Renaissance.[111] Bishop Fox's personal experience of the infiltration of Renaissance design can be illustrated by a comparison between his pastoral staff of purely Gothic design, presumably made at his first elevation to a bishopric in

---

[110] Ibid.

[111] Illus. in G. Cook, *Medieval Chantries and Chantry Chapels* (London, 1947), pp. 13 and 14, and Biddle, 'Early Renaissance' (as above n. 36a), pp. 281–7.

1487, and the luscious Renaissance arabesque scrolls of his standing salt and cover, made while he was bishop of Durham, 1494–1501. Both are now at Corpus Christi College, Oxford. The rehousing of the bones of the Anglo-Saxon kings and bishops (Fig. 149), the frieze, and the inscriptions associated with this translation, are attributed to *c*.1525–30, and show Fox as patron of a fairly austere classicism. The carver responsible may have had access to Flemish engravings, but his achievement hardly suggests a more intimate link with his source material. It could be said that his work stands in the same relationship to the Renaissance as that of the painter of the Round Table. Perhaps this prominent reinterment of the Anglo- Saxon kings and bishops was executed in anticipation of Henry VIII's visit in 1522. Nor is it impossible that the idea of painting the Round Table in the Great Hall also originated with Bishop Fox. The two commissions are complementary: the array of Anglo-Saxon kings and bishops in the cathedral underlined the antiquity and ancient prerogatives of the see; the Round Table recalls Winchester's ancient and traditional importance as a centre of secular, royal power.

The only manuscript of Malory's *Morte Darthur* remained until recently in the library of Winchester College.[112] This very text may well have been one source from which the iconography of the table was laid out (see above, Chapter 8). Among other likely sources, Robert Fabyan's *Chronicles* of 1516, newly published when the painting of the table was mooted, was the first to question the claims of Arthur's conquests in France.[113] This work may have influenced the decision to omit the fleurs-de-lys from Arthur's crown on the table.[114]

The ancient roots of chivalry were of great importance to the early Tudor monarchs, in whose minds Arthur and the Garter were inextricably related. Henry VII himself thought indeed that King Arthur had founded the Order of the Garter,[115] and in the 1520s Arthur's links with chivalry were being re-emphasized. Thomas Wriothesley's Statutes and Ordinances of the Garter were composed and illustrated between 1519 and 1521,[116] and on 23 April 1522, at the annual

---

[112] Now BL, Add MS. 59678; see *William Caxton: an Exhibition to Commemorate the Quincentenary of the Introduction of Printing into England*, British Library (London, 1976), no. 74, p. 74.

[113] A. W. Pollard and G. R. Redgrave, *Short-Title Catalogue of Books printed in England, Scotland and Ireland 1475–1640* (London, 1926), no. 10659, p. 232, quoted by Kendrick, *British Antiquity*, p. 41. The whole of Kendrick's Chapter III, 'The Tudor Cult of the British History' (pp. 34–44), is fundamental to the understanding of the material available to the painter of the Round Table.

[114] See, 'The crown', pp. 293–304.

[115] See *CSP Venetian*, i, *1202–1509*, no. 709 (p. 281); quoted by Kendrick, *British Antiquity*, p. 42 and n. 2.

[116] Bound with, inter alia, Wriothe's 'Garter Book' in the possession of the Duke of Buccleugh and Queensbury; see also Wagner, 'Medieval Rolls'.

assembly on the Feast of St George, the official revisions were put forward under the king's name. Later that summer Henry and Charles V went straight to Winchester from the Garter ceremonies at Windsor, having a few days earlier in London seen a pageant which included King Arthur (Chapter 12).

The author of the text of the Black Book of the Garter, which must have been drafted before 1529, reflects informed opinion in the 1520s about the origins of chivalry.[117] Casting back, for the institution of knighthood, to Dionysius the Great holding an assembly of forty days at the foot of Mount Olympus, he gives his narrative a classical prototype in the Olympic games. Thereafter a knightly bout of jousting and feasting could claim, with some justification, to be in the classical tradition. And when, after an interminable list of intermediaries, Arthur himself is seen on stage, he is wearing a mantle of classical civilization, rather than dwelling in the wattle and daub of Brut:

> *Arthur* who for the Excellency of his Actions, has been deservedly noted and famous, and in whose Reign, the Riches and Powers of the *Britains* largely encreased, began that noble Tower [at Windsor], and there instituted (as they call it) his round Table. This was (if we may believe Authors) a Seat made of an extraordinary Wood, drawn round into a Circle and beautifully adorned, which *Arthur* had set apart for those select Knights, which he had chosen and united for himself; and was still farther ennobled, by the consecrating Hand of the then Archbishop of *Canterbury*. These were twenty eight of the best Knights joined together: Which Number does not much differ from that, which is now observed by this military Society, ... For in this Order are twenty six over which as Sovereign the King of *England* for the Time being, always presides, ... These [Arthur's knights] he ordered when they were either to banquet together, or take Counsel about any Business in War, to sit together in a Circle, that so no Envy might arise at one's being preferred before [an]other , ... After this Manner our Sovereign [the third Edward] at first instituted his Knights, that when they were called upon, either to eat or consult together, they should sit at, or stand round the same Table together, following in this Method, the Example of the illustrious Knights of the noble *Arthur*, ...

So the continuity between Arthur's company and the Knights of the Garter is maintained, but to the author of the Black Book the Winchester Round Table does not appear to be a known relic. He was writing from Windsor, so perhaps there was

[117] Anstis, *Register ... of the Order of the Garter*, as above, n. 53, where my reasons for assigning this work to a date before 1529 are given. The quotation which follows is from vol. i, pp. 19–20, 25.

rivalry with Winchester and he deliberately omitted mention of the table (see Chapter 11).

It may be said, therefore, that although Caxton and Leland knew and quoted the table at Winchester as one of the 'proofs' of Arthur's authenticity (see above, pp. 29–30 and below, pp. 394, 483–4), its importance was not unanimously accepted. The Black Book at Windsor gave the Round Table no mention, even at the moment when the paint was still fresh upon it. What must have struck those who saw the table in 1522 was the parallel between the seated king at its head and the actual monarch seated among his Knights of the Garter at Windsor a few days before.

The image of the king among his knights in the Black Book of the Garter (Plate XXVI) was painted some twelve years later and by a more fluent hand,[118] but its relationship to the image on the Round Table is strong – even if John Brown or his understudy took as his immediate model nothing more sophisticated than a penny from his purse.

Conclusion

When in 1976 we undertook the study of the Round Table as part of the project to preserve and understand it, the documentary evidence of Henry VIII's visit to Winchester in 1516, and the evidence, both documentary and dendrochronological, of repairs to the table immediately after that visit, were unknown. Faced with a range of occasions in 1486, 1522, and 1554 my choice was unequivocally for 1522. As knowledge stood in 1976 this implied that the table was painted at the behest of Bishop Fox as part of a campaign, including also the new tombs of the Anglo- Saxon kings and bishops, designed to interest the king and establish in his eyes the ancient importance of Winchester.

The factor of Henry's visit in August 1516, however, shifts the emphasis from Bishop Fox to the king himself (see below, p. 440). Henry emerges as the initiator of the project, and the plan for his visit in 1522 now appears to have been made with foreknowledge of what he was going to be able to show Charles V. The painting of the table could have been the last stage in its reinstatement – done, perhaps in 1517 – or it could have been a secondary embellishment made in immediate anticipation of Henry's further visit with Charles V in 1522. The visual evidence, as here

---

[118] See Erna Auerbach, 'The Black Book of the Garter', *Report of the Friends of St George's*, 5 (1972–3), 149–53, with illustrations. For the interweaving of the cult of chivalry and royalty in the sixteenth century, see especially Roy Strong, 'Queen Elizabeth and the Order of the Garter', *Archaeological Journal*, 119 (1962), 145–69.

collected, does not admit of further refinement. We can be reasonably confident, however, that this painting was carried out between 1516 and 1522.

This new facet in our understanding is in keeping with what we are piecing together in other fields of historical research about Henry VIII as architect of the events of his reign. As John Guy has said, 'It was Henry VIII himself who directed government strategy after 1529. His influence was never again eclipsed by that of a ministerial *alter rex* ....'[119] Already, more than ten years earlier, we now see Henry taking an initiative independently of Wolsey, an initiative that is a fair pointer to the way he will work in his critical later years – by directing attention to historical research whereby the case for independence from Rome can be bolstered by the citation of ancient and national roots. The image of a seated king on the Round Table in Winchester Great Hall is not only a prime example of the interest in British history evinced by Henry VIII and his advisors: it is a card in the game of international diplomacy that engaged the papacy, the Holy Roman Empire, and the French and English monarchies during most of Henry VIII's reign. The Roman Emperor had Charlemagne; Francis of France claimed Julius Caesar. Henry VIII called out the Table Round presided over by King Arthur, his own imperial ancester – '*Emperoure hymself thorow dygntye of his hondys*'.

---

[119] John Guy, 'The Privy Council: Revolution or Evolution?, in C. Coleman and D. Starkey, *Revolution Reassessed: Revisions in the History of Tudor Government and Administration* (Oxford, 1986), pp. 59–85, esp. p. 69.

Solutions and Meanings

The evidence on which to attempt some account of the origin of the Winchester Round Table and its transmutation from furniture to symbol has now been gathered. In the first three chapters we have explored the setting of the table in literature, in the history of furniture, in Winchester Castle and in the Great Hall — itself one of the finest buildings of the English Middle Ages. In the next six chapters the Winchester table and its painting have themselves been interrogated to reveal as much as we have been able to discover of their purpose, character, and date.

Our next task is to see whether it is possible to identify in historical terms the moments at which the three principal events in the life of the Winchester Round Table took place: its making (Chapter 10), its hanging on the wall (Chapter 11), and its painting (Chapter 12). In doing this, we shall explore the role of the table in the context of each event, and the changes in meaning which are revealed.

10

The making of the Round Table

For anyone looking at the Round Table, the first question will always be, When was it made? Few perhaps assume that it was really made for King Arthur in the sixth century AD, although in the nineteenth century and far into the twentieth the keepers of the hall were always ready to tell visitors that the table was an authentic relic of that distant and mythical age.[1] There were however always those who from at least the sixteenth century had realised that the table was unlikely to be so old,[2] although few were prepared even to guess at its real age, let alone at the purpose for which it had been made.

A more critical approach began with John Milner at the end of the eighteenth century. Milner thought the table no older than the twelfth century: this view 'whilst it takes off six centuries from its supposed antiquity, still leaves it an existence of seven centuries and a half, enough to render it a curious and valuable monument.'[3] Edward Smirke's pioneering study of the Great Hall on the basis of the public records, presented in a paper given at the 1845 meeting of the Archaeological Institute in Winchester, assigned to the table 'a respectable, but moderate antiquity' of four or even as many as six centuries, with the tentative suggestion that it might have

---

[1] Nicholas Griffiths, who drew many of the figures for this book, remembers a visit as a schoolboy to the Great Hall on a Saturday in 1961 or 1962, when 'a tall chap in a blue uniform and a peaked cap' told him that the table 'had to be King Arthur's.' The hall keeper's logic was that the table was too big to have come in through any of the doors or windows; that there was no record of it having been brought in in pieces and reassembled; therefore the hall must have been built around it; that we know the hall was built by William the Conqueror; and that the only king before the Conqueror who could have had the table made was King Arthur. Comments and questions that arose during the investigation of the table in 1976–9 showed that these and other tales, some even stranger, were well embedded locally, and that oral memory even of events concerning the table in the 1930s to 1950s could be uncertain; see above, pp. 146–7.

[2] See above, pp. 28–30, and below, p. 491, 493. See also Milner (as next note), 2nd edn., ii, 183.

[3] John Milner, *The History ... of Winchester*, 2 vols., 1st edn. (Winchester, n.d. but 1798 [date of dedication], i, pp. 73–80, ii [also n.d.], pp. 171–3; 2nd edn. (Winchester, 1809), i, pp. 73–80, ii, pp. 182–4; 3rd edn. (Winchester and London, 1839), i, pp. 56–61; ii, pp. 204–5.

been made in the reign of Henry III or Edward I.[4] Smirke's view has held the field, reflected in successive generations of local histories and guidebooks, and emphasised by the authority of the Royal Archaeological Institute's programme for their summer meeting at Winchester in 1924 ('no older than the thirteenth century')[5] and by Lloyd Woodland's *Story of Winchester* in the 'Medieval Towns' series in 1932 ('a piece of Early English carpentry which it would be hard to match anywhere').[6] The purpose for which the table may have been made was also now being addressed. About 1900 T. W. Shore had asserted that the table had probably been 'constructed as the symbol of a tournament actually held [at Winchester] in the 13th century'[7]. And about the same time Melville Portal argued that 'we may reasonably assume that the Round Table was connected with the Court festivities ... in the time of one of the Edwards'.[8]

When the table was moved from the east wall of the hall to the west in 1873, and the back inspected for the first time since the early sixteenth century, the mortices visible in the underside of each of the twelve radial 'spokes' of the frame demonstrated at once that the great disk had in actual fact once been the top of a round table standing on twelve legs (Figs. 34 and 167).[9] This did not solve the problem of its date, even if the sophistication of the carpentry hinted at something made more recently than the 'Dark Ages'.[10]

When the table was again taken down just over a century later in 1976, the study of medieval carpentry had advanced to the point where Cecil Hewett (who had himself been responsible for much of this advance) was able to suggest after only a short inspection that the table had probably been made between 1250 and 1350 by a carpenter who was experienced in the construction of mill-wheels using the up-to-date device of a clasp-arm assembly (Figs. 43–6, 49, cf. Figs. 56–9).[11]

---

[4]   Edward Smirke, 'On the Hall and Round Table at Winchester', *Proceedings at the Annual Meeting of the Archaeological Institute ... at Winchester, September MDCCCXLV* (London, 1846), pp. 44–80, at p. 67.

[5]   *Archaeological Journal*, 81 (1924), 374–5; this was probably the opinion of Sir William Portal in his talk to the members of the Institute on their visit to the hall.

[6]   W. Lloyd Woodland, *The Story of Winchester*, The Medieval Towns Series (London, 1932), p. 281.

[7]   T. W. Shore, 'King Arthur and the Round Table at Winchester', *Proceedings of the Hampshire Field Club* 4 (1898–1903), 187–204, at p. 199. More than a century earlier *The Winchester Guide* (new edition, J. Wilkes, Winton, 1780), p. 7, had suggested that the table might have been used on the occasion of tilts and tournaments for entertaining the combatants.

[8]   Melville Portal, *The Great Hall Winchester Castle* (Winchester and London, 1899), p. 92.

[9]   T. H. Wyatt, 'On The Old Hall and New Assize Courts at Winchester', R.I.B.A. *Sessional Papers* 10 (1873–4), 157–69, at p. 159; Portal, *The Great Hall Winchester Castle* (as above, n. 8), p. 90; see also above, pp. 89–94.

[10]   But it probably influenced the dating proposed by Portal in 1899 (n. 8), at the Royal Archaeological Institute's meeting in 1924 (n. 5), and by Lloyd Woodland in 1932 in his specific attribution of the carpentry to the Early English period (n. 6).

[11]   See above, pp. 117–20.

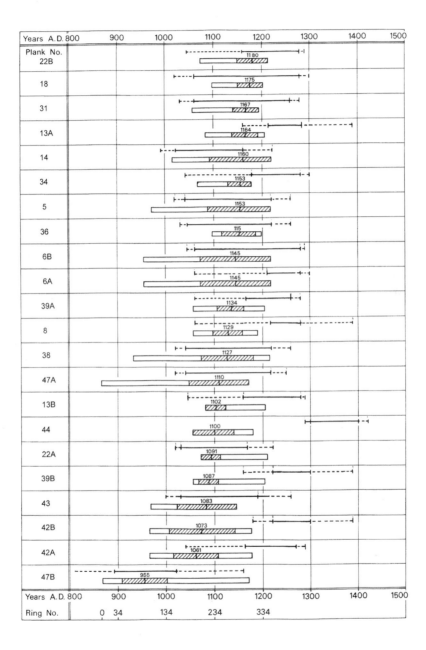

150 Dating the Round Table: radiocarbon dates and tree-ring dates compared for the twenty-two planks from the surface of the table dated by both methods.

Table 17
Tree-ring dating and radiocarbon determinations for the Round Table: basic data

Plank number HAR number[1]	Ring span of ^{14}C sample[2]	Centre ring of ^{14}C sample	Age BP	Error ± 1σ	Calibrated ^{14}C date (AD)[3]			Tree-ring date 1990 for ^{14}C sample	
					68.2% (1σ) confidence	95.4% (2σ) confidence	Centre date (2σ)	of rings spanned	of centre ring
RAD 5 HAR 2129	222–352	287	888	65	1040–1220	1020–1260	1140	1088–1218	1153
RAD 6A HAR 2130	207–351	279	793	51	1210–1285	1060–1300	1180	1073–1217	1145
RAD 6B HAR 2291	207–351	279	820	56	1160–1280	1040–1290	1165	1073–1217	1145
RAD 8 HAR 2298	231–295	263	780	55	1215–1285	1060–1390	1225	1129–1161	1129
RAD 13A HAR 2062	271–325	298	773	52	1215–1285	1160–1390	1275	1137–1191	1164
RAD 13B HAR 2297	215–257	236	820	52	1160–1280	1040–1290	1165	1081–1123	1102
RAD 14 HAR 2121	235–353	294	940	57	1020–1160	990–1220	1105	1101–1219	1160
RAD 18 HAR 1825	283–335	309	833	83	1060–1280	1020–1300	1160	1149–1201	1175
RAD 22A HAR 1770	205–245	225	924	49	1030–1170	1020–1220	1120	1071–1111	1091
RAD 22B HAR 2046	283–345	314	825	51	1160–1280	1040–1290	1165	1149–1211	1180
RAD 31 HAR 2047	274–328	301	850	54	1060–1260	1030–1280	1155	1140–1194	1167
RAD 34 HAR 2292	263–311	287	813	52	1180–1280	1040–1300	1170	1129–1177	1153
RAD 36 HAR 2048	249–319	284	880	52	1040–1220	1030–1260	1145	1115–1185	1150
RAD 38 HAR 2295	207–315	261	890	56	1040–1220	1020–1260	1140	1073–1181	1127
RAD 39A HAR 2061	240–296	268	834	36	1165–1260	1060–1280	1170	1106–1162	1134
RAD 39B HAR 2294	201–241	221	747	57	1220–1300	1160–1390	1275	1067–1107	1087

Plank number HAR number[1]	Ring span of ^{14}C sample[2]	Centre ring of ^{14}C sample	Age BP	Error ± 1σ	Calibrated ^{14}C date (AD)[3]			Tree-ring date 1990 for ^{14}C sample	
					68.2% (1σ) confidence	95.4% (2σ) confidence	Centre date (2σ)	of rings spanned	of centre ring
RAD 42A HAR 1827	149–241	195	840	49	1160–1270	1040–1290	1165	1015–1107	1061
RAD 42B HAR 2293	139–275	207	743	51	1220–1300	1180–1390	1285	1005–1141	1073
RAD 43 HAR 2124	156–278	217	915	67	1030–1190	1000–1260	1130	1022–1144	1083
RAD 44 HAR 2296	194–274	234	603	51	1300–1400	1290–1420	1355	1060–1140	1100
RAD 47A HAR 1828	180–306	243	893	56	1040–1220	1020–1250	1135	1046–1172	1109
RAD 47B HAR 1829	43–135	89	1077	61	890–1020	770–1160	965	909–1001	955
VRT 130 HAR 2060	16	–	310	54	1490–1650	1450–1670	1560	–	–
VRT 132A HAR 1771	8	–	490	52	1330–1460	1300–1500	1400	–	–
VRT 132B HAR 2059	25	–	360	54	1470–1640	1440–1650	1545	–	–
VRT 135 HAR 1826	Not known	–	715	58	1240–1390	1210–1400	1305	–	–
RIM 125A HAR 1802	Not known	–	530	117	1290–1480	1270–1650	1460	–	–
RIM 125B HAR 2049	Not known	–	485	55	1330–1470	1300–1620	1460	–	–
RIM 126 HAR 2050	Not known	–	455	56	1405–1490	1320–1640	1480	–	–

[1]The number of the radial plank (RAD), vertical (VRT) or rim (RIM), see Figs. 43 and 81. The radials are numbered from top left to top right as seen from the back of the table..
[2]Table 2.
[3]Stuiver et al. (1998); OxCal v.3.5 Bronk Ramsey (2000).

Two other investigations put in hand at the same time aimed at establishing the date of the wood used to make the table, one by tree-ring dating, the other by radiocarbon. The results obtained do not agree with each other, but both fall within the estimate of 1250 to 1350 suggested by Cecil Hewett for the carpentry (Fig. 151).

Professor A. C. Barefoot shows in Chapter 5 that the latest surviving tree-ring on the 49 planks of the table sampled for tree-ring dating was growing in the year 1219 (Tree 2). This ring is a heartwood ring, the carpenter having removed the sapwood and an unknown quantity of heartwood in preparing this plank for use in the table (Fig. 92*b*). An estimate of the number of missing heartwood and sapwood rings has therefore to be added to the year 1219 to arrive at some idea of the date at which the tree from which this plank came was felled. Professor Barefoot estimates that the tree may have been felled in the years 1250 to 1265. But this is still not the end of the matter. The boards obtained from the tree may have been seasoned for a number of years and have been in store for an even longer period. The tree-ring date can therefore only show that Tree 2, the latest identified tree used for the table, was felled some considerable time after 1219, perhaps in 1250–6, and that its timber may have been in store for some time thereafter. Taking into consideration the length of time some of the boards used for the table had been in store, Professor Barefoot suggests a construction date 'well after 1250/65 at the earliest'.[12]

The radiocarbon dating was undertaken at the Atomic Energy Research Establishment at Harwell by Mr R. L. Otlet and Miss Jill Walker. They describe in Chapter 6 how they have been able to suggest a radiocarbon 'stand-alone' date of AD 1298 to 1341 for the felling date of two of the groups of planks sampled for radiocarbon dating (Table 12; weighted mean, but at 95.4% confidence), and how they have produced a felling date of AD 1311 to 1371 for Tree 1a, which they consider to be the latest of the trees felled to provide the planks of the table (Table 13; pooled mean, 95.4% confidence; cf. p. 231).

These results from dendrochronology and radiocarbon dating show that there can now be no doubt that the table was made in the second half of the thirteenth or first half of the fourteenth century, no earlier than about 1250 and not much later than about 1350 (Fig. 151). This result should be compared that of AD 1260–1390 obtained for the linen of the shroud of Turin.[13] The Round Table result is useful, but in historical terms it leaves most questions unanswered. Assuming that the table was made by royal order, was it Henry III (1216–72), his son Edward I (1272–1307), his grandson Edward II (1307–27), or even his great–grandson Edward III (1327–77) who had it made? And for what purpose, or for what occasion?

The disagreement between the tree–ring and radiocarbon dates is at its sharpest in the felling dates proposed for Tree 1a. Tree–ring dating indicates a felling date of

---

[12] See above, pp. 182, 193, and cf. below pp. 389–90 and Table 20).

[13] P. E.Damon [with twenty other authors], 'Radiocarbon Dating of the Shroud of Turin', *Nature* 337 (1989), 611–15, at p. 614 ('Conclusions').

*c.*1233 or *c.*1236–41 (Table 6, Planks 39 and 13, respectively). Radiocarbon dating proposes a felling date of AD 1311 to 1371 (Table 13), a difference of a hundred years or more. Chapters 5 and 6 demonstrate the care their authors have taken to control and verify both sets of results. Clearly, however, with this level of disagreement both cannot be right. Is it possible to choose between them?

As Chapter 5 shows Professor Barefoot's work of the later 1970s has stood up to subsequent matching with the suite of tree-ring curves available by 1990, subject to a four-year shift towards an older (i.e. earlier) date as a result of the redating of the only master curves available to him in the late 1970s for dating the 25-plank curve (Table 5).[14]

The radiocarbon dating proposed in Chapter 6 has been subjected by Mr Otlet and Miss Walker to checks from both 'equal-age' samples (Table 9) and paired samples (Tables 10 and 11), and has within broad limits stood up to these controls.

A deeper problem arises however because the radiocarbon dating challenges not only the felling dates of the individual trees indicated by tree-ring dating (Table 13, cf. Table 6), but also compromises the internal coherence of the 25-plank curve. This is most clearly seen by noting those planks detailed in Table 13 which belong to the 25-plank curve (indicated by asterisks on Tables 1–3.2). These are radial planks (RAD) 8, 13, 18, 22, 31, 34, 36, 39, and 44.[15] If the 'six boards which next matched most easily' (indicated by + on Tables 2 and 3.2) are included, radiocarbon samples from RAD 5, 42, 43, and 47 must also be taken into consideration. In other words, of the 22 results listed on Table 13 eleven (including for these purposes RAD 44) come from the 25-plank curve and another 6 from the planks 'next most easily matched'. Yet the radiocarbon dates indicate that these planks derive from trees whose dates are very different to those given by tree-ring dating. Acceptance of the radiocarbon results thus involves not only contradicting the tree-ring dates but also deconstructing the 25-plank curve which is verified against a suite of 18 other curves (Table 5).

Modern radiocarbon calibration as used in Chapter 6 (see, for example, Figs. 90*a* and 90*b*) relies on ascertaining the radiocarbon age of individual rings from long-lived trees reaching back thousands of years.[16] It is difficult therefore to accept that any one set of radiocarbon results can contradict the placing of rings in a curve which has been shown to agree at very high level of probability with other independently verified English and North European curves (Tables 5).

---

[14] See above, pp. 183–93.

[15] RAD 44 is omitted from Table 13 for the reason explained on p. 224.

[16] See, for example, Baillie, *Tree-ring Dating* (as above, p. 209, n. 18) *passim.*

How then to explain the miss-match between the radiocarbon and the tree-ring results? The first point which should be made is that at the 68.2% (1 sigma) confidence range 13 of the 22 radiocarbon determinations (59 %) lie within or overlap the tree-ring dating of the individual planks (Tables 17 and 18; cf. Fig. 150). A further 6 results (27.3%) lie within or overlap the 95.4% (2 sigma) confidence range, and 3 (13.6%) lie outside the 95.4% range. By normal probability theory these figures should be 15 at the 68.2% (1 sigma) range and a further 6 at the 95.4% (2 sigma) range, with only one result outside that range in a set of twenty-two. This same relationship between the tree-ring dates of the Round Table planks and the radiocarbon results from the same planks can be seen between the expected dates and the results of other radiocarbon dates produced by the Harwell laboratory for the Winchester project in the 1970s (Table 18). It would clearly be wrong to expect a higher degree of precision for the Round Table results than for these other sets.

The 22 radiocarbon results are shown in Fig. 93 aligned to felling date. If these same results (excluding RAD 44, as explained[17]) are aligned to A. C. Barefoot's Ring 380, as in Fig. 94, and tested against the dating of Ring 380 to AD 1250, they give a date of AD 1290 to 1350 at 95.4% confidence, but fail the X^2 test at 5%, i.e. we can be 95% certain that the results do not all correspond.[18] The same exercise, ignoring RAD 39B and RAD 42B (which give consistently poor agreement) in addition to RAD 44, gives a slightly different date of AD 1285 to 1330 at 95.4% confidence but passes the X^2 test. A third exercise assumes that there was an offset of 0.5% in the Harwell laboratory on this set of samples. Such an offset would have had the effect of shifting the results obtained some 40 years towards a younger, i.e. more recent, age-range. Allowing for this offset produces an older date for Ring 380 of AD 1255 to 1301 at 95.4% confidence, and passes the X^2 test.

[17] See above, n. 15.

[18] I am grateful to Dr Christopher Bronk Ramsey, Deputy Director of the Radiocarbon Accelerator Unit at Oxford and author of the OxCal programme used in Chapter 6, for his advice on this and the following statistical tests. I am also grateful to Professor Michael Tite, Director of the Research Laboratory for Archaeology, University of Oxford, and Professor Richard Bradley, University of Reading, for much helpful advice and information. Birthe Kjølbye-Biddle, Winchester Research Unit, devised and compiled Tables 17 and 18 and revised Figs. 150 and 151. I am especially indebted to her detailed discussion of the many questions arising from the use of radiocarbon dates in medieval archaeology.

Table 18

Winchester radiocarbon dating determinations by the Harwell laboratory

Subject	Basis for expectation of date	Number of determinations	Results, calibrated dates AD[1]		
			Within or overlaps the 1 σ range	Within or overlaps the 2 σ range	Outside the 2 σ range
Theoretical expectation	–	–	68.2%	95.4%	4.6%
Winchester Round Table, radial planks	Dendrochronological determinations	22	59.1%	86.4%	13.6%
Winchester Round Table, rim and verticals	Written evidence	7	28.6%	71.4%	28.6%
Winchester 'Equal-age' samples[2]	Written evidence	5	40%	100%	0
Winchester Lower Brook Street[3]	Archaeological stratigraphy, written evidence	85		12.9%	27.1%
Winchester Lower Brook Street[4]	Archaeological stratigraphy, written evidence,	85	60%	72.9%	27.1%
Winchester Old Minster[5]	Archaeological stratigraphy, written evidence, and 3 dendrochronological determinations	46	54.3%	78.2%	21.7%
Totals	(As above)	186	55.4%	78.0%	22.0%

[1]Using OxCal 3.5 Bronk Ramsey (2000)

[2]Table 9 (p. 220), excluding the Old Minster samples and the 'Trusty Servant' shutter which have too wide an expected date.

[3]Dates processed in the 1970s. These dates were compiled and analysed by Birthe Kjølbye-Biddle on behalf of English Heritage, see D. Jordan, D. Haddon-Reece and A. Bayliss. *Radiocarbon Dates from Samples Funded by English Heritage before 1981*, (London, 1994) pp. 212–32.

[4]See n. 3.

[5]Dates processed in the 1970s. M. Biddle and B. Kjølbye-Biddle, *The Anglo-Saxon Minsters at Winchester*, Winchester Studies 4.1, forthcoming.

The laboratory argues that these results were not subject to any systematic offsetting at the time they were obtained (Figs. 95a and 95b),[19] but other laboratories have

[19] See above, pp. 233–4.

reported offsets, most notably the British Museum Research Laboratory which identified a systematic error in its results for the great majority of samples dated between 1980 and 1984.[20] It is common knowledge that radiocarbon laboratories do not always produce the same date for the same object. This is especially true of dates produced in the 1960s and 1970s, but would probably not be the case today. The most famous case in the period of the Round Table is the dating of the Shroud of Turin. Three laboratories (Arizona, Oxford and Zurich) produced dates of 1220 to 1300, 1280 to 1390, and 1280 to 1400 (95% confidence) from samples of the same material obtained under carefully controlled and independently refereed conditions.[21]

The set of determinations made by the Harwell laboratory for 'Lindow Man', a well preserved body found at Lindow Moss in Cheshire in 1984, illustrates another discrepancy.[22] Six samples from the body itself were measured at Harwell between September 1984 and February 1986.[23] These results were consistent among themselves in indicating a late Roman age (AD 410 to AD 570 at 95% confidence). A second series of determinations made later by the Oxford laboratory indicated a date in the middle part of the 1st century AD (AD 0 to AD 130 at 95% confidence).[24] The Oxford authors of the 1989 paper have 'no hypothesis to offer which can explain the differences between the Oxford and Harwell dates for Lindow Man, *both series being internally consistent*' (my emphasis). The discussion which follows, embracing the options of abandoning either the Oxford or the Harwell results, or of selecting a point within the range of the Oxford and Harwell dates, or of rejecting both, mirrors the discussion of the contradiction between the radiocarbon dates and the tree-ring dates for the Round Table. In the end the authors of the 1989 article decided in favour of a date 'in the 1st century AD or thereabouts', but admit that the 'specific discrepancy between Oxford AMS and Harwell small counter dates on the body has not been resolved'.[25]

[20] M. S. Tite, S. G. E. Bowman, J. C. Ambers and K. J. Matthews, 'Preliminary Statement on an Error in British Museum Radiocarbon Dates (BM-1700 to BM-2315)', *Antiquity* 61 (1987), 168; also in *Radiocarbon* 30(1) (1987), 132. See further the explanation of the reason for the error and the steps taken to counteract it, as set out by S. G. E. Bowman, 'Radiocarbon Chronology' in John C. Barrett, Richard Bradley and Martin Green, *Landscape, Monuments and Society* (Cambridge, 1991), pp. 3–5.

[21] P. E. Damon *et al.*, as above, n. 13. The authors note that 'the spread of measurements for sample 1 [the sample taken from the Shroud] is somewhat greater than would be expected from the errors quoted' (p. 613). The dates quoted here have been recalibrated using OxCal v3.5 Bronk Ramsey (2000).

[22] I. M. Stead, J. B. Bourke and Don Brothwell, *Lindow Man. The Body in the Bog* (London, 1986).

[23] R. L. Otlet, A. J. Walker, and S. M. Dadson, 'Report on Radiocarbon Dating of the Lindow Man by AERE, Harwell', in Stead *et al.* (as last note), pp. 27–30. The dates quoted here have been recalibrated using OxCal v3.5 Bronk Ramsey (2000).

[24] J. A. J. Gowlett, R. E. M. Hedges and I. A. Law, 'Radiocarbon Accelerator (AMS) Dating of Lindow Man', *Antiquity*, 63 (1989), 71–9. The dates quoted here have been recalibrated using OxCal v3.5 Bronk Ramsey (2000).

The present discussion of the Round Table discrepancy ends on very much the same note. All the evidence suggests that the tree-ring date should be accepted but no certain explanation of the discrepancy can be put forward. The possibilities which have been suggested, notably of a specific offset in the radiocarbon results would not be accepted by our colleagues whose careful presentation in Chapter 6 leads to the results under question here. One of the problems may well be that results which would be perfectly acceptable, and both useful and important, in the study of prehistory cannot reasonably be subjected to the much finer resolutions which are possible on the basis of written and other evidence when dealing with the Middle Ages. The point has already been made that at the broader level of the period 1250 to 1350 all the dating methods show broad agreement. Whatever the answer, the two dating exercises on the Round Table have raised important questions for the scientific dating of medieval artefacts. From this point onwards, however, the making of the table will be considered only in relation to the tree-ring dating proposed in Chapter 5.

One approach, on the assumption that the table was made for the hall in which it is known to have hung since at least 1463 or 1464[26], is to ask whether the table could have been made as part of the original fitting up or decoration of the hall by Henry III. Following the completion of the hall in 1235, works took place on several occasions over the next thirty years or so, notably in 1235–6, 1239, 1256, and 1268–9, and of these the works of 1256 and 1268–9 would fit with the dating suggested by the carpentry and by the tree-ring dating (Fig. 151). Another approach would be to ask whether there was some event which took place at Winchester in the years between 1250 and 1350 in connection with which the table might have been made. There is such an event, a royal tournament held at Winchester in April 1290 at a crucial moment in Edward I's reign.

These possibilities require investigation in some detail if a choice is to be made between them, but the later the date is set, the greater the allowance which has to be made either for the amount of heartwood trimmed off by the carpenter in preparing the planks for the top of the table or for the time the wood remained in store, or both. A date in the period 1250 to 1300 is therefore more likely than a date after 1300. This is reinforced by the destruction of the royal apartments in the castle by fire in 1302.[27] The Great Hall was spared, but the royal apartments were not rebuilt. Thereafter the castle was very rarely used as a royal residence, perhaps only in 1330 when

---

[25] Gowlett *et al.* (as last note), 77–8.
[26] See below, pp. 393–6.
[27] See above, p. 69.

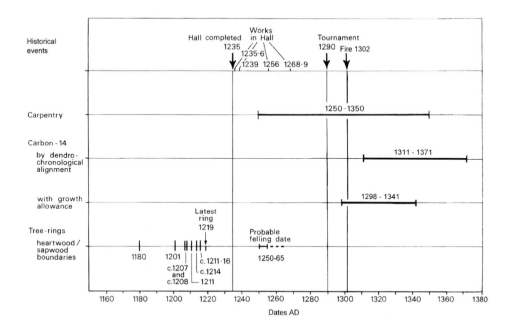

151 Dating the Round Table: the results of the different dating methods compared. For carpentry, see above, p. 117; for the Carbon-14 dates, p. 231; for the tree-ring date, p. 192.

Edward III stayed there when Parliament was held at Winchester for the first time since the fire.[28] The absence of the royal family makes it unlikely that a feast such as that for which this exceptional table was probably made would have been held in the castle after 1302.

Winchester as an 'Arthurian' city

A round table is so unusual and distinctive a piece of furniture that it is probably safe to assume that the Winchester table was made in emulation of the Round Table of King Arthur.[29] Is there anything therefore about Winchester which makes the city a likely setting for the creation of an 'Arthurian' table?

The association of Arthur with Winchester began, as does almost everything Arthurian, with Geoffrey of Monmouth. In his *Historia Regum Britanniae*, finished in 1135,[30] Geoffrey was especially concerned with Winchester and its church, for which he provided a fabulous and entirely non-historical past. Winchester is one of the places he 'mentioned oftenest in the *Historia*, nearly as often as York or London,' 'the most obvious reason' being, as J. S. P. Tatlock argued, 'that there was someone at Winchester who was worth pleasing'.[31] This was Henry of Blois, brother of King Stephen, appointed bishop of Winchester only six years before in 1129 and an 'extremely able and ambitious young man'.[32] It is all the more striking therefore, as Tatlock said,

> that Geoffrey gives Arthur no connection with [Winchester] (save to appoint a bishop and to besiege Modredus there); and this in spite of the prominence of the city all through the *Historia*, and the later appearance of Arthurian associations in Winchester. Here we have merely an example of the prodigious later vogue of Geoffrey's Arthur. The preservation [in Winchester] of his father's dragon-ensign [VIII.17], the Arthurian bishop long before St. Augustine [IX.15], the refuge taken by Modredus and his sons [XI.1, 3, 4], and the city's

---

[28] PRO, E372/176; cf. *Calendar of Close Rolls 1330–3*, p. 5.

[29] See above Chapters 1 and 2, and especially pp. 9–15 and 57.

[30] For the dates of the successive dedications, see D. R. Howlett, 'The Literary Context of Geoffrey of Monmouth: an Essay on the Fabrication of Sources', *Arthuriana* 5.3 (Fall 1995), 25–69, at 34–44, 52–4.

[31] J. S. P. Tatlock, *The Legendary History of Britain. Geoffrey of Monmouth's Historia Regum Britanniae and its Early Vernacular Versions* (Berkeley and Los Angeles, 1950), pp. 36–7, 39.

[32] Tatlock, *Legendary History*, p. 37. For Henry, see now Nicholas Riall, *Henry of Blois, Bishop of Winchester: a Patron of the Twelfth-Century Renaissance*, Hampshire Papers 5 (Winchester, 1994).

history as an ancient capital gave a sort of justification in later centuries for Arthur's Round Table appearing there, if it needed any.[33]

Only these few passages tell of Arthur and the city, yet Winchester's importance in Geoffrey is clear enough. It was at Winchester that Arthur's father, Uther Pendragon, was acclaimed and *suscepit dyadema regni Britanniae et in regem sublimatus* ('received the diadem of the kingdom of Britain and was made king').[34] Later writers were to embroider these hints.

The earliest of these whose work survives was Wace, a Norman Jerseyman, who translated Geoffrey's Latin prose into Old French verse in 1155.[35] Wace adds little to Geoffrey's few passages on Winchester, but after his account of Arthur's battle against Mordred outside Winchester and of Mordred's flight via [South]hampton to Cornwall he has a more decisive statement of Arthur's capture of the city:

> Li reis Arthur Wincestre asist,
> La gent venqui, la cité prist.

> King Arthur besieged Winchester
> Defeated the people and took the city.[36]

Arthur was now again in control of Winchester where his father Uther Pendragon had been acclaimed king.[37] Yet Wace's most famous and most influential addition to Geoffrey's original story is quite unaffected by the importance of Winchester to Uther

---

[33] Tatlock, *Legendary History*, pp. 38–9, 330. The references in square brackets are to the books and chapters of Geoffrey's *Historia*, as given in the standard editions and translations, e.g., Acton Griscom (ed.), *The Historia Regum Britanniae of Geoffrey of Monmouth* (London, 1929), and Lewis Thorpe (trans.), *Geoffrey of Monmouth. The History of the Kings of Britain*, The Penguin Classics (Harmondsworth, 1966). The new single text editions, e.g. Neil Wright (ed.), *The Historia Regum Britannie of Geoffrey of Monmouth*, i, Bern, Burgerbibliothek, MS. 568 (Cambridge/Woodbridge, 1985) and ii, *The First Variant Version: a Critical Edition* (Cambridge/Woodbridge, 1988), give references by section numbers.

[34] *Historia*, VIII.16 (Griscom (ed.), p. 419; Wright (ed.), ii, cap. 135).

[35] Judith Weiss (ed.), *Wace's Roman de Brut. A History of the British. Text and Translation*, Exeter Medieval English Texts and Studies (Exeter, 1999). Her text is in essence that of Ivor Arnold (ed.), *Le Roman de Brut de Wace*, Société des anciens textes français, 2 vols. (Paris, 1938, 1940), whose line numbers she retains. Wace was preceded by Geffrei Gaimar who translated the *Historia* into rhyming Old French couplets at an early date, perhaps almost as soon as it appeared, but his version is lost: Howlett, 'Literary Context' (as above, n. 30), pp. 47–55. Wace was followed *c.*1200 by another poet whose Anglo-Norman text added nothing to the role of Winchester; Alexander Bell (ed.), *An Anglo-Norman Brut*, Anglo-Norman Texts 21–2 (Oxford, 1969).

[36] Weiss (ed.), lines 13187–8.

[37] Weiss (ed.), lines 8365–8402.

and Arthur. In the first appearance of the Round Table in literature, in the great period of peace following Arthur's wars, Wace does not say where it was made:

> Fist Artur la Runde Table
> Dunt Bretun dient mainte fable.

> Arthur had the Round Table made,
> About which the British tell many a tale.[38]

The coronation of Arthur at Caerleon which follows in the text not long after the making of the Round Table might give one to think that the table was made at Caerleon, but this is never said. At his coronation feast at Caerleon, Arthur dined seated in his chair upon the dais and the lords and princes sat around the board, according to the usage of the country, each in his order and degree.[39] This is the very antithesis of the spirit and purpose of the Round Table, where

> all [were] equal, all leaders; they were placed equally round the table and equally served. None of them could boast he sat higher than his peer; all were seated near the place of honour, none far away.[40]

Fifty years later, about the end of the twelfth or beginning of the thirteenth century, Layamon of King's Arley on the Severn translated Wace's Norman French into partly alliterative, partly rhyming Middle English verse.[41] Layamon greatly expanded Wace, giving a much fuller account of the founding of the Round Table and

> in a passage of remarkable beauty he launched as upon a great river flowing towards posterity the story of how Arthur after his last battle was carried away by two maidens in a boat, to Argante in Avallon, to be healed of his wounds. 'And afterwards I will return to my kingdom and dwell among the Britons with great joy'.[42]

---

[38] Weiss (ed.), lines 9751–2; for discussion, see above, John Fleming in Chapter 1, pp. 9–10.

[39] Weiss (ed.), lines 9753–60, her translation.

[40] On this distinction between round and high tables, see above, Simon Jervis in Chapter 2, pp. 39–47.

[41] Howlett, 'Literary Context' (as above, n. 30), pp. 57–8.

[42] Gwyn Jones, 'Introduction' to Eugene Mason (trans.), *Wace and Layamon; Arthurian Chronicles*, Everyman's Library (London and New York, 1962, reptd. 1976), p. xi.

To this Layamon added feasts, armings, similes, descriptions of natural background, and of rapid and warlike action: 'he had a brave poetic imagination which he exercised on a variety of transmutable material, and for the most part transmuted it for good'.[43] But he added little about Winchester, apart from a tendency to repeat the name where once would do.[44] For Layamon, as for Wace and Geoffrey before him, Caerleon was Arthur's city not Winchester. As for the table, which Layamon never calls round, a carpenter in Cornwall made it for the king.[45]

Not long after Wace wrote, Chrétien de Troyes, the greatest of all the authors of Arthurian romance, portrayed Winchester as Arthur's capital. In general, Arthur plays an inactive role in Chrétien's stories; he is the focal point of chivalry, and his court is the greatest in the world, but his character is often that of a *roi fainéant*. The one exception to this is *Cligés*, the least Arthurian of Chrétien's works, in which Alexander, son of the Greek emperor, hears of Arthur's fame and sets out to visit his court. He and his company land near Southampton, and learn that Arthur is at Winchester:

> Et quant il furent atorné,
> De soz Hantone sont torné,
> Si ont le droit chemin tenu
> Tant qu'a Guincestre sont venu,
> Ou li rois estoit a sejor.
> Einçois qu'il fust prime de jor
> Furent a cort venu li Gré;
> Au pié descendent del degré.
> Li escuier et li cheval
> Remestrent an la cort aval,
> Et li vaslet montent amont
> Devant le meillor roi del mont
> Qui onques fust ne ja mes soit.[46]

Once ready, they left Southampton and, following the direct route, came to Winchester where the king was staying. Before six o'clock in the morning the

---

43 Jones (as last note), p. xii.

44 G. L. Brook and R. F. Leslie (ed.), *Layamon: 'Brut'*, Early English Text Society, 2 vols., o. s., 250, 277 (Oxford 1961, 1978), e.g. lines 14161, 14164, 14183, 14195, 14201; cf. his constant repetition of the name of Arthur, often with the epithet, 'noblest of kings', giving an Old English, not to say Homeric, character to his verse.

45 Brook and Leslie (ed.) (as last note), lines 11422–54.

46 Chrétien de Troyes, *Cligés*, ed. Stewart Gregory and Claude Luttrell, Arthurian Studies 28 (Cambridge and Rochester, N.Y., 1993), ll. 299–311.

Greeks had arrived at court. They dismount at the foot of the steps; and their squires and horses remain in the courtyard below while the youths go up into the presence of the best king who ever was or ever may be in the world.[47]

Here for the first time Winchester appears as the natural place for Arthur to be holding court. Chrétien may have visited England possibly in the entourage of Henry de Blois, Bishop of Winchester, whose nephew, Henry, count of Champagne, was his patron.[48] If so, Chrétien was in a good position to reflect the reality of the later twelfth century when in Henry II's time Winchester was still the principal royal city of the kingdom. As has been well said, Alexander's reception 'smacks too much of twelfth-century royal Winchester to be mistaken for the "ancient court" of King Arthur.[49]

Winchester continues to figure in the romances, including the precursors of the great cycle of stories that modern scholars know as the Vulgate Cycle,[50] but it is not until the appearance in the years around 1230 of this vast composition in Old French Prose, also known as the Prose Lancelot, that a new episode is actually set in Winchester. Consisting of three separate tales, *Lancelot*, *The Quest of the Holy Grail*, and *The Death of King Arthur*, it is the story of Lancelot, his birth and Grail adventure, his love for Arthur and his adultery with Guinevere, of his conversion and repentance, his fall back into adultery, and his final climb from sin towards a kind of sainthood, and of how these actions brought about the destruction of the company of the Round Table.

The *Mort Artu*, the third and final part of the story of Lancelot, was composed by an unknown Frenchman, perhaps from Champagne, writing about 1230–5. It opens with the renewed affair between Lancelot and Guinevere and ends with Arthur's mortal wound in battle against his bastard son Mordred on Salisbury Plain and Lancelot's repentance and conversion to the service of Jesus Christ. At his dying order Arthur's squire threw Excalibur into a lake where a hand rose from the water to catch the sword. Arthur's sister Morgan and her companions then bore the dying

---

[47] Chrétien de Troyes, *Arthurian Romances* trans. D. D. R Owen, Everyman Classics (London 1993), pp. 96–7.

[48] As argued by Urban T. Holmes jr. and M. Amelia Klenke, *Chrétien, Troyes, and the Grail* (Chapel Hill, 1959), pp. 14–15, 23–5; cf. Urban T. Holmes jr., *Chrétien de Troyes* (New York, 1970), pp. 24–5.

[49] Constance Bullock-Davies, 'Chrétien de Troyes and England', *Arthurian Literature* 1 (Cambridge, 1981) pp. 1–61; at pp. 12–13.

[50] For a full list of references, see under 'Winchester' in G. D. West, *An Index of Proper Names in the French Arthurian Verse Romances* (Toronto, 1969), and idem, *An Index of Proper Names in the French Arthurian Prose Romances* (Toronto, 1978), in both cases *s.v.* Winchester.

Arthur out to sea in a boat. When news of Arthur's death and of the death of Guinevere reached him, Lancelot, sad and grief-stricken, took a great army to Winchester to rescue the city from the sons of Mordred and in a final battle outside the city defeated them. Losing his way after the battle, Lancelot came to an ancient chapel where his brother Hector eventually found him. They stayed there four years in the service of Christ until first Hector and then Lancelot died. Lancelot's body was carried at his wish to the castle of the Joyeuse Garde and buried beside his son Galahad, and on the tomb was inscribed, 'Lancelot del Lac, who was the finest knight that ever entered the Kingdom of Logres, except for his son Galahad'.

The *Mort Artu* opens at Camelot where Arthur orders the adventures of the Quest for the Holy Grail to be written down. And then,

> li rois, por ce qu'il veoit que les aventures del roiaume de Logres estoient si menees a fin qu'il n'en avenoit mes nule se petit non, fist crier un tornoiement en la praerie de Wincestre, por ce qu'il ne vouloit pas toutevoies que si compaignon lessassent a porter armes.[51]

> since the king saw that the adventures of the kingdom of Logres were so nearly ended that very little more could happen, he had a tournament proclaimed on the meadow at Winchester, because he in no way wished that his knights should cease to bear arms.

The days before the tournament see the renewed affair between Lancelot and Guinevere, but all that concerns us here is that Lancelot delays his departure from Camelot so that he may appear at the tournament in disguise and unrecognised. A day is set aside for the tournament and many of Arthur's knights go there (§ 6).

It takes two days or so to reach Winchester (§ 6–10, 15). Lancelot, although leaving Camelot after Arthur and riding by night, is recognised and arranges to borrow the shield and other equipment of a newly dubbed knight (*un de ces escuz me prestez a porter a cele assemblee de Wincestre et les couvertures et touz les autres apareillemenez autresi,* § 12) so that he may not be recognised (§ 11–12). Lancelot's squire will also bear the same arms and caparisons (§ 16). Lancelot sends his squire on ahead to Winchester to find out who is going to be supporting those inside the castle and who were joining those outside. The squire reported back that there were a great number of people both inside and out because knights had come from everywhere, *ausi li privé com li estrange,* 'both familiar ones and strangers', but the greater force was

---

[51] Jean Frappier (ed.), *La Mort Le Roi Artu: roman du XIIIe siècle* (Paris, 1954), § 3. In what follows, Frappier's section numbers are given in the body of the text.

inside since the companions of the Round Table were there: Bors and Lionel and Hector were inside, the kings of Scotland, Ireland, Wales, of North Wales and many other great men were outside:

> mes toutevoies n'ont il pas ausi bones genz con cil dedenz, car il sont trestuit chevalier coqueilli et estrange; si ne sont pas coustumier de porter armes, si comme sont cil del roialme de Logres, ne si bon chevalier ne sont il mie (§ 16).

> but no way do they have as good people as those inside for they are all foreigners, gathered from all sides, not used to bearing arms like those from the kingdom of Logres, and they are not such good knights.

Lancelot then rode on with his companions

> qu'il vindrent en la praerie de Wincestre qui ja estoit toute couverte de josteeurs, et estoit ja li tornoiemenz si pleniers qu'il estoient assemblé et d'une part et d'autre (§ 16).

> until they came to the meadow of Winchester which was already completely covered with jousters, and there were already so many participants that they had formed into one side and the other.

Arthur and a great company of knights now climbed the main tower of the city (*en la plus mestre tor de la vile*) to see the tournament (§ 17). Lancelot joined the party outside, because 'it would not be honourable to join the stronger side'. A melée then ensued between the two parties on the tournament field (§ 18–20). This was not literally an attack by the party 'outside' the castle on the part 'inside'; the identifications were made up simply to provide two groups between whom combat could take place on the field. Fighting in disguise, Lancelot carried out so many deeds of valour and prowess that he was regarded as the finest knight on either side, the just winner of the tournament. But Lancelot had been badly wounded early in the fight by his cousin Bors and as soon as he saw that those 'inside the city' had lost the day, he left the field at speed and disappeared (§ 20–1). No one had recognised the knight who had won the tournament, for he had carried a shield completely red and a red caparison and worn a lady's silk sleeve on his helmet (§ 23, 25, 28).

The tournament at Winchester is the great set-piece of the early part of the *Mort Artu*. Tournaments at Tanebourc and Camelot follow, but they are dismissed in a few lines (§ 43, 66). The essentials of the Winchester tournament are these. Arthur himself calls the tournament. He decrees that it should be held, not at his principal seat at Caerleon, but at Winchester, two days or so away. No reason is given for the choice of Winchester; the importance of the city is accepted fact, emphasised at the end of the *Mort Artu* when in battle outside the city Lancelot defeats the sons of Mordred (§ 196–8) and King Bors (as he had then become) enters the city and buries his brother Lionel 'in a way befitting a king' (§ 201). The tournament was to take place on the *praerie de Wincestre* (§ 3, 16), a meadow, evidently outside the city. Usually called a *tornoiement* (§ 3, 5, 6, 9, etc.), the occasion is also a great *assemblé* (§ 12, 26, 28, etc.) of kings, the companions of the Round Table, and other knights, both natives and strangers. The combatants are divided into two groups, the party 'inside the castle' and the party 'outside', but since everything takes place on the tournament field, this is a device (possibly emphasised by the construction of some temporary 'castle'?). Disguise is a key element in the story. Arthur and many (non-participant) knights climb a tower to get a better view. There is a *melée*, a free-fight between the parties, in which one knight is judged to have won the tournament. The whole event lasts for one day only and people depart the following day. The tournament is not described as a Round Table and there is no mention of a feast following it. The Round Table is not mentioned, except to describe the company of knights of the Round Table.

The *Mort Artu* was written about sixty years before the Winchester tournament of 1290. As we shall see, the latter shares some features with the tournament of the *Mort Artu*, but these are not striking enough to suggest that the Winchester tournament was modelled on the *Mort Artu*. The key elements are that it is Arthur who calls the tournament and that it is to be at Winchester.[52]

The mythical tournament of the *Mort Artu* of the 1230s was not the first to have taken place outside Winchester. The *Histoire de Guillaume le Maréchal*, 'the first medieval "biography" of a layman who was not a king', is a Middle French poem written sometime between 1226 and 1229. It speaks of the royal garrison at Winchester in 1141 riding out daily to do *chevalerie*, in the sense of virtuosity in military games of horsemanship and arms.[53] The similarity in date of the two poems may suggest that one has influenced the other, but even if this were so it only serves to emphasise the sense that

---

[52] There is a description of a tournament at Winchester in Robert of Blois' romance *Biausdous*, written about 1250, but Robert seems to have had no English associations, and to be imitating Chrétien de Troyes' romances, particularly *Cligés*. See Gisèle Andrée Lamarque, '*Le Roman de Biausdous*, a Critical Edition', unpublished dissertation, University of North Carolina at Chapel Hill, 1968 (Dissertation Abstracts 69–1634), ll.3901–4684, I owe this reference to the kindness of Dr. Richard Barber.

[53] David Crouch, *William Marshal: Court, Career and Chivalry in the Angevin Empire 1147–1219* (London, 1990), pp. 28 and n. 4, 183; for the text, see Paul Meyer (ed.), *L'histoire de Guillaume le Maréchal, comte de Striguil et de Pembroke, regent d'Angleterre 1216 à 1219: poème français*, 3 vols., Société de l'histoire de France 255, 268, 304 (Paris, 1891–1901), i, lines 174–8.

Winchester was regarded in the first part of the thirteenth century as a proper place for such knightly conduct.

Edward I and Queen Eleanor will have been well aware of this, for both read romances. Eleanor employed two scribes and a painter for whom gold, vermilion, gum, ink and vellum were bought *ad libros regine* or *ad opus regine ad libros scribendos* ('for the queen's books' or 'for the queen's work for writing books').[54] Girard of Amiens dedicated to her his *Escanor*, a French Arthurian romance of great length and complexity,[55] and the royal accounts show that by May 1288 her books included *romancias* and that *un romanz* of Isembart had been written and illuminated for her in France about 1281.[56] Edward appears to have owned a Prose Tristan or a Palamède which he took with him on the crusade and left or loaned in Italy perhaps in 1273.[57]

This section began with the question whether there was anything about Winchester which makes the city a likely setting for the creation of an 'Arthurian' table. The answer would seem to be this. Up to the time of the writing of the *Mort Artu* in the 1230s Winchester was an important city of the Arthurian world but it was not in any special sense Arthur's own city. That city was Caerleon. The Round Table itself was associated with Cornwall if anywhere, not with Winchester. From the time of the *Mort Artu*, however, it was possible to see Winchester as a proper place for holding a tournament, above all because Arthur had chosen the city himself, but also because it had been the scene and occasion of the valorous deeds of Lancelot of the Lake, 'the noblest man in the world and the finest knight alive'.[58] The tradition that would lead by the end of the Middle Ages to the idea that the Round Table began at Winchester probably owes more however to the actual presence of a round table hanging in Winchester Castle hall than it does to thirteenth-century ideas of the role of the city in Arthur's world. There is a real sense in which the making of a round table was the making of Arthurian Winchester.

[54] This should not be taken to mean that she wrote them herself: Parsons (ed.), *Court and Household* (as below, n. 85), pp. 13–14.

[55] J. D. Bruce, *The Evolution of Arthurian Romance from the Beginnings down to the Year 1300*, 2 vols. (Baltimore and Göttingen, 1928), ii, pp. 275–6, 283–5.

[56] Parsons (ed.), as below, n. 85 p. 13.

[57] Loomis, 'Edward I, Arthurian Enthusiast' (as below, n. 72), p. 115; see also V. H. Galbraith, 'The Literacy of the Medieval English Kings', *Proceedings of the British Academy* 21 (1935), 201–35.

[58] Frappier (ed.), as above n. 51, § 30.

A table made for the Great Hall?

In a city with an Arthurian tradition such as Winchester, a round table might perhaps have been made as an appropriate element in the furnishing of Henry III's new hall, completed in 1235. All the evidence suggests, however, that Henry's hall was designed and decorated as a statement of royal majesty.[59] There were upper and lower ends. The lower end, as defined by the service doors, lay to the east, the upper end to the west. In 1235–6, immediately after its completion, a bench and a seat for the king's use were made at the head of the hall.[60] The dais itself was laid with glazed tiles in 1237–8,[61] in 1241 the floor before the dais was paved,[62] and in 1256 and 1258–9 the upper and lower steps were tiled.[63] Beside the dais to the north a doorway framed in Purbeck marble opened westwards into the royal apartments (Plate XII). A Wheel of Fortune painted on the west wall above the royal seat in 1235–6 reminded all who saw the king in state of the transience of royal power (cf. Plate III; Figs. 4–6).[64] A few years later in 1239 a *mappa mundi*, a circular Map of the World, was painted on the east wall of the hall, facing the king and echoing the Wheel of Fortune above his head.[65] The same year four images, probably statues, were ordered for the south porch; in 1256 an image of St. George was placed over the entrance to the hall; and in 1268–9 an image of St Edward was set at the door of the hall, but whether St. George and St. Edward the Confessor were at the great south porch leading to the king's apartments, or at one of the other entrances to the hall is not recorded.[66] None of these embellishments hints at Arthur or at the supposed equality of honour implied by the use of a round table. The hierarchical arrangement of the Winchester hall, with an upper and lower end and a high seat, reflects the use of a rectangular high table across the upper end, just such a table as was made in Purbeck marble for West-minster Hall, probably in the reign of Henry III (Fig. 21).[67]

---

[59] See above, pp. 71–5; but cf. Simon Jervis in Chapter 2, p. 42.

[60] PRO, E372/80, rot. 10^d: *in quodam banco et quodam*[sic] *sede ad opus regis faciendis ad capud aule regis Wint' versus orientem*, 110s. 3d.; cf. E352/29. In 1252–3 the king's seat was repainted, E372/92, rot. 15.

[61] This seems to be the meaning of PRO, E372/82, rot. 7^d: *in desio eiusdem aule tam coloribus quam aluinde emendando.*

[62] PRO, E372/85: *in aula pauanda ante desiu.*

[63] In 1256 a tile pavement was made on the upper step (*Calendar of Liberate Rolls 1256*, p. 343) and in 1258–9 the lower step was tiled (E372/103).

[64] See above, pp. 74, and below, p. 409.

[65] See above, p. 74–5, and below, p. 413–14.

[66] See above, p. 75.

[67] H. M. Colvin (ed.), *The History of the King's Works*, i (1963), pp. 544–5. When this volume of *The History* was written, the fragments of the Purbeck marble table shown in Fig. 21 had not been found and the date of the making of the table was unknown. See also above, pp. 41–2; and cf. p. 372, n. 124.

The dates of these works are shown in Fig. 151 at 1235, 1235–6, 1256, and 1268–9, but the nature of the works done gives no grounds for suggesting that the Round Table might have been made for the original furnishing of the hall. To the contrary, they suggest that a round table would have been alien to the spirit of Henry's hall as first conceived. The decoration of Henry III's houses is well documented and neither at Winchester nor elsewhere does it suggest that King Henry had any special interest in King Arthur.

Table 19

Edward I's expenditure on repairing the *domus regis*, the royal apartments of Winchester Castle, 1283–1301[1]

1283–4	12th year	20	3	10¼[2]
1284–5	13th year	120	0	3[3]
1286–7	15th year	15	0	4[4]
1287–8	16th year	32	8	4½
1289–90	18th year	75	8	11[5]
1291–2	20th year	44	14	3½
1292–3	21st year	29	6	7½
1293–4	22nd year	18	9	11
1299–1300	28th year	24	7	8½
1300–1	29th year	279	7	9[6]
Total, 1283–1301		£659	8	0¼[7]

[1]Exchequer years, ending 29 September.

[2]PRO, E101/491/15. Includes work on the castle walls and the bridge. The total is incomplete and may be accounted for within the expenditure of another account.

[3]Includes work on the great bridge over the ditch on the west side of the castle.

[4]Includes repair of bridges.

[5]Includes further work on the great bridge.

[6]Includes work on the castle walls.

[7]PRO, E372/130, 132, 133, 135, 146 (rot. 5(2)d for 1291–2, 1292–3, and 1293–4; rot.5(1)d for 1299–1300), and E372/147, rot. 7d (for 1300–1), respectively. For 1286–7 (E372/132), cf. PRO, E101/491/16 and E101/561/1. For 1289–90 (E372/135), cf. PRO, E368/61, m. 45r. These figures revise those given in Colvin, *History of the King's Works* (as above, n. 67), ii. p. 862.

But is it possible that the table was made for some special event held at Winchester in Henry III's reign? During his fifty-six years on the throne, Henry visited Winchester (where he had been born) perhaps a hundred times, on at least eighteen occasions for the Christmas feast.[68] Obviously, the table could have been made for one of these visits. Nevertheless, the king's evident lack of interest in the story of Arthur must make this unlikely. The interests of his son and successor, Edward I (1272–1307), provide a more likely context and a specific occasion.

In the thirty-five years of his reign Edward visited Winchester only eleven times, but on four of these visits he stayed one or two weeks, at Christmas 1270 for three weeks, and in 1306 for three months, when awaiting the birth of his third and last child by his second wife Margaret.[69] Edward kept the castle in good repair until the fire of 1302 in the royal apartments put an end to the use of the castle as a royal residence.[70] Thereafter he and his successors usually stayed either at the bishop of Winchester's palace of Wolvesey or occasionally in the prior's lodging at the cathedral.[71] Edward's work at the castle consisted mainly of roofing, glazing, and repairing walls, his father having done all that was needed to reconstruct the defences and the royal apartments on modern lines. Even so, Edward on several occasions had to spend heavily, usually on repairs to the *domus regis*, 'the king's houses', that is to say the royal apartments (Table 19). In 1283 the work included reroofing the Great Hall and in 1289 the walls and entrance of the hall and its windows were repaired.

Unlike his father, Edward I was a passionate Arthurian[72]. He was also so keen an organiser of tournaments and participant that 'the thirty yars after 1267 are likely to have been the golden age of the tournament in England.'[73] Given the Arthurian

[68] PRO, MS Itinerary of Henry III (originally Chancery Lane, Round Room, Press 17, no. 5; now Kew, Map Room, Open Shelves).

[69] PRO, MS Itinerary of Edward I (originally London, Chancery Lane, Round Room, Press 17, nos. 6–7; now Kew, Map Room, Open Shelves). In 1306 the king and queen stayed at the bishop's palace at Wolvesey.

[70] See below, p. 387.

[71] But, for Edward III's stay at the castle in 1330, see above, p. 69.

[72] R. S. Loomis, 'Edward I, Arthurian Enthusiast', *Speculum* 28 (1958), 114–27; Juliet Vale, *Edward III and Chivalry. Chivalric Society and its Context 1270–1350* (Woodbridge, 1982), pp. 14–24. Michael Prestwich, *Edward I* (London, 1988), pp. 120–2, adopted a minimal view: the figure of Arthur 'was probably no more than a conceit [Edward] toyed with occasionally'; but Richard K. Morris has widened and strengthened the case: 'The Architecture of Arthurian Enthusiasm: Castle Symbolism in the Reigns of Edward I and His Successors', in Matthew Strickland (ed.), *Armies, Chivalry and Warfare in Medieval Britain and France, Proceedings of the 1995 Harlaxton Symposium*, Harlaxton Medieval Studies 7 (Stamford, 1998), pp. 63–81.

[73] N. Denholm-Young, 'The Tournament in the Thirteenth Century', in R. W. Hunt, W. A. Pantin, and R. W. Southern (ed.), *Studies in Medieval History Presented to Frederick Maurice Powicke* (Oxford, 1948), pp. 240–68, at pp. 258–60, 263–8; the quotation is from p. 264.

associations of Winchester, the table might have been made at any point in Edward's reign, but one occasion stands out as being the most likely. In 1290, at 'something of a climacteric in his personal as well as his political life',[74] Edward held at Winchester a tournament to celebrate the arrangements he had made for the marriage of his son and two of his daughters. It is to this tournament, apparently unknown so far to tournament history,[75] that we must now turn.

The tournament of 1290

In August 1289 after an absence of three years in Gascony Edward returned home to England. His mind had long been on the marriage of his children. Margaret was betrothed to John of Brabant as early as 1278, and in May 1287 Pope Honorius IV had granted a general act of dispensation allowing Edward to make these marriages outside the prohibited degrees of affinity or consanguinity.[76] By the spring of 1290 'Edward, at the height of his influence' was ready to secure 'the succession to his kingdom as part of a domestic settlement'.[77] Two weeks after Easter, on Monday 17 April, a family gathering took place at Amesbury in Wiltshire where Edward's mother, Eleanor of Provence, had been a nun for the last four years. In addition to the queen mother and her son, the gathering included Edward's queen, Eleanor of Castile, his brother, Edmund Earl of Lancaster, his uncle, William of Valence, and Gilbert de Clare. The archbishop of Canterbury, John Pecham, and the bishops of Bath and Wells, Durham, Exeter, Winchester and Worcester were also present, together with Henry de Lacy, earl of Lincoln, Otto de Grandson, William de Braose, John de St John, John of Berwick, and Maistre William de Lue, soon to become bishop of Ely.[78]

Edward had long intended to go on crusade, but before he could leave the future of the realm had to be secured.[79] The most important of the three unions now in

---

[74] I owe this phrase to Arnold Taylor in a letter written on 17 February 1990, in the 750th anniversary year of the Winchester tournament.

[75] Cf., for example, Denholm-Young, 'The Tournament in the Thirteenth Century'; Vale, *Edward III and Chivalry*, pp. 14–24; Juliet R. V. Barker, *The Tournament in England 1100–1400* (Woodbridge, 1986). It had however been noted by L. F. Salzman, *Edward I* (London, 1968), p. 92, in a work probably written forty years before but until then unpublished: as this book was, unusually for Salzman, without references, the tournament was not followed up.

[76] F. M. Powicke, *Henry III and the Lord Edward* (Oxford, 1947), ii, p. 732.

[77] Ibid.

[78] Thomas Rymer, *Foedera, conventiones, litterae, et cujuscunque generis acta publica*, I.ii (London, 1816), p. 742. William de Lue (of Louth) was elected bishop of Ely on 12 May and consecrated on 1 October; he died 25 March 1298. Edward's children were probably also at Amesbury, for they were all at Winchester three days later: see below, p. 364.

[79] Powicke, *Henry III and the Lord Edward*, pp. 732–3.

prospect was the impending betrothal of the king's son, the six-year old Edward of Caernarvon, to Margaret, the seven-year old queen of Scotland, known as the 'Maid of Norway', daughter of King Eric of Norway, and grand-daughter of Alexander III of Scotland and his wife Margaret, sister of Edward I.[80] Scarcely less crucial was the forthcoming marriage of Joan of Acre, now just 18, to Gilbert de Clare, Earl of Gloucester: 'the king's greatest subject was ... to marry the king's second surviving daughter'.[81] The third marriage would be that of Margaret, still not 15, to John, heir of Duke John of Brabant.[82]

After witnessing Gilbert de Clare's sworn adhesion to the king's will concerning the succession to the English crown,[83] and writing to King Eric of Norway with news of a further papal dispensation issued at Rome the previous year,[84] the royal family left Amesbury on 18 April, passed the night at Stockbridge, and arrived in Winchester on Wednesday 19 April (Fig. 152).[85] The royal apartments in the castle had been extensively repaired the previous year, probably in anticipation of this visit,[86] and during the previous weeks the lists had been prepared for the tournament to be held the next day, Thursday 20 April.[87] Two days later Edward and his family left for Chichester which they reached that day, arriving back in Westminster on 28 April (Fig. 152).

---

[80] Powicke, ibid., pp. 668–9, 732–3, and Appendix G, pp. 788–90; M. H. Keen, *England in the Later Middle Ages* (London and New York, 1973), pp. 1, 27–30. See also Prestwich, *Edward I*, pp. 360–2. Negotiations with Scotland and Norway over the betrothal had begun at least as early as April 1289; they were concluded on 28 August 1290 by a ratification of the agreement: Ranald Nicholson, *Scotland: The Later Middle Ages* (Edinburgh, 1974), pp. 29–34. The importance of the year 1290 is emphasised by Dr Keen's decision to commence his political history of the late Middle Ages in England from the death of Margaret of Scotland that year and with it the collapse of Edward's dynastic plans; see further below, p. 391.

[81] Powicke, *Henry III and the Lord Edward*, ii, pp. 732–3, and Appendix G, pp. 788–90. For Gilbert, see Michael Altschul, *A Baronial Family in Medieval England: the Clares, 1217–1314*, Johns Hopkins University Studies in Historical and Political Science 83.2 (Baltimore, 1965), pp. 34–9, 94–156, and for his marriage to Joan of Acre, pp. 37–9, 148–9. For Joan, see M. A. E. Green, *Lives of the Princesses of England*, 6 vols. (London, 1849–55), ii (1849), pp. 318–62.

[82] For John of Brabant, see below, pp. 370–71. For Margaret, see Green, *Lives of the Princesses* (as last note), ii, pp. 363–401.

[83] Printed in Rymer, *Foedera* (as above, n. 78), I. ii, p. 742, and done at Amesbury on Monday 17 April 1290 in the presence of those listed above on p. 361, and signed by the archbishop and the five other bishops.

[84] Rymer, *Foedera* (as above, n.)78, I. ii, p. 731.

[85] PRO, MS Itinerary of Edward I (as above, n. 69); J. C. Parsons (ed.), *The Court and Household of Eleanor of Castile in 1290*, Pontifical Institute Studies and Texts 37 (Toronto, 1977), pp. 62, 101 [from BL, Add. MS. 35,294, ff. 3ʳ, 9ʳ].

[86] See below, p. 364–6.

[87] See below, p. 367–9.

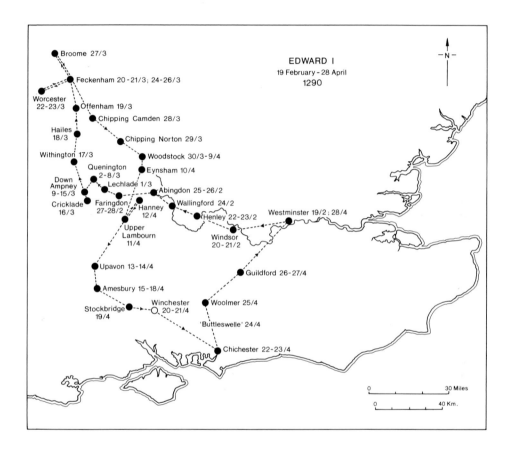

Broome 27/3

Feckenham 20-21/3; 24-26/3

Worcester
22-23/3
Offenham 19/3

Chipping Camden 28/3

Hailes
18/3
Chipping Norton 29/3

Withington 17/3
Woodstock 30/3-9/4

Quenington
2-8/3
Eynsham 10/4

Down
Ampney
9-15/3
Lechlade 1/3

Cricklade
16/3
Abingdon 25-26/2

Faringdon
27-28/2
Hanney
12/4
Wallingford 24/2

Henley 22-23/2
Westminster 19/2; 28/4

Upper
Lambourn
11/4
Windsor
20-21/2

Upavon 13-14/4
Guildford 26-27/4

Amesbury 15-18/4

Stockbridge
19/4
Winchester
20-21/4
Woolmer 25/4

'Buttleswelle' 24/4

Chichester 22-23/4

EDWARD I
19 February - 28 April
1290

− N −

0   30 Miles

0   40 Km.

152 Itinerary of Edward I, 19 February to 28 April 1290.

Most of those who had been at Amesbury seem also to have been at Winchester: the king and queen, their children, Edward of Caernarvon and his five sisters, Gilbert de Clare, and probably also Edmund of Lancaster, William of Valence, Otto de Grandson and the other magnates, as well as the archbishop and the five bishops, although we have no specific written evidence of their presence.[88] They were now joined by John of Brabant.[89]

The preparation of the castle

Already in May 1288 the sheriff of Southampton had been ordered to repair the 'houses' of Winchester castle.[90] The order was repeated in April 1289[91] and at the same time the keeper of the Forest of Asshele (West Bere, Ashley, near Winchester) was instructed to provide the sheriff with twelve oaks fit for timber for the works at the castle.[92] Work began in the last week of February 1289 and continued throughout the building season until October. The particular account for this work survives.[93] From it, by calculating the total man-weeks devoted to each of the named works, it is possible to get some idea of the timing of the works done, their nature, and their relative importance:

[88] The king and queen, their son Edward and their five daughters (Eleanor, Joan, Margaret, Mary, and Elizabeth) made offerings in the cathedral on 20 April at the feretory of St. Swithun, at the heart burial *Sancti Aylmarici* (presumably Bishop Aymer de Valence, the king's uncle, who died in 1260, but he was never a saint and the offering was presumably for masses for his soul) and at the relics in the treasury: PRO, C47/4/4/ f. 41 (I owe this reference to the kindness of Dr A. J. Taylor). The children were still with their parents on Sunday, 23 April 'at the church of St. Richard' (i.e. Chichester cathedral) and again on 29 April at Westminster, see Green, *Lives of the Princesses* (as above, n. 81), ii, p. 414; cf. Parsons (ed.), *Court and Household*, (as above, n. 85), pp. 9–10. It has not proved possible, using the published itineraries, to tell whether Archbishop Pecham and the other bishops were also at Winchester, nor to show that Edmund of Lancaster and William of Valence were there, although this seems likely. After Chichester, the royal children went direct to Sheen to await the king's coming on his way to London (PRO, C47/4/5, p. 21). Since Sheen was Otto de Grandson's principal residence outside London (as Dr Taylor points out to me), it seems likely that he accompanied them there having gone on to Winchester from Amesbury.

[89] We do not know whether John of Brabant had been at Amesbury. His expenses for travelling to and from Winchester do not mention Amesbury, suggesting perhaps that he had not been there, although he had visited the queen-mother at Amesbury on what appears to be a previous occasion: see below, p. 370.

[90] *Calendar of Close Rolls 1279–88*, p. 506.

[91] *Calendar of Close Rolls 1288–96*, p. 7.

[92] Ibid. For the forest of West Bere, see Kate Gilbert, *The History of Ashley* (Winchester, 1992), pp. 20–1.

[93] PRO, E101/491/17.

The hall in the *dunione*	59 man-weeks
The great bridge	44 man-weeks
The king's stables	40 man-weeks
The almonry	35 man-weeks
St. Thomas's chapel	32 man-weeks

None of the other works involved more than eight man-weeks: Richard Foun's chamber (less than 8), the house next to St. Thomas's and the king's hall (5 man-weeks each), the king's small chapel and garden (4 man-weeks), the scullery (4 man-weeks), the queen's great chamber (2 man-weeks), and the tower beyond the gate (less than 1 man-week). This shows that while very little was done on the king's hall (presumably the Great Hall) and on the other royal apartments in the bailey, the principal royal residence, a great deal was done on the hall in the *dunione* ('the dungeon', that is, the 'keep' forming the upper ward). Much effort was also devoted to what one might describe as the public buildings of the castle: the great bridge leading to the principal entrance on the west, the stables, the almonry, and St Thomas's chapel, the principal of the five places of worship. The importance of the stables is emphasised by the work done on Richard Foun's chamber, for he was the master of the king's great horses with a key role in the tournament that was to take place the following spring.[94]

Over the period 20 February to 22 October the man-weeks contributed by each trade were:

carpenters	100	plumbers	about 28
slaters	90	labourers	24
masons	75	sawyers	23
glaziers	47	smiths	2

The only trades which required a master were carpentry and plumbing. The carpenters worked from April to September, with up to ten (including assistants) employed at any one time and Master Peter present for three weeks in June (probably working on the hall in the *dunione*) and again for five weeks in July and August (probably working on the great bridge). He must, as *The History of the King's Works* says, have done his work well for the bridge was described in the fourteenth century

[94] See below, p. 372, but see also Martin Biddle and Beatrice Clayre, *Winchester Castle*, Winchester Studies 6. i (forthcoming), where this work is fully described.

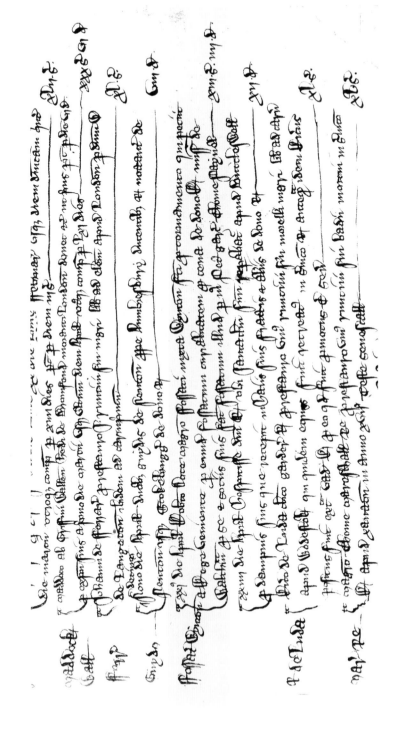

153 Record of the payment of a reward to Robert Dote and his companions for making the ditched enclosure for the tournament at Winchester, April 1290 (PRO, C47/4/5).

as 'the finest timber bridge of any castle or town in England'.[95] One or two plumbers were at work from May to July, but a master plumber was present only in July. Two or three slaters with two or three assistants were involved throughout the building season, with two or three masons, a similar number of masons' assistants, and two or three glaziers from May to October. Purchase of laths and nails suggests that the king's stable, the almonry, and the hall in the *dunione* (the upper ward) were reroofed.

The preparation of the tournament place

Almost everything that is known about the Winchester tournament of April 1290 is to be found in the Wardrobe Controller's book for the eighteenth year of Edward's reign, covering the period from November 1289 to November 1290.[96] The single most important entry concerns the making of the tournament place (Fig. 153).[97] Against a marginal heading, *Fossatum Wynton'*, it reads:

> xxj° die Aprilis, Roberto Dote, magistro fossati iuxta Wynton' facti pro tornia-
> mento, qui petiit a rege veniente per eundem fossatum curialitatem pro cena, de
> dono regis misso de Waltham, pro se et sociis suis facientibus fossatum illud,
> per manus Petri garcionis Thome Paynel,
> xiij.s.iiij.d.

[95] Colvin (ed.), *The History of the King's Works* (as above, n. 67), ii, p. 862.

[96] PRO, C47/4/5. Dr A. J. Taylor, the historian of Edward I's castles, was the first to notice the information about the Winchester tournament contained in this MS. and to bring it to the writer's attention. Dr Kate Gilbert followed up Dr Taylor's information by transcribing the relevant entries in the MS and with great generosity Dr Taylor subsequently checked and extended her transcriptions. Professor Benjamin F. Byerly and Mrs Catherine Ridder Byerly were at that time engaged on a full transcript of the MS. for a third volume in their PRO series of *Records of the Wardrobe and Household*, of which they had already published the volume for 1285–6 in 1977 and that for 1286–9 in 1986. Following Professor Byerly's death in 1990, Dr Taylor made available copies of some of the relevant entries from the Byerlys' transcript as a further control on the information extracted for the present study. Dr Gilbert also examined the other wardrobe accounts listed under 17–19 Edward I, and those marked 'temp. Edward I' (i.e. those in E101/352, plus C47/3/22–3, C47/4/4, and B.L., Add MS. 60,313), except for the rolls relating to messengers, falconers, and soldiers' wages. In references to C47/4/5 the pencil foliation of the MS has been followed. The 'Byerly' numbers refer to the corresponding entries in their projected volume *Records of the Wardrobe and Household 1289–90*, which has not yet been published, but Mrs Byerly has very generously checked the numbers against the typescript, adding those not previously available, and has made several corrections to both transcriptions and interpretations. I am very greatful to her.

[97] PRO, C47/4/5. f. 45 (Byerly 2828).

> 21 April, [paid to] Robert Dote, master of the earthwork next to Winchester made for the tournament, who asked the king as he came by that earthwork for the favour of a dinner for himself and his fellows making that earthwork, of the king's gift sent from Waltham, by the hands of Peter the servant of Thomas Paynel,
>
> 13s.4d. [1 mark]

The entry is dated on the day after the tournament, and the order was sent from Waltham, presumably Bishop's Waltham in Hampshire, 8 miles south-east of Winchester on the direct road to Chichester, where the king had arrived by 22 April. It looks as if the king had passed by the tournament site on leaving Winchester on 21 April, had spoken with Robert Dote, and had later sent an order to make the gift, either as a mark of appreciation for a job well done or because Dote and his men were by then levelling the site.[98]

Ellis de Hauville, marshal of the household, was paid his expenses for going and returning from London to Winchester for provisioning the tournament (*usque ad torniamentum Wynton' pro munitione eiusdem*),[99] an indication that he may have been responsible for setting up the tournament field and all that went with it. Payments were also made to Gilbert de Birdsall, knight, for guarding on the king's behalf the lists made at Winchester for the tournament (*listas factas ibidem pro tornamento*),[100] and to William Arnold, a Gascon knight, for eight days with his serjeants-at-arms guarding the tournament (*ad custodiendum turniamentum*).[101]

This is the sum total of the information we have regarding the tournament place: it was next to (*iuxta*) rather than in Winchester and its construction involved digging and the construction of lists (*listae*). These are the essential elements of a tournament field, which consisted of a ditched and banked enclosure within which a

---

[98] The king made other gifts on passing through the city: on 20 April 1290, the Wardrobe paid 40s. to the Black Friars *pro putura ... per tres dies quando rex transitum fecit per eandem villam* ('for the food allowance ... for three days when the king made his progress through that town'): PRO, C47/4/4, f. 40ᵛ (Byerly 1162). This was a customary payment to the various orders of friars when the king was visiting a city, and on this occasion he also paid 30s. to the Franciscans and 20s. to the Carmelites. I am grateful to Mrs Catherine Byerly for the proper identification of this entry.

[99] PRO, C47/4/5, f. 6ᵛ, cf. f. 21 (Byerly 1629, 1924); see also the Wardrobe counter-roll for 1289–90, B.L., Add. MS. 60,313, m.4. I am grateful to Dr David Howlett for his comment that the word *munitio* has the meaning in this context of 'provisioning', 'furnishing', or 'supplying', e.g. a town or fortified place.

[100] PRO, C47/4/5, f. 5ᵛ, cf. f. 21 (Byerly 1614, 1923); see also the Wardrobe counter-roll for 1289–90, B.L., Add. MS. 60,313, m. 3.

[101] PRO, C47/4/5, f. 15, cf. f. 34ᵛ (Byerly 1759, 2362).

stout timber fence, sometimes double, surrounded the lists, with a stand for specta-tors along one or more sides.[102]

A level site would have been needed. The type of site chosen was typically a flat water meadow between a castle or city and a river or wood, as at the famous tourna-ments of Le Hem in Picardy in 1278 and Chauvency (now dép. Meuse) near Montmédy in 1285, on the marches of France, Luxembourg and the Empire.[103] At Winchester just such a site could have been found in the water meadows beside the Itchen to north or south of the walled city. Immediately outside the north wall, a tradition of combat survived into the seventeenth century in the legend of the fight in Hyde Meadows between Guy of Warwick and Colebrand the Dane, told in the medieval chroniclers and put into verse by Michael Drayton.[104] The name Dane-mark, applied to a part of Hyde Meadows as early as 1280 in the form *denemarche*, meaning 'boundary in a valley',[105] may have contributed to the fiction that the fight with Colebrand the Dane took place here, but a tradition of the use of the area for a famous tournament could have been another factor. In 1280, when the king claimed from the abbot of Hyde three acres of meadow land outside the city wall, a jury found that the king had a valid claim to one acre of ground called Denemarche, which was enclosed by a ditch and worth 3*s.* a year.[106] It is tempting to see this small enclosed piece of royal meadow as an existing tournament field and the site of the

---

[102] Richard Barber and Juliet Barker, *Tournaments, Jousts, Chivalry and Pageants in the Middle Ages* (Woodbridge, 1989), pp. 193–4. The rear endpaper shows a diagram of the arrangement of lists and stands, with a double fence, from René d'Anjou's treatise on the tournament written in the 1450s. Although two centuries later than the Winchester tournament, this gives a good idea of what was probably involved. It should be compared with a painting from the same treatise showing the lists with a mêlée about to start, ibid. pp. 182–3. The lists at the Field of Cloth of Gold in 1520 provide a particularly good example, although the tilt is a late innovation: see the useful analysis by Sydney Anglo, 'The Hampton Court Painting of the Field of Cloth of Gold Considered as an Historical Document', *Antiquaries Journal* 46 (1966), 287–307, at pp. 300–2, Fig. 2.

[103] Vale, *Edward III and Chivalry* (as above, n. 72), p. 7.

[104] For the early form of the legend, see Antonia Gransden, *Historical Writing in England*, ii, *c.1307 to the Early Sixteenth Century* (London and Henley, 1982), pp. 313 n. 25, 493. Henry Knighton gives the legend as it was in the later 14th century: J. R. Lumby (ed.), *Chronicon Henrici Knighton*, 2 vols., Rolls series (London, 1889, 1895), i, pp. 19–27. Thomas Rudborne gives the legend as it was in Winchester by *c.*1450: H. Wharton (ed.), *Anglia Sacra* (London, 1691), i, p. 212. For the state of the legend at the end of the 18th century, see Anon., *The History and Antiquities of Winchester*, 2 vols. (Winchester, 1773), ii, pp. 15–20, and cf. Milner, *History ... of Winchester* (as above, n. 3), 1st edn. (1798), i, pp. 144–8, ii, p. 210; 2nd edn. (1809), i, pp. 144–8, ii, p. 221; 3rd edn. (1839), i, pp. 109–12, ii, pp. 236. Early versions such as Knighton (as above, this note, p. 25) placed the fight in the Chilcomb valley to the south-east of Winchester, but Rudborne located it in Hyde Mead, as did Drayton in 1612, *Poly-Olbion* (ed. J. W. Hebel, Oxford, 1933), Song XII, line 160.

[105] Martin Biddle (ed.), *Winchester in the Early Middle Ages*, Winchester Studies 1 (Oxford, 1976), pp. 236–7.

[106] Derek Keene, *Survey of Medieval Winchester*, Winchester Studies 2 (Oxford, 1985), pp. 946–7, Fig. 113.

tournament of 1290. If the ditches of Robert Dote's *fossatum* are one day found in the course of archaeological work in this area, the problem will have been solved.

The participants

Apart from the immediate royal family, most of whom seem to have been in Winchester for the occasion and were presumably at the tournament,[107] we know very little about those who were present as either participants or spectators. Of the two men who were to marry the king's daughters, we know most of John of Brabant, who was then 20. Our only source is again the Wardrobe account for 18 Edward I. John of Brabant, son and heir of John I, duke of Brabant, had been betrothed to Edward's daughter Margaret since 1278 when she was only three. He had been living in England at the king's expense since 1285 to learn English court and society manners and had been provided with a household and a large retinue of servants. As a keen huntsman and a frequent participant in tournaments he had expensive tastes, but not excessively so by the standards of his rank and times.[108] During the period of the Winchester tournament John received both his usual allowance and special payments for his expenses, all of which were paid to him through his clerk, Roger de Stalham, who had been seconded to John's household from the Wardrobe. John's expenses for 42 days during the period 12 March to 30 July (nearly one-third of the time) spent on frequent absences from court for hunting in various parks and forests and for travelling, included eight days travelling to see Eleanor of Provence, his future grandmother-in-law, at Amesbury and eight days travelling to and from London to Winchester for the tournament (*ad torniamentum*).[109] On 15 July John also received expenses for taking his father, Duke John of Brabant, from Westminster to Dover, the duke having come over for his son's wedding to Margaret at Westminster the week before.[110]

John of Brabant also received several advances on his immediate expenses *contra torniamentum Wynton'*, both for travelling and for staying there, amounting in all to the

---

[107] See above, p. 364.

[108] See Byerly and Byerly, *Records of the Wardrobe and Household 1286–9* (as above, n. 96), pp. xvi–xvii. John's household counter-roll of necessary expenses for 1286–9 (PRO, E101/352/6) is printed by the Byerlys, ibid. pp. 401–13.

[109] PRO, C47/4/5, f. 13ᵛ (Byerly 1733). His visit to Queen Eleanor cannot have been for the family meeting on 17 April, three days before the Winchester tournament, unless he was double-claiming. The order of the entries suggests that it was on some earlier occasion in March or April.

[110] PRO, C47/4/5, f. 23 (Byerly 1998), a payment of £10 on 15 July and £2 later. These payments may be advances (even if the second payment was in arrears) on his final settlement recorded on f. 13ᵛ (see last note), which includes expenses for six days taking his father to Dover.

very large sum of £85.[111] He received in addition an advance of £8 13*s.* 4*d.* (13 marks) for four tuns of wine consumed at the tournament (*pro .iiij. doleis vini que expendidit apud turniamentum Wynton'*).[112]

The king also paid the expenses of his nephew, John of Brittany, son of Duke John of Brittany. Edward had made John a grant of a thousand marks (£666 13*s.* 4*d.*) for his expenses in taking part in the tournament (*in turniamento excercendo*). In a series of complex transactions, John received some of the money from various citizens of Winchester including John de Drokenesford (Droxford, Hants)[113] and Thomas de Michel, and was later repaid *pro debito quod ... debuit de turniamento Wynton'*, presumably so that he could in turn repay the sums borrowed, a vivid indication that a young nobleman could be bailed out by rich burgesses.[114] John received further payments towards the king's grant from the foreign merchants, Lapis Boneti of Pistoia of the merchant society of the Amanati, Robert de Laumbres (Lumbres?) and Peter Renome, both merchants of Flanders, John de Southez, draper of Douai, and William Mauques of Bezas (dép. Gironde),[115] from the London apothecary Richard of Montpellier, the queen's spicer,[116] and from various royal officers, sometimes through his clerk, Peter Guerier, or his chaplain, Robert of Provins.[117]

We have very little information about other participants in the tournament. For Gilbert de Clare, earl of Gloucester, then aged about 47, who was to marry the 18-year old Joan of Acre on 30 April, ten days after the tournament, we have no

[111] PRO, C47/4/5, f. 21 (Byerly 1921–2), f. 21ᵛ (Byerly 1951), and f. 22 (Byerly 1962).

[112] PRO, C47/4/5, f. 22ᵛ (Byerly 1989).

[113] A Winchester family of this name appears in the 14th century: Keene, *Survey of Medieval Winchester* (as above, n. 106), p. 1218. A John de Droxford, appointed usher of the Wardrobe in 1288 and treasurer in 1295, is perhaps the same man: Byerly and Byerly, *Records of the Wardrobe and Household 1285–6* (as above, n. 96), p. xviii; idem, *1286–9*, p. xi. He later went on to become bishop of Bath and Wells: Parsons (ed.), *Court and Household* (as above, n. 85), p. 74 and n.

[114] PRO, C47/4/5, f. 46ᵛ (Byerly 2871), f. 47 (Byerly 2881), and f. 48ᵛ (Byerly 2914).

[115] Sometimes referred to as Raymond William Marchesio, of Bezas, cf. Byerly and Byerly, *Records of the Wardrobe and Household 1286–1289* (as above, n. 96), index.

[116] For the family, see Parsons (ed.), *Court and Household* (as above, n. 85), p. 97 and n; cf. Byerly and Byerly, *Records of the Wardrobe and Household 1285–1286* (as above, n. 96), p. xxxiv, and many references ibid. *1286–1289*, index.

[117] PRO, C47/4/5, f. 47 (Byerly 2881) and f. 48ᵛ (Byerly 2914). On f. 47 the king's grant is described as *pro expensis suis in turn' excercendo* and in the same entry his debt is described as *de turn' Wynton'*, i.e. the grant was for a single tournament at Winchester. In the summary account of the payment of the full 1,000 marks on f. 48ᵛ the grant is described as *in subsidium expensarum quas fecit ad turniamenta et alibi*, with *turniamenta* written out in full in the plural. The wardrobe payments are however dated in June and July, indicating payment in arrears after the Winchester tournament, with no indication that more than one tournament was involved.

information at all, and his presence at Winchester can only be inferred.[118] The Clare household accounts do not survive[119] and since Gilbert's expenses do not appear on the Wardrobe account, it must be assumed that he paid his own way, except when present with the court at Winchester where he and his companions will have been lodged and victualled as part of the royal household and not accounted for separately.

The only other participant of whom we know is Henry de Beaumont (*de Bello Monte*), brother of Lady de Vesci,[120] and that is only because he was taken ill (*infirmus, infirmatus*) and his expenses while absent from court were covered by the king. The payments were made to Martin Ferrand, the queen's squire (*scutifer*), for Henry's expenses in staying on at Winchester after the king's departure and in later returning to the court at Westminster, and covered bread and wine, with fodder, hay and oats for his horses, and other necessaries.[121]

Two entries record advances made to Roger Lisle (*de Insula*), keeper and buyer of the Great Wardrobe.[122] On 19 April he spent 21s. 8d. on the purchase of wax from William Apothecary of Winchester, the money received in William's name by Adam Payn.[123] And on 20 April Roger purchased also at Winchester four cloths-of-gold,[124] two from John de Stok'[125] for 28s. each and two from Richard Gabriel[126] for 24s. each.

Other entries deal with the activities of Richard Foun or Fohun. His chamber, which appears to have been near the stables, was repaired in 1289.[127] In February

---

[118] But for the Clares as a tourneying family, and for Gilbert in particular, see Barker, *The Tournament in England* (as above, n. 75), pp. 117–19.

[119] Altschul, *A Baronial Family* (as above, n. 81), p. 232, but cf. ibid. n. 114 for a single fragment.

[120] For the Vesci family, see Parsons (ed.), *Court and Household* (as above, n. 85), pp.46–8.

[121] PRO, C47/4/5, f. 21 (Byerly 1920), a prest of 60s. dated 20 April 1290, i.e. on the actual day of the tournament; cf. f. 46ᵛ (Byerly 2862), a (further?) payment of 38s. 5½d. An additional payment of 37s. is recorded on the Wardrobe gift roll, E101/352/21, m. 2 (Byerly 3748).

[122] Byerly and Byerly, *Records of the Wardrobe and Household 1286–1289* (as above, n. 96), pp. iii, ix, xiii.

[123] PRO, C47/4/5, f. 23ᵛ (Byerly 2008).

[124] PRO, C47/4/5, f. 21 (Byerly 1918). The amount of material represented by a *pannus* of cloth, in this case *panni ad aurum*, seems not to be known: Constance Bullock-Davies, *Menestrellorum multitudo: Minstrels at a Royal Feast* (Cardiff, 1978), p. xxiv. On the occasion brilliantly reconstructed by Dr Bullock-Davies, the so-called Feast of Swans held at Westminster at Pentecost 1306 in honour of the knighting of Edward of Caernarvon, 4 *panni ad aurum* (the same amount of cloth-of-gold that was purchased at Winchester in 1290) were bought for hanging on the wall of Westminster Hall behind King Edward and the Prince as they sat at the banquet, at the table shown here in Fig. 21: ibid. p. xxviii n.

[125] Member of Parliament and citizen, see Keene, *Survey of Medieval Winchester* (as above, n. 106), p. 1359.

[126] Bailiff in 1280–2 and mayor in 1300–2, see Keene, *Survey of Medieval Winchester* (as above, n. 106), p. 1240.

[127] See above, p. 364.

1290, as keeper of the king's great horses and coursers (*custos magnorum equorum regis et cursorum*) Richard received 20*s.* for his winter robe for the year.[128] On 17 April at Amesbury, just before the tournament, he received an advance of £20 to cover the expenses of the king's destriers and coursers.[129]

The king's riding horses were the responsibility of another official, Adam de Riston, the keeper of the king's palfreys (*custos palefridorum regis*). On 19 April he received an advance of £10 against the expenses of taking the king's palfreys back to London from Winchester.[130]

These are the only individuals so far identified as having been present at Winchester for the tournament. Yet it was a major royal occasion attended by the whole court and by distinguished visitors, and accompanied by very large numbers of retainers and servants. The cost of their lodging and keep will in most cases have been covered by the daily expenditure of the household for 19, 20, and 21 April. The full publication of the Wardrobe accounts for the year 1290 will probably add much to the picture already obtained, which deals essentially with the additional and exceptional rather than the standing daily expenses of the court.[131] Some idea of the scale of the event can perhaps be gauged from the consumption in three days by John of Brabant's household alone of four tuns of wine, equivalent to 1008 gallons.

The event and the table

Preparations for the tournament and for the marriages which followed shortly afterwards must have been under way for some time. Edward's plans for the marriages of his children went back to the 1270s and their initial success was marked by the betrothal of Margaret to John of Brabant in 1278 and of Joan of Acre to Gilbert de Clare in 1283. In 1289 negotiations began with Scotland and Norway for the marriage of Edward of Caernarvon to Margaret of Scotland. That same year preparations were made to put Winchester Castle in good repair to receive the royal court and the king's guests. The choice of Winchester must have been quite deliberate, for the court could easily have returned from Amesbury to London rather than make the considerable detour to Winchester. Yet the visit to Amesbury was an equal cause of

---

[128] PRO, C47/4/5, f. 38 (Byerly 2484).

[129] PRO, C47/4/5, f. 20ᵛ (Byerly 1913).

[130] PRO, C47/4/5, f. 20ᵛ (Byerly 1915). For Riston's title, see ibid. f 5ᵛ (Byerly 1615).

[131] For the operation of the household of Edward I, see the Byerlys' introductions to the two published volumes of the *Records of the Wardrobe and Household*, as above, n. 96. For the publication of the Wardrobe accounts for 1290, see also above, n. 96. For the payment of minstels for the year, see below, n. 178.

the detour (Fig. 152), and the king's wish to involve the queen mother in the final stages of the implementation of his great plan is a sufficient indication of the careful planning of the whole series of events.

The selection of Winchester was perhaps personal; Edward and his family may simply have liked the palace and its castle. But the city's supposed Arthurian past was probably a significant element in the king's choice. At all events, plans for the tournament were probably known at least by the spring of 1289 when the castle began to be put in order.

The particular accounts for the work at the castle contain enough detail to let us see what was done.[132] The most interesting work is the renovation of the hall in the *dunione*, the upper ward at the south end of the castle (Figs. 23–4). However, this hall was probably not being prepared for the use of the royal family. Modern apartments for the king and queen existed west and south of the Great Hall in the lower ward at the north end of the castle, where Henry III had spent heavily on rebuilding, extending, and decorating the king's and queen's apartments (Figs. 23–4).[133] Henry seems by contrast to have done little to the buildings inside the upper ward, to judge by the amount of work which had to be done to the hall there in 1289, although he had rebuilt the two eastern towers of the ward. This suggests that the hall in the *dunione* was being got ready to accommodate some of the other guests for the forthcoming tournament, perhaps for the future husbands of the young princesses. It is important to consider this, since it might otherwise perhaps be thought that the Round Table was originally made for the hall in the *dunione*.[134]

[132] See above, pp. 364–7.

[133] See above, pp. 68, 70–5.

[134] Dr Arnold Taylor has called attention (in letters of 8 and 10 November 1990) to two entries in the particular account (PRO, E101/491/17):

In .xvj. columpnis ligneis emptis ad aulam in donione, .iij.s. In cariagio predictarum columpn' de villa Wynton' usque castrum predictum, .ij.d.

In bordis emptis ad aulam in donione, .iiij.s. .v.d. In cariagio eorundem de villa usque castrum, .ij.d.

The question is whether these entries could refer to the purchase of the legs of the table and the boards for its top. Both lots are described as *emptis ad aulam in donione*, the direct meaning of which is that they were required for work on the hall itself, perhaps for posts in the roof and for boarding below the leads. The phrase might have included works done in finishing the hall, even the construction of a table, but there seems no need to assume this. A second difficulty is that the table required twelve not sixteen supports with a thirteenth of different form and not certainly of timber at the centre (see Figs. 50 and 55). On balance, it would seem that the *columpne* and boards bought *ad aulam* were probably not for making the Round Table, but this cannot wholly exclude the possibility that the table was made for the hall in the *donione* and later moved to the Great Hall.

There is no mention of the making of the table in the particular accounts. This may be because it was silently included within the 100 man-weeks worked by the carpenters in 1289 and did not merit special mention; or because it was made by contract and accounted for elsewhere; or because the table was not made in 1289.

Yet the tournament and the context in which it was held provide an obvious occasion for a feast at which the central players might have been seated at a round table of Arthurian inspiration. That a feast followed the tournament cannot be doubted. Whether it was an occasion of Arthurian character is another question.

Edward's marriage to Margaret of France, Canterbury, 1299

To explore this question we must look at another royal celebration, the character of which is much disputed. Edward's marriage to his second wife, Margaret of France, at Canterbury nine years later is best described by the continuator of the chronicle of Gervase of Canterbury. Writing with obvious local knowledge either as an eye-witness himself or drawing on eye-witness accounts, the continuator describes the treaty of peace with France, a key element in which was that King Edward would marry Margaret, the sister of the king of France, and his son Edward of Caernarvon would marry the king's daughter, Isabella.[135] The continuator then writes about Margaret's arrival in England and the marriage on Thursday 10 September 1299. The archbishop performed the ceremony in the cloister door of the cathedral next to the door of the martyrium of St Thomas (*in ostio ecclesiæ versus claustrum, juxta ostium martyrii Sancti Thomæ*) and afterwards celebrated the nuptial mass at Becket's shrine.[136] There was then a dispute between the archbishop, the prior and other clerics about who should have the cloth carried over the bridal pair during the ceremony. The king ordered the cloth to be given to the Earl of Lincoln as an independent party

[135] William Stubbs (ed.), *The Historical Works of Gervase of Canterbury*, ii, *The Minor Works: comprising the Gesta Regum with its Continuation, the Actus Pontificum, and the Mappa Mundi ... edited from the MS. C.C.C. 438*, Rolls Series (London, 1880), pp. 316–8. For the continuation of Gervase, see Antonia Gransden, *Historical Writing in England*, i, *c.550 to c.1307* (London, 1974), pp. 422–3, 448–9. For the journey of Margaret of France and the friendship which grew up between her and her step-daughter Mary, who was much the same age as her step-mother, see Green, *Lives of the Princesses* (as above, n. 81), pp. 424–6.

[136] Traditionally the rite of marriage consisted of two parts, the betrothal and the marriage proper. The betrothal, which took place at the church door, often in the porch (as Professor Eamon Duffy points out to me), included much of what we think of as essential to the marriage service today, the exchange of rings, the joining of hands, and the making of vows. The marriage service, essentially a service of blessing and including a celebration of the eucharist (the nuptial mass), took place in the church, in front of the main altar or, as here, at another exceptionally important altar; see further, F. L. Cross and E. A. Livingstone (ed.), *The Oxford Dictionary of the Christian Church*, 3rd edn. (Oxford, 1997), s.v. 'Matrimony', 'Nuptial Mass'.

until a decision could be made, and then returned to Chartham until evening.[137] The queen meanwhile dined in state in the archbishop's palace with the archbishop, the bishops of Durham, Winchester and Coventry, the dukes of Burgundy and Brittany, the earls of Warenne, Lincoln, Pembroke, Warwick, Lancaster, and Hereford, the Earl Marshal of England, and almost all the leading nobles of the kingdom. The continuator of Gervase goes on to describe how on Saturday two days later the queen heard mass celebrated in the archbishop's chapel by the bishop of Coventry and Lichfield. Following the custom of other women Margaret gave her wax taper (*cereum*) to the celebrant who immediately took it to the altar at the shrine of St. Thomas. The continuator says nothing else about the wedding or the festivities which followed it.

Another account, very short and without the touches of local knowledge, is given in a chronicle associated with the name of William Rishanger, a monk of St. Albans, but written after 1327.[138] 'Rishanger' briefly describes the peace treaty, the arrival of Margaret accompanied by the duke of Burgundy with *non modica multitudine Gallicorum* ('no small crowd of Frenchmen') and by the count of Brittany with the nobles subordinate to him and almost all the princes living 'this side of Spain', and gives an account of the marriage itself.[139] He then goes on to say that he will not describe the *sublimitas* of the guests from many countries, nor the *convivii apparatus*, nor the expense, lest he should seem to have written a *panegyricon*. The rejoicing lasted four days, after which the foreigners were given licence to depart, honoured with great and varied gifts.

From his view-point at St. Albans, 'Rishanger' knew only the essential facts about the event at Canterbury some years before. His reticence was not shared by the anonymous author of the *Annales Angliae et Scotiae* preserved in another St. Albans manuscript.[140] This gives an account, three times as long, of the French treaty, of the arrival of Margaret in England, and of the marriage. It then gives a long description of the feast and the games which followed lifted word for word from Geoffrey of Monmouth's *Historia Regum Britanniae*.[141] *The Annales* include about one third of the

---

[137] A few miles south-west of Canterbury. Since there was not a royal house at Chartham, the king was presumably staying in the prior's manor-house there.

[138] H. T. Riley (ed.), *Willelmi Rishanger ... et quorundam anonymorum chronica et annales*, Rolls Series 28.2 (London, 1865), p. 192. For Rishanger, see Gransden, *Historical Writing in England*, i (as above, n. 135), pp. 4–5, but the authorship of the *Chronica* is in fact obscure.

[139] Rishanger gives the date of the marriage as 12 instead of 10 September; the continuator of Gervase dated it 9 September.

[140] Riley (ed.), *Willelmi Rishanger ... chronica et annales* (as above, n. 138), pp. 394–7.

[141] First observed and demonstrated with parallel texts by Laura Keeler, 'The *Historia Regum Britanniae* and Four Mediaeval Chroniclers', *Speculum* 21 (1946), 24–37, at pp. 27–31.

words in 'Rishanger's' account, including some key phrases, and give the same (incorrect) date of 12 September for the marriage, but also introduce two obvious errors, referring to the king's palace at Canterbury, which did not exist, and describing Edward as *tertius*, 'the Third'.

The *Annales* cover only the years from 1292 to 1300, and half the text deals with the years 1299 and 1300. Their nineteenth-century editor thought that they had been used by 'Rishanger'.[142] If so, 'Rishanger' dropped the long section borrowed from Geoffrey of Monmouth, presumably because he did not accept it as a valid description of the festivities which followed the wedding. If the reverse is true and the *Annales* are no more than a later elaboration of 'Rishanger's' account, then the passage borrowed from Geoffrey of Monmouth is included simply to pad out the annalist's account of an event about which he had no independent information, a common device of medieval chroniclers.[143] Either way, there are no grounds for accepting the *Annales* account of the Canterbury marriage, and in particular no reason for believing that the festivities which followed were of an Arthurian character.

Professor Keeler thought that the author of the *Annales* might have had one of three motives for using this passage from Geoffrey of Monmouth. First, 'being a monk unfamiliar with wedding festivities at court, yet desiring to do justice to the magnificence of his sovereign's nuptials, he turned to what he did know.'[144] This was Geoffrey's description of the festival which Arthur held during the Pentecostal season to celebrate his triumphs, 'the elaborate splendor of the service, the fashionable attire, the charming witty ladies, the knightly sports, the rich awards – all ... simply lifted across the centuries from the *HRB* to the pages of the St Albans annals.' Or, second, wishing to give colour to his narrative, he may 'have found in this picture of lavish court splendor the bright hues he desired.' Or, third, he may have been influenced by the idea of Alfonso the Wise of Castile (1252–84), brother-in-law of Edward I, that history in chronicles 'should be written not by monks in their cloister, but by high officials of the palace who took active part in the stirring scenes they recorded,' and wishing to uphold the reputation of St. Albans for historical writing, 'turned for assistance to the pages of a familiar dependable source'.

---

[142] Riley (ed.), *Willelmi Rishanger ... chronica et annales* (as above, n. 138), pp. xxiv–xxv, xxxi–xxxiii. Gransden, *Historical Writing in England*, ii (as above, n. 135), pp. 4–5, does not mention the 'Annales', but she describes the MS. in which the text is preserved (B. L., Cotton Claudius D.VI) as 'a volume of historical pieces from St. Albans' which suggests 'the possibility that Rishanger was making drafts and collecting documents for a full-scale continuation of Matthew Paris' *Chronica Majora*' (ibid. p. 5, n. 22, with further references).

[143] See, for example, with reference to the Feast of Swans, Bullock-Davies, *Menestrellorum multitudo* (as above, n. 124), pp. xxix; and cf. below, p. 388, and n. 166.

[144] Keeler, 'Four Mediaeval Chroniclers' (as above, n. 141), pp. 30–1 The quotations which follow are taken from pp. 28 and 30–1 of Professor Keeler's article.

Lodewijk van Velthem, Canterbury and Winchester

In 1958, in his influential study, 'Edward I, Arthurian Enthusiast', Roger Loomis plumped for the first of these suggested motives, arguing that the St. Albans monk 'knew only that there had been some effort to reproduce the festivities of King Arthur's time.'[145] But there is no evidence that the author of the *Annales* did know this. Loomis took this line because he believed that he had identified a description of the Canterbury wedding in a completely different source, a description couched in explicitly Arthurian terms.

Lodewijk van Velthem, a Brabançon priest, was a prodigious translator of French Arthurian romances into Dutch. He also composed a rhyming continuation in Dutch of the *Speculum Historiale* of Vincent of Beauvais, covering the years 1248 to 1316.[146] By the marriage of his daughters, Eleanor to the Count of Bar and Margaret to John, son of Duke John of Brabant, the English king had become something of a Brabançon national hero,[147] a fact recalled by van Velthem himself: 'since Arthur received the empire, there never was king so powerful in war as he was always.'[148] This was why van Velthem devoted large parts of his continuation to an account of Edward's deeds, including an elaborate account of a festivity called a 'Round Table'.

Most of what van Velthem wrote about Edward consists of a series of romantic adventures set in an Arthurian mould in the flimsiest of historical contexts.[149] This is romance not history, but the very fact that van Velthem thought it appropriate to place Edward in an Arthurian world has its own significance. Relevant here are the festivities held to celebrate King Edward's wedding to the daughter of the Spanish king: her entry to London, followed by a feast, a tournament, and a second feast, which van Velthem describes in six chapters of 566 lines of rhyming verse.[150] None

---

[145] Loomis (as above, n. 72), pp. 120–1

[146] Lodewijk van Velthem, *Voortzetting van den Spiegel Historiael (1248–1316)*, ed. H. Vander Linden, W. de Vreese, and P. de Keyser, Commission royale d'histoire 38 (Brussels, 1906–38). The *Speculum Historiale* had been translated into Dutch rhyme by Jacques de Maerlant and it was this that Van Velthem continued.

[147] 'Le roi était ... pour les Brabançons une sorte de héros national': G. Huet, 'Les traditions arturiennes chez le Chroniqueur Louis de Velthem', *Le Moyen Age*, 26 (1913), 173–97, at pp. 175, n.1., 196. In the present context, and especially for the betrothal and marriage of Edward's daughter Margaret to John, son of Duke John I of Brabant, see above, p. 362, and below, p. 391.

[148] Van Velthem, *Voortzetting* (as n. 146), iii (1938), p. 64: Book V, cap. 26, lines 1718–21.

[149] For an analysis of van Velthem's treatment of Edward's Welsh campaigns, see Th. M. Chotzen, 'Welsh History in the Continuation of the 'Spiegel Historiael' by Lodewijk van Velthem', *Bulletin of the Board of Celtic Studies* 7 (1935), 42–54. For Arthurian traditions in the *Voortzetting*, and in particular for an analysis of the sources Van Velthem used, his knowledge of Edwardian affairs, and the contributions of his own imagination, see Huet (as above, n. 147), pp. 183, 193–4, 196.

[150] Van Velthem, *Voortzetting* (as above, n. 146), i (1906), pp. 295–321: Book II, cap. 15–20, lines 1072–1637.

of the details correspond to the realities of Prince Edward's marriage to Eleanor of
Castile in 1254, long before he became king. That is not the point: 'the chronological and geographical confusion is shocking to the sober historian but amusing for
the mere *littérateur* to contemplate'.[151] And so it doubtless was for the contemporary
Brabançon readers for whom van Velthem wrote.

Van Velthem begins his account in Chapter 15 of Book II, *Hoe die coninc Edeward
een wijf nam, ende vander feeste die men daer dreef* ('How King Edward took a wife, and
concerning the festivities which took place there'), with 'King' Edward's request to
the king of Spain for the hand of one of his daughters in marriage, Edward's journey
to Spain, and his return to England with his bride.[152] London gave her a joyful entry:

Dansen, reyen, singen, springen,	Dancing, roundels, singing, leaping—
Hets nieman diet mochte vort bringe[n],	there is no one who could describe
Die feeste die de stede dreef.	the celebrations of the citizenry.
(1112–14)	

of which van Velthem gives a brilliant account told, he claims, from a Latin description (1115–30). The king gave a great feast to celebrate the wedding:

Ende spelen, dansen, drinken, eten,	And games, dancing, drinking, eating—
Dit was nieman daer wederseit.	none of these were denied anyone there.
(1137–8)	

And during the feast plans were laid to hold a Round Table of knights and squires:

Binnen der feeste ward daer geleit	In the course of the feast there was prepared
Ene tafelronde van ridderen ende cnapen,	a Round Table of knights and squires,
Dat wie so wille, mochter […] wapen	such that whoever wished might ... take
Dragen ende joesteren mede.	up weapons and joust with them.
Daer was gemaect na den sede	According to custom there was enacted
Een spel va[n] Artur den coninc,	a play of Arthur the King,
Ende geordineert also die dinc,	and things were arranged accordingly,
Ende ut gescoren die beste saen,	and the best (men) chosen without delay

---

[151] Loomis, 'Edward I, Arthurian Enthusiast' (as above, n. 72), 119.

[152] Book II, Chapter 15, lines 1072–1106. Subsequent references are given by lines only. Professor David F.
Johnson, Florida State University, Tallahassee, generously provided the English translation of the passages
which follow, and Professor Geert H. M. Claassens, Leuven University, kindly vetted them for him.

Ende genoemt daer sonder waen

Na die heren van ouden stonden

Diemen hiet vander tavelronden.

(1139–49)

and there named (without doubt)

after the lords who, in the olden days.

had once belonged to the Round Table

Chapter 16, *Hoe die tavelronde began, ende vanden heren vander tavelronde* ('How the Round Table began and of the knights of the Round Table'), opens with the taking of parts:

Doe daer dat spel *was* op geleit,

Alse hier vore es af geseit,

So vercoes der elc den sinen:

Haer vromicheit sal daer nu scinen.

Daer was Lanceloet ende Walewein,

Ende Perchevael ende Eggrawein,

Ende Bohort ende Gariet,

Ende Lyoneel ende Mordret,

Ende .i. Keye was daer gemaect.

(1184–92)

When that play began,

as described here above,

each man chose his part:

their virtue shall now become apparent.

There was Lancelot and Gawain

and Perceval and Agravain,

and Bors and Gareth,

and Lionel and Mordred,

and a Kay, too, was created there.

Proclaimed all over England, a great assembly including many ladies and maidens having gathered (1202–15), the Round Table began at dawn:

Recht int opgaen vander sonnen

Beg1an die tavelronde aldaer:

Het was scone weder ende claer.

(1199–1201)

Just as the day dawned

the Round Table began there:

the weather was fair and bright.

The knights of the Round Table had the better of their opponents except for Kay who, true to form, having been set on by twenty young knights, was thrown from his horse (1216–50). At the end, the king and queen turned from the field to the hall:

Die coninc ende die coninginne

Warens blide in haren sinne

Dat dit also was gevallen.

Die coninc geboet doen hem allen,

Dat genoech waer. "Laet ons eten

Varen te hove. Dit spel vermeten

Es recht na Arturs wise comen.

The king and the queen

were very pleased

that it had turned out thus.

The king sent word to them all

that enough was enough. "Let us ride

to court and eat. This splendid play

has turned out in true Arthurian fashion.

Nu laet ons dit vort begomen	Now let us continue in the
Dies gelike dat hi plach.	same way as they were wont to do.
Elc doet tsine oft hi mach!"	Let each man play his part as he is able!"
Dus geloefdense noch alle daer	Thus all present vowed publicly
Dit te volbringen openbaer.	that they would do so.
(1256–67)	

In Chapter 17, *Van den etene, ende vanden genen die daer boetscap bringen* ('Of the eating and of those who bring messages'), van Velthem describes the feast held after the tournament. The king bade all the knights who had assumed Arthurian names to sit at the table with him:

De coninc es tere tafel geseten,	The king sat down to table,
Entie heren vander tavelronden	and at the same time he had
Dede die coninc ter selver stonden	the lords of the round table
In sittene sitten oec daer mede,	seated with him in chairs
Gelijc dat coninc Artur dede	just as King Arthur had done
Alse hi feeste hilt, dat wi gelesen	when he held a feast, as we
Dicke hebben Gelijc oec desen,	have often read. In similar fashion
So dede Edeward nu, godweet.	then, Edward now ordered
Die ridders sitten daer gereet.	his knights to take their seats.
(1271–9)	

After the first course the king ordered one of the squires to rap on a window for silence and announced in conformity with ancient custom that before any more food was brought in he must hear news [of some adventure] (1288–96). The knights replied:

"God geve datse ons moete vromen!"	"May God grant us that pleasure!"
Spraken die heren die daer saten.	Said the lords who were seated there.
(1297–8)	

Shortly afterwards a squire rode up to the table spattered with blood and addressed the king and the knights sitting beside him. The squire challenged them, else God destroy them, to take revenge on the Welsh for what they had done to him (1294–1333). The knights reply with one voice. The king with their encouragement agreed to act once the meal was over (1334–45).

In Chapter 18, *Vanden selven meer* ('More of the same'), the second course is brought in *met groter feeste*, but before the third can arrive the king knocked on the wall with a rod and spoke:

"Noch soude gerne niemare horen,
Wilse ons yeman bringen voren
Eer wi mer vorward aten."
(1356–8)

"I should eagerly wish to hear some news,
if anyone would offer some
before we continue with our meal."

After a short delay, another squire rode in on a sumpter, bound hand and foot, the bridle in his arms:

Dese maecte groet gecarm
Ende quam aldus in dien zale
Vore die tafle, daer altemale
Die vander tavelronden sijn geseten.
(1365–8)

This man lamented loudly
and entered thus the hall
and stood before the table, where all
the lords of the round table are seated

The squire called on *Lanceloet van Lac, edel man* (1383) to unbind him, and when he was unbound gave Lancelot a letter (1397–9). In this the king of Ireland called Lancelot a false knight and a traitor and challenged him to single combat on the Welsh coast. Lancelot was hesitant, but Gawain spoke for the knights and the king promised his help:

"Gelijc dat Artur in allen lande
Voer om die vander tavelronde,

Al dier gelijc willic ter stonde
Met elken ridder oec nu varen.
Van allen sticken die si selen baren
In dit spel, al sonder vresen,
Daer willic een geselle af wesen.
Oec willic dat gi dat oec mi
Geloeft, ende doet alse ridderen vri."
(1427–35)

"Just as Arthur himself rode
through every land
  with the knights of the round table
in the same way I shall now
set out with every knight.
Of all the feats of arms they will perform
fearlessly in this play,
I wish to be a witness.
I also desire that you pledge the same
to me, and do so as noble knights."

And so the feast continued:

Dit late wi nu aldus wesen,
Ende scriven vander feesten vord
Die gi genoech niet hebt gehord.
(1443–5)

We leave this for what it is,
and turn instead to describe the feast
about which you have not heard enough.

Chapter 19, *Vanden derden bode, die wonderlijc gemaect was* ('Of the third messenger who was wonderfully made'), opens with the third course. Afterwards the king again called for silence, saying that he must have news before any more food was brought (1446–55). Shortly after, a *lelike creature*, a 'dreadful creature' (1458), appeared, with a nose a foot long and more than a palm broad, ears like an ass, braided hair hanging down to her girdle, a goitre under her chin, a long red neck, and other ghastly features. This damsel, *dese joncfrouwe* (1485), rode up to the table on a lame horse and addressed Perceval first:

"Wetti," seitsi, "wien ic groette
Vor alle die sijn in dien zale?
Dat es den here Perchevale.
Hem so groetic vor u allen!"
(1495–8)

"Do you know," she said, "whom I greet
before all those who are in this hall?
Sir Perceval it is.
I greet him before all of you!"

Perceval is to go to Leicester and take the castle there from its lord who is attacking his neighbours (1512–23). Then she addresses Gawain: he is to go to 'Cornuaelge' to help the city put an end to the struggle which had broken out between the people and their lords (1524–38). Gawain and Perceval stand and declare their determination to carry out their tasks and the damsel then leaves the hall (1539–55).

In Chapter 20, *Vander joncfrouwe noch, ende hoe dat hof sciet* ('More about the damsel, and how the court dispersed'), the *lelike joncfrouwe*, the 'loathly damsel' (1573), took off her disguise:

Alse dese joncfrouwe was uter zale,
Const si daer die pade wale.
Si was ontslopen saen,
Ende heeft die paruren af gedaen
Daer si mede ontliesent was.
Dese joncfrouwe, daer ic af las,
Was .i. van des coninc cnapen:
Entie coninc had dese wapen,
Ende dit ansicht, ende dit hoeft

Once the damsel had left the hall,
she knew the way very well.
She soon slipped away,
and removed her garments
with which she was disguised.
This damsel was, as I read it,
one of the king's squires:
for the king had had this livery
and this countenance [mask],
	as well as the head [wig]

Heymelike doen maken, des geloeft,	secretly made, you may be sure,
So dat na een joncfrouwe sceen.	so he looked like a damsel.
Ende alle dese worde overeen	And all these words together
Die dese boden brochten vort,	that these messengers delivered,
Haddensi vanden coninc gehort,	they had heard from the king
Ende gevest oec harde wale.	and memorized very carefully.
Doent geruechte inden zale	When the commotion in the hall
Leden was, vraechdemen daer nare	had died down, people began to wonder
Waer die lelike joncfrouwe ware.	where the loathly damsel had gone.
(1556–73)	

The king then spoke: these adventures were all part of the celebrations, but as knights of the Round Table all must now stand by their vows to undertake the challenges put by the messengers. The knights accepted, and it was agreed that within fourteen nights they would be in 'Cornuaelge' before the city, and would go from there to Wales and Ireland. And so the court broke up (1579–1637).

In Chapters 23–6 van Velthem tells the story of the expeditions to Cornwall, Wales, and Ireland, and finally against Leicester. There, after the capture of the castle, the king gives a great feast for the knights of the Round Table. Then the knights go their way.

The essential elements are these. During a marriage feast, a tournament (confusingly itself called a 'Round Table') is announced and proclaimed throughout the land. A great assembly having gathered, the Round Table begins at dawn. The knights who take part have assumed the names of Arthur's knights of the Round Table. After the tournament, the king gives a great feast in a hall where the knights with Arthurian names sit together with him at table. Three times during the feast messengers, blood-spattered, bound hand-and-foot, or tricked up as a loathly damsel, ride into the hall and issue challenges to the knights sitting at table with the king, first to them all, next to Lancelot, finally to Perceval and to Gawain. The king then reveals that the messengers were squires in disguise and had been part of the festivity, but that nevertheless the knights must stand by the vows they made in response to the challenges.

The squires were disguised. The context suggests that the knights may also have been dressed in some distinctive way to take their Arthurian parts both on the tournament field and at table. How otherwise could Kay have been created (1192) and set upon during the tournament? And how could the messengers have addressed specific knights at table, such as Lancelot, Perceval and Gawain? The king himself was probably not dressed as Arthur. It is never suggested that Arthur was present and the king, clearly identified as Edward, calls on matters to be done, or as having been done, in 'Arthur's way.' The table at which they feast is never described. It might be assumed from the context that the table was round, but van Velthem does not say so. He does, however, reiterate the phrase *heren vander tavelronden* in close association with the actual table at which the knights were sitting:

De coninc es tere tafel geseten,	The king sat down to table,
Entie heren vander tavelronden	and at the same time he had
Dede die coninc ter selver stonden	the lords of the Round Table
In sittene sitten oec daer mede,	seated with him in chairs
Gelijc dat coninc Artur dede	just as King Arthur had done
Alse hi feeste hilt, dat wi gelesen	when he held a feast, as we
Dicke hebben.	have often read.
(1271–7)	

Ende quam aldus in dien zale	And thus entered into the hall
Vore die tafle, daer altemale	to stand before the table where all
Die vander tavelronden sijn geseten.	the members of the Round Table
(1366–8)[153]	were seated.

As Huet argued many years ago, van Veltham's tale of the wedding and of the campaigns which follow the tournament and feast are completely contrary to historical fact.[154] Loomis took a less sceptical view of the feast following the tournament, arguing that 'though utterly anachronistic on the occasion of Edward's first marriage in 1254, [it] would have been quite possible and appropriate on the occasion of his second marriage in 1299 to Margaret, sister of Philip IV of France'.[155] Loomis supported this assertion (it is no more) by reference to the 'remarkable confirmation' to be found in the passage from Geoffrey of Monmouth inserted by the St Albans annalist into his account of the wedding. But this is circular: as we have seen, there is nothing to make us believe the *Annales* account of the Canterbury festivities, just as there is nothing to suggest that van Velthem's account reflects the same event.

There is no sign that van Velthem had any one particular moment in mind other than 1254, and that is historically and contextually impossible. All that seems relevant is that van Velthem wanted to place Edward in an Arthurian context, and that this may reflect the reality that Edward did from time to time lay on festivities of an

---

[153] For the full context of these quotations, see above pp. 381, 382.
[154] 'Les traditions arthuriennes', (as above, n. 147), p. 176.
[155] Loomis, 'Edward I, Arthurian Enthusiast' (as above, n. 72), p. 120.

Arthurian kind. As van Veltham says, the 'play of Arthur the King' was enacted *na den sede*, 'according to custom' (line 1143).

The factors new to the equation since Loomis wrote over forty years ago are two. First, the Winchester Round Table can now be shown to be a table of Edward's time and probably of Edward's making. Second, the Brabançon connection which Loomis stressed can now be related directly both to the occasion for which the table may have been made (a celebration of two impending marriages, one of them between Margaret of England and John of Brabant) and to the presence of John of Brabant himself as a participant in the Winchester tournament.

The commitment of the Brabançons both to Margaret and to her father cannot be doubted.[156] There was no such link either at the time of the 1254 wedding which van Velthem pretends to describe, or on the occasion of the 1299 wedding, a very Anglo-French affair, which Loomis wanted to see as van Velthem's model.

This is not to argue, and this cannot be stressed too strongly, that van Velthem is describing the Winchester feast. But it is to suggest that memories of the Winchester event, carried back by the Brabançons, by John himself and by members of his *familia*, may have influenced van Velthem's creation of the Arthurian milieu in which he placed his romance of Edward's deeds. Van Velthem gives us a description of the kind of event for which the Round Table may have been made. The table itself is the strongest argument that something of the kind van Velthem describes may actually have taken place in Winchester Castle hall. For why, in that age, have a round table without the knights?

The hall itself, once described as 'the finest surviving aisled hall of the 13th century' in England,[157] and evidently one of the finest of its time, has its own evidence to contribute to the view that the Round Table was intended for use in the way its shape implies. Although the hall was built long before in the reign of Edward's father,[158] its magnificent marble columns, soaring arcades, transomed windows, and paintings of the Map of the World and of the Wheel of Fortune on its gable walls, provided as fine a feasting hall as any castle of romance.[159] Standing within a castle believed to have been built by Arthur, Edward could have found no finer setting for a feast at the Round Table.

[156] See, for example, J. F. Willems (ed.), *Rymkronyk van Jan van Heelu betreffende den Slag van Woeringen van het Jaer 1288*, Collection de chroniques belges inédites (Brussels, 1836). Written in 1291–2, just after her marriage, van Heelu addressed his chronicle to Margaret (lines 1–16), hoping 'that a eulogistic life of her father-in-law [Duke John I] would encourage the English princess to learn Flemish' (Vale, *Edward III and Chivalry* (as above, n. 72), p. 22).

[157] Margaret Wood, *The English Medieval House* (London, 1965), 39–40.

[158] See above, pp. 70–1.

[159] Morris, 'The Architecture of Arthurian Enthusiasm' (as above, n. 72), pp. 79–81.

Edward I and the making of the Round Table

The question should then be asked, whether any of Edward I's other visits to Winchester might have been the occasion for making the Round Table. His visits in the second half of the reign, after 1290, offer few possibilities. Edward was in Winchester in August 1293 and again August 1294, but in the aftermath of the Winchester tournament of 1290 and the collapse of his plans these visits seem unlikely to have seen a celebration of the kind for which a round table might have been needed. Edward's visit early in May 1302, the first with his new wife Margaret of France, is a possibility, and the fire from which they narrowly escaped on that occasion does not mean that some great celebration may not have been intended or even have taken place.[160] Yet there is no evidence for any event comparable to the tournament of 1290, nor was there any special occasion to mark. Edward's long visit to Winchester from 17 February to 16 May 1306, when he and Margaret lodged at the bishop's palace of Wolvesey awaiting the birth of their third child, seems an unlikely moment. A feast might perhaps have been planned in anticipation of the birth, in the event that of their first daughter on 4 May, but it has left no record. In setting aside the visits of 1293, 1294, and 1306, and in not emphasising the possibility of 1302, the lesson of the recent discovery of the tournament of 1290 must be remembered. Until the riches of the Wardrobe and Household records for the later years of Edward's reign have been revealed by the publication of indexed transcripts new evidence may always emerge, although this becomes less likely with the amount of attention now being paid to courtly activities and dress, for which these records are the principal source.

By contrast, the first half of Edward's reign offers several possibilities. Edward visited Winchester as king five times in the years before 1290. Two of these visits, in January 1276 and from 20 December to 10 January 1279/80 were not in the tournament season, but the Round Table could have been made for the Christmas or New Year feast on the latter occasion.[161] The visit of October 1281 would be an unusual although not an unprecedented time of year for a tournament. But the visit in 1285 deserves particular attention. Substantial repairs had been done at the castle in the year ending 29 September 1285, both to the royal apartments and to the great bridge (Table 19). Edward stayed at Winchester from 7 to 12 September, spent the

---

[160] Thomas Hog (ed.), *F. Nicholai Triveti ... Annales*, English Historical Society (London, 1845), p. 395, n. 2, quoting from the MS. of the Annals in Merton College, Oxford.

[161] For a late example of such feasts in Arthurian romance, see for example those at Carlisle: Mary Hamel (ed.), *Morte Arthure: a Critical Edition* (New York and London, 1984), lines 64–77 (Christmas), 78–230 (New Year's Day), composed at the very end of the 14th century.

next three weeks in the north-east of the county (at Wootton, Woodmancott, Micheldever and Overton), and was then back in Winchester from 3 to 16 October when Parliament was held and the series of police regulations known as the Statute of Winchester were passed.[162] Echoes of this visit are still to be found in the Wardrobe and Household accounts for the following year as outstanding claims were gradually cleared up. These show that it had been a major royal occasion at which John of Brittany and John of Brabant had both been present, and for which Princess Mary had come from Amesbury to be with her parents.[163]

Edward's visit to Winchester of 3–5 May 1278 may provide another possible occasion. Edward and Eleanor had come to Winchester direct from Glastonbury where they had been present at the translation of the supposed remains of Arthur and Guinevere to a new marble tomb before the high altar of the abbey.[164] Precisely because this seems a possible occasion for an Arthurian feast in 'Arthur's city', the records of the Wardrobe and Household have been searched by Dr Arnold Taylor, who found only one conceivably relevant entry. This is the king's order on Good Friday 15 April to the sheriff of Southampton and Wiltshire for the provision of swans (pro cignis querendis), and on the same day to the sheriff of Somerset and Dorset perhaps for the same (but not specified) purpose.[165] This may recall the Feast of Swans in 1306, but the records of that feast give no hint that it was an event in an Arthurian mould.[166]

---

[162] PRO, MS Itinerary of Edward I (as above, n. 69). For the Statute of Winchester, dated 8 October 1285, see *Statutes of the Realm*, Record Commission, i (London, 1810), pp. 96–8; M. Powicke, *The Thirteenth Century* 2nd edn. (Oxford, 1962), pp. 357, 369, 374–5; Prestwich, *Edward I* (as above, n. 72), pp. 280–1, 523. Milner claims that on this occasion Edward held 'a great military solemnity creating at one time forty-four knights' (*History ... of Winchester* (as above, n. 3), 1st edn. (1798), i, pp. 269–70; 2nd edn. (1809), i, pp. 269–70; 3rd edn. (1839), pp. 204–5). The sources Milner gives both refer to the Statute of Winchester but neither mentions the creation of knights. No evidence to support Milner's statement has yet been found. Should it emerge, the visit of 1285 would have to be carefully considered as a possible occasion for the making of the table, although the festive and dynastic character of 1290 would still make that the most likely context.

[163] Byerly and Byerly, *Records of the Wardrobe and Household 1285–1286* (as above, n. 96), Nos. 41, 93, 222, and 273; see also, Nos. 14, 22, 43, 88, and 201.

[164] Loomis, 'Edward I, Arthurian Enthusiast' (as above, n. 72), pp. 115–16; Morris, 'The architecture of Arthurian Enthusiasm' (as above, n. 72), pp. 67–9 (with further references); Prestwich, *Edward I* (as above, n. 72), p. 120; James P. Carley, *Glastonbury Abbey: the Holy House at the Head of the Moors Adventurous* Woodbridge, 1988), pp. 36–7, 124–5; James P. Carley (ed.), *The Chronicle of Glastonbury Abbey* (Woodbridge, 1985), pp. 242–7.

[165] A. J. Taylor in a letter to the author, 24 August 1985. The reference is to PRO, E101/308/4.

[166] For descriptions of the feast, see H.R. Luard (ed.), *Bartholomaei de Cotton ... Historia Anglicana*, Rolls Series (London, 1859), pp. 176–7, and the passage from the continuation of the *Flores Historiarum* discussed by Gransden, *Historical Writing in England*, i (as above, n. 135), pp. 453–4. Bullock-Davies, *Menestrellorum multitudo* (as above, n. 124), pp. xxix–xxxviii, quotes, translates and compares three descriptions of the feast, and on p. xxxvii refutes Loomis, 'Edward I, Arthurian Enthusiast' (as above, n. 72), pp. 121–6. In a similar critical vein, see Prestwich, *Edward I* (as above, n. 72), 121.

We are left with four occasions in Edward's reign on which a feast involving Arthurian elements such as a round table might have been held at Winchester, 1278, 1279, 1285 and 1290. Of these, 1279 is the least likely. May 1278, in the immediate aftermath of the translation at Glastonbury, the most dramatic of Edward's known public assertions of his interest in Arthur, may seem a strong candidate, but the order to obtain swans is irrelevant and there was no special feast, for example Pentecost or Trinity Sunday, to be marked. The extended visit in 1285 offers a more likely occasion. There is no evidence that a tournament was held but there will probably have been a major feast, although not perhaps of the kind for which an Arthurian celebration might have been appropriate. Further research in the Wardrobe and Household records may yet throw light on these earlier occasions, but the holding of the Winchester tournament in April 1290 at a moment of great political and family success offers the most likely occasion for the making of the Round Table which still hangs in Winchester Castle hall.

To what extent can the tree-ring result (Chapter 5) be reconciled with this conclusion? The year 1289/90, being further away from the latest recorded ring of 1219, appears less likely than 1278 or 1279. Put another way, to reach 1289/90 larger allowances must be made for the missing heartwood or sapwood or both, and/or for seasoning and storage. Consider the following figures in Table 20 which are based on two assumptions, first, that the missing years are accounted for by missing heartwood rings and by the period in seasoning and storage, and, second, that the allowance for the missing sapwood rings remains constant.

Table 20

Tree-ring dating the Round Table: reconciliation of the date of the latest surviving ring with felling date and construction date: possible solutions

Latest ring	Missing hardwood	Missing sapwood	Felling date	Seasoning and storage	Construction date
1219	20	25	1264	5	1269
1219	25	25	1269	10	1279
1219	30	25	1274	15	1289

Different assumptions could be made: for example, that the figure for sapwood is variable and was in this case at the upper limit of its likely range, say 40 years rather than 25, and/or that the wood had remained much longer in store. In either case the effect might be to reduce the number of missing heartwood rings needed to reach 1289/90 or one of the earlier possible occasions in the later thirteenth century. Although timber was usually used green in medieval building works, planks intended for panelling (wainscot) and fine joinery were seasoned. Professor Barefoot's dating of the individual trees used in the making of the table has shown that timber of this quality could be stored for many years.[167] The gaps between the planks forming the top of the Winchester table are very small indeed, and may only have opened up since the introduction of central heating into the Great Hall in the early nineteenth century. The wood must therefore have been well seasoned before being cut and pegged. This seasoning would probably have taken a year or so for each inch of thickness of the baulks from which the boards were to be cut.[168]

The tree-ring result cannot be used to discriminate between 1278, 1279, and 1290, let alone between 1285 and 1290. Yet it has rendered the great service of telling us that these possibilities are compatible with the age of the wood of the table as established by a scientific investigation quite independent of the written sources.

In the current state of research into the written records, the conclusion of this enquiry is that the table was probably made in 1289, perhaps by Peter the master carpenter engaged on the works at Winchester castle that year.[169] The table reflected the latest technology in the engineering of large wheels for water-mills and the tread-wheels of great cranes (Figs. 56–9).[170] The top of the table was made of seasoned boards so well cut and pegged edge to edge that they have scarcely moved in seven centuries. The table stood on twelve legs of unknown but probably simple form, steadied presumably by a rail near the floor, its heavy centre supported by a pillar of stone but more probably of timber (Figs. 46, 50). Eighteen feet (5.5 m) in diameter and weighing about three-quarters of a ton,[171] the table would have seated twenty in comfort with a little less than three feet (0.83 m) for each place (cf. Fig. 168).[172] A hanging of leather or more probably of cloth, a tablier, seems to have hung from its rim, to judge from the small nails revealed by X-ray around the circumference (Figs. 103–4).[173] The surface may have

---

[167] See above, p. 182.

[168] See above, p. 152.

[169] This is the conclusion also of Dr Arnold Taylor, as he wrote to me on 17 February 1990. Master Peter does not otherwise occur in Colvin (ed.), *The History of the King's Works* (as above, n. 67), vols. i or ii.

[170] See above, pp. 117–20.

[171] Allowing for the approximate weight of the rim, supporting timbers and ironwork added in 1516, and for the weight of the pine boards and encircling iron ring put on in 1873: see above, p. 105.

[172] When HM the Queen lunched at a replica table set on the floor of the castle hall in 1979, twenty-four guests (including Her Majesty) were seated at a table 18 feet in diameter (Fig. 168). Since the number of 24 knights (excluding King Arthur) may be an innovation of the repainting of the table in 1516 (see above, pp. 281–3), twenty is taken here as the kind of number for which the table may have been made. Gill Rushton, Winchester Archivist in the Hampshire Record Office, kindly checked the records of the Queen's visit in 1979.

[173] See above, pp. 127, and for parallels, Figs. 17–20.

been permanently covered with some material fastened by these same nails and decorated, as seems to have been the case after 1348,[174] or it may have been spread with a fine textile as occasion arose, perhaps with cloth-of-gold.[175] Whether made by Peter or another master for 1290, or possibly for 1285 or even 1278 or 1279, the Round Table now hanging on the west wall of the Great Hall of Winchester castle is the grandest piece of moveable furniture to have come down to us from the English Middle Ages.

The aftermath of the Winchester tournament

Joan of Acre married Gilbert de Clare in Westminster Abbey on Sunday, 30 April 1290, in a private ceremony conducted by the king's chaplain.[176] Margaret married John of Brabant two months later in Westminster Abbey on Saturday, 8 July,[177] in 'an event which enabled Edward and his magnates to indulge all their tastes in feudal magnificence.'[178] The treaty governing the betrothal of Edward of Caernarvon to Margaret of Scotland was ratified at Northampton at the end of August.[179]

Then on 26 September came the death in the Orkneys of young Edward's betrothed, Margaret of Scotland, the 'Maid of Norway,' news of which cannot have reached Edward until mid October.[180] By this time Queen Eleanor, long unwell, had

---

[174] See below, pp. 465–6.

[175] The four cloths-of-gold purchased in Winchester on 20 April 1290, the day of the tournament, may be recalled, but they might equally well have been purchased for hanging on the wall of the castle hall: see above, and n. 124.

[176] Green, *Lives of the Princesses* (as above, n. 81), pp. 330–1; Parsons (ed.), *Court and Household* (as above, n. 85), p. 134, lines 28–9.

[177] Green, *Lives of the Princesses* (as above n. 81), pp. 370–2; A.J. Taylor, 'Military Architecture', in A. L. Poole (ed.), *Medieval England* (Oxford, 1958), pp. 98–127, at p. 98, n. 1; Parsons (ed.), *Court and Household* (as above, n. 85), p. 147, n. 11.

[178] Powicke, *Henry III and the Lord Edward* (as above, n. 76, p. 732). The many references to minstrels under the year 1290 give some idea of the scale of the festivities at the two weddings, especially that of Margaret: Constance Bullock-Davies, *Register of Royal and Baronal Domestic Minstrels 1272–1327* (Woodbridge, 1986). The *Register* also records the standing payments and gifts of robes made to musicians of the royal household in 1290, but gives no specific information about minstrels present at Winchester in April that year, suggesting (as with the daily expenses of the household) that the records we have of that event relate to the exceptional items of expenditure only.

[179] Rymer, *Foedera* (as above, n. 78), p. 738.

[180] Keen, *England in the Later Middle Ages* (as above, n. 80), p. 27. The news cannot have reached Edward until mid October at the earliest, for it was not until 7 October that the bishop of St. Andrew's had written to inform the king that she was unwell but getting better: Nicholson, *Scotland* (as above, n. 80), pp. 34–5; E.L.G. Stones and Grant G. Simpson, *Edward I and the Throne of Scotland 1290–1296*, 2 vols. (Glasgow, 1978), i, pp. 4–5, ii, pp. 3–4.

become seriously ill.[181] Edward was at Clipstone in Nottinghamshire until 11 November, but now hurried to her at Harby in the same county, a few miles west of Lincoln. He reached her a week before she died on 28 November 1290. At each place where her funeral cortege paused overnight on its sad slow journey to Westminster, twelve in all, Edward ordered crosses to be erected, and these, together with the tombs of her entrails in the cathedral at Lincoln, of her heart in the Dominican Church in London, and of her body at Westminster formed 'a monumental display more elaborate than that accorded to any English king or queen before or since.'[182]

The years of careful negotiation which on King Edward's death would have culminated in the union of the English and Scottish crowns had come to naught with Margaret's death, and Edward's personal life now entered into 'the desolation of his greatest sorrow.'[183] It was to be nine years before Edward remarried. Under the terms of the same treaty with France in 1299 Edward of Caernarvon was betrothed to the French king's daughter, but it was not until January 1308, eighteen years after Margaret's death and six months after his accession to the throne as Edward II, that he eventually married Isabella of France.

---

[181] As revealed by many entries in her household roll: Parsons (ed.), *Court and Household* (as above, n. 85), pp. 23–7.

[182] Colvin, *History of the King's Works* (as above, n. 67), i, pp. 479–85, at p. 479; on Eleanor's death, her funeral, and the crosses, see also the essays in David Parsons (ed.), *Eleanor of Castile 1290–1990: Essays to Commemorate the 700th Anniversary of her Death* (Stamford, 1991).

[183] Powicke, *Henry III and the Lord Edward* (as above, n. 76), p. 733.

11

The Hanging of the Table

When John Hardyng produced a revised version of his verse chronicle of the history of England in 1464, he rewrote his account of Arthur's last battles, placing the crucial conflict not in Cornwall but at Winchester,

> Wher many Prynces and lordes in that case
> Were slayne on both sides for evermore
> Of the Round Table that longe hade been afore
> Many worthy knyghtes there were spended
> For Arthure love that myght not be amended.

Hardyng then added the lines,

> The Rounde Table at Wynchestre beganne
> And ther it ende and ther it hangeth yet
> For ther were slayne of that Round Table thanne
> The knyghtes all that euer dide at it sitt
> Of Britayne borne save Launcelot ...[1]

---

[1] BL, Harleian MS. 661, fol. 55r, 55v. For John Hardyng and his chronicle, see Antonia Gransden, *Historical Writing in England*, ii, *c. 1307 to the Early Sixteenth Century* (London, 1982), pp. 274–87. The second version of Hardyng's chronicle was published by Henry Ellis (ed.), *The Chronicle of John Hardyng* (London, 1812; reprinted, New York 1974) from the edition printed by Richard Grafton in 1543. The verses quoted here from the Harleian MS. appear on Ellis, p. 146. See also Felicity Riddy, 'John Hardyng's Chronicle and the Wars of the Roses', *Arthurian Literature* 12(1993), 91–108.

These lines are not in Hardyng's first version, presented to Henry VI in 1457.[2] They occur only in the second version, which he continued down to 1464, but of which he may have presented an early copy to Edward IV at Leicester in 1463.[3]

Hardyng uses the term 'Round Table' in two of its senses (see above, p. 22), the companionship of knights, and the table itself at which they sat, changing his subject in mid-sentence. But by 1464, and perhaps by 1463, he had learnt or seen for himself that the table was hanging in Winchester. As far as we know, this is the first mention of the actual table, and it provides a crucial fixed point in its study, but it does not tell us how long the table had been hanging nor why it was hung up. Nor does Hardyng tell us that the table was hanging in the Great Hall, although that seems a safe assumption.

This is the darkest period in the history of the table. In the two centuries between 1290 and 1516, we have only Hardyng's verse of 1463–4; Caxton's Prologue of 1485, in which 'at Wynchester, the Round Table', is one of the 'many remembraunces' of Arthur which 'ben yet of hym and shall remayne perpetuelly';[4] Henry VII's comment of 1506; and two mentions in Welsh poems (see below, p. 419–22). In this chapter we have to try to see whether it is possible to discover how the table changed from a piece of furniture into an ikon and when this change took place. That there is a problem to be solved, is clear enough. The X-rays show that the Tudor design is the first to have been painted on the table. The table hanging up by 1463–4 must therefore, it seems, have been a huge, bare disc, an awesome, indeed gaunt remembrance, more impressive perhaps than the painted table of today. But is this conceivable? Is it likely that such an antiquity would have been left undecorated, without some explicit identification such as was provided in the early sixteenth century: 'Thys is the rounde table of Kyng Arthur ...'? This problem must be tackled after some attempt has been made to discover when and why the table was first hung up.

Hardyng wrote the original version of his chronicle 'to please Henry VI and the Lancastrian faction; he wrote the second to please Edward IV and the Yorkists'.[5] The changes Hardyng made with change of patron are complex, with additions but

---

[2] The first version of Hardyng's chronicle is only known from BL, Lansdowne MS. 204, probably the actual manuscript presented to Henry VI in 1457, where the passage parallel to that quoted here from the second version appears on fols. 85v-86r. For the first version in general, see C. L. Kingsford, 'The First Version of Hardyng's Chronicle', *English Historical Review* 27 (1912), 461–82, 740–53.

[3] Kingsford, 'First Version', 466; cf. Gransden, *Historical Writing*, ii, p. 277.

[4] James W. Spisak (ed.), *Caxton's Malory* (Berkeley and Los Angeles, 1983), i, p. 2.

[5] Gransden, *Historical Writing*, ii, p. 277; cf. Kingsford, 'First Version', 465–6, 469.

also with deletions which made the later version substantially the shorter. The mention of the Round Table was one of these additions, but to what end? The associated changes are interesting. Arthur fought three battles against Mordred, at Dover, at Winchester, and in Cornwall. In the first version the crucial battle is the third one, in Cornwall, 'In whiche batayle the floure of all knyghthode/ Ded was'.[6] Hardyng follows at what seems like a natural point with his valediction on the collapse of Arthur's kingdom. But in the later version, the Winchester battle becomes the pivot. Although Arthur is still alive and has yet to chase Mordred to Cornwall, it is at Winchester that Hardyng pauses to mourn the passing of the Round Table. In this second version there is no valedictory verse after the Cornish battle: it has all been said.

An historian's first reaction to Hardyng's mention of the Round Table is to ask if the new information reflects a new situation: had the table been hung up in the course of works in the Great Hall between 1457 and 1463–4, the dates of Hardyng's two editions? Or does the added information in some way mirror the political situation: does Hardyng strengthen his new-found case for the Yorkist Edward by bringing in Arthurian connections irrelevant to the Lancastrian Henry? Although the badges on the tie-beams of the Great Hall used to be taken as evidence for extensive repairs in the reign of Edward IV, it now looks as if they belong to a century earlier (see below, p. 414–16). There is, in fact, no evidence that Edward IV did anything at all to the hall. Nor does Hardyng give any indication that he regarded Arthur as a key figure in Edward's claim to the thrones of England or Scotland, introducing him in verses on 'the Kynges tytle to all his landes' only to illustrate a proverb commenting on Edward's supposed rights to Castile and Leon:

> By small hackeneys greate coursers men chastice
> As Arthure did by Scottes wanne all fraunchese.[7]

Hardyng's changed emphasis on Arthur's battle at Winchester suggests a simpler explanation. Sometime after completing his first edition in 1457, he saw or heard for the first time of the table at Winchester. Imagining that its presence there could be taken as a relic of that company of knights, he revised his account of Arthur's last battles to place the destruction of the Round Table not in Cornwall but at Winchester:

---

[6] Ellis, p. 419. I am grateful to Dr. Kate Gilbert for comments on Hardyng's changes of emphasis which I have followed here.
[7] Ellis, p. 419.

For ther were slayne of that Round Table thanne
The knyghtes all that euer dide at it sitt
Of Britayne borne save Launcelot ..[8].

'And ther it hangeth yet': the 'yet' suggests that Hardyng thought the table had been hanging there a considerable time, perhaps ever since the battle. Hardyng provides the first known mention of the Winchester table and tells us it was already hanging. This is vital information for the situation in 1463–4, but tells us nothing of how or when it came to be hanging. For this we have to turn to the evidence of the table itself.

As we have seen in Chapter 4, a series of six vertical spars were fixed across the back of the table at some date after its original construction. A raised rim was added to the front, possibly but not certainly on the same occasion. It is natural to think that these verticals were added when the table was hung up, to counter the stresses which arose from the change of plane. But this is not the case (see above, p. 131). Before the verticals were added, the table had suffered a long period of brown rot which can only have attacked the table while it was hanging, with more or less the same sector upwards as now, where water could drip on to it. Since the verticals probably date from the repairs of 1516 (see below, p. 441), they were evidently added to strengthen an already decayed table, rather than to hold it firmly together when first raised out of the horizontal. The table was thus originally hung up without strengthening and remained hanging long enough to be seriously weakened by rot, before being taken down and repaired in 1516. The degree of damage caused by the rot provides a very rough index to the length of time the table had been hanging before 1516: a period long enough for the outer ends of two of the radials to be completely destroyed (Fig. 66). No span can be put to this except to suggest that a considerable period, of decades rather than years, had probably intervened. That the table was in need of repair in 1516 is shown by the very fact that repairs were then undertaken, probably on the king's personal intervention (see below, p. 440). And Paulo Giovio, as we shall see, says quite specifically that the table was much decayed before being restored. His account is second-hand and was not published until 1548, but probably derives from one of those who accompanied Charles V in 1522 (see below, p. 404–5).

The evidence of the table itself thus shows that it had been hanging in the Great Hall for long enough before 1516 to become badly decayed. Hardyng's claim, written in or before 1463–4, that the table 'hangeth yet', fits well into this picture,

[8]   See above, n. 1.

but the new evidence still does not tell us how long the table had been hanging in the Great Hall, and when and why it had originally been hung up. What are the possible known occasions when this might have happened? The danger is to suppose that the hanging was a particularly significant event, or that it necessarily happened in connection with other, recorded, works of repair or alteration. The decision to clear the floor by putting the table on the wall may not have seemed of much consequence at the time. An added difficulty is that the survival of records of payment for works at the castle is much poorer for the fourteenth and especially fifteenth centuries than it seems to have been for the age of Henry III and Edward I.

The fire of 1302 in the royal apartments brought an end to the use of the castle as a royal residence. As far as we know, the royal rooms were never repaired and simply fell into ruin. But the Great Hall, undamaged in the fire, was kept in repair (see above, pp. 76–80): in 1314 the cost of repairs was put at 100s.; in 1348–9 the hall was re-roofed at a cost (including some other works) of over £300; in 1389 the aisle roofs were re-leaded at a cost of £7 6s. 8d; in 1394–5 the walls and windows were repaired at a cost which is unlikely to have exceeded £26 13s. 4d. and may have been less; and in 1425–8 the hall was re-roofed with shingles, a material which must imply that this operation dealt with the steeply pitched 'middle roof' rather than the gently sloping leaded roofs of the aisles. Probably there were other repairs, particularly in the fifteenth century, of which no record survives: an allowance of £80 made in 1450 for work at the castle is unspecific, but could have included work on the hall. The frequency with which its roofs needed repair in the sixteenth century suggests either that the fifteenth-century records are defective or that the maintenance of the hall was then neglected for long periods. This is a typical medieval pattern: it left its results in the brown rot which attacked the table as a result of water dripping on to it from a leaky gable window or a hole in the middle roof.

At some date in the fourteenth or fifteenth centuries the hall roof was completely remodelled: the gables which originally covered the windows were taken down, the aisle walls were raised, the aisle roofs were laid to a flatter pitch, tie-beams were inserted between the arcades, and the high roof above them remade (Figs. 26–7). The date of those works, on the assumption they belong together, is indicated by the style of the openwork tracery filling the spandrels between the tie-beams and their supporting braces (Fig. 29). This tracery has been cogently compared to high-quality work of the mid fourteenth century, such as the panelling in the lower part of the lantern at Ely, a dating which goes well with the known period of heavy expenditure on re-roofing the Great Hall in 1348–9 (see above, p. 78). But there is a problem: below each tie-beam, and carved in one piece with it, there is a badge which has usually been identified as the *rose en soleil* and attributed to

Edward IV (1461–83). These badges are, however, very unlike Edward's *rose en soleil* as carved elsewhere in Winchester (Fig. 28c), and Beatrice Clayre has concluded in Chapter 3 that the tie-beams and their spandrels, and with them the rest of the major remodelling of the Great Hall, should probably be dated to 1348–9 (see above, pp. 78–80).

We shall return in a moment to the problem of the badges. First we have to consider whether the recorded works of 1348–9, supposing that they are to be identified with the major remodelling revealed by the structure of the hall, do provide a possible moment for the hanging of the table. The operation itself was awkward and must have involved a lot of cordage as it did in 1873–4 (Figs. 33–4), but the table was not given any special treatment. The stretcher and pedestal were removed, the legs broken out without much care, sometimes damaging the mortices or leaving the treenails in position (Figs. 60a, 63), and the table was hoisted up the wall and secured in position, with (as the rotted areas show) more or less the same segment uppermost as now. We have no evidence at all of the means used to raise it, or of the supports used to hold it in position once raised. No trace of suspension devices such as survive from the Tudor repairs of 1516 can be seen. Presumably the table was held in position by brackets much like those still used below the table, but with the addition of further brackets or perhaps simple iron clamps to hold its top against the wall.[9] If the table was originally hung, as seems reasonable, on the east wall of the hall, all traces of early fixings in the wall itself will have been destroyed when Wyatt pierced his arches through to the new courts in 1873.

An operation such as this will not have taken long or cost much: it is no surprise that no record of it survives. It might have been done as part of any of the recorded works, or as part of some other operation of which no record survives. But the fourteenth century in general, and the remodelling attributed to 1348–9 in particular, seem to offer a likely context for the hanging of the table. After 1302 the hall was used little, if at all, for royal ceremonial. It lay now in what by the end of the century was called 'the sheriff's ward', and from here the sheriff and his deputies administered the county. Courts of assize and *nisi prius* had probably been held in the hall since at least the reign of Edward I. New statutes of 1344 and 1350 required in addition the appointment of justices to meet at least four times a year for the peace of the county and it was in the hall that they met. The Great Hall became the shire

---

[9] The anonymous 18th-century sketch of the table from Warner's collections (Fig. 119) has on its back a sketch elevation of the east wall of the hall showing the table apparently held in position by four brackets or clamps. There is no other evidence for the use of four brackets, and from 1789 onwards there seem to have been only the two lower ones (Fig. 163), as now. But the Warner collection sketch suggests that the Tudor fixing involved four brackets and this may itself be a reflection of the pre-Tudor arrangement.

hall, the seat of justice, and thus the first home of the county and of the legal functions which still occupy this area today.

The remodelling of the hall in 1348–9 may be a reflection of this changing use, modernising the building by removing the low roofs between the side gables to provide an airier and lighter space. The clearance of the floor by removing the Round Table, now no longer needed for ceremonial and festive occasions, could well have taken place at this time. That the table was hung up at some moment we know for sure, for it was not originally made to be a symbol hanging on the wall. The works of 1348–9 offer a possible occasion and a reason, provided we accept that the table had by this date already become something more than a piece of old furniture to be thrown away.

If we accept 1348–9 as a possible date, it may be worth looking beyond Winchester for a wider context in which the preservation of the Round Table may have been significant. It was in 1348 that Edward III instituted at Windsor his Order of the Garter, 'perhaps the most brilliant inspiration of the Age of Chivalry', a fellowship of knights which took as its model the fellowship of the knights of King Arthur's Round Table.[10] Four years earlier in January 1344 Edward had announced at Windsor his intention

> mensam rotundam inciperet, eodem modo et statu quo eam dimisit dominus Arthurus quondam rex Angliae, scilicet ad numerum trecentorum militum ...[11]

> to found a Round Table in the same manner and form as the Lord Arthur once King of England had established it, namely for the number of three hundred knights ...

---

[10] For the foundation of the Garter, see May McKisack, *The Fourteenth Century 1307–1399* (Oxford, 1959), pp. 250–3; the quotation is taken from p. 251. See Juliet Vale, *Edward III and Chivalry. Chivalric Society in its Context 1270–1350* (Woodbridge, 1982), pp. 76–92: the first formal celebration of St George's Day seems to have been in April 1349. The most recent account is Hugh E. L. Collins, *The Order of the Garter, 1348–1461. Chivalry and Politics in Late Medieval England* (Oxford, 2000), pp. 6–33. See also Peter Begent and Hubert Chesshyre, *The Most Noble Order of the Garter* (London, 1999), pp. 7–18.

[11] Vale, *Edward III and Chivalry*, pp. 67–8, quoting Adam Murimuth, *Continuatio chronicarum*, ed. E. M. Thompson, Rolls ser. (London, 1889), p. 232; Juliet R. V. Barker, *The Tournament in England 1100–1400* (Woodbridge, 1986), pp. 67–8, 92–4. For the walled structure known as the Round Table, 200 feet in diameter, begun in the upper bailey at Windsor in 1344, see H. M. Colvin (ed.), *The History of the King's Works* ii, *The Middle Ages* (London, 1963), pp. 870–2, Plan IV (Windsor Castle). For Edward's abortive Round Table project, see now Collins, *Order of the Garter*, as above, n. 10, pp. 6–10.

Edward's Order of the Round Table was a romantic idea abandoned almost as soon as it was begun under the pressure of events abroad, but its Arthurian inspiration as a centre of chivalry in the principal royal castle of the realm survived to influence the foundation of the Garter four years later.[12]

The 1340s were thus years in which the idea of King Arthur's Round Table was much in men's minds both as an institution and, inevitably, as the actual table which was its setting and its symbol. Here then is a context in which the preservation in the royal hall at Winchester of a round table with obvious Arthurian symbolism and a supposed Arthurian origin can be set; a context perhaps in which its destruction would have been unthinkable. Both local developments and the wider world of ideas point to the years 1348–9 as the moment when the Winchester table may have been raised from utilitarian object, however exalted, to the status of symbol set high on the wall.

Is it possible to discern the men who played some part in the working out of this complex interaction? In 1344, as treasurer of the exchequer, William Edington was one of those responsible for authorising the issue of writs and other guarantees in connection with the construction of the hall of the Round Table at Windsor.[13] In 1346 Edington was consecrated bishop of Winchester, a city he had known well since moving there as clerk to the household of Bishop Orleton in 1333.[14] A few years later Edington seems to have become the first prelate of the Order of the Garter.[15] The selection of the bishop of Winchester for this post, always afterwards to be held by his successor, is a further and probably significant link between Winchester and Windsor in the transition from Round Table to Garter (see Appendix I).

During these years William of Wykeham, later to be Edington's successor in the see, was passing through the first stages of his career, probably in the service of Sir John Scures, then sheriff of Hampshire and constable of Winchester Castle.[16] When

---

[12] Colvin (ed.), *King's Works*, ii, p. 871; M. H. Keen, *England in the Later Middle Ages* (paperback edn., London, 1975, reprinted 1986), pp. 134–7.

[13] PRO, SC 1/40/92 and 41/163. Although appearing under Winchester in the new *Index* (1969) to *Lists and Indexes* 15 (1902, revised 1968), these documents concerning the works of *la sale de la table rounde* probably both refer to Windsor and are to be dated in January or February 1344. This correction is due to Dr A. J. Taylor who kindly provided a photocopy and transcription of 40/92, discussed the problems raised, and suggested the possible role of William of Wykeham.

[14] S. F. Hockey (ed.), *The Register of William Edington Bishop of Winchester 1346–1366*, i, Hampshire Record Series 7 (Winchester, 1986), pp. vii–viii.

[15] See below, Appendix I, pp. 513–18.

[16] G. H. Moberly, *Life of William of Wykeham*, 2nd edn. (Winchester and London, 1893), p. 9 quoting from 'Heath's' MS. 'Life of Wykeham' (*ibid*. Appendix E, p. 324).

Scures gave up these offices in 1338, Wykeham may have continued in post as secretary to the constable of the castle, but about 1347 he was taken into the royal service, where by 1349 he had rendered sufficient service to be presented by the king to the living of Irstead in Norfolk.[17] By 1356 Wykeham was surveyor of the works at Windsor, where in the next five years he undertook what was in effect the demolition and reconstruction of the castle, including the removal of whatever had been completed of the hall of the Round Table twelve years before.[18] He was to be one of the great builders of the century, first at Windsor for the king, and then from 1367 as bishop of Winchester.[19]

The works undertaken on the castle hall at Winchester in 1348–9 were carried out and accounted for by the sheriff of Hampshire, Henry Sturmy.[20] It seems quite likely that the bishop of Winchester, as had happened before and would happen again,[21] played some role in their conduct. Edington, from his experience of the abortive Order of 1344 and his new role as prelate of the Garter, and young Wykeham, now in the royal service but still with active interests in Hampshire,[22] were ideally placed to have advised and acted in the matter of the Round Table and the respective claims of Winchester and Windsor. It may well have been they who arranged for the hanging of the Round Table high on the east wall of Winchester Castle hall.

Before passing on to the crucial question of what the table looked like on the wall, there is another problem to be dealt with. Although it now seems reasonably certain that the table was made in Winchester (see Chapter 10), the question still arises from time to time whether it might not have been brought to Winchester from

[17] Moberly, *Life*, pp. 11–13. The sources need to be used with care: see James Tait's comments in the bibliography of his notice of Wykeham in *DNB* xxi (1900), pp. 1141–6, at p. 1146, and T. F. Tout, *Chapters in the Administrative History of Medieval England* iii (1928), 235–9. For the significance of Wykeham's appointment to Irstead, see Tout, *Chapters*, pp. 235–6.

[18] H. M. Colvin (ed.), *The History of the King's Works* i, ii (London, 1963), 166–7, 877–82.

[19] For Wykeham's building as bishop, see now John Harvey, 'The Buildings of Winchester College', in Roger Custance (ed.), *Winchester College. Sixth Centenary Essays* (Oxford, 1982), pp. 77–127; Gervase Jackson-Stops, 'The Building of a Medieval College', in J. Buxton and P. Williams (ed.), *New College, Oxford 1379–1979* (Oxford, 1979), pp. 147–92; and J. N. Hare, 'Bishop's Waltham Palace, Hampshire, William of Wykeham, Henry Beaufort and the Transformation of a Medieval Episcopal Palace', *Archaeological Journal*, 145 (1988), 222–52.

[20] See above, p. 78, and PRO, SC 1/40/85.

[21] For example, in 1233 when the bishop lent the king money for the works of the Great Hall (*Cal Lib R 1226–40*, pp. 221, 232), or in 1516–7 when the bishop was involved in the repair of the hall and the Round Table (see below, pp. 438–9).

[22] Moberly, *Life*, p. 13. In 1352 Wykeham was acting in a land transaction between Henry Sturmy and Edington (*ibid.*, p. 20). These men were clearly well known to each other.

elsewhere, perhaps from Windsor after 1344, for use or display in the hall. The table has however never been taken apart since it was first permanently put together as the undisturbed signatures of the adzing from plank to plank show (see above, p. 117; Fig. 54), so if it has been moved, it (or at least its top) was moved in one piece, 18 feet in diameter and weighing three-quarters of a ton. This could certainly have been done, although it would have been arduous over more than short distances. The table could have come into the hall through one of the windows: by taking out the tracery and removing the sill wall an opening 24 feet high could easily have been made, much as a slot was cut in the back partition of the Nisi Prius court in 1873 to take the table through (Fig. 34). To move the table any distance a special cart would have been needed, and such wains made to move specific loads are recorded from time to time in medieval building accounts and elsewhere. Indeed at Windsor in 1344 heather and sand were strewn on the bridges *ne frangerentur cum magno cariagio tabule rotunde* ('lest they should be broken by the great cart bearing the Round Table').[23]

This phrase presents a problem. Taken at face value, it suggests that the (*or a*) Round Table was being (or was to be) transported on the medieval equivalent of a low-loader. If so, it may mean that preparations had been made in 1344 to move the table from Winchester to Windsor, from Arthur's legendary capital to the castle of Edward III's birth, where the king intended to create a *siège d'honneur* of the most splended kind as a centre of a newly instituted Order of Chivalry. On this interpretation the Winchester table would have been the centrepiece of the new *sale de la table rounde*, the vast circular arena then under construction in the upper bailey of Windsor castle for the ceremonial connected with the holding of tournaments.

This is much the most likely meaning of *cum magno cariagio*, but the noun *cariagium* is also used in the abstract as a heading in building accounts to signify costs of carriage in general. If that were its meaning here, we should perhaps translate the whole clause to mean 'so that the bridges should not be broken by the heavy carriage of materials for building the Round Table', the reference being to the circular building then being built in the upper bailey. With an adjective such as *magnum*, however, the noun could be taken as concrete, in the sense of 'a large (wheeled) vehicle'.[24]

In either case, Edward's plans were still-born. The works of the 'hall of the Round Table' at Windsor were abandoned and the Round Table remained at Winchester. There is in fact no evidence that the Round Table was ever taken away

[23] Barker, *Tournament in England*, p. 90.

[24] I have been greatly helped in the interpretation of *cariagium* and its implications by Dr A. J. Taylor (letter of 28 Oct. 1990), to whom I owe several phrases in this and the preceding paragraph.

from Winchester, let alone brought there in the first place, and the fact that it could have been moved, does not mean that it was. It cannot in any case have been made for the Round Table hall at Windsor in 1344, for it is now quite certain that the Winchester table is at least half a century older, and perhaps more. To go on to suggest that it must therefore have come from some other unspecified place and event stretches credulity. It is an option which need not be pursued.

A much more important question, one of the most significant and difficult in this study, is what the table looked like when it was raised high on the wall. The evidence provided by the X-rays, the paint sections, and the detached fragment is conclusive (Chapter 7): the wooden surface of the table was not painted until given its present design in the Tudor period. In other words, when first hung up the table was a bare wooden disc, the surface patterned only by the radiating joints of its planks (Fig. 52). This is perhaps the most surprising result of the whole investigation. If the table hung as a gaunt unpainted disc, if it was raised into position in that state, this can only underline the significance already then attached to it as a piece of antiquity: an imposing sight, and an evocative one.

Evocative, but quite unmedieval: in the western world medieval art and display abhorred a vacuum. The cool presentation of so large an unadorned, uncluttered surface is out of place in that time and culture. This is a dissonance harsh enough to suggest that such a view of the table may be quite wrong. The question must be rephrased: although the wooden surface was unpainted, was the table undecorated? Is it possible that the top was ornamented by a painted cover? Several pieces of evidence may point in this direction.

The edge of the table is hidden behind an iron band put on in 1874 (Fig. 73), but the X-rays provided a picture of much of the concealed detail. They revealed amongst other features a series of small nails hammered in radially around the edge of the table at intervals of four to six inches, and sometimes in small groups (see above, p. 127 and Figs. 103–4). Unfortunately it is impossible to tell from the X-rays whether the nails are hammered into the raised rim added to the front of the table in the Tudor period (see below, p. 127), into the ends of the planks forming the surface, or into the felloes forming the rim of the frame on the back of the table. But it is possible to draw some conclusions. If the nails were hammered into the felloes, they would be absent from the X-rays in the area where felloe 142 was replaced in the Victorian period, but they continue round uninterrupted. This is also true in the case of the adjacent felloe 117 which was probably replaced in the Tudor period.[25]

---

[25] The evidence is to be seen on X-rays A14, AA12, AA13, BB10, BB11 deposited with the project records in the Hampshire Record Office. For the position of felloes 117 and 142, see Fig. 43.

Supposing therefore that the nails are pre-Victorian, they must have been hammered into the ends of the planks or into the edge of the raised rim added to the front. In fact, however, the outer ends of the nails (their heads are usually missing) can often be seen to run with the line of the edge of the original table where this diverges slightly on the X-rays from the line of the outer edge of the added rim. So it is reasonably certain that the nails were hammered into the ends of the planks.

There seems to be only one possible function for these nails around the edge of the table, and that is to fix some added material either directly or through some reinforcing, no traces of which remain. The most obvious use of such a material would have been to form a valance, a *tablier* hanging in folds around the edge of the table when in use (see above, p. 47 and, for examples, Figs. 18, 19). But it is also possible that the nails may have held the edges of some material stretched over the surface of the table, or have performed both functions simultaneously.

There is one written source, the earliest actual description of the table we have, which specifically mentions the state of the surface before its Tudor repainting. The historian and antiquary Paulo Giovio (1483–1552), biographer of Pope Leo X and bishop of Nocera from 1528, published at Venice in 1548 his *Descriptio Britanniae, Scotiae, Hyberniae, et Orchadum ...*, the first (and only published) part of an intended description of the empires and peoples of the known world.[26] His villa at Como, designed to contain his famous museum, was decorated with frescoes by his friend Vasari, whom he incited and helped to write *The Lives of the Most Famous Artists*. Although widely travelled, Giovio seems never to have visited England. But the 1548 edition of his *Description of Britain* is printed in one with a chronicle from Brutus to 1547 and notes (*elogia*) on the famous English scholars of his age, both written by George Lily,[27] son of that William Lily (*c.*1468–1522) who played, as we shall see in Chapter 12, an important part in the entry of Charles V into London in 1522. Giovio had his own contacts with the court of Charles V, attending his coronation at Bologna in 1530, his triumph at Naples in 1535, and his festival at Milan in 1541. Whether from Lily or from someone who had accompanied Charles V to England in 1522, Giovio was well placed to learn something of the Round Table. He describes the traditional history of Britain, the deeds of Vortigern, Hengist, and Arthur and the founding of the Round Table:

[26] For Paulo Giovio, see L. Rovelli, *L'Opera storica ed artistica di Paolo Giovio* (Como, 1928); *Enciclopedia italiana* xvii (Milan, 1933), pp. 277–8; and F. Chabod, 'Paolo Giovio', *Scritti sul Rinascimento* (Turin, 1967), pp. 241–67, with further references.

[27] For George Lily, see T. D. Kendrick, *British Antiquity* (London, 1950), p. 41; and G. K. Hunter's life of his nephew, *John Lyly: the Humanist as Courtier* (London, 1962), pp. 26–30, 36. Lily's *elogia* occupy fols. 45r-54v and his chronicle fols. 57–end of the 1548 edition of Giovio's *Descriptio* (see next note).

Custoditur religiose adhuc ea mensa admirandae uirtutis testimonio memorabilis, ostentaturque claris hospitibus, uti nuper Carolo Cesari apud Vintoniam urbem, sed exesis multa carie circa margines Procerum nominibus, quae dum ab imperitis inflicta maiestati uetustatis iniuria insulso iudicio reponerentur, pene effectum est, ut ueluti suspecta fide, magnam partem dignitatis amiserit.[28]

That table is still reverently preserved in the town of Winchester, a notable witness of admirable valour, and is shown to distinguished visitors, as recently to the Emperor Charles. But the names of the knights around the edge, which had been badly eaten away by decay, were then renewed by unskilled hands so insensitively and with such damage to its ancient grandeur, that the table looks like a fake and has lost much of its credibility.

This is certainly the reaction of someone who had seen the freshly painted table, but less certain that this person had also seen for himself the table in its decayed state. More probably the information about the decay of the edge and its effect on the names had come in answer to a question aroused by suspicion of its fresh appearance – *ueluti suspecta fide*. Taken at face value Giovio's description implies that the names of the knights were visible around the edge of the table before it was restored. Since we now know that the wooden surface had not previously been painted, the names can only have been painted on some cover overlying the wood. But this is probably not an eye-witness account; more probably it is hearsay, and to that extent less reliable.

There is another hint. Caxton's mention of the Round Table in 1485, like Hardyng's twenty years before, identifies it as King Arthur's Round Table.[29] Giovio's informant saw the table after it was painted and thus identified, but Hardyng and Caxton saw it, or heard about it, before it was painted. On what was their identification based? On the obvious fact of it being a round table? On some local tale told by the hall keeper? Or on some identifying inscription like that which now encircles the central rose?

None of this material is easy to evaluate, but on balance it supports the idea that the table was in some way decorated when it was first hung on the wall. This can never be more than a possibility, perhaps a probability, but it may be worth going

---

[28] Paolo Giovio, *Descriptio Britanniae, Scotiae, Hyberniae, et Orchadum ex libro ... de Imperiis et Gentibus cogniti orbis* (Venice, 1548), fol. 6r-6v (sig. b. ii r-v); now republished in E. Travi and M. Penco (ed.), *Dialogi et Descriptiones*, Opera Pauli Iovii ix (Roma, 1984), pp. 89–128, at p. 93, with new introduction, pp. 67–72.

[29] See above, nn. 1 and 4

further to inquire what sort of cover might have been used and even to see if we can obtain any hint of how it may have been decorated.

There are only two kinds of material at all likely to have been used: textile and leather. For cloth to have been used it would probably have to have been a closely woven material, gessoed or otherwise prepared to take the painted decoration, and pasted down to the planked surface.[30] Even when tightly stretched, there would have been a tendency for it to become detached and sag, so that tacks or even battens might have been used to keep it in place, possibly disguised as part of the design (see below, p. 422). A very careful check was made of the X-rays in case some textile might have been left attached to the table when the raised rim was added to the front in the Tudor repairs. Remarkably some textile was found hidden behind the rim (Fig. 108), but rather than a closely woven fabric, it was a wool, now disintegrating, in a loose tabby weave.[31] It would have been unsuitable for painting upon and its presence is unexplained.

It is more likely that the table was covered with leather. Theophilus wrote his book *On Divers Arts* somewhere in what is now north-west Germany in the first half of the twelfth century. In it he provides detailed instructions for covering the jointed wooden panels of altars, doors, and shields with damp raw hide stuck down with cheese glue. He explains how the hide, when it has dried out, can be covered with as many as three coats of gesso, which is rubbed down until smooth and white. This prepared surface can then be painted red and varnished, so that it is 'made bright, beautiful, and completely lasting'.[32] Theophilus describes how the wooden panels are first glued together and then carefully smoothed with a two-handled draw knife, a process comparable to the careful smoothing of the Round Table planks, after assembly.[33]

At Valère, in Sion, Switzerland, the thirteenth-century doors of the rood-screen are still covered with red leather glued down to the wood and overlain by splendidly scrolled ironwork.[34] Such surviving examples are very rare. One is the door from Högby church, Östergötland, now in the Statens Historiska Museum in Stockholm.

---

[30] Theophilus, writing in the first half of the twelfth century, notes that ordinary unused cloth stuck down with cheese glue can be used to cover wooden panels if skins are not available: see below, n. 32, *De Diversis Artibus*, ed. Dodwell, p. 17 (Bk. I, cap. xvii); *On Divers Arts*, ed. Hawthorne and Smith, p. 27 (Bk. I, cap. 19).

[31] Miss Elisabeth Crowfoot kindly confirmed this identification originally made by Mrs R. M. Eldredge. Theophilus's phrase *cum panno mediocri et novo*, translated by Hawthorne and Smith, p. 27, as 'medium weight new cloth', might possibly include material such as this, but it seems improbable.

[32] *On Divers Arts: the Treatise of Theophilus* ed. John G. Hawthorne and Cyril Stanley Smith (Chicago, 1963), pp. 26–9. For the Latin text with facing translation, see *De Diversis Artibus*, ed. C. R. Dodwell, Nelson's Medieval Texts (London, 1961), pp. 16–20 (Bk. I, cap. xvii–xxi).

[33] See above, p. 117, Fig. 54.

Another is the door now in the Chapter House vestibule, Westminster Abbey, once covered with what is probably cow hide. In England popular superstition has sometimes assumed that the skin occasionally found on church doors was human, usually from a flayed Dane.[35] Even if a few examples may be human (and I, for one, will continue to doubt this until we have additional positive scientific identifications), the majority must be examples of the practice described by Theophilus and seen at Valère.

As Theophilus indicates in mentioning altar panels and shields, as well as doors, skin or leather covered all manner of objects in the Middle Ages, especially furniture. Surviving examples include chests, choir stalls, and cupboards.[36] In the sixteenth and seventeenth centuries leather was used for hangings, screens, bed-covers, and for panelling rooms, as well as for covering terrestial and celestial globes and on tables. The technique used in panelling rooms is particularly interesting: a number of leather panels of identical size were seamed together and the resultant sheet was fixed to the wall with leather covered nails and a narrow leather border. Apart from nailing all round the edges, the leather in effect was hung, and for a time supplanted tapestry because of its rich effect.[37] Surviving examples and records of the craft show that the use of gilded and embossed panels of this kind reached the height of its development and popularity in the sixteenth and seventeenth century and went out of use soon after 1700, but the use of leather for mural decoration is much earlier. The technique began in Spain, traditionally at Cordoba (hence *cordovan* or 'cordwan' leather, and 'cordwainers', who were workers in Spanish leather), using tawed hair-sheep skin, but in the fourteenth century there was a change to the use of bovine (calf) leather which was much better adapted to embossing by hand stamping. The focus of this evolution seems to have been Flanders, where Spanish-Arab *cordouaniers* were established in Mechlin (Malines) before 1305.[38] The gorgeous effect came from the combination of gilding and embossing, enhanced by painted colour.

Very little mural leatherwork has survived from a date earlier than about 1500, although the earliest known pieces are difficult to date,[39] but there are sufficient

---

[34] Albert Naef, *Chillon: La Camera Domini* (Geneva, 1908), pp. 55–7, Figs. 46, 49, 50. I owe this reference and knowledge of the Högby, Östergötland, door to Dr A. J. Taylor.

[35] M. J. Swanton, 'Dane-Skins': Excoriation in Early England', *Folklore* 87 (1976), 21–8; P. V. Addyman and Ian H. Goodall, 'The Norman Church and Door at Stillingfleet, North Yorkshire', *Archaeologia* 106 (1979), 75–105, pp. 103–4.

[36] E.g. Naef, *Chillon*, pp. 58–9; Penelope Eames, *Medieval Furniture* (London, 1977), pp. 111, 115–16, 171, 177.

[37] J. W. Waterer, 'Leather', in Charles Singer et al. (ed.), *A History of Technology* ii (Oxford, 1956), Chapter 5, esp. pp. 178–80.

[38] J. W. Waterer, *Spanish Leather. A History of its Use from 800–1800 for Mural Hangings...* [etc.] (London, 1971), pp. 31–2, 55; the Spanish contribution is usefully summarized on pp. 41–2.

[39] See, for example, Waterer, *Spanish Leather*, pls. 1–5 and the comments on them.

indications of its once widespread use. The most famous surviving example is in the Alhambra of Granada, where the ceilings of three chambers opening off the *Sala de los Reyes* (The Hall of the Kings) at the east end of the Court of the Lions are decorated with paintings on leather. The cupola of the central chamber displays ten figures, perhaps kings of the Nazari dynasty, hence the name of the adjacent hall; to either side the other cupolas present scenes of courtship and chivalry from some as yet unidentified romance. There is general agreement that these paintings belong to the late fourteenth century and show the influence of Christian taste on the Islamic Nazarine kingdom, but much else about them remains unclear.[40] Not so their technique, which has now been minutely studied, not least because of the problems presented by their conservation.[41] The rooms are vaulted with cupolas formed of planks of a species of poplar pegged edge-to-edge with tin-coated iron nails and suspended from a framework of wooden ribs – the similarity to the construction of the Round Table is striking. The wooden vaults are lined with sheep skin, stuck to the wood with wheat flour paste and fixed in the angles of the leather and at the edges with small bamboo-cane tacks which pegged the leather without perforating it. The leather was then coated with fish glue and on to this were laid seven coats of plaster and glue in equal parts, the latter probably mixed with egg-yolk to counteract the possible absorption of humidity. On to this plaster thin sheets of decorative relief were fixed and gilded. The outlines of the figures were then graved into the prepared leather and the paintings were made and waxed against humidity.

One of the glories of the Alhambra, these paintings are all that survive of a tradition of painted leather ceilings which 'represented extraordinary luxury and was a sign of the artistic feeling and good taste of the owner'.[42] Yet their technique was already outmoded. Innovations in Flanders, already described, using bovine leather and hand embossing, marked the route that would eventually be taken, not least in Spain, towards the full development of the use of embossed, gilded and painted leather for interior decoration.

By 1380 King Charles V of France had gilded leather hangings – 'carreaux de cuir tanné ouvré à or' – and in 1423 an inventory of the wardrobe of Henry VI of England included a leather 'carpet', perhaps a cover for some kind of furniture such as a bed or table.[43] As early as 1308, when the tomb of King Sæberht, legendary

---

[40] Oleg Grabar, *La Alhambra: Iconografía, Formas y Valores* (Madrid, 1980), pp. 80–3, 198 (originally published as *The Alhambra* (Harmondsworth, 1978)).

[41] Jesús Bermúdez Pareja, *Pinturas sobre piel en la Alhambra de Granada*, Publicaciones del Patronato de la Alhambra 1 (Granada, 1987), pp. 49–62, 139–50 (English translation).

[42] Ibid., p. 115 (cf. p. 25).

[43] Waterer, *Spanish Leather*, pp. 28, 31, 59.

founder of Westminster Abbey, was rebuilt in a new position on the south side of the High Altar, the vault over the tomb was decorated with paintings which may have used leather in a way similar to that in the painted cupolas of the Alhambra.[44]

Thus, if the Round Table was covered rather than left bare when hung on the wall, the possibility that its cover was leather, embossed, gilded, painted, or all three, should probably not be dismissed out of hand.

Remembering always the extent to which this entire discussion is based on a supposition, can we go further and get any idea of what such a decorated cover (*if ever there was one*) might have shown? Further enquiry can only be speculative, but it raises in an acute form the question of the source of the present – Tudor – design.

The obvious analogue is the Wheel of Fortune, as John Fleming suggests (see above, pp. 25–8, Plate III and Figs. 4–6), where the ruling monarch is enthroned like Arthur at the top and the spokes of the Wheel frame panels which taper to the centre. A Wheel of Fortune was painted on the west wall of the Great Hall in 1235–6 (see above, p. 74) and, since traces of a thirteenth-century scroll border were discovered below whitewash on this wall in 1874,[45] may well have remained visible long enough to influence the Tudor painting of the table. But there is a striking difference: on the Round Table only the ruling king, *Regno*, is shown: the falling, fallen, and future kings – *Regnavi*, *Sine Regno Sum*, and *Regnabo* – are omitted (Fig, 6, where the words are in Spanish). Perhaps this is a direct tribute to Arthur, the once and future king, designed to contrast with the still visible control of Fortune over lesser monarchs on the opposite wall. The inclusion of the 'lesser' kings would also be contrary to the fundamental principle of the Round Table, that the seats are all of equal status.

But there is a more profound reason why Arthur alone is shown. On Trinity Sunday night before his last battle and death

---

[44] Waterer, *ibid.*, p. 48n., states this as a fact, but recent personal inspection of the very fragmentary paintings on the vault of the tomb, with a 15x lens, revealed no certain traces of leather but only under the paint a light brown, ?crystalline, layer which might be the decayed remains of leather. For Saeberht (king of the East Saxons, reigned from before 604 to 616 or 617) and his tomb, see Pamela Tudor-Craig in Christopher Wilson *et al.*, *Westminster Abbey*, The New Bell's Cathedral Guides (London, 1986), p. 106. For the related question of the use of vellum or canvas strips to provide suspension for the gesso base of medieval panel paintings (including the mid thirteenth-century Westminster Retable) over joints in their timber components, see Paul Binski 'What was the Westminster Retable?', *Journal of the British Archaeological Association* 140 (1987), 152–74 at p. 153 with further references.

[45] Melville Portal, *The Great Hall. Winchester Castle* (Winchester and London, 1899), p. 93. It may be relevant that the scroll formed a straight border of the kind which appears on the edges of the Hereford map (Jancey, *Mappa Mundi* (as below, note 57), pp. 6, 8, 10, 12), although in the Great Hall, the map would have been in the opposite gable.

kynge Arthure dremed a wondirfull dreme, and in hys dreme hym semed that he saw uppon a chafflet [scaffold, platform] a chayre, and the chayre was faste to a whele, and thereuppon sate kynge Arthure in the rychest clothe of golde that myght be made. And the kynge thought there was undir hym, farre from hym, an hydeous depe blak watir, and therein was all maner of serpentis and wormes and wylde bestis fowle and orryble. And suddeynly the kynge thought that the whyle turned up-so-downe, and he felle amonge the serpentes, and every beste toke hym by a lymme. And then the kynge cryed as he lay in hys bed,

'Helpe! helpe!'.[46]

This is the text of Malory's *Morte Darthur* as preserved in the Winchester manuscript and published by Caxton in 1485 (see above, p. 278 and Table 15). Malory's source for the dream was at least a century older, the English poem in eight-line stanzas known as *Le Morte Arthur* composed somewhere in the north-west Midlands towards the end of the fourteenth century. It provides an even more striking image of the king on the wheel:

Hym thowht he satte in gold All gledde
As he was comely Kynge with crowne,
Vpon A whele that full wyde spredd,
And All hys knyghtis to hym bowne.
The whele was ferly Ryche And Rownd,
In world was neuyr none halfe so hye;
There-on he satte Rychely crownyd
With many A besaunte broche And be;
he lokyd downe vpon the growND,
A blake water ther vndyr hym he see,
With dragons fele there lay vn-bownde,
That no man durst hem nyghe nyee.
he was wondyr ferd to falle
A-monge the fendys ther that faught;

[46] Eugene Vinaver (ed.), *The Works of Sir Thomas Malory*, 2nd edn. (Oxford, 1967; repr. 1973), iii, p. 1233, and cf. p. 1649; James W. Spisak (ed.), *Caxton's Malory* (Berkeley and Los Angeles, 1983), p. 587 (*Morte Darthur*, Bk. xxi. 3). The first person to draw attention to the parallel between the Winchester Round Table and Arthur's Trinity Sunday dream seems to have been A. A. Barb, '*Mensa Sacra*. The Round Table and the Holy Grail', *Journal of the Warburg and Courtauld Institutes* 19 (1956), 40–67 at n. 98 (p. 66). See further, Alan H. Nelson, 'Mechanical Wheels of Fortune, 1100–1547', *Journal of the Warburg and Coutauld Institute*, 43 (1980), 227–33.

The whele over-tornyd ther with-All
And eueryche by A lymme hym caught.[47]

Here are most of the attributes of the Arthur of the table: a wheel, 'full wyde spredd', 'ferly Ryche and Rownd', 'neuer none halfe so hye', on which he sat and from which he could look 'downe vpon the grownd'. Arthur himself is clad all in gold, 'Rychely crownyd/ With many A besaunte broche And be', 'And All hys knyghtis to hym bowne'.

This English poem is in turn derived from a French prose romance, the *Mort Artu*, written in the earlier part of the thirteenth century. Here Fortune placed Arthur

seur une roe. En cele roe avoit sieges dont li un montoient et li autre avaloient. Li rois regardoit en quel leu de la roe il estoit assis et voit que ses sieges estoit li plus hauz. La dame li demandoit: "Artus, ou ies tu?". "Dame, fet il, ge sui en une haute roe, mes ge ne sei quele ele est." "C'est, fet ele, la roe de Fortune ...".

on a wheel, on which there were seats, some rising and some falling. The king looked to see at which part of the wheel he was sitting, and saw he was at the highest point. The lady asked him:

'Arthur, where are you?'
'My Lady,' he replied, 'I am on a high wheel, but I do not know what kind of a wheel it is'.
'T'is the Wheel of Fortune,' she replied.[48]

It is this French version with its rising and falling seats which inspired medieval artists to illuminate manuscripts of the *Mort Artu* with pictures of Fortune's Wheel on which they showed the falling, fallen, and future kings, as well as the present ruler

[47] J. Douglas Bruce (ed.), *Le Morte Arthur. A Romance in Stanzas of Eight Lines*, EETS Extra ser. 88 (London, 1903; repr. 1959), lines 3172–87 [stanzas 398–400].

[48] For this section of *Mort Artu* (*La Mort le Roi Artu*), a work which forms the fifth and last part of the Vulgate Cycle (the modern name for the most complete account of the Matter of Britain, composed *c.*1215–30 in French prose), see H. O. Sommer (ed.), *The Vulgate Version of the Arthurian Romances*, 8 vols. (Washington, 1908–16), vi, p. 361; J. Frappier (ed.), *La Mort le Roi Artu, roman du XIIIe siècle*, 3rd edn. (Geneve and Paris, 1964), pp. 226–7 (cap. 176, lines 61–7), and for an English version, J. Cable (trans.), *The Death of King Arthur* (Harmondsworth, 1971), p. 205, from which the translation here is taken. For an account of the development of the Death of Arthur theme from Geoffrey of Monmouth to Malory, see Eugène Vinaver (ed.), *The Tale of the Death of King Arthur by Sir Thomas Malory* (Oxford, 1955), pp. vii–xi.

(cf. Plate III, Figs. 4–6).[49] The English *Morte Arthur* and Malory's *Morte Darthur* have but one king; it is their descriptions which come closest to the king on the Round Table (*Frontispiece*). Of the two, it is perhaps the poem, with its details of the king's jewellery and 'All hys knyghtis to hym bowne' which may have inspired the painter of the Winchester table.

When exactly this inspiration took effect is another matter. The *Morte Arthur* in the form we have it is not to be dated much if at all before 1400. But a simpler version of the king at the top of the wheel could have been inspired by the *Mort Artu* at an earlier date. The very fact that the table seems to have had a right-way up, a top, which was preserved in the Tudor painting (see above, pp. 137–8, 396), suggests that the previous decoration had something to indicate which was the top, and the king's figure would have done this very well. The Tudor painting could then in its turn have been influenced by more recent versions of Arthur's dream, whether in the *Morte Arthur* or in Malory.

If the table was decorated before being painted in the Tudor period, the simplest solution is thus to imagine that it had a design similar to that of the Tudor painting. But if so, it cannot have been exactly the same. Quite apart from questions of content, style, and composition, as discussed by Pamela Tudor-Craig in Chapter 9, the red and white rose is impossible before 1485, and the roll-call of knights is post-Malory (Chapter 8). Twenty-four names could easily have been found at an earlier date, but they would have been spelt differently and the list would not have been quite the same. The Wheel of Fortune, whether the idea or the actual painting in the Great Hall, probably did influence the Tudor design, and may have influenced a predecessor, but it does not provide the whole answer. No Wheel of Fortune had so many spokes – eight seems to have been common, sometimes six or ten – and the spokes radiate not from a rose but a hub. What then might be the origin of an arrangement of multiple panels widening outwards from a central rose?

Precisely such a pattern is implicit in the design of the badge carved on the tie-beams of the Great Hall roof, where a central rose is surrounded by a series of tapering rays (Fig. 28). The six badges are not exactly the same. Three have 16 rays,

---

[49] There is another English version, the 14th-cent. alliterative romance known as the *Morte Arthure* (the minor variations in the titles of the various versions are critical in distinguishing between them), which contains a long and very different description of Arthur's dream and sets him on the wheel in the company of several other kings in different positions of fortune: Erik Björkman (ed.), *Morte Arthure*, Alt- und Mittelenglische Texte 9 (Heidelberg and New York, 1915), lines 3260–93, and esp. for Arthur's clothing and the wheel, lines 3349–81. This poem is derived principally from Wace (see above, pp. 9–13; 350–1), but the dream is a new element, greatly elaborated from the version in the *Mort Artu*. For the latest edition, see Mary Hamel (ed.), *Morte Arthure*, Garland Medieval Texts 9 (New York, 1984).

the others 10, 14, or 18; four have 5 petals to the rose, the others 4 or 6; and the centres of the roses are all slightly different. But the principle is the same and each pair of rays defines in the field between them a panel which widens outwards from the rose, as in the painted design of the Round Table.

In the late seventeenth century, John Aubrey noted that the table was divided 'like a sea chart' (see below, p. 492), a comment which takes us straight to the related ideas of the compass rose and the wind rose. On a compass rose the rhumb lines radiate from a central point, defining the segments of a circle. Despite the name, an actual flower seems never to have been drawn at the meeting point of the rhumb lines, although a top mark (later a fleur-de-lys) indicates the 'uprightness' of the design, as does the king on the Round Table.[50] Compass roses were drawn directly on to sea charts, hence Aubrey's comment. The first known example occurs in the Catalan Atlas of 1375, the next in Sentuzo Pongeto's chart of 1404, but it is not until the second half of the fifteenth century that the compass rose became commonplace.[51] They then have 32 lines radiating from the centre, but this was apparently an innovation of Petrus Roselli in 1456–68, and previously only sixteen lines were shown.

It is the number sixteen which relates the compass rose directly to the wind rose then in use. The classical world recognized more than one system of winds.[52] The fundamental four-fold division corresponded to the four quarters of the heavens as astronomically defined by sunrise, sunset, noon, and celestial pole, and to the four quarters as defined by contrasting winds. These could be sub-divided. The Tower of the Winds in Athens shows the winds personified on the eight faces of an octagon, and there was also the twelve-fold division of Aristotle. Aristotle's was the scholastic system of the Middle Ages, one version of which *secundum magistrum Elyam de Derham* ('according to Master Elias of Dereham') is preserved for us in a copy drawn by the St Alban's monk Matthew Paris before 1259.[53] Matthew also produced his own version of the twelve-fold system,[54] but went further and drew a diagram which

---

[50] Heinrich Winter, 'A Late Portolan Chart at Madrid and Late Portolan Charts in General', *Imago Mundi* 7 (1950), 37–46, esp. fig. on p. 38.

[51] Tony Campbell, 'Portolan Charts from the Late Thirteenth Century to 1500', in J. B. Harley and David Woodward (ed.) *The History of Cartography* i (Chicago, 1987), pp. 371–463, at pp. 395–7. Professor P. D. A. Harvey kindly provided this and other references in the course of discussing this problem.

[52] For the classical winds, see Harley and Woodward, *History of Cartography*, pp. 145–6, 153, 248–9, and for Aristotle's winds, Fig. 8.14.

[53] E. G. R. Taylor, 'The *De Ventis* of Matthew Paris', *Imago Mundi* 2 (1937), 23–6, illustration facing p. 23, after BL, Cotton MS. Nero D.i, fol. 184r; see Richard Vaughan, *Matthew Paris*, 2nd edn. (Cambridge, 1979), pp. 255–6.

[54] Vaughan, *Matthew Paris*, p. 255 and Pl. XX*d*, after Corpus Christi College, Cambridge, MS. 385, Part II, p. 152.

seems to be the earliest surviving example of the adaptation of this system to the sixteen-fold division then in use by seamen in northern waters.[55]

There are two quite separate issues here: the existence by the mid thirteenth century of the sixteen-fold division of the winds to which we shall return, and the interest in the subject taken by Elias of Dereham. Elias was in charge of the completion of the Great Hall in Winchester Castle in the 1230s and his interest in the winds has suggested that he might also have been consulted about the *mappa mundi* painted in the hall in 1239, apparently by Master Nigel 'chaplain and painter in the king's hall and chapel' (see above, pp. 74–5). Matthew's version of Elias's diagram of the winds consists of a large blank circle surrounded by three narrow concentric bands, the outermost divided into the twelve winds. This blank circle would surely have contained a map of the world, a *mappa mundi*, just as Matthew's own diagram of the twelve winds contained a T-shaped world diagram,[56] and like the Hereford World Map was also contained within a narrow border divided into the twelve winds.[57] The point seems not to have been made that the top of the Hereford Map is gabled just as such a map would have had to be to fit on to a gable wall, whether of the hall at Winchester or the king's chamber at Westminster.[58] All this suggests that at Winchester from 1239 onwards there was a diagram of the winds, labelled in segments around the perimeter of a world map exactly as the knights' names were eventually to be written around the edge of the Round Table.

To return to the sixteen winds. Three of the six badges on the tie-beams of the Great Hall have sixteen rays; the other three badges have 10, 14, and 18 rays respectively.[59] To discover whether the number sixteen might be significant in this context we have to look at the possible origins and meaning of this badge – the irradiated rose.[60] Edward I was the first king of England to use the rose as one of his badges, a golden rose on a green stalk (a *rose or, stalked vert*, in heraldic terms). Henry IV

[55] Vaughan, *Matthew Paris*, pp. 255–6; BL, Cotton MS. Nero D.i, fol. 184v; discussed in Taylor, '*De Ventis*'.

[56] Vaughan, *Matthew Paris*, Pl. XXd.

[57] N. J. Morgan in Jonathan Alexander and Paul Binski (ed.), *Age of Chivalry. Art in Plantagenet England 1200–1400*, Exhibition Catalogue, Royal Academy of Arts (London, 1987), No. 36; N. J. Morgan, *Early Gothic Manuscripts 1250–85*, A Survey of Manuscripts Illuminated in the British Isles iv. 2 (London, 1987), no. 188. See also Peter Wiseman, 'Julius Caesar and the Hereford World Map', *History Today* 37 (Nov. 1987), 53–7; and, with convenient large-scale illustrations from the lithograph made from drawings and published in 1869, Meryl Jancey, *Mappa Mundi. The Map of the World in Hereford Cathedral. A Brief Guide* (Hereford, 1987). For a full discussion, see now P. D. A. Harvey, *Mappa Mundi. The Hereford World Map* (Hereford and London, 1999); see also, David Woodward, 'Medieval *Mappaemundi*', in Harley and Woodward, *History of Cartography*, pp. 286–370.

[58] Vaughan, *Matthew Paris*, p. 247.

[59] I am most grateful to Dr Beatrice Clayre for her careful recording of these badges from a specially erected scaffold and to Mr John Crook for his photographs (see Fig. 28 and above, pp. 78–80).

combined a red rose with the sun in splendour to make a *rose en soleil*; Edward IV bore the white rose and sun – again the *rose en soleil*; Edward V and Richard III used the white rose; and Henry VII and his successors used the red and white rose combined (the Tudor rose), as on the Round Table. A sun badge may first have been used by Edward III in the form of sunbeams issuing from a cloud. Richard II bore the sun in splendour, usually with a face and with alternating wavy and straight rays. Richard III also used the sun in splendour, and Henry IV and Edward IV, as we have seen, combined the rose and sun.

There is no *contemporary* evidence that Edward III used the sunburst of gold rays issuing from a cloud, which is principally attributed to him on the basis of a College of Arms manuscript of the sixteenth century.[61] On any grounds, therefore, the Winchester badges pose a problem, if correctly assigned to the mid fourteenth century by the dating of the timber-work with which they are integral (see above, p. 78). There is, however, another interpretation of Edward III's supposed sunburst badge. Long ago A. C. Fox-Davies suggested that it was not a sunburst at all but rather 'an attempt to pictorially represent the name "Windsor" by depicting "winds" of "or"'.[62] Here the sixteen rays of three of the six Winchester badges may have something to contribute, if they reflect, as now seems possible, the sixteen-wind system of contemporary seamen's practice. Such a canting badge, alluding to Edward's birth at Windsor, although to us an atrocious pun, would be quite typical of at least later medieval heraldry. Early forms of the name Windsor (*Windesores* in Domesday Book, with variant spellings *Windesoris, Windesor(e), Wyndesore, Wyndesor'*, down to 1600)[63] seem

---

[60] J. H. and R. V. Pinches, *The Royal Heraldry of England* (London, 1974); A. C. Fox-Davies, *Heraldic Badges* (London, 1907); A. C. Fox-Davies, *A Complete Guide to Heraldry* (1st edn., London, 1909; rev. by J. P. Brooke-Little, London, 1985). I am grateful to Mrs Rosemary Pinches for her comments and advice in letters to Dr Beatrice Clayre on the problem of the rose irradiated badge in general and the Winchester badges in particular.

[61] College of Arms, MS. I.2, made 1510–25 and published by Joseph Foster, *et al.*, *Banners, Standards and Badges from a Tudor Manuscript in the College of Arms* (London, n.d.). I am grateful to Mrs Pinches for this reference.

[62] Fox-Davies, *Heraldic Badges*, (London and New York, 1907), p. 53. C. W. Scott-Giles, *The Romance of Heraldry* (London, 1965), p. 88. disagreed, pointing out that the badge was described as a sunburst at an early date [when?], and suggesting that Edward III may have adopted it either by taking Richard I's sun-badge as its basis, or simply, without thought of precedent, taking the rays of the sun as the natural symbol of monarchy. The Winchester badges, apparently datable to the mid fourteenth century by their associated tracery, provide an entirely new element in the discussion and seem to require a better-founded explanation than that offered by Scott-Giles.

[63] Margaret Gelling, *The Place-Names of Berkshire* i (Cambridge, 1973), pp. 26–7; in fact the name, as the form *Windlesoran* and variants from the mid eleventh century onwards show, is derived from the OE words *windels* and *ora*, with the meaning 'river-bank with a windlass'. But this is no objection to the use of the apparent form of the name in the kind of pun discussed here.

to offer no objection, even if the word 'wind' would normally have been pronounced to rhyme with 'behind', 'bind', 'find', 'mind', and so forth, before the present pronunciation became common in polite speech in the eighteenth century.[64]

There remains the problem of the rose, but if the Winchester rays *are* winds, the centre of the badge would not in any case be a cloud. It might seem to be going too far to believe that this badge is in literal form a wind-rose, but that does seem to be where this line of argument leads.

If we accept this interpretation of the Winchester badges, what are the implications? First, that the tie-beams of the roof are acceptably dated to the reign of Edward III. Second, that in Winchester of all places, with its strong Arthurian traditions, a statement was being made of the claims of Windsor to an equally strong, if not stronger, link with Arthur and his Round Table. This is precisely what was being claimed at the time: that Windsor Castle had been built by King Arthur and was the place where the Round Table had originally been founded.[65] These beliefs, enhanced by his own birth in the castle, were powerful elements in Edward III's attachment to Windsor, in his founding there of the still-born Order of the Round Table in 1344, and in his creation at the castle in 1348 of the Most Noble Order of the Garter. In the face of such beliefs, the Round Table at Winchester may have been something of an embarrassment, not to be destroyed, but certainly to be made to tell an appropriate tale.

Is it possible, however, that the badges on the tie-beams were only one part of an even more direct attempt to call attention to the claims of Windsor? We have already noted that these badges provide an analogue for the basic design of the Tudor painting on the Round Table: a central rose surrounded by radiating panels. Although the painted segments on the table reverse the tapering rays of the badges, there is an obvious relationship between the widening panels of the table with their perimeter inscriptions, the widening fields defined by the rays of the badges, and the inscribed segments of wind-roses such as those drawn by Matthew Paris, or to be found in sectors around the perimeter of medieval world maps such as the Hereford map and such, probably, as the map painted in the hall in 1239.

Indeed the Great Hall with this map, the Wheel of Fortune, and the badges of the roof provides a rich context within which to explore not only the sources of the Tudor design painted on the Round Table, but also the question of what design

---

[64] *OED*, s.v. 'wind'.

[65] Jean Froissart, *Chroniques*, ed. S. Luce, L. Mirot, *et al.*, Société de l'histoire de France iii (Paris, 1872), p. 37, relying on Jean Le Bel, *Chronique*, ed. J. Viard and E. Déprez, Société de l'histoire de France ii (Paris, 1905), p. 26; discussed by Vale, *Edward III and Chivalry*, p. 77.

might have been painted on a covering over the surface of the table when it was first hung up.

The most likely treatment of the cover was probably close to that of the badges in the roof: a central rose surrounded by rays with, if we accept the evidence of Giovio, names of knights written around the edge between the ends of the rays. Whether the figure of Arthur was shown, reflecting the Wheel of Fortune on the west wall of the hall, or whether this was a Tudor innovation, must remain open, although there seems to have been something to indicate the uprightness of the design. The question of whether there was an identifying inscription like that now written around the central rose must likewise remain open.

When one looks today from the table to the badges on the underside of the tie-beams, the resemblances are striking. They would once have been more so had the table stated the main theme now only reflected in the badges. From this arises the possibility that the decoration of the table and the making of the badges were done at the same time and originally presented a unified programme intended to provide an appropriate setting for the hanging table, while at the same time calling attention by its canting design to Windsor as the place where the Round Table had begun and where, whether as Round Table or as Garter, it had now been refounded.

There are two good parallels for such a decoration on a round table, although both are much later in date, and both show a sun, not winds. One is the table from Schloss Clappenburg painted with a calendrical design of 1497 (Plate VII); the other is the disc – I take it to be a table top – on which are laid out the volumes of Jacob Mennel's 'History of the Imperial House', published in 1518 (Fig. 161).

Two points remain. In examining the names of the twenty-four knights which appear on the table today, it became clear that the last half dozen or so were the obscurest of the lot and it looks possible that one or more of them might have been chosen because of a recent appearance in print (see above, p. 282). If these six or so names at the end of the list represent an addition to a sequence of better known knights, including all the most famous names, is it possible that this sequence provides the roll-call of those knights whose names appeared on the postulated original decoration? If so, the names have been revised to conform with Malory or post-Malory forms. Some may even have been replaced or their order changed, particularly if, as Giovio indicates, the original names were badly decayed.

Finally, to return to our starting point, if some such original design as that suggested here had indeed pointed to Windsor, Hardyng may have been making a most pointed remark when he claimed that

The Rounde Table at Wynchestre beganne.

Is this, at last, the political message of Hardyng's additional lines: that attention should now be redirected back from Windsor, so favoured by Henry VI, to Winchester?

This long and speculative review of the most obscure period in the history of the table has revealed a complex pattern of evidence and suggestion within a wide range of possible sources for elements in a putative predecessor of the present painted design. It may be as well to distinguish the main threads in this tangled skein:

1   The table had been hanging for a long time before being taken down, repaired, and painted in the Tudor period.

2   The table may first have been hung up in 1348–9, the date at which the hall seems to have been remodelled.

3   The table may have been hung up as a bare, undecorated disc, but this seems improbable in a medieval context.

4   There are reasons for believing, to the contrary, that when it was hung up the table was provided with a decorated cloth or, more likely, leather cover.

5   By considering the origins of the present design on the table and the possible significance of the badges on the tie-beams, some ideas emerge as to what the principal elements of the original design might have been.

6   These ideas may suggest that an attempt was being made in 1348–9, while preserving the table, to draw attention to Windsor as the place where the Round Table had begun and where, in the sense of Edward III's Order of the Garter, it remained.

7   The offices held at various stages in their careers by William Edington, bishop of Winchester 1346–66, and by the young William of Wykeham, bishop 1367–1404, may suggest that they played a role in making the Winchester table into an ikon which reflected the transition to Windsor.

8   The appointment of the bishop of Winchester as prelate of the Garter *ex officio* may have been intended as a permanent and public demonstration of approval and acceptance of this transition, an act of legitimation.

For nearly two centuries, from 1348 until 1516, the Round Table hung on the east wall of Winchester castle hall. During these years, water coming in through the gable window gradually rotted the uppermost parts of its wooden frame and, as we can now perceive, will have loosened the glue of its cloth or leather cover and gradually destroyed the painted decoration. Here then, it seems, is the explanation of Paolo Giovio's statement that 'the names of the knights around the edge ... had been badly eaten away by decay' before the restoration which preceded Charles V's visit in 1522 (see above, p. 405).

Welsh poets and the Tudor king, voices from the periphery and the centre, cast unexpected light on the appearance of the table in the last years of the fifteenth and first years of the sixteenth century. Some time between 1509 and *c*.1513 Rhys Nanmor wrote a poem in Welsh to Lewis Môn, a smith then living in the neighbourhood of Temple Bar in London, praising a buckler (a small, round shield) which he was thanking for or requesting. One of the features of the buckler was that it was

> Llawn hoelion Bord Gron Caerwynt
> Llonaid grât llun deigr ydynt

> Full of rivets like the Round Table of Winchester,
> A grate full, they are like tears.[66]

Welsh bucklers were covered on the outside with concentric rings of metal plates fastened to a leather base by iron rivets with small domed brass heads, the point of the simile.

Rhys Nanmor was a 'family poet' who wrote primarily in honour of Sir Rhys ap Thomas, the chief Welsh supporter of Henry VII. Sir Rhys was created a Knight of the Garter on 23 April 1505 and continued in favour after the accession of Henry VIII, distinguishing himself in the invasion of France in 1513. Rhys Nanmor's poems to Sir Rhys ap Thomas cover the years from *c*.1485 to *c*.1513. He wrote an elegy for Prince Arthur in 1502, and a poem to welcome Henry VIII to the throne in 1509, but there is no evidence of anything written by him after 1513.[67]

---

[66] Ifor Edwards and Claude Blair, 'Welsh Bucklers'. *Antiquaries Journal* 62 (1982), 74–115, at pp. 78 (translation) and 95 (Welsh text): Winchester appears here under its Welsh name, *Caerwynt*, a better reading of which would be the lenited form *Gaerwynt*. I am most grateful to my friend Nicholas Griffiths for first drawing my attention to this reference, and to Professor Ellis Evans for translating and elucidating for me the standard edition of the works of Lewis Môn (Eurys I. Rowlands (ed.), *Gwaith Lewys Môn* (Cardiff, 1975)), where the poem of Rhys Nanmor, his relationship to Lewis Môn, and the question of whether Lewis Môn the smith and Lewis Môn the poet are one and the same is discussed on p. xiv. I owe an especial debt to Dr Gruffydd Aled Williams for his detailed and generous response to my enquiries, for examining the manuscript copies of Rhys Nanmor's poem, for pointing out and commenting on Tudur Aled's couplet on the Round Table, and for his general guidance. It can be taken that everything of value in the paragraphs which follow are due to him, while the errors are mine.

[67] *Dictionary of Welsh Biography Down to 1540* (henceforth *DWB*) (London, 1959), s.nn. Rhys ap Thomas (pp. 840–1), and Rhys Nanmor (p. 843). M. G. Headley, 'Barddoniaeth Llawdden a Rhys Nanmor' ['The Poetry of Llawdden and Rhys Nanmor'], University of Wales (Bangor), unpublished MA thesis (1938), p. li. The poem by Rhys Nanmor to Lewis Môn is included on pp. 158–62 of this thesis, for knowledge of which I am indebted to Professor Evans and Dr Williams.

Lewis Môn was also a poet, or so it seems, as well as being a smith and 'acting as a squire' for Henry VIII 'over Canterbury', for he must surely be the same as the Lewis Môn who composed an elegy on Rhys Nanmor.[68] This Lewis Môn wrote in honour of the Penrhyn family, died in 1527, and was buried at Valle Crucis abbey.[69] But when was he working in London? The chronology of Rhys Nanmor's poems suggests that it was at the very beginning of Henry VIII's reign, between 1509 and *c.*1513.

If this is correct, the rivets of which Rhys Nanmor writes must have been visible on the front of the table, for it was not until 1516 that the table was taken down and repaired from the back with up to a hundred iron spikes. If Rhys Nanmor was still writing as late as 1516, he might possibly have heard of (or even seen) the repairs of the table and have been inspired to his comparison by the bright metal of the new spikes seen from the back. Indeed, in one type of Welsh buckler, the concentric metal rings are crossed by narrow laths which radiate from the centre and are fastened together by rivets placed at the points where rings and laths intersect.[70] The effect is remarkably like the back of the Round Table where spikes transfix the vertical spars as they intersect with the radials of the original structure (Figs. 40, 43, 62).

But this is a curious comparison. Rhys Nanmor's words would refer more naturally to a series of dome-headed nails applied to the front of the table to hold down a cloth or leather cover, such as is argued above had once existed (pp. 407–9). No trace of the holes for such nails has been seen on the X-rays, but being only in the surface of the table, the holes would probably have been filled in when the table was painted and would now be invisible. In fact, if the 'rivets' were nailed in over the radials or ledges, their holes would probably also be invisible on the X-rays, due to the relative radio-opacity of those areas where the X-rays had to pass through several layers of wood.

There is fortunately no need to make the odd assumption that Rhys Nanmor was referring to the back of the table during the short time it was visible late in 1516, for he had probably seen it, or heard of its appearance some time before. In 1492 Sir Rhys ap Thomas was party to an indenture binding him to bring his men to Winchester by 9 June 1492 en route for Portsmouth and the expedition to France of that year.[71]

---

[68] Mary Headley (see last note) took this view, but Eurys Rowlands left the question unresolved (as n. 66, p. xiv).

[69] *DWB*, s.n. Lewis Môn (p. 545).

[70] Edwards and Blair, 'Welsh Bucklers' (as n. 66), p. 83 (Type 2), and see Pl. XVIa.

[71] J. M. Lloyd, 'The Rise and Fall of the House of Dinefwr (The Rhys Family) 1430–1530', University of Wales (Cardiff), unpublished MA thesis (1963), p. 27, referring to the text of the indenture (PRO, E101/72/6) given in an Appendix to the thesis (p. 121).

Sir Rhys was probably in Winchester again in 1509. The evidence comes from another poem by Rhys Nanmor which refers to the passing of Henry VII and to the expectations aroused by the accession of Henry VIII.[72] The poem is addressed to Sir Rhys and makes two references to Winchester:

Am aer aparawnt y mae'r hynt, am ŵr
Ym Merwig a Chaer Wynt

The jouney(?) concerns an heir apparent,
it concerns(?) a man in [both] Berwick and Winchester.

This is certainly cryptic; the second reference is quite precise:

Offrwn I'r Grog goffraid yn Wyntmestr

Make an offering of a chestful [i.e. of money]
to the Rood/Cross at Winchester.

These verses show that Sir Rhys ap Thomas was in Winchester in 1492 and *c.*1509, that Rhys Nanmor knew of the second visit, and thus may have seen the Round Table for himself, or been told about it by someone in Sir Rhys's entourage, or even by Sir Rhys himself.

Another poem requesting a buckler, addressed to Richard Herbert, constable at Aberystwyth castle, by the poet Tudur Aled (fl. 1450–1526), clinches the matter. It contains the following couplet:

Fo eurwyd graens y Ford Gron
Wrth aelwyd a myrthylion.

The grains of the Round Table have been gilded
By means of a hearth and hammers.[73]

---

[72] I owe this information entirely to Dr Williams. The poem is presented in Mary Headley's thesis (as n. 67), pp. 233–44, and the two quotations appear on pp. 239 and 242, respectively.

[73] I again owe this reference and comments upon it to Dr Williams. See T. Gwynn Jones (ed.), *Gwaith Tudur Aled* (Cardiff, 1926), ii, p. 456.

The phrase 'the grains of the Round Table' is here used metaphorically to refer to the rivets on the buckler, the word *graens* being borrowed from English 'grains'.

The poem was probably composed before 13 October 1513 when Richard Herbert was knighted, for the poet nowhere greets Herbert as 'Sir Richard' or refers to his knighthood, a highly unlikely omission given the conventions of poems in the Welsh eulogistic tradition.[74]

The evidence of these Welsh poems seems conclusive: the Round Table as it was known to Welshmen prior to the repairs of 1516 was notable for presenting an appearance comparable to that of a Welsh buckler and in particular for being decorated with a great number of gilded 'grains', or 'rivets'. There can be little doubt that these were gilded dome-headed nails used to fasten down the decorated cover of leather or cloth. They may have been mainly around the edge, under the raised rim added in 1516, but it seems more likely that they were at least in concentric rings and perhaps in radial lines, and thus comparable in pattern to the riveting of Welsh bucklers. If, as already noted, the nails were placed over the radial spokes, concentric ledges, and felloes of the frame, their removal prior to painting would probably have left no observable trace.

The last words in this complex matter may perhaps be left to King Henry VII. In January 1506 Philip of Burgundy, king of Castile, archduke of Austria, was wrecked on the south coast of England while on his way from the Low Countries to Spain.[75] With him were his queen Joanna, sister of Catherine of Aragon, and a great part of his court. On 13 January King Philip's ship managed to make harbour at Melcombe Regis, near Weymouth in Dorset, but his fleet, or what survived of it, was scattered from Falmouth to Wight. When Henry learnt of the disaster, he sent Sir Thomas Brandon to escort the king archduke with appropriate dignity towards Windsor; and a few days later he despatched Henry, prince of Wales, to meet Philip

---

[74] W. G. Lewis, 'Astudiaeth o Ganu'r Beirdd i'r Herbertiaid hyd ddechrau'r Unfed ganrif ar Bymtheg' ['A Study of Poetry Addressed to Members of the Herbert Family up to the Beginning of the Sixteenth Century'], University of Wales (Bangor), unpublished Ph.D. thesis (1982), i, pp. 244–6 (for a new edition of the poem), and ii, p. 255 (for the date).

[75] The wreck and Philip's subsequent sojourn in England are dealt with in all the standard histories of the period, e.g.: J. D. Mackie, *The Earlier Tudors 1485–1558* (Oxford, 1952), pp. 184–7; S. B. Chrimes, *Henry VII* (paperback edn., London, 1977, repr. 1987), pp. 289–91; R. B. Wernham, *Before the Armada. The Growth of English Foreign Policy 1485–1588* (London, 1966), pp. 55–7. More detailed accounts from specific points of view are given by M. L. Bruce, *The Making of Henry VIII* (London, 1977), pp. 179–93, and Garrett Mattingly, *Catherine of Aragon* (London, 1950), pp. 65–70. All depend on two basic sources: an English account, probably written by a herald, printed in James Gairdner (ed.), *Memorials of King Henry the Seventh*, Rolls ser. (London, 1858), pp. 282–303, cf. p. lv; and a description in French by a Flemish member of Philip's suite published in L. P. Gachard (ed.), *Collection des Voyages des Souverains des Pays-Bas* i (Brussels, 1876), pp. 389–480. This Franco-Flemish account seems to have been written down as soon as events happened (Gachard (ed.), p. xxiii) and is the only one to preserve details of the Garter dinner at Windsor on 9 February (ibid. pp. 424–5).

at Winchester. The prince was fourteen, on his first diplomatic mission. Bishop Fox received King Philip at Winchester and dined him magnificently in his palace of Wolvesey on 30 January. Prince Henry arrived – *grandement et noblement acompagnié* – at vespers (about 5 pm). Such was the immediate accord between the young prince and his brother-in-law, the king archduke, that to one observer at least they seemed *frères et bons amis*. The next morning after dinner (rather before noon) they set out for Windsor, to be greeted by King Henry a mile or so before the castle.

For the English king, Philip's enforced visit was an occasion for display, courtesy, and hospitality. It was also an opportunity for diplomacy: a commercial treaty (unfavourable to the Netherlands but open to indefinite delay), arrangements for the marriage of King Henry to Margaret of Savoy, daughter of the Emperor Maximilian, and for the betrothal of Mary Tudor to Philip's son, Charles of Ghent, the future Emperor Charles V (arrangements pleasing to both sides and readily ratified by Maximilian who was under no obligation to do so), and a secret and unlimited alliance 'binding themselves to be friends of friends and enemies of enemies without excepting any prince in Christendom and notwithstanding any alliance previously contracted.'[76] The Treaty of Windsor, sworn and signed on 9 February 1506, countered the Treaty of Blois entered into the year before by Louis XII of France and Ferdinand of Aragon.[77] Windsor laid the foundations of the friendly relations between England and the Empire which endured for the next two decades – and provided the setting for the meetings of Henry VIII and Charles V described in the next chapter.

The signing of the Treaty of Windsor on 9 February 1506 was solemnized by mass in St George's Chapel, at which King Philip was admitted to the Order of the Garter and Prince Henry to the Golden Fleece. Returning from mass, the two kings and the prince of Wales dined together alone in a small chamber, the kings wearing the Garter and the prince wearing the Fleece. After regretting the absence of the Emperor Maximilian, Henry VII went on:

> Toutesfois, puisqu'il ne peult estre, je vous prometz que ceste assemblée ne plaira guère à noz ennemis, et qu'ilz ne s'en esjoïront de riens: aussi n'est-elle point faicte à leur advantaige. Vous avez veu à Wincestre la table ronde pendue en l'église, et en a-l'on beaucop parlé et escript: mais j'espère que l'on parlera cy-après de ceste-icy, et que l'on dira, longtemps après noz déceps, que à ladicte table furent faictes la vraye amitié perpétuelle d'entre l'empire de Romme, le royaulme de Castille, Flandres, Brabant et du royaulme d'Engleterre. Et vous prometz que la table en sera mise en lieu où elle

[76] Mattingly, *Catherine of Aragon*, p. 68.
[77] Ibid.; Chrimes, *Henry VII*, p. 288; Mackie, *Earlier Tudors*, p. 154.

pourra estre veue, et escript le jour et la noble compagnye qui ont mengié dessus, affin qu'il soit à tous jours mais mémoire de l'amitié et alliance qui y a esté faicte.

Nevertheless, although that cannot be, I promise you that this gathering will in no way please our enemies, and that they will have nothing to rejoice about: this was not done for their good. Hung up in the church at Winchester you saw the Round Table about which so much has been said and written: I hope that in time to come people will speak of this table at which we sit here, and that long after our passing they will say that it was at this table that true and lasting friendship was made between the Holy Roman Empire, the kingdom of Castile, Flanders, Brabant, and the kingdom of England. I promise you that this table will be put where it will be able to be seen and that the date and the noble company who dined at it will be written upon it, so that it may for ever be a memorial of the friendship and alliance which have been made at it.[78]

As far as we know, the table used for this Windsor dinner was not preserved as Henry promised, or if it was, has not survived, but the pictures we have of other Garter dinners à trois suggest that it too was probably a round table (Plate X). Henry would scarcely have made his promise in these terms, referring directly to the Round Table at Winchester which Philip (and perhaps the prince of Wales) had seen only ten days before, if the Winchester table had been a blank uninscribed and thus unidentified disk. Henry VII, or at least his reported speech, is perhaps our clearest witness that the Round Table at Winchester was indeed decorated and inscribed before it was painted for the first time some ten years later.

[78] Gachard (ed.), pp. 424–5. Henry's statement that the Round Table was hanging 'in the church' is by far the earliest expression of the view that the Great Hall was a chapel, an idea not finally quashed until well into the 19th century (see above, p. 87; below, p. 497, 502). That Henry could take this view shows how completely all memory of the use of the castle as a royal palace had faded since the fire of 1302 had destroyed the royal apartments leaving only the Great Hall of the palace intact.

12

The Painting of the Table

O n Friday, 6 June 1522, towards 7 in the evening, Henry VIII and Charles V, Emperor-elect of the Romans, made their entry into London.[1] Riding side-by-side, on identical mounts and dressed identically, except that Henry wore the Order of the Fleece and Charles the Garter, the two young rulers – Henry was 30, Charles 22 – approached the drawbridge at the south end of London Bridge.[2] Here the Bridge Gate was guarded by the figures of two giants, Hercules and Samson, who held aloft between them an iron chain from which hung a tablet inscribed in gold on blue with the names of Charles's lands and dominions. Under these, perhaps on another tablet, were written the verses:

> Carolus, Henricus, vivant defensor uterque
> Henricus fidei, Carolus Ecclesie.

On each of the pageants which followed, on the Great Cross in Cheap, and in every street these lines celebrating friendship, equality, and shared power were repeated in golden letters. Sometimes they were in English:

---

[1] The entry has been analysed in detail by Sydney Anglo, *Spectacle, Pageantry, and Early Tudor Policy* (Oxford, 1969), Chapter V, and by Jean Robertson, 'L'Entrée de Charles Quint à Londres, en 1522', in J. Jacquot (ed.), *Les fêtes de la Renaissance* ii, *Fêtes et cérémonies au temps de Charles Quint* (Paris, 1960), pp. 169–81, who both give full references to the principal sources. For the itinerary of the visit, which offers some problems in its later stages, see below, pp. 429–32.

[2] The identical apparel of the two rulers is noted by most observers, but see especially Alonso de Santa Cruz, *Crónica del Emperador Carlos V,* ed. Ricardo Beltrán y Rózpide and Antonio Blázquez y Delgado-Aguilera (Madrid, 1920), p. 515 ('no sólo en las voluntades mas aun en las cabalgaduras y vestiduras iban conformes'), and Charles's own comments in a letter of 9 June 1522 to the seigneur de la Chaulx quoted by L. P. Gachard in *Biographie Nationale ... de Belgique* iii (Brussels, 1872), col. 540.

Long prosperitie
To Charles and Henry Princes moste puissant.
The one of fayth
The other of the Churche Chosen defendant.[3]

The allusions were topical. Henry had received the title *Fidei Defensor* from Pope Leo X only the year before, and felt himself at last equally honoured with the kings of Spain and France, Charles *rex Catholicus* and Francis *rex Christianissimus*, whose titles had been bestowed by the pope in 1494 and in the fourteenth century, respectively. Henry's title, long sought, had in the end been awarded following the publication of the king's book, *Assertio Septem Sacramentorum* ('The Defence of the Seven Sacraments'), against Martin Luther in the summer of 1521. The application to Charles of the unofficial title *Defensor Ecclesie* was a neat reference to the Imperial Edict of the Diet of Worms issued on 26 May 1521 which placed Luther under the ban of the empire.[4] The author of the couplet was that William Lily (*c.*1468– 1522), high master of St Paul's and celebrated Latinist, who wrote verses for six of the following pageants and an *acclamatio* of the emperor which was perhaps delivered at the Great Cross in Cheap.[5]

From the giants, the streets lined by the livery companies and by the clergy, the route of the procession was punctuated at intervals by a series of eight pageants. At the middle of London Bridge Jason and Medea celebrated the Order of the

3 The Latin and English texts are those given in Edward Hall, *The Vnion of the Two Noble and Illustre Famelies of Lancastre & Yorke*, (London, 1548), Henry VIII, fol. 98r. The other English versions (e.g. those given in the Pynson pamphlet and in the Corpus MS., for which see below, nn. 5 and 6) appear to be subsequent translations rather than (as here) the actual text displayed in the streets. The Latin couplet was also set up in Guildhall, over the door of the council chamber, where it was still to be seen long afterwards: John Speed, *The History of Great Britaine* (London, 1611), p. 758, quoted in Walter Scott (ed.), *A Collection of Scarce and Valuable Tracts* [Somers Tracts], i (London, 1809), p. 32. The couplet also appeared in Winchester, see below, p. 431.

4 For *Fidei Defensor*, see Anglo, *Spectacle, Pageantry*, pp. 173–4, 205, and J. J. Scarisbrick, *Henry VIII* (London, 1968), pp. 115–17. For the Spanish title, see Henry Kamen, *Spain 1469–1714. A Society of Conflict* (London and New York, 1983), p. 35. The French title was first used in certain 14th-cent. papal documents and exclusively attributed to the French kings from the 15th cent. onwards: *Grand Larousse Encyclopédique* 3 (Paris, 1960), s.v. 'Chrétien'. For the *Assertio* and the Edict, see Scarisbrick, *Henry VIII*, pp. 110–15; and V. H. H. Green, *Renaissance and Reformation* 2nd edn. (London, 1964), pp. 117–26, esp. p. 123, respectively. For this interpretation of *Defensor Ecclesie* in relation to Charles, see Speed, *History of Great Britaine*, pp. 758–60.

5 C. R. Baskerville, 'William Lily's Verse for the Entry of Charles V into London', *Huntingdon Library Bulletin* 9 (1936), 1–14, gives the text of the verses as printed by Richard Pynson. For Lily, see Anglo, *Spectacle, Pageantry*, pp. 182, 187–9, 199–200, with further references. Since he was godson of William Grocyn, a Wykehamist, and his home was at Odiham in Hampshire, less than 25 miles from Winchester, Lily may himself have been educated at Winchester: Michael McDonnell, *The Annals of St Paul's School* (London, 1959), pp. 58–9.

Golden Fleece, of which Charles was head, as Henry was head of the Garter. At the conduit in Gracechurch Street there were three scenes of Charlemagne, from whom Charles was descended. In a central tower Charlemagne, holding two swords and two 'Crowyns imperyall off golde', offered one to Henry and the other to Charles, as his heirs.[6] At Leadenhall the pageant was a genealogical tree growing from John of Gaunt, duke of Lancaster, and surmounted by images of king and emperor, showing generation by generation how their lineage sprang 'owt off the howse off englonde'.[7]

The fourth pageant, at the conduit in Cornhill, took the form of a castle across the street, with towers to either side filled with trumpeters, shawms, and sackbuts. Between the towers was a palace

> where satte the ryght noble and victorious emprowr Kynge Arthur with a crowne imperiall in complett harnes and a swerde in hys hande with the rounde table before hyme. Whiche was accompanyed with all the noble prynces thatt were under his obeisaunce ...[8]

On Arthur's right were the kings of Scotland, Denmark, Gotland, North Wales, and Iceland, and the earls of Cornwall and Salisbury; on his left the kings of Ireland, South Wales, Little Britain, Orkney, and Norway, and the earls of Gloucester and Chester.[9]

> Also ther was a childe goodly apparelde whiche saluted the emprowr in laten versis laudyng and resemblyng hym in noblenes to the seyd Arthur.[10]

---

[6] Corpus Christi College, Cambridge, MS. 298, 'The descrypcion of the pageantes made in the Cyte of London att the receyving of the most excellent pryncys Charlys the fyfte Emperour & Henry the viij Kyng off englonde'. Much (but not all) of this MS. was printed by R. Withrington, *English Pageantry* i (Cambridge, Mass., 1918), pp. 175–8. Quotations from fol. 137ᵛ given below are by permission of the Master and Fellows of Corpus. The then Librarian, Dr. R. I. Page, kindly made arrangements for study of the MS. The phrase quoted here is from Withington, *Pageantry*, p. 176.

[7] Withington, *Pageantry*, p. 177.

[8] Corpus Christi College, Cambridge, MS. 298, fol. 137ᵛ.

[9] For Arthur's conquests and dominion, see Geoffrey of Monmouth, *The History of the Kings of Britain*, trans. Lewis Thorpe (Harmondsworth, 1966), pp. 212–28, and the scathing comments of William of Newburgh: P. G. Walsh and M. J. Kennedy (ed.), *The History of English Affairs*, Book I (Warminster, 1988), pp. 32–5.

[10] Corpus Christi College, Cambridge, MS. 298, fol. 137ᵛ.

The fifth pageant, at the Stocks, displayed the isle of England set amid the blue waves of a silver sea. There were two images

one in a castell lyke to the emprowr in visage, and the other in an herbar wyth rosys lyke to the Kynges grace with ii swerdys nakyd in ther handys.[11]

The images were mechanical. They beheld each other, cast away their swords, and embraced 'in tokennyng off love and pease', whereon an image of the Father in heaven 'all in burnyd golde' appeared with the text, *Beati pacifici qui filii dei vocabuntur* ('Blessed are the peacemakers, who will be called the children of God').[12]

At the Great Conduit in Cheapside, in the sixth pageant, a maiden appearing out of a great rose offered a white rose to the emperor, a red rose to the king. Above, in the top of each of four towers, were ladies representing the four cardinal Virtues.

The seventh pageant, at the Standard in Cheapside, showed Alfonso the Wise (king of Castile 1252–84) from whose breast sprang a tree in whose topmost branches sat Charles, Henry, Catharine his wife, and Mary their daughter. This Spanish tree balanced the English tree springing at Leadenhall from John of Gaunt.

The procession now passed the Great Cross in Cheap which was new gilded at vast cost for the event. Here too the couplet *Carolus Henricus vivant* was displayed and it was perhaps here that a boy delivered Lily's acclamation *Ad Carolum .5. Germani Imperatorem* ('To Charles the Fifth, Emperor of Germany').[13]

The eighth and last pageant, presenting the Assumption of the Virgin Mary, with the Archangels Michael and Gabriel, the twelve Apostles, St George, St John the Baptist, and a troop of English saints – King Edmund, Edward the Confessor, Erkenwold of London, Dunstan, Becket, and the still uncanonized Henry VI – was built like a heaven with clouds, sun, moon, stars, and the hierarchies of angels.

After the singing of the *Te Deum* in St Paul's, Charles went in procession to his lodging at Blackfriars. A few days later, emperor and king removed first to Richmond (9 June), then to Hampton Court (10 June), and finally to Windsor (11–20 June). Here on 16 June a treaty was signed for a combined assault on France and for her subsequent dismemberment. On the Feast of Corpus Christi (19 June), mass was

---

[11] Withrington, *Pageantry*, p. 177.

[12] Matthew 5.9; cf. the Vulgate, *Beati pacifici quoniam filii Dei vocabuntur*, whence the Authorised Version, '... for they shall be called the children of God.'

[13] For the Great Cross and its gilding, see Anglo, *Spectacle, Pageantry*, p. 200. There is some uncertainty about where the acclamation was delivered (cf. ibid. pp. 199–200; Robertson, 'L'Entrée', p. 178; and for the two variant texts, Baskerville, 'William Lily's Verse', pp. 5–6, 10), but the great expense of £100 on gilding the cross suggests that it was here *in foro* that the acclamation was delivered.

celebrated in St George's Chapel at a chapter of the Garter, to which Charles had been elected in 1508, and a second, secret, treaty was sworn.[14]

On 20 June, Henry and Charles left Windsor for Winchester, travelling and hunting via Farnham and Alresford, and arriving on 24 June (Fig. 154).[15] The problems of accommodating the enormous entourage were impossible – the emperor had originally intended to bring to England 2,044 persons and 1,126 horses, but in the event this was reduced by leaving out the 'grande chappelle' and a few others, a total of not more than twenty-six persons.[16] Provisions were scarce and the plague was in Winchester.[17] The two rulers stayed only two nights, 24 and 25 June. The city mended a bridge and repaired the 'shemelles' (shambles, i.e. meat market), while the mayor sat with the king's clerk of the market to try to cope with the problem of provisions.[18] Henry and Charles were probably entertained at the College, for the bursar spent £5 2s. 7 ½d. on beer, fish, capons, pheasants, and 'golls'.[19] And they also saw the Round Table. The Spanish chronicler Alonso de Santa Cruz, writing about 1551, says they went

> hasta una casa de placer del Obispo de Winchester, donde se muestra la tabla redonda de los caballeros de Artu[ro] ...

> to a pleasure house of the bishop of Winchester, where the Round Table of the knights of Arthur can be seen.[20]

Alonso's meaning is slightly obscure: he may be confusing the bishop's rural retreat (*casa de placer*) at Waltham (where Henry and Charles went after leaving Winchester) with the bishop's palace of Wolvesey in Winchester (where Henry and

---

[14] *LP Henry VIII* 3.ii (1521–3), nos. 2322, 2333 (1–25); *CSP Spanish* ii (1509–25), nos. 427, 430–5; Gachard, *Collection des Voyages* (as next note) ii, p. 66; Gachard in *Biographie Nationale ... de Belgique* iii, col. 541; Robertson, 'L'Entrée', p. 180; Anglo, *Spectacle, Pageantry*, pp. 203– 6.

[15] For the itinerary, see PRO, E101/419/7, fol. 24ᵛ. See also L. P. Gachard (ed.), *Collection des Voyages des Souverains des Pays-Bas* ii (Brussels, 1874), pp. 32, 66, and Manuel de Foronda y Aguilera, *Estancias y Viajes del Emperador Carlos V* (Madrid, 1914), pp. 201–5.

[16] *LP Henry VIII* 3.ii (1521–3), no. 2288 (4), (5); Anglo, *Spectacle, Pageantry*, p. 181.

[17] *CSP Spanish* ii (1509–25), no. 441.

[18] Winchester Chamberlain's roll for 13–14 Henry VIII (1521–2), HRO, W/E1/59; J. S. Furley's transcript (in Local Studies Library, Jewry Street, Winchester), fols. 682, 686.

[19] Bursar's account roll for 13–14 Henry VIII (1521–2), WCA 22180. For 'golls', read perhaps 'galls', from *gallina*, 'hen' or 'chicken'?

[20] *Crónica*, as above, n. 2, p. 516.

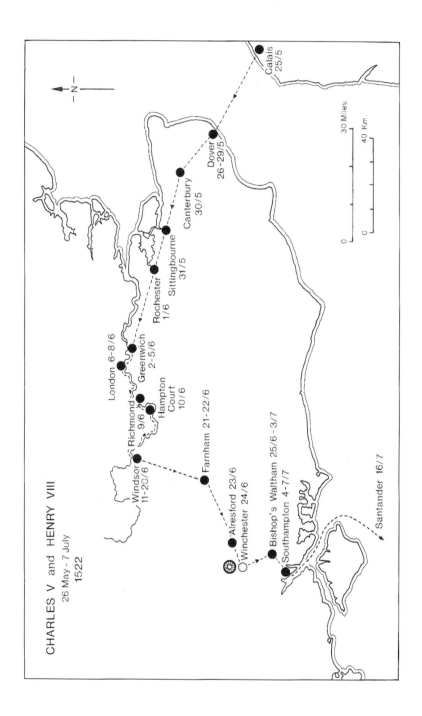

CHARLES V and HENRY VIII
26 May - 7 July
1522

Calais 25/5

Dover 26 - 29/5

Canterbury 30/5

Sittingbourne 31/5

Rochester 1/6

London 6 - 8/6

Greenwich 2 - 5/6

Hampton Court 10/6

Richmond 9/6

Windsor 11 - 20/6

Farnham 21 - 22/6

Alresford 23/6

Winchester 24/6

Bishop's Waltham 25/6 - 3/7

Southampton 4 - 7/7

Santander 16/7

30 Miles
40 Km.
0

154 Itinerary of the Emperor Charles V and Henry VIII, 26 May to 7 July 1522.

430

Charles probably stayed on 24 and 25 June), while by *donde* ('where') he probably means no more than 'in Winchester', for the table was to be seen not in the bishop's house, but in the Great Hall of the castle. It is Paulo Giovio who states quite clearly that Charles was shown the Round Table (see above, pp. 404–5). Although Giovio, whose book was published in 1548, was writing like Alonzo de Santa Cruz many years after the visit of 1522, his source, as we saw in Chapter 11, may well have been George Lily, son of that William Lily who wrote the verses for Charles's entry into London. At Winchester, below the Round Table, William Lily's couplet appeared again, as John Trussell (1580–1648), mayor of Winchester in 1624 and 1633, noted a century later in his 'Origin of Cities'. The visit, he wrote, 'is manifested by a scotcheon which, affirmed by many that had seen and redd this distich, was inscribed

> Carolus Henricus vivant defensor uterque
> Henricus fidei Carolus ecclesiae.'[21]

Trussell's words seem to imply that the 'scotcheon' (escutcheon) was no longer legible when he wrote, although a label which probably represents it was still visible below the table as late as the middle of the eighteenth century (Figs. 30 and 120). Nevertheless, Trussell's version is identical to the London text (punctuation and capitals apart) and there can be no doubt that the couplet was put up for the visit of 1522, and was intended to bring the table into that celebration of shared inheritance and power which was the theme of the London entry.

The problems of provisioning and accommodation at Winchester – to say nothing of the plague – were such that Henry quickly took Charles on to Bishop's Waltham, keeping only his household servants and sending the court and council to Chichester so that they would not eat up everything around Southampton where the emperor's fleet was due. The Spanish entourage were lodged 'in poor villages at least four Spanish leagues distant from each other', wrote Martin de Salinas, ambassador of the archduke and infante Ferdinand, who had been a notably sour commentator throughout the visit.[22] By 1 July he was himself at Winchester, which he seems to include among the villages, leading 'a miserable life', and unable to attend to business. But he admitted that the emperor was in good health and had 'much pleasure in the society of the king of England'.[23]

---

[21] HRO, Trussell MS., p. 38; Tom Atkinson's transcript (also in HRO), p. 38.
[22] *CSP Spanish* ii (1509–25), no. 441.
[23] Ibid.

Henry and Charles stayed in the bishop's palace at Waltham for over a week. The Treaty of Waltham was signed on 2 July and the next day Charles completed and signed his will, a necessary act before his sea voyage.[24] The imperial fleet entered Southampton Water the same day and there, or on the 4th, the two rulers parted, Charles embarking at once, his entourage following in great haste and at great loss and extraordinary expense, or so Martin de Salinas complained.[25]

The fleet did not sail until dawn on 7 July, arriving at Santander nine days later on 16 July. It felt, the emperor wrote to his aunt, Margaret of Austria, regent of the Netherlands, as if he had been in England a thousand years.[26]

The repair and painting of the Round Table, 1516

The Round Table, as Charles saw it in Winchester that June, had recently been restored. Looking up at it the emperor cannot have failed to remark in King Arthur the likeness of his bearded host (see above, pp. 315), just as in the London entry his own and Henry's visage had appeared in pageant after pageant (see above, pp. 427–8; and Figs. 156–7).

But to what extent was this Winchester likeness deliberately contrived for the occasion? That the table was newly painted is quite certain, Giovio (or rather his source) complaining that the work had been so incompetently done as to undermine its credibility as an authentic relic (see above, p. 405). Trussell took a similar view, possibly from reading Giovio, but more likely relying on independent evidence:

> The antiquitie of the round Table, att least the veritie of this that hangethe to bee the right table, is by mutch the more brought within the Daunger of suspect by how mutch the Characters of the Knights names theron inscribed make showe to bee but of late tymes Desciphered: where the truthe is when Henry the eight gaue entertaynment in this Cittie to the Emperor Charles ... that table was then new paynted, & the knights names super or circumscribed as they now are fixt upon the Wall.[27]

Charles's visit may have been the occasion for the painting of the table: that seems to be what Giovio's informant – and, for what it is worth, Trussell – believed.

---

[24] Ibid., no. 442; Karl Brandi, *The Emperor Charles V*, trans. C. V. Wedgwood (London, 1954), p. 177.

[25] *CSP Spanish* ii (1509–25), nos. 443, 446.

[26] Quoted by Robertson, 'L'Entrée', p. 180. I have not been able to trace the original text of this letter.

[27] HRO, Trussell MS., p. 37; Atkinson's transcript, p. 37.

Certainly, the couplet below the table can only have been set up in 1522, but that does not date the painting. There is in fact independent evidence that the table was repaired in 1516.

In August that year, a writ under the privy seal was issued to the collectors of customs and subsidies in the port of Southampton instructing them to pay £66 13s. 4d. to William Greme for the repair of the hall and Round Table in Winchester Castle.[28] This payment was a 'prest', an advance, equivalent to a round sum of 100 marks of 13s. 4d. each. In due course Greme's account was audited at the exchequer and enrolled among the foreign accounts, so-called because they related to the expenditure of funds issued by treasurers – in this case the customers of Southampton – who were external or *forinsecus* to the central exchequer.[29]

Greme accounted here for the expenditure of the money *inter festum Sancti Bartholomaei apostoli anno viii^{vo} et ultimum diem Januarii tunc proxime sequentem*, that is between 24 August 1516 and 31 January 1517. The money had been provided (Fig. 155):

> ad reparandam et emendendam aulam domini Regis infra castrum Regis de Wynchestre et le Round Table ibidem,

> for the restoration and repair of the king's hall within the king's castle of Winchester and the Round Table there,

but the words used to describe what it was actually spent on are slightly different (Fig. 155):.

> super et circa reparacionem aule et aliarum domorum infra castrum predictum per superius Thome Coke in hac parte per dominum Ricardum Wynton Episcopum unum consiliariorum domini Regis per mandatum domini Regis assignatum,

> on and about the repair of the hall and other houses within the said castle by the above [*sic*] Thomas Coke appointed to this task by the lord Richard, bishop of Winchester, one of the king's councillors, acting on the king's order.

---

[28] The writ does not survive but the collectors subsequently presented it at the exchequer of receipt to be allowed against their account and on 29 January 1517 the transaction was entered in the Exchequer, Receipt Rolls (Pells): PRO, E401/1053. The accountant's name is here spelt Greme, but is elsewhere sometimes spelt Grene (cf. next note). Greme is probably correct, see below, n. 33.

[29] Exchequer, Foreign Account Rolls: PRO, E364/120, where the name is spelt Grene. The main entry is on rot. 13^v, and the basic facts are repeated in the index written in the V-shaped section at the bottom of rotulet.

155 Account of William Greme for £66 13s. 4d. spent on the repair of the hall of Winchester Castle and the Round Table, 1516–17 (PRO, E364/120, rot. 13v).

The scope of the work is set out twice more, once in the index at the foot of the membrane carrying the main entry, and once in the related entry on the Receipt Roll. In both places the repair of the hall and the Round Table are mentioned together, in words virtually identical to the first description in the main account. In all three cases this probably reflects the wording of the original writ under the privy seal. Why then are the words used to describe what the money was actually spent on rather different, omitting the Round Table, but including 'other houses'?

The main text continues with an abstract of the payments made, taken from a *quaterna papiri* (a 'quarto' of four leaves or eight pages), of which the following is a shortened translation:

wages of carpenters, masons, stone-cutters, plumbers, glasiers, tilers, labourers, and other artificers working on the repair of the hall, houses, and walls   £29 12s. 6d.

purchases of timber, lead, stone, lime, sand, clay, glass, iron, tiles, nails, and other things needed for the repair of the premises   £33 13s. 5d.

hewing and sawing of timber, carriage of stone, lime, tiles, lead, and other necessaries   £1 13s.

wages of the accountant (i.e. William Greme), 76 days at 6d. a day   £1 18s.

Total   £66 16s. 11d.

The accountant was in 'superplusage', having spent 3s. 7d. more than the £66 13s. 4d. he had received. Unfortunately the original *quaterna papiri* probably no longer exists, so that the details of expenditure, the names and wages of the craftsmen, and the items purchased must remain unknown.[30] We can only assume that the initial purpose – to repair hall and table – was carried through, and that the vagaries in the enrolled copy of Greme's account represent only the chances of the immensely repetitive and formalised way in which it was drawn up: it refers, for example, to the

[30] Edward Smirke, 'On the Hall and Round Table at Winchester', as above, p. 92, n. 71, p. 79, was the first to discover and quote from this roll. There should be a further reference in the King's Remembrancer's Memoranda Rolls (PRO, E159), as the text of PRO, E364/120, rot. 13ᵛ, actually states, but we have not been able to locate it. I am most grateful to Dr. Beatrice Clayre who traced Smirke's reference to E364/120 in the PRO and discovered the new material on E401/1053.

156 Henry VIII, *c.*1520–2, artist unknown (National Portrait Gallery, 4690).

157 Charles V, 1522, by Bernaert van Orley (Museum of Fine Arts, Budapest)

above (*superius*) Thomas Coke, although he has not been mentioned before in this document, another sign that the clerk concerned was extracting from the paper before him without much care or thought.

To obtain some idea of the overall scale of this expenditure, we have to find out what £66 16s. 11d. was worth in early Tudor terms. A very approximate indication can be obtained by using a price index which has been compiled on the basis of the work of a number of scholars for the period from the 1260s to the 1990s.[31] This suggests that the sum of £66 16s. 11d. spent in 1516 might be equivalent to something like £35,000 in the 1990s. This figure suggests that there was ample provision within £66 16s. 11d. for the cost of taking the table down, repairing and reinforcing its woodwork, painting the front, and rehanging it, even if, regretably, the particular payments for this work are now lost within the very generalized account which is all that survives.

Clearly, however, this evidence cannot prove that the Round Table was repaired (and hence probably painted) in 1516. The names of those involved can tell us a good deal more. The customers of Southampton, Sir John Dawtrey and Richard Palshyd, need not detain us long. They were frequently called on, as here, to make payments for royal works and other concerns out of the profits of the port, and Dawtrey was well known to Bishop Fox.[32] William Greme, the accounting officer under the writ, was bailiff of Winchester in 1512–13 and mayor in 1522–3.[33] But Richard Fox, bishop of Winchester from 1501 until his death in 1528, is the key figure. He had been secretary to Henry VII, had baptised Prince Henry in 1491, and when the young man came to the throne in 1509 had become his friend as he had been his father's. Bishop successively of Exeter, Bath and Wells, Durham, and Winchester, much of his life was spent in politics, diplomacy, and administration. 'the bishop of Winchester is *alter rex*', reported the Venetian ambassador at the start of the new reign.[34] In 1516 Fox resigned the keepership of the privy seal, an office he had held for twenty-nine years, and retired to Winchester, to the care of

[31] Nicholas Mayhew, *Sterling: the Rise and Fall of a Currency* (London, 1999), pp. 279–81.

[32] H. M. Colvin (ed.), *The History of the King's Works* iii, *1485–1660*, Pt. II, pp. 493–4, 496–8; for [Sir] John Dawtrey, who was sheriff of Hampshire from 1516/17 to 1517/18 and died *c*.1520, see P. S. and H. M. Allen (ed.), *Letters of Richard Fox 1486–1527* (Oxford, 1929), pp. 59–75, 99–103.

[33] Derek Keene, *Survey of Medieval Winchester*, Winchester Studies 2 (Oxford, 1986), ii, p. 1249. His name is spelt Greme in E401/1053, Grene in E364/120 (see above, nn. 28–9), and Gryme in the Pipe Roll for 1518–19 (E372/364) and in the Winchester City Account Rolls for 1514–15. His office of bailiff in 1512–13 and association in the City Records and in the Pipe Rolls with his fellow bailiff for the year, David Anderson, leave no doubt that Grene, Greme, and Gryme refer to one and the same man. The credit for sorting out this problem belongs to Dr. Beatrice Clayre.

[34] *CSP Venetian* ii (1509–19), no. 64 (24 April 1510).

his bishopric, his monasteries, and the foundation of his college of Corpus Christi at Oxford. But he was still constantly called back to court, and to attend to matters great and small. As in 1513 he had had to oversee the collection of transports and victuals at Portsmouth and the construction of new brewhouses for supplying the army in France,[35] or in 1515 to devise the painting of the windows of King's College Chapel, Cambridge,[36] so in August 1516 he was commanded to arrange for the repair of the hall and Round Table at Winchester.[37]

As his agent to oversee the work, Fox appointed Thomas Coke, his registrar.[38] Coke was a wealthy Winchester citizen, a trader 'on a notable scale' in stone and timber, town clerk from 1512 to 1525, and member of parliament at the time of his death in 1529.[39] Fox's team was thus a local one, composed of men he was well used to working with. This was just the time when, as we now know, Fox was building his chantry chapel in the cathedral, having completed over the previous ten years or so the reconstruction and vaulting of the presbytery.[40] He clearly had a skilled body of overseers, craftsmen, and clerks at his disposal, and probably drew on them for the task of repairing hall and table.

[35] Allen and Allen (ed.), *Letters of Richard Fox*, pp. 59–75; for the brewhouses, see p. 74, and Colvin (ed.), *The History of the King's Works* iii, *1485–1660*, Pt. II, p. 493.

[36] Robert Willis and J. W. Clark, *The Architectural History of the University of Cambridge* i (Cambridge, 1886), pp. 498–9; H. Wayment, *The Windows of King's College Chapel, Cambridge* (London, 1972), p. 3 and Appendix B. Fox may also have had a hand in the iconography of the glazing programme for Henry VII's Chapel at Westminster, as Hilary Wayment suggests (ibid. p. 2; I am grateful to Dr Phillip Lindley for his comments on this suggestion). Direct documentary evidence is lacking, but Fox was involved in the abbey as one of Margaret Beaufort's executors who awarded the contract for her tomb to Pietro Torrigiano, the first great Italian Renaissance sculptor to work in England.

[37] Fox had great experience in the devising and administration of building works, large and small: Colvin (ed.), *The History of the King's Works* iii, *1485–1660*, Pt. I, pp. 30 (Fox's comments on Humphrey Coke, master carpenter of the king's works), 193 (King's College Chapel windows), 209 (Henry VII's Almshouses, Westminster), 340, 344 (the sea-banks and harbour works at Calais); and see Edmund C. Batten, 'The Life of Bishop Richard Fox', prefaced to *The Register of Richard Fox, while Bishop of Bath and Wells, A.D. 1492–4* (privately printed, 1889), *passim* (for his works at Norham castle, Winchester Cathedral, Corpus Christi College, Oxford, and at his other foundations). For the latest views on the chronology of Fox's extensive works at Winchester Cathedral, see below, n. 40.

[38] *LP Henry VIII* 3.ii (1521–3), no. 2472. For a letter to Fox from Coke and William Hawles 'your seruauntis', see Allen and Allen (ed.), *Letters of Richard Fox*, pp. 159–60.

[39] Keene, *Survey of Medieval Winchester* i, pp. 298n., 323–4, 410 (Table 36); ii, p. 1197. With Fox, Viscount Lisle, the mayor, and justices he was a commissioner to collect the subsidy of 1523: *L P Henry VIII* 3.ii (1521–3), nos. 3282 (p. 1523), 3504; for his death, see ibid. 4.iii (1529–30), p. 2692.

[40] Angela Smith, 'The Chantry Chapel of Bishop Fox', *Winchester Cathedral Record* 57 (1988), 27–32; Phillip Lindley, 'The Sculptural Programme of Bishop Fox's Chantry Chapel', ibid. 33–7, esp. p. 33; Martin Biddle, 'Early Renaissance at Winchester', in John Crook (ed.), *Winchester Cathedral. Nine Hundred Years 1093–1993* (Winchester and Chichester, 1993), pp. 257–304, at p. 263 and n. 41.

According to Greme's account, work began on 24 August 1516, the writ under the privy seal having presumably been issued a short while before. The occasion of the writ was most likely Henry VIII's first visit to Winchester as king. In the course of the late summer progress, a feature of the early years of his reign, Henry stayed at Farnham Castle for a few days early in the month before moving on to Southampton where he had arrived by Sunday, 10 August. Some time in the previous week he made an 'offring at his comyng into Wynchester at the high aulter vi*s*. viii*d*. and at Saint Swythuyn' shryne other vi*s*. viii*d*.',[41] while the city spent 4*s*. on wafers for the queen and 10*s*. 8*d*. on 'fylberdes', 'cake', and 'ipocras'.[42] Without the actual writ under the privy seal, we cannot know whether it was issued in Winchester, or a few days later in Southampton, but the timing suggests that Henry saw the Round Table during his visit and at once decided on its repair. He had perhaps seen the table before, but not as king; now he was able to get something done.[43]

But what was done? Was the table repaired and painted, or was it only repaired and the painting left to a later occasion? As we have seen, the summary account of the money spent gives no clue, and cannot even prove that anything was actually done to the table itself on this occasion. But since the table was apparently already decorated, and those decorations were in a sad state, 'the names of the knights around the edge ... badly eaten away by decay', as Paolo Giovio recorded (see above, p. 405), it is inconceivable that the king would have wanted the table repaired without being redecorated. Indeed, it was probably the decay of the decoration which caught Henry's eye: the true state of the woodwork would only have become clear when the table was taken down. In the last resort, the best evidence that the table *was* restored at this time is probably the writ specifying the repair of the table issued under the king's privy seal during or shortly after his visit to Winchester in the week before 10 August 1516 and acted upon by 24 August. The vagaries of the

---

[41] PRO, E36/215, fol. 463 (cf. *LP Henry VIII* 2.ii (1517–18), p. 1472).

[42] Winchester chamberlain's roll for 7–8 Henry VIII (1515–16): HRO, W/E1/55; Furley's transcript (in Local Studies Library, Jewry Street, Winchester), fol. 645. Filberts are nuts of the cultivated hazel (*corylus avellana*); hippocras is a cordial of wine flavoured with spices: it cost 8*s*. on this occasion – more than two weeks wages for a labourer.

[43] Henry's first known visit to Winchester was as prince of Wales to greet King Philip of Castile in January 1506: he may have seen the table on this occasion (see above, pp. 422–4). He may have been in Winchester again in September 1507, but de Puebla's letter of 5 October, sometimes taken as evidence for the prince's presence in the city during the previous month, does not actually say he was there: *CSP Spanish* i (1485–1509), no. 552. The Venetian ambassador reported King Henry's return from Winchester 'where the court is' in a letter of 17 July 1510 (*LP Henry VIII* 1.i (1509–13), no. 531), but this is certainly an error for Windsor where the king was throughout the first half of the month (cf. ibid. nos. 528, 546 (43, 57–9, 62–3)), and there is no evidence he was at Winchester either earlier or later the same year.

surviving summary of the account are not sufficient reason to suppose that an integral part of the king's writ was ignored.

Considerable repairs were needed (see above, pp. 130–1, 138): part of the rim of the frame (felloe 117) had to be replaced and the general condition of the table was such that six stout vertical spars were halved and nailed to the back of the frame to strap it together. The edge was reinforced and the outer ends of the planks covered and held down by the addition of a raised rim to the front of the table. Vertical iron straps, projecting well above the table, were attached to the two central verticals to take some of the weight when it was put back on the wall, and the two adjacent verticals were pierced to take ropes to be used when raising the table into position (Figs. 43, 63).

The new pieces were oak and unlike the original work, which was pegged except for the scarfs of the felloes, the new pieces were all fixed by large iron spikes or nails which served to bind the whole structure together (Fig. 62). There were more than a hundred of these spikes and their use is the best evidence that these various additions all belong to the same phase of repair. In terms of 'stratigraphic' sequence, we know this work was carried out *after* a (probably lengthy) period of rot when the table was already in a hanging position, but *before* the table was used as a target in 1642 (see above, p. 138–42).

There are only two ways of dating these repairs in calendar years: by an assumption that they belong to the one supposed work of repair in 1516; or by scientific means. Unfortunately, the ring-sequences preserved by the new timbers are too short to be matched, and so cannot be dated dendrochronologically. We do however have a series of radiocarbon dates both for the verticals applied to the back and for the raised rim added to the front (see above, Chapter 6 and pp. 215–17, 231–2 and Table 8). At the 95 per cent confidence level – i.e. with only a 1 in 20 chance that the real date falls outside the range quoted – the results are

> for the verticals: AD 1472 to 1660
> for the rim: AD 1436 to 1515.

The range for the rim falls earlier than that for the verticals because no sapwood was found and hence there is no way of knowing how many years should be added to bridge the interval between the rings dated and the felling date of the tree from which the rim timber was taken. In the case of the verticals, where we do know where the sapwood began, the range quoted is likely to be well distributed about the actual felling date. There is clearly some support in the radiocarbon dates for the view that the addition of the verticals and the raised rim took place at the same time and that this could have been in 1516.

As already suggested, the poor condition of the woodwork will only have emerged when the table came down: the real reason for ordering the repair will have been the state of the surface decoration. This must have been stripped off as part of the repair, leaving (as the X-rays have shown) a clean disk, which was then framed by the addition of a raised rim. Here we have a setting which demanded decoration. It would have been as odd at this date to have left a blank disk, as it would have been two centuries before (see above, p. 403). This suggests that the table was both repaired *and* painted in 1516.

But how well do the indications of date established by Pamela Tudor-Craig in Chapter 9 fit with 1516? The evidence is best set out in a list, showing those features for which a date can be suggested.

The seated figure	1489–1544 (on the penny coin)
The double rose	1486–1603 (perhaps *c*.1500–30)
Crown: hoops	by1520–1 at the latest
points	by 1505–9 (and also *c*.1520)
Orb: form	by 1526
profile hand holding	1520–6
Sword	1521? (if reference is to Pope Leo X's gift of that year)
Beard	by July 1519
Canopy	1515–32 (exact match in 1515)

Perhaps the first point to be made is how clearly the art-historical approach points to a date around 1520. This is a remarkable achievement and one which can probably not be refined given that parallel occurrences can only tell us the date *by* which a feature appears. It is almost certainly asking too much of this evidence to say whether it points to 1522 rather than 1516, or vice-versa. Clearly, if Arthur's sword were a reference to Pope Leo X's gift of 1521, that would be decisive. But the sword is an Arthurian commonplace. Arthur with drawn sword, orb, hooped crown, and substantial beard appears in a glass window of about 1450 in St Mary's Hall, Coventry (Fig. 123).[44] The value of this image is that it shows how Arthur could be

---

[44] Roger Sherman Loomis and Laura Hibbard Loomis, *Arthurian Legends in Medieval Art* (London and New York, 1938), p. 40, Pl. 16. The 'orb' in this window is an extraordinary object, like a papal tiara surmounted by a cross patée.

158 Francis I, *c.*1530, by Joos van Cleve (The Royal Collection).

shown already in the fifteenth century: it provides rich parallels for the figure of Arthur on the Round Table, but is not a source.

The Arthur of Coventry, like many Arthurs, is shown bearded, and this too is a commonplace.[45] The exact date at which King Henry first grew a beard is thus not critical for the date of the painting, for the painter could have made Arthur in other respects as much like Henry as possible. Likenesses of Henry and Charles were a feature of the London pageants of 1522, and thus provide an obvious context for the painting of the table that year: their similar clothing was an occasion for comment (see above, p. 425), and is preserved in a contemporary double portrait in which both are bearded (Pl. XXVIII).[46]

The dating of the painting on the Round Table to 1522 might seem also supported by the use of the hand in profile to hold the orb (see above, pp. 305–7), but here again we cannot be sure that this way of holding the orb could not have appeared earlier. Indeed this representation of Arthur, although traditional, is in some ways very up-to-date, as the appearance of the Renaissance form of the canopy, best paralleled in 1515, also suggests.

If we had no record of the repairs of 1516, the painting would be dated to 1522 with confidence, and with an abundance of parallels in the figures of Arthur and Henry in the pageants of the London entry. But the problem is in reality less simple. Pamela Tudor-Craig, who first wrote Chapter 9 before the records of the 1516 repairs had been relocated and the role of Bishop Fox in the work demonstrated, showed how the style and details of the painting could be related to works undertaken under his patronage for the cathedral (see above, pp. 329–30). When this is considered anew, in the light of Bishop Fox's now certain involvement in the repairs of 1516, and when the unlikelihood of the table having been left unpainted after the

---

[45] Although Arthur is beardless in the wall painting at La Manta of about 1430 (Loomis and Loomis, *Legends in Medieval Art* (as last note), Pl. 14), and in some representations of him as one of the Nine Worthies (e.g. ibid. Pls. 11, 15), he is bearded in the four representations of him in the Runkelstein wall paintings of c.1400 (ibid. Pls. 60, 186, 199, 200), in the Metropolitan Museum tapestry of about the same date (ibid. Pl. 12), and in other versions of the Nine Worthies (ibid. Pls. 13, 394(?)).

[46] Exhibited for the first time at the Henry VIII Exhibition at Greenwich in 1991: David Starkey (ed.), *Henry VIII. A European Court in England* (London, 1991), p. 56 (Item V.1). The painting belonged to the antiquary James West (?1704–72) and was purchased at his sale in 1773 by Horace Walpole for £7 7s.: W. S. Lewis (ed.), *The Yale Edition of Horace Walpole's Correspondence* i (London, 1937), p. 305. In Walpole's *Description of Strawberry Hill* (1774), it was described as 'Henry VIII aged 29, and Charles V, aged 20', with the implication that Walpole believed the painting to date from 1520. Henry and Charles met twice that year (see below, pp. 448–9), but Charles was not then bearded. The emphasis in the London entry of 1522 on the portraits of the two rulers, and their contrived similarity in dress, suggest that the double portrait was probably painted in relation to that visit. I am most grateful to the owners of the painting for their generosity in allowing it to be reproduced here and to Mr Christopher Foley for the Walpole reference and for his help in general.

repairs is recalled, it must seem probable that the painting was done that year. The evidence falls short of proof, but the position may become clearer if examined in the context of the politics of the first quarter of the sixteenth century.

England and the Habsburgs

For quarter of a century, since the treaty of 1496 with the Netherlands government later known as the *Intercursus Magnus*, the whole thrust of English foreign policy had been pro-Habsburg. For both sides, trade and a need to contain the power of France had been sufficient grounds.[47]

Henry VII, more anxious to avoid risks than to seize chances, had sought a good understanding with France: she should not be provoked nor actively opposed unless real English interests were threatened. Henry VIII at first abandoned this principle. England joined the Holy League against France in 1511 and in 1513 invaded French territory, but the next year peace was signed, and the English alliance with France, so carefully fostered by Henry VII, was restored and even enhanced.

England was not a party to the Treaty of Noyon in August 1516 between Francis, Charles, and Maximilian, but all wanted England's goodwill. In a spectacular diplomatic stroke, Wolsey concluded a new Anglo-French treaty in 1517. The next year he expanded this into the Treaty of Universal and Perpetual Peace whereby the Emperor Maximilian, Charles of Burgundy and Spain, Francis I of France, Henry of England, and the Pope joined in pledging themselves to everlasting friendship and to joint action against the Turk. The negotiation of this pact in London cast Henry VIII 'in an almost imperial role'.[48] Although Henry's imperial pretensions were cut short by Charles' election as Emperor in June 1519, the diplomatic successes of the previous two years set the scene for England's seeming role as middle man[49] in 1520 when in a set of close-packed encounters, Henry met Charles at Dover in late May, Francis on the Field of Cloth of Gold in June, and Charles again at Gravelines early in July.

Charles V now ruled not only the Netherlands, inherited from his father Philip of Burgundy (*d.*1506), but Spain, Naples, and parts of the New World, inherited from his maternal grandfather Ferdinand of Aragon (*d.*1516), and the Austrian and

---

[47] For what follows, see principally R. B. Wernham, *Before the Armada. The Growth of English Foreign Policy 1485–1588* (London, 1966), Chapters II–IV and VI–VIII, but cf. also J. J. Scarisbrick *Henry VIII* (London, 1968), especially pp. 70–4, 79–88, 95–9 for foreign policy in the period 1513–22.

[48] Wernham, *Before the Armada* p. 94.

[49] On this see especially Scarisbrick, *Henry VIII*, p. 81.

other lands of the Empire, in succession to his paternal grandfather, Maximilian I
(*d.*1519). With French control of Milan and Genoa threatening the routes between
his Spanish kingdoms and the Austrian and imperial lands, the sea lanes between the
Netherlands and Spain were of paramount importance. If England were neutral,
French ships operating out of Channel and Breton ports might threaten imperial
traffic. If England were hostile, the English fleet might close the Channel to imperial
ships.[50]

Charles needed England's friendship. The meetings of 1520 laid the foundation
of an understanding. By 1521, 'the imperial lion was beginning to prowl and Henry
and Wolsey prepared to play jackal to him'.[51] In August Wolsey concluded a secret
treaty with Charles at Bruges by which Henry was to declare war upon France, keep
the Channel open for imperial ships, and invade France from Calais in 1523. Charles
for his part promised to plan for the conquest and division of France, to invade from
Spain in 1523, and to marry the Princess Mary, Henry's only legitimate child.

The Bruges treaty was confirmed and elaborated by further agreements
concluded at Windsor and Bishop's Waltham during Charles' visit to England the
next year (see above, p. 432). England had now chosen sides and in August 1522
marched into northern France. Charles, for his part, had 'achieved all that he had
worked for'.[52]

This is the background against which the painting of the Round Table must be
read. The table had been called upon in 1506 at another juncture of English and
Netherlandish affairs (see above, pp. 422–4). Now in 1522 it apeared again in a
wider imperial context. Was there some special significance in Arthur's table which
made it a particularly appropriate symbol in English dealings with the Empire?
Within a few years the whole political scene had moved: Charles V's capture of
Francis I (Fig, 158) at the Battle of Pavia in February 1525 changed the balance of
power. Charles no longer needed a war to dismember France, nor an English
marriage. In English eyes, Charles was now too strong. Later that year England and
France were in direct negotiation and in 1527 signed The Eternal Peace, the start of
a decade of Anglo-French entente, profoundly influential in the political, cultural,
and artistic life of England.[53] But it also marked the end of the role of the Round
Table in contemporary affairs. Henceforth, the table was an object of antiquarian
interest not a political image. Whatever it was which had given the table some

---

[50] Wernham, *Before the Armada*, p. 95.

[51] Ibid. p. 96; cf. Scarisbrick, *Henry VIII*, pp. 82–94.

[52] Ibid. p. 95.

[53] For the events of 1527, and the celebrations which marked the conclusion of the treaties, see now Starkey
(ed.), *Henry VIII* (as n. 46), pp. 54–99.

contemporary symbolic force in the affairs of nations early in the century, lost its significance when England's long alliance with the Habsburgs came to an end.

To explore this role we must examine the five meetings between Habsburg and Tudor monarchs which took place between 1506 and 1522, and contrast them with the single meeting between Tudor and Valois, the encounter on the Field of Cloth of Gold in 1520.

When Henry VII entertained Philip of Burgundy at Windsor in 1506 the Round Table – 'about which so much has been said and written' – provided the type and suggested a way to commemorate the dinner at which King Henry, King Philip, and the young Henry sat together after signing the Treaty of Windsor, the *Intercursus Malus*, and attending mass in St George's Chapel (see above, pp. 422–4). Whether the comparison was already intended when Philip was shown the Round Table during his overnight stop in Winchester a few days before, we may never know for sure, but the contrivance of the parallel and the interest of Philip's father, the Emperor Maximilian, in matters Arthurian suggest that the coincidence may have been deliberate.

Henry VIII met the Emperor Maximilian only once, during the French campaign of 1513, but he met his grandson Charles, son of Philip of Burgundy, no less than four times, in 1513, in May and July 1520, and in 1522.

Henry set siege to Thérouanne in August 1513, where he was joined by Maximilian with a small Burgundian force.[54] Together they watched the defeat of the French force on 16 August at the Battle of the Spurs – so called by the French because their cavalry galloped away so fast – at which the Emperor and his men-at-arms wore the red cross of St George, the uniform of Henry's men. Eight days later Henry and Maximilian entered Thérouanne together in triumph.

While his army then advanced on Tournai, Henry diverted to Lille where Maximilian, Margaret of Austria, and the young Prince Charles of Castile were staying with their court. Henry entered Lille in state, wearing his crown, 'all the strets ... sett on bothe sydes with burnying torches and diuerse goodly pagiantes pleasant to beholde',[55] but after three days of festivities left to prosecute the siege of Tournai. The city surrendered on 23 September after a week's bombardment. Two days later Henry made his entry in magnificence, followed in the evening by Maximilian,

---

[54] For what follows, see G. C. Cruickshank, *Army Royal. Henry VIII's Invasion of France 1513* (Oxford, 1969), esp. pp. 90–1, 114–18, 139–41, 146–9. More details can be found in Jasper Ridley, *Henry VIII* (paperback edition, London, 1987), pp. 64–71, but the principal contemporary account of the campaign from the English point-of-view is that by John Taylor: BL, Cotton MS. Cleopatra C. v, fols. 64 ff., printed in *LP Henry VIII*, i, 1291.

[55] Hall, *The Vnion* (as above, n. 3), Henry VIII, fol. 35v.

Margaret, and Charles. A few days later Maximilian left for Germany and on 13 October Henry departed for Calais and home.

Although there were ceremonial meetings, triumphant entries, jousts, and sustained festivities, notably after the fall of Tournai, we have no record of the subjects of any pageants or festive structures, apart from the splendours of Henry's travelling camp and the magnificence of his tents.[56] For all its show, and it was great, this was a military campaign, attended by order and soldierly display (Plate XXVII). For our present purpose, its significance is two fold: it was the only time that Henry met the old Emperor Maximilian, 'the last of the knights', and it was Henry's first meeting with the emperor's young nephew, the future Emperor Charles V.[57]

Henry and Charles met on three subsequent occasions: in July 1520 and June 1522 the figure of Arthur was explicit; in May 1520 at Dover (and again in May 1522), Arthur's name and relics of his knights infused the castle with his presence.

Dover Castle 'is the key of England', wrote Matthew Paris in the thirteenth century. No fortification in the British Isles has a longer recorded history; its legendary history begins with Julius Caesar.[58] In Henry VIII's reign, the people in the castle pointed out Arthur's Hall and Guinevere's Bedchamber to a sceptical John Leland, and showed him Gawain's gigantic bones, claiming they also possessed relics of Craddock.[59] Half a century earlier Malory had followed *Le Morte Arthur*, itself composed towards the end of the fourteenth century (see above, pp. 410–11), in placing Gawain's burial 'in a chapell within Dover castell',[60] while Caxton, in his Preface to Malory, written in 1485, had recalled the 'many remembraunces' of Arthur and his knights which 'ben yet ... and shall remayne perpetually', among which 'in the Castel of Douer ye may see Gauwayns skulle and Cradoks mantel'.[61]

[56] Cruickshank, *Army Royal*, pp. 43–5.

[57] For somewhat differing evaluations of Henry's success and the degree to which he was outfoxed by Maximilian in this campaign, see Cruickshank, *Army Royal*, pp. 206–7; Wernham, *Before the Armada*, pp. 86–8; and Ridley, *Henry VIII*, p. 69.

[58] H. M. Colvin (ed.), *The History of the King's Works* ii (London, 1963), pp. 629–41; iii (London, 1975), pp. 242–8. For the legendary history, as set down by an Elizabethan writer, see William Darell, *The History of Dover Castle* (London, 1786).

[59] John Leland, *Assertio Inclytissimi Arturii ...* (London, 1544), ed. Thomas Hearne, *Joannis Lelandi ... Collectanea*, 2nd edn., v (London, 1774), pp. 25, 26, and cf. p. 7. See also E. M. R. Ditmas, 'The Cult of Arthurian Relics', *Folklore* 75 (1964), 19–33, at pp. 31–3.

[60] Eugène Vinaver (ed.), *The Works of Sir Thomas Malory*, 2nd edn. (Oxford, 1967; repr. 1973), iii, pp. 1232, 1250–1; cf. J. Douglas Bruce (ed.), *Le Morte Arthur. A Romance in Stanzas of Eight Lines*, EETS Extra ser. 88 (London, 1903; repr. 1959), lines 3136–9 [stanza 394].

[61] James W. Spisak (ed.), *Caxton's Malory* (Berkeley and Los Angeles, 1983), i, p. 2. Marcus Binney (*Country Life*, 5 Jan. 1984) has wondered whether these relics were in origin the product of thirteenth-century Arthurianism.

However sceptical Leland may have been in the 1540s, these names and relics were the stuff of Arthurian story. The young emperor Charles was lodged in the castle for a night in May 1520, when Henry came to greet him,[62] and was accommodated there again for several days in May 1522, once more in Henry's company.[63] Charles will not have been left in ignorance of the great past around him. Indeed, he can have been housed only in the keep which was described in the sixteenth century as the *regale palatium* ('royal palace'), and which was then linked by a gallery 80 ft long to the principal royal hall, known since the fourteenth century as 'Arthur's Hall'. The remains of this hall, and a second structure known as 'Arthur's Lesser Hall', still survive against the curtain-wall of the Inner Bailey, although Arthur's Gate and the gallery have long since vanished.[64]

One must certainly not make too much of the Arthurian character of Dover in relation to Charles' visits. But seen in the context of the specific display of the figure of Arthur soon afterwards, in July 1520 at Calais, and in June 1522 at London and Winchester, the stories of Dover take on the role of prologue.

The round house at Calais, 1520

Six weeks after their meeting at Dover in May 1520, Charles and Henry met on English territory at the half-way point between Calais and Gravelines. Henry escorted Charles back to the English border, and after crossing over into imperial territory, Charles escorted Henry into Gravelines for an evening of sumptuous feasting and entertainment. The next day, 11 July, Henry escorted Charles and his aunt, Margaret of Savoy, back into English territory and on to their lodgings in the

---

[62] Oxford, Bodleian Library, MS Ashmole 1116, f.100^r; Hall, *The Vnion* (as above, n. 3), Henry VIII, fol. 72. MS Ashmole 1116 contains among other items an anonymous narrative (fols. 100–3^v) of Henry's meetings in 1520 with Charles (in May and July) and with Francis (in June). J.G. Russell suggested that it may have been written by Christopher Barker, herald to the king's brother-in-law, Charles Brandon, Duke of Suffolk, for the duke's part in the feats of arms at the Field of Cloth of Gold is 'closely marked and praised' (J.G. Russell, *The Field of Cloth of Gold* (London, 1969), p. 122). Russell printed the narrative as his Appendix C (pp. 209–15). MS Ashmole 1116 continues (fols. 103^v-5) with 'the poesies and writings that were in the rownd howse made at Callais for the feasting and banqueting of the Emperor Charles the Vth', which was not printed by Russell. On this MS, see further n. 80, below.

[63] Hall, *The Vnion* (as above, n. 3), Henry VIII, fol. 93^v; Anglo, *Spectacle, Pageantry* (as above, n. 1), pp. 183–4.

[64] Colvin (ed.), *King's Works* (as above, n. 32) ii, Pl. 40, B; iii, pp. 245–6. The location and names of these structures (except for the gallery, by then demolished) can also be seen on the plan of Dover Castle published in 1786 in William Darrell, *Dover Castle* (as above, n. 58), facing p. 1.

Staple Hall at Calais. Henry himself lodged at the Exchequer of Calais, beside which, as Edward Hall later wrote,

> for solas was builded a banquetyng house, 80. foote round, after a goodly deuise, builded upon Mastes of shippes in suche maner as I think was neuer sene, for in it was the whole sp[h]ere portrated whiche by reason of the great winde that blewe, could not be achieued.[65]

The wind destroyed this marvellous house, so that the emperor and the lady Margaret supped with the king and queen at the Exchequer under straitened circumstances on the 12th. Two days later they returned into imperial lands.[66]

In 1520 the round wooden theatres of Elizabethan London were still far in the future (*The Theatre* 1576, *The Curtain* 1577, *The Rose* 1587, *The Swan* c.1595, *The Globe* 1599), but Stow was entirely right in 1580 to describe the round house at Calais as 'like a theatre',[67] a comparison made even more striking in 1989 by the discovery of *The Rose and The Globe*.[68] It is as a theatre-like structure, the beginnings of English theatre design, that the Calais round house has attracted most attention in recent years,[69] and it is here that we must begin.

The round house was built on a specially cleared site in front of the Exchequer. Like the London theatres of the later sixteenth century,[70] it was a polygon, with sixteen sides each 24 feet in length. If this figure is accurate (and it was the easiest to

[65] Hall, *The Vnion* (as above, n.3), Henry VIII, fol. 84ᵛ.

[66] MS Ashmole 1116, fol. 103. The dates of the Calais meeting in this account are those originally envisaged (i.e. 4–8 July) whereas the days of the week are correct for the actual dates (10–14 July) as given (with further errors) in Hall.

[67] John Stow first made this comparison as an insertion into his quotation from Richard Turpin's description of the round house at Calais (*The Chronicles of England to 1580* (London, 1580), p. 927). It was copied by him in his new edition of Raphael Holinshed (*The Third Volume of Chronicles ... first compiled by Raphaell Holinshed, and by him extended to the yeare 1577. Now ... continued to the yeare 1586 by John Stow and others* (London, 1586), p. 861), and appears in all later editions of both Holinshed and Stow (e.g. Edmund Howes, London, 1631, p. 507). Stow had not made the comparison in any of the editions of his *Summarie of English Chronicles* or its *Abridgement* prior to 1580, and it must reflect the construction of the London playhouses in 1576 and 1577. Sanuto (or his source) had made the comparison to an *amphiteatro* and to a *theatro* already in 1520 (*I diarii di Marino Sanuto*, ed. F. Stefani (Vienna, 1879–1902) (hereafter, 'Sanuto'), vol. xxix, cols. 251, 254; translated and abridged in *CSP Venetian* iii (1869), no. 50 (p. 32), but Stow is most unlikely to have known this.

[68] Jean Wilson, *The Archaeology of Shakespeare* (Stroud, 1995), pp. 159–83.

[69] Richard Hosley, 'The Theatre and the Tradition of Playhouse Design', in Herbert Berry (ed.), *The First Public Playhouse: The Theatre in Shoreditch 1576–1598* (Montreal, 1979), pp. 47–79; John Orrell, *The Human Stage. English Theatre Design, 1567–1640* (Cambridge, 1988), esp. pp.31–8, 43, 50–1.

measure or pace on the ground), the round house measured 121 feet between opposite faces of the polygon. The roof was carried on a massive central 'piece', 134 feet
long, composed of eight great masts lashed together with ropes and bound with iron.
This 'mainmast' supported a canvas roof which, raised and held in position by ropes
rigged from the top of the mast down to the top of the polygon, formed 'a handsome and well proportioned covering, like a pavilion,'[71] a 'great canvas marquee',[72]
or a circus 'top'.

The central 'piece' was clearly a 'made mast' of the kind used for the largest
ships of the time. Like the Calais 'mainmast', these were composed of several
different pieces of timber held together by rope or iron bands placed around the
mast at intervals and known as 'wooldings'. The only English medieval mast known
to have survived into modern times was of this kind. Found at Woolwich, it possibly
came from Henry VII's 600–ton *Sovereign* built in 1488, rebuilt in 1509, and finally
laid up in 1521. Strictly contemporary with the Calais mast, the surviving stump of
the Woolwich mast measured 4 ft 4 in (1.32 m) in diameter at the base and
consisted of a central pine spindle surrounded by eight thick oak baulks or 'filling
pieces', bound together by iron bands.[73]

Only 10 ft of the Woolwich mast survived, and little is known of the length of
such medieval masts, but the main mast of the 1000–ton *Regent* built *c*.1512 was
specified as 114 ft (34.8 m) and a mainmast actually available for her at Bristol was
107 ft 3 in long (32.7 m). A century earlier, a visiting Italian galley captain dining
aboard Henry V's *Grace Dieu* took measurements which suggest that her mainmast
was possibly 190 ft (57.9 m) long. The keel of the *Grace Dieu* now lying in the
Hamble suggests that contemporary Mediterranean shipwrights would have given
her a mast of at least 180 ft (54.9 m).

The structure of the Calais mast and its length of 134 ft were recorded by
Richard Turpin in the *Chronicle of Calais*.[74] The evidence of contemporary ships'

[70] As Sidney Anglo was the first to observe in modern times (*Spectacle, Pageantry*, p.159). Stow had made the
comparison in 1580 and Sanuto or his source in 1520 (see above, n. 67).

[71] Sanuto, col. 251; *CSP Venetian* iii (1869), no. 50 (p. 32).

[72] Colvin (ed.), *King's Works*, (as above, n. 32) iii, p. 343.

[73] This and the next paragraph rely on Ian Friel, *The Good Ship* (London, 1995), pp. 86–92, Fig. 5.2, and Table 6
(p. 203). Dr Friel's Figs. 4.5 and 5.1 give a very good idea of the probable appearance of the Calais mast
which he regards as 'very similar to the type of great mast used in the largest English ships', and at '134 foot ...
certainly ... very large for its day, but not impossibly so' (letter of 2.x.1996).

[74] J. G. Nichols (ed.), *The Chronicle of Calais*, Camden Soc., o.s. 35 (London, 1846), p. 29. Turpin's manuscript
survives only in a transcript by John Stow, now BL, MS Harl. 542. This was used by Stow in his *Chronicle* of
1580, with further additions from Bodleian, MS Ashmole 1116, and from Hall's *The Vnion* of 1548. The
details of the mast were recorded by Turpin himself.

mainmasts shows he can be believed. He also noted that it had cost £6 13s. 4d. to set it upright. This may be a suspiciously round figure – it equals 10 marks of 13s. 4d. – but it reveals the size of the problem. At 134 ft the mast would have been almost as high as the tower of Winchester Cathedral. If set 20 ft to 25 ft into the ground (which seems a minimum to hold it fast and provide a 'toe' against which to haul it upright), and if 15 ft protruded as a pinnacle above the canvas, the top of the pavilion would have been about 90 ft to 100 ft above the ground. If the walls of the polygon, themselves hung on sixteen 'princypals made of greate mastes,' were 40 ft to 50 ft high, as the measurements of the internal galleries suggest, the canvas roof would have risen to a peak at about twice the height of the walls. This produces a reasonable shape. Indeed, the Elizabethan theatres were high-walled in relation to their diameter, as the reconstructed Globe shows.

The Calais Round House was thus an extraordinary structure. Well might the Latin inscription at the entrance exclaim:

> Miraris hospes, vnde moles haec nova.

> Visitor, you marvel, whence came this vast new house.[75]

The answer is that it came from England, was floated over in parts, and was erected, probably in a very short time, at the Exchequer in Calais.

Inside, all round the perimeter, rose three tiers of balconies, each raked from back to front to allow those at the back to see over the heads of those in front. The structural similarity of the whole to an Elizabethan theatre is again obvious. The decoration was elaborate in the extreme.[76] Above, painted on an inner canvas ceiling rising from the perimeter to the central mast and possibly rigged so as to form a dome, were painted the four elements of Aristotle's cosmography, earth, water, air and fire. These rose in superimposed concentric zones: at the lower level, above the uppermost tier of balconies, a natural landscape populated with buildings and animals; above this the sea, filled with ships, fish, and monsters; then the sky, scattered with clouds, winds, birds, the sun, the moon, the planets, and the stars, and

---

[75] See below, pp. 453–4. Its timbers may in fact have been floated over from England, just as ship's masts were towed to where they were needed, attached to a great iron swivel (Friel, as n. 73, p. 92). Ian Friel points out to me that the erection and rigging of the masts and canvas roof of the round house are likely to have been the work of sailors not shipwrights. Further research into contemporary naval accounts may yet reveal more about how the Calais house was designed and built.

[76] For this and the next two paragraphs, see Anglo, *Spectacle, Pageantry*, pp.160–1.

inscribed with philosophical propositions; and at the top, around the central mast, a sphere of flames.

The mast itself was surrounded by timber stages for organs and other instruments, their players, and singing men, with space for the enactment of pageants.

Windowless and covered, the round house was lit by cornucopias serving as candle holders, each fixed to one of the lesser masts at the sixteen interior angles. At a higher level chandeliers hung from the ceiling, alternating at the angles with silk-clad wickerwork figures of 'grete men' and women bearing torches. Throughout there were mottoes celebrating friendship and amity,[77] and all around were hung the arms of England ancient and the imperial eagle, alternating with a device of two naked swords, whose significance had been made clear in the entrance.[78]

The entrance was the key, although later commentators have ignored it in favour of the round house.[79] The sources, rich and complementary, come from all the interested parties: English ('Ashmole'), imperial (*Le triumphe*), French (*L'ordonnance*), and Venetian ('Sanuto'), an indication of the political significance of the building in contemporary eyes.[80] An inscription set somewhere on the entrance made clear the purpose of the whole house:

> Miraris hospes, unde moles haec nova.
> Templum est dicatum regie concordiae
> Quod hunc in usum condidere gratiae.[81]

> Visitor, you marvel, whence came this vast new house.
> It is a temple dedicated to royal concord:
> To this one intent the Graces assembled it.

---

[77] Bodleian, MS Ashmole 1116, fos. 104ᵛ-5, gives the text of 39 of these mottoes 'at the lowest storie' and 'the second storye'.

[78] Sanuto, col. 254, lines 1–3. The translation in *CSP Venetian* iii (1869), no. 50 (p. 34), is obscure.

[79] Hosley (see above n. 69), pp. 64, 73, shortened Sanuto's description of the entrance and did not attempt to show it in his reconstruction drawings (Figs. 3–5); Orrell (as above, n. 69) also omits the entrance from his reconstruction, but in a key passage put forward an interpretation of its significance, suggesting (in a memorable phrase) that the round house asserted 'a Tudor/Imperial equality contained in a vessel of cosmic order', while the entrance presented 'the balanced symbolism' which was carried through into the theatre itself. Anglo provides the longest description and discussion, combining material from the different sources, and arguing that the whole was an appeal 'to fulfil the chivalric ideal of life' represented by Arthur 'as an international figure of chivalry' (*Spectacle, Pageantry*, pp. 161–3).

The entrance consisted of a covered passage or vestibule 30ft long and over 15ft wide with decorated portals at either end.[82] The outer portal ruled by the figure of Arthur was by far the most elaborate, like one of those triumphal arches which were

---

[80] The only English source which gives any details of the entrance is Oxford, Bodleian, MS Ashmole 1116, ff.103ᵛ-5 [hereafter, 'Ashmole']. This lists the Latin 'posies and writings that were in the rownd howse made at Callais,' and forms part of a much longer document (ff.73–132ᵛ; see above n. 62) of court procedures and precedents finely written on paper bearing a watermark of a style first known to have been used in 1564 (C.M. Briquet, *Les Filigranes*, ed. J.S.G. Simmons (Amsterdam, 1968), i, 269–70, iii, No.4433). Ashmole is therefore a copy and not an original: see further, n. 86. The imperial account was published three months after the meeting: *Le triumphe festifz* (printed by Jean de Buyens, Arras, 27 October 1520; copy in the British Library, Dept. of Printed Books, C.33.e.28; hereafter *Le triumphe*). This consists of four un-numbered printed pages, with the arms of Charles V on f.4ᵛ. Although written in French, the arms show that it was an imperial production: Arras was at that time in imperial territory and did not become part of France until 1640. The meeting at Calais was of special interest to the French, who were not invited, and their account was also published in 1520: *L'ordonnance et ordre du tournoy, ioustes & combat* (printed by J. Lescaille, Paris, 1520; copy in the British Library, Dept. of Printed Books, C.33.d.22(1); hereafter *L'ordonnance*). After a long description of the Field of Cloth of Gold (ff.1–27), *L'ordonnance* continues with 'Les devises et dictz des Roys & personsnages miz et apposez au dessus des portes du festin faict a Callays' (ff.27ᵛ-8), indicating the position of each 'devise et dict', and providing the only known text of the French poem set below Arthur on the outer portal. The Venetian account was copied by Marino Sanuto the Younger (1466–1535), chronicler and hereditory legislator of Venice, in his diary, probably (since it is clearly an eye-witness description) from a report written by a Venetian at the court of Henry VIII, possibly Lodovico Spinelli. For the text, see *I diarii di Marino Sanuto*, ed. F. Stefani, 58 vols. (Venice, 1879–1902), xxix (1890), cols. 225–54 (hereafter, 'Sanuto'). This provides a long description of the Field of Cloth of Gold (cols. 225–50) followed by an account of the Calais meeting (cols. 250–4), including a minutely detailed section on the round house and its entrance (cols. 251–3) with the text of six of the mottoes. The whole was translated from one of the MS copies of Sanuto's diary by Rawdon Brown in his *CSP Venetian*, iii (1869), no.50, pp.14–34, but Rawdon Brown improved the Latin of the mottoes and his translation is not wholly satisfactory.

[81] Ashmole, f.104ʳ, followed by colon and a space and on the next line *Cui adhereo preest* (on which, see below, pp. 460–1). Kenneth Painter suggests to me that there may be in these lines a reminiscence of some of the language of Horace, *Odes* II, 15 (lines 1–2, 20). 'Ashmole' begins with an eight-line Latin poem introduced by a rubricated heading *De concordia Charoli Imperatoris et Henrici Angliae regis*, but gives no indication where or whether this was displayed in the round house. Ashmole then divides the remaining 'posies and writings' into three groups by rubricated headings: *In substuccionem Calesiensem*, 'the lowest storie', and 'the second storye'. Comparison with *Le triumphe*, *L'ordonnance*, and Sanuto shows that the ten of the eleven mottoes following the heading *In substuccionem Calesiensem* on f.104 were displayed in the entrance (for the eleventh, see below, n. 86). Since the poem *Miraris hospes* ... comes first after the heading, it was probably also at the entrance, and its content suggests it may have been the first thing the visitor saw. The rubric *In substuccionem Calesiensem* is corrupt: *substructionem*, 'under-building, foundation, substructure', presumably means here the entrance, a markedly lower element before the towering mass of the round house. 'On the Calais fore-building' is probably the meaning.

[82] Sanuto, col. 253. No other source provides these measurements. Throughout the description of the entrance which follows here, the details have to be pieced together from the four separate sources, none of which is complete.

so notable a feature of the pageant architecture of royal entries, as at Bruges for the young Charles in 1515, or at London in 1522 for the Emperor Charles and Henry VIII.[83] We will pass through this portal, returning to it later, and look first at the vestibule to which it led, and then at the inner portal opening into the round house.

The vestibule was lined by six columns or pillars, three to either side, on which were set gilded statues of kings and emperors.[84] *Le triumphe* alone records that the rulers had distinctive features or attributes. Each was accompanied by a motto of friendship.[85] The sources do not record that the statues were named, but three (and perhaps all) held shields bearing their arms. It is again only *Le triumphe* which lists in sequence *en entrant* the three to the right and the three to the left.[86]

On the right side

1. A statue holding a sceptre
Motto: *Amico fideli nulla est comparatio*
'A faithful friend is beyond compare'.[87]

2. The second holding a shield, *azure* a '*croix ancré*' and 5 fledglings *or* [King Edward the Confessor]

[83] Sydney Anglo, *La tryumphante Entree de Charles Prince des Espagnes en Bruges 1515* (Amsterdam and New York, n.d.); for London, see above, pp. 425–8.

[84] *Le triumphe*, f.2', line 13; cf. Sanuto, col.253, who says *sei statue regali dorate tre per lai*, but gives no other details of them. The other sources provide information about the vestibule as follows; 'Ashmole', mottoes only; *L'ordonnance*, mottoes and some locations; *Le triumphe* mottoes, with the location and attributes of the figures.

[85] The three sources which give the mottoes do not always agree. The most reliable text is *Ashmole*, the English source, which gives ten of the twelve, omitting only the second and third on the left. The mottoes are usually correct in *L'ordonnance*, but often corrupt in *Le triumphe*. The mottoes are commonplaces; where sources have been found, they come from Cicero, *De amicitia*, or from the Vulgate or the Apocrypha.

[86] *L'ordonnance* groups the mottoes three by three, by side, but does not say which side was which, and disagrees as to both sequence and side. Comparison between *Le triumphe* and 'Ashmole' shows that 'Ashmole' lists the mottoes in a logical order: outer portal (centre, left, right) vestibule left (1, [2, 3]), inner portal (left, centre, right), vestibule right (3, 2, 1), i.e., down the left side of the vestibule, across the inner portal from left to right, and back up the right side of the vestibule. 'Ashmole' has a different version on the left side of the vestibule: the motto *Diliges amicum tuum sicut te ipsum*, the first on the left, is followed by an otherwise unknown motto (*Amicitia principis est ad benevolentiam coniungendam*), and there is no third motto. This may suggest that 'Ashmole' copies a draft in which the left side of the vestibule was still being worked out. The general agreement on sequence between 'Ashmole' and *Le triumphe* confirms that the latter probably preserves the actual order as constructed.

[87] 'Ashmole', *L'ordonnance*; *Le triumphe* ... *nuliae* ... . Book of Jesus ben Sira 6.15 (Apocrypha, *Ecclesiasticus* 6.15).

Motto: *Verae amicitiae sempiternae sunt*
'True friendships are everlasting'.[88]

3. An emperor keeping watch, carrying a sceptre hanging downwards, his left hand carrying arms, above a shield with a sword in each quarter[89]
Motto: *In amicis nil requiritur sed voluntas.*[90]
'Goodwill is all that is asked for among friends'.

On the left side

1. An uncrowned king holding a sceptre and carrying a shield, *azure* three crowns *or* [Arthur[91]]
Motto: *Diliges amicum tuum sicut teipsum*
'You shall love your friend as you love yourself'.[92]

2. The second holding his sceptre in both hands lest it escape him
Motto: *Amicitiam natura ipsa peperit*
'Nature herself created the bond of friendship'.[93]

3. An emperor with a black beard, appearing roused like a watchman surprised
Motto: *Nullus diligit vivere sine amicis*
'No-one chooses to live without friends'.[94]

At the end of the vestibule, an inner portal opened into the interior of the round house, or as Sanuto calls it, the *theatro*.[95] Above the door there were three statues. In the centre stood a crowned, winged and clothed figure of a blindfold God of Love, his quiver by his side, holding a bow, with a dart in his right hand,[96] saying:

---

[88] 'Ashmole'; *L'ordonnance* with plurals in *-e*; *Le triumphe* with plurals in *-i*. Cicero, *De amicitia* 9.32.

[89] *Le triumphe*, f. 2ᵛ, line 21: *vng escu de to' les cartiers despaye*. The interpretation of these arms as showing a sword in each quarter is uncertain. Mr P. L. Dickinson, Richmond Herald, suggests to me that *despaye* might be a variant of the term *diaspré*, possibly denoting a plain quarterly shield with diapering, or (on the suggestion of Mr. John Goodall) *desplayé*, meaning a shield with all the quarterings displayed.

[90] 'Ashmole'; *L'ordonnance*, *In amicis non res queritur sed voluntas*; *Le Triumphe*, as *L'ordonnace* but beginning *In amicte ...*

[91] C.W. Scott-Giles, 'Some Arthurian Coats of Arms', *Coat of Arms* 8 (1964–5), 333. Mr Dickinson points out to me that this shield was also associated with early English kings such as Edmund the Martyr, and that the arms *Azure three crowns in pale Or* are attributed to Beli Mawr.

[92] 'Ashmole'; *L'ordonnance*, *Le triumphe ... teipsum*. Cf. *Leviticus* 19.18; *Matthew* 19.19, 22.39; *Mark* 12,31, 33; etc.

[93] *L'ordonnance*; *Le triumphe*, ... *pepetit*; not in 'Ashmole'. Cicero, *De amicitia* 5.19.

[94] *L'ordonnance*; *Le triumphe*, with errors; not in 'Ashmole'.

[95] Sanuto, col. 254; cf. col. 251, *amphiteatro, theatro*.

Inveni hominem secundum cor meum
'I have found a man after my own heart'.[97]

Clearly this is not the usual Blind Cupid, but a much more formidable figure, a princely God of Love of the kind first found unblindfold in allegorical epics of the *Roman de la Rose* type, and subsequently as a blindfold figure in illustrations of the *Ovide Moralisé* and their derivatives.[98]

To the left, in the position of honour on the God's right,[99] stood a *Landsknecht* holding a pike, and in one hand a scroll with the words:

Intus pax habitat nos pro foribus vigilamus
'Peace dwells within; we stand watch before her gates'.[100]

To the right, on the God's left, was an English archer with his buckler, drawing on his bow and arrow, with a scroll bearing the motto:

Stet procul hinc qui pacem violare velit
'Let him stand well away, who might wish to break the peace'.[101]

The inner portal, the God of Love supported by typical soldiers of the Empire and of England, was the final defence before entry to the Temple of Concord

[96] The description given here is that of *L'ordonnance* (Sig. fii^r): *vng roy couronne a poinctes, qui a vng petit auberion esmaille dor, vng bas de chausses et soulliers en laboureur, les yeulx bandez, aiant sa trousse a son coste. Et a main droicte vne fleche quil gecte degeet, et de laultre main tient larc auec des aelles, qui ne dit riens.* Sanuto, col. 253, says simply *un dio di amor vestito con questo ditto a piedi*, while *Le triumphe* (f. 2^v) has only *cupido aueugle couronne tenant arc et trouse a vng dart en sa dextre disant ...* .

[97] 'Ashmole', *Le triumphe*, Sanuto; *L'ordonnance* says that the figure *ne dit riens*. Cf. *Acts* 13.22.

[98] Erwin Panofsky, *Studies in Iconology* (Torchbook edn, New York and Evanston, 1962), pp. 95–128, cf. esp. pp. 101–3 with p. 114, and illustrations 73–4 (Pl. XLIII) with 82 (Pl. XLVI) and 86–7 (Pl. XLVIII). The Calais figure seems to have been very similar to a picture of 'Blind Cupid', Venus and the Three Graces in a 14th-century French MS (Paris, BN, ms. Fr. 373, f. 207) illustrated by Panofsky, ibid., illustration 86.

[99] *Le triumphe* and *L'ordonnance* both say to the left, and this agrees with the sequence of mottoes in Ashmole. Sanuto, col. 253, says that the statues which flanked the *dio di amor* were both *a man destra*, a error which invalidates his evidence on this point. A position to the God's right, placing the *Landsknecht* in the position of honour by comparison with the English archer, agrees with the arrangement of the outer portal, see below, pp. 458–60.

[100] 'Ashmole', *L'ordonnance*, *Le triumphe* ... *pro foris* ...; Sanuto ... *pro servis* ... .

[101] 'Ashmole'; *Le triumphe* ... *hic pacem qui* ...; *L'ordonnance*, *Estet procul hic pacem qui violare velit* ; Sanuto *Qui violat pacem hinc procul habeat*.

(*templum ... regie concordiae*). The outer portal thirty feet away at the entrance to the vestibule was a much grander affair, *fort gorgiasement et triumphament faict*,[102] a triumphal arch for a triumphal entry, where Arthur presided over the personifications, arms, and badges of the Emperor and of England.

Above the outer portal stood three statues of life-size, *bien painct et bien dore*.[103] At the centre, *un peu plus haut*,[104] was the figure of King Arthur in royal apparel, holding his sceptre in one hand and the Round Table in the other.[105] Below his feet a scroll bore three royal crowns *per traverso*.[106] Below was written in French:

> Moy Artus roy chef de la table ronde
> Principal chef de tous cueurs vallereux
> Vueil receuoir de volunte parfonde
> Tous nobles cueurs par effect vertueux
> Princes puissans preux et audacieux
> Ayans honneur soubz vostre seigneurie
> Suyuez mes faitz et ma cheuallerie.[107]

> I, King Arthur, head of the Table Round,
> Principal leader of all valorous hearts,
> Wish to receive with profound good will
> All noble hearts made virtuous by deed.
> Puissant princes, valiant and brave,
> You who have honour at your command,
> Follow my deeds and my knightliness.

---

[102] *Le triumphe*, f. 2^r, line 25.

[103] *Le triumphe*, f. 2^r, line 27.

[104] *L'ordonnance*, Sig. fi^v.

[105] *Le triumphe*, f. 2^r, lines 28–9: *vng roy artus qui tenoit vne table ronde a tous bons cheualiers et droicturiers a soustenir et deffendre tout le monde*. These words, which appear to be a comment by the author of *Le triumphe* rather than a description of anything shown on the table held by Arthur, may paraphrase the French poem which follows and which *Le triumphe* does not quote.

[106] Sanuto, col. 253. Cf. the arms on the shield held by the first king on the left in the vestibule, above p. 456.

[107] The text is preserved only in *L'ordonnance*, Sig. fi^v, except that Sanuto (*I diarii*, col. 253), stating specifically that the verses were in French, gives the sense of the first three lines in Italian. The use of French, the language of Arthurian romance, would in no way diminish the role of Arthur in this bid for English influence, and underlines the surviving importance of Arthurian material as a political metaphor. I am most grateful to my colleague, Dr Roger Pensom, for his comments.

Beneath these verses, there was a golden shield bearing on a blue field two drawn swords held by two hands, interlaced with a scoll bearing the motto:

> *Cui adhereo preest*
> 'Whom I support, wins'.[108]

It was, Sanuto noted, a motto which 'induced much comment' (*dil quale è stato ditto assai*).[109]

To the left, in the position of honour on Arthur's right, were the symbols of the Empire and of the Emperor Charles V, King Henry's guest.[110] Next to Arthur stood a black eagle holding in its claws a banner with the emperor's arms. Beside the eagle stood Hercules, club in hand, and below his feet a scroll with Charles's badge, the Pillars of Hercules and his motto *Plus ultra*, 'More Beyond'.[111] Below was the motto:

> *Amicus fidelis est protectio fortis*
> 'A faithful friend is a strong defence'.[112]

To the right, on Arthur's left, were the symbols of England and of Henry Tudor. Next to Arthur reared the Red Dragon holding a banner with the arms of England. Beside the dragon stood a crowned king in armour, sword (or spear) in hand, bearing on a shield his arms, quartered first and third *or* a lion *de genses* (probably for *gules*, the

---

[108] *Le triumphe*, ff. 2^r-v, and Sanuto, col. 253, both describe this shield and quote the motto. For the text and its meaning, see below, pp. 460–1.

[109] Sanuto, col. 253.

[110] *Le triumphe* and *L'ordonnance* both say to the left. Sanuto, col. 253, says to the contrary that Hercules stood *a man destra* and the Man-at-Arms *a man sinistra*. A position to Arthur's right, placing Hercules and the emperor's symbols in the position of honour, agrees with the arrangement of the inner portal, see above, p. 457 and n. 99. Sanuto, or his source, or a copyist, made an error in giving the positions on the inner portal: the agreement of *Le triumphe* and *L'ordonnance* seems conclusive for the arrangement of both portals.

[111] *Le triumphe*, f. 2^v; cf. the engraving of the emperor's arms on f. 4^v. Charles V's motto, *Plus Ultra*, 'More Beyond', and his emblem showing the motto on a scroll spanning and interlacing the Columns of Hercules (the Straits of Gibraltar), was designed by the humanist Ludovico Marliano (M. Fernández Alvarez, *Charles V* (London, 1975, p. 71). Ludovico or Luigi Marliano (before 1484–1521), born at Milan, the philosopher and celebrated mathematician, bishop of Tui (Túy) in Galicia, was Charles V's doctor. His invention of Charles's motto and emblem is recorded by Paolo Giovio, *Dialogo dell' Imprese* (8vo, Venice, 1557), p. 14.

[112] 'Ashmole'; *L'ordonnance*, *Le triumphe* omit *est*; Sanuto, *Fidelis amicus protector fortis*. Book of Jesus ben Sira 6.14 (Apocrypha, *Ecclesiasticus* 6.14).

heraldic colour red), second and fourth *azure* three crowns *or*.[113] Below on a scroll was the motto:

> *Verus amicus est alter ego*
> 'A true friend is your other self'.[114]

This armed warrior supporting Arthur's left cannot be simply a 'man-at-arms', but like Hercules supporting Arthur's right a figure of power and significance. His arms, England quartering Arthur, are those usually attributed to Brutus the Trojan, the mythical first king of Britain. It is the British History which is important here and not the saints, hence no St. George.

The key to all this, not only to the imagery and symbolism of the round house and its entrance, but to the intent of the whole meeting at Calais, was the motto, *Cui adhereo preest*. Set immediately above the outer portal, below the figure of Arthur and Arthur's verses of welcome, it occupied the most prominent position possible.

The text of the motto is recorded by 'Ashmole', *Le triumphe*, and Sanuto; it is omitted by *L'ordonnance*. 'Ashmole' gives the Latin motto without explanation, *Le triumphe* explains it, but on the basis of a reading so inaccurate as to be almost meaningless,[115] and Sanuto gives the text remarking only that it caused much comment.[116] Giovio, writing thirty years later but probably relying on a contemporary source, provides the only near-contemporary comment we have:

> Nec multo post Caesar, quod iam enata essent semina orientis belli inter se et Galliae Regem, ab Hispania rediens in Britanniam divertit, non obscura obtrectatione eius colloquii: ita ut tres simul Reges coire voluisse crederentur. Sed uterque, praemoliens bellum et iam arma parans, Britannum [*for* Britannicum] socium sibi asciscere contend-

---

[113] *Le triumphe*, f. 2ᵛ, lines 2–4, has the fullest description: *vng roy courone portant son escu escartels premier et tiece cartier dor vng leon de genses, les deux otstres dazur a trois couronnes dor et disoit en son dictier* (*Verus amicus est alter ego*). *Et auoit les armes dangleterre a vng petit escuchen prez de luy et art' tenant vne banniere de denotre armes dangleterre ...* Sanuto, col. 253, is clearer: *uno armato da homo d'arme con lanza in mano, et soto i piede un scrito con l'arme vechie de Ingaltera, di sotto questo ditto ... Tra questa imagine e quella regia* [*sc.* Arthur] *era quel drago rosso che porta questo Re con la bandiera in mano, overo l'arma de Ingaltera*. *L'ordonnance* (Sig. fiᵛ) says only that the figure was *tout arme aiant une espee en la main*. I am most grateful to Richmond Herald for his identification of these arms as those usually attributed to Brutus.

[114] 'Ashmole', *L'ordonnance*, *Le triumphe*; Sanuto has *Amicus fidelis ...*, probably by confusion with the previous motto.

[115] 'Ashmole', Sanuto, *Cui adhereo preest*; *Le triumphe*, *Cui adhereor pre me est*, 'cest a dire deuant est cely a qui ie adhere'. The version printed by Giovio in 1552 includes two diphthongs (*Cui adhæreo præest*). *Cui adhereo preest* seems likely to have been the spelling on the Calais portal.

[116] See above, p. 459.

ebat. Nam ille, belli et pacis arbiter existimari cupiens, dudum animi sui argumentum tam aptum quam insolens in foribus ligneae domus supra armatum ingentem sagittarium, habitu Britannico scite perpictum, praetulerat hoc titulo: CUI ADHAEREO PRAEEST.

Not long afterwards [i.e. after the meeting of Henry and Francis on the Field of Cloth of Gold] the Emperor-elect, perceiving that the seeds of a coming war between himself and the French king were already in the air, turned aside on his journey back from Spain to visit Britain. He did this not out of some hidden jealousy of that meeting, but because the three kings might be supposed to have wanted to meet together at the same time. But each was preparing for war and was already arming himself, and was engaged in a struggle to secure the British king as an ally. The latter, wanting to be seen as the arbiter of war and peace, had recently set out his position, as apt as it was impertinent, at the entrance to the wooden house. There, above the huge armed figure of an archer painted clad in British costume, was the motto: WHOM I SUPPORT WINS.

Whether written by Giovio himself or taken more or less verbatim from his source, this is an accurate analysis of the political situation, even if the text does conflate the meetings of June and July 1520.[117] It is an analysis which was followed by all later writers, Flemish, French and English, in the seventeenth and eighteenth centuries, until the motto and its significance were gradually forgotten.[118] As for the translation of the motto, the French *Qui i'accompagne est maistre* of François de Mezeray gets the sense very well: of the two contending kings, the one I support will win, or in the argot of the later twentieth century, 'Arthur's friend rules, OK!.'

The Arthur of Calais was not simply 'an international figure of chivalry', and his appeal was not by any means an appeal 'to fulfil the chivalric ideal of life'.[119] Nor, though nearer the mark, was he a figure of 'Tudor/Imperial equality', even if the round house itself was in some sense 'a vessel of cosmic order in which equality was contained'.[120] Rather, at one level, the figure of Arthur at Calais stands for England, not wholly unlike the John Bull of later years, or even the defiant Tommy of Low's famous cartoon, 'Very well, alone!', of June 1940. At another level Arthur is Henry: 'Whom Henry supports, wins.'

[117] See below, Appendix II, pp. 519–20.
[118] For further discussion and references, see Appendix II.
[119] Anglo, *Spectacle, Pagentry*, pp. 161–3.
[120] Orrell, as above, nn. 69, 79.

Whether the Arthur of Calais was actually in the likeness of Henry, cannot now be known. But the concentration upon likeness two years later in the London entry of June 1522 and during the visit (Plate XXVIII), and the appearance of Henry as Arthur four years earlier in 1516 in the painting of the Winchester table, may suggest that at Calais the face that looked down over the entrance to the round house was that of Henry himself. How much more pointed then the motto: 'Whom I support, wins!'

Arthur's choice is made explicit on the inner portal where the God of Love standing in the central position declares in the first person, *Inveni hominem secundum cor meum*, 'I have found a man after my own heart'. Not two men, but one: Charles is Arthur's chosen ally. No such imagery appeared at Guisnes, whatever the expressions of friendship between Henry and Francis. The imagery of Calais has a different tone, more personal, more perhaps familial. What then was the role which Arthur played between Habsburg and Tudor?

At Calais in July Arthur is the reigning figure. He commands the entrance, welcoming the princes, offering his support. He declares his allegiance without equivocation. In the tortuous balance of power between the Empire and France, the side with Arthur's support will prevail.

At Guisnes in June, Arthur appeared only as one of the Nine Worthies in a company of maskers which went to the French queen at Ardres on the last Sunday. The company, the first of four each comprising ten maskers, was led by Hercules, more splendidly dressed than the rest. When they devisored and showed their faces, Hercules was revealed as Henry himself.[121]

There was only one other possible Arthurian reference at Guisnes. A gallery *faicte et couverte de verdure* led from the castle of Guisnes to the English palace so that Henry could pass to and fro at his pleasure without appearing in public.[122] Something about this green corridor made the French author of *L'ordonnance* describe it as *difficile comme la maison de dedalus ou le iardin de morgue la fee du temps des chevaliers errans* ('difficult as the house of Daedalus or the garden of Morgan le Fay in the time of the knights errant').[123] Emphasising the secret and private character of the passage (which the

---

[121] Edward Hall, *The Vnion of the Two Noble and Illustre Famelies of Lancaster and York* (London, 1548), f. 83ʳ [reprinted, The Scholar Press (Manston, 1970), f. 83ʳ]; cf. Anglo, *Spectacle, Pagentry*, pp. 157–8. See also Edward Hall, *Chronicle* (London, 1809), p. 619.

[122] *L'ordonnance*, f. 12ʳ; Sanuto, *I diarii*, col. 233 (cf. *CalSPVenetian*, p. 3 (1869), p. 20); Hall, *Chronicle* (1809), p. 606.

[123] *L'ordonnance*, f. 12ʳ. The house of Daedalus, the labyrinth of King Minos, refers to the hidden and concealing nature of the covered gallery. Morgan le Fay was Arthur's sister. Cf. Stephen Bamforth and Jean Dupèbe (ed.), "Francisci Francorum regis et Henrici Anglorum Colloquium" by Jacques Dubois', *Renaissance Studies* 5.1–2 (1991), 222 (lines 90–3), 228.

French writer will have seen only from the outside), these comparisons are probably no more than descriptive. They emphasise that at the Field of Cloth of Gold, Arthur had no role to play.

Why should this have been so? What was there in July 1520 at Calais, and in June 1522 in London and at Winchester, which made the figure of Arthur so potent an image at Henry VIII's meetings with Charles V, Emperor-elect of the Romans? The answer lies in Austria where at the beginning of the sixteenth century Arthur played a far from insignificant role in the imagery of the Habsburg court.

Maximilian and Arthur

The single most dramatic statement of Habsburg interest is the magnificent bronze statue of Arthur in the Hofkirche in Innsbruck (Fig. 159). The emperor Maximilian (1493–1519) had begun to plan the construction of his tomb as early as 1502, but died before it was completed and was buried in the chapel of the castle of Wiener Neustadt where he had been born nearly sixty years before in 1459. Maximilian had developed the concept of his monument, but apparently had not thought seriously where it was to be placed, and it was his successor but one as emperor of Germany, Ferdinand I (1521–64), who brought the monument as near completion as was possible.[124]

Maximilian's intention seems to have been that his monument should be a dynastic celebration, a political memorial and a political testament as much or even more than a tomb.[125] Around the sarcophagus, itself decorated with marble reliefs of the emperor's most famous victories, were to stand forty larger than life bronze statues of his ancestors, encompassing the continuity of the imperial idea, from Julius Caesar, the founder of the empire of Antiquity, and Charlemagne, the renewer of the empire in Christian dress.[126] To these were added the heirs of the House of Habsburg and their related lines, Maximilian's own family, and his relations by marriage, representing the extension of Habsburg policy towards a European imperium – Burgundy, Portugal, Spain, and England, here represented by King Arthur to whom Maximilian sought to claim relationship through his mother-in-law, Margaret of York.

Only twenty-eight of these figures were ever cast, ten or so in Maximilian's lifetime, the first bronze statues of such a size to be cast north of the Alps since the

---

[124] Erich Egg, *Die Hofkirche in Innsbruck: das Grabdenkmal Kaiser Maximilians I. und die silberne Kapelle* (Innsbruck, Wien, München, 1974), p. 14.

[125] Ibid. p. 13.

[126] Ibid. p. 12.

159 'King Arthur of England', statue by Peter Vischer, 1513, for the monument of the Emperor Maximilian I in the Hofkirche, Innsbruck.

160 'King Arthur of England, count of Habsburg', copy of a design by Gilg Sesselschreiber, *c.*1502–8, for a statue of Arthur for the monument of the Emperor Maximilian I in the Hofkirche, Innsbruck.

465

161 Jacob Mennel presents the five books of his *Fürstlichen Chronik* to the Emperor Maximilian I, 1518.

Roman period. The first of these, cast in 1510, was King Ferdinand of Portugal (*d.* 1383). The second and third, both cast in Nuremberg in 1513 by Peter Vischer the Elder (*c.*1460–1529), were Theoderich, king of the Ostrogoths (454–526), and King Arthur 'of England'. Arthur, 'determined and tense, his form rounded and forbidding [is] a virile hero of legend who unites the bright idealism of the Apostles with the muted other-worldliness of the "self-portrait"' (Fig. 159).[127] Such is the quality and early Renaissance style of both the Theoderich and the Arthur that the pair have often with reason been attributed to lost designs by Albert Dürer, but this 'work of the highest significance could without doubt be the achievement of Vischer's own development'.[128]

Such a *tour de force* had not been achieved without difficulty. Designs for the various statues had been made by several hands.[129] Two for the Arthur survive in copies made by Jörg Kölderer. One shows 'Artus kunig zu Enngellanndt' in full armour, robed and crowned, with open visor, a pastiche of the arms of England below: it is not an heroic figure.[130] The second, from an original design by Gilg Sesselschreiber drawn *c.*1508–12, is altogether more accomplished (Fig. 160).[131] In full armour, his visor closed, crowned, wearing an order which is (rightly) neither the Garter nor the Fleece, Arthur holds a sceptre in his right hand and in his left the strap of a shield bearing the Royal Arms of England.[132] Above his head is an inscription which encapsulates the whole purpose of his presence here: *Kunig Artus zu Enngllandt Graue zu Habspurg*, 'King Arthur of England, Count of Habsburg'. It is a remarkable claim.

---

[127] Gert von Osten and Horst Wey, *Painting and Sculpture in Germany and the Netherlands 1500–1600* (Harmondsworth, 1969), pp. 24–5, Pl. 12.

[128] Ibid. 25. See also V. Oberhammer, *Die Bronzestandbilder des Maximiliangrabmales in der Hofkirche zu Innsbruck* (Innsbruck, 1935), i, pp. 404–19, Abb. 229–30, 232. The coats of arms of both statues, cast probably by Stefan Godl in Innsbruck, were added *c.*1533 (Egg, *Die Hofkirche*, p. 32). Arthur's shield shows the Royal Arms of England with the quartering reversed.

[129] Pierre du Colombier, 'Les Triomphes en images de l'empereur Maxmilien 1er', in J. Jacquot (ed.), *Les fetes de la Renaissance*, ii, *Charles Quint* (Paris, 1960), 99–112, at p. 100.

[130] Kunsthistorisches Museum, Vienna, Pergamentrolle Inv. Nr. 5333, from Schloss Ambras near Innsbruck; reproduced in Egg, *Die Hofkirche*, rear end-paper.

[131] Vienna, Österreichisches Nationalbibliothek, Cod. 8329, fol. 27r. See Oberhammer, *Die Bronzestandbilder*, p. 197, 252–3, Abb. 87; von Osten and Wey, *Painting and Sculpture*, Pls. 13, 14.

[132] France Modern quartering England, adopted by Henry IV in 1405 and in use until 1603. On an escutcheon in the middle of the quartered shield is a lion rampant, the earliest known English arms, used by Richard I from his accession in 1189 until the striking of a new Great Seal in 1195 when the three lions passant guardant were adopted. This curious escutcheon perhaps reflects a recognition that Arthur must antedate any coat of arms showing France Modern, first adopted by Charles V of France (1364–80). Be that as it may, Sesselschreiber or some herald had been doing their homework.

Two other huge works of art were created by Maximilian's command, both engravings on wood for printing and eventual wide distribution, the *Ehrenpforte* or 'Triumphal Arch' and the *Triumphzug* or 'triumph'. The Triumphal Arch, one of the largest prints ever produced, was devised by Johann Stabius, court historian and mathematician, after the model of the ancient triumphal arches of the Roman emperors. The design was a team-effort carried out in 1512–15,[133] the overall appearance of the structure by Jörg Kölderer and the individual scenes and architectural elements by Dürer, who sub-contracted much of the work to his pupils. It was engraved in 1515–17 on 192 wood blocks. Although displaying Maximilian's genealogy in the form of a family tree, together with events from his public and private life, and busts of emperors, kings, and ancestors, Arthur does not appear. This is strange given Kölderer's role in the design, for he was also involved at this time in the development of the design for Maximilian's tomb-monument. In addition, Henry VIII does appear in a scene showing the meeting of Maximilian and Henry at Thérouanne in 1513 (cf. Plate XXVII).[134] Arthur's absence is perhaps to be explained by the fact that he could not be fitted into the family tree, where the degree of relationship would have had to be made explicit,[135] but he could perhaps have been placed among the Roman emperors or the Holy Roman emperors,[136] although this too would have required a perhaps unacceptable degree of precision.

Maximilian's *Triumphzug*, 'Triumph Car', was designed after the Roman manner on the analogy of the *Triumph* of Andrea Mantegna, , painted in 1490–5.[137] The initial scheme was worked out in a series of miniatures begun by Jörg Kölderer and his assistants in 1512/13 and finished in July 1515.[138] The engraving on 132 separate woodblocks took a further five years. It was completed in 1519 after Maximilian's death, but not published until 1526.[139] The subject is a long procession among which a series of 'floats', each set on a horse-borne litter, precede Maximilian's triumphal car.

---

[133] du Colombier, 'Les Triomphes', 99, 102, 107. A copy is displayed in the British Museum, next to the entrance to the restaurant (Dept. of Prints and Drawings, E.5–1; see Campbell Dodgson, *Catalogue of Early German and Flemish Woodcuts* (London, 1903), p. 311). For a complete reproduction see [Anon.], *Maximilian's Triumphal Arch; Woodcuts by Albrecht Dürer and Others*, Dover Publications (New York, 1972), which contains at reduced size all the plates from the edition by Eduard Chmelarz ('Die Ehrenpforte des Kaisers Maximilian I.', *Jahrbuch der Kunsthistorischen Sammlungen des Allerhöchsten Kaiserhauses* 4 (1886), pp. 289–319, plates to original size in *Supplementband* (1885–6)), with an introduction based on Chmelarz's essay of 1886, and further information from Joseph Meder, *Dürer-Katalog* (Vienna, 1932).

[134] [Anon.], *Maximilian's Triumphal Arch*, Pl. 20 (a, lower).

[135] Ibid. Pls. 27–8.

[136] Ibid. Pls. 12, 13, 16.

[137] For Mantegna's *Triumph*, see Andrew Martindale, *The Triumphs of Caesar by Andrea Mantegna* (London, 1979); du Colombier, 'Les Triomphes', 104–4.

The floats carry funerary statues representing 'the bold emperors, kings, arch-dukes, and dukes whose coat of arms and name Emperor Maximilian bears and whose land he rules',[140] engraved by Hans Springinklee, a pupil of Dürer's. On the third float the four figures are, King Odobert of Provence, King Arthur of England, King John of Portugal, and Godfrey of Bouillon, 'king' of Jerusalem.[141] Arthur is in full armour ('ganntz harnasch'[142]), crowned not helmeted, a sceptre in his right hand, his left grasping the hilt of his sword, with before him a shield bearing the three lions of England. The earlier miniature shows 'Artus kunig zu Engelland' as a standing armoured figure, bearded, crowned, with a sceptre in his right hand and his left hand resting on a shield with the three 'lions'.[143] The miniature is quite different in detail to the woodcut, but the attributes are the same. Neither the woodcut, the miniature, nor the statue in the Hofkirche show Arthur wearing the hooped crown imperial. This was an English conceit; in Austria the hooped crown was reserved to the Holy Roman emperors.

These extraordinary claims, that Arthur had been Graf von Habsburg and that Maximilian bore Arthur's arms and ruled over the land that Arthur had ruled, have no basis in historical fact. They represent Maximilian's devotion to the Arthurian ideal, an ideal which permeates his autobiographical writings (Fig. 161).[144]

Maximilian gave an account of his early life and deeds in three biographies *à clef*, cast in the form of Arthurian romances. Because he was always too poor to under-take great works of architecture or sculpture (with the exception of his unfinished tomb at Innsbruck), Maximilian decided in middle age to idealise his deeds and perpetuate his memory using the new technology of the printing press and the

---

[138] Franz Winzinger, *Die Miniaturen zum Triumphzug Kaiser Maximilians I.* (*Faksimileband* and *Kommentarband*), Veröffentlichungen der Albertina 5, ed. Walter Koschatzky (Graz, 1972); see also Franz Unterkirchen (ed.), *Maximilian I. 1459–1519 Austellung*, Österreichische Nationalbibliothek, Graphische Sammlung Albertina, Kunsthistorisches Museum (Waffensammlung), 23. Mai bis 30. September 1959, Biblos-Schriften 23 (Wien, 1959), Kat. Nr. 246 (p. 86).

[139] For a complete reproduction, see Stanley Appelbaum, *The Triumph of Maximilian I. 137 Woodcuts by Hans Burg-kmair and Others*, Dover Publications (New York, 1964); see also du Colombier, 'Les Triomphes', 99.

[140] Translation quoted from Appelbaum, *The Triumph*, p. 14.

[141] Appelbaum, *The Triumph*, pp. 14–15, Pl. 108.

[142] Winzinger, *Die Miniaturen, Kommentarband*, p. 51.

[143] Winzinger, *Die Miniaturen, Faksimileband*, Pl. 31 (left) [in colour], *Kommentarband*, Bild 31: Albertina-Katalog 258, Inv. Nr. 25.234; *Maximilian I. Austellung*, Kat. Nr. 246. This miniature shows a different group of figures: Ladislaus (king of Hungary and Bohemia, 1440–57); John (king of Portugal, 1385–1433), Albrecht (Roman king of Hungary and Bohemia, 1438–8), and Arthur, king of England.

[144] Hans Rupprich, 'Das literarische Werk Kaiser Maximilians I.', in E. Egg (ed.), *Ausstellung Maximilian I. Innsbruck* (Innsbruck, 1969), 47–55 [pagination following catalogue]. For Jacob Mennel and his *Fürstlichen Chronik* shown in Fig. 161, see above, p. 53, n. 64.

woodcut: 'his books would include woodcuts and engravings from South Germany's leading artists, set to the rhetoric of her humanists, orators and poets in the mode of Dürer, Celtis and Peutinger.'[145]

The first, *Weisskunig*, told in prose the story of Maximilian's life and that of his parents from before his birth in 1459 until his early manhood.[146] Maximilian is the young White King (or Wise King), surrounded by figures of the contemporary world lightly disguised by names which were meant immediately to be deciphered. 'Knights calling themselves the King of Troy and the King of Europe perform deeds of great courage, while observing rituals known to them and their audiences from the literature they cherish', romances such as *Parsifal* and *Tristan*.[147]

Weisskunig was left unfinished and not published until 1775, but *Theuerdank* was published in 1517. A verse romance in which Maximilian is the hero Theuerdank, the 'Great Thinker', it gives 'an encoded and fictionalised account' of the most important event in his life, his journey to the land of his bride-to-be, Mary of Burgundy, and his next eight years as ruler of the duchy.[148]

Freydal ('the White [Wise] and Happy Youth'), the third of these tales, tells in verse a story devoted entirely to chivalric combat games and masquerades. The Youth is set difficult and dangerous tasks by three royal maidens; when eventually he returns to his father's court, he is sent as ambassador to a powerful queen; she is one of the three maidens of his previous encounters, whom he now marries.[149] The text was left unfinished, but the 265 woodcuts show sixty-four different series of joust, combat and masquerade based on actual events in Maximilian's life, 'a striking testimony to the sheer diversity of his chivalric expertise'.[150]

As the underlying theme of the Arthurian story is the knight finding moral and ethical renewal for himself and his society, so the theme of Maximilian's trilogy is his

---

[145] Gerhard Benecke, *Maximilian I (1459–1519). An Analytical Biography* (London, 1982), pp. 16–17, from whom the quotation is taken; William Henry Jackson, 'The Tournament and Chivalry in German Tournament Books of the Sixteenth Century and in the Literary Works of Emperor Maximilian I', in Christopher Harper-Bill and Ruth Harvey (ed.), *The Ideals and Practice of Medieval Knighthood*, Papers from the First and Second Strawberry Hill Conferences (Woodbridge, 1986), 49–73, at p.58.

[146] A. Schultz (ed.), 'Der Weisskunig', *Jahrbuch der Kunsthistorischen Sammlungen des Allerhöchsten Kaiserhauses* 6 (1888), 1–558; H. Th. Musper *et al.* (ed.), *Kaiser Maximilians I. Weisskunig*, 2 vols., (Stuttgart, 1956).

[147] Gerhild S. Williams, 'The Arthurian Model in Emperor Maximilian's Autobiographic Writings *Weisskunig* and *Theuerdank*', *Sixteenth-Century Journal* 11.4 (1980), 3–22, at pp. 14–15.

[148] S. Laschitzer (ed.), 'Der Theuerdank', *Jahrbuch der Kunsthistorischen Sammlungen des Allerhöchsten Kaiserhauses* 8 (1888), 1–580; Rupprich, 'Literarische Werk', 52–3. Comment quoted from Jackson, 'Tournament and Chivalry', 58.

[149] Quirin von Leitner, *Freydal. Des Kaisers Maximilian I. Turniere und Mummereien* (Vienna, 1880–2); P. Krenn, 'Heerwesen, Waffe und Turnier unter Kaiser Maximilian I.', in Egg (ed.), *Ausstellung Maximilian I. Innsbruck*, pp. 86–92; Rupprich, 'Literarische Werk', p. 52.

[150] Jackson, 'Tournament and Chivalry', 59.

struggle against allegorical adversaries, reflecting his perception of himself 'as a knight and ruler in the Arthurian tradition.'[151] Gerhild Williams has shown in a fundamental study how 'the basic image, the guiding concept and catalyst of his life and his autobiography, Maximilian found in the idea and ideal of King Arthur and his Knights of the Round Table'.[152] Here lies the explanation of the appearance of the figure of Arthur in Maximilian's artistic endeavours, and the justification, if one were needed, of the heroic nobility of the bronze Arthur among the real and imagined ancestors of the Hofkirche grave monument (Fig. 159). Given Maximilian's all-encompassing family genealogy, it was thus only natural for him to see Arthur as a Habsburg.[153] 'In true medieval fashion, emperors, princes, knights, and martyrs preceded Maximilian in a long line of excellence which pointed forward to him as its zenith, its momentary fulfillment.'[154] In a not dissimilar way later ages came to look back to Maximilian as *der letzte Ritter*, 'the last of the knights.' However, despite Arthur's inclusion among the Hofkirche bronzes and in the Triumphzug, he does not appear in the 'Genealogy', or on the fundamentally genealogical and historical *Ehrenpforte*. These omissions may suggest reasonable uncertainty amongst Maximilian's scholarly advisors as to the grounds for claiming Arthur as one of his 'ancestors'. If the cost of the Innsbruck bronze is an indication, this uncertainty may not have been shared by Maximilian.

Maximilian's *imitatio Arthurii* in jousts, tournies, courtly conduct, art and literature[155] invites comparison with the attitudes and actions of King Edward I of England as we have explored them in Chapter 10:

> In late medieval Europe the Arthurian Model continued to provide a strong conceptual basis for identification with a political ideal and a potent vehicle of imperial propaganda. It proved flexible enough to be adapted to imperial, knightly, princely and even bourgeois ambitions. ... Maximilian was aware of its potential and used it to interpret his own life and, in so doing, tried to influence his audience in their acceptance of his ambitions.[156]

---

[151] Williams, 'The Arthurian Model', p. 18, and cf. pp. 6 and 10.

[152] Ibid. p. 4.

[153] S. Laschitzer (ed.), 'Die Genealogie des Kaisers Maximilian I.', *Jahrbuch der Kunsthistorischen Sammlungen des Allerhöchsten Kaiserhauses* 7 (1888), 1–201; idem (ed.), 'Die Heiligen aus der Sipp-, Mag- und Schwägerschaft Kaiser Maximilians I.', ibid., 4 (1886), 70–288, 5 (1887), 117–261.

[154] Williams, 'The Arthurian Model', p. 3.

[155] Again, I owe this phrase to Gerhild Williams: 'The Arthurian Model', p. 20.

[156] Williams, 'The Arthurian Model', p. 22.

Here, in a study of Maximilian's literary works, undertaken independently of any consideration of the use of Arthurian imagery by an English ruler to influence Habsburg policy, we have the complete explanation of why in 1520 the image of Arthur played so prominent a role at Calais in Henry VIII's reception of Maximilian's successor. Arthur was precisely the right image to use at this juncture, precisely the right figure to whom to attribute the motto *Cui adhaereo praeest*, 'Whom I support wins.'

The appeal was made of course not to Maximilian but to his grandson, the young Charles. But the meeting was held in the aftermath of Charles's election as emperor, and it was in this context that Maximilian had structured his claim to an Arthurian inheritance. We have no indication that Charles was particularly influenced by Maximilian's Arthurianism, but he must have been fully aware of it, briefed by his advisors on the significance of England's use of the figure of Arthur, if in no other way.

The question remains, how did Henry's advisors know that Arthur was a figure of significance for the Habsburgs? As so often seems to be the case, the king's own knowledge may have been decisive. Henry and Maximilian met only once, at Thérouanne, Lille and Tournai during the French war of August and September 1513, when they were together on and off for nearly six weeks (Pl. XXVII).[157] This was the moment when all Maximilian's great artistic and literary endeavours were under way: Peter Vischer cast the bronze Arthur for the grave monument the same year, the designs for the 'Triumphal Arch' and the 'Triumph Car' were complete, the compilation of *Weisskunig*, *Theuerdank*, and *Freydal* had been in progress for some years. Arthur was an obvious point of contact between Tudor and Habsburg and could have been the subject of one of 'the diuerse goodly pagiantes pleasant to beholde' which decorated the streets of Lille.[158]

Whether it was from this meeting, or from the reports of ambassadors, the English obviously thought they knew the power of an appeal to the shared figure of Arthur, and that they should emphasise the place of Arthur in the tapestry of British history. From this emerged the programme for the decoration of the entrance to the Round House at Calais. The Habsburg significance of the Arthurian connection is made plain by the virtual absence of the figure of Arthur from the meeting with the French at the Field of Cloth of Gold the previous month before.

Thus the Round Table at Winchester fits into a pattern of English display in meetings with the Empire. This might seem to suggest that the table is most likely to have been painted for the visit of Charles to Winchester in 1522, but in fact there is

---

[157] See above, pp. 447–8.
[158] See above, p. 447.

no evidence for this. Everything points, as we have seen, to the painting of the table in 1516. If this is so, all that was done in 1522 was to add the verses still legible in the seventeenth century on the wall below the table:

> Carolus Henricus vivant defensor uterque
> Henricus fidei Carolus ecclesiae,

which had been translated in the streets of London that same summer of 1522:

> Long prosperitie
> To Charles and Henry Princes moste puissant.
> The one of fayth
> The other of the Churche chosen defendant.

Although it was convenient for Charles to set sail from Southampton at the end of his visit, taking him a further step on his voyage to Spain, it may be significant that already in April 1522, when the details of the visit were first being worked out, Winchester was to be last stopping point. There was no really suitable accommodation in Winchester for Henry or Charles, let alone both of them, as proved to be the case, and it may well be that the principal intention of the visit was to display to Charles the most venerable and potent symbol of the Arthur of Britain, to whose ancestry Henry might seem to have by far the better claim. Here is Arthur as Henry, the figure whose support at Calais two years before was put forward as the decisive fulcrum of the balance of power.

As for the painting of the table in 1516, this was at a moment when it seemed to Henry and to Wolsey that there was some hope that Henry might be elected emperor. Maximilian had twice offered to abdicate in Henry's favour, and however unlikley such an outcome may have been, Henry's interests at that time were imperial. For some decades the image of Arthur had been becoming ever more imperial in English hands, his wearing of the hooped imperial crown the decisive attribute. Whether this carried any weight at all with Charles may be doubted: Norfolk had no success in 1531 when he tried to impress Charles's ambassador with the imperial role of Arthur by showing him Arthur's seal then preserved at Westminster. But by this time the role of the Round Table as one of the most powerful political symbols of the age was falling rapidly into oblivion.[159]

---

[159] David Starkey's paper, 'King Henry and King Arthur', appeared after this chapter was written; we cover some of the same ground and share similar views on the role of Arthur in Anglo-Habsburg meetings: see *Arthurian Literature* 16 (1998), 171–96.

Symbol and Epilogue

The meaning of the Winchester table has changed from age to age. At the end of the thirteenth century, so Chapter 10 has argued, it was made in the likeness of King Arthur's table of amity and fellowship to grace a feast held after a tournament celebrating the culmination of King Edward I's plans for the future of his dynasty and of the English crown.

Sixty years later his grandson King Edward III had the legs of the table broken out and its top hung on the wall of Winchester castle hall, a symbol, no longer a functioning piece of furniture. The table was now apparently decorated for the first time (Chapter 11), its surface covered with a painted leather or cloth in a design which seems to have echoed the Wheel of Fortune on the opposite wall of the hall and to have foreshadowed, perhaps in some detail, the painting we see on the table today. Edward III's intention seems to have been simultaneously to celebrate King Arthur's table and at the same time by curious punning to direct attention away from Winchester to Windsor where at this very moment he was engaged in founding the Order of the Garter in the castle where both he and, so it was then believed, King Arthur had been born.

Hanging and decaying for the next two centuries, memory of the table's purpose was lost as it became ever more closely identified with the literary original of which it was never more than a realisation. In the early 1460s John Hardyng appears to have believed that the Winchester table was truly the table at which the company of the Round Table had begun, 'and ther it hangeth yet'. In 1506 Henry VII seems also to have thought of the Winchester table as a relic of those who had actually sat around it, a suitable model to follow in creating a memorial of the Garter dinner held at Windsor that year after the investiture of King Philip of Spain.

A decade later, the ready wit of his son Henry VIII saw in the table a symbol which could be used to bolster the claim that the realm of England was an empire (Chapter 12). Henry's bid for election as Holy Roman Emperor failed, as it always must. But the English king's knowledge of things Habsburg, in particular of the Emperor Maximilian's belief that King Arthur too must have been a Habsburg, allowed Henry to see how the figure of Arthur could be used in his own attempt to become arbiter of Europe, holding the balance between the Emperor Charles V and Francis I of France.

When the long association of England and the Empire faltered and fell way in the 1520s in favour of a closer (although short-lived) rapprochement with France, the figure of King Arthur ceased to play any role in the iconography of contemporary politics. The Winchester table now became an object of no more than antiquarian interest and speculation. In the last two chapters we explore this afterlife. Beatrice Clayre and Roger Davey, now the County Archivist of East Sussex but previously Deputy County Archivist of Hampshire, trace in Chapter 13 the way in which over the centuries the County of Hampshire, owner of the Great Hall since 1642 and thus custodian of the Round Table, has discharged its duty of care for such an odd and venerable antiquity.

The table remained during these centuries an object of curiosity seen by many, for it hung on the wall of the castle hall above the judges in the Nisi Prius Court. In Chapter 14 the late Clive Wainwright, for many years a Keeper in the Department of Furniture and Woodwork at the Victoria and Albert Museum and latterly Senior Research Fellow in the Research Department, reviews the reactions of travellers and others who over the last four hundred and fifty years have visited and described the table, ranging from the sceptic to the credulous, the antiquary to the romantic.

Already in the eighteenth century, traditionally as early as 1720, the ideals of the Round Table began again to be exercised through the foundation of one of London's oldest clubs, now The Honourable Society of Knights of The Round Table. With its headquarters at Simpson's in the Strand since 1828 for over a century and still dining regularly at the Athenaeum and in other London clubs and halls, the Honourable Society fosters good fellowship and better international understanding by means of charitable activities supported by its hundred or so Brother Knights. Since 1921 the association of the Honourable Society with Winchester and the Round Table has been celebrated by an annual pilgrimage.

During the twentieth century, the idea of the round table took on a wholly new lease of life as an expression of supposed equality and hoped-for amity and common purpose in seating negotiators at the councils of the nations. It was at this time that the Winchester Round Table became the symbol of the Round Table Movement, adopted by the National Association of Round Tables (still then known as the Central Council) in April 1929. The Winchester table has since then taken on new life around the world as the symbol of one of the best recognised and highly respected movements of common purpose, an ever-present invitation to recall childhood's half-remembered tales of King Arthur and his knights of the Round Table and their deeds of chivalry in an age long ago.

13

The County and the Round Table

Responsibility for the care of the Round Table has always been linked with the maintenance of the Great Hall of Winchester Castle in which the table has been preserved. Until the first half of the sixteenth century, the necessary works were carried out under the supervision of royal officers (see above, pp. 70–80), but in the latter part of the century the situation became less clear. A survey in January 1572 stated that the queen had had the south aisle of the Great Hall repaired, while the City of Winchester had since 1559 spent £14 on repairs to the 'middle roffe'. The north aisle, meanwhile, was in urgent need of repair.[1] The city, which was involved because the corporation had been granted the office of constable of the castle in 1559,[2] now disputed its liability for the hall. Litigation about who should repair the north aisle was in progress in 1576–7,[3] and judgement was clearly given against the city, since in most years between 1578 and 1601 the city chamberlain made payments for repairs to the hall in general, the north aisle being specifically mentioned in 1578–9 and 1600–1601.[4]

In 1602, however, the county took over responsibility for maintaining the building, and a rate was levied for the necessary works.[5] The reason for the change is not immediately obvious, but the answer would seem to lie with the Poor Relief Act of 1601, under which the Justices of the Peace (who administered Hampshire through the Court of Quarter Sessions) had the duty to levy rates for the relief of the poor prisoners of the King's Bench and Marshalsea.[6] The Great Hall had long been used for holding the Assizes and Quarter Sessions, and this seems to have been considered sufficient justification for the application of the poor prisoners' funds to

---

[1] BL, Cotton MS. Titus B, ii, fol. 243.

[2] PRO, C66/946, item 36.

[3] HRO, W/B1/1, fol. 193v and W/B1/3, fol. 6v.

[4] HRO, W/E1/101–114.

[5] HRO, letter book of Sir Henry Whithed, 4M53/141, fol. 4.

[6] Statute 43 Eliz., cap. 2, s.14.

its maintenance. Indeed the same funds continued to be used for this purpose until the eighteenth century. The records of Quarter Sessions refer many times to repairs of the Great Hall from 1623 onwards, but it was to be over a century before the Round Table itself was specifically mentioned.

In 1607 the castle passed into private ownership for the first time when James I granted it to Sir Benjamin Tichborne as a reward for his services. Only the Great Hall and a small piece of land to the north of it were excluded and remained in crown hands.[7] Following Tichborne's death in 1629, his sons surrendered the castle to the chancellor of the exchequer and the attorney general 'for the use of his majesty',[8] but the evidence suggests that Charles I's lord treasurer, Richard Weston, Earl of Portland, was interested in acquiring it as his family seat. Portland was lord lieutenant of Hampshire at the time and before his death in 1635 had spent considerable sums on repairing and beautifying the buildings at the castle.[9]

In March 1635, King Charles I granted the castle to Portland's son, Jerome, and his wife, Frances, who was the daughter of Esmé Stuart, Earl of March and Duke of Lennox.[10] The Great Hall was included in the grant and it seems to have been this which provoked Trussell's outburst in his poem 'The Complaint of the Castell of Winchester'. He grieves that the hall

> which through the Counties cost and cyttes care has hitherto been kept in good repayer

was now

> to private use converted and not free as hitherto yt was for the whole sheer att tymes for publick service to appeare.

And he fears that it would be used for stabling 'Flanders Coatch mares' and other livestock, and that 'Arthures Table' would

---

[7] PRO, C66/1613.

[8] PRO, Crest 35/710.

[9] 'A Relation of a Short Suruey of the Westerne Counties in Which is Breifely Described the Cities, Corporations, Castles, and Some Other Remarkables in Them Obseru'd in a Seuen Weekes Journey Begun at Norwich, and Thence into the West on Thursday August 4th, 1635 ...', ed. L. G. Wickham Legg, in *Camden Miscellany* 16, Camden Society 3rd ser. 52 (1936), p. 51. The Lieutenant was one Hammond, his Christian name unknown.

[10] PRO, C66/2643.

bee flunge mongst hoggs, doggs, cowes, sowes and coatch horse dung & their unrecoverablie to lye and rote and have her glorye drownd, her name forgotte.[11]

Fortunately Jerome and Frances soon surrendered the castle to the crown and Sir William Waller, to whom it was granted in 1638, recognized the importance of the Great Hall to the county and in 1642 sold it (and consequently the Round Table) for £100 to Sir Henry Worsley and other Justices of the Peace for Hampshire.[12]

Both the table and the hall suffered damage during the Civil War. The table was used as a shooting target (see above, pp. 138–42) and during the siege of the castle by Oliver Cromwell in 1645 the hall was hit by a round of mortar fire which killed three soldiers (see above pp. 142). The damage must have been extensive because, before the hall could again be used for the courts, over £200 had to be spent in 1646 on repairs.[13] It was spared in 1651, however, when much of the rest of the castle was pulled down on the orders of the Council of State, concerned that Winchester Castle should never again pose a serious threat to the Commonwealth,[14] and was again repaired by the justices in 1654.[15]

The survival of the hall was placed in jeopardy by Charles II's decision in 1682 to build a hunting lodge in Winchester, designed by Sir Christopher Wren. The city authorities, delighted by this proposal, gladly gave the king the site of the old castle, which they had purchased from Waller in 1656.[16] The justices for their part granted Charles the Great Hall on condition that he provided them with alternative accommodation in the city.[17] Since the hall stood only about ten feet away from the proposed new palace, it is almost certain that it would have been pulled down to make way for other buildings in Wren's grand plan, but it is impossible to know what the fate of the Round Table might have been. Charles died in 1685, however, before the building was completed. All work was stopped. For several years there was uncertainty over the future of the new building and the various pieces of land bought to make a great park around it. The justices, meanwhile, in the absence of any alternative accommodation, continued to use the Great Hall. The date when it

[11] J. Trussell, 'The Complaint of the Castell of Winchester', in his 'Benefactors of Winchester', Bodleian Library, MS. Top. Hants C.5., pp. 91–2.

[12] PRO, C66/2806; C54/3257. See also HRO, W/K1/14 for a copy of part of these letters patent conveying the Great Hall of the castle to Sir William Waller and his heirs, 1638; and HRO, Q1/4, p. 195.

[13] BL, Add. MS. 24, 861, fols. 6–7.

[14] *CSP Domestic 1649–50*, pp. 180, 197, 241, 243, 245, 294, 304–5, 320, 323; *CSP Domestic 1650*, pp. 178, 471, 479, 488; *CSP Domestic 1651*, pp. 11, 57.

[15] HRO, Q1/3, p. 229.

[16] PRO, C54/3888; HRO, W/F2/5, fols. 370–1; HRO, W/B1/6, fols. 142v, 152.

[17] *CSP Domestic 1683*, i, pp. 22, 84, 99.

was formally returned to the county remains unknown: the lack of any record of payments for repairs suggests this may not have happened until some ten years after Charles' death.

In subsequent years the Quarter Sessions orders and accounts frequently mention payments to contractors for carpenters' work, painting, and the like, which may well have covered maintenance of a minor kind to the Round Table. In 1743 Robert Malpas was paid one guinea for 'drawing a perspective of the East End of the County Hall and King Arthurs Table'.[18] Malpas's drawing was presumably the original of the published view engraved by Richard Benning (Figs. 30 and 120), which is the earliest known illustration of the hall, and of which the date and artist are otherwise unknown. Benning also engraved William Godson's printed *Map of Winchester*, published in 1750, which included a very similar representation of the table (Fig. 121).

Thin-sections of the paint (see above, pp. 246, 251) have shown that the Round Table was repainted only once. This probably happened in 1789. Melville Portal said so categorically, quoting as his source 'Sessions Books and Bills',[19] but unfortunately neither of these sources now survives in the official custody of the county. The bills (or vouchers to accounts) were presumably destroyed many years ago, while the Quarter Sessions minute book for the years 1783–91 is also missing. References in the order books and account books show, however, that substantial alterations were made to the hall in 1789–90 at a cost of over £1,000. The precise nature of the works is not clear, but they included blocking up the original main door of the hall and altering the windows on the north side. Apparently, the internal arrangements for the courts were also substantially changed, since large sums were paid for carpentry.[20] Among payments made to the contractors was one on 20 July 1789 to 'Cave and Son, painters' of £8 14s. William Cave the elder (1737–1813) and his son of the same name (died 1817) were highly regarded in Winchester as artists and interior decorators and did much skilled work throughout the city.[21] Their firm undertook all the painting at the Great Hall, routine as well as specialised, from 1766 to 1824, and the repainting of the Round Table was almost certainly done by one or other of them.

---

[18] HRO, Q10/3/1, fol. 23r. Robert Malpas and Catherine his wife were described as *peregrini* (travellers) when their child was baptised at the Roman Catholic chapel in Winchester in 1735. They settled locally, however, and the last reference to them occurs in a baptism of 1745. See *Publications of the Catholic Record Society* 42: *Hampshire Registers* i (1948), pp. 154–9.

[19] Portal, *Great Hall*, p. 90.

[20] HRO, Q1/21, fol. 152r; also HRO, Q10/3/2, fols. 66r-70v.

[21] B. Carpenter Turner, 'A Notable Family of Artists: The Caves of Winchester', *Proceedings of the Hampshire Field Club*, 22.1 (1961), 30–4. See further above, pp. 319–22.

The Caves were further connected with the table in that James Cave (d. 1834), second son of William the elder, made a drawing of it which was engraved by John Pass of Pentonville and first published in 1796 (Fig. 144). James Cave was also the artist who prepared most of the drawings for John Milner's *History of Winchester*, first published in 1798–9, which includes an engraving of the Round Table also made by Pass after a drawing by James Cave (Fig. 164). Dr Milner was the Roman Catholic priest of Winchester and a famous controversalist, in addition to being a noted anti-quary (see above, p. 87), and the Caves were members of his congregation. In November 1788 Milner had written a letter to the *Gentleman's Magazine* in which he asserted that the Round Table had been 'for the last time new painted' for the visit of the Emperor Charles V in 1522.[22] In his *History*, however, he altered the wording to suggest that it appeared to have been 'first painted' at that time,[23] thus indirectly supporting the view that repainting had taken place between 1788 and 1798.

Until the early nineteenth century the hall was probably heated by charcoal, procured by the hall-keeper. In 1825 it was agreed to construct two underground stoves to circulate hot air by means of iron pipes into both courts.[24] In 1840, £350 was spent installing Perkins patent apparatus in the centre of the hall (the octagonal feature shown on Fig. 31) to distribute piped hot water to all points of the building.[25] The brick-lined feature in the west wall of the hall, popularly known as 'the king's ear', was probably a duct for circulating either hot air or hot water.

The next major treatment of the table came in 1873–4 when it was moved from the east to the west wall of the Great Hall in the course of extensive rebuilding (see above, pp. 89–94), Thomas Henry Wyatt, the architect of the works, described the operation in a paper delivered to the Royal Institute of British Architects in May 1874:

> This table was only taken down from its eastern position at the last moment, when it became necessary to open the communication between the old Hall and the new buildings. I need hardly say that it was lowered and subsequently raised to its present resting place with the greatest care and anxiety to your humble servant ... . Before it was again raised it was secured on the outer edge with a wrought iron hoop or band five inches wide, like the tyre of a wheel, securely key-wedged together.[26]

[22] *Gentleman's Magazine*, 58 (1788), 970. Milner dated the visit to 1512 in error for 1522 (see above, pp. 429–31).

[23] John Milner, *The History ... of Winchester*, 1st ed. (Winchester, 1798–9)), ii, p. 172.

[24] *Hampshire Chronicle*, May 1825.

[25] HRO, Q1/39, p. 502; *Hampshire Chronicle*, 6 January 1840.

[26] T. H. Wyatt, 'On the Old Hall and New Assize Courts at Winchester', *RIBA Sessional Papers 1873–4*, no. 10, p. 159.

Official records of the time are largely silent about the table, although the works generally are well documented. However, it is clear from contemporary newspaper reports that cleaning and restoration were carried out while the table was down.[27] The iron band mentioned by Wyatt was the subject of a committee minute which rejected on grounds of expense the estimate of Messrs Hill and Sons of Islington (the main contractors) for a half-inch thick band, and proposed instead one not more than one-eighth of an inch in thickness. (Figs. 73, 103–4).[28] The table was photographed during the move by a local man, William Savage, and a careful drawing was made (Figs. 33–4, 167).[29]

In 1889 the newly created Hampshire County Council took over the administrative functions of the Magistrates of Quarter Sessions, thus inheriting responsibility for the Great Hall and the Round Table. For some years there is little mention of the table in official records, except that it was first floodlit in 1932. Investigations in 1938 into the condition of the table and in 1948 as to the advisability of removing the top coat of paint have been fully described above, pp. 146–7. For nearly thirty years thereafter the table remained undisturbed, until the exhaustive investigations of 1976 upon which this book is based.

---

[27] *Hampshire Chronicle* and *Hampshire Advertiser*, both for 14 March 1874.

[28] HRO, Q14/2, 27 Dec. 1873.

[29] Prints of the two photographs are preserved with the drawing in two large volumes of plans relating to the Great Hall; HRO, 31M60/2, 33. The prints can also be found in Melville Portal's own specially bound copy of Smirke's article of 1845 (see above, p. 92, n. 71), now in the possession of Mr Richard Sawyer. A drawing made from the photograph of the back of the table appeared in Portal, *Great Hall*, p. 89 and in various editions of local guides. For Savage's claim to have photographed the table, see his *Guide to the Ancient City of Winchester*, 9th ed. (1875), p. 74.

14

Travellers to the Round Table

C harles V was only the first of many visitors to the Round Table of whom we have some record. Charles's visit in 1522, a key moment in the history of the table, did not appear in print until the middle of the century (see above, pp. 404–5), by which time the first Englishman to record his impression of the table had already been to Winchester. In 1540 the antiquary John Leland visited the city in the course of his travels through England. Leland was particularly interested in Arthur, and his famous *Itinerary* includes a number of descriptions of places associated with him. He was especially keen to establish the truth about the historical Arthur by examining the surviving Arthurian relics as tangible proofs of his existence. He made a careful examination of the tomb of Arthur at Glastonbury and was shown the famous cross discovered when Arthur's body had been exhumed there in 1190 or 1191. It was Leland's fascination with Arthur which led him to write the *Assertio inclytissimi Arturi regis Britanniae* – the 'Assertion of the Most Famous Arthur, King of Britain', published in 1544. In the chapter entitled *Orbicularis Arturii mensa* ('Arthur's Round Table') he says:

> Venté Simenorum in castro fama notissimo appendet muro aulé regié mensa, quam & rotundam a maiestate Arturiana vocant. Quid? Quod nec memoria, nec societas Orbicularis chori recentioribus séculis ex animis nobilium, excidit. Eadueardus Longus, vt fama refert, Orbicularem illam societatem plurimi fecit, fabricata in eos vsus, si credere dignum est, tabula sphérica, & tripodibus ex auro solido.[1]

[1] John Leland, *Assertio inclytissimi Arturii regis Britaniae* (London, 1544), fol. 10v. The English edition is *A Learned and True Assertion of the Original Life, Actes, and Death of the Most Noble, Valiant, and Renowned Prince Arthure, King of Great Brittaine...* trans. Richard Robinson, (London, 1582), from which (fols. 10v-11r) the translation, or more accurately, paraphrase here is taken. It is obvious from Leland's description of Winchester in his *Itinerary* that he visited the city in 1540 or shortly thereafter, although he does not describe the table in that book. For a full discussion of Leland's interest in Arthur, see Joseph Ritson, *The Life of King Arthur from Ancient Historians and Authentic Documents* (London, 1825); and T. D. Kendrick, *British Antiquity* (London, 1950), pp. 44–64, 85–95.

At *Venta Symeno* alias *Winchester* in ye castle most famously knowne, standeth fixed ye table at the walle side of ye kinges Hal, which (for ye maiesty of *Arthure*) they cal ye round table. And wherefore? Because neyther the memorie nor felowship of the round Trowpe of Knightes as yet falles out of Noble mens mindes, in the latter age of the world. *Kinge Edward* sirnamed the longe, as fame telleth, made much of that rounde order of Knightes. To those vses was the round table instituted and framed, (if it be worthie of credit) and that it was with three feete made of perfect gold.

Leland was nineteen years old in 1522, when Henry VIII showed the newly painted table to Charles V. When Leland himself saw it later it must still have been in an almost perfect condition. His observations provide us therefore with a important insight into the period of the painting of the table and the whole Tudor cult of Arthur. His writings on Arthur and the table were also crucial as a source for many of the later commentators with whom I shall be dealing.

In Winchester Cathedral on 25 July 1554 Mary Tudor married Philip, king of Naples and Jerusalem. Eighteen months later Philip was to succeed his father, the emperor Charles V, as King Philip II of Spain. A great concourse of Spanish courtiers accompanied Philip to England for the wedding, many of whom wrote descriptions of the journey to Winchester, the marriage ceremony, and the feast which followed.[2] Two days after the wedding, some of them went:

> á ver la Tabla redonda questá en el castillo deste lugar, que fué del Rey Artus, que dicen que esta' [allí] encantado, y los doce Pares que comían con él están escritos sus nombres al rededor segun se asentaban.

> to see the Round Table which is in the castle of this place, which belonged to King Arthur – who, they say, is enchanted [there]; and the names of the twelve Peers who ate with him are written round it in order as they sat.[3]

---

[2] Martin A. S. Hume, 'The Visit of Philip II', *English Historical Review* 7 (1892), 253–80; Ronald Hilton, 'The Marriage of Queen Mary and Philip of Spain', *Proceedings of the Hampshire Field Club* 14.i (1938), 46–62; Sheila Himsworth, 'The Marriage of Philip II of Spain with Mary Tudor', ibid. 22.ii (1962), 82–100. C. V. Malfatti, *The Accession, Coronation, and Marriage of Mary Tudor as Related in Four Manuscripts of the Escorial* (Barcelona, 1956), notes in his introduction (p. viii) that there are no fewer than forty-nine manuscript 'memoirs' of Philip's visit, together with a very considerable number of documents in the archives at Simancas.

[3] Anon (?Don Pedro Enriquez), 'Carta primera de lo sucedido en el viaje de S. A. á Inglaterra, Año de 1554' ([Seville], 1554); reprinted from a copy in the Escorial in Pascual de Gayangos (ed.), *Viaje de Felipe Segundo á Inglaterra por Andrés Muñoz...y replaciones varias relativas al mismo suceso*, Sociedad de Bibliófilos Españoles 15 (Madrid, 1877), pp. 85–101, at p. 97; adapted from a translation in Himsworth, 'The Marriage of Philip II of Spain with Mary Tudor', pp. 89–95, at p. 93.

None of the other accounts printed at the time mentions the Round Table. But Julian del Castillo included a much more elaborate description in his *Historia de los reyes Godos* ('History of the Gothic Kings'), which was published in Burgos in 1582. Del Castillo's minutely detailed account of how Philip was dressed for the wedding can only have been written by an eyewitness; so too his description of the Round Table:

> ... y en el año de mil y quinientos y cinquenta y quatro, estando biudo el Catholico Rey nuestro don Philippe, ... se caso en Inglaterra, y Ciudad o Villa de Hunchistre, donde esta la tabla redonda delos veyntiquatro caualleros que instituyo y ordeno el Rey Artus de Inglaterra como atras se toco: la qual mesa es de veyntiquatro girones, lo ancho dellos a la parte de fuera, y las puntas adentro, que van a dar todos a la Rosa de Inglaterra que esta en medio, y el Rey Artus pintado con una espada en la mano: y en lo ancho de los girones hazia fuera, estan escritos los nombres de los caualleros della, y los girones son blancos y verdes: y es fama comun que el Rey Artus esta encantado en aquella tierra, en figura de cueruo, y ay entre ellos grandes penas contra el que mata cueruo, y que ha de boluer a Reynar: y cierto dizen que su Magestad el Rey don Philippe nuestro Rey juro, que si el Rey Artus viniesse en algun tiempo, le dexaria el Reyno.

And in the year 1554 our Catholic King, don Philip, being a widower ... was married in England, and [in] the city or town of Winchester, where the round table of the twenty-four knights is to be found, which was instituted and ordained by King Arthur of England as has already been mentioned. This table has twenty-four segments, the widest parts of which are to the outside and the points to the inside, which all meet at the Rose of England which is in the middle, and King Arthur painted with a sword in his hand. And at the widest part of the segments towards the outside, the names of its knights are written, and the segments are white and green. And it is common knowledge that King Arthur is enchanted in that land, in the form of a raven (and there are among them great penalties against any who should kill a raven) and that the king will return to Reign again. And some say that his Majesty, King Philip, our King, swore that if King Arthur should come at any time he would hand the Kingdom over to him.[4]

---

[4] Julian del Castillo, *Historia de los reyes Godos* ... (Burgos, 1582), fols. 156r–156v, translated by Dr Beatrice Clayre. A second edition, enlarged and edited by Gerónimo de Castro y Castillo, the author's son, was published in Madrid in 1624: its variations in this passage (p. 356) add nothing, but were followed by Charles B. Millican, *Spenser and the Table Round* (Cambridge, Mass., 1932), pp. 35–6. This passage comes in an account of King Philip, but in an earlier part of the book (fol. 54r) del Castillo describes the foundation of the Round Table in the context of the resistance of Spain and Britain to barbarian attacks on the Roman empire. According to the *Enciclopedia Universal Ilustrada Europeo-Americano*, xii (Madrid, 1979), Julian del Castillo was born near Burgos in the middle of the century, but later moved to Madrid, where he had duties at court and was appointed by Philip III to be his chronicler.

This is the earliest precise description of the painting on the Round Table we have, and as such is a key record of what the table looked like after its repainting at the beginning of the century.

There is another Spanish description, less easy to follow, which was probably also derived from an eyewitness account of the wedding in 1554, but which survives, so far as we know, only in the 'Epitome Cronológico' compiled by Diego de Vera in or after 1650 and never published:

> Fue este Principe [King Arthur] el que instituyo la celebre Caballería de la Tabla redonda senalando en ella xxiiii Caballeros los mas famosos y Valientes de sus Exercitos (de que despues se inventaron tantos desaçiertos y patranas como contienen los molestos y cansados libros de Caballeria) la preeminençia de los tales era comer con el Rey a una mesa y esta era redonda partida en 24 [*changed to 25 in MS.*] girones ô partes distintas gravadas de Blanco y Verde que en el Centro se juntaban en punta y se iban ensanchando a la circumferencia formandose de todas una Rosa y en cada tabla ô division de estas estaba escrito el nombre de el Caballero, y tambien Arturo tenia la suya Con su nombre. Conservabase esta tabla (segun dizen) en Hunchriste Población de Ingalaterra quando el Catholico y prudentisimo Rey Phélipe II se caso con la Reyna Maria, y oy dizen se conserva.

> It was this prince [King Arthur] who founded the famous order of the knights of the round Table, indicating on it 24 of the most famous and Valiant Knights of his armies (about whom at a later date so many erroneous and longwinded stories were invented, such as are found in the tiresome and boring books of Chivalry), whose privilege it was to eat with the King at a table which was round and divided into 24 [*changed to 25 in MS.*] segments or distinct parts, decorated in White and Green, which come together in a point at the Centre and which widen towards the circumference, forming all together a Rose. And in each table or division was written the name of the Knight, and Arthur also had his own [division] with his name. It was said that this table was preserved in Winchester, a Town in England, when the wise and Catholic King Philip II married Queen Mary, and they say it is still preserved there today.[5]

Diego de Vera may have been drawing on Julian del Castillo's published description, but the strange spelling of Winchester they both use ('Hunchistre', 'Hunchriste') is no guide, for Spanish has no 'w' and when 'h' is used as a phonetic equivalent something of this kind must result. More probably de Vera was copying from another of the many unpublished contemporary accounts of the journey to England in 1554.

The 'common knowledge' that Arthur is enchanted 'in that land', in the form of a raven, is a story that was still told in Cornwall in the nineteenth century, but was apparently unknown elsewhere. Cervantes mentions it several times, thrice in *Don*

Quixote, first published in 1605, and once in *Persiles y Sigismunda*, first published in 1617. He probably took it from Julian del Castillo's book, which had been published several years before.[6]

A later visitor was John Lesley (or Leslie; 1526–96), bishop of Ross, afterwards bishop of Coutances, who came to England with Mary Queen of Scots in 1568, but was imprisoned in the Tower in 1572. He was moved in June to the bishop of Winchester's castle at Farnham in Surrey, where he remained until November, and was banished the next year. He began his *History of Scotland* while in England and in 1571 presented part of it written in Scots to Queen Mary. He finished it after his departure and published it in Latin in Rome in 1578.

Lesley must have seen the table between 1568 and 1572, most probably (on parole?) when he was at Farnham in 1572. He lists Arthur's conquests of many lands, including Scotland, all of which he rejects, but accepts that Arthur was a truly great king and describes his creation of an order of twenty-four noble knights of equal standing bound together in love (*pares pari omnes amore*):

> Cum omnes simul accumberent, ne quis forte se primo in loco constitutum gloriose praedicaret, aut ad infimum locum deturbatum invide cogitaret, mensam rotundam ad corone formam effingendam curauit. Locum in quo ii omnes accumbere solebant, rotundam Arthuri Tabulam, & nostrates & Britanni appelant. Eandem ego mensam (si accole falsa quadam maiorum superstitione conflictati, non errent) in Wintoniensi castro, ad eternam rei memoriam solenniter conseruatam, militumque equestrium nominibus vndique notatam, non ita pridem aspexi.[7]

5   Diego de Vera, 'Epitome cronológico real y universal de todos los imperios y monarquías del mundo desde el primer instante del tiempo hasta el año de 1650 de nuestra salud', Madrid, Biblioteca Nacional, MS. 1300, fol. 237v. The passage quoted here comes in a section dealing with the early British kings and follows an account of King Arthur. We are grateful to Dr Beatrice Clayre for locating the MS. and providing the transcript and translation and to Susana Puch and Dr. Paloma García-Bellido for help in checking the MS and the text. Diego de Vera was secretary and gentleman of the chamber to Cardinal Sandoval, archbishop of Toledo (d.1665). His 'Epitome' has previously been known in Round Table studies only from the translation into French of the passage in question given in Leroux de Lincy (ed.), *Le Roman Brut* (Paris, 1836), p. 166, and quoted by Edward Smirke, 'On the Hall and Round Table at Winchester', *Proceedings at the Annual Meeting of the Archaeological Institute of Great Britain and Ireland at Winchester, September 1845* (London, 1846), p. 63, but it is also quoted by Juan Antonio Pellicer (ed.), *El ingenioso hidalgo Don Quixote de la Mancha*, 2nd edn., (Madrid, 1797), I.i, pp. 130–1.

6   Del Castillo gives the raven story twice, on fols. 54r and 156r-156v. It is fully discussed with further references in R. S. Loomis, 'Arthurian Tradition and Folklore', *Folklore* 69 (1958), 1–25, at p. 16. See also Pellicer, *Don Quixote*, I.i, pp. 129–30.

This passage from the second, Latin part of the *History* was translated into Scots by Father James Dalrymple in 1596:

> Quhen thay al satt doune to the table, that na man war proud, or throuch vane glore began to crak hich gif he war in the first place sett, or began to Jnvie gif he saw him selfe set laicher than he walde; he caused a round table to the forme of a croune be maid. The place in quhilke al thir vset to sit, baith our countrey men, and the britonis vset to name King Aarthures round table. The sam selfe table (gif our countrey men throuch sum superstitioune of our forbearis have not erret) haue my self seine; quhair it is solemnelie keiped, perpetuallie to be remembered of; in the castel of Wintoune, and ouer al noted w^t the names of his weirlie knychtes; quhilke I sawe nocht lang syne.[8]

William Camden, the herald and antiquary, described the table in 1586, in the first edition of his *Britannia*:

> De mensa illa circulari, siue orbiculari muro hic appensa, quam vulgus hominum tanquam Arthurianam mensam suspicit, nihil est quod dicam, nisi recentioris esse aetatis. Superioribus enim saeculis, cum virtutis bellicae exercendae gratia, militares decursiones, (*Torneamenta* vocant) frequenter haberentur; huiusmodi mensis vsi erant, ne quod discrimen inter nobiles ex ambitione foret: & veteri sane, vt videtur, instituto, Gallos enim antiquos circularibus mensis circumsedisse, Armigerosque eorum scuta ferentes a tergo adstitisse, memorat in libro Deipnosop. 4. Athenaeus.[9]

The later Latin editions follow this text, but the English editions differ slightly, as the several editors used different translations. These differences do not significantly change Camden's meaning. The 1637 edition reads:

7   John Lesley [Leslie], *De origine, moribus, et rebus gestis Scotorum libri decem* (Rome, 1578), p. 146. The version of Books 8–10, written by Lesley in Scots in 1568–70, while in England, and presented to Queen Mary in 1571, was published by the Bannatyn Club in 1830: John Leslie, *The History of Scotland*, ed. T. Thomson (Edinburgh, 1830). For details of Lesley's life, see the introduction to the Bannatyne Club edition, pp. i–vii, the *DNB*, and Cody's edition given in the next note.

8   John Lesley [Leslie], *The Historie of Scotland ... Translated into Scottish by Father James Dalrymple ... 1596*, ed. E. G. Cody, i, Scottish Text Society 5 and 14 (published in one volume; Edinburgh and London, 1888 for 1884 (5)), pp. 223–4.

9   William Camden, *Britannia* (London, 1586), p. 129.

As concerning that round table there, hanging up against the wall which the common sort useth to gaze upon with great admiration, as if it had beene King Arthurs table, I have nothing to say but this, That, as a man which vieweth it well may easily perceive, it is nothing so ancient as King Arthur. For, in latter times when for the exercise of armes and feates of warlike prowesse, those runnings at tilt, and martiall justlings or torneaments, were much practiced: they used such tables, least any contention or offence for prioritie of place should through ambition arise among Nobles and Knights assembled together. And this was a custome of great antiquitie, as it may seeme. For, the ancient Gaules, as Athenéus writeth, were wont to sit about round tables ....[10]

The *Britannia* was so widely read, both in Europe and England, that from 1586 every scholar was aware of Camden's thoughts concerning the Round Table.

The next mention was in a discourse read to the Elizabethan Society of Antiquaries in 1598 by Francis Tate (1560–1616), of Magdalen College, Oxford, and the Middle Temple. Tate seems to have written twenty-eight discourses for this society on a variety of subjects between 1590 and 1601.[11] That which particularly interests us here was read on 2 November 1598 and was entitled 'Of the Antiquity of Arms in England'. In it Tate says:

Although some authores wright doutefully of kinge Arthur, yet our historyes doe agree that his bodey was fownd buryed at Glastenbury, in the tyme of kinge Henrye the second, with a Crose of leade whereon was writen his name. And at Winchester there doth remayne at this daye, a great rownde table, whereon are writen the names of divers knightes, which are taken to bee the knightes of the rownde table instituted by king Arthur. I have a Frenche book wherein, king Arthur beinge set downe to be one of the nyne worthyes, there is also printed the arms of his knights.[12]

It is not possible to ascertain whether Tate had actually examined the table himself. He may well have heard about it at first hand from Camden, who was a member of the same society, and had, for instance, read a 'Discourse on Epitaphs' to the Society in November 1600.[13]

---

[10] Ibid., trans. Philemon Holland (London, 1637), p. 265.

[11] May McKisack, *Medieval History in the Tudor Age* (Oxford, 1971), p. 68.

[12] This discourse was not printed until 1773, when it appeared in the third revised edition of Thomas Hearne, *A Collection of Curious Discourses...* (London, 1773), i, p. 168.

[13] Printed ibid., p. 310.

There was considerable literary as well as antiquarian interest in the subject of Arthur during the opening decades of the seventeenth century. The poet Drayton alludes to the table in 1612:

> The Knights whose martiall deeds farre fam'd that *Table-round*;
> Which, truest in their loues; which, most in Armes renown'd
> The Lawes, which long vp-held that Order, they report;
> The *Pentecosts* prepar'd at *Carleon* in his Court,
> That Tables ancient seate; her Temples and her Groues,
> Her Palaces, her Walks, Baths, Theaters, and Stoues;
> Her Academie, then, as likewise they prefer:
> Of *Camilot* they sing, and then of *Winchester*.[14]

Later in the same poem, Drayton writes of the personified River Itchen:

> And, for great *Arthurs* seat, her *Winchester* preferres,
> Whose old *Round-table*, yet she vaunteth to be hers:
> And swore, th'inglorious time should not bereaue her right;
> But what it could obscure, she would reduce to light.
> For, from that wondrous Pond, whence shee deriues her head,
> And places by the way, by which shee's honoured,
> (Old *Winchester*, that stands neere in her middle way,
> And *Hampton*, at her fall into the *Solent* sea).
> Shee thinks in all the Ile not any such as shee,
> And for a Demy-god she would related bee.[15]

The table was certainly seen by a soldier called Hammond late in August 1635:

> From hence I march'd downe again to see what manner of Hall, and Table, that braue and warlike worthy Brittish Prince kept aboue 1000 yeeres since, which are both fit for so royall a Prince; what the one exceeded in Longitude, the other did in Rotundity: For I found the Hall 50 Paces long and very broad, with 2 Rowes of goodly Marble Pillers: For the other, his Table as they call it, with his whole Jury of couragious warlike knights round about it, shew'd no end of his bounty.[16]

---

[14] M. Drayton, *Poly-Olbion...* (London, 1612), p. 28 (Song IV, lines 299–306).
[15] Ibid., p. 62 (Song II, lines 233–42).
[16] As above, p. 478, n. 9, p. 51.

The table was mentioned in two places in John Evelyn's famous diary. Evelyn, who was in Winchester in connection with the events of the Civil War, made the following entry for 3 October 1642:

> ... I went to the siege of *Portsmouth* beleagur'd by Sir William *Waller*, The Rebellion now spreading its Disloyal Effects in all places almost of the Kingdon [sic], & this considerable Towne & Harbour delivered, by the Tretchery of Coll: *Goring* the Governor, who embarked for *France*: Hence I went to *Southampton* & *Winchester*, Where the Castle, Schole, Church, and K *Arthurs* Round Table: with portraictures of his Romantique Heros, and the monuments of the Saxon kings are shew'd ....[17]

In another description of the same visit he says:

> On the 6t I went from Portsmouth to [Southampton], lay at Winchester, where I visited the Castle, Schole, Church & K: Arthyrs round table; but especially the Church and its Saxon Kings Monuments, which I esteemed a worthy antiquity.[18]

As we have seen in Chapter 4, the Round Table was damaged in the Civil War, but none of the contemporary tracts gives an account of this incident. Thirty years later, in 1672, Elias Ashmole mentioned the damage in discussing the table:

> At the upper end of the great Hall in *Winchester Castle*, I remember to have seen a large Round Table hang against the wall, called King *Arthurs Round Table*, and affirmed by the Inhabitants (who had taken up the report upon vulgar Tradition) to have been as ancient as that Kings time; but it carried no very great show of antiquity to a judicious eye; however it seemed to have been set up, either in the room of one more ancient, or else by some who were perswaded, there was once such an *Order of Knights*, which had been denominated thence. This old Monument was broken to pieces (being before half ruined through age) by the Parliaments Soldiers, in the beginning of the late unhappy War, because looked upon as a relique of Superstition (as were those little gilded Coffers with Inscriptions, that did preserve the bones of some of the *Saxon* Kings and Bishops, deposited by Bishop *Fox* in the top of the Walls on both sides the upper part of the Quire of the Cathedral Church of that city) though guilty of nothing but the crime of reverend Antiquity.[19]

---

[17]   E. S. De Beer (ed.), *The Diary of John Evelyn* (Oxford, 1955), i, p. 52.

[18]   Ibid., ii p. 79.

[19]   Elias Ashmole, *The Institution, Laws & Ceremonies of the Most Noble Order of the Garter* (London, 1672), p. 95.

Ashmole's statement that the damage was done 'in the beginning' of the war must be taken with his description of the damage to the 'gilded coffers'. A contemporary description of the sack of the cathedral on 12 December 1642 states that:

> These monsters of men, to whom nothing is holy, nothing is sacred, did not stick to prophane and violate these cabinets of the dead and to scatter their bones all over the pavement of the church.[20]

It would thus seem likely that the table was damaged at the same time as the coffers, although it is of course possible that it was still further damaged when the castle was taken again in 1645.

Ashmole's account relies to some extent upon Camden's, virtually repeating verbatim in places the texts of the various English translations. He was also able to rely upon a contemporary account by his friend John Aubrey (1626–97). Aubrey's material was never published, but was included in his manuscript compilation, the *Monumenta Britannica*. Aubrey circulated the *Monumenta*, which he intended to publish, to his friends for comment and alteration, and it is annotated by both Ashmole and Evelyn. It contains the following important passages about the Round Table:

fol. 255
> Mensa rotunda Regis Arthuri.
> Owen's Epigr. lib. VI. Ep. 40.
> Inscribi septem Sapientum nomina jussit
> In tereti sapiens Delphicus orbe Deus.
> Sic Arthure sagax, Eques unusquisque tuorum
>
> In tereti mensa primus Eximus erit.

fol. 256
> In the hall at Winton castle where the Assizes are held, which is good Gothick architecture, of about Hen. 3., at ye east end over the Judges seate is affixed a great round Table, known by the name of K. Arthurs round Table, with divisions like a sea chart, & in every division in modern Gothique charr: of the Kts names. The diam: is about 21, or 22 feete.

---

[20] G. N. Godwin, *The Civil War in Hampshire (1642–45)*, 2nd edn. (Southampton and London, 1904), pp. 47–50.

The divisions of the Table are 26.

This is the round Table of K. Arthur wt xxiiij of his namyd knights. viz. Sr Galahalt. Sr Lancelot deu Lake. Sr Gauen. Sr Poyvale. Sr Lyonell, Sr Trystram de Lyens. Sr Garethe, Sr Beddvere, Sr Blubrys. Sr Lacote maletayle, Sr Bucane, Sr Plomyd, Sr Bors de gauis, Sr Safer, Sr Pellens, Sr Kay, S Ectorde marys, S dagonett, S^r degore S Brumear. S Lybius dyscony. Sr Alymare, Sr Mordred.

fol. 258 [original letter to Aubrey, bound in] Sep: 19

Sr,

I have here sent you the names of the knights of King arthurs round table as I have coppyed them from the Picture att my Lady Nortons Beginning at King Arthurs Left hand.

Sr Galahalt, Sr Launcelot du Lake; Sr Gaven, Sr Poyvale, Sr Lyonell, Sr Tristram de Lyens, Sr Garethe, Sr Bedduere, Sr Blubrys, Sr Lacotemale Tayle, Sr Bucane, Sr Plomyd, Sr Lamorall, Sr Bors de gavys, Sr Sater, Sr Pellens, Sr Kay, Sr Sertor de Marys, Sr Dagonett Sr Degore Sr Brumear, Sr Lybyns d'yscony, Sr Alymare, Sr Mordred. I have got another coppy from that table that is at Winchester which I doe not find to differ in the Orthography of any of the names but that of Sr Garethe which seems to bee garetz but tis soe ill a hand that tis writt in that I can not bee positive butt that, that which seems too mee to bee tz may bee an awkward th. The Diameter of the winchester Table is Eighteen foot, But seems to mee to bee soe far from being (as they pretent) King Arthurs; that I dont take it to bee above 200 years old. Bee yt how it will it is Enough for mee that It gives me an opportunity of assyring you that I am yr most Humble Servant

An: Henley.[21]

Several points need to be made about this material. 'An: Henley', the author of the letter transcribed by Aubrey, was Anthony Henley (d. 1711), the wit and politician, whose father, Sir Robert Henley, lived not far from Winchester at the Grange near Alresford and often entertained Aubrey there. While staying with Henley not long after the letter was written, Aubrey wrote *Villa; or, a Description of the Prospect of*

---

[21] Bodleian, MS. Top Gen. c. 24, fols. 255–8. The epigram which Aubrey quotes is from John Owen, *Epigrammatum* (Amsterdam, 1647), p. 141. The *Monumenta* has now been published in facsimile: *John Aubrey's Monumenta Britannica*, ed. John Fowles, 2 vols. (Sherborne, 1980–2).

Easton Piers, his own house in Wiltshire. This he described as '*A trifle of mine* Writ 1671 in my solitude at Sir R Henley's in Hants'.[22]

The 'Picture att my Lady Nortons' mentioned by Henley would be of great interest if it could be found; whether it was of the Winchester table or another round table is unclear, but the similarity of the knights' names to those on the Winchester table suggests that it is indeed a picture of the Winchester table. When it was painted and by whom is impossible to say.

Lady Norton may have been the widow of Sir John Norton who lived at Rotherfield Park, East Tisted. He died in 1686 and is buried in East Tisted church under an elaborate monument erected 'by the piety of his wife, Lady Dorothy'. Sir Richard Norton who died in 1645, a staunch royalist, had been sheriff of Hampshire on several occasions. The Nortons were related by marriage to other Hampshire families, such as Sir Henry Whithed and William Kingsmill of Shalden, many of whom had served their county as justices or as sheriff. On Lady Dorothy Norton's death in 1703, the estate passed to John Norton's niece, Elizabeth, who married Francis Paulet of Amport, and it remained in the Paulet family until 1808 when it was sold to James Scott. It is very likely that a picture of the Round Table should have belonged to a family such as the Nortons with their long association with the administration of the county. Living at the Grange, near Alresford, not far from Rotherfield Park, Anthony Henley would almost certainly have known Lady Norton.

There is little difference between Aubrey's list of knights' names and Henley's, except that Aubrey mentions only twenty-three names (see above, pp. 270–4). He speaks of 'xxiiij of his namyd knights', however, and when the two lists are compared, it is apparent that Aubrey omitted Henley's Sir Lamorall, i.e., Sir Lamorak. It is curious that Aubrey did not amend his list in the light of the Henley letter, but he must have used a source other than Henley, because in addition to the knights' names, Aubrey also quotes the inscription around the centre of the table. That source was almost certainly the evidence of his own eyes. No one other than Aubrey at that date would have described the Great Hall as 'good Gothick architecture, of about Hen. 3.' and the description of the table, with the analogy of a sea chart, is the work of an eyewitness. Since Winchester lay on the route from Easton Piers to Alresford, Aubrey could have visited the city many times. The differences between Aubrey's and Henley's spelling of the knights' names are no more than might arise between any two transcriptions. The names are difficult enough to read today, being mostly on their side or upside-down, and in the 1670s, after the

---

[22]   Michael Hunter, *John Aubrey and the Realm of Learning* (London, 1975), p. 239.

162 John Aubrey's water-colour of the Round Table, *c.* 1670.

damage inflicted during the Civil War, they may well have been even more difficult to decipher. Henley, as we have seen, writes of the names on the table being in 'soe ill a hand'. Henley also took his list from the Norton picture and not directly from the Winchester table, although he observes that the names in the picture do not 'differ in the Orthography' (see further above, pp. 270–4).

The Aubrey manuscript includes a water-colour (Fig. 162) which seems to be the earliest known representation of the table. It pre-dates by half a century the one now preserved in the Bingley papers in the Hampshire Record Office (Fig. 119; see above, p. 270), although the Norton painting, if it survived, would be even earlier. Did Aubrey paint the one in the manuscript himself? It is crude, but is of a similar character to others in the Aubrey manuscripts which probably were painted by Aubrey. It could not have been painted from the descriptions quoted above, and so must have been painted by someone who had either seen the table or had a very good description to work from. Oddly, it shows only sixteen divisions rather than the actual twenty-four, and the two names written on the rim to indicate the position of the names are Sir Safer and Sir Kay, which are not adjacent on the actual table. The water-colour appears on a page of the manuscript which faces Aubrey's own description. Was it perhaps done by Aubrey at Winchester as a crude *aide-mémoire* to supplement the list of names which he also transcribed? Whatever the explanation, and despite its crudeness, this coloured representation is a document of considerable importance for the history of the table.

Aubrey also mentions the table in the section of the *Monumenta Britannica* entitled 'Barrows'. He says, in a note written about 1690, 'Sr Gawen was a Knight of ye Round-Table as can be read ['seen' written above in MS.] in the Limbe about the Round-Table in the Castle-hall at Winchester'.[23] This final note and the material quoted above make Aubrey without doubt the most serious investigator of the Round Table prior to the eighteenth century.

It might have been expected that William Stukeley, whose interests in Merlin, Druids, and barrows were very close to Aubrey's, would have noticed the table, but he published only a brief reference to it written on about 9 September 1723, when he drew a view of Winchester to go with his description of the city. He said of the table, 'In the higher part of the city is the castle, which overlooks the whole: here is a famed round table, where king Arthur's knights used to sit'.[24] I could find no further mention of the table in Stukeley's surviving manuscripts and sketch-books.

[23] Bodleian, MS. Top Gen. c. 25, fol. 22.
[24] W. Stukeley, *Itinerarium Curiosum* (London, 1776), i, p. 191.

Two eighteenth-century travellers left a record of their reactions to the table. In 1738, Edward Harley (1689–1741), the second Earl of Oxford, wrote an account for his wife of a journey through Hampshire:

> Near the King's house stands an ancient large building which is called King Arthur's Hall. It is a good room, the length is better than one hundred and eight feet, the height I take to be about thirty feet. There are five arches, each arch distant from one another eighteen feet. There is nailed up against the wall at the end of the hall the top of what they call Arthur's Round Table, and the places marked where his knights sat. This I do not very strictly believe, but that there was a King Arthur and that he had many knights is most certain [twenty four *note in MS.*]. The use that this room is now put to is a Court of Justice, which is made use of when the Judges come their circuits to Winchester.[25]

Harley's tempered scepticism contrasts well with the scarcely concealed wish of Dr Richard Pococke that it were all true. Pococke arrived in Winchester at the end of September 1754:

> The walls of the town are defended by a deep fossee, and at the south corner of the town are some remains of an old castle, which was likewise encompassed by a deep fossè. The county hall was the chapel of the castle, which is a fine Gothic building as it appears within. It is 110 feet long and 55½ broad. This, with the castle is said to have been built by King Arthur, and at the west end of the outside of the chapel I saw some very old pillars. For King Arthur lived at this place. They have a table hung up at the west [*sic*] end of this room, which they call King Arthur's round table, but it is supposed to be a table of much later date, used in the time of justs and turnaments, being convenient to sit at in order to avoid disputes in relation to precedency. The names of the twenty-four knights are round it: Sr Galahallt, Sr Lancelot Duelake, Sr Gavey, Sr Pribald, Sir Lyonell, Sir Tristram Delyens, Sir Gavetbe, Sir Bedewere, Sr B. Bibrys, Sir Lametemale Tayte, Sir Bicane, Sir Oplomyds, Sir Lamorak, Sir Boro de Ganys, Sir Sater, Sir Pellens, Sir Kay, Sir Edorde Marys, Sir Degonet, Sir Degare, Sir Brumear, Sir Lybyns Dillong, Sir Allymore, Sir Mordrede.
>
> At the top is the figure of a king, sitting, with these words – 'King Arthur.' In the middle a rose is painted, with these words round it: 'This is the round table of King Arthur and twenty-four of his Knights.'[26]

---

[25] Historical Manuscripts Commission, *Portland VI*, Harley MSS. iv, 1723–45 (London, 1901), p. 174.

[26] *The Travels through England of Dr. R. Pococke*, ed. J. J. Cartwright, ii, Camden Society 3rd ser. 44 (1889), p. 122.

The visitors with whom I have dealt so far have been in the main antiquaries and topographers with an interest in how the table related to the historical Arthur. But the two most important eighteenth-century commentators were much more specifically involved with the history of Winchester itself. By this I do not mean that their interests related narrowly to the city, but that they were for personal reasons involved with Winchester. The first was Thomas Warton, Fellow of Trinity College, Oxford; Professor of Poetry; Poet Laureate. He was educated at Winchester College and in later life frequently went to stay with his brother Joseph, who was the headmaster there. In 1762 Thomas published the second edition of a fascinating work in two volumes which, although entitled *Observations on the Fairy Queen of Spenser*, contains much else besides. It includes, for instance, the first publication of Warton's new and exciting ideas concerning the history and chronology of Gothic architecture. In his discussion of the relationship of the Arthurian legends to the Fairy Queen, Warton has this to say about the Round Table:

> On Arthur's round table, as it is called, in the castle at Winchester, said to be founded by Arthur, are inscribed in antient characters, the names of twenty-four of his knights, just as we find them in MORTE ARTHUR. This table was hanging there, in the year 1484, and was even then very old, being at that time, by tradition, called *Arthur's round table*. I presume, that in commemoration of Arthur's institution, and in direct imitation of his practice, in later ages, a round table, inscribed with his knights, was usually fixed in some public place, wherever any magnificent turney was held, on which probably the combatants were afterwards seated. It is well known that tournaments were frequently celebrated in high splendour at Winchester; and this is perhaps one of those very tables... Harding, in his *Chronicle* of english kings from Brutus to Edward IV, in whose reign he wrote, tells us that Uther Pendragon, Arthur's father, founded the *round table* at Winchester, chiefly for the recovery of *Sangreal*, but in commemoration of his marriage with Igerne. Joseph of Arimathea is likewise introduced on this occasion.

> And at the day he weddid her and cround,
> And she far forth with child was then begonne,
> To comfort her he set the ROUND TABLE
> At *Winchester* of worthiest knights alone,
> Approved best in knighthood of their sone,
> Which TABLE ROUND, *Joseph of Arimathie*,
> For brother made of the SAINT GRAL only.[27]

[27] Thomas Warton, *Observations on The Fairy Queen of Spenser* (London, 1762), i, pp. 43–5.

163 John Carter's sketch of the Round Table, 1789.

Warton also wrote several poems on Arthurian subjects, including an ode on 'The Grave of King Arthur' which was published in 1777. In this same year he also published a sonnet 'On King Arthur's Round Table at Winchester':

> Where Venta's Norman Castle still uprears
> Its rafter'd hall, that o'er the grassy foss,
> And scatter'd flinty fragments, clad in moss,
> On yonder steep in naked state appears;
> High-hung remains, the pride of warlike years,
> Old Arthur's Board: on the capacious round
> Some British pen has sketched the names renown'd,
> In marks obscure, of his immortal peers.
> Though join'd by magic skill, with many a rime,
> The Druid-frame, unhonour'd, falls a prey
> To the slow vengeance of the wizard Time,
> And fade the British characters away;
> Yet Spenser's page, that chants in verse sublime
> Those Chiefs, shall live, unconscious of decay.[28]

Warton also wrote *A Description of the City, College, and Cathedral of Winchester* which he published anonymously in 1760. Large parts of this *Description* were reprinted in 1773, without credit, in another anonymous work which is now known to be the production of Richard Wavell, entitled *The History and Antiquities of Winchester*. Wavell reproduces Warton's discussion of the history of the table practically verbatim:

> Over the court of Nisi Prius, above the judge's seat, hangs what is commonly called king Arthur's round Table, which is eighteen feet in diameter. This piece of antiquity is said to be upwards of twelve hundred years standing; though some authors affirm, that it is of a much later date. However, it is of higher antiquity than it is commonly supposed to be; for Paulus Jovius, who wrote above two hundred years ago, relates, that it was shewn to emperor Charles the Fifth, and that, at that time, many marks of its antiquity had been destroyed; the names of the knights were then just written afresh, and the table, with its whole ornaments, newly repaired. Tilts and tournaments are supposed to have been established at Winchester by king Arthur, and were often

---

[28] Thomas Warton, *Poems* (London, 1777), p. 82.

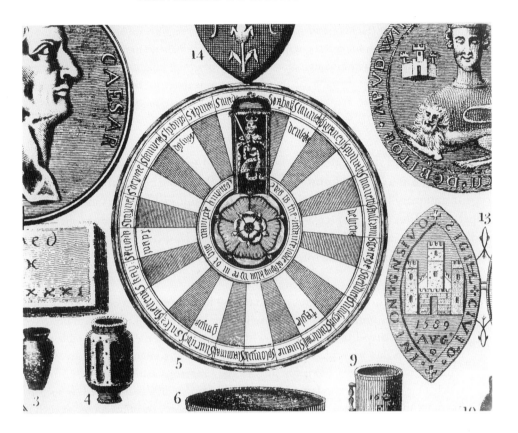

164 James Cave's drawing of the Round Table, engraved by J. Pass for John Milner's *History of Winchester*, published 1798.

held here before the king and parliament. This table might probably have been used on those occasions, for entertaining the combatants; which, on that account, was properly inscribed with the names of Arthur's twenty-four knights. The names of the knights inscribed on the table, are much the same as those we find in an old romance, called Morte Arthur, viz. Sir Lancelot du Lake, Sir Tristram, Sir Pelleas, Sir Gawain, Sir Garethe, etc.[29]

Like Warton, John Milner was closely involved with the city of Winchester, to which he came as a Roman Catholic priest in 1779. In collaboration with the architect and antiquary John Carter he designed and had built in 1792 the Gothic Revival chapel of St Peter (see Chapter 3). In 1803 he was appointed vicar apostolic of the Midland District and titular bishop of Castabala and moved from Winchester to Wolverhampton. In 1788 he wrote to the *Gentleman's Magazine*:

In this [Winchester] castle Arthur is said to have held his martial sports, and seated his knights, as at his principal palace. In proof of this, a huge round table is still preserved in the ancient chapel of the castle, now the county hall, as the identical table round which his knights were placed at their feasts to avoid contentions for precedency: certain it is, that it was shewn for such to the Emperor Charles V in 1512 [*sic*], at which time it was, for the last time, new painted; that it was described as such by Hardinge the poet in the reign of Edw. IV; and that it was generally reputed as such in the beginning of the twelfth century.[30]

By 1798, when he published his notable *History ... and Antiquities of Winchester*, Milner had changed his mind about the date of Charles V's visit and the date of the painted decoration. His final discussion of the table runs as follows:

The chief curiosity in this ancient chapel, now termed the County Hall, is Arthur's Round Table, as it is called. This hangs up at the east end of it, consisting of stout oak plank, which, however, is perforated with many bullets, supposed to have been shot by Cromwell's soldiers. It is painted with the figure of that prince, and the names of his twenty-four knights, as they have been collected from the romances of the 14th and

29 [Richard Wavell], *History and Antiquities of Winchester...* (Winchester, 1773), i, p. 5. For the authorship and interrelations of the *Description* and the *History*, see J. M. G. Blakiston, 'Thomas Warton's *Description of Winchester* and its Derivates', *Proceedings of the Hampshire Field Club* 35 (1979), 227–38.

30 *Gentleman's Magazine* orig. ser. 58 (1788), pt. ii, 970. For Giovio's account see above, pp. 404–5. Milner goes on to give the passage from John Lesley quoted above (pp. 487–8), attributing his visit to 1139(!) as evidence for an early twelfth-century reference to the table.

15th centuries. The costume and characters that are here seen, are those of the reign of Henry VIII, when this table appears to have been first painted, the style of which has been copied each time that it has been since new painted. At the time we are speaking of, and even in the middle of the 15th century, this table was certainly believed to have been actually made and placed in the castle by its supposed founder, the renowned British prince Arthur, who lived in the early part of the 6th century. ... We have reason ... to suppose that the real founder, or at least the great improver of the castle, king Stephen, and not the pretended founder of it, Arthur, made the present table, which supposition, whilst it takes off six centuries from its supposed antiquity, still leaves it an existence of seven centuries and an half, enough to render it a curious and valuable monument.[31]

In 1789 John Carter, who was later to collaborate with Milner over the chapel of St Peter, did a sketch of the table (Fig. 163; see above, pp. 270, 274). A note on this drawing shows that it was carried out for a '____ Bull Esq'. This must surely be the Richard Bull mentioned in Carter's obituary:

> The following year, 1781, brought him [Carter] acquainted with John Soane esq. the Architect to the Bank; his great friend the Rev. Dr. Milner, who about that time left the College of Douay in France ... and his eminent and learned patrons Sir Henry Charles Englefield, Richard Bull, esq. and the Hon. Horace Walpole, afterwards Lord Orford, (to whose notice he was introduced by Mr. Bull.)[32]

In 1788 Carter is known to have made three sketches of Walpole at Strawberry Hill for Richard Bull's extra-illustrated copy of Walpole's *Description of Strawberry Hill*.[33] The drawing of the Round Table was presumably commissioned by Bull for his private collection rather than for publication.

By the close of the eighteenth century the subject of Arthur was becoming the focus of scholarly interest and research. The Society of Antiquaries of London discussed him in their meetings just as the Elizabethan Society of Antiquaries had

---

[31] John Milner, *The History ... of Winchester* (Winchester, 1798–9), ii, pp. 171–3; for the engraving of the table published by Milner, see Fig. 164 and above, p. 481.

[32] *Gentleman's Magazine* orig. ser. 87, (1817), pt. ii, 363.

[33] Catalogue for 'The Age of Horace Walpole in Caricature: an Exhibition of Satirical Prints and Drawings from the Collection of W. S. Lewis', Sterling Memorial Library, Yale University, October–December 1973, caption to pl. I. Bull's copy of Walpole's *Description* was also illustrated with Carter water-colours of Strawberry Hill which had been shown at the Royal Academy. See W. S. Lewis, *Horace Walpole* (London, 1961), pls. 35, 39, 40, 47, 53.

165 Engraving of the Round Table from Edward Smirke's paper to the Congress of the [Royal] Archaeological Institute at Winchester in 1845, probably after a drawing by O. B. Carter.

166 Photograph by William Savage (?1817–87) of a painting of the Round Table made sometime after 1789 and engraved to illustrate the successive editions of Savage's *Winchester Guide* between ?1854 and 1884.

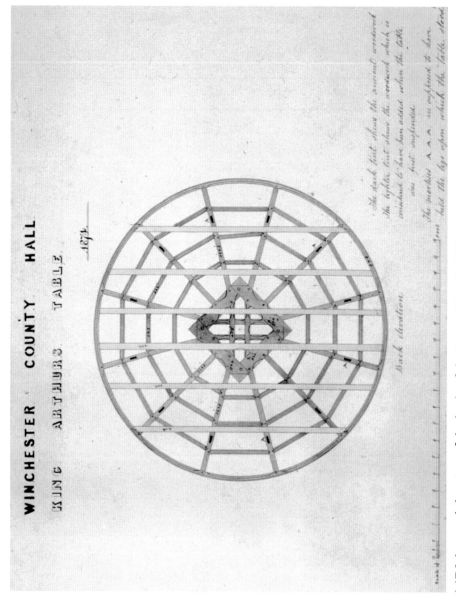

167 Measured drawing of the back of the Round Table, 1874.

done two centuries before, in Camden's day. Papers published by the Society in *Archaelogia* during the closing years of the eighteenth century mentioned, among other things, Arthur's tomb and the so-called Round Tables at Caerleon and Penrith. Stukeley, Warton, Carter, and Milner had all been fellows themselves.

The table was described by the indefatigable topographer John Britton, as one might expect,[34] but he did little more than paraphrase Milner's description and add the Warton sonnet quoted above. The table was described at some length by Charles Ball in 1818,[35] but he again bases his description upon Milner's. It is probable that the table is also described in some of the wide range of topographical publications which are such a feature of the opening decades of the nineteenth century. I have examined a considerable number but by no means all. In any case, Warton and Milner (Fig. 164) had discussed the table so thoroughly that they would very probably have been the principal sources for all but the most thorough and scholarly commentators, as they were for Britton and Ball.

The most careful examination to have yet been carried out took place in 1845, when the congresses of both the [Royal] Archaeological Institute and the British Archaeological Association took place – separately – in Winchester, with most of England's leading archaeologists, medievalists, and antiquaries in attendance. Two papers on the table were read to these congresses, and all attending would have had an opportunity to examine it. The paper given to the Archaeological Institute by Edward Smirke discussed both the Great Hall and the Round Table and included an engraving of the table (Fig. 165). Smirke examined very carefully all the evidence relating to the table, and much of his analysis still stands today. He dealt with many of the sources from which I and the other authors of this book have quoted. His discussion of the table takes up twenty-three pages and is thus far too long to quote in full. He concludes by saying:

> ... but I must leave the determination of the precise date to those whose curiosity and leisure may induce them to search for decisive evidence among the records of the Exchequer.
>
> In the mean time, we must be content to assign to this curious work of art a respectable, but moderate, antiquity. With some allowance for repaintings and reparation, it is, at all events, impossible to deny to it an age of about four centuries: – it is possible that this may be extended to as many as six; – but the chances, in the present state of the evidence, are in favour of some early, intermediate, date.[36]

[34] E. W. Brayley and John Britton, *The Beauties of England and Wales...*, vi (London, 1805), pp. 91–2.

[35] Charles Ball, *An Historical Account of Winchester...* (Winchester, 1818), pp. 54–5, 146.

[36] Smirke, as above, n. 5, p. 67.

168 Her Majesty the Queen Elizabeth II lunching at a round table beneath the Round Table, 12 April 1979.

The paper given to the British Archaeological Association was read by Charles Roach Smith, but had been written by Alfred John Kempe. Entitled 'The Table at Winchester, called Arthur's Round Table, and its connection with the origin of the Order of the Garter', it added nothing to Smirke's observations, but in the discussion following, J. R. Planché observed that

> the round table under consideration had evidently been painted under a Tudor dynasty, from the colours (white and green) which formed the compartments, and that it was so by Henry VII, as that prince was proud of his Cambrian descent, and had named his eldest son (born at Winchester) Prince *Arthur*. The scraping of the table, if allowed, would probably discover the previous coats of paint, and might lead to a better guess at its age, as most probably it was always decorated with the colours of the reigning family, and would, therefore, have been red and blue in Edward III's time; red and white in Richard II's; blue and white in Henry V's; and murray and blue in Edward IV's.[37]

In 1845 an article in the *Gentleman's Magazine* discussed the table at some length, but it added no new material to that published on the occasion of the two archaeological congresses. The author – who signed himself A. J. K. – was again Alfred John Kempe, who noted that his article was prompted by the Winchester congresses: much of it was even in the same words.[38] Apart from William Savage's Winchester Guide first issued about 1854 (Fig. 166), there seem to have been no further significant publications concerning the Round Table until 1873. In that year it was removed from the east wall to the west wall of the Great Hall, and this opportunity was taken to examine the way in which it was constructed. The comments of the architect in charge of the operation are described in Chapters 3 and 13.

In 1899 and 1900 two scholarly treatments of the Round Table were published, one by Melville Portal and the other by T. W. Shore.[39] Their conclusions did not differ in any significant way from those reached by earlier authors. Both Shore and Portal did include, however, for the first time a view of the back of the table, showing the way in which it is constructed, drawn from the photograph taken in 1873 (Fig. 34; compare Fig. 167).

[37]   *Transactions of the British Archaeological Association, at its second Annual Congress, Held at Winchester August 1845* (London, 1846), pp. 473–6.

[38]   'Notes on the Table called Arthur's Round Table, Preserved at Winchester', *Gentleman's Magazine* new ser. 24 (1845), 236–40.

[39]   Melville Portal, *The Great Hall Winchester Castle* (1899); T. W. Shore, 'King Arthur and the Round Table at Winchester', *Proceedings of the Hampshire Field Club* 4.3 (1900), 186–204.

When one considers the highly sophisticated scientific analytical techniques which we now have at our disposal and compares them with the slender hearsay evidence, imprecise manuscript references, and obvious visual examination upon which Camden, Aubrey, and Smirke had to rely, it is remarkable that they came to any specific conclusions at all. It is fascinating to see whether in the final analysis we have been able to add any significant facts to those surmised by them and their contemporaries.

The year 1900 seems a sensible point at which to end, since little has been written about the Winchester table between then and now. Not everyone today is happy about the application of modern technology and scholarship to this problem. Here is a comment made at the time of the BBC 'Horizon' TV film of the 1976 investigation.

> Now its [Winchester Castle's] notable feature is King Arthur's Round Table hanging on the wall like a huge dartboard – not King Arthur's at all, but a tribute to him probably by Edward III [*sic!*] (there never is any shortage of experts to transmute golden myth into leaden reality)![40]

[40]   John Lucas, 'Of Captains and Kings', *The Sunday Telegraph*, 31 July 1977.

169 The Round Table rehung, February 1980.

Appendix I

The Bishop of Winchester and the Foundation of the Order of the Garter

(see above, Chapter 11, p. 400)

The role played by the bishop of Winchester, in the person of William Edington, in the foundation of the Order of the Garter seems never to have been explored.[1] Edward III returned from the Crécy campaign and the capture of Calais in the autumn of 1347, landed at Sandwich on 12 October, and proceded directly to London which he reached on the 14th.[2] The Garter badge and the Garter motto had been 'an integral part of [his] campaign from its inception, not merely a retrospective commemoration of its success'.[3] Eighteen months later the first formal celebration of St George's day took place in the chapel at Windsor.[4]

[1] D'A. J. D. Boulton, *The Knights of the Crown. The Monarchical Orders of Knighthood in Later Medieval Europe 1325–1520* (Woodbridge, 1987), pp. 96–166, comments that the reason for the annexation of the office of prelate to the see of Winchester is unknown, but adds that 'the historic importance of the see and its associations with the Arthurian tradition probably played a part in its selection for the honour' (p. 148). For the early history of the Order, see now Hugh E. Collins, *The Order of the Garter 1348–1461. Chivalry and Politics in Late Medieval England* (Oxford, 2000).

[2] *Calendar of Close Rolls, Edward III*, viii, *1346–9*, pp. 396–7; T. Rymer, *Foedera* (ed. J. Caley and F. Holbrooke, London, 1825), III.i, p. 139. I am grateful to Dr W. M. Ormrod for these references which show that the story that Edward proceeded along the south coast from Sandwich via Portsmouth and Southampton to Winchester, retailed by Martin and followed by Moberly, cannot be corroborated from the contemporary sources (G. H. Moberly, *Life of William of Wykeham*, 2nd edn. (Winchester and London, 1893), p. 12, quoting (inaccurately) Thomas Martin, *Historica Descriptio Complectens Vitam ... Guillielmi Wicami* (London, 1597), Bk. 1, Cap. 2 (Sig. B4v)). The point is of some interest in demolishing the tale that it was on this occasion in Winchester that Edward chanced to meet and at once recruited the young William of Wykeham to his service. If Wykeham was then, as Martin alleges, Edington's secretary (*Edintonio Episcopo tum erat a consiliis et epistolis*), Edward could as well have met him in London during the Michaelmas legal term of 1347, when both Edward and Edington were present with few interuptions, as Dr Ormrod has demonstrated (letter of 25 Feb. 1991). For Edington and Wykeham, see further, W. M. Ormrod, *The Reign of Edward III. Crown and Political Society in England 1327–1377* (London, 1990), pp. 86–94.

[3] Juliet Vale, *Edward III and Chivalry* (Woodbridge, 1982), pp. 77–9; the quotation is taken from p. 77.

[4] Ibid. pp. 83–4; Boulton, *Knights of the Crown*, as above n. 1, p. 116.

Edward's two collegiate foundations, St George's Windsor and St Stephen's Westminster, were founded on the same day, 6 August 1348. The chapel at Windsor was rededicated to the Blessed Virgin Mary and St George, that at Westminster to the Virgin and St Stephen. Each foundation was originally to have twenty-four secular priests. And in each case the arrangements were placed in the hands of the archbishop of Canterbury (John Stratford, d. 23 August 1348, formerly bishop of Winchester, 1323–33) and the bishop of Winchester (William Edington, 1346–66).[5]

Edward issued letters patent for the foundation of the college of St George in the chapel of Windsor castle on 6 August 1348.[6] Since chapel and college were clearly intended to provide the setting for the annual celebration of the feast of the Order on St George's day, the foundation of the college can be taken as the earliest surviving indication of Edward's clear intention to establish the Order.

The buildings of the new college were not begun until April 1350, perhaps owing to the Black Death.[7] The repair and refurbishment of the existing chapel in the lower bailey, henceforth to be known as St George's Chapel, was completed by the installation of the new windows of painted glass in March 1353. The vestry and chapter house were completed by 1352, the warden's lodge by 1353, the treasury and the lodgings of the canons and vicars by 1355, and the cloister in 1356–7. To mark the completion of the college buildings, the Feast of St George was celebrated in the castle in 1358 with great splendour and solemnity.

Meanwhile, the statutes of the college had taken over four years to complete. The king petitioned the pope to confirm the consecration, endowment, and statutes in 1349.[8] Papal letters of approval, not dispatched until 30 November 1350, granted a faculty to the archbishop of Canterbury (now Simon Islip, 1349–66) and the bishop of Winchester (William Edington) to settle the ordinances and statutes.[9] These letters were accompanied and followed by further faculties to the archbishop and bishop allowing them to appropriate certain benefices (31 January 1351) and grant exemption from ordinary jurisdiction to the college (12 February

[5] For St Stephen's, see *The Victoria History of the Counties of England, London*, i (1909), p. 566; *Calendar of Entries in the Papal Registers Relating to Great Britain and Ireland. Petitions to the Pope*, i, *1342–1419*, pp. 186–7; *Calendar of Entries in the Papal Registers Relating to Great Britain and Ireland. Papal Letters*, iii, *1342–62*, p. 330. For St George's, see below.

[6] *Calendar of the Patent Rolls Preserved in the Public Record Office, Edward III*, viii, *1348–50*, p. 144.

[7] For Edward III's works in creating the college, see H. M. Colvin (ed.), *The History of the King's Works*, ii (London, 1963), pp. 872–5.

[8] *Calendar of Papal Registers. Petitions to the Pope*, i, *1342–1419*, pp. 187–8.

[9] *Calendar of Papal Registers. Papal Letters*, iii, *1342–62*, p. 395.

1351).[10] The ordinances and statutes were finally completed on 30 November 1352.[11]

Although Windsor lay within the diocese of Salisbury, the existing castle chapel was apparently free from the bishop's control: the choice of the bishop of Winchester to join the archbishop in settling the ordinances and statutes of the college was therefore clearly deliberate and may have been indicated in Edward's petition of 1349.[12] Edington thus played a central role in the creation of the college – perhaps the key role after the king – and may have drafted the statutes himself.[13] A greater question is whether the bishop played a similar role in the foundation of the Order.

The original statutes of the Garter have not survived. Edward probably made provisions for the governance of the order in a set of statutes and ordinances, but the earliest set of statutes to survive was issued in French by Henry V on 22 April 1415.[14] The bishop of Winchester is named only in Article 19, and then only in passing:

> Lesquelz nominacions escrira le chief prelat dudit ordre, c'est assavoir l'evesque de Wyncestre pour le temps estant, ou en son absence le doion ou registreur, ou le plus ancien residencier dudit College en leur absence.[15]

---

[10] Ibid. pp. 383–4, 399. For the texts of these and other relevant letters, see now P. N. R. Zutshi (ed.), *Original Papal Letters in England 1305–1415* (Vatican City, 1990), nos. 227, 229–30, 232–3, 241. I owe this reference to the kindness of Professor C. N. L. Brooke.

[11] A. K. B. Roberts, *St George's Chapel, Windsor Castle, 1348–1416. A Study in Early Collegiate Administration* (Windsor, n.d. [1947]), p. 107, cf. pp. 17–18, 143, 145, 238.

[12] For the status of the existing chapel, see J. H. Denton, *English Royal Free Chapels 1100–1300: A Constitutional Study* (Manchester, 1970), pp. 129–30, and for that of the new foundation, ibid., pp. 116–17. Edington's role in the foundation of the college at St Stephen's seems to have been equally deliberate, for St Stephen's lay also outside his diocese. Dr Ormrod has suggested ('Edward III's Government of England, 1346–1356' [Oxford D. Phil. thesis, 1984], pp. 222–61, esp. pp. 232–3) that Edington's attempts as treasurer (an office he held from 1344–56) to produce greater cohesion between the various departments of finance in the later 1340s were related to the use of the canonries of St Stephen's for officials of the Exchequer of Receipt, or Lower Exchequer.

[13] Roberts, *St George's Chapel*, as above n. 11, p. 107, took the view, without quoting further evidence, that the statutes were drawn up by William Edington at the king's request, but the matter falls short of proof.

[14] College of Arms, MS Arundel 48, the significance of which was first recognised by Lisa Jefferson, 'MS Arundel 48 and the Earliest Statutes of the Order of the Garter', *English Historical Review* 109 (1994), 356–85. Dr Jefferson's discovery has been corroborated by references in the Treasurer's Account of the College of St. George for 1415–16 (see her chapter, 'The Statutes of the Order', in Peter Begent and Herbert Chesshyre, *The Order of the Garter* (London, 1999), pp. 52–72 and is now accepted (see, for example, Collins, *The Order of the Garter*, as above, n. 1, pp. 15–17). I am most grateful to Dr Jefferson for her crucial comments on the text of earlier versions of this appendix.

[15] MS Ashmole 48, f. 187ᵛ, as printed by Jefferson, 'MS Arundel 48', 380, lines 162–5.

This is the earliest occurrence of this description of the office, yet the wording refers to the *chief prelat* as if to an established position (it has not been defined elsewhere in the statutes) and then qualifies it by defining the holder as the bishop of Winchester 'for the time being'. There is no other evidence for the use of this description in the earlier fifteenth century, but there is also no known document which grants the office to the see of Winchester.[16] The statutes of 1415 leave the impression that they refer in passing to an existing situation. The use of the title (if it has already become such) is however a different matter from the question of the association of the bishop of Winchester with the Order from its earliest days.

Edington's personal attendance at the St George's day feasts might be followed in detail from his itinerary or from records of the annual issue to him of Garter robes from the Great Wardrobe. Both sources are incomplete. The earliest occasion on which Edington's presence at Windsor on 23 April appears in his itinerary is 1360.[17] The accounts of the Great Wardrobe are missing for the years 1349–60.[18] By 1361 the issue of robes for the feast of St George had become an annual item, and from 1364 an issue to the bishop of Winchester was a normal feature. These sources do not, therefore, provide a safe indication of practice, or of the bishop's presence, in the earliest years of the Order.[19]

Edington's gift to the college of £200 to endow his obit, received in 1361–2, provides another indication of his close association with both the chapel and the Order.[20]

Edington was, however, present at Windsor on one of the earliest feasts of the Garter. On St George's Day 1350, as recorded in the first notice of a feast of the Garter by a contemporary chronicler,

---

[16] Jefferson, 'MS Arundel 48', 372–3 and 372, n. 1.

[17] S. F. Hockey (ed.), *The Register of William Edington, Bishop of Winchester, 1346–1366*, Hampshire Record Series 7 (Winchester, 1986), pp. xxiii–xxvi, at p. xxiv. The itinerary provided by Dom Hockey omits all reference to the bishop's periods of residence in Southwark: these can easily be established by noting the place and date printed to the right below each entry throughout the register. The itinerary only records, of course, those places where Edington carried out episcopal functions of the kind normally entered in an episcopal register. It cannot therefore provide a complete personal itinerary. For a specific problem regarding the bishop's movements, see below p. 517.

[18] PRO, *List of Foreign Accounts*, Lists and Indexes 11 (1900), p. 104.

[19] Vale, *Edward III and Chivalry*, pp. 77–8, 82; Ashmole, *Institution*, p. 236; John Anstis, *The Register of the Most Noble Order of the Garter*, 2 vols. (London, 1724), i, pp. 11–15, 171, 310; G. F. Beltz, *Memorials of the Order of the Garter* (London, 1841), p. 7; N. H. Nicolas, *History of the Orders of Knighthood of the British Empire*, 4 vols. (London, 1842), ii, Appendix, pp. xv–xviii, xix*–xlviii*; N. H. Nicolas, 'Observations on the Institution of the Most Noble Order of the Garter', *Archaeologia* 31 (1846), 1–163, esp. pp. 134–40.

[20] Roberts, *St George's Chapel*, p. 45, cf. pp. 65, 149.

a solemn mass [was] sung by the bishops of Canterbury, Winchester, and Exeter, and [afterwards the whole company] sat together at a common table, to the honour of the holy martyr to whom the noble fraternity was especially dedicated, calling their company 'St. George de la Gartière'.[21]

Edington's presence at Windsor on this occasion appears to be confirmed by the strictly contemporary evidence of entries on the fine roll warranted 'by bill of the treasurer' and dated 20 and 25 April 1350.[22] The bishop's register records institutions and admissions at Southwark on 21, 24, and 25 April, but these actions do not necessarily imply the bishop's presence there on those days, for he may have authorised them some days before and left it to his officials to issue the necessary documents.[23]

Article 19 of the statutes of 1415 suggests that the role of the bishop of Winchester 'for the time being' as prelate of the Garter was by then an established fact. What might possibly be new is the description of 'chief' prelate, as if to suggest there may have been other bishops who might claim this role. The other evidence we have supports the impression that the association of the Order with the bishop of Winchester in the person of William Edington goes back to its earliest days. The records of St George's chapel support this impression, and the presence of the bishop at the Garter ceremonies of 1350 appears to confirm it. The choice of the bishop of Winchester to draw up the statutes of the college in association with the archbishop of Canterbury appears to have been deliberate, an element in the shift of emphasis from Edward's still-born Order of the Round Table of 1344 to his successful foundation of the Order of the Garter in 1348–9.

Without Edward III's original statutes and ordinances we may never be sure whether there was some specific assignment of the office to the bishop of Winchester 'for the time being'. It is equally possible that the long service of Edington in the office gave rise *de facto* to a presumption that it pertained to the see of Winchester. In adding the adjective 'chief', the statutes of 1415 may simply have been giving force to an existing situation.

For Edward I Winchester had been the city of Arthur. Now Edward's grandson, Edward III, wished to affirm that Windsor rather than Winchester was the castle founded by Arthur, the seat of chivalry, and (not incidentally) his own birthplace.[24] In

---

21 E. M. Thompson (ed.), *Chronicon Galfridi le Baker de Swynebroke* (Oxford, 1889), pp. 108–9; translated by Boulton, *Knights of the Crown*, pp. 116–17.

22 *Calendar of Fine Rolls*, vi, Edward III, 1347–56, p. 231 (*bis*). I owe this reference to Dr Ormrod.

23 Hockey (ed.), *Register of William Edington*, i, nos. 747–9. I am grateful to Professor Brooke for his advice on the significance of these entries in the register.

such a transition, the choice of the bishop of Winchester as prelate of the new Order would be both an expression of continuity with the ancient claims of Winchester and a validation of the status of Windsor.[25]

---

[24] See, for example, the words of Froissart and Jean Le Bel quoted by Boulton, *Knights of the Crown*, as above, n. 1, pp. 102, 105.

[25] See above, pp. 415–16. I am most grateful to Dr A. J. Taylor for his comments on an earlier version of this appendix and for his suggestion that one should explore the role of William of Wykeham in the changes through which the table went at this time. I am also much indebted to Dr W. M. Ormrod, who read this appendix in an earlier draft and made several important corrections and suggestions which I have followed. The responsibility for any errors which remain is, of course, my own. This appendix originally appeared under the title 'Why is the bishop of Winchester prelate of the Garter?,' in *Winchester Cathedral Record* 60 (1991), pp. 18–22.

Appendix II

Calais and Guisnes 1520: the confusion of the sources

(see above, Chapter 12, p. 461)

The picture was long confused by writers who conflated the details of the reception of Charles V at Calais in July with the meeting of Henry and Francis on the Field of Cloth of Gold between Guisnes and Ardres the previous month, in particular by assigning the key motto, *Cui adhereo preest*, to Guisnes rather than to Calais.

Paolo Giovio began the confusion in Book 20 of his *Historiarum sui temporis*, published at Florence in 1552.[1] Giovio's intended text of this book, which dealt with the year 1520, was never completed and exists only in a short 'compendium', hence probably the confusion.[2] Giovio introduces the meeting between Henry and Francis *constituto in finibus Morinorum loco* ('at an agreed place in the territory of the Morini [the pre-Roman tribe inhabiting the Pas-de-Calais]') and describes the *lignea domus* erected there by Henry, but without mentioning Guisnes. He goes on to refer to Henry's subsequent meeting with Caesar (i.e. the emperor-elect Charles V), and to Henry's wish to play arbiter, but without mentioning Calais. Giovio then says that Henry had made his intention clear by the motto *Cui adhaereo praeest* (as he spells it) set up in *foribus ligneae domus supra armatum ingentem sagittarium, habitu Britannico scite perpictum* ('at the entrance to the wooden house, above a huge armed archer painted in British dress'). In the context of Giovio's text, the reference to the wooden house places the motto at Guisnes. A second confusion is introduced by the British archer who occupied at Calais only a secondary position, above and to one side of the inner door of the vestibule of the round house (see above, p. 457).

---

[1]   *Opera Pauli Iovii*, ed. Dante Visconti (Rome, 1964), iv [= *Historiarum sui temporis*, Bk. 2, Pt. i], p. 6.

[2]   F. Chabod, 'Paolo Giovio', in his *Scritti sul Rinascimento* (Turin, 1967), pp. 243–67, esp. 243–4, and 243 n.2.

Giovio's sketch of his intended Book 20 gave rise to a long history of error. In England the confusion was perpetuated by Lord Herbert in 1649,[3] and followed over a century later by A. C. Ducarel.[4]

On the Continent, Giovio's version was followed by Emmanuel van Meteren *c.*1600[5] and copied by François de Mezeray in 1646.[6] The matter began to be sorted out by Bernard de Montfaucon, who referred specifically to the confusion. De Montfaucon used a wide range of sources, including perhaps *La description* and the notebooks of Peiresc (a long section from one of which he transcribed), but he did not mention the key problem of the motto *Cui adhaereo praeest* and its location.[7] Despite Montfaucon, the error continued to be perpetuated in local histories.[8]

---

[3] Edward Herbert, *The Life and Raigne of King Henry the Eighth* (London, 1649), p. 98.

[4] A.C. Ducarel, *Anglo-Norman Antiquities Considered in a Tour through Part of Normandy* (London, 1767), Appendix 3, 'A Description of the Basso Relievos Representing the Interview of Henry VIII ... with Francis I', p. 43.

[5] Emmanuel van Meteren, *Historia Belgica* (Antwerp, *c.*1600), p. 424.

[6] François de Mezeray, *Histoire de France* ii (Paris, 1646), p. 405 [2nd edn (Paris, 1685), p. 914].

[7] Bernard de Montfaucon, *Monumens de la Monarchie Française* iv (Paris, 1732), pp. 163–206.

[8] For example in Abbé Lefebvre, *Histoire générale et particulière de la ville de Calais* ii (Paris, 1766), p. 221.

Index